CAMBRIDGE
EDUCATIONAL SERVICES®

AMERICA'S PREMIERE TESTING READINESS PROGRAM

Victory
for the
SAT Test

S T U D E N T   T E X T

Our Mission: Progress Through Partnership

Cambridge Educational Services partners with educators who share the significant mission of educational advancement for all students. By partnering together, we can best achieve our common goals: to build skills, raise test scores, enhance curriculum, and support instruction. A leading innovator in education for twenty years, Cambridge is the nation's premier provider of school-based test preparation and supplemental curriculum services.

If you have purchased Cambridge SAT Software:

SOFTWARE LICENSE AGREEMENT AND LIMITED WARRANTY

BY OPENING THE SOFTWARE PACKAGE, YOU ARE AGREEING TO BE BOUND BY THE FOLLOWING AGREEMENT. THIS LEGAL DOCUMENT IS AN AGREEMENT BETWEEN YOU AND CAMBRIDGE PUBLISHING, INC. (CP). CP IS WILLING TO LICENSE THIS SOFTWARE TO YOU ONLY ON THE CONDITION THAT YOU ACCEPT ALL THE TERMS CONTAINED IN THIS LICENSE AGREEMENT. IF YOU DO NOT AGREE WITH THESE TERMS AND CONDITIONS, CP IS UNWILLING TO LICENSE THIS SOFTWARE TO YOU AND YOU SHOULD REMOVE THIS SOFTWARE FROM YOUR COMPUTER.

1. GRANT OF LICENSE: In consideration of the price you paid for this product and your agreement to abide by the terms and conditions of this Agreement, CP grants to you a non-exclusive right to use and display the enclosed software program (hereinafter "the SOFTWARE") on a single computer (i.e., with a single CPU) at a single location.
2. OWNERSHIP OF THE SOFTWARE: You own only the magnetic or physical media on which the SOFTWARE is recorded or fixed, but CP retains all rights, title, and ownership to the SOFTWARE recorded on the enclosed CD copy and all subsequent copies of the SOFTWARE.
3. COPY RESTRICTIONS: This SOFTWARE and the accompanying printed materials are the subject of copyright. You may not copy the Documentation or the SOFTWARE, except when you make a single copy of the SOFTWARE for backup or archival purposes.
4. USE RESTRICTIONS: You may not network the SOFTWARE or otherwise use it on more than one computer at the same time. You may not distribute copies of the SOFTWARE or the Documentation to others. You may not reverse-engineer, disassemble, decompile, modify, adapt, translate, or create derivative works based on the SOFTWARE or the Documentation without the prior written consent of CP.
5. TRANSFER RESTRICTION: The enclosed SOFTWARE is licensed only to you and may not be transferred to anyone else without prior written consent of CP. Any unauthorized transfer of the SOFTWARE shall result in the immediate termination of this Agreement.
6. TERMINATION: This license will terminate automatically without notice from CP if you fail to comply with any of its provisions. All provisions of this Agreement as they apply to warranties, limitation of liability, remedies or damages, and ownership rights shall survive termination.
7. MISCELLANEOUS: This Agreement shall be construed in accordance with the laws of the United States of America and the State of Illinois and shall benefit CP, its affiliates, and assignee.
8. LIMITED WARRANTY AND DISCLAIMER OF WARRANTY: CP warrants that the SOFTWARE, when properly used in accordance with the Documentation, will operate in substantial conformity with the description of the SOFTWARE set forth in the Documentation. CP does not warrant that the SOFTWARE will meet your requirements or that the operation of the SOFTWARE will be uninterrupted or error-free. CP warrants that the media on which the SOFTWARE is delivered shall be free from defects in materials and workmanship under normal use for a period of ninety (90) days from the date of your purchase. Your only remedy and CP's only obligation under the limited warranties set forth in this Agreement is at CP's election.

See Cambridge SAT CD-ROM for complete Software License Agreement and Limited Warranty

---

Cambridge Publishing, Inc.
www.CambridgeEd.com

© 1994, 1995, 1996, 1997, 2000, 2003, 2004, 2005, 2010, 2012 by Cambridge Publishing, Inc.
All rights reserved. First edition 1994
Eleventh edition 2012

Printed in the United States of America
15 14 13 12   1 2 3 4 5

ISBN-13: 978-1-58894-150-3

SFI — Certified Chain of Custody
Product Line Contains At Least
20% Certified Forest Content
www.sfiprogram.org
SFI-00756

TABLE OF CONTENTS

How to Use This Book.. vii

OFFICIAL PRE-ASSESSMENT/COURSE PLANNING | 1

Official Pre-Assessment Administration.. 3
How to Use the Official Pre-Assessment Reports 5
Setting a Test Score Target.. 9
Overcoming Test Anxiety 25
Overall Time Management.. 33
Planning a Course Schedule 37

TEST MECHANICS, CONCEPTS, AND STRATEGIES | 39

Critical Reading: Passages | 41

Course Concept Outline.. 41
Test Mechanics.. 43
Lesson 53
Quizzes 75
Review 103
Strategy Summary 121

Critical Reading: Sentence Completions | 125

Course Concept Outline.. 125
Test Mechanics.. 127
Lesson 135
Quizzes 147
Review 157
Strategy Summary 165

Math: Multiple-Choice | 167

Course Concept Outline.. 167
Test Mechanics.. 171
Lesson 183
Quizzes 227
Review 243
Strategy Summary 249

Math: Student-Produced Responses | 253

Course Concept Outline.. 253
Test Mechanics.. 255
Lesson 267
Quizzes 275
Review 287
Strategy Summary 293

Writing 295

Course Concept Outline..295
Test Mechanics..299
Lesson...315
Quizzes...333
Review...351
Strategy Summary..361

PRACTICE TEST REINFORCEMENT 365

Directed Study Practice Test 367

Section 1: Writing..369
Section 2: Math..372
Section 3: Writing..382
Section 4: Critical Reading...397
Section 5: Math..408
Section 6: Critical Reading...416
Section 8: Math..429
Section 9: Critical Reading...436
Section 10: Writing..447

Practice Test I 455

Section 1: Writing..457
Section 2: Critical Reading...458
Section 3: Math..466
Section 5: Critical Reading...470
Section 6: Math..476
Section 7: Writing..480
Section 8: Critical Reading...486
Section 9: Math..492
Section 10: Writing..496

Practice Test II 499

Section 1: Writing..501
Section 2: Math..502
Section 3: Critical Reading...506
Section 4: Math..514
Section 6: Writing..518
Section 7: Critical Reading...524
Section 8: Math..530
Section 9: Critical Reading...534
Section 10: Writing..540

Practice Test III 543

Section 1: Writing..545
Section 2: Critical Reading...546
Section 3: Math..554
Section 4: Writing..558
Section 5: Critical Reading...564
Section 7: Math..570
Section 8: Critical Reading...574
Section 9: Math..580
Section 10: Writing..584

OFFICIAL POST-ASSESSMENT

587

Official Post-Assessment Administration...589
How to Use the Official Post-Assessment Reports 591
Planning for Further Study 593

APPENDIX A: BEYOND THE SAT TEST

595

Application Preparation...597
Six Way to Jumpstart Your College Admissions Essays 603

APPENDIX B: ANSWERS AND EXPLANATIONS

615

Test Mechanics, Concepts, and Strategies

617

Critical Reading: Passages 619
Critical Reading: Sentence Completions..621
Math: Multiple Choice...623
Math: Student-Produced Responses 625
Writing...627

Practice Tests

631

Practice Test I...633
Practice Test II 665
Practice Test III..699

APPENDIX C: TEST ANSWER SHEET

733

Test Answer Sheet..735

APPENDIX D: PROGRESS REPORTS

737

Test Mechanics, Concepts, and Strategies...739
Practice Test Reinforcement...745

Error Correction and Suggestion Form 753

Item Index...771

HOW TO USE THIS BOOK

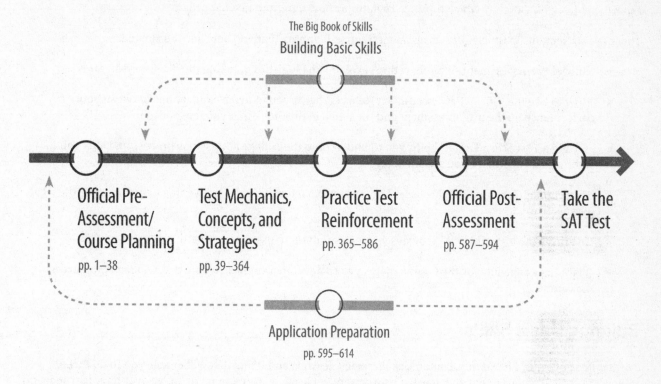

This course is organized into seven parts, which are outlined in the diagram above:

- **Official Pre-Assessment/Course Planning.** A diagnostic pre-assessment and score reports help you identify your starting point and prepare for the course.

- **Building Basic Skills.** This review material, found in *The Big Book of Skills, 11th Edition,* serves as a refresher on topics you may not have studied in a while.

- **Test Mechanics, Concepts, and Strategies.** Items resemble those on the real tests, which your instructor will use to teach tested concepts and applicable strategies.

- **Practice Test Reinforcement.** Four full-length SAT practice tests allow you to practice your skills in a testing format.

- **Official Post-Assessment and Action Plan.** A diagnostic post-assessment helps you to see how far you've come, and recommended courses of action help you to continue your study after the course.

- **Application Preparation.** Tips and sample essays help you prepare your college applications.

- **Take the SAT Test.** After you complete the course you will take the SAT test, using everything you will learn throughout this course to succeed on test day.

The following introduction will briefly explain how to use each part of this volume.

Official Pre-Assessment/Course Planning

In order to know where to begin preparing for the real test, you have to find out what you already do well and what you could learn to do better. The pre-assessment serves this purpose. First, you will take an official test under actual testing conditions. Then, with the help of your instructor, you will examine your Student Summary report and determine exactly which topics to review, for how long, and in what order.

There are six sections in Official Pre-Assessment/Course Planning that will help get you started:

- "Official Pre-Assessment Administration" explains the logistics of taking the pre-assessment.

- "How to Use the Official Pre-Assessment Reports" helps you to make connections between your performance on the pre-assessment and the items in this book that you most need to study.

- "Setting a Test Score Target" helps you to understand the college admissions process and aids you in setting goals for where you should apply.

- "Overcoming Test Anxiety" discusses how to approach test days, from planning to maintaining the right perspective.

- "Overall Time Management" provides strategies for you to use when scheduling your study time.

- "Planning a Schedule for the Course" helps you to develop a study schedule that will aid your success in the course.

Building Basic Skills

The Big Book of Skills, 11th Edition, contains skills review lessons and items that will enable you to do three things: (1) review material that you may have forgotten; (2) learn material that you may never have learned; and (3) master the skills required to answer the more difficult multiple-choice items on the real test. Your teacher may have already reviewed this material with you, or your teacher may integrate portions of it while you work through the material in this book.

Test Mechanics, Concepts, and Strategies

Test Mechanics, Concepts, and Strategies make up the heart of this course. This part of the book contains items that look like those found on the real SAT test. When compared with items on the real tests, the items in this part of the book have similar content, represent the same difficulty levels, and can be solved by using the same problem-solving skills and alternative test-taking strategies.

There are five chapters in Test Mechanics, Concepts, and Strategies, each chapter representing a core component of the exams:

- Critical Reading: Passages

- Critical Reading: Sentence Completions

- Math: Multiple-Choice

- Math: Student-Produced Responses

- Writing

Each of the above chapters begins with a Course Concept Outline, which acts as a syllabus, listing the concepts that are tested for each item type. The items in each chapter are organized to correspond with the respective outline. For each concept in the outline, there is a group of items. The group contains a greater number of items if the item type appears with great frequency on the real test, and it contains a lesser number of items if the item type appears with less frequency. Although the concepts are not grouped in this way on the real SAT test, we organize the lessons in this manner so that the concepts are emphasized and reinforced. After you learn the concepts, you will be able to practice applying this conceptual knowledge on the practice tests.

Practice Test Reinforcement

In the Practice Test Reinforcement portion of this book, there are four full-length SAT practice tests. In these tests, the items not only mimic the real test in content and difficulty level, but they are also arranged in an order and with a frequency that simulates the real test.

The first test is arranged as a Directed Study Practice Test. You will see the test problems alongside the correct answers and explanations. This format allows you to work through a test with some guidance before tackling a practice test that functions like the real exam. After you complete the Directed Study Practice Test, you will complete three additional practice tests with time restrictions. You may complete these items in class or your instructor may assign them as homework. Either way, adhering to the time restrictions forces you to pace yourself as you would on the real test. If you complete all four of the practice tests, any test anxiety you may have will be greatly reduced. Answers and explanations to Practice Tests I–III are located in Appendix B of this book. Perforated essay response and bubble sheets for Practice Tests I–III are located in Appendix C of this book.

Official Post-Assessment and Action Plan

In order to know how far you've come since the pre-assessment, you have to take a second official SAT test. You will take this post-assessment under actual testing conditions. You will then receive a second Student Summary report to help you determine final areas for review.

This section contains three "Winning Strategies" sections to help you see how far you've come:

- "Official Post-Assessment Administration" explains the logistics of taking the post-assessment.

- "How to Use the Official Post-Assessment Reports" shows you how to use the Student Summary report you will receive to identify areas of study, as well as particular items in your textbook, upon which to focus as you continue to prepare for the real test.

- "Planning for Further Study" includes advice on how to make the most of an effective and concrete action plan. You will learn how to maximize your remaining course time and prioritize material to be reviewed before you take the actual SAT test.

Application Preparation

Appendix A provides a short guide that will help you beyond the course:

- "Application Preparation" teaches you how to highlight your unique qualities to maximize your chances of admission into your first-choice school.

- "Six Ways to Jumpstart Your College Admissions Essays" gives examples of actual college admissions essay questions/responses and shows you how to ace the essay.

Official Pre-Assessment/ Course Planning

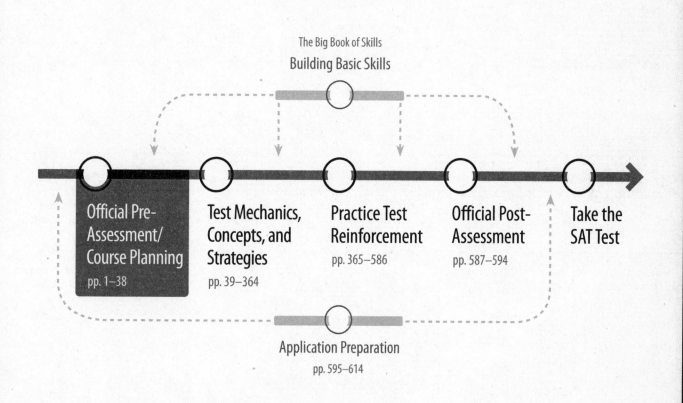

The Big Book of Skills
Building Basic Skills

Official Pre-Assessment/ Course Planning
pp. 1–38

Test Mechanics, Concepts, and Strategies
pp. 39–364

Practice Test Reinforcement
pp. 365–586

Official Post-Assessment
pp. 587–594

Take the SAT Test

Application Preparation
pp. 595–614

CAMBRIDGE
VICTORY FOR THE
SAT TEST

OFFICIAL PRE-ASSESSMENT ADMINISTRATION

At the beginning of the course, you will take a pre-assessment. This pre-assessment consists of an official, retired SAT test. Perforated test answer sheets for the pre-assessment are located in Appendix C of this book for programs not utilizing the Cambridge Assessment Service. When you take the pre-assessment, you should bring the following items to the classroom, in addition to anything else your teacher instructs you to bring:

1. Sharpened, soft-lead No. 2 pencils

2. A calculator that is approved for use on the test. This includes any four-function, scientific, or graphing calculator, except for the following:

   - Pocket organizers or PDAs

   - Handheld or laptop computers

   - Electronic writing pad or pen-input devices

   - Calculators built into any electronic communication device, such as a cell phone

   - Models with a QWERTY (typewriter) keypad (Calculators with letters on the keys are permitted as long as the keys are not arranged in a QWERTY keypad.)

   - Models that use paper tape, make noise, or have a power cord

     (For more detailed information on calculator usage, go to *http://www.collegeboard.com/student/testing/sat/testday/bring.html*.)

3. A watch (to pace yourself as you work through each test section)

If your program has ordered pre-assessment reports, you will receive these reports with your pre-assessment results. These reports will help you determine the areas in which you need the most study and enable you to target the skills that are necessary to lay a foundation for success in the course. You can then utilize the course time to prepare in those areas so that when you take the real test, you are ready to do your best. You will learn more about how to read and use the reports in the "How to Use the Official Pre-Assessment Reports" section on page 5.

HOW TO USE THE OFFICIAL PRE-ASSESSMENT REPORTS

Now that you have taken the pre-assessment, you and your teacher will use the results to recognize your individual strengths and weaknesses. Having this valuable information will allow you to create a realistic study plan for the course so that you can effectively manage your time.

You will receive the results of your official pre-assessment in the form of a Student Summary and Student Item Analysis. These reports provide details about your performance and will help you determine where to focus your efforts during the course by strategically targeting those skills that will help you to improve in your areas of weakness. Review the details of the sample Student Summary and Student Item Analysis below so that you are familiar with their contents.

Student Summary

Raw scores are calculated by adding one point for each item answered correctly and subtracting ¼ point for each multiple-choice item answered incorrectly. Results are converted and then reported on a scale of 200-800 points. No points are subtracted for omitted items.

The sum of the Critical Reading, Math, and Writing scores

According to the test-writers, a student's score usually falls within a range of 30-40 points above or below his or her actual ability. Colleges receive this range along with the actual test score.

Calculated by factoring together the writing score and the essay score. An overall scaled score is reported on a scale of 200-800 points.

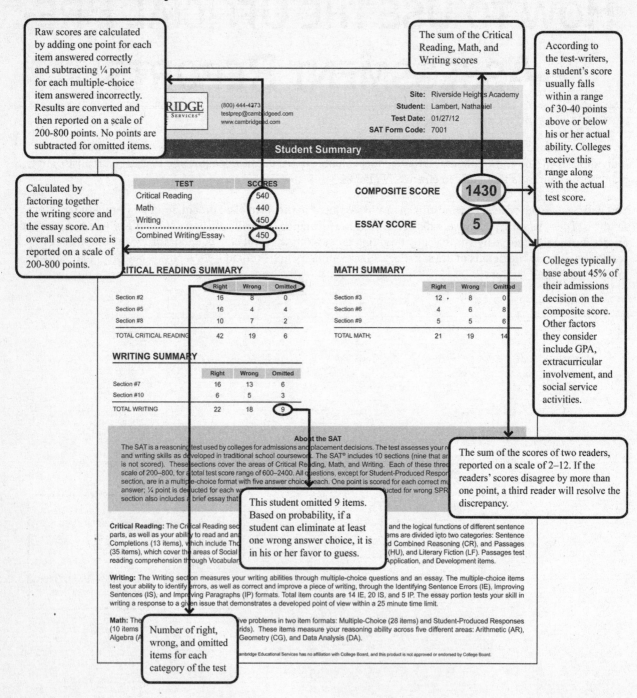

Site: Riverside Heights Academy
Student: Lambert, Nathaniel
Test Date: 01/27/12
SAT Form Code: 7001

(800) 444-4273
testprep@cambridgeed.com
www.cambridgeed.com

Student Summary

TEST	SCORES
Critical Reading	540
Math	440
Writing	450
Combined Writing/Essay	450

COMPOSITE SCORE — 1430

ESSAY SCORE — 5

CRITICAL READING SUMMARY

	Right	Wrong	Omitted
Section #2	16	8	0
Section #5	16	4	4
Section #8	10	7	2
TOTAL CRITICAL READING	42	19	6

MATH SUMMARY

	Right	Wrong	Omitted
Section #3	12	8	0
Section #6	4	6	8
Section #9	5	5	6
TOTAL MATH;	21	19	14

WRITING SUMMARY

	Right	Wrong	Omitted
Section #7	16	13	6
Section #10	6	5	3
TOTAL WRITING	22	18	9

Colleges typically base about 45% of their admissions decision on the composite score. Other factors they consider include GPA, extracurricular involvement, and social service activities.

The sum of the scores of two readers, reported on a scale of 2–12. If the readers' scores disagree by more than one point, a third reader will resolve the discrepancy.

This student omitted 9 items. Based on probability, if a student can eliminate at least one wrong answer choice, it is in his or her favor to guess.

Number of right, wrong, and omitted items for each category of the test

About the SAT

The SAT is a reasoning test used by colleges for admissions and placement decisions. The test assesses your re... and writing skills as developed in traditional school coursework. The SAT® includes 10 sections (nine that ar... is not scored). These sections cover the areas of Critical Reading, Math, and Writing. Each of these three... scale of 200–800, for a total test score range of 600–2400. All questions, except for Student-Produced Respon... section, are in a multiple-choice format with five answer choices each. One point is scored for each correct mu... answer; ¼ point is deducted for each w... ...ucted for wrong SPR... section also includes a brief essay that...

Critical Reading: The Critical Reading sec... ...and the logical functions of different sentence parts, as well as your ability to read and ana... ...ems are divided into two categories: Sentence Completions (13 items), which include Tho... ...d Combined Reasoning (CR), and Passages (35 items), which cover the areas of Social... ...(HU), and Literary Fiction (LF). Passages test reading comprehension through Vocabulary... ...Application, and Development items.

Writing: The Writing section measures your writing abilities through multiple-choice questions and an essay. The multiple-choice items test your ability to identify errors, as well as correct and improve a piece of writing, through the Identifying Sentence Errors (IE), Improving Sentences (IS), and Improving Paragraphs (IP) formats. Total item counts are 14 IE, 20 IS, and 5 IP. The essay portion tests your skill in writing a response to a given issue that demonstrates a developed point of view within a 25 minute time limit.

Math: The... ...ive problems in two item formats: Multiple-Choice (28 items) and Student-Produced Responses (10 items... ...rids). These items measure your reasoning ability across five different areas: Arithmetic (AR), Algebra (A... ...Geometry (CG), and Data Analysis (DA).

...ambridge Educational Services has no affiliation with College Board, and this product is not approved or endorsed by College Board.

Student Item Analysis

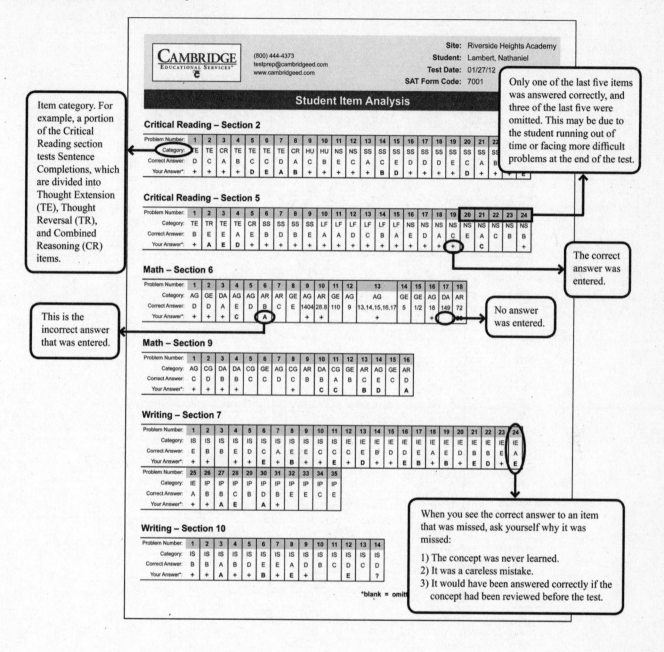

SETTING A TEST SCORE TARGET

As a high school student, the next significant hurdle for you in reaching your academic and career goals is applying to and getting accepted into a college or university. This section prepares you to take significant practical steps toward successful admission to the college or university of your choice.

Colleges and universities use a variety of approaches in selecting which students are accepted to attend their schools. To you as a student, the admissions process may seem complex ("Why must I complete all these forms, tests, and recommendations?"), the criteria for admission may appear mysterious ("Why did the university select student 'A' and not student 'B'?"), and the entire process may be emotionally frustrating ("Why haven't I heard back from college 'X,' why did I get denied by university 'Y,' and why was I placed on a waiting list by university 'Z'?").

To gain helpful strategies for applying to a college or university, read through this section carefully to see what we have learned over the years. We have advised tens of thousands of students, interviewed college admissions officers across the country, and attended annual college advisors' conferences. In the following pages, we have compiled the most valuable statistics and advice we have gleaned from a variety of sources.

This section is designed for a range of students—from those who are already actively working on their applications to those who are only starting to think about applying to college. Therefore, some of the points that are made are very general, while other points are very specific. You may already be familiar with some of the information, while other points and tips may surprise you. Whatever your current stage in the college application process, the following information and strategies will be helpful for both applying to and getting into the college of your choice.

Embrace the College Application Process as Truly Important

Applying for college is a really big deal! When you embark on the college application process, you take the important first step on a personal and career path that may influence the rest of your life. Decisions that you make about colleges at this stage of your life influence how much money you will make, where you may live, and what jobs will be available to you 5, 10, 20, 30, or even 40 years from now. Just imagine the different pathways that your life might follow depending on whether you do or do not get into college. Compare your career prospects depending on whether you are or are not accepted by your first-choice school. Or consider whether your life satisfaction might change if you can't enter the specialty program in which you have invested your dreams. **Be realistic, but don't be afraid to dream big.**

Now, this is not to say that not getting into a certain school or a specific program spells ultimate disaster. Not all high school students dream of becoming psychologists, engineers, or biochemists. And not every student needs to receive a degree in an advanced subject from one of the very best schools to achieve personal or career success. But to many high school students, success or failure in the admissions process does influence, to varying degrees, future potential. Indeed, you do not have to look far into the future to appreciate the effect that the admissions decision will have on your everyday life. The time, energy, and money that you invest in the college application process at this point may determine, at the very least, where you are likely to live for the next four years, how you will spend your time, and who will become your friends and acquaintances over those years.

Appreciate How Much the Application Process Might Cost You

You must also appreciate the financial commitment that you are making when applying to colleges and universities. With your high school years falling away, you can fully anticipate a future with challenging academic studies, new friendships, exciting vocational preparation, and a flood of life experiences as a college student. You will live among other students from all over the nation and the world, be introduced to cutting-edge research, experience enthusiasm for college athletics, learn from intelligent instructors and professors, and engage with a variety of new social networks.

But with the dream of attending college comes the sobering reality that a college degree comes with a financial price tag. You must understand the pieces of the financial puzzle and work diligently to piece that puzzle together so the financial system benefits you. While every college maintains a unique system for providing financial aid, most colleges use a basic pattern for establishing costs; determining a student's needs; and providing scholarships, grants, loans, and other financial aid. When you understand the basic system that colleges use to assist college students in paying for college, you can begin to proactively help yourself.

First of all, the fees that you pay to take the SAT test, if you request ten score reports to be sent to schools that interest you, could be over $100. The test itself costs $49, which includes four score reports sent to the schools of your choice; each additional score report is $10.50. Furthermore, colleges and universities charge an average of about $40 to apply.[1] Assuming that you apply to ten schools, you could easily spend over $400 on application fees. In addition, you could spend at least $100 on administrative details, such as document preparation, copying, and postage. When you add up to $400 for test preparation, you could easily be committed to a total of over $1,000 just to apply to colleges.

On top of the application expenses, you may need to send a non-refundable acceptance deposit by a certain deadline after you receive an acceptance notice. You may find yourself in the uncomfortable position of having to pay this deposit in order to ensure that you have reserved a spot at your chosen college or university even though you have not yet heard from some other schools. And **don't forget the cost of travelling to visit prospective schools.**

These initial sums of money, however, pale in comparison to the cost of tuition, which can exceed $40,000 each year at private institutions (see "Tuition at Selected Colleges and Universities" on the next page). When the expense of room and board for four years is taken into account, the expense to obtain your college degree could easily exceed $200,000. (Fortunately, there are many more affordable options, such as state colleges and universities.) The costs accompanying a college education can be broken down into the following major components. Your own personal needs may differ depending on your situation.

- *Tuition:* Tuition is the cost for providing instruction and includes the expenses for professors, classrooms, equipment, learning resources, and an array of support services needed to manage and maintain a college.

- *Room and Board:* Room and board is the expense charged for living in college housing and eating meals provided by the college food service. Students may also have options to provide their own room and board through other means (e.g., renting private housing).

- *Fees:* Fees are special costs assigned for services, activities, or projects that are not covered by tuition. These fees may cover technology enhancements, laboratory needs, student activities, health services, athletic attendance, special building projects, etc. At some colleges, tuition and fees are communicated as a single cost.

---

[1]U.S. News & World Report Education, "Top 10 Highest College Application Fees," http://www.usnews.com/education/articles/2011/09/14/top-10-highest-college-application-fees (accessed June 18, 2012).

- **_Transportation:_** Transportation costs incurred by students include traveling to or from college at the start or end of each semester, on breaks, or on holidays. Costs may also be realized when acquiring a private vehicle, insurance, maintenance, and parking. **Parking fees alone at some schools are exorbitant.**

- **_Books and Supplies:_** Books and supplies include required textbooks, class resources, materials, or equipment. The costs for books and supplies vary per class and academic program. Although you can certainly purchase books at your college or university's bookstore, **consider saving on book costs by obtaining ISBN numbers and ordering books online.**

- **_Incidentals:_** Other costs to you as a student might include various general living expenses, health insurance, clothing, recreation, etc.

Most colleges provide a breakdown of these expenses for prospective students. Financial aid departments can communicate a detailed estimate of these various costs.

TUITION AT SELECTED COLLEGES AND UNIVERSITIES
(Expenses only—does not include Room and Board)*

Oberlin College (OH)	$43,210
Williams College (MA)	$43,190
Duke University (NC)	$41,958
Indiana University (Bloomington)	$9,028 in-state; $27,689 out-of-state
University of Georgia	$9,472 in-state; $27,682 out-of-state

*U.S. News & World Report, "Best Colleges 2012," http://colleges.usnews.rankingsandreviews.com/best-colleges (accessed June 18, 2012).

Do not let these numbers frighten you. We are not trying to dissuade you from pursuing a college or university degree. In fact, we applaud students who accept the challenge of obtaining a college or university education. We are simply trying to dramatize a point—namely, that the decision to apply to college has significant financial implications for you as an individual and perhaps for your family. But for many, the investment in preparing for, applying to, and studying at a college or university will be rewarded by four years of rich college experiences, deep new learning, and a great start on a rewarding career path.

Consider Your Academic, Career, and Personal Goals

REFLECTION
On a separate sheet of paper, write down some thoughts about what academic, career, and personal successes you'd like to achieve in the next 20 years of your life. Include the salary you would like to earn in the next 10 or 20 years. (Use the chart on the following page as a point of reference.) List some ways that getting into a college or university of your choice might help you achieve these academic, career, and personal goals.

The following chart displays a range of salaries (high, average, low) for several occupations[2].

Occupation	OCCUPATION/SALARY RANGES (in USD/year)		
	25th Percentile	Median	75th Percentile
Physician (Family and General Practitioners)	$125,800	$163,510	>$166,400
Lawyer	$75,200	$112,760	$165,470
Marketing Manager	$80,900	$112,800	$151,260
Human Resources Manager	$77,240	$99,180	$130,090
Electrical Engineer	$66,880	$84,540	$105,860
Registered Nurse	$52,980	$64,690	$79,020
Technical Writer	$47,970	$63,280	$81,110
Accountant	$47,990	$61,690	$81,290
Librarian	$43,390	$54,500	$67,860
Police Patrol Officer	$40,830	$53,540	$69,070
Secondary School Teacher	$42,670	$53,230	$67,210
Graphic Designer	$33,200	$43,500	$58,600
Administrative Assistant	$24,710	$30,830	$38,160
Customer Service Representative	$24,150	$30,460	$38,750
Construction Laborer	$22,730	$29,280	$39,850

Note that higher-paying occupations often require a college or university degree. Recent U.S. Census Bureau information indicates that individuals with a bachelor's degree earn on average almost twice as much annually as high school graduates without further education[3]. **Be aware that job location also plays a major role in determining salary.** For additional salary information, visit www.salary.com or www.payscale.com.

Determine a Path toward Paying for College

Colleges expect students to pay for college using the following basic formula:

College Payment = Family Portion + Student Portion + College Aid + Federal Student Aid + State Student Aid

---

[2]Bureau of Labor Statistics, "National Cross-Industry Estimates," May 2010, United States Department of Labor, http://www.bls.gov/oes/oes_dl.htm (accessed June 18, 2012).

[3]Weinberg, Daniel H, "Evidence From Census 2000 About Earnings by Detailed Occupation for Men and Women," *Census 2000 Special Reports* CENSR-15 (May 2004): 3, http://www.census.gov/prod/2004pubs/censr-15.pdf (accessed June 21, 2012).

And here is a breakdown of its components:

- **Family Portion:** The Free Application for Federal Student Aid (FAFSA) form determines each student's "Expected Family Contribution." In general, this is a calculation of how much the government estimates that a parent or parents will pay. Among other factors, the "Expected Family Contribution" takes into consideration marital status, income levels, number of family members who will attend college or career school during the year, and current financial assets.

- **Student Portion:** A student's portion is established through a percentage calculated from his or her savings from work, gifts, or other sources.

- **College Aid:** Colleges choose to award grants, scholarships, waivers, assistantships, and work-study funding through their own endowments and financial resources. Colleges have various formulas to determine aid.

- **Federal Student Aid:** The federal government provides a number of resources for college students. Such federal student aid typically comes through grants, work-study, and loans. According to the U.S. Department of Education[4], the federal government provides more than $150 billion in these types of student aid every year to nearly 14 million students. When received from the federal government, financial aid can be used by eligible students not only for tuition, fees, books, supplies, and transportation, but also for such items as dependent child-care expenses.

- **State Student Aid:** States may offer additional financial aid to their legal residents through grants or loans. Each state varies in the type and amounts of aid offered.

The following terms often appear in the context of financial aid:

- **Grants:** Grants do not have to be repaid and are generally awarded based on financial need demonstrated by the family and/or student.

- **Scholarships:** Scholarships do not have to be repaid and are presented based on a variety of factors, including, but not limited to, accomplishments in academics, athletics, or extracurricular activities; musical or artistic talent; or leadership.

- **Loans:** Loans are funds used for education that are repaid to the lending institution, usually with interest. A "Stafford Loan" is administered by the government.

- **Employment:** College students can earn funds by working in exchange for wages. Work-study programs may be subsidized by colleges or by governmental agencies.

Here are some quick tips to assist your search for financial aid:

- Thoroughly explore the FAFSA website immediately. The website (www.fafsa.ed.gov) contains valuable information about funding sources for college and university. See www.fafsa4caster.ed.gov to anticipate aid levels even if you are not yet applying to schools. Help in understanding the federal aid application process is also available at 1-800-4-FED-AID. **Completing the FAFSA is also a requirement for many state-funded programs.**

- Determine and maintain your eligibility for federal financial aid, as well as state-sponsored college aid programs. Read thoroughly the FAFSA (or state) guidelines to determine and maintain your eligibility.

---

[4]U.S. Department of Education, Federal Student Aid, Student Experience Group *Funding Education Beyond High School: The Guide to Federal Student Aid 2011–12*, Washington, D.C., 2010.
http://studentaid.ed.gov/students/attachments/siteresources/Funding_Education_Beyond_HS_2011-12.pdf (accessed June 18, 2012).

Among other factors, eligibility is based on the following general criteria: having a high school diploma, GED, or equivalent; being a U.S. citizen or eligible noncitizen; possessing a valid Social Security number; and complying with Selective Service registration. Review all eligibility requirements in full on the FAFSA website.

- Submit your FAFSA application and paperwork according to necessary deadlines. There are no exceptions offered by the federal government for the FAFSA application dates and deadlines. Note that there are both federal and state deadlines; be sure to comply with both. Go to www.fafsa.ed.gov to verify the submission schedule for federal aid.

- Check with your high school counselor about financial aid funded by the state in which you claim legal residency. Generally, states maintain websites that provide information about state-funded financial aid.

- Start early to search for available scholarships. Talk to your high school counseling office about scholarship options. Ask a variety of college financial aid offices for a list of scholarships or scholarship websites that they recommend. At https://studentaid2.ed.gov/getmoney/scholarship/v3browse.asp, there is a searchable index of available scholarships. Remember to search for any and all possible scholarships for which you might apply. A wide variety of scholarships are granted that target particular groups of students. The following are some general categories which you might consider when searching for a more targeted scholarship (note that this is not an exhaustive list): ethnicity, academic performance level, athletic ability, civic group affiliation, parents' employers, religious affiliation, political connection, local or regional area, gender, community service, and special talent or ability.

- Communicate and negotiate with colleges for financial aid. Directly ask about other financial aid sources if you need them. Be assertive about your own needs. Remember that college-based financial aid counselors deal with thousands of students in a short period of time, so assert yourself, voice your needs, and be persistent. If there are special circumstances in your family that affect your ability to pay for college, clearly articulate those. Depending on your need, move up the organizational chain of command to negotiate for more scholarship and grant money. You may also benefit from talking to multiple colleges.

- Remember that student loans, whether they come from the federal government, state government, or private financial institutions, must ultimately be repaid. Always read repayment information carefully when applying for student loans.

- All colleges address student financial needs and financial aid differently. As with all information in this section, check directly with each school you are considering to obtain unique and necessary information, paperwork, and deadlines for securing financial aid and scholarships.

Solve the Puzzle of How and Why Colleges Select Students for Admission

During the application process, you may for a time feel like a lab specimen placed under a microscope. Why do colleges and universities invest so much time and energy in assessing each and every student who applies? Why do schools ask so many questions, need transcripts and test scores, and require references? Why does it matter to a college or university which students are accepted to study in its programs? Why does it seem some schools open wide their doors for almost anyone to attend while others only allow a select few students to study at their institution? Some answers to these questions are simple, but others are more complex.

First, colleges and universities are selective because of their own financial needs. A college or university has to be run in the same way as any other business. It has paid employees, it owns or rents property, it operates a library, it buys furniture and office equipment, it pays utility bills, etc. As a student, your tuition and fees pay for many of these expenses. A college or university, therefore, is absolutely dependent upon a steady flow of tuition income. At the same time, most colleges and universities must limit the number of students they can allow to attend. This limit may be due to the amount of total spaces available for student housing, the quantity of classrooms on hand, or even the number of students that its board of directors allows based on various college rules and regulations. So, admissions directors make decisions about whether you will be accepted in the context of budgetary constraints. The college needs you as a student to start paying tuition and to continue paying tuition (or to have someone else—parents, a scholarship, state or federal aid, etc.—pay tuition). A college simply cannot afford to have large numbers of students dropping out of school. Therefore, one of the primary concerns of a college admissions officer is to ensure that those applicants who are accepted are committed to completing a course of study.

Second, schools worry about their reputations and how potential students might help or hinder that reputation. Colleges and universities desire future alumni who will make their school look good to others. It should not be surprising to learn that as an applicant, if you show considerable professional promise, you will be considered more favorably than others. A school that graduates successful B.A. and B.S. students gets a reputation for being a good school, and such a reputation tends to attract more highly qualified applicants.

Third, colleges and universities also want to be socially responsible to the needs of individuals and the wider society. They meet this responsibility in some fairly obvious ways, such as by actively seeking applicants from groups who are under-represented in the professional community and by establishing programs to train professionals for positions of special need.

Regardless of the various filters that schools use to evaluate potential students, the admissions process should benefit both the student and the college. The process is ideally designed to create a positive mutual relationship between students and institutions. Unfortunately, for decades, there have been more interested students than available spots at certain accredited colleges and universities. For a great number of schools, especially in specialty programs, there are actually far more applicants than available seats. Given the mismatch between the number of available seats and the number of applicants, the application process has turned into a rigorous competition.

TOP RANKED SCHOOLS AND PERCENTAGE OF APPLICANTS ACCEPTED (FALL 2010)*

Harvard University	7%	University of Pennsylvania	14%
Princeton University	9%	California Institute of Technology	13%
Yale University	8%	Massachusetts Institute of Technology	10%
Columbia University	10%	Dartmouth College	12%
Stanford University	7%	Duke University	16%

*U.S. News & World Report, "Best Colleges 2011," http://colleges.usnews.rankingsandreviews.com/best-colleges/rankings/national-universities/data (accessed June 18, 2012).

With the strategies provided in this section, you will have the information to create a solid college application—that is, an application that will give a college an affirmative reason for accepting you. Each college and university is unique in its admissions criteria. No single source of information (not even this textbook) can guarantee your acceptance to the college or university of your choice. But solid information regarding the process is helpful. In addition to this student textbook, you may also want to consider some other sources. For general information about the accredited colleges in the United States, you should refer to the *College Handbook*. This book can be found in either your school's library or your local bookstore. The *College Handbook* is published by the College Board and contains summaries of more than 3,800 colleges, universities, and technical schools. Use this handbook for general guidance. Additionally, check out the website or request an information packet from each school in which you have even a passing interest. Read the information carefully; it will provide listings of faculty members and their qualifications, descriptions of any special programs, information about student activities and campus life, financial aid information, and much more. Email or call the admissions department if you desire additional information or have other questions.

REFLECTION

A. On a separate piece of paper, create a list of ten colleges or universities to which you might consider applying.

B. Put a star next to each college or university that you consider to be selective (accepts fewer students than apply—use the *College Handbook* for help in this process).

C. Place a check mark next to those colleges or universities that you have a strong desire to attend. Call or email for more information about their admissions and application process.

Making the Admissions Process Work for You

There is no one single admissions process used by every college and university. Rather, each institution has its own customized admissions process, which differs from that of every other college in the country.

There are approximately 2,300 four-year colleges and universities in the U.S. We are unable to talk about the exact details of the admissions process for every school, not only because of the sheer number of institutions but because colleges and universities regard the mechanics of the decision-making process as a highly sensitive, even secretive, matter. As a result, they don't share the details of that process with outsiders. We can, however, help clarify this fuzzy process with a few important generalizations. By researching college and university admissions processes, we have discovered some patterns you can expect. You can also help yourself by researching the specific admissions policies and statistics of the schools in which you are interested. In any event, you are ultimately incapable of exercising much control over the way a college makes its decision. The good news, as you will see, is that you do not need "inside" information to create an effective application.

So, how do colleges or universities select which applicants to accept for enrollment? As a general practice, university personnel make the decision based on some combination of the following:

SELECTION FOR ADMISSION

+ NUMERIC EDUCATIONAL DATA
  (GPA, SAT test score, Class Rank)

+ PERSONAL ACHIEVEMENTS (academic and non-academic)
  (Extracurricular Activities, Athletics, Clubs, Community Service, Jobs, etc.)

+ REFERENCES FROM KEY PEOPLE
  (Teachers, Coaches, Advisors, Administrators, Employers, Clergy, etc.)

+ SPECIAL STATUS CHARACTERISTICS
  (Unique Talents, Abilities, Geographical Location, Ethnicity, Socioeconomic Status, State Residency, Family Who Are Alumni, etc.)

+ GOALS AND ASPIRATIONS
  (Career Goals, Dreams, or Ambitions Provided Through Personal Statement)

Don't undervalue the importance of your extracurricular activities, especially community service initiatives, in the application process. Currently, the trend indicates that schools are searching for students who have not only achieved academic success but who have balanced school with other interests and activities that have helped them become well-rounded individuals. Involvement in community service, clubs, athletics, the arts, or unique employment may help differentiate you from other students with equivalent SAT test scores and GPA.

Who ultimately makes the decision to accept you as a student? Again, colleges and universities answer this question differently. Faculty committees may be required to gather and make decisions by majority vote or unanimous agreement before an applicant is accepted. A professional admissions officer or a Dean of Admissions may make the decisions. A committee of members drawn from both administration and faculty may choose who receives an acceptance letter. Other students may even have some input into the decisions. However, we encourage you not to dwell on these different possibilities. This particular factor—who makes the decision to accept your application—is completely out of your control. Instead, focus your time and energy on what you *can* control.

In order to successfully compete with your peers, you must portray yourself as an attractive candidate; you must convince those making the admissions decision that you will help them satisfy their need for a qualified and unique student body. This persuasive approach to acceptance must be a guiding force as you create your application.

Because each college and university has a unique admissions process and criteria, it is important that you communicate directly with an admissions counselor at each school to which you are applying. For example, some public universities base most of the admissions decision on an applicant's grades, with the other factors being considered primarily for students who are applying for scholarships. Discuss the specifics of how the school weighs the factors listed above and what you can do to help yourself in the process.

REFLECTION

Your SAT test score and GPA are important (see the next section) but so are other life experiences.

On a separate sheet of paper, create a list of fifteen unique experiences you have had, personal qualities that you exhibit, or accomplishments you have achieved (awards, community service projects, unique international travel, employment promotions, musical or artistic accomplishments, student government or volunteer positions, etc.)

Determine to Elevate Your SAT Test Score and Your GPA

Despite the variety of formal admissions selection processes, one generalization is significant to remember:

> *"Every college relies to some extent on an applicant's grade point average (GPA) and standardized test score, but there are few (if any) colleges that rely solely on these quantitative factors."*

This statement contains two important ideas; let us examine each of them.

First of all, most colleges do use a student's grade point average and SAT test score to help determine his or her viability as a future student. Schools do differ, though, on how they rely on these numbers. Many schools use a formula that blends the two together into what is called an index. This formula is designed to weigh the two numbers so that they give admissions officers some idea of how applicants stack up against each other.

How each college uses this type of index varies from school to school. Some schools have a fairly mechanical admissions process that places great emphasis on the index or some variation on its form. For example, a school may choose to set a minimum index below which applications receive little or no consideration. Such schools may also have a second, higher minimum that triggers an automatic acceptance. In this case, students with indices that exceed the higher minimum are accepted unless there is some glaring weakness in the application that otherwise disqualifies them. (As you prepare to apply, it would be helpful to research the SAT test score ranges of students who are typically accepted at the institutions with which you have an interest. This will help you determine whether you are already a good fit for these schools as far as test scores are concerned or whether you need to study harder in order to elevate your SAT test score.) On the other hand, there are schools that claim to minimize the importance of the SAT test and the GPA. They claim that the SAT test score is the very last factor at which they look when making decisions. Such schools tend to have a very flexible admissions process.

Most schools fall between the two ends of the spectrum. Typically, schools use the test scores and grades as a screening device to determine how much attention will be given to an application. Applications with very low test scores and grades will receive little attention. The schools reason that unless there is something obvious and compelling in the application to offset the low numbers, the applicant should be rejected. Applications with very high test scores and grades will also receive little attention. The reasoning is that unless there is something obvious and compelling in the application to reject the applicant, he or she should be accepted. Based on this theory, the applications with average test scores and grades will receive the greatest attention. These applications are provided by candidates who are at least competitive enough for that particular school but who do not command an automatic acceptance. It is in this pool of candidates that competition is the most intense.

The following table illustrates what happens at most colleges. The fractions represent the total number of accepted applicants divided by the total number of applicants.

GPA	SAT TEST SCORE (Percentile)			
	61–70%	71–80%	81–90%	91–100%
3.75+	$\frac{2}{19}$	$\frac{49}{101}$	$\frac{102}{116}$	$\frac{72}{79}$
3.50–3.74	$\frac{6}{112}$	$\frac{75}{275}$	$\frac{301}{361}$	$\frac{120}{129}$
<3.49	$\frac{10}{160}$	$\frac{90}{601}$	$\frac{375}{666}$	$\frac{201}{250}$

The twelve categories in the table show how this particular college responded to applications with certain SAT test scores (shown in percentile terms) and GPAs. The category in the upper right-hand corner represents candidates who scored above the 90th percentile with GPAs above 3.75. The table shows that 72 of the 79 applicants who satisfy these conditions were accepted and seven were rejected.

What is obvious from the table is that some candidates with higher numbers were rejected in favor of candidates with lower numbers. For example, of those candidates with scores between the 81st and 90th percentiles, 74 more candidates were accepted with a GPA below 3.50 than were accepted with a GPA between 3.50 and 3.74.

Why would a college reject an applicant with higher numbers for one with lower numbers? The answer lies in our analysis of the admissions process. Apparently, there were factors in the applications of those who were accepted that suggested to the admissions committee that such applicants would better meet the social and economic goals of the institution. Those factors are unquantifiable—motivation, commitment, leadership, experience, and so on.

As you prepare your applications, you may already, of course, be saddled with your GPA and your SAT test score. Aside from hard work, there is nothing that you can do to change those factors. If you still have an opportunity, work hard to elevate your GPA. Besides that, the only remaining control you will have over your application will be those unquantifiable factors, and we will advise you on how to maximize their impact.

Send in Your Applications at the Right Time

There is one final point about the mechanics of the application process that you must understand: early and rolling admissions. Early admissions and rolling admissions are devices used by many colleges to regulate the release of acceptance notifications to potential students.

A typical college application season opens in October and closes in May or June. Applications from students are received throughout this season, and decisions are made on an ongoing basis with the intent of targeting an entering class. Based on its admissions history, a college will estimate the expected range of SAT test scores and GPAs of the students that it will accept in the upcoming year. Then, as it receives applications (e.g., on a monthly basis for rolling admissions or by a specific deadline for early admissions), the college or university will act on each application accordingly. Students with very strong applications compared with the target group receive acceptances; students with weak applications receive rejections. Applications in the middle may be carried over, and the applicants will receive either an application pending notification—also known as a deferral notice—or no notification at all.

The early or rolling admissions process has advantages for both the college and the applicant. From the applicant's point of view, the earlier you know the decision about an application, the better. Once you know whether you have been accepted or rejected, you can begin to make additional important decisions about your future. After you've received official notification of your admission into a school and decided to accept that offer, you can move forward in acquiring scholarships and loans, securing housing, making travel plans, looking for student employment opportunities, and scheduling personal trips and opportunities prior to leaving for college. Some students accept an early application simply to relieve the anxiety of waiting to hear from other schools. From the college's point of view, the configuration of the entering class begins to take shape as early as possible, allowing the university time for establishing the budget, hiring new faculty or instructors, arranging for student housing needs, and planning for student orientation.

If the college or university has an early decision or early action plan, students may apply earlier and receive the college's admissions decision before the typical spring notification date. If students choose to apply early using one of these plans, they should be aware that early decision plans (but not early action plans) are binding and they may be required to withdraw their other applications, should they be accepted. Some plans also only allow students to apply for early decision or early action at one school.

Whether you are following an early decision or early action plan or simply applying early during the traditional admissions season, be aware of the advantages of applying as soon as possible. Obviously, for most schools there are more seats available earlier in the admissions season rather than later. We do not mean to imply that you will be rejected if you apply late in the season. In fact, it is impossible to exactly quantify the advantage that earlier applications may have over later applications. Still, if you want to maximize your chances of acceptance, apply early. Also, be aware that if you are attempting to acquire a special scholarship for a college or university, the date of admissions application and notification might be tied directly to that scholarship. You should read all scholarship information carefully with this in mind.

REFLECTION
From the list of colleges that you created earlier, list those schools that allow for early or rolling admissions. You may need to contact the schools directly to determine this.

Utilize a Sophisticated Approach to Determine Where to Send Applications

Given the time, energy, and financial commitment that you will be making to apply to schools, one of the most obvious questions in your mind will be, "Where should I apply?" You should apply to a group of schools that, given your financial resources, will maximize your chances of gaining admission to the schools that will best help you reach your future goals.

To apply to a college, you must send in a non-refundable application fee. Essentially, you are gambling with your money. You pay the application fee in advance of knowing whether you will win or lose (gain admission or not). So, hedge your bets. In such a "gambling" situation, a person has several choices. Some options will be long shots; other options will be almost sure things; and still other options will lie somewhere in between these two extremes. The long shots will pay handsome dividends, and the sure things will pay a reasonable return. The other options will obviously pay somewhere in between.

Given these considerations, you should select two or perhaps three "long shot" schools. As the term "long shot" implies, the odds of your being accepted to these schools are not extremely high, but the potential payoff justifies the gamble. These may be highly selective schools or ones that typically require SAT test scores and GPAs above what you have earned. On the other extreme, you should also select one or two "sure thing" schools. In this case, you may have to apply to either a school in your geographical area that does not enjoy a reputation as a standout school, a school that is located in another part of the country but is looking for students with your characteristics, or a smaller school currently in need of students. Given that you've now gambled on a few "long shot" schools and a few "sure thing" schools, the rest of your applications should go to your "good bet" schools—schools for which the chances for acceptance are 40 to 75 percent.

Now, let us assume that you have the resources to apply to ten schools and that you have both an above average GPA and an above average SAT test score. Depending on your exact GPA and SAT test numbers, you may very well have a chance at one of the top colleges. But those colleges are your "long shot" schools (colleges that are very selective). You are almost a "sure thing" at many schools (colleges that are not selective), and there is a long list of schools in the middle (colleges that are selective) at which your application will likely receive serious consideration but is not guaranteed for acceptance.

This strategy of "stacking" your applications will maximize your chances of acceptance at one of your desired schools, while minimizing your chances of not getting into any school at all. Of course, the details of this strategy will be unique for you as an individual with distinct aspirations. For students who are lucky enough to have a high GPA and a top SAT test score, the middle- and bottom-tier schools collapse into a single tier. At the other extreme, those students who have a GPA and SAT test score that are below what most schools accept will have to work with the second and third tiers.

As you prepare to implement this strategy, make a realistic assessment of your chances. Candidates unfortunately tend to overestimate the importance of what they believe to be their own interesting or unique factors. For example, we often hear candidates who make such statements as, "Well sure my GPA is a little low, but I had to work part-time while I was in school," and "I know my SAT test score is not that good, but I was a member of the high school Student Council." These points are valid and are usually taken into consideration by admissions officers. However, the most important concern is how much weight these points will be given since such statements are true of most everyone who is applying to college. For example, if you are thinking of applying to a program that requires an average GPA of 3.8 and an average SAT test score in the 90th percentile and you do not meet these requirements, then it will be difficult for you to obtain admission to that program unless your application has some other strikingly unique characteristics.

As you consider where to apply, you will probably want to know which undergraduate schools are the best in the country. Since there is no single criterion for "best school" that would be accepted by everyone, it is arguable whether this classification can be made objectively. However, even though no unequivocal classification can be made, it is possible to make an approximation as to the best schools in the nation. The "U.S. News & World Report" 2012 rankings[5] list the top 25 national universities and top 25 national liberal arts colleges. (Entries on the list may change each year, as may the rankings. This particular report is published annually, so check out the most recent one available.)

TOP 25 NATIONAL UNIVERSITIES

1. Harvard University (MA)
1. Princeton University (NJ)
3. Yale University (CT)
4. Columbia University (NY)
5. California Institute of Technology
5. Massachusetts Institute of Technology
5. Stanford University (CA)
5. University of Chicago (IL)
5. University of Pennsylvania
10. Duke University (NC)
11. Dartmouth College (NH)
12. Northwestern University (IL)
13. Johns Hopkins University (MD)
14. Washington University in St. Louis (MO)
15. Brown University (RI)
15. Cornell University (NY)
17. Rice University (TX)
17. Vanderbilt University (TN)
19. University of Notre Dame (IN)
20. Emory University (GA)
21. University of California—Berkeley
22. Georgetown University (DC)
23. Carnegie Mellon University (PA)
23. University of Southern California
25. University of California—Los Angeles

TOP 25 NATIONAL LIBERAL ARTS COLLEGES

1. Williams College (MA)
2. Amherst College (MA)
3. Swarthmore College (PA)
4. Pomona College (CA)
5. Middlebury College (VT)
6. Bowdoin College (ME)
6. Carleton College (MN)
6. Wellesley College (MA)
9. Claremont McKenna College (CA)
10. Haverford College (PA)
11. Davidson College (NC)
12. Washington and Lee University (VA)
12. Wesleyan University (CT)
14. U.S. Military Academy (NY)
14. U.S. Naval Academy (MD)
14. Vassar College (NY)
17. Hamilton College (NY)
18. Harvey Mudd College (CA)
19. Grinnell College (IA)
19. Smith College (MA)
21. Bates College (ME)
21. Colby College (ME)
21. Colgate University (NY)
24. Oberlin College (OH)
25. Bryn Mawr College (PA)

[5]U.S. News & World Report. "Best Colleges 2012," http://colleges.usnews.rankingsandreviews.com/best-colleges (accessed June 18, 2012).

Define Your SAT Test Target Score

Now that you have researched the schools you are interested in and have some idea of what schools qualify as "long shots," "sure things," and "good bets" for you, you have a better idea of the SAT score that you need to shoot for. Review the following ways of making sure you know where you stand, and then complete the action steps.

Test

Your first step is to take the official SAT pre-assessment that is part of your Cambridge course. After you take this test, you will receive a score report that gives you a very accurate measure of where you stand. To begin the process of setting a test score goal, fill in your pre-test scores below:

TEST SECTION	SCORE
Critical Reading	
Math	
Writing	
Essay	
Composite	

As you use these scores to make a plan for improvement throughout this course, remember that if you had a bad test day (for example, if you were ill or distracted by personal problems), your scores may not be reflective of your true abilities. Be sure to take this into account as you set a goal for your post-test and your real SAT.

Research

Now, make a list of schools that you are interested in attending and research the average scores and GPAs of admitted students so that you can get an idea of how you stack up. Fill in the score that you estimate you need for each school. If you are interested in applying for scholarships, make sure you also research the scores each school requires for scholarship eligibility.

School: _____	Average SAT Score of Admitted Students:	_____
	Average GPA of Admitted Students:	_____
	Scholarship Score Requirement:	_____
	Estimated SAT Score Needed:	_____
	Additional Points Needed:	_____
School: _____	Average SAT Score of Admitted Students:	_____
	Average GPA of Admitted Students:	_____
	Scholarship Score Requirement:	_____
	Estimated SAT Score Needed:	_____
	Additional Points Needed:	_____
School: _____	Average SAT Score of Admitted Students:	_____
	Average GPA of Admitted Students:	_____
	Scholarship Score Requirement:	_____
	Estimated SAT Score Needed:	_____
	Additional Points Needed:	_____
School: _____	Average SAT Score of Admitted Students:	_____
	Average GPA of Admitted Students:	_____
	Scholarship Score Requirement:	_____
	Estimated SAT Score Needed:	_____
	Additional Points Needed:	_____
School: _____	Average SAT Score of Admitted Students:	_____
	Average GPA of Admitted Students:	_____
	Scholarship Score Requirement:	_____
	Estimated SAT Score Needed:	_____
	Additional Points Needed:	_____

Once you have this chart filled in for several schools, you should have a good idea of the difference between your pre-test score and the score you will need to get into your schools of interest. Fill in this information below:

| Pre-Test Date: _____ | Score: _____ |

Action

How do you translate these numbers into an action plan? See your Student Summary report. The second page of the report, the item analysis, gives you valuable information for every question on the pre-test. You'll see your answer, the correct answer, and the type of question that was asked. With a little analysis, you can see exactly where your weaknesses are and make a plan to address them. The "How to Use the Official Pre-Assessment Reports" section earlier in this book gives you visual examples and specific ideas on using the score report to maximum advantage in targeting a higher score. Also, make sure to review the "Planning a Course Schedule" section on page 37.

OVERCOMING TEST ANXIETY

Test anxiety can manifest itself in various forms—from the common occurrences of "butterflies" in the stomach, mild sweating, or nervous laughter, to the more extreme occurrences of overwhelming fear, anxiety attacks, and unmanageable worry. It is quite normal for students to experience some mild anxiety before or during testing without being greatly affected. On the other hand, more intense worry, fear, or tension can prevent students from performing successfully on standardized tests. Some experts who study human performance propose that light stress may actually help to focus a person's concentration on the task at hand. However, stress that reaches beyond minimum levels and remains for a long period of time can block a student's ability to quickly recall facts, remember strategies, analyze complex problems, and creatively approach difficult items. When taking a test, being calm and collected promotes clear and logical thinking. The following strategies provide practical hints and methods to help alleviate debilitating test anxiety.

Plan—Have a Study Plan and Stick to It

Putting off important test review assignments until the last minute naturally causes high stress for anyone who is seriously anxious about test day. Even the brightest student experiences nervousness when he or she walks into a test site without feeling ready. Prepared test-takers are more relaxed, confident, and focused, so you should begin to review materials earlier rather than later in order to reduce anxiety.

Be warned that it is almost impossible to successfully cram for standardized tests. Waiting until the day or week before the test to begin studying will only serve to elevate your anxiety level. While cramming at the last minute may have worked for you in the past with quizzes or less comprehensive tests, it will not work to prepare you for long, comprehensive, standardized tests. Such comprehensive tests require extended and intensive study methods. Trying to cram will leave you feeling frustrated, unprepared, overwhelmed, and nervous about the pending test day.

So, the key to combating test anxiety is to plan ahead so that you are not unprepared. Do not procrastinate—develop a study plan, start early, and stick to it. A study plan is a written set of daily goals that will help you track the content and the sequence of your test review. This plan will help you tell yourself what, when, where, and how much you will study. (See the "Overall Time Management" section on page 33 for a further description of how to organize your time effectively.)

By planning your work and working your plan, you can alleviate any unnecessary anxiety. Here are some tips on how to produce your study plan:

Record a Plan on Paper

A written study plan is more concrete and dependable than one that simply rattles around in your head. So, you should use a piece of paper and a pencil to write out a plan for reviewing all of the materials that are necessary to succeed on the test. Record important items and dates on your calendar (Overall Time Management), and post the study plan in a place where you will see it often (e.g., your bedroom door or your refrigerator). When you accomplish one of the goals on your plan (e.g., taking a timed practice exam or reviewing a certain number of items), designate its completion with a checkmark. This system of recording your goals will give you a sense of achievement.

Break the Test into Pieces

Standardized tests are segmented into multiple sections according to subject-area. However, you should not try to learn all of the material related to a particular subject-area in one sitting. The subject matter that is covered is far too broad to learn in a few short minutes, so you should not try to learn every test strategy at once or review the whole test in one day. Instead, you should break the test into smaller portions and then study a portion until you are confident that you can move on to another. You should also vary the sections that you study in order to ward off boredom. For example, on Monday, study a math section, and on Tuesday, study a reading section.

In addition to breaking the test into smaller portions, you should always remember to review sections that you have already studied. This review will keep all of the sections fresh in your mind for test day. No two students are capable of learning at an identical rate. Some students can learn huge chunks of information at once, while other students need to review smaller amounts of information over a greater period of time. Determine the amount of material that you can comfortably and adequately cover in one day; then, attack that amount of material on each day.

For most students, the study plan is determined by the class schedule. The class schedule and sequence have been developed to help you improve your test score. So, follow the guidance of your class instructor and mold your personal study plan around the schedule.

Do Some Studying or Preparation Every Day

Yes. It is very important that you study something every single day. Once you get the "study snowball" rolling, the momentum will help you overcome the temptation to quit. Be consistent. It is far better to study sixty minutes per day for seven straight days than to study seven straight hours only once per week.

Study at the Same Time and Place

Find somewhere quiet to study, where there are few distractions, the lighting is good, and you feel comfortable. Avoid studying in bed or in a lounge chair; simulate the test conditions by studying at a desk or table. Turn off the television or the radio. Shut down the computer, unless of course you are using it as a study tool. Give yourself uninterrupted quality time to study. Find a consistent time when you can study and lock it into your schedule. Do not let yourself off the hook. Study each day at the same time and place so that you can become accustomed to your work environment.

Set Goals and Reward Yourself

Set a weekly goal for the amount of time that you will study and the amount of material that you will review. When you meet these weekly goals, reward yourself. Offer yourself special incentives that will motivate you to reach your next goal.

Find a Study Partner or Someone to Hold You Accountable for Your Progress

There really is strength in numbers. Find at least one person who will help you stay on course with your goals. Have this person ask you, every few days, whether or not you are sticking to your plan. Consider finding a "study buddy." Push each other to set and reach high test preparation goals.

Early and consistent test preparation means that you will walk calmly and confidently into the testing center on test day, knowing that you have done your very best to prepare for the test.

Prepare Positively—Replace Anxiety with Positivity

Positive thinking helps overcome test anxiety. For years, psychologists have studied how attitudes affect and alter achievement. These studies suggest that students with positive attitudes consistently score higher than students with negative attitudes.

Here are some practical ways to create a positive mindset:

Talk Positively to Yourself

Success comes in a "can," not a "cannot." So, learn to think positively by mentally replacing "cannot" with "can." Negative statements such as, "I will never pass this test," "I know I can't get this," or "I'm not smart enough to get a good score," are counterproductive, and they hinder both studying and the test-taking process. In order to eliminate negative thoughts, you must first take note of them when they occur and then take steps to remove them from your mind. As soon as you recognize a negative thought, immediately replace it with a positive thought. It is quite easy. Whenever you hear phrases such as "I can't do this" or "I'm not smart enough," think to yourself, "I *can* do this," "I *will* understand this," or "I *am* smart enough." Furthermore, as you walk into the classroom on the day of the test, repeatedly say to yourself, "I have studied, I will do my best, and I will succeed."

Think Positively About Yourself

Think positively with the help of visualization. Try this: while in a relaxed mood, close your eyes and envision yourself walking into the test room, perfectly calm and confident. Now, imagine yourself taking each section of the test without any difficulty and with great calmness. See yourself answering the items quickly and correctly. Watch yourself exiting the test area with confidence because you know that you performed extremely well. With these visualization techniques, you can mentally and emotionally practice taking the test in a confident and calm manner. You can practice visualizing yourself at any time and for any given situation. Many students find that it works well close to bedtime. Coaches encourage their peak performing athletes to use daily visualization exercises in order to increase their abilities in running, jumping, shooting, etc. Every single day, from now until the test day, practice visualization and picture yourself taking the test quickly, easily, confidently, and calmly. Visualization can help you exude a positive attitude and overcome test anxiety. Get the picture?

Act Positively Toward Yourself

On the day of the test, act positively. Even if you do not "feel" completely confident, you should stride into the test site with your head held high and a bounce in your step. Show both yourself and your peers that you are at ease and in complete control of the situation. Present yourself as someone who knows that he or she will be successful. Acting confidently will actually help you feel confident.

Practice these strategies in order to instill a positive mental attitude. Positive thinking means believing in yourself. Believe that you can achieve your highest goal under any circumstances. Know that you can do it. Dare to try.

Put Away Negative Thoughts—They Fuel Test Anxiety

Since you will be practicing positive thinking, you should also learn to recognize and eliminate distorted, or twisted, thinking. Avoid thinking any of the following distorted things about yourself:

"I must always be perfect." The reality is that everyone makes mistakes. In testing situations, perfectionists mentally fuss and fume about a single mistake instead of celebrating all of the items that they answered

correctly. Dwelling on mistakes wastes time and creates more tension. Push mistakes behind you and move forward to the next set of items. Remember that we all reserve the right to learn and grow.

"I failed the last time, so I'll fail this time." Past failure does not lead to future failure. People do get better the more that they practice. Because you did poorly on something in the past does not guarantee a poor performance either this time or in the future. Use this test as an opportunity for a fresh start. Forget yesterday's failures and realize that today is a brand new beginning.

"I have been anxious when taking tests before; therefore, I'll always be anxious." This twisted logic implies that you have no control over your behavior; however, that is not the case. You can change and learn to control your anxiety. It might take time and hard work to build calmness and confidence, but it is certainly within your reach.

Power Up Physically—Release Stress with Physical Exercise

Physical exercise is an excellent way to both reduce anxiety levels and cope with the effects of stress. Start a regular program of physical fitness that includes stretching and cardiovascular activities. If necessary, check with a doctor or a health professional in order to develop a customized fitness program.

Practice Being Calm—Learn to Mentally and Physically Relax

You may not realize that mental and physical relaxation play significant parts in the studying process. By setting aside time for clearing your mind and body of stress and anxiety, you will refresh your mental and physical energy reserves. Spend quality time studying and reviewing for the test. Then, spend time relaxing your mind and body so that you are re-energized for your next study session.

Practice the following relaxation exercises to calm the body and mind:

Physical and Mental Relaxation Exercise

Pick a quiet room where there are few distractions. Shut off all intrusive lights. Sit in a chair or lie down in a bed. If you wear glasses, take them off. Get comfortable, loosening any tight or binding clothing. Close your eyes, and take a deep breath. Blow out all of the air in your lungs, and then breathe in deeply. Now, focus on your tense muscles and consciously relax them. Start by focusing on your toes, your feet, and your calves. Tense and release your muscles to fully relax them. Move upward through each muscle group in your body, up to and including your facial muscles. Continue to breathe slowly, steadily, and fully during this exercise. Repeat this process, while consciously relaxing tense muscles, until you relax your entire body. Then, rest in this state for a few minutes. If you wish, begin meditating after your body is in a relaxed state. Concentrate on something monotonous until your mind becomes quiet. You may choose to concentrate on a sound, a word, or an object. Observe your thoughts without controlling them. Gently refocus on the sound, word, or object. Passively observe your thoughts when they come, then gently refocus back upon the sound, word, or object. When you are finished, open your eyes, and remain still for another minute or two before rising.

Breathing Exercise

Deep and relaxed breathing will calm your nerves and reduce stress. Whenever you start feeling anxious, take time out to perform this simple breathing exercise. Place your hands upon your stomach and breathe in slowly and deeply through your nose, feeling your rib cage rise. Pause and hold your breath for a second, thinking to yourself, "I am calm." Release your breath slowly and fully, blowing it out through your mouth. Repeat this exercise eight to ten times. Perform this exercise whenever you feel nervous or anxious.

Prepare—Do Not Leave Important Items Until the Last Minute

You are going to want to remain as relaxed as possible on the day of the test. In order to eliminate the last-minute, frantic rush to find that "one thing" that you cannot locate, make a list of the items that you need for the day of the test. Set out those important items the night before in order to efficiently and effectively speed you on your way toward the testing center.

Determine the Items That You Are Expected to Bring

Carefully read the test materials so that you know exactly what you should and should not bring to the test center.

Gather the Items That You Need

On the night before the test, gather all of the necessary items so that you can avoid the anxiety of trying to find them at the last minute.

Know the Directions to the Test Center

If you have not been to the test center before, make sure that you are provided with clear and specific directions as soon as possible. If necessary, drive to the test center the day before the test so you are sure of where you are going. If you are at all confused about how to get to the test center, call the center immediately and clarify the directions.

Decide Whether to Study the Night Before the Test

Should you study the night before the test? Well, as mentioned earlier, you certainly should not attempt to cram for the test. You may want to review a few strategies, but you do not want to attempt to learn large amounts of new material. Instead, take some time to review, and then find some entertaining activity to occupy your time. Go to the gym or see a movie with friends. Laughing is always a great way to reduce stress, so you may want to find something humorous to do or watch.

Sleep Well

A good night of sleep will help reduce stress on test day. Do not stay out late on the night before the test.

Get to the Test Site Early

Your anxiety level will increase if you arrive at the test center late. So, arrive early. Take a few minutes to relax and compose yourself. You may also need time to locate the restrooms and drinking fountains. However, do not arrive at the test center too early. Students typically get nervous and anxious when they have to wait for a long period of time with nothing to do except think about the upcoming test. So, find the balance between "too early" and "too late" that works best for you.

Watch Your Diet

What you choose to eat can be a physical cause of stress. Therefore, control your eating habits in order to maintain lower stress levels. Eat a healthy meal on the day of the test. Restrict your intake of sugar, salt, and caffeine. Remember that sugar and caffeine are found in coffee, cola, cocoa, and tea. These substances trigger a stress response in your body. High levels of sugar and caffeine are associated with nervousness, dizziness, irritability, headaches, and insomnia. Additionally, smoking has been found to decrease a person's ability to handle stress. Cigarettes act as a stimulant because of their nicotine content and will serve to increase stress levels.

Dress Comfortably

The good news is that you are going to a test, not a fashion show. So, wear comfortable clothes to the testing center; choose clothes that are not overly binding or tight. Dressing in layers is always a good idea since testing rooms are notoriously either too hot or too cold.

Pause—Release Physical and Mental Anxiety Before the Test

As already stated, relaxation allows you to focus your full attention and energy on the task at hand, rather than be distracted by tension and stress. You must release as much tension and anxiety as possible right before taking the test. Try the physical or mental exercises given earlier in this section.

Release and Relax

Having arrived early at the test site, take the last few minutes to relax. Do not attempt to study or review at this point. Instead, use the breathing technique you learned earlier. Try to gradually slow the pace of the "in-and-out" motion of your breathing. Visualize yourself at a place that you find peaceful and relaxing, such as the beach, the woods, or some other favorite spot. Continue this technique for a few minutes until you feel yourself becoming relaxed and calm.

Massage Tension Away

While waiting for the test, sit comfortably in your chair. Notice places in your body that feel tense—generally the shoulders, neck, or back. Gently massage tense areas for a few minutes.

Press On—Concentrate on the Current Item, Not the Last or Next One

Dwelling on answers to previous items will only elevate test anxiety, so do not worry about those sections or items that you have finished.

Focus on One Item at a Time

Your task on any test is to correctly answer each item, one item at a time. Good test-takers focus only on the item with which they are currently working. Poor test-takers worry about items that they just completed or about items in the upcoming section. Try to stay "in the moment" by concentrating on one item at a time.

Proudly Depart—Walk Out with Your Head Held High

Know That You Have Done Your Best

If you have followed the strategies listed in this section, attended test preparation classes, and spent time reviewing and studying on your own, you have most likely done your very best to prepare for the test. As you walk out of the test site, remind yourself that you have indeed put forth your best effort.

Watch the Labels

After the test, never label yourself as a "failure," "loser," or "underachiever." Instead, if you do not feel that you did as well as you expected, use the experience to learn about the test and about yourself. Students are able to retake standardized tests, so reflect upon what you can do better next time, not upon how poorly you think you did this time.

Perspective—Keep Life in Perspective

Yes, the test you will take is important, but other things in life are important too. Remember that this test is a means to an end—getting into college—and not the end itself.

NOTE: Some test-takers, even after applying all of the above strategies, still experience debilitating stress. Intense anxiety or stress that causes nausea, headaches, overwhelming emotional fears, or other severe symptoms may need special attention and care that goes beyond the strategies in these pages. If you suffer from these debilitating stress symptoms, ask your counseling office about what resources are available to help overcome severe test anxiety.

OVERALL TIME MANAGEMENT

High school students live hectic and exciting lives. In order to succeed in high school, you must learn how to manage your time, which really means that you must learn how to manage yourself by becoming a proactive student. To be proactive means to act assertively and decisively in order to prepare for upcoming events or situations. To be proactive also means to make wise decisions about how to plan the use of your time.

Classes and homework take up a great deal of the day, but there are also opportunities for recreation, extracurricular activities, and personal development. While jobs, athletics, friends, clubs, concerts, and other activities may take time away from your academic life, learning to manage your time and juggle multiple responsibilities is essential for succeeding in high school. This section focuses on how to better manage your time by using such powerful tools as the *PLAN* method and pyramid scheduling.

Scheduling for Success—Have a PLAN

The *PLAN* method presents four elements for maximizing your time:

> *PRIORITIZE* tasks according to their long-term benefit.
> *LIST* those tasks according to their priority.
> *ARRANGE* those tasks on a schedule.
> *NEGOTIATE* your schedule if those tasks become overwhelming.

P...Prioritize

Though involvement in many activities is important, it is necessary to determine which of these activities are the most important. Students who *prioritize* their tasks arrange them in an optimum order that is based on level of importance: more important tasks take precedence over less important tasks. So, in order to prioritize, you need to identify activities that will benefit you most in the long run.

Different students have different priorities. While most students do not study during all of their free time, successful students generally prioritize academics over other activities. These students devote a majority of their free time to studying so that they can reinforce what they have already learned in class. In order to effectively prioritize your tasks, you must first identify your own long-term goals. With a better understanding of your goals for the future, you can more effectively prioritize your activities in the present.

Here are some questions that you should ask yourself in order to better determine your long-term goals:

- What clubs or social service organizations would I like to join?
- What sports would I like to play?
- With whom do I want to be friends?
- What type of impact would I like to have on my community?
- What special accomplishments do I want to achieve?
- What types of positive things do I want people to say about me?
- Whom do I want to impress? How will I impress them?
- What will make me a happy and fulfilled person?
- Do I want to go to college? If so, which college and what major might I choose?
- What career would I like to pursue?
- In what additional ways can I prepare for this career?

L...List

Every week, make a *list* of the tasks that you want to accomplish, placing the most important tasks at the top of your list.

A...Arrange

Each day, ***arrange*** all of your tasks on a daily schedule, prioritizing the most important tasks over tasks that are less important. The key to prioritization is to maintain a clear understanding of what is most important so that you can remain focused on the most significant tasks at hand.

N...Negotiate

In any given term, there are weeks that are especially busy and may prove to be overwhelming. Typically, chapter tests and final exams require considerable amounts of study time. The following are seven tips on how to better ***negotiate*** the details of your schedule in accordance with the potential added pressures of exam time.

1. Anticipate weeks with heavy workloads and note them on your schedule.
2. Meet with your teachers to discuss any problems that you might have with completing class work.
3. Form a study group to help prepare for tests.
4. Get plenty of rest; you will need rest and energy during stressful times.
5. Do not wait until the last week of the term to complete major projects; procrastination is unproductive.
6. Attempt to get time off from your job during the most hectic times.
7. Say no to distractions such as watching television and reading frivolous books or magazines.

Manage Your Time by Using Pyramid Scheduling

A pyramid consists of a large base, or foundation, which transitions into progressively narrower levels until finally reaching a small point at the top. In a similar fashion, pyramid scheduling begins with organizing your long-term projects and then moves on to your more immediate tasks until finally reaching your daily schedule. Purchase an annual calendar or planner so that you can schedule months, weeks, and days, approaching your scheduling process in the following manner:

Schedule the Entire Term

During the first week of each term, organize all of your major assignments and responsibilities on the calendar. After you have received a syllabus for each of your classes, reference all important dates that coincide with any of the following:

- Class assignments, such as reading selections and projects
- Tests and exams
- Quizzes
- Holidays and vacations
- Personal obligations, such as birthdays and family gatherings
- Job commitments
- Extracurricular activities, such as athletic events and student government meetings

Schedule Each Month

Two days before the beginning of each month, review your monthly schedule for all assignments, tests, and quizzes. Then, reference any important dates for monthly activities that do not already appear on your calendar, such as:

- Additional assignments
- Sporting events or concerts that you plan to attend
- Personal commitments, such as work and social engagements
- Study blocks for major projects, exams, tests, or quizzes

Schedule Each Week

On Sunday night of each week, review your weekly schedule for all assignments, tests, and quizzes. Look for any personal appointments or special commitments that may be scheduled for the upcoming week. Then, on a weekly calendar, outline a schedule for that upcoming week so that you will have sufficient time for studying and completing assignments. Each day of the weekly schedule should be divided up into mornings, afternoons, and evenings so that you can reference the most important times for certain daily activities, such as:

- Classes
- Class assignments, such as reading selections and projects
- Tests and exams
- Quizzes
- Holidays and vacation days
- Personal commitments, such as work and social engagements
- Employment commitments
- Extracurricular activities
- Study sessions

Schedule Each Day

On the night before each school day, create a schedule that outlines important times for the following daily activities:

- Class schedule
- Study times
- Job schedule
- Free time
- Additional appointments, tasks, or responsibilities

Finally, Remember to Stick to Your Schedule

The most difficult—but most important—part of your plan is the actual implementation of the plan. Unless emergencies arise, stick to your schedule. Do not change your schedule unless it is absolutely necessary to accommodate and prioritize new activities. Remember that time management is really about self-management. So, remain disciplined so that you can follow your schedule without falling prey to distractions.

Successful students are able to manage themselves by learning and using valuable time management tools. If you start to use these tools now, you can be successful in high school and beyond. Always remember to schedule your work and work your schedule.

PLANNING A COURSE SCHEDULE

The most significant aspect of an effective study plan is that it is a written plan. A written study plan is more concrete than one that you simply draw on from memory. So, when creating your plan, write out a day-by-day schedule for reviewing all of the materials that are necessary for success in the course. This written format will provide a clear and dependable guide for study. The schedule should be prioritized according to the time that you need to devote to each of the different subjects, based on the amount of time that you have.

Consider how you can plan your study time so that it corresponds with the course topics. In addition to assignments given in class, you may wish to devote extra study time to your particular areas of weakness. The "to do" list you created based on your Student Summary report is a good place to start. Use the empty calendars that follow to develop a plan of action with your teacher, determining what topics you will study each day and allotting time to study those sections of the book and complete the relevant exercises. Remember that it is not necessary for you to do everything all at once. Instead, picking a few things to focus on each week will help you to better manage your time.

Using the following empty calendars, fill in your assignments and study plan for each day. Your teacher can help you set goals for each subject.

MONTH: _____						
Sunday	**Monday**	**Tuesday**	**Wednesday**	**Thursday**	**Friday**	**Saturday**

Test Mechanics, Concepts, and Strategies

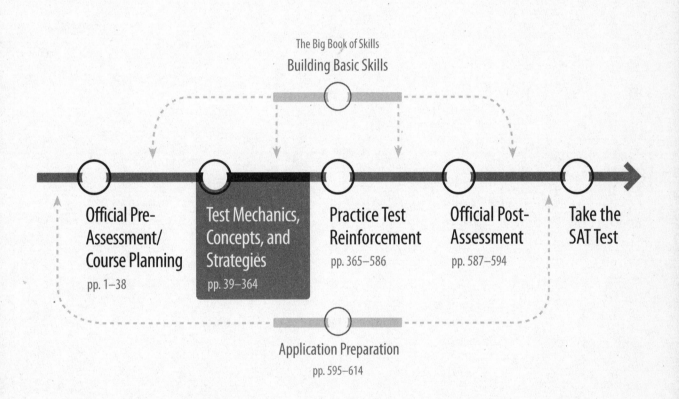

The Big Book of Skills
Building Basic Skills

Official Pre-Assessment/ Course Planning
pp. 1–38

Test Mechanics, Concepts, and Strategies
pp. 39–364

Practice Test Reinforcement
pp. 365–586

Official Post-Assessment
pp. 587–594

Take the SAT Test

Application Preparation
pp. 595–614

CAMBRIDGE
VICTORY FOR THE
SAT TEST

Critical Reading: Passages

Course Concept Outline

I. Test Mechanics (p. 43)

A. Overview (p. 43)

B. Anatomy (Items #1-4, pp. 44-45)

C. Pacing (p. 46)

D. Time Trial (Items #1-3, pp. 47-48)

E. Game Plan (p. 49)

1. Quickly Preview the Test Section, but Skip the Directions (p. 49)
2. Personalize the Passage Order (p. 49)
3. Read Any Introductory Notes (p. 49)
4. Preview the Passage (p. 49)
5. Preview the Item Stems (p. 51)
6. Read the Passage (p. 52)
7. Answer the Items (p. 52)

II. Lesson (p. 53)

A. Preliminaries[1]

1. What Is Tested
2. Directions
3. Item Profiles

B. Facts about Passages

1. Four Passage Topics, Unfamiliar Subjects
2. Passages Test Comprehension, Not "Speed-Reading"

---

[1] Some concepts in this Course Concept Outline are not illustrated through examples in your student text but may be covered by your instructor in class. They are included here to provide a complete outline of your course.

C. Item-Types (p. 53)

   1. Applying Item-Types to Long Passages (p. 53)
     a) Main Idea (Items #1–2, p. 54)
     b) Explicit Detail (Items #3–5, p. 54)
     c) Vocabulary (Item #6, p. 54)
     d) Development (Items #7–8, p. 55)
     e) Implied Idea (Items #9–11, p. 55)
     f) Application (Items #12–13, p. 56)
     g) Voice (Items #14–15, p. 56)
   2. Applying Item-Types to Short Passages (Items #16–29, pp. 56–58)

D. Strategies (p. 58)

   1. Three Reading Comprehension Levels
     a) General Theme
     b) Specific Points
     c) Evaluation
   2. Using the Three Comprehension Levels
   3. Five Steps to Approaching Passages (p. 58)
     a) Label Passages as "Easy" or "Hard"
     b) Preview First and Last Sentences of Passage
     c) Preview Item Stems
     d) Read the Passage
     e) Answer the Items (Items #30–41, pp. 58–60)
   4. Item-Type Strategies (p. 61)
     a) Main Idea Clues (Items #42–43, p. 61)
     b) Explicit Detail Clues (Item #44, p. 62)
     c) Vocabulary Clues (Items #45–49, p. 62)
     d) Development Clues (Items #50–51, p. 62)
     e) Implied Idea Clues (Items #52–53, p. 63)
     f) Application Clues (Item #54, p. 63)
     g) Voice Clues (Item #55, p. 63)

E. Further Use of Reading Strategies (p. 63)

   1. Humanities (Items #56–75, pp. 63–67)
   2. Literary Fiction (Items #76–90, pp. 67–70)
   3. Social Studies (Items #91–97, pp. 71)
   4. Natural Sciences (Items #98–112, pp. 72–74)

F. Pre-Assessment Examples

III. Quizzes (p. 75)

   A. Quiz I (Items #1–18, pp. 75–81)

   B. Quiz II (Items #1–17, pp. 82–87)

   C. Quiz III (Items #1–18, pp. 88–93)

   D. Quiz IV Brain Buster (Items #1–29, pp. 94–102)

IV. Review (Items #1–60, pp. 103–119)

V. Strategy Summary (p. 121)

TEST MECHANICS

Overview

Critical Reading sections include two types of items: Passages and Sentence Completions. The Passages part of the section consists of one or more reading selections followed by several items. You read the selection and answer the items based upon what is stated or implied in the selection.

Reading selections (also called "passages") come in different lengths (ranging from 100 words to 850 words) with varying numbers of items (anywhere from 1 to 15). Sometimes, selections use paired passages on the same topic and pose questions asking you to compare and contrast the two points of view presented.

The reading passages are selected from four general content areas: Humanities, Literary Fiction, Social Studies, and Natural Sciences. In most cases, the passage will be about a topic with which you are not familiar. The test-writers choose unusual topics so that Passages items will be a test of reading skill and not of knowledge. Of course, you may find a topic that you know something about, but even so, your knowledge is probably not going to help you very much, though familiarity with a topic is a definite advantage.

Critical Reading sections have a 20- or 25-minute time limit, depending on the number of items. Given the time limit, you obviously need to work quickly. The exam, however, is not a test of "speed-reading." Instead, the exam is a test of reading <u>comprehension</u>.

Anatomy

DIRECTIONS: The passage below is followed by a set of items based on its content. Answer the items on the basis of what is stated or implied in the corresponding passage.

The directions make Passages items sound easy: read this and answer the items. So, the directions aren't very helpful, and you can ignore them from now on.

Items #1–4 are based on the following passage.

This passage is adapted from a government publication about the history of alcohol abuse.

The movement to prohibit alcohol began in the early years of the nineteenth century with the formation of local societies in New York and Massachusetts to promote temperance in
5 consumption of alcohol. Many of the temperance societies were affiliated with Protestant evangelical denominations and met in local churches. As time passed, most temperance societies modified their goal to call for complete abstinence from all
10 alcoholic beverages.
In 1919, largely in response to the lobbying efforts of the Anti-Saloon League, the Eighteenth Amendment to the Constitution was passed banning the production, transportation, and sale of all
15 alcoholic beverages. The Amendment, also known as the Prohibition Amendment, provided for concurrent enforcement by both federal and state law. By January 1920, in addition to the federal Volstead Act, the nation had laws in thirty-three
20 states prohibiting alcohol entirely.
Prohibition, however, proved unworkable as bootleggers and speakeasies quickly organized to satisfy the public's continuing thirst for alcohol. Thirteen years later, the "Noble Experiment,"
25 doomed by the impracticality of enforcement, ended with the repeal of the Prohibition Amendment.

Many of the passages, particularly longer ones, will include an introductory note telling you where the passage comes from. A note may provide some useful information, so read it.

Typically, reading passages discuss an unfamiliar topic. Even if you know something about Prohibition, that information may or may not be helpful since you'll be asked about this particular passage.

This passage is organized chronologically. The first paragraph talks about the "early years of the nineteenth century," in other words, the early 1800s.

The second paragraph starts with 1919. Then, the passage briefly traces the events leading up to Prohibition.

The third paragraph explains why Prohibition failed: people wanted to drink, so bootleggers and illegal clubs satisfied that demand. Eventually, Prohibition was repealed.

1. The passage is primarily concerned with the

(A) social problems caused by alcohol abuse
(B) founding of anti-alcohol temperance societies
(C) origins of Prohibition and its subsequent failure
(D) efforts to enforce Prohibition legislation
(E) decision to repeal the Eighteenth Amendment

1. **(C)** *This is a common type of Passages item: the item asks you to identify the main idea of the passage. The passage discusses the origins and failure of Prohibition.*

2. According to the passage, in the early nineteenth century, temperance societies originally

(A) encouraged moderation in alcohol use
(B) demanded the repeal of the Eighteenth Amendment
(C) supported efforts to enforce the Volstead Act
(D) refused to align with religious groups
(E) pressed for an amendment banning alcohol

2. **(A)** *This item asks about something that is specifically stated in the passage. The author clearly states that the temperance societies were originally founded to "promote temperance" as opposed to complete prohibition.*

3. The passage implies that Prohibition failed because

(A) religious organizations withdrew their support for the program
(B) the repeal of the Eighteenth Amendment was only experimental
(C) too many states passed laws prohibiting the sale of alcohol
(D) widespread demand for alcohol made enforcement impossible
(E) the Constitution did not include an anti-alcohol amendment at the time

3. **(D)** *This item requires that you "read between the lines" of the passage. In the third paragraph, the author does not specifically say why Prohibition failed, but you can figure it out from what's said: people simply refused to quit consuming alcohol, even illegally.*

4. In line 17, the word "concurrent" means

(A) unsuccessful
(B) shared
(C) practicable
(D) intermittent
(E) temporary

4. **(B)** *This item asks you for the definition of a term in the context of the passage. The passage states that the federal government and the states were given "concurrent" authority and that the states, as well as the federal government, passed laws against alcohol. So, "concurrent" must mean something like "joint" or "shared."*

Pacing

The mix of short and long Critical Reading: Passages varies, as does the number of Sentence Completions items included in the Critical Reading test sections. The following table, however, gives some rough estimates as to how much time you would want to spend on a particular passage and its corresponding questions, regardless of the Critical Reading test section in which the passage is located.

PASSAGES IN CRITICAL READING TEST SECTIONS					
Type of Reading Selection	Approximate Number of Words	Time Spent Reading Selection	Number of Items	Time Spent on Items	Total Time
Short Single-Paragraph	125	1 minute	2	2 minutes	3 minutes
Short Double-Paragraph	250	2 minutes	4	4 minutes	6 minutes
Long Single-Passage	750	3 minutes	12	12 minutes	15 minutes
Long Double-Passage	800	3 minutes	13	13 minutes	16 minutes

Time Trial

(3 Items—5 minutes)

> **DIRECTIONS:** The passage below is followed by a set of items based on its content. Answer the items on the basis of what is stated or implied in the corresponding passage.

Items #1–3 are based on the following passage.

This passage is excerpted from an essay exploring the possible reasons for extinction of salmon runs in New England rivers.

Folklore holds that Atlantic salmon were once so abundant in New England rivers that early colonists walked across the backs of the fish as they ran up the rivers in spring. Then, according to the
5 received wisdom, at the turn of the nineteenth century, increasing pollution in the rivers and the construction of large main stem dams across rivers caused salmon to become severely depleted. For this reason, restoration programs to "bring back the
10 salmon" have been, and continue to be, an extensive and ongoing effort supported by a variety of lobbying groups.

If the theory were accurate, then there should be considerable archaeological evidence that
15 salmon played a significant role in the diets of the aboriginal peoples of New England; but in site after site, although bones of numerous other fish species have been recovered, no salmon bones have been found. It's more likely that the accounts of salmon
20 were intentionally embellished by early writers, who were, in reality, promoters with strong motives for presenting to the folks back in the old country a favorable image of New England as a place of natural abundance. Since salmon was a much
25 esteemed fish at home, its inclusion and description was important.

In fact, salmon did not begin to colonize New England streams until a period of climatic cooling known as the Little Ice Age (C.E. 1550–1800). At the
30 end of this period, the climatic warming created less favorable environmental conditions for salmon, and hence their range retracted. The idea that initial colonization did not occur until this time, and then only as a temporary range expansion, explains the
35 lack of salmon in prehistoric sites and the depletion of the fish at the end of the eighteenth century.

It is fashionable in western culture today to view human impact on the natural environment as often the major contributing factor in
40 environmental change. It is also fashionable to suggest that science can fix or undo anthropogenic environmental change. While humans unarguably have impacts on the natural environment, and have done so for as long as their four-million-year
45 evolutionary history on the Earth, the environmental ideology that grants omnipotence to humans over the environment can prevent us from recognizing that natural environmental fluctuations in climate and species distributions or extinctions
50 are probably more substantive on a long-term scale than human induced ones.

While authorities such as D. W. Lufkin have stated that "the circumstances leading to the demise of *Salmo salar* are relatively simple to identify" and
55 have cited dams, pollution, logging practices, and over-fishing, causes behind its demise are more complex, with ecological and climatological bases. If pollution and dams were the major cause of the extinctions, then why were the runs not made
60 extinct on the Penobscot, a heavily dammed and polluted river in Maine? Why did salmon runs become extinct downstream of the dams on the Connecticut River? The general lack of success in salmon restoration programs over the last two
65 centuries suggests a more fundamental ecological cause for impoverished salmon runs in New England than an anthropogenic one.

1. The primary purpose of the passage is to

   (A) propose a long term plan for restoring salmon runs to the rivers of New England
   (B) undermine the theory that human activity caused the extinction of salmon runs in New England rivers
   (C) demonstrate that anthropogenic factors are often more powerful than natural ones in shaping the environment
   (D) provide evidence that the disappearance of *Salmo salar* was caused by the damming and pollution of the rivers
   (E) refute the contention that climatological factors played an important part in the collapse of the salmon runs

2. The author cites the lack of salmon bones in archaeological digs as evidence that

   (A) the salmon population in New England rivers declined sharply after the end of the Little Ice Age
   (B) aboriginal Americans, who consumed other fish species, refused to eat the abundant salmon
   (C) salmon were not available to aboriginal Americans before the time of the arrival of the first colonists
   (D) anthropogenic factors were largely responsible for the extinction of the salmon runs
   (E) salmon stocks had been largely depleted by the time of the arrival of the first colonists

3. It can be inferred that D. W. Lufkin would most likely

   (A) agree with the author that the primary causes of the depletion of salmon stocks are climatological
   (B) accept the author's contention that early reports about the abundance of salmon were greatly exaggerated
   (C) reject the author's thesis and insist that the causes of salmon extinction are anthropogenic
   (D) disagree with the author that salmon stocks have declined precipitously since the end of the eighteenth century
   (E) argue that the decline of salmon stocks began before the arrival of the first colonists to New England

Game Plan

Quickly Preview the Test Section, but Skip the Directions

Last-minute adjustments to the test format are theoretically (but not practically) possible, so check the test section before you start to work, especially the number of passages, the number of items, and the time limit. And yes, the test-writers always tell you to "read the directions carefully." But they don't tell you that you have to read them during the test. Instead, become familiar with them <u>before</u> test day. That way, you won't waste 30 seconds or more (enough time to answer an item) re-reading directions you are already familiar with.

Personalize the Passage Order

Remember that you don't have to do the items in the order in which they are presented in the booklet. For some sections, like the math section, doing problems in order (more or less) makes good sense. But in a Critical Reading section with Passages items, it is a sound strategy to make a choice about the order in which you're going to work through the section. You may decide to do the reading passages in the order presented, or you may want to change the order.

What factors should you consider? First, you may find a topic that seems familiar to you. Of course, you can't expect that you'll already know the answers to the items, but familiarity is a definite advantage. Second, you'll feel more comfortable with some topics than with others. Do you like biology but hate literature or like social science but hate art? Then do the passages with topics that you like first.

Aside from topics, there are some formal characteristics that you can consider. You have both long and short passages. Most students prefer the short passages. And you have single-passages and double-passages, and most students prefer the single-passages.

This sets up the following personalized order for completion of the passages:

1. Choose familiar topics to do first.
2. Otherwise, choose your favorite topics to do first.
3. Choose your second favorite topic to do second, and so on.
4. Otherwise, choose short, single-passages.
5. Otherwise, choose short, double-passages.
6. Otherwise, choose long, single-passages.
7. Last, do long, double-passages.

When you choose your passages, you should number them in the margin of your test booklet. For example, if the section has two short single-passages and two long single-passages, you'll look first to see whether the topics are helpful. Then, you'll formulate an order for the remaining passages and number all the passages "1" through "4."

Read Any Introductory Notes

Many passages, particularly longer ones, will include an introductory note telling you where the passage comes from and maybe some other information. Sometimes, this information is useful for getting a better understanding of the passage. Therefore, before starting on a passage and items, always read any introductory notes.

Preview the Passage

Before you begin reading a particular passage, take 15 to 30 seconds to preview key sentences. Key sentences are the first and last sentences of the passage and the first sentence of each paragraph. Why preview? First sentences are often topic sentences, so reading a series of topic sentences will tell you what the author is trying to say, and it can give you an outline of the development of the passage. Sometimes, though not always, the last sentence is a conclusion. Note that for short single-paragraph passages, you will probably skip this step.

To see how this can work, preview the following passage about solar energy, in which only the key sentences are visible.

At the present time, 98 percent of world energy consumption comes from sources such as fossil fuels.

5

Our energy consumption amounts to about one-ten thousandth of the energy we receive from the sun.

10

15

It is often stated that the growth rate will decline or that energy conservation measures will preclude any long-range problem.

20

The only practical means of avoiding the problem of thermal pollution is the use of solar energy.

25

30

To see what you can learn from just a few sentences, think about these questions:

What's the passage about?

- Gas mileage.
- Space exploration.
- Solar energy.

What is a common attitude about energy conservation?

- That it doesn't work.
- That it might work.
- That it will probably work.

What's the author's view on solar energy?

- It doesn't work.
- It's unnecessary.
- It's absolutely essential.

And the answers are that the passage is about solar energy, which the author believes to be necessary, even though a lot of people think conservation could solve all our problems.

Preview the Item Stems

Additionally, before reading a particular passage, you <u>may</u> find it helpful to preview the item stems, which are presented either as questions or incomplete statements. If a stem mentions a key word or phrase, make a mental note and look for it as you read the selection. See what you would learn from the following items, in which only the item stems are visible.

1. According to the passage, the most important disadvantage of nuclear energy is

(A)
(B)
(C)
(D)
(E)

Previewing would tell you to look for certain information in your reading. The first stem uses the phrase "most important disadvantage of nuclear energy." So, you know that the passage will discuss disadvantages of nuclear energy. When you find the "most important" one, mark that reference so that you can answer this item.

2. According to the author, shifting climate patterns will have all of the following effects EXCEPT

(A)
(B)
(C)
(D)
(E)

The second stem tells you that the author discusses "shifting climate patterns," probably in some detail since the passage mentions multiple effects. Each time you find one of the effects, mark it so that when you answer this item you can eliminate those choices that mention such effects. ("EXCEPT" means to look for the one NOT mentioned in the passage.)

3. The author's attitude toward scientists who deny that average temperatures are rising can best be described as

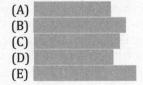

(A)
(B)
(C)
(D)
(E)

The third stem lets you know that the passage discusses average temperatures and a theory advanced by some scientists. If you find that reference in your reading, you'll have the answer to this item.

4. Which of the following best describes the main point of the passage?

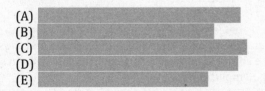

(A)
(B)
(C)
(D)
(E)

Finally, the last stem tells you to look for the main idea. That, in and of itself, is not particularly helpful because you're always reading for the main idea—even if you don't get a question that asks about it. So, some stems are not very helpful while others are.

Read the Passage

Keep the following points in mind when reading a passage:

- Read the passage quickly but carefully. You'll probably need about one minute to read a short single-passage and twice that for short double-passages; and you'll probably need about two to three minutes to read a long single-passage and slightly more for long double-passages. This is about 300 to 350 words a minute.

- Read the passage for important themes. Many of the items will ask about important themes of the passage, such as the main point, the purpose of a particular paragraph, or the author's intention.

- Do not try to memorize details. If you need detailed information, you can always go back to the passage to find it. This is an "open-book" test.

- Pause at the end to summarize your reading. One of the most helpful reading techniques is to summarize in your own words what you have just read. What is the main point? What did the author do in the first paragraph? In the second paragraph? What did the author prove?

Answer the Items

Keep the following points in mind when answering the accompanying items:

- Identify the question being asked. Passages items fall into one of seven categories such as "Main Idea," "Explicit Detail," and "Vocabulary." Specific item-types have characteristic kinds of answers. If you identify the category first, it will be easier to find the right answer. You'll learn more about the seven item-types later in the Critical Reading: Passages Lesson.

- Answer the question being asked. One of the most common mistakes made by examinees is to read the item stem carelessly and then answer the "wrong" question. That is, they respond to what they think they read rather than what is actually on the page. Since wrong answers often sound plausible, if you make this mistake, you're probably going to find a pretty good answer—to the wrong question.

- Read the answer choices carefully. You'll learn how to recognize the seven Passages item-types and what the correct answer to each should look like. Do this experiment: estimate how many words are in a typical long single-passage selection and then how many are in the answer choices. The answer choices are just about as long as the passage itself. That means reading comprehension doesn't stop at the end of the last sentence of the passage. It continues all the way through to the last word of the last answer choice to the last item.

- Pay attention to thought-reversers. Thought-reversers are words in the item stem like "NOT," "BUT," and "EXCEPT." These words turn the question upside down. What is normally the right answer is now a wrong answer, and what is normally a wrong answer is the right answer.

- Do not spend too much time on any one item. Remember that you get +1 for the hardest question and +1 for the easiest. With Passages items, the easiest ones can theoretically be the last in the group and the hardest ones can be the first. So, if you sense that you're spinning your wheels, make an educated guess (if you can eliminate at least one answer choice) and then move along.

LESSON

The passages and items in this section accompany the in-class review of the skills and concepts tested by the Passages part of the SAT Critical Reading test sections. You will work through the items with your instructor in class. Answers are on page 619.

> **DIRECTIONS:** Each passage below is followed by a set of items based on its content; items following a pair of related passages may also be based on the relationship between the two passages. Answer the items on the basis of what is stated or implied in the corresponding passage(s).

Item-Types

Applying Item-Types to Long Passages

Items #1–15 are based on the following passage.

To broaden their voting appeal in the Presidential election of 1796, the Federalists selected Thomas Pinckney, a leading South Carolinian, as running mate for the New Englander
5 John Adams. But Pinckney's Southern friends chose to ignore their party's intentions and regarded Pinckney as a Presidential candidate, creating a political situation that Alexander Hamilton was determined to exploit. Hamilton had long been wary
10 of Adams' stubbornly independent brand of politics and preferred to see his running mate, who was more pliant and over whom Hamilton could exert more control, in the President's chair.

The election was held under the system
15 originally established by the Constitution. At that time, there was but a single tally, with the candidate receiving the largest number of electoral votes declared President and the candidate with the second largest number declared Vice President.
20 Hamilton anticipated that all the Federalists in the North would vote for Adams and Pinckney equally in an attempt to ensure that Jefferson would not be either first or second in the voting. Pinckney would be solidly supported in the South while Adams
25 would not. Hamilton concluded if it were possible to divert a few electoral votes from Adams to

Pinckney, Pinckney would receive more than Adams, yet both Federalists would outpoll Jefferson.

Various methods were used to persuade the
30 electors to vote as Hamilton wished. In the press, anonymous articles were published attacking Adams for his monarchical tendencies and Jefferson for being overly democratic, while pushing Pinckney as the only suitable candidate. In private
35 correspondence with state party leaders, the Hamiltonians encouraged the idea that Adams' popularity was slipping, that he could not win the election, and that the Federalists could defeat Jefferson only by supporting Pinckney.

40 Had sectional pride and loyalty not run as high in New England as in the deep South, Pinckney might well have become Washington's successor. New Englanders, however, realized that equal votes for Adams and Pinckney in their states would defeat
45 Adams; therefore, eighteen electors scratched Pinckney's name from their ballots and deliberately threw away their second votes to men who were not even running. It was fortunate for Adams that they did, for the electors from South Carolina
50 completely abandoned him, giving eight votes to Pinckney and eight to Jefferson.

In the end, Hamilton's interference in Pinckney's candidacy lost him even the Vice Presidency. Without New England's support,
55 Pinckney received only 59 electoral votes, finishing third to Adams and Jefferson. He might have been President in 1797, or as Vice President a serious contender for the Presidency in 1800; instead, stigmatized by a plot he had not devised, he served
60 a brief term in the United States Senate and then dropped from sight as a national influence.

Main Idea

1. The main purpose of the passage is to

   (A) propose reforms of the procedures for electing the President and Vice President
   (B) condemn Alexander Hamilton for interfering in the election of 1796
   (C) describe the political events that led to John Adams' victory in the 1796 Presidential election
   (D) contrast the political philosophy of the Federalists to that of Thomas Jefferson
   (E) praise Thomas Pinckney for his refusal to participate in Hamilton's scheme to have him elected President

2. Which of the following titles best describes the content of the passage?

   (A) The Failure of Alexander Hamilton's Plan for Thomas Pinckney to Win the 1796 Presidential Election
   (B) The Roots of Alexander Hamilton's Distrust of John Adams and New England's Politics
   (C) Important Issues in the 1796 Presidential Campaign as Presented by the Federalist Candidates
   (D) The Political Careers of Alexander Hamilton, John Adams, and Thomas Pinckney
   (E) Political and Sectional Differences between New England and the South in the Late 1700s

Explicit Detail

3. According to the passage, which of the following was true of the Presidential election of 1796?

   (A) Thomas Jefferson received more electoral votes than did Thomas Pinckney.
   (B) John Adams received strong support from the electors of South Carolina.
   (C) Alexander Hamilton received most of the electoral votes of New England.
   (D) Thomas Pinckney was selected by Federalist party leaders to be the party's Presidential candidate.
   (E) Thomas Pinckney received all 16 of South Carolina's electoral votes.

4. According to the passage, Hamilton's plan included all of the following EXCEPT

   (A) Articles published in newspapers to create opposition to John Adams
   (B) South Carolina's loyalty to Thomas Pinckney
   (C) Private contact with state officials urging them to support Thomas Pinckney
   (D) John Adams' reputation as a stubborn and independent New Englander
   (E) Support that the New England states would give to John Adams

5. The passage supplies information that answers which of the following questions?

   (A) How many electoral votes were cast for John Adams in the 1796 Presidential election?
   (B) Under the voting system originally set up by the Constitution, how many votes did each elector cast?
   (C) Who was Jefferson's running mate in the 1796 Presidential election?
   (D) What became of Alexander Hamilton after his plan to have Thomas Pinckney elected President failed?
   (E) How many more electoral votes did Jefferson receive in the 1796 Presidential election than Pinckney?

Vocabulary

6. In line 12, the word "pliant" most nearly means

   (A) assertive
   (B) public
   (C) national
   (D) popular
   (E) yielding

Development

7. Why does the author refer to the election procedure established by the original Constitution?

(A) To prove to the reader that New England as a whole had more electoral votes than the state of South Carolina

(B) To persuade the reader that Thomas Pinckney's defeat could have been avoided

(C) To alert the reader that the procedure used in 1796 was unlike that presently used

(D) To encourage the reader to study Constitutional history

(E) To remind the reader that the President and Vice President of the United States are chosen democratically

8. The overall development of the passage can best be described as

(A) refuting possible explanations for certain phenomena

(B) documenting a thesis with specific examples

(C) offering an explanation of a series of events

(D) making particular proposals to solve a problem

(E) attacking the assumption of an argument

Implied Idea

9. The passage implies that some electors voted for John Adams because they were

(A) in favor of a monarchy

(B) persuaded to do so by Hamilton

(C) afraid South Carolina would not vote for Pinckney

(D) concerned about New England's influence over the South

(E) anxious to have a President from their geographical region

10. Which of the following can be inferred from the passage?

(A) Thomas Pinckney had a personal dislike for Jefferson's politics.

(B) The Federalists regarded themselves as more democratic than Jefferson.

(C) The Hamiltonians contacted key Southern leaders to persuade them to vote for Adams.

(D) Electors were likely to vote for candidates from their own geographical region.

(E) New England states cast more electoral votes for Jefferson than did the South.

11. It can be inferred that had South Carolina not cast any electoral votes for Jefferson, the outcome of the 1796 election would have been a

(A) larger margin of victory for John Adams

(B) victory for Thomas Jefferson

(C) Federalist defeat in the Senate

(D) victory for Thomas Pinckney

(E) defeat of the Federalist Presidential candidate

Application

12. The electors who scratched Pinckney's name from their ballots behaved most like which of the following people?

(A) A newspaper publisher who adds a special section to the Sunday edition to review the week's political events
(B) A member of the clergy who encourages members of other faiths to meet to discuss solutions to the community's problems
(C) An artist who saves preliminary sketches of an important work even after the work is finally completed
(D) A general who orders his retreating troops to destroy supplies they must leave behind so the enemy cannot use the supplies
(E) A runner who sets too fast a pace during the early stages of a race and has no energy left for the finish

13. Hamilton's strategy can best be summarized as

(A) divide and conquer
(B) retreat and regroup
(C) feint and counterattack
(D) hit and run
(E) camouflage and conceal

Voice

14. The tone of the passage can best be described as

(A) witty
(B) comical
(C) scholarly
(D) frivolous
(E) morose

15. The author's attitude toward Hamilton's plan can be described as

(A) angry
(B) approving
(C) analytical
(D) regretful
(E) disinterested

Applying Item-Types to Short Passages

Items #16–22 are based on the following passage.

The sixteenth-century revival of learning was naturalistic, a rejection of the dominant supernaturalistic strain of thought. Perhaps the influence of classic Greek literature has been
5 overestimated by some historians, and undoubtedly the change in thinking was mainly a product of contemporary conditions; but there can be no doubt that educated people, enamored of the new viewpoint, turned eagerly to Greek literature. This
10 interest in Greek thought was not in literature for its own sake, but in the spirit it expressed. The mental freedom that animated Greek expression aroused new readers to think and observe in a similar untrammeled fashion. Sixteenth-century
15 history of science shows that the young physical sciences borrowed points of departure from the new interest in Greek literature. As Windelband said, "the new science of nature was the offspring of humanism."

16. The author's primary purpose is to

(A) connect sixteenth-century science and Greek thought
(B) distinguish modern thinking from Greek thinking
(C) contrast Greek naturalism with Greek supernaturalism
(D) show the relevance of Greek thinking to modern science
(E) demonstrate that sixteenth-century science utilized Greek myths

17. According to the author, the most important influence on the revival of learning in the sixteenth century was

(A) ancient Greek literature
(B) sixteenth-century scientific thought
(C) existing historical conditions
(D) supernaturalistic thinking
(E) humanistic interpretation of Greek thought

18. In line 14, the word "untrammeled" most nearly means

(A) unhistorical
(B) uninteresting
(C) irresponsible
(D) unrestricted
(E) irreverent

19. The author cites Windelband as an authority on

(A) ancient Greek life
(B) classical Greek texts
(C) modern science
(D) sixteenth-century thought
(E) supernaturalism

20. The author implies that scholars have debated the extent to which

(A) ancient Greek thought was truly characterized by intellectual freedom
(B) supernaturalism in the sixteenth century interfered with scientific progress
(C) humanism represented a radical departure from earlier supernaturalistic thinking
(D) renewed interest in Greek thinking valued ancient literature for its own merits
(E) Greek literature inspired the sixteenth-century revival in learning

21. The discussion of ancient Greek literature presupposes that it is possible to

(A) distinguish the "spirit" of literature from actual written words
(B) be influenced by literature without having to read the texts
(C) trace the roots of any intellectual movement back to ancient times
(D) analyze a scientific question without the history that gave rise to the question
(E) find direct influences of ancient writings in all modern writings

22. It can be inferred that the author's attitude toward Windelband's conclusion is one of

(A) condemnation
(B) indifference
(C) mistrust
(D) approval
(E) regret

Items #23–29 are based on the following passage.

Are republics less likely than monarchies to make war? Sparta, Rome, and Carthage, all republics, often engaged in war. Sparta was little better than a well regulated camp, and Rome never
5 tired of conquest. Carthage was the aggressor in the very war that destroyed it. In later times, Venice figured often in wars of ambition, until Pope Julius II gave a deadly blow to the power and pride of that haughty republic. In Britain, the representatives of
10 the people compose one branch of the national legislature. Few nations have been more frequently engaged in war, and there have been almost as many popular as royal wars. The cries of nations and representatives have forced monarchs to enter
15 and continue wars contrary to their inclinations. Is any of this surprising? Are not the former administered by humans as well as the latter?

23. The author's primary purpose is to

(A) demonstrate that republics do not ordinarily engage in war
(B) deny that war is a valid instrument of foreign policy
(C) condemn several ancient republics for their aggressive tendencies
(D) criticize Britain for allowing its monarchs to initiate wars
(E) show that republics are as likely as monarchies to wage war

24. In line 16, the word "former" refers to

(A) nations
(B) people
(C) republics
(D) representatives
(E) monarchies

25. In line 13, the word "popular" most nearly means

(A) very well-liked
(B) completely victorious
(C) supported by people
(D) brutally devastating
(E) cautiously started

26. The author develops the thesis of the passage primarily by

(A) citing examples to answer a question
(B) finding a contradiction in a theory
(C) personally attacking the proponent of a claim
(D) challenging the evidence presented for a conclusion
(E) redefining key terms in the discussion

27. The author implies that republics are

(A) more likely than monarchies to wage war
(B) less likely than monarchies to initiate a war
(C) equally as likely as monarchies to act defensively
(D) just as likely as monarchies to be involved in war
(E) more likely than monarchies to fight a war of aggression

28. Which of the following would be most appropriate for the author to take up in a continuation of the selection?

(A) contrasting different military tactics used by republics and monarchies
(B) studying the changing value over time of war as a tool of national policy
(C) analyzing moral implications of initiating a war without adequate reason
(D) reviewing some examples of unjust wars started by monarchies
(E) comparing justifications given by republics and monarchies for war

29. It can be inferred that the author's attitude toward the actions of Venice is

(A) laudatory
(B) neutral
(C) disapproving
(D) indifferent
(E) speculative

Strategies

Five Steps to Approaching Passages

Answer the Items

Items #30–34 are based on the following passage.

The liberal view of democratic citizenship that developed in the seventeenth and eighteenth centuries was fundamentally different from that of the classical Greeks. The pursuit of private interests
5 with as little interference as possible from government was seen as the road to human happiness and progress rather than the public obligations and involvement in the collective community that were emphasized by the Greeks.
10 Freedom was to be realized by limiting the scope of governmental activity and political obligation and not through immersion in the collective life of the *polis*. The basic role of the citizen was to select governmental leaders and keep the powers and
15 scope of public authority in check. On the liberal view, the rights of citizens against the state were the focus of special emphasis.

Over time, the liberal democratic notion of citizenship developed in two directions. First, there
20 was a movement to increase the proportion of members of society who were eligible to participate as citizens—especially through extending the right of suffrage—and to ensure the basic political equality of all. Second, there was a broadening of
25 the legitimate activities of government and a use of governmental power to redress imbalances in social and economic life. Political citizenship became an instrument through which groups and classes with sufficient numbers of votes could use the state's
30 power to enhance their social and economic well-being.

Within the general liberal view of democratic citizenship, tensions have developed over the degree to which government can and should be
35 used as an instrument for promoting happiness and well-being. Political philosopher Martin Diamond

has categorized two views of democracy as follows. On the one hand, there is the "libertarian" perspective that stresses the private pursuit of
40 happiness and emphasizes the necessity for restraint on government and protection of individual liberties. On the other hand, there is the "majoritarian" view that emphasizes the "task of the government to uplift and aid the common man
45 against the malefactors of great wealth." The tensions between these two views are very evident today. Taxpayer revolts and calls for smaller government and less government regulation clash with demands for greater government involvement
50 in the economic marketplace and the social sphere.

30. The author's primary purpose is to

(A) study ancient concepts of citizenship
(B) contrast different notions of citizenship
(C) criticize modern libertarian democracy
(D) describe the importance of universal suffrage
(E) introduce means of redressing an imbalance of power

31. It can be inferred from the passage that the Greek word "*polis*" (line 13) means

(A) family life
(B) military service
(C) marriage
(D) private club
(E) political community

32. The author cites Martin Diamond in the last paragraph because the author

(A) regards Martin Diamond as an authority on political philosophy
(B) wishes to refute Martin Diamond's views on citizenship
(C) needs a definition of the term "citizenship"
(D) is unfamiliar with the distinction between libertarian and majoritarian concepts of democracy
(E) wants voters to support Martin Diamond as a candidate for public office

33. According to the passage, all of the following are characteristics that would distinguish the liberal idea of government from the Greek idea of government EXCEPT

(A) The emphasis on the rights of private citizens
(B) The activities that government may legitimately pursue
(C) The obligation of citizens to participate in government
(D) The size of the geographical area controlled by a government
(E) The definition of human happiness

34. A majoritarian would be most likely to favor legislation that would

(A) eliminate all restrictions on individual liberty
(B) cut spending for social welfare programs
(C) provide greater protection for consumers
(D) lower taxes on the wealthy and raise taxes on the average worker
(E) raise taxes on the average worker and cut taxes on business

Items #35–41 are based on the following passage.

Park Service strategies to restore natural quiet to the Grand Canyon include both short-term and long-term actions. A limit has been imposed on the number of aircraft operating in the park, and a
5 curfew has been enacted in the Zuni and Dragon corridors. The immediate benefit will be a dramatic reduction in noise levels in some of the most scenic and most sensitive park areas. The Park Service has also increased the number of flight-free zones in the
10 park. In the long-term, the air tour industry must be encouraged to conduct operations using quieter aircraft. Many of the current air tour craft will be phased out and replaced with more noise-efficient designs that incorporate quiet aircraft technology.
15 Additional encouragement will be provided by rewarding companies that invest in new technology. For example, special air tour routes will be established where only quiet aircraft would be permitted to operate.

35. The author's primary concern is to

(A) debate the impact of governmental financial incentives
(B) describe strategies for reducing noise levels in the Grand Canyon
(C) discourage the operation of air tours over the Grand Canyon
(D) discredit the motives of those who oppose noise pollution control
(E) dispute the effectiveness of government noise reduction plans

36. The passage mentions all of the following as strategies for controlling noise pollution in the Grand Canyon EXCEPT

(A) economic incentives for tour companies to buy new aircraft
(B) a curfew on flights over especially sensitive park areas
(C) a total ban on tour flights over the park areas
(D) restrictions on the number of flights over the park
(E) establishment of more flight-free zones in the park

37. In line 6, the word "dramatic" most nearly means

(A) theatrical
(B) suddenly noticeable
(C) slowly developing
(D) permanent
(E) speculative

38. The author mentions the Zuni corridor in order to

(A) illustrate the impact of a flight-free zone
(B) demonstrate the effect of curfews on critical areas
(C) highlight the value of phasing out older aircraft equipment
(D) underscore the advantage of providing incentives
(E) prove the importance of reducing park noise levels

39. The passage implies that the Park Service believes that

(A) tourism is more important than controlling noise
(B) some reduction in park noise levels is desirable
(C) curfews are more effective than flight-free zones
(D) quieter air tour equipment is not presently available
(E) only natural noise levels in the park are acceptable

40. Which of the following would most interfere with the plan to control noise by offering financial incentives to air tour operators?

(A) Special air tour routes would not be sufficiently profitable to pay for the cost of purchasing quiet technology.
(B) The availability of air tours attracts numerous visitors to the Grand Canyon who would not visit were the tours not offered.
(C) The air tourism industry has indicated a willingness to adopt new technology if it is profitable to do so.
(D) Special air tour routes ordinarily include some of the park's most remote and most beautiful scenery.
(E) Many tourists who visit the park on foot or as members of horseback tours complain about the noise of overflights.

41. The author's attitude toward the proposals for reducing noise pollution in the park is one of

(A) skepticism
(B) reluctance
(C) approval
(D) enthusiasm
(E) ignorance

Item-Type Strategies

Items #42–55 are based on the following passage.

The Aleuts, residing on several islands of the Aleutian Chain, the Pribilof Islands, and the Alaskan Peninsula, have possessed a written language since 1825, when the Russian missionary Ivan
5 Veniaminov selected appropriate characters of the Cyrillic alphabet to represent Aleut speech sounds, recorded the main body of Aleut vocabulary, and formulated grammatical rules. The Czarist Russian conquest of the proud, independent sea hunters was
10 so devastatingly thorough that tribal traditions, even tribal memories, were almost obliterated. The slaughter of the majority of an adult generation was sufficient to destroy the continuity of tribal knowledge, which was dependent upon oral
15 transmission. Consequently, the Aleuts developed a fanatical devotion to their language as their only cultural heritage.

The Russian occupation placed a heavy linguistic burden on the Aleuts. Not only were they
20 compelled to learn Russian to converse with their overseers and governors, but they had to learn Old Slavonic to take an active part in church services as well as to master the skill of reading and writing their own tongue. In 1867, when the United States
25 purchased Alaska, the Aleuts were unable to break sharply with their immediate past and substitute English for any one of their three languages.

To communicants of the Russian Orthodox Church, knowledge of Slavonic remained vital, as
30 did Russian, the language in which one conversed with the clergy. The Aleuts came to regard English education as a device to wean them from their religious faith. The introduction of compulsory English schooling caused a minor renaissance of
35 Russian culture as the Aleut parents sought to counteract the influence of the schoolroom. The harsh life of the Russian colonial rule began to appear more happy and beautiful in retrospect.
Regulations forbidding instruction in any
40 language other than English increased its unpopularity. The superficial alphabetical resemblance of Russian and Aleut linked the two tongues so closely that every restriction against teaching Russian was interpreted as an attempt to
45 eradicate the Aleut tongue. From the wording of many regulations, it appears that American administrators often had not the slightest idea that the Aleuts were clandestinely reading and writing in their own tongue or that they even had a written
50 language of their own. To too many officials,

anything in Cyrillic letters was Russian and something to be stamped out. Bitterness bred by abuses and the exploitations that the Aleuts suffered from predatory American traders and
55 adventurers kept alive the Aleut resentment against the language spoken by Americans.

Gradually, despite the failure to emancipate the Aleuts from a sterile past by relating the Aleut and English languages more closely, the passage of
60 years has assuaged the bitter misunderstandings and caused an orientation away from Russian toward English as their second language, but Aleut continues to be the language that molds their thought and expression.

Main Idea Clues

42. The author is primarily concerned with describing

(A) the Aleuts' loyalty to their language and American failure to understand the language
(B) Russian and American treatment of Alaskan inhabitants both before and after 1867
(C) how the Czarist Russian occupation of Alaska created a written language for the Aleuts
(D) American government attempts to persuade the Aleuts to use English as a second language
(E) the atrocities committed by Russia against the Aleuts during the Czarist Russian occupation

43. Which of the following titles best fits the passage?

(A) Aleut Loyalty to Their Language: An American Misunderstanding
(B) Failure of Russian and American Policies in Alaska
(C) Russia's Gift to the Aleuts: A Written Language
(D) Mistreatment of Aleuts During Russian Occupation
(E) The Folly of American Attempts to Teach Aleuts English

Explicit Detail Clues

44. According to the passage, which of the following was the most important reason for the Aleuts' devotion to their language?

(A) Invention of a written version of their language
(B) Introduction of Old Slavonic for worship
(C) Disruption of oral transmission of tribal knowledge
(D) Institution of compulsory English education
(E) Prohibition against writing or reading Russian

Vocabulary Clues

45. In line 19, the word "linguistic" infers relation to

(A) orthodoxy
(B) commerce
(C) language
(D) laws
(E) culture

46. In line 34, the word "renaissance" most nearly means

(A) resurgence
(B) rejection
(C) repeal
(D) reassessment
(E) reminder

47. In line 48, the word "clandestinely" most nearly means

(A) secretly
(B) reliably
(C) openly
(D) casually
(E) exactly

48. In line 58, the word "sterile" most nearly means

(A) germ-free
(B) unproductive
(C) fortunate
(D) ill-timed
(E) dominant

49. In line 60, the word "assuaged" most nearly means

(A) failed
(B) created
(C) intensified
(D) eased
(E) formed

Development Clues

50. The passage is developed primarily by

(A) testing the evidence supporting a theory
(B) describing causes and effects of events
(C) weighing the pros and cons of a plan
(D) projecting the future consequences of a decision
(E) debating both sides of a moral issue

51. Why does the author mention that the Russians killed the majority of adult Aleuts?

(A) To call attention to the immorality of foreign conquest
(B) To urge Russia to make restitution to the children of those killed
(C) To stir up outrage against the Russians for committing such atrocities
(D) To explain the extreme loyalty that Aleuts feel to their language
(E) To prove that the Aleuts have a written language

Implied Idea Clues

52. Which of the following statements about the religious beliefs of the Aleuts can be inferred from the passage?

    (A) Prior to the Russian occupation they had no religious beliefs.
    (B) American traders and adventurers forced them to abandon all religious beliefs.
    (C) At no time in their history have the Aleuts had an organized religion.
    (D) Aleut leaders adopted the religious beliefs of the American officials following the 1867 purchase.
    (E) The Russians forced Aleuts to become members of the Russian Orthodox Church.

53. The passage implies that

    (A) the Cyrillic alphabet was invented for the Aleut language
    (B) all of the Cyrillic characters were used in writing the Aleut language
    (C) Russian and the Aleut language have some similar speech sounds
    (D) English is also written using the Cyrillic alphabet
    (E) the Cyrillic alphabet displaced the original Aleut alphabet

Application Clues

54. Distributing which of the following publications would be most likely to encourage Aleuts to make more use of English?

    (A) Russian translations of English novels
    (B) English translations of Russian novels
    (C) An English-Russian bilingual text devoted to important aspects of Aleutian culture
    (D) An Aleut-English bilingual text devoted to important aspects of Aleutian culture
    (E) A treatise about religions other than the Russian Orthodox Church written in English

Voice Clues

55. The author's attitude toward the Aleuts can best be described as one of

    (A) understanding and sympathy
    (B) callousness and indifference
    (C) condemnation and reproof
    (D) ridicule and disparagement
    (E) awe and admiration

Further Use of Reading Strategies

Humanities

Items #56–62 are based on the following passage.

The figure dangling from the electric sign or propped against the side of the ticket-booth is quintessentially Charlie Chaplin, and the splayed feet, moustache, derby hat, and rattan cane make up
5 a universal symbol of laughter. It is impossible to dissociate Chaplin from Keystone comedy where he began. The Keystone touch is evident in all his later work, often as its most precious element. He enters from a corner of the screen and becomes entangled
10 in a force greater than himself. He advances to the center where he spins like a marionette in a whirlpool until the madness of the action ejects him at the opposite end of the screen. He wanders in a stranger and exits unchanged. "I am here today"
15 was his legend. With its emotional overtone of "gone tomorrow," it was both faintly ironic and exactly right. There is always something about Chaplin and his characters that slips away.

56. The author's attitude toward Chaplin can best be described as

    (A) condescending
    (B) admiring
    (C) judgmental
    (D) inconsistent
    (E) unflattering

57. In line 15, the word "legend" most nearly means

(A) endearing habit
(B) personal history
(C) exaggerated story
(D) descriptive caption
(E) peculiar character

58. The author implies that Chaplin's movie characters are

(A) independent and heroic
(B) similar from film to film
(C) borrowed from other actors
(D) wooden and lifeless
(E) minor role players

59. With which of the following statements would the author most likely agree?

(A) It is possible to detect the influences of an artist's earlier work in later works.
(B) An artist's earlier work is a more important indicator of talent than later work.
(C) Chaplin's work at Keystone represents the most important accomplishments of his career.
(D) The number of times a character can appear in films is limited, as people will eventually tire of the character.
(E) Chaplin appeals primarily to unsophisticated movie-goers who are amused by stock characters.

60. The passage mentions all of the following as helping to define Chaplin's movie character EXCEPT

(A) mode of dress
(B) color themes
(C) body posture
(D) on-screen antics
(E) action sequence

61. The author's primary concern is to

(A) introduce the reader to Chaplin's most important films
(B) analyze audience reaction to Chaplin's film characters
(C) explore the effect of Chaplin's personal life on his work
(D) compare Chaplin's work with that of other comic actors
(E) discuss some of the important features of Chaplin's work

62. The author compares Chaplin's movie character to a marionette (line 11) in order to

(A) suggest that Chaplin was not aware of his role
(B) demonstrate that Chaplin once worked at Keystone
(C) emphasize that the character was not in control
(D) illustrate the variety of roles played by Chaplin
(E) elicit sympathy for the character from the reader

Items #63–71 are based on the following passage.

When we speak casually, we call *Nineteen Eighty-Four* a novel, but to be more exact we should call it a political fable. This requirement is not refuted by the fact that the book is preoccupied with
5 an individual, Winston Smith, who suffers from a varicose ulcer, or by the fact that it takes account of other individuals, including Julia, Mr. Charrington, Mrs. Parsons, Syme, and O'Brien. The figures claim our attention, but they exist mainly in their relation
10 to the political system that determines them. It would indeed be possible to think of them as figures in a novel, though in that case they would have to be imagined in a far more diverse set of relations. They would no longer inhabit or sustain a fable, because a
15 fable is a narrative relieved of much contingent detail so that it may stand forth in an unusual degree of clarity and simplicity. A fable is a structure of types, each of them deliberately simplified lest a sense of difference and
20 heterogeneity reduce the force of the typical. Let us say, then, that *Nineteen Eighty-Four* is a political fable, projected into a near future and incorporating historical references mainly to document a canceled past.

25   Since a fable is predicated upon a typology, it
must be written from a certain distance. The author
cannot afford the sense of familiarity that is induced
by detail and differentiation. A fable, in this respect,
asks to be compared to a caricature, not to a
30 photograph. It follows that in a political fable there
is bound to be some tension between a political
sense dealing in the multiplicity of social and
personal life, and a fable sense committed to
simplicity of form and feature. If the political sense
35 were to prevail, the narrative would be drawn away
from fable into the novel, at some cost to its
simplicity. If the sense of fable were to prevail, the
fabulist would station himself at such a distance
from any imaginary conditions in the case that his
40 narrative would appear unmediated, free or bereft
of conditions. The risk would be considerable: a
reader might feel that the fabulist has lost interest
in the variety of human life and fallen back upon an
unconditioned sense of its types, that he has
45 become less interested in lives than in a particular
idea of life. The risk is greater still if the fabulist
projects his narrative into the future: The reader
cannot question by appealing to life conditions
already known. He is asked to believe that the
50 future is another country and that "they just do
things differently there."
    In a powerful fable, the reader's feeling is
likely to be mostly fear: He is afraid that the
fabulist's vision of any life that could arise may be
55 accurate. The fabulist's feeling may be more various.
A fable such as *Nineteen Eighty-Four* might arise
from disgust, despair, or world-weariness induced
by evidence that nothing, despite one's best efforts,
has changed and that it is too late now to hope for
60 the change one wants.

63. In line 15, the word "contingent" most nearly
means

(A) dependent
(B) essential
(C) boring
(D) unnecessary
(E) compelling

64. In drawing an analogy between a fable and a
caricature (lines 28–29), the author would
most likely regard which of the following pairs
of ideas as also analogous?

(A) The subject of a caricature and the topic of
a fable
(B) The subject of a caricature and the main
character in *Nineteen Eighty-Four*
(C) The subject of a fable and the artist who
draws the caricature
(D) The artist who draws the caricature and a
novelist
(E) The minor characters in a fable and a
photographer

65. Which of the following would be the most
appropriate title for the passage?

(A) A Critical Study of the Use of Characters in
Nineteen Eighty-Four
(B) *Nineteen Eighty-Four*: Political Fable
Rather Than Novel
(C) *Nineteen Eighty-Four*: Reflections on the
Relationship of the Individual to Society
(D) The Use of Typology in the Literature of
Political Fables
(E) Distinguishing a Political Fable from a
Novel

66. According to the passage, which of the
following are characteristics of a political
fable?

(A) It is widely popular at its time of
development.
(B) The reader is unlikely to experience fear
as his reaction to the political situation
described.
(C) Its time frame must treat events that occur
at some point in the future.
(D) Its characters are defined primarily by
their relationship to the social order.
(E) It is similar to a caricature.

67. Which of the following best explains why the author mentions that Winston Smith suffers from a varicose ulcer?

(A) To demonstrate that a political fable must emphasize type over detail
(B) To show that Winston Smith has some characteristics that distinguish him as an individual
(C) To argue that Winston Smith is no more important than any other character in *Nineteen Eighty-Four*
(D) To illustrate one of the features of the political situation described in *Nineteen Eighty-Four*
(E) To suggest that *Nineteen Eighty-Four* is too realistic to be considered a work of fiction

68. The "tension" that the author mentions in line 31 refers to the

(A) necessity of striking a balance between the need to describe a political situation in simple terms and the need to make the description realistic
(B) reaction the reader feels because he is drawn to the characters of the fable as individuals but repulsed by the political situation
(C) delicate task faced by a literary critic who must interpret the text of a work while attempting to describe accurately the intentions of the author
(D) danger that too realistic a description of a key character will make the reader feel that the fable is actually a description of his own situation
(E) conflict of aspirations and interests between characters that an author creates to motivate the action of the narrative

69. The author's attitude toward *Nineteen Eighty-Four* can best be described as

(A) condescending
(B) laudatory
(C) disparaging
(D) scholarly
(E) ironic

70. The author uses the phrase "another country" in line 50 to describe a political fable in which

(A) political events described in a fable occur in a place other than the country of national origin of the author
(B) a lack of detail makes it difficult for a reader to see the connection between his own situation and the one described in the book
(C) too many minor characters create the impression of complete disorganization, leading the reader to believe he is in a foreign country
(D) the author has allowed his personal political convictions to infect his description of the political situation
(E) an overabundance of detail prevents the reader from appreciating the real possibility that such a political situation could develop

71. The author's primary concern is to

(A) define and clarify a concept
(B) point out a logical inconsistency
(C) trace the connection between a cause and an effect
(D) illustrate a general statement with examples
(E) outline a proposal for future action

Items #72–75 are based on the following two passages.

Passage 1

Comedy appeals only to the intelligence, for laughter is incompatible with emotion. Depict some fault, however trifling, in such a way as to arouse sympathy, fear, or pity, and it is impossible to laugh.
5　On the other hand, a vice—even one that is, generally speaking, of an odious nature—can be made ludicrous by a suitable contrivance. So long as it leaves our emotions unaffected, it is funny. This is not to say that the vice itself is ludicrous but only
10　that the vice, as embodied in a particular character, is ludicrous. The only requirement is that it must not engage our feelings.

Passage 2

Absentmindedness is always comical. Indeed, the deeper the absentmindedness the higher the
15 comedy. Systematic absentmindedness, like that of Don Quixote, is the most comical thing imaginable; it is the comic itself, drawn as nearly as possible from its very source. Take any other comic character, however unconscious he may be of what
20 he says or does: He cannot be comical unless there is some aspect of his person of which he is unaware, one side of his nature which he overlooks. On that account alone does he make us laugh.

72. The author of Passage 1 implies that laughter

(A) is not an emotional reaction
(B) counteracts feelings of dread
(C) can correct a vice
(D) is triggered only by a vice
(E) endures longer than emotion

73. The author of Passage 1 discusses vice primarily in order to

(A) advise the reader on how to avoid certain behavior
(B) make it clear that comedy does not engage the emotions
(C) provide an example that the reader will find amusing
(D) demonstrate that emotions are more powerful than intelligence
(E) argue that vice becomes more acceptable if it is portrayed in a humorous fashion

74. In context, "deeper" (line 14) means

(A) complete
(B) complex
(C) courageous
(D) futile
(E) insignificant

75. Which of the following best describes the logical connection between the views expressed in the two passages?

(A) Passage 2 provides examples that show that the views of Passage 1 are incorrect.
(B) Passage 2 redefines a key term that is used by the author of Passage 1.
(C) The two passages reach the same conclusion based on different evidence.
(D) The two passages both cite systematic research for their conclusions.
(E) The two passages discuss different aspects of the topic.

Literary Fiction

Items #76–90 are based on the following two passages.

Passage 1

Shortly after sunrise, just as the light was beginning to come streaming through the trees, I caught the big bright eyes of a deer gazing at me through the garden hedge. The expressive eyes, the
5 slim black-tipped muzzle, and the large ears were perfectly visible, as if placed there at just the right distance to be seen. She continued to gaze while I gazed back with equal steadiness, motionless as a rock. In a few minutes she ventured forward a step,
10 exposing her fine arching neck and forelegs, then snorted and withdrew.

Trembling sprays indicated her return, and her head came into view; several steps later, she stood wholly exposed inside the garden hedge, gazed
15 eagerly around, and again withdrew, but returned a moment afterward, this time advancing into the middle of the garden. Behind her I noticed other pairs of eyes.

It then occurred to me that I might possibly
20 steal up to one of them and catch it, not with any intention of killing it, but only to run my hand along its beautiful curving limbs. They seemed, however, to penetrate my conceit and bounded off with loud, shrill snorts, vanishing into the forest.

25 I have often tried to understand how so many deer, wild sheep, bears, and grouse—nature's cattle and poultry—could be allowed to run at large through the mountain gardens without in any way marring the beauty of their surroundings. I was,
30 therefore, all the more watchful of this feeding flock, and carefully examined the garden after they left, to see what flowers had suffered; I could not, however,

detect the slightest disorder, much less destruction.
It seemed rather that, like gardeners, they had been
35 keeping it in order. I could not see one crushed
flower, nor a single blade of grass that was bent or
broken down. Nor among the daisy, gentian, or
bryanthus gardens of the Alps, where the wild sheep
roam at will, have I ever noticed the effects of
40 destructive feeding or trampling. Even the burly,
shuffling bears beautify the ground on which they
walk, decorating it with their awe-inspiring tracks,
and writing poetry on the soft sequoia bark in boldly
drawn hieroglyphics. But, strange to say, man, the
45 crown, the sequoia of nature, brings confusion with
all his best gifts and with the overabundant,
misbegotten animals that he breeds, sweeps away
the beauty of the wilderness like a fire.

Passage 2

The night was intolerable for Antoine. The
50 buffalo were about him in countless numbers,
regarding him with vicious glances. It was only due
to the natural offensiveness of man that they gave
him any space. The bellowing of the bulls became
louder, and there was a marked uneasiness on the
55 part of the herd. This was a sign of an approaching
storm.

Upon the western horizon were seen flashes of
lightning. The cloud that had been a mere speck had
now become an ominous thunderhead. Suddenly the
60 wind came, and lightning flashes became more
frequent, showing the ungainly forms of the animals
like strange monsters in the white light. The colossal
herd was again in violent motion. It was a blind rush
for shelter, and no heed was paid to buffalo wallows
65 or even deep gulches. All was in the deepest of
darkness. There seemed to be groaning in heaven
and earth—millions of hoofs and throats roaring in
unison.

As a shipwrecked sailor clings to a mere
70 fragment of wood, so Antoine, although almost
exhausted with fatigue, stuck to the saddle of his
pony. As the mad rush continued, every flash
displayed heaps of bison in death's struggle under
the hoofs of their companions.
75 When he awoke and looked around him again it
was morning. The herd had entered the strip of
timber which lay on both sides of the river, and it
was here that Antoine conceived his first distinct
hope of saving himself.
80 "Waw, waw, waw!" was the hoarse cry that
came to his ears, apparently from a human being in
distress. Antoine strained his eyes and craned his
neck to see who it could be. Through an opening in
the branches ahead he perceived a large grizzly bear
85 lying along an inclined limb and hugging it
desperately to maintain his position. The herd had
now thoroughly pervaded the timber, and the bear
was likewise hemmed in. He had taken his
unaccustomed refuge after making a brave stand
90 against several bulls, one of which lay dead nearby,
while he himself was bleeding from several wounds.

Antoine had been assiduously looking for a
friendly tree, by means of which he hoped to escape
from captivity. His horse, by chance, made his way
95 directly under the very box-elder that was sustaining
the bear and there was a convenient branch just
within his reach. He saw at a glance that the
occupant of the tree would not interfere with him.
They were, in fact, companions in distress. Antoine
100 sprang desperately from the pony's back and seized
the cross-limb with both his hands.

By the middle of the afternoon the main body
of the herd had passed, and Antoine was sure that
his captivity had at last come to an end. Then he
105 swung himself from his limb to the ground, and
walked stiffly to the carcass of the nearest cow,
which he dressed, and prepared himself a meal.
But first he took a piece of liver on a long pole to
the bear!

76. The word "sprays" (line 12) refers to

(A) minute droplets
(B) light mist
(C) thin legs
(D) heavy showers
(E) small branches

77. In context, "steal up" (line 20) means

(A) acquire unlawfully
(B) prepare for action
(C) promise faithfully
(D) approach undetected
(E) confine within a boundary

78. In the first two paragraphs, the author of
Passage 1 is primarily concerned with

(A) recounting an experience
(B) exploring a theory
(C) teaching a lesson
(D) offering an opinion
(E) criticizing a plan

79. In context, "conceit" (line 23) means

(A) arrogance
(B) selfishness
(C) fanciful notion
(D) dissatisfaction
(E) clever plan

80. According to the passage, the deer and the sheep are alike in that they both

(A) are wary of human beings
(B) inhabit remote Alpine gardens
(C) feed without causing destruction
(D) live untamed in wilderness regions
(E) strike beautiful and dramatic poses

81. The "boldly drawn hieroglyphics" (lines 43–44) are probably

(A) claw marks
(B) park signs
(C) rare flowers
(D) hoof prints
(E) graffiti

82. The author compares the deer to gardeners (lines 34–37) in order to

(A) encourage the reader to learn more about deer
(B) refute the idea that deer are aggressive
(C) illustrate the similarity between deer and humans
(D) emphasize that deer are not destructive
(E) dramatize the need for wildlife protection

83. In context, "wallows" (line 64) means

(A) shallow depression
(B) deep cave
(C) rugged cliff
(D) low hill
(E) open plain

84. By "the natural offensiveness of man" (line 52), the author of Passage 2 probably refers to man's

(A) frequent rudeness
(B) disagreeable odor
(C) uncontrolled aggression
(D) distasteful behavior
(E) primitive nature

85. All of the following are true of the comparison drawn in the third paragraph of Passage 2 EXCEPT

(A) Antoine, like a shipwrecked sailor, is in a desperate situation.
(B) The herd of buffalo are like the storm driven sea.
(C) Antoine's pony supports him the way that debris might support a shipwrecked sailor.
(D) The struggle to survive leaves both Antoine and the shipwrecked sailor exhausted.
(E) The environment is filled with dangerous creatures that threaten a sailor the way Antoine fears the buffalo.

86. The tone of the first two paragraphs of Passage 2 is

(A) frivolous
(B) suspenseful
(C) animated
(D) reserved
(E) lighthearted

87. The phrase "unaccustomed refuge" (line 89) suggests that the bear

    (A) preferred open areas to confined spaces
    (B) rarely climbed a tree for safety
    (C) did not often encounter buffalo
    (D) was fearful of the presence of a human
    (E) had been surprised by the storm

88. In context, "dressed" (line 107) means

    (A) adorned
    (B) clothed
    (C) bound
    (D) embellished
    (E) prepared

89. The mood of Passage 2 moves from

    (A) joy to despair
    (B) hopelessness to hope
    (C) happiness to gloom
    (D) excitement to torpor
    (E) apprehension to courageousness

90. The information provided in Passage 2 most directly challenges Passage 1 in its description of

    (A) wild animals as gentle and non-destructive
    (B) human beings as able to survive dangerous threats
    (C) gardens as suitable habitats for wild animals
    (D) bears as being unable to climb trees
    (E) the effect of storms on fragile landscapes

Social Studies

Items #91–97 are based on the following passage.

Considerable advances have been made in healthcare services since World War II. These include better access to healthcare (particularly for the poor and minorities), improvements in physical
5 plants and facilities, and increased numbers of physicians and other health personnel. All have played a part in the recent improvement in life expectancy. But there is mounting criticism of the large remaining gaps in access, unbridled cost
10 inflation, the further fragmentation of service, excessive indulgence in wasteful high-technology "gadgeteering," and breakdowns in doctor-patient relationships. In recent years, proposed panaceas and new programs, small and large, have
15 proliferated at a feverish pace and disappointments have multiplied at almost the same rate. This has led to an increased pessimism—"everything has been tried and nothing works"—that sometimes borders on cynicism or even nihilism.
20   It is true that the automatic "pass through" of rapidly spiraling costs to government and insurance carriers produced for a time a sense of unlimited resources and allowed a mood to develop whereby every practitioner and institution could "do his own
25 thing" without undue concern for the "Medical Commons." The practice of full-cost reimbursement encouraged capital investment and now the industry is overcapitalized. Many cities have hundreds of excess hospital beds; hospitals have
30 proliferated a superabundance of high-technology equipment; and structural ostentation and luxury were the order of the day. In any given day, one-fourth of all community beds are vacant; expensive equipment is underused or, worse, used
35 unnecessarily. Capital investment brings rapidly rising operating costs.
      Yet, in part, this pessimism derives from expecting too much of healthcare. Care is often a painful experience accompanied by fear and
40 unwelcome results; although there is room for improvement, it will always retain some unpleasantness and frustration. Moreover, the capacities of medical science are limited. Humpty Dumpty cannot always be put back together again.
45 Too many physicians are reluctant to admit their limitations to patients; too many patients and families are unwilling to accept such realities. Nor is it true that everything has been tried and nothing works, as shown by the prepaid group practice
50 plans at the Kaiser Foundation and Puget Sound. However, typically such undertakings have been drowned by a veritable flood of public and private moneys that have supported and encouraged the continuation of conventional practices and
55 subsidized their shortcomings on a massive, almost unrestricted scale. Except for the most idealistic and dedicated, there were no incentives to seek change or to practice self-restraint or frugality. In this atmosphere, it is not fair to condemn as failures all
60 attempted experiments; it may be more accurate to say that many never had a fair trial.

91. In line 15, the word "feverish" most nearly means

(A) diseased
(B) rapid
(C) controlled
(D) timed
(E) temperate

92. According to author, the "pessimism" mentioned in line 37 is partly attributable to the fact that

(A) there has been little real improvement in healthcare services
(B) expectations about healthcare services are sometimes unrealistic
(C) large segments of the population find it impossible to get access to healthcare services
(D) advances in technology have made healthcare service unaffordable
(E) doctors are now less concerned with patient care

93. The author cites the prepaid plans (lines 47–50) as

(A) counterexamples to the claim that nothing has worked
(B) examples of healthcare plans that were overfunded
(C) evidence that healthcare services are fragmented
(D) proof of the theory that no plan has been successful
(E) experiments that yielded disappointing results

94. It can be inferred that the sentence "Humpty Dumpty cannot always be put back together again" means that

(A) the cost of healthcare services will not decline
(B) some people should not become doctors
(C) medical care is not really essential to good health
(D) illness is often unpleasant and even painful
(E) medical science cannot cure every ill

95. With which of the following descriptions of the system for the delivery of healthcare services would the author most likely agree?

(A) It is biased in favor of doctors and against patients.
(B) It is highly fragmented and completely ineffective.
(C) It has not embraced new technology rapidly enough.
(D) It is generally effective but can be improved.
(E) It discourages people from seeking medical care.

96. Which of the following best describes the logical structure of the selection?

(A) The third paragraph is intended as a refutation of the first and second paragraphs.
(B) The second and third paragraphs are intended as a refutation of the first paragraph.
(C) The second and third paragraphs explain and put into perspective the points made in the first paragraph.
(D) The first paragraph describes a problem, and the second and third paragraphs present two horns of a dilemma.
(E) The first paragraph describes a problem, the second its causes, and the third a possible solution.

97. The author's primary concern is to

(A) criticize physicians and healthcare administrators for investing in technologically advanced equipment
(B) examine some problems affecting delivery of healthcare services and assess the severity of those problems
(C) defend the medical community from charges that healthcare has not improved since World War II
(D) analyze the reasons for the healthcare industry's inability to provide quality care to all segments of the population
(E) describe the peculiar economic features of the healthcare industry that are the causes of spiraling medical costs

Natural Sciences

Items #98–104 are based on the following passage.

Like tropical reef corals, deep-sea corals have hard skeletons built from calcium and carbonate ions extracted from seawater. Oxygen and oxygen isotopes in carbonate ions can be used to determine
5 the water temperature when the skeleton was formed. The absolute abundance of an isotope is difficult to measure, so studies focus on the ratio of the rare oxygen isotope ^{18}O to the common isotope ^{16}O. This ratio is inversely related to water
10 temperature during formation of carbonates, so higher ratios mean lower temperatures. Some corals live for decades or centuries, so their skeletons contain a natural record of climate variability, like tree rings and ice cores. The ratio
15 can be used as a proxy for data that cannot be obtained by direct measurement. The information gathered would be useful in determining the extent to which global warming may be a problem.

98. The passage is primarily a discussion of how

(A) scientists use proxies to study changing climate conditions
(B) natural climate records generate data about global warming
(C) coral reefs extract chemicals from the ocean to build reefs
(D) deep-sea coral reefs can provide information about climate change
(E) global warming threatens deep-sea and tropical corals

99. In line 15, the word "proxy" most nearly means

(A) conclusion
(B) substitute
(C) theory
(D) instrument
(E) proof

100. A finding that the ratio of the ^{18}O isotope to the ^{16}O had been increasing for a certain period would most strongly support the conclusion that

(A) the water temperature in the surrounding area had decreased
(B) global warming had intensified for those years
(C) climate variations for the period were insignificant
(D) ocean water temperature around the reef had increased
(E) other natural records show increases as well

101. The author mentions tropical reef corals in line 1 in order to

(A) prevent a possible misunderstanding
(B) provide the reader with a point of reference
(C) highlight an important difference for the reader
(D) introduce the reader to a key distinction
(E) indicate to the reader the main thesis of the passage

102. The author's attitude toward climate change can best be described as

(A) alarmed
(B) complacent
(C) concerned
(D) fearful
(E) optimistic

103. According to the passage, studies use the ratio of the ^{18}O isotope to the ^{16}O isotope because

(A) it is difficult to determine how much of any given isotope was in the environment
(B) direct measurements of ocean temperatures cannot be taken at great depths
(C) rare oxygen isotopes are found with sufficient frequency to permit direct measurements
(D) carbonate ions can absorb either the oxygen isotope ^{18}O isotope to the ^{16}O isotope
(E) deep-sea corals do not lie at or near the surface but at the bottom of the ocean

104. It can be inferred that scientists determine the approximate years in which various parts of a deep-sea coral were formed

(A) without referring to the oxygen isotope content of carbonate ions
(B) by relying on the ratio of the ^{18}O isotope to the ^{16}O isotope
(C) by calculating the availability of the ^{18}O isotope in the environment
(D) by calculating the availability of the ^{16}O isotope in the environment
(E) by relying on the ratio of the ^{16}O isotope to the ^{18}O isotope in the skeleton

Items #105–112 are based on the following passage.

Galaxies come in a variety of sizes and shapes: majestic spirals, ruddy disks, elliptically shaped dwarfs and giants, and a menagerie of other, more bizarre forms. Most currently, popular theories
5   suggest that conditions prior to birth—mass of the protogalactic cloud, its size, its rotation—determine whether a galaxy will be large or small, spiral or elliptical; but about 10 percent of all galaxies are members of rich clusters of thousands of galaxies.
10   The gravitational forces of fields of nearby galaxies constantly distort galaxies in the crowded central region of rich clusters. In addition, rich clusters of galaxies are pervaded by a tenuous gas with a temperature of up to 100 million degrees. Galaxies
15   are blasted and scoured by a hot wind created by their motion through the gas. In crowded conditions such as these, environment becomes a more important determinant of the size and shape of a galaxy than heredity. In fact, if our galaxy had
20   happened to form well within the core of a cluster such as Virgo, the Sun would probably never have formed, because the Sun, a second- or third-generation star located in the disk of the galaxy, was formed from leftover gas five billion years or so
25   after the initial period of star formation. By that time, in a rich cluster, the galaxy may well have already been stripped of its gas.
    As a galaxy moves through the core of a rich cluster, it is not only scoured by hot gas; it
30   encounters other galaxies as well. If the collision is one-on-one at moderate to high speeds of galaxies of approximately the same size, both galaxies will emerge relatively intact, if a little distorted and ragged about the edges. If, however, a galaxy coasts
35   by a much larger one in a slow, grazing collision, the smaller one can be completely disrupted and assimilated by the larger.

    Under the right conditions, these cosmic cannibals can consume 50 to 100 galaxies. The
40   accumulative effect of these collisions is to produce a dynamic friction on the large galaxy, slowing it down. As a result, it gradually spirals in toward the center of the cluster. Eventually, the gravitational forces that bind the stars to the infalling galaxy are
45   overwhelmed by the combined gravity of the galaxies in the core of the cluster—just as the ocean is pulled away from the shore at ebb tide by the Moon, the stars are pulled away from their infalling parent galaxy. If there is a large galaxy at the center
50   of the cluster, it may ultimately capture these stars. With the passage of time, many galaxies will be torn asunder in the depths of this gravitational maelstrom and be swallowed up in the ever-expanding envelope of the central cannibal galaxy.
55   Galactic cannibalism also explains why there are few if any bright galaxies in these clusters other than the central supergiant galaxy. That is because the bright galaxies, which are the most massive, experience the greatest dynamical friction. They are
60   the first to go down to the gravitational well and be swallowed up by the central galaxies.
    Over the course of several billion years, 50 or so galaxies may be swallowed up, leaving only the central supergiant and the 51st, the 52nd, etc.,
65   brightest galaxies. Given time, all the massive galaxies in the cluster will be absorbed, leaving a sparse cluster of a supergiant galaxy surrounded by clouds of small, dim galaxies.

105. In line 3, the word "menagerie" most nearly means

(A) odd mixture
(B) open environment
(C) uniform collection
(D) flat area
(E) simple structure

106. It can be inferred from the passage that the physical features of a galaxy that does not belong to a rich cluster are determined primarily by the

(A) size and rotation of the protogalactic cloud
(B) intensity of light emanating from the galaxy
(C) temperature of the interstellar gas
(D) age of the protogalactic cloud
(E) speed at which the protogalactic cloud is moving through space

107. The author implies that the currently accepted theories on galaxy formation are

(A) completely incorrect and misguided
(B) naive and out-of-date
(C) speculative and unsupported by observation
(D) substantially correct but in need of modification
(E) accurate and adequate to explain all known observations

108. According to the passage, a cluster with a central, supergiant galaxy will

(A) contain no intermediately bright galaxies
(B) have 50–100 galaxies of all sizes and intensities
(C) consist solely of third- and fourth-generation stars
(D) produce only spiral and disk-shaped galaxies
(E) be surrounded by galaxies of all sizes and shapes

109. According to the passage, the outcome of a collision between galaxies depends on which of the following?

(A) The relative velocities of the galaxies
(B) The relative ages of the galaxies
(C) The relative sizes of the galaxies
(D) The relative velocities and ages of the galaxies
(E) The relative velocities and sizes of the galaxies

110. According to the passage, as a galaxy falls inward toward the center of a cluster, it

(A) collides with the central core and emerges relatively intact
(B) absorbs superheated gases from the interstellar medium
(C) is broken apart by the gravitational forces of the core
(D) is transformed by collisions into a large, spiral galaxy
(E) captures unattached stars that have been ejected from the galaxy's core

111. The passage provides information that will answer which of the following questions?

(A) What is the age of our sun?
(B) What proportion of all galaxies are found in clusters?
(C) Approximately how many galaxies would be found in a rich cluster?
(D) What type of galaxy is ours?
(E) At what velocity does our solar system travel?

112. The tone of the passage can best be described as

(A) lighthearted and amused
(B) objective but concerned
(C) detached and unconcerned
(D) cautious but sincere
(E) enthusiastic and enlightened

QUIZZES

This section contains three Critical Reading: Passages quizzes. Complete each quiz under timed conditions. Answers are on page 619.

Quiz I

(18 items; 30 minutes)

DIRECTIONS: Each passage below is followed by a set of items based on its content. Answer the items on the basis of what is stated or implied in the corresponding passage..

Item #1 is based on the following passage.

In 1800, after two thousand years of public and private construction projects, travel in Europe had hardly improved at all. A few bridges had been built, and a post-road extended from Madrid to St.
5 Petersburg; but the diligence that rumbled from Calais to Paris required three days to cover the one hundred and fifty miles. Travelers to Marseilles met with rough roads and hardships like those of the Middle Ages. Italy was almost as remote from the
10 north of Europe as when carriage roads were first built. Indeed, because of the violence of revolutionary wars during the last ten years of the eighteenth century, conditions had actually deteriorated.

1. As used in line 5, the word "diligence" refers to

   (A) a positive mental attitude
   (B) a heavy wheeled conveyance
   (C) an unimproved roadway
   (D) a lengthy journey
   (E) perseverance in adversity

Item #2 is based on the following passage.

Before there was a Federal Constitution, the Articles of Confederation provided for a union of the former British colonies of what is now called the United States. From the beginning, however, many
5 Americans recognized the inadequacies of the Articles as a national government, and a movement for a new national government began outside the Congress. Representatives of Maryland and Virginia, meeting at Mt. Vernon to discuss trade problems
10 between the two states, agreed to invite delegates from all states to discuss commercial affairs at a meeting in Annapolis, Maryland, in September 1786. Although delegates from only five states reached the Annapolis Convention, that group
15 issued a call for a meeting of all states to discuss necessary revisions of the Articles of Confederation. Responding to this call, every state except Rhode Island selected delegates for the Federal Convention at Philadelphia.

2. The author states that the convention to create a new national government was primarily a response to

   (A) the Annapolis Convention
   (B) a trade meeting at Mt. Vernon
   (C) the Federal Convention
   (D) the Continental Congress
   (E) Rhode Island's delegates

Item #3 is based on the following passage.

In America today, most people are living longer. The reasons are simple: advances in medicine and healthcare, better nutrition and healthier lifestyles, and a major reduction in
5 environmental pollutants. By the year 2020, one in six Americans—53 million men and women—will be age 65 or older. This is the same generation that overloaded schools, challenged the healthcare system, and overburdened the transportation
10 network. The nation is not ready for this surge in the senior population. Many of these seniors will need housing and healthcare services that may be neither available nor affordable unless the nation acts now. If the situation is dire now, it will be
15 desperate in the year 2020.

3. The author regards the situation created by the aging population as a

(A) passing phenomenon
(B) historical precedent
(C) long-term challenge
(D) fortunate development
(E) governmental crisis

Item #4 is based on the following passage.

Manufactured homes evolved from the mobile home and tend to have certain distinctive features such as a lower pitch to the roof because they are built in the factory and towed to a final location.
5 They have little or no roof overhangs because of highway width limitations and are long and narrow due to hauling restrictions. However, many of the differences between manufactured and site-built homes are disappearing. Manufacturers are using
10 siding and roofing that are the same as those used on other types of housing. They have developed hinged roofs that can be delivered flat and set up on site with a normal roof pitch and overhangs. Newer manufactured homes can also be set on permanent
15 foundations, thereby avoiding the skirting that is usually associated with manufactured housing. Furthermore, manufactured homes are larger than ever, as multi-section units have become available.

4. The author implies that the feature of manufactured homes that is LEAST likely to change is the

(A) overhangs at the edges of the roofs
(B) quality of the siding material used
(C) type of foundation used for support
(D) size and shape of individual sections
(E) pitch of the roof of the finished home

Item #5 is based on the following passage.

Many volcanoes are associated with movement of tectonic plates. Where the plates move apart, as along the Atlantic mid-ocean ridge, a rift forms and allows magma to escape from deep within the Earth.
5 The temperature of the magma is about 1200°C; but due to the cold deep ocean water, the magma solidifies into a mixture of minerals and volcanic glass. The resulting basalt formations are slowly broken down due to "weathering." Once believed to
10 be a chemical process, new evidence suggests that microbial organisms may partly be responsible for "weathering." Microscopic examinations of weathered basalts show pits, channels, and other patterns that are unlike chemical weathering. These
15 weathered rocks also contain large amounts of carbon, phosphorus, and nitrogen, byproducts of biological activity, as well as traces of nucleic acids. No living cells have been discovered in the rocks, but objects have been found that resemble cellular
20 structures.

5. It can be inferred that the pits and channels in the basalt (line 13)

(A) were created when the basalt was cooled by ocean water
(B) are generally the products of organic activity
(C) resulted from chemical processes at high temperatures
(D) exhibit the size and shape of cellular structures
(E) inhibit the functioning of chemical processes

Item #6 is based on the following passage.

Imagine the telecommunication cables of a large city: millions of calls flash down fiber optic cables at incredible speeds. Multiply that many-fold and that's the brain. As a neuron receives messages
5 from surrounding cells, an electrical charge builds up. This charge travels down the axon to the end, where it triggers the release of chemical messengers that are called neurotransmitters, which move from the axon across a tiny gap to the
10 dendrites or cell bodies of other neurons. There, they bind to specific receptor sites on the receiving end of the dendrites of nearby neurons and either open channels through the cell membrane into the receiving nerve cell's interior or start other
15 processes that determine what the receiving nerve cell will do.

6. The author's primary purpose in the passage is to

(A) present new scientific findings
(B) describe the structure of the brain
(C) discuss methods of improving brain function
(D) propose a model for telecommunications
(E) outline a biochemical process

Item #7 is based on the following passage.

About 50 percent of nitrogen that is applied to crops as fertilizer is taken up by plants; the remainder washes off or is blown off the soil. Run-off of nitrogen and phosphate from fertilizers
5 results in "eutrophication" of surface waters. Eutrophication is a natural process in which a water body is enriched by the addition of excessive nutrients, which causes excessive algae growth and depletes oxygen. Many species cannot survive in
10 these conditions, and large "dead zones" appear from decaying matter undergoing anaerobic degradation.

7. The author uses the word "excessive" (line 7) to describe nutrients that are

(A) present in fertilizers and that cannot be absorbed by crops
(B) in surface water above what is needed to maintain a balance of life
(C) applied to crops only to be blown off later
(D) present in surface water and that are not absorbed by algae
(E) made from chemicals and that pollute water and create dead zones

Item #8 is based on the following passage.

It is sometimes more noble to be wrong than to be right. We feel respect for consistency, even in error, and we lament the virtue that is debauched into a vice. At least the person who acts consistently
5 but wrongly can be said to have a measure of integrity, while the person who acts virtuously one day and villainously the next is at best weak and at worst hypocritical. And is that not what it means to have integrity? The word echoes its root: a whole.
10 The person who has integrity consistently values virtue even though it may be unattainable.

8. The author would most likely accept which of the following as an example of integrity?

(A) An enemy soldier who fights bravely and fairly
(B) A professor who teaches that all morals are relative
(C) A merchant who donates to charity to generate goodwill
(D) A lawmaker who supports a bill only to please voters
(E) An artist who paints portraits that flatter the subject

Items #9–10 are based on the following passage.

As a debater, Abraham Lincoln was consistently an actor, a caricaturist, and a satirist. In an early political debate, he mimicked his opponent so accurately and with such bitter ridicule that the
5 man was reduced to tears. At the bar, his famous "Skin the defendant alive" meant an outpouring of personal ridicule. Personal ridicule was usually presented with a guileless air. As he rose to respond to Douglas in one of those rightly famous debates,
10 Lincoln deadpanned, "I was not aware until now that Mr. Douglas's father was a cooper. And I have no doubt that he was a very good one." Lincoln bowed gravely to Douglas and continued, "He has made one of the best whiskey casks I have ever seen."

9. In line 11, the word "cooper" most nearly means

(A) satirist
(B) debater
(C) barrel maker
(D) defendant
(E) offspring

10. In lines 13–15, Lincoln implies that Douglas

(A) was an excellent debater
(B) had the intelligence of a cask
(C) deserved to be skinned alive
(D) was not as famous as his father
(E) should not have used personal ridicule

Items #11–18 are based on the following passage.

The healthcare economy is replete with unusual and even unique economic relationships. One of the least understood involves the peculiar roles of producer or "provider" and purchaser or
5 "consumer" in the typical doctor-patient relationship. In most sectors of the economy, the seller attempts to attract a potential buyer with various inducements of price, quality, and utility, and the buyer makes the decision. Where
10 circumstances permit the buyer no choice because there is effectively only one seller and the product is relatively essential, government usually asserts monopoly and places the industry under price and other regulations. Neither of these conditions
15 prevails in most of the healthcare industry.

In the healthcare industry, the doctor-patient relationship is the mirror image of the ordinary relationship between producer and consumer. Once an individual has chosen to see a physician—and
20 even then there may be no real choice—it is the physician who usually makes all significant purchasing decisions: whether the patient should return "next Wednesday," whether X-rays are needed, whether drugs should be prescribed, etc. It
25 is a rare and sophisticated patient who will challenge such professional decisions or raise in advance questions about price, especially when the ailment is regarded as serious.

This is particularly significant in relation to
30 hospital care. The physician must certify the need for hospitalization, determine what procedures will be performed, and announce when the patient may be discharged. The patient may be consulted about some of these decisions, but in the main it is the
35 doctor's judgments that are final. Little wonder, then, that in the eyes of the hospital, the physician is the real "consumer." Consequently, the medical staff, not the administration, represents the "power center" in hospital policy and decision-making.
40 Although usually there are in this situation four identifiable participants—the physician, the hospital, the patient, and the payer (generally an insurance carrier or government)—the physician makes the essential decisions for all of them. The
45 hospital becomes an extension of the physician; the payer generally meets most of the bona fide bills generated by the physician/hospital; and for the most part the patient plays a passive role. In routine or minor illnesses, or just plain worries, the
50 patient's options are, of course, much greater with respect to use and price. In illnesses that are of some significance, however, such choices tend to

evaporate, and it is for these illnesses that the bulk of the healthcare dollar is spent. We estimate that
55 about 75 to 80 percent of healthcare expenditures are determined by physicians, not patients. For this reason, economy measures directed at patients or the public are relatively ineffective.

11. In line 1, the phrase "replete with" most nearly means

(A) filled with
(B) restricted by
(C) enriched by
(D) damaged by
(E) devoid of

12. The author's primary purpose is to

(A) speculate about the relationship between a patient's ability to pay and the treatment received
(B) criticize doctors for exercising too much control over patients
(C) analyze some important economic factors in healthcare
(D) urge hospitals to reclaim their decision-making authority
(E) inform potential patients of their healthcare rights

13. The author's primary concern is to

(A) define a term
(B) clarify a misunderstanding
(C) refute a theory
(D) discuss a problem
(E) announce a new discovery

14. It can be inferred that doctors are able to determine hospital policies because

(A) it is doctors who generate income for the hospital
(B) most of a patient's bills are paid by health insurance
(C) hospital administrators lack the expertise to question medical decisions
(D) a doctor is ultimately responsible for a patient's health
(E) some patients might refuse to accept their physician's advice

15. According to the author, when a doctor tells a patient to "return next Wednesday," the doctor is in effect

(A) taking advantage of the patient's concern for his health
(B) instructing the patient to buy more medical services
(C) warning the patient that a hospital stay might be necessary
(D) advising the patient to seek a second opinion
(E) admitting that the initial visit was ineffective

16. The author is most probably leading up to

(A) a proposal to control medical costs
(B) a discussion of a new medical treatment
(C) an analysis of the causes of inflation in the United States
(D) a study of lawsuits against doctors for malpractice
(E) a comparison of hospitals and factories

17. The tone of the passage can best be described as

(A) whimsical
(B) cautious
(C) analytical
(D) inquisitive
(E) defiant

18. With which of the following statements would the author most likely agree?

(A) The quality of healthcare given to an individual patient is compromised by doctors hoping to reduce costs.

(B) In the doctor-patient relationship, the patient is able to reduce costs by physician-shopping.

(C) Insurers and the government pay large sums of money to reimburse hospitals for services not performed and other fraudulent practices.

(D) Efforts to reduce the cost of healthcare will be most effective if they are aimed at the physician.

(E) Most of the cost of healthcare is for expensive tests and treatments that are completely unnecessary.

Quiz II

(17 items; 30 minutes)

DIRECTIONS: Each passage below is followed by a set of items based on its content. Answer the items on the basis of what is stated or implied in the corresponding passage.

Item #1 is based on the following passage.

The French are great optimists. They seize upon every good thing as soon as it appears and revel in even fleeting pleasure. The English, on the other hand, are apt to neglect the present good in
5 preparing for the possible evil. However badly things may be going otherwise, if the sun breaks through the clouds for even a moment, the French are out in holiday dress and spirits, carefree as butterflies, as though the sun will shine forever. But
10 no matter how brightly the sun is shining, if there is a wisp of cloud on the horizon, the English venture forth distrustfully with umbrellas in hand.

1. The author of the passage uses weather as

(A) an example of a force of nature
(B) an illustration of pleasant and unpleasant traits
(C) an excuse to write about French and English habits
(D) a symbol of good and bad fortune
(E) a measure of a society's values

Item #2 is based on the following passage.

It has been half a century since nuclear energy was introduced to the public in a most dramatic, but unfortunately, most destructive way—through the use of a nuclear weapon. Since then, enormous
5 strides have been made in developing the peaceful applications of this great and versatile force. Because these strides have always been overshadowed by the focus of public attention on military uses, the public has never fully understood
10 or appreciated the gains and status of the peaceful atom.

2. The author implies that had a nuclear weapon not been used

(A) people would be more receptive to peaceful uses of nuclear power
(B) governments would be less likely to deploy nuclear weapons
(C) public support for nuclear weaponry would be undermined
(D) the security of nations having nuclear arsenals would be weakened
(E) military and non-military uses of nuclear power would be limited

Item #3 is based on the following passage.

In 1964, the Surgeon General announced that cigarette smoking was a significant health hazard, yet smoking still kills over 400,000 people annually in the United States alone—more deaths each year
5 than from AIDS, alcohol, cocaine, heroin, homicide, suicide, motor vehicle crashes, and fires combined. We have made gains in preventing and controlling tobacco use; but despite the massive education campaigns and years of litigation, as well as
10 substantial price hikes designed to curb smoking, the incidence of smoking has increased. There is no disagreement that the best option for any person using tobacco products is to stop, and when asked, most smokers say they want to quit. Unfortunately,
15 very few of them are able to break the habit.

3. The author cites deaths from non-smoking causes (lines 5–6) primarily to

(A) show that smoking is not as serious a problem as many people believe
(B) demonstrate that many health hazards other than smoking require attention
(C) illustrate the variety of diseases that pose a danger in modern society
(D) dramatize the seriousness of the health problem presented by the use of tobacco
(E) stress the importance of encouraging people to discontinue the use of tobacco

Item #4 is based on the following passage.

We think of invasive non-native plants as overgrowing an entire ecosystem, but plants can also change entire ecosystems by modifying ecosystem traits and processes. In Florida,
5 Australian paperbark trees, with spongy outer bark and highly flammable leaves and litter, have increased the frequency of fire. This has helped paperbark replace native plants on at least 400,000 acres. In the arid Southwest, the deep roots of
10 Mediterranean salt cedars deplete soil water. On the island of Hawaii, the nitrogen-fixing firebush has invaded nitrogen-poor areas. As there are no native nitrogen fixers, native plants have adapted to the nitrogen-poor soil. However, introduced species
15 cannot tolerate it, so a wave of invasive plants are taking over areas that are prepared by the firebush.

4. Which of the following best summarizes the main point of the passage?

(A) Non-native plant species can devastate an ecosystem by overgrowing native plant species.
(B) Non-native plants can change an ecosystem without directly displacing native species.
(C) Native plant species are often unable to adapt to significant changes in an ecosystem.
(D) The introduction of non-native plant species carries a significant environmental risk.
(E) Plants such as the Australian paperbark tree are not able to survive in their native habitats.

Item #5 is based on the following passage.

For indigenous people of the United States, the continuance of cultural values and traditions depends on the transmission of language, but many languages are dying and many more have become
5 extinct already. Of the 85–100 indigenous languages that used to exist in California, half are gone. As for the other half, the vast majority have five or fewer speakers, all over 70 years old. The languages are silent at home and in the community, and so the
10 most effective way to get a critical mass of new fluent speakers of an endangered language is through the school, the same institution that was used to destroy those very languages in the past.

5. Which of the following most nearly captures the meaning of "critical mass" (line 10)?

(A) A sufficient number
(B) At least five or more
(C) Five or fewer
(D) Eighty-five to 100
(E) More than 70

Item #6 is based on the following passage.

In 1986, a Wall Street Journal article used the phrase "glass ceiling" to refer to an invisible, but impenetrable, barrier preventing women from reaching the highest level of business. Subsequent
5 research confirmed the existence of such a barrier. Ninety-seven percent of the senior managers of Fortune 500 companies are male. Where there are women in high places, their compensation is lower than that of men in comparable positions. Nor is the
10 glass ceiling likely to disappear soon. There are relatively few women in the "pipeline," the positions most likely to lead to the top. In short, the world at the top of the corporate hierarchy does not look anything like America.

6. The author regards the existence of the "glass ceiling" (line 2) as

(A) well documented
(B) theoretically possible
(C) relatively unlikely
(D) entirely speculative
(E) virtually impossible

Item #7 is based on the following passage.

In politics, the hero does not live happily ever after. The last chapter is merely a place where the writer imagines that the polite reader has begun to look furtively at the clock. When Plato came to the
5 point where it was fitting to sum up, his assurance turned into stage fright. Those sentences in the Republic are so absurd that it is impossible either to live by them or to forget them: "Until philosophers are kings, or kings have the spirit of philosophy, and
10 political greatness and wisdom meet in one, cities will never cease from ill." Whenever we make an appeal to reason in politics, the difficulty in this parable recurs, for there is an inherent difficulty in using reason to deal with an unreasoning world.

7. The author uses the phrase "inherent difficulty" (line 13) to indicate that

(A) Plato's instructions in the Republic have no application to current events
(B) it is unrealistic to expect that political leaders will be philosophers
(C) political leaders rarely have the personal characteristics to be heroic
(D) the practical world can only be ordered according to the principles of reason
(E) political greatness and wisdom coexist only when a political leader is also a philosopher

Item #8 is based on the following passage.

Zora Neale Hurston, author of four novels, a folk opera, and nearly 100 short stories, loved a good lie. When her late-model car aroused suspicion among poor country folk whose lives she was
5 researching, she pretended to be a bootlegger. She lied on official documents like marriage licenses, giving her age at the time of her second marriage as 31 rather than 48. Her letters sometimes seem to be written by different people, and her autobiography,
10 in which she claims to have been born in Eatonville, Florida, rather than Notasulga, Alabama, is full of misinformation. So, Hurston's own statements and writings are not likely to settle any of the debates over the details of her life.

8. The author implies that Hurston's writings are not a good source of information about the details of her life because

(A) details of an author's personal life are not usually available
(B) autobiographical information cannot be independently verified
(C) writers of fiction cannot be trusted to portray events accurately
(D) official documents are more reliable than family histories
(E) Hurston's descriptions of the details of her life are unreliable

Items #9–10 are based on the following passage.

Recently, six Magellanic penguins that were taken from the wild arrived at the San Francisco Zoo. The 46 long-time resident Magellanic penguins, which had spent relatively sedentary lives of
5 grooming and staying in burrows, began to simulate migratory behavior when they watched the new penguins swimming around the 130-by-40-foot 40 foot pool. All 52 birds now swim almost all of the time, resting on the artificial island in the middle of
10 the pool only at night. Indeed, when the pool is drained for cleaning, the penguins refuse to leave, walking around it instead of swimming.

9. In line 4, the word "sedentary" most nearly means

(A) sheltered
(B) aquatic
(C) uninteresting
(D) inactive
(E) spontaneous

10. Which of the following conclusions can be most reliably drawn from the information above?

(A) Migratory behavior in animals is acquired rather than innate.
(B) Animals in zoo environments rarely exhibit active behavior.
(C) Magellanic penguins in the wild spend most of their time swimming.
(D) The close quarters of a zoo environment suppress animal migratory behavior.
(E) Animals sometimes mimic the behavior they see in other animals.

Items #11–17 are based on the following passage.

Man, so the truism goes, lives increasingly in a man-made environment. This puts a special burden on human immaturity, for it is plain that adapting to such variable conditions must depend very heavily
5 on opportunities for learning, or whatever the processes are that are operative during immaturity. It must also mean that during immaturity, man must master knowledge and skills that are neither stored in the gene pool nor learned by direct
10 encounter, but that are contained in the culture pool—knowledge about values and history, skills as varied as an obligatory natural language or an optional mathematical one, as mute as levers or as articulate as myth telling.
15 Yet, it would be a mistake to leap to the conclusion that because human immaturity makes possible high flexibility, therefore anything is possible for the species. Human traits were selected for their survival value over a four- to five-million-
20 year period with a great acceleration of the selection process during the last half of that period. There were crucial, irreversible changes during that final man-making period: the recession of formidable dentition, a 50 percent increase in brain
25 volume, the obstetrical paradox—bipedalism and strong pelvic girdle, larger brain through a smaller birth canal—an immature brain at birth, and creation of what Washburn has called a "technical-social way of life," involving tool and symbol use.
30 Note, however, that hominization consisted principally of adaptations to conditions in the Pleistocene era. These preadaptations, shaped in response to earlier habitat demands, are part of man's evolutionary inheritance. This is not to say
35 that close beneath the skin of man is a naked ape, that civilization is only a veneer. The technical-social way of life is a deep feature of the species adaptation. But we would err if we assumed *a priori* that man's inheritance placed no constraint on his
40 power to adapt. Some of the preadaptations can be shown to be presently maladaptive. Man's inordinate fondness for fats and sweets no longer serves his individual survival well. Furthermore, the human obsession with sexuality is plainly not fitted
45 for survival of the species now, however well it might have served to populate the upper Pliocene and the Pleistocene eras. Nevertheless, note that the species responds typically to these challenges by technical innovation rather than by morphological
50 or behavioral change. Contraception dissociates sexuality from reproduction. Of course, we do not know what kinds and what range of stresses are

produced by successive rounds of such technical innovation. Dissociating sexuality and reproduction,
55 for example, surely produces changes in the structure of the family, which in turn redefine the role of women, which in turn alters the authority pattern affecting the child, etc. Continuing and possibly accelerating change seems inherent in such
60 adaptation. This, of course, places an enormous pressure on man's uses of immaturity, preparing the young for unforeseeable change—the more so if there are severe restraints imposed by human preadaptations to earlier conditions of life.

11. The primary purpose of the passage is to

(A) refute some misconceptions about the importance of human immaturity
(B) introduce a new theory of the origins of the human species
(C) describe the evolutionary forces that formed the physical appearance of modern humans
(D) discuss the importance of human immaturity as an adaptive mechanism
(E) outline the process by which humans mature into social beings

12. It can be inferred that the obstetrical paradox is puzzling because

(A) it occurred very late during the evolution of the species
(B) evolutionary forces seemed to work at cross purposes to each other
(C) technological innovations have made the process of birth easier
(D) an increase in brain size is not an ordinary evolutionary event
(E) a strong pelvic girdle is no longer necessary to the survival of the species

13. Which of the following statements can be inferred from the passage?

(A) Human beings are today less sexually active than were our ancestors during the Pleistocene era.
(B) During the Pleistocene era, a fondness for fats and sweets was a trait that contributed to the survival of humans.
(C) Mathematics was invented by human beings during the latter half of the Pleistocene era.
(D) The use of language and tools is a trait that is genetically transmitted from one generation to the next.
(E) During immaturity, human beings gain knowledge and learn skills primarily through the process of direct encounter.

14. As used in line 32, the term "preadaptations" refers to traits that

(A) were useful to earlier human beings but have since lost their utility
(B) appeared in response to the need to learn a natural language and the use of tools
(C) humans currently exhibit but that developed in response to conditions of an earlier age
(D) are disadvantageous to creatures whose way of life is primarily technical and social
(E) continue to exist despite evolutionary pressures that threaten to erase them

15. The author mentions contraception to demonstrate that

(A) human beings may adapt to new conditions by technological invention rather than by changing their behavior
(B) sexual promiscuity is no longer an aid to the survival of the human species
(C) technological innovation is a more important adaptive mechanism than either heredity or direct encounter
(D) conditions during the upper Pliocene and Pleistocene eras no longer affect the course of human evolution
(E) morphological change is a common response to new demands placed on a creature by its environment

16. With which of the following statements would the author LEAST likely agree?

(A) The technical-social way of life of humans is an adaptive mechanism that arose in response to environmental pressures.
(B) The possibility of technical innovation makes it unlikely that the physical appearance of humans will change radically in a short time.
(C) Technological innovations can result in changes in the social structures in which humans live.
(D) New demands created by changes in the social structure are sometimes met by technological innovation.
(E) The fact that humans have a technical-social way of life makes the species immune from evolutionary pressures.

17. The author is most probably addressing which of the following audiences?

(A) Medical students in a course on human anatomy
(B) College students in an introductory course on archaeology
(C) Psychologists investigating the uses of human immaturity
(D) Biologists trying to trace the course of human evolution
(E) Linguists doing research on the origins of natural languages

Quiz III

(18 items; 30 minutes)

DIRECTIONS: Each passage below is followed by a set of items based on its content. Answer the items on the basis of what is stated or implied in the corresponding passage.

Item #1 is based on the following passage.

A dictionary, while it sets forth the spelling, pronunciation, and meaning of individual words, does not serve as a model of style for good writing. I think it was Jonathan Swift who proposed forming
5 an academy of learned scholars who would settle the true spelling, accentuation and proper meaning of words and the purest, most simple, and perfect phraseology of language. It has always seemed to me, however, that if some great master of style
10 could give an example of good composition, which might serve as a model to future speakers and writers, it would do more to fix the orthography, idiomatic usage, and sentence structure than all the dictionaries and institutes that have ever been
15 made.

1. Which of the following best describes the main point of the passage?

   (A) Good writers know instinctively how to use words to create clear and unambiguous sentences.
   (B) An academy of scholars would provide more authoritative guidance to writers than a dictionary.
   (C) An example of good writing would serve as a reference for spelling, meaning, and sentence structure.
   (D) Examples of good writing by accomplished authors would make the use of dictionaries unnecessary.
   (E) Dictionaries do not include models of good writing for authors to follow.

Item #2 is based on the following passage.

Goethe's *Faust* can hardly be said to be a play designed primarily for the galleries. In general, it might be ranked with *Macbeth* or *She Stoops to Conquer* or *Richelieu*. One never sees it fail,
5 however, that *Faust* will fill the gallery with people who would never dream of going to see one of the other plays just mentioned; and the applause never leaves one in doubt as to the reasons for Goethe's popularity. It is the suggestiveness of the love
10 scenes, the red costume of Mephistopheles, the electrical effects, and the rain of fire, that give the desired thrill—all pure melodrama of course. *Faust* is a good show as well as a good play.

2. The author implies that the people mentioned in line 5 would not attend a performance of *Macbeth* because

   (A) *Macbeth* is considered to be inferior to *Faust* as a work of literature
   (B) the production of *Macbeth* would not include suggestive scenes and special effects
   (C) the galleries would be filled with theatergoers who do not understand the play
   (D) melodrama is not intended to appeal to people who are hoping to be entertained
   (E) certain themes in *Macbeth* might not be suitable for all audiences

Item #3 is based on the following passage.

Unlike most cells, which have a short lifespan, nerve cells, which are generated during gestation or a short time after birth, live a long time. Brain neurons can live over 100 years. In an adult, when
5 neurons die because of disease or injury, they are not usually replaced. However, recent research shows that in a few brain regions, new neurons can be born. In general, though, to prevent their own death, living neurons must constantly maintain and
10 remodel themselves. If cell cleanup and repair slows down or stops for any reason, nerve cells cannot function well and eventually die.

3. The author mentions the findings of recent research (lines 6–8) primarily as

(A) proof of the theory that nerve cells are formed during gestation or shortly after birth
(B) an example of the kind of cell cleanup and repair that is needed to preserve nerve cells
(C) further evidence for the notion that neurons are susceptible to disease and injury
(D) a qualification on the general rule that neurons are not replaced
(E) a counterexample to the principle that nerve cells live a long time

Item #4 is based on the following passage.

Chukar partridge chicks can run up a tree by flapping their wings. The beating wings serve the same purpose as spoilers on racecars: to provide better traction. Similarly, feathered dinosaurs may
5 have flapped their primitive wings to better run up inclines, helping them to catch prey. Thus, the "proto-wing" may have offered a non-flight-related survival benefit, and only later did this wing-beating behavior lead to the aerial possibilities of wings.
10 This evolutionary path of primitive birds toward flight is different from two previous models: the arboreal model, in which birds first launched themselves from trees, and the cursorial model, in which they took off from the ground.

4. The author of the passage primarily intends to

(A) offer a third alternative to an either/or challenge
(B) provide a counterexample to refute a popular theory
(C) point out a contradiction in a competing position
(D) attack the proponent of a plan rather than its merits
(E) shift the burden of proof to an opponent of a plan

Items #5–6 are based on the following passage.

A democracy is beyond question the freest government because everyone is equally protected by the laws and equally has a voice in making them. I do not say an equal voice. Some people have
5 stronger lungs than others and can express more forcibly their opinions of public affairs. Others may not speak very loudly, yet they have a faculty of saying more in a short time; and in the case of others, who speak little or not at all, what they do
10 say contains good sense and so carries a lot of weight. So, all things considered, every citizen has not, in this sense of the word, an equal voice. But the right being equal, what is the problem if it is unequally exercised?

5. Which of the following best describes the relationship between the question posed in lines 12–14 and the rest of the paragraph?

    (A) The question is rhetorical in that the author believes that it has already been answered.
    (B) The question is unanswerable because the author has failed to define key terms.
    (C) The question is open-ended, and the answer depends on how one defines "democracy."
    (D) The question is ambiguous because the answer depends on the reader's preference.
    (E) The question is unfair because it presupposes that the reader accepts the author's position.

6. In line 7, the word "faculty" most nearly means

    (A) ability
    (B) teachers
    (C) tendency
    (D) language
    (E) conclusion

Items #7–8 are based on the following passage.

The transportation sector is responsible for a large majority of air pollutants in urban areas. Biofuels, because of the oxygen they contain, can reduce carbon monoxide emissions that result from
5 incomplete combustion. Ground-level ozone (smog) is a result of a complex reaction triggered by ultraviolet radiation, but the principal ingredients are carbon monoxide, hydrocarbons, and nitrogen oxides. The addition of biofuels to gasoline products
10 reduces incomplete combustion and therefore carbon monoxide and unburned tailpipe hydrocarbon emissions. On the other hand, a 10-percent-ethanol gasoline is more volatile than pure gasoline or ethanol, so hydrocarbon evaporation
15 from the fuel system may be higher. Furthermore, nitrogen oxide formation increases with combustion temperature, so its production increases slightly with oxygenated fuels. However, the overall impact of using biofuels is to
20 substantially reduce pollutant emissions.

7. The author regards the use of biofuels as

    (A) entailing some environmental costs but on the balance beneficial
    (B) preferable in every regard to conventional fuels such as gasoline
    (C) inefficient and actually likely to result in an increase in pollution
    (D) able to do little to reduce pollution but likely to cause no environmental harm
    (E) able to reduce pollution but probably only by insignificant amounts

8. In line 13, the word "volatile" most nearly means

    (A) extremely unstable
    (B) evaporating quickly
    (C) environmentally favorable
    (D) completely burned
    (E) chemically complex

Items #9–10 are based on the following passage.

In the decade following World War I, millions of Americans believed in the existence of a radical conspiracy to overthrow the United States government and that a "Red revolution" might begin
5 at any moment. Newspaper headlines shouted news of strikes and Bolshevist riots. Properly elected members of the Assembly of New York State were expelled because they had been elected as members of the Socialist Party. The Vice President cited as a
10 dangerous manifestation of radicalism in women's colleges the fact that Radcliffe debaters upheld the affirmative in a debate that labor unions are essential to successful collective bargaining. It was an era of lawless and disorderly defense of law and
15 order, of unconstitutional defense of the Constitution, of suspicion and civil conflict— literally, a reign of terror.

9. The most important feature of the logical development of the passage is the

(A) presentation of competing theories
(B) use of examples
(C) definition of important terms
(D) introduction of statistics
(E) refutation of an argument

10. By the use of the word "shouted" (line 5), the author intends to suggest that the newspapers

(A) accurately reported important events
(B) overlooked evidence of a conspiracy
(C) incited strikes and civil unrest
(D) invented stories about Bolsheviks
(E) exaggerated the danger of revolution

Items #11–18 are based on the following passage.

The uniqueness of the Japanese character is the result of two seemingly contradictory forces: the strength of traditions and selective receptivity to foreign achievements and inventions. As early as
5 the 1860s, there were counter movements to the traditional orientation. Yukichi Fukuzawa, the most eloquent spokesman of Japan's "Enlightenment," claimed, "The Confucian civilization of the East seems to me to lack two things possessed by
10 Western civilization: science in the material sphere and a sense of independence in the spiritual sphere." Fukuzawa's great influence is found in the free and individualistic philosophy of the Education Code of 1872, but he was not able to prevent the
15 government from turning back to the canons of Confucian thought in the Imperial Rescript of 1890. Another interlude of relative liberalism followed World War I, when the democratic idealism of President Woodrow Wilson had an important
20 impact on Japanese intellectuals and, especially, students; but more important was the Leninist ideology of the 1917 Bolshevik Revolution. Again, in the early 1930s, nationalism and militarism became dominant, largely because of failing economic
25 conditions.
Following the end of World War II, substantial changes were undertaken in Japan to liberate the individual from authoritarian restraints. The new democratic value system was accepted by many
30 teachers, students, intellectuals, and old liberals, but it was not immediately embraced by the society as a whole. Japanese traditions were dominated by group values, and notions of personal freedom and individual rights were unfamiliar. Today,
35 democratic processes are evident in the widespread participation of the Japanese people in social and political life, yet there is no universally accepted and stable value system. Values are constantly modified by strong infusions of Western ideas, both
40 democratic and Marxist. School textbooks espouse democratic principles, emphasizing equality over hierarchy and rationalism over tradition, but in practice these values are often misinterpreted and distorted, particularly by youth who translate the
45 individualistic and humanistic goals of democracy into egoistic and materialistic ones.
Most Japanese people have consciously rejected Confucianism, but vestiges of the old order remain. An important feature of relationships in
50 many institutions such as political parties, large corporations, and university faculties is the *oyabun-kobun*, or parent-child relationship. A party leader,

supervisor, or professor, in return for loyalty, protects those subordinate to him and takes general
55 responsibility for their interests throughout their entire lives, an obligation that sometimes even extends to arranging marriages. The corresponding loyalty of the individual to his patron reinforces his allegiance to the group to which they both belong. A
60 willingness to cooperate with other members of the group and to support without qualification the interests of the group in all its external relations is still a widely respected virtue. The *oyabun-kobun* creates ladders of mobility that an individual can
65 ascend, rising as far as abilities permit, so long as he maintains successful personal ties with a superior in the vertical channel, the latter requirement usually taking precedence over a need for exceptional competence. Consequently, there is
70 little horizontal relationship between people even within the same profession.

11. As used in line 48, the word "vestiges" most nearly means

(A) institutions
(B) superiors
(C) traces
(D) subordinates
(E) virtues

12. Which of the following is most like the relationship of the *oyabun-kobun* described in the passage?

(A) A political candidate and the voting public
(B) A gifted scientist and his protégé
(C) Two brothers who are partners in a business
(D) A judge presiding at the trial of a criminal defendant
(E) A leader of a musical ensemble who is also a musician in the group

13. According to the passage, Japanese attitudes are NOT influenced by which of the following?

(A) Democratic ideals
(B) Elements of modern Western culture
(C) Remnants of an earlier social structure
(D) Marxist ideals
(E) Confucianism

14. The author implies that

(A) decisions about promotions within the vertical channel are often based on personal feelings
(B) students and intellectuals do not understand the basic tenets of Western democracy
(C) Western values have completely overwhelmed traditional Japanese attitudes
(D) respect for authority was introduced into Japan following World War II
(E) most Japanese workers are members of a single political party

15. In developing the passage, the author does which of the following?

(A) Introduces an analogy
(B) Defines a term
(C) Presents statistics
(D) Cites an authority
(E) Issues a challenge

16. It can be inferred that the Imperial Rescript of 1890

(A) was a protest by liberals against the lack of individual liberty in Japan
(B) marked a return in government policies to conservative values
(C) implemented the ideals set forth in the Education Code of 1872
(D) was influenced by the Leninist ideology of the Bolshevik Revolution
(E) prohibited the teaching of Western ideas in Japanese schools

17. Which of the following is the most accurate description of the organization of the passage?

(A) A sequence of inferences in which the conclusion of each successive step becomes a premise in the next argument

(B) A list of generalizations, most of which are supported by only a single example

(C) A chronological analysis of historical events leading up to a description of the current situation

(D) A statement of a commonly accepted theory that is then subjected to a critical analysis

(E) An introduction of a key term that is then defined by giving examples

18. Which of the following best states the central thesis of the passage?

(A) The value system of Japan is based upon traditional and conservative values that have, in modern times, been modified by Western and other liberal values.

(B) Students and radicals in Japan have used Leninist ideology to distort the meaning of democratic, Western values.

(C) The notions of personal freedom and individual liberty did not find immediate acceptance in Japan because of the predominance of traditional group values.

(D) Modern Japanese society is characterized by hierarchical relationships in which a personal tie to a superior is often more important than merit.

(E) The influence on Japanese values of the American ideals of personal freedom and individual rights is less important than the influence of Leninist ideology.

Quiz IV Brain Buster
(29 items; 30 minutes)

> **DIRECTIONS:** Each passage below is followed by a set of items. Read the passage and choose the best answer for each item. You may refer to the passage as often as necessary to answer the items.

Items #1–9 are based on the following passage.

President Roosevelt's administration suffered a devastating defeat when, on January 6, 1936, the Agricultural Adjustment Act of 1933 was declared unconstitutional. New Deal planners quickly pushed
5 through Congress the Soil Conservation and Domestic Allotment Act of 1935, one purpose of which was conservation, but which also aimed at controlling surpluses by retiring land from production. The law was intended as a stopgap
10 measure until the administration could formulate a permanent farm program that would satisfy both the nation's farmers and the Supreme Court. Roosevelt's landslide victory over Landon in 1936 obscured the ambivalent nature of his support in
15 the farm states. Despite extensive government propaganda, many farmers still refused to participate in the Agricultural Adjustment Administration's voluntary production control programs, and the burdensome surpluses of 1933
20 were gone not as the result of the AAA, but as a consequence of great droughts.

In February of 1937, Secretary of Agriculture Wallace convened a meeting of farm leaders to promote the concept of the ever normal granary, a
25 policy that would encourage farmers to store crop surpluses (rather than dump them on the market) until grain was needed in years of small harvests. The Commodity Credit Corporation would grant loans to be repaid when the grain was later sold for
30 a reasonable profit. The conference chose a Committee of Eighteen, which drafted a bill, but the major farm organizations were divided. Since ten of the eighteen members were also members of the American Farm Bureau Federation, the measure
35 was quickly labeled a Farm Bureau bill, and there were protests from the small, but highly vocal, Farmer's Holiday Association. When debate on the bill began, Roosevelt himself was vague and elusive and didn't move the proposed legislation into the
40 "desirable" category until midsummer. In addition, there were demands that the New Deal's deficit

spending be curtailed, and opponents of the bill charged that the AAA was wasteful and primarily benefited corporations and large-scale farmers.
45 The Soil Conservation and Domestic Allotment Act had failed to limit agricultural production as the administration had hoped. Farm prices and consumer demand were high, and many farmers, convinced that the drought had ended the need for
50 crop controls, refused to participate in the AAA's soil conservation program. Without direct crop controls, agricultural production skyrocketed in 1937, and by late summer there was panic in the farm belt that prices would again be driven down to
55 disastrously low levels. Congressmen began to pressure Roosevelt to place a floor under farm prices by making loans through the CCC, but Roosevelt made such loans contingent upon the willingness of Congress to support the
60 administration's plan for a new system of crop controls. When the price of cotton began to drop, Roosevelt's adroit political maneuver finally forced congressional representatives from the South to agree to support a bill providing for crop controls
65 and the ever normal granary. The following year Congress passed the Agricultural Adjustment Act of 1938.

1. The primary purpose of the passage is to

   (A) analyze the connection between changes in weather conditions and the movement of agricultural prices
   (B) call attention to the economic hardship suffered by farmers during the 1930s
   (C) discuss the reasoning that led the Supreme Court to declare the Agricultural Adjustment Act of 1933 unconstitutional
   (D) describe the events that led to the passage of the Agricultural Adjustment Act of 1938
   (E) pinpoint the weaknesses of the agricultural policies of Roosevelt's New Deal

2. Which of the following is NOT a statement made by the author about the Soil Conservation and Domestic Allotment Act?

(A) It was intended to be a temporary measure.
(B) It aimed at reducing agricultural production.
(C) It aimed at soil conservation.
(D) It was largely ineffective.
(E) It was drafted primarily by the Farm Bureau.

3. According to the passage, the Roosevelt administration wanted agricultural legislation with all of the following characteristics EXCEPT

(A) it would not be declared unconstitutional by the Supreme Court
(B) it would be acceptable to the nation's farmers
(C) it would dismantle the Agricultural Adjustment Administration
(D) it would provide loans to help farmers store surplus grain
(E) it would provide for direct control of agricultural production

4. According to the passage, all of the following were impediments to the passage of the Agricultural Adjustment Act of 1938 EXCEPT:

(A) initial lack of clear Presidential support.
(B) prosperity enjoyed by the nation's farmers.
(C) opposition to the idea of a Farm Bureau bill.
(D) doubts about the constitutionality of the bill.
(E) lack of clear support for the bill in farm states.

5. The author implies which of the following conclusions?

(A) Roosevelt's ability to gain passage of the Agricultural Adjustment Act of 1938 depended on the large harvests of 1937.
(B) Secretary of Agriculture Wallace alienated members of the American Farm Bureau Federation by proposing an ever normal granary.
(C) The Agricultural Adjustment Act of 1933 was declared unconstitutional because it was written by the Farm Bureau.
(D) The Commodity Credit Corporation was created to offer farmers incentives for taking land out of production.
(E) The compulsory production controls of the Agricultural Adjustment Act of 1933 were effective in eliminating surpluses.

6. It can be inferred from the passage that the Farmer's Holiday Association opposed the bill drafted by the Committee of Eighteen because

(A) the bill was not strongly supported by President Roosevelt
(B) the Farmer's Holiday Association opposed the American Farm Bureau Federation
(C) the Roosevelt administration had incurred excessive debt to finance its New Deal
(D) its membership consisted primarily of large-scale farmers
(E) none of its members had been invited to participate in the meeting convened by Wallace

7. It can be inferred that loans granted by the Commodity Credit Corporation would encourage farmers to store surplus grain by

(A) providing farmers a financial incentive to take arable land out of production
(B) implementing a comprehensive program of mandatory soil conservation practices
(C) conditioning financial assistance on a promise to participate in the Agricultural Adjustment Administration's program
(D) relieving farmers of the need to sell grain in order to obtain immediate cash
(E) encouraging farmers to construct long-term storage facilities for agricultural products

8. The passage provides information that would help answer which of the following questions?

      I. Who was Secretary of Agriculture during Roosevelt's second term?
     II. Who was Roosevelt's major opponent in the 1936 Presidential election?
   III. Who was President of the American Farm Bureau Federation in 1937?

    (A) I only
    (B) II only
    (C) I and II only
    (D) I and III only
    (E) I, II, and III

9. Which of the following best describes the author's treatment of Roosevelt's farm policies?

    (A) Scholarly but appreciative
    (B) Objective but critical
    (C) Analytical but abrasive
    (D) Biased and condemnatory
    (E) Noncommittal and indifferent

Items #10–17 are based on the following passage.

    The present day view of alcoholism as a physical disease was not a scientific discovery; it is a medical thesis that has developed only slowly over the past 200 years and amidst considerable
5 controversy. Historically, the moral perspective of the Judeo-Christian tradition has been that excessive use of alcohol is a willful act, one that leads to intoxication and other sinful behavior; but in the early nineteenth century, Benjamin Rush, a
10 founder of American psychiatry, proposed that "the habit of drunkenness is a disease of the will." By the late nineteenth century, physicians generally viewed the habitual use of drugs such as opiates, tobacco, and coffee as a generic disorder stemming
15 from biological vulnerability, either inherited or acquired.
    Prohibition represented a triumph of the older morality over a modern medical concept. Where physicians who championed the disease concept of
20 alcoholism emphasized the need for treatment, the Temperance Movement stressed that alcohol itself was the cause of drunkenness and advocated its control and eventually its prohibition. Scientific interest in alcoholism, dampened by Prohibition,
25 revived toward the middle of the twentieth century, not because of any new scientific findings but because of humanitarian efforts to shift the focus from blame and punishment to treatment and concern.
30   The early 1960s witnessed a growing acceptance of the notion that, in certain "vulnerable" people, alcohol use leads to physical addiction—a true disease. Central to this concept of alcoholism as a disease were the twin notions of
35 substance tolerance and physical dependence, both physical phenomena. Substance tolerance occurs when increased doses of a drug are required to produce effects previously attained at lower dosages; physical dependence refers to the
40 occurrence of withdrawal symptoms, such as seizures, following cessation of a drinking bout. In 1972, the National Council on Alcoholism outlined criteria for diagnosing alcoholism. These criteria emphasized alcohol tolerance and physical
45 dependence and treated alcoholism as an independent disorder, not merely a manifestation of a more general and underlying personality disorder.
    In 1977, a World Health Organization report challenged this disease model by pointing out that
50 not everyone who develops alcohol-related problems exhibits true alcohol dependence. This important distinction between dependence and

other drug-related problems that do not involve dependence was not immediately accepted by the
55 American Psychiatric Association. The early drafts of the 1980 edition of its *Diagnostic and Statistical Manual of Mental Disorders* described a dependence syndrome for alcohol and other drugs in which tolerance and dependence were important, but not
60 essential, criteria for diagnosis, but at the last moment, the inertia of history prevailed, and tolerance and dependence were both included not as necessary to diagnose dependence but as sufficient indicators in and of themselves.
65   It was not until 1993 that the American Psychiatric Association modified this position. In the fourth edition of the *Manual*, tolerance and withdrawal symptoms are the first two of seven criteria listed for diagnosing alcohol and other drug
70 dependence, but the clinician is not required to find whether either is present or in what degree in order to make the diagnosis.
        Despite the consensus among health professionals, we should not forget that the moral
75 perspective on alcoholism is still very much alive. It perhaps does not surprise us that the Reverend D. E. Todd wrote an essay entitled "Drunkenness a Vice, Not a Disease" in 1882, but we should be concerned that the book *Heavy Drinking: The Myth of*
80 *Alcoholism as a Disease* was published in 1988. Even as late as the mid-1970s, sociologists were reporting that the term "alcoholic" was commonly used in the United States as a synonym for "drunkard," rather than as a designation for
85 someone with an illness or a disorder. Apparently, in the mind of nonprofessionals, the contradictory notions of alcoholism as a disease and alcoholism as a moral weakness can coexist quite comfortably.

10. The author's primary concern is to

(A) refute the notion that drunkenness is a serious social problem
(B) argue that alcoholism is less serious than it was 200 years ago
(C) explain the evolution of the idea that alcoholism is a disease
(D) give an example of the way that medical terminology changes over time
(E) propose that the medical community treat alcoholism as a disease

11. According to the passage, members of the Temperance Movement

(A) agreed with doctors that alcohol abuse was a serious problem
(B) agreed with doctors that the solution to alcohol abuse was treatment
(C) agreed with doctors that drunkenness should be treated as a disease
(D) disagreed with doctors that alcoholism was a serious problem
(E) disagreed with doctors that traditional morality proscribed drunkenness

12. The author mentions Benjamin Rush in order to

(A) mark the beginning of the evolution of the disease concept of alcoholism
(B) highlight the seriousness of habitual use of certain drugs
(C) discredit a central tenet of the religious view of alcoholism
(D) encourage physicians to treat alcoholism as a physical disease
(E) refute the notion that alcoholism is a moral weakness

13. It can be inferred that the concepts of tolerance and dependence helped to establish the disease model of alcoholism because they

(A) prove that alcoholism is not a manifestation of a fundamental personality disorder
(B) are necessary but not sufficient findings to diagnose alcoholism
(C) demonstrate that alcohol abuse is similar to abuse of opiates and other drugs
(D) are evidence of physical addiction which is an affliction of the body
(E) allow a physician to prescribe specific treatments for alcoholism

14. The author regards the essay "Drunkenness a Vice, Not a Disease" as

(A) misguided and dangerous
(B) incorrect and harmful
(C) insightful and beneficial
(D) outdated but harmless
(E) corrupt but benign

15. The author implies that all of the following are true EXCEPT

(A) historically, alcoholism has been regarded as a weakness of the will rather than a disease
(B) in modern times, the medical community has disagreed over the exact definition of alcoholism
(C) the medical profession may make terminological distinctions that are not understood by the general population
(D) it is now generally accepted by health care professionals that alcoholism is a disease
(E) the long-held view that alcoholism is a moral problem has finally been totally discredited

16. According to the fourth paragraph, the draft versions of the 1980 *Diagnostic and Statistical Manual of Mental Disorders* were similar to the final 1993 version in that they

(A) listed tolerance and dependence as both necessary and sufficient conditions for the diagnosis of alcoholism
(B) did not specify tolerance and dependence as essential elements of alcoholism
(C) suggested that alcoholism might be a generic, biological disorder
(D) argued that viewing alcoholism as a disease might actually encourage drunkenness
(E) described alcoholism as a disease that had no fixed set of symptoms

17. With which of the following statements would the author most likely agree?

(A) Shifting public opinion will force physicians to return to the view that alcoholism is a moral weakness.
(B) A physician should not make a finding of alcoholism in a patient in the absence of either tolerance or dependence.
(C) The determination to classify a problem as a disease depends in part on whether it is susceptible to medical treatment.
(D) New scientific findings on the workings of tolerance and dependence warranted a shift to the disease model of alcoholism.
(E) Consensus within the medical community cannot be established in the absence of consensus in the community which it serves.

Items #18–23 are based on the following passage.

Most thinkers have distinguished three political entities: the individual, society, and state. It is normal to begin with the individual and then to consider society as the embodiment of his nature as
5 a social being. Thus, the individual is considered to be both logically and historically prior to society and society both logically and historically prior to the state. But in James Burnham's vision of the future state, the logical priority of the individual
10 over the state is inverted. Burnham changed his mind on many points of detail between one book and the next, primarily because he thought that what was happening in national and world politics at any given moment was decisive. But his general
15 sense of the form political power would take didn't move far from the version of it he gave in *The Managerial Revolution*. In that book he predicted that the weaknesses of capitalism would eventually prove fatal, but the downfall of capitalism would not
20 be the victory of the proletariat followed by a Marxist paradise. Capitalism would be replaced by autocracy even more extreme than that in Stalin's Russia. Under this autocracy, the instruments of production would be controlled by the state, and
25 the state, in turn, would be controlled by a ruling elite of managers.

Burnham argued that managers would control the instruments of production in their own corporate favor and the economy of state
30 ownership would provide the basis for domination and exploitation by a ruling class of an extremity and absoluteness never before known. The masses would be curbed or constantly diverted so that they would, as we say, go along with the managerial
35 arrangements. In Burnham's future state, history has come to an end because existence has removed itself from historical process and become pure essence, its attributes those of official meaning. Perfection is defined as the state of completeness in
40 accordance with the terms prescribed for it by the state, as a proposition in logic or a theorem in mathematics might be faultless.

In *We*, Yevgeny Zamyatin envisaged a one-world state, but Burnham allowed for three states.
45 Three superstates would divide the world between them and would enter into shifting alliances with one another. In 1941, Burnham thought the three would be the United States, Europe, and Japan. The superpowers would wage war over marginal
50 territory. "Ostensibly," Burnham said, "these wars will be directed from each base for the conquest of the other bases. But it does not seem possible for any one of these to conquer the others; and even two of them in coalition could not win a decisive
55 and lasting victory over the third."

By 1947, several of Burnham's predictions had already proved false, a result of his irrepressible tendency to assume that present conditions would persist unchanged indefinitely; but a more damning
60 indictment of his vision is the hypocrisy concealed behind the attack on power. Burnham was infatuated with the image of totalitarianism; he was fascinated by the power he attacked and he despised the democracy he should have defended.
65 Ultimately, Burnham voiced the secret desire of the English intelligentsia to destroy the old, egalitarian version of Socialism and usher in a new hierarchical society in which the intellectual could at last get his hands on the whip.

18. The author's treatment of James Burnham's writing can best be described as

(A) analytical and condemnatory
(B) insightful and neutral
(C) speculative and jaded
(D) cynical and detached
(E) uncertain and hostile

19. The statement that Burnham inverted the logical priority of the individual over the state means that Burnham believed that

(A) the state came into existence before a society of individuals
(B) history culminated in the existence of an all-powerful government
(C) individuals can reach perfection only as social beings
(D) the existence of individuals can be deduced from the existence of a state
(E) people are seen as aspects of the state and not as individuals

20. The author criticizes Burnham for

(A) extrapolating from existing political and
    social conditions
(B) failing to show how a totalitarian state
    could evolve from a democracy
(C) thinking that democracy is a form of
    government superior to oligarchy
(D) reversing the normal relationship between
    the individual and society
(E) predicting that the world would evolve
    into a three-world state rather than a one-
    world state

21. According to Burnham, in the completely
autocratic state, history will have come to an
end because

(A) the state will define the social forms that
    individuals must conform to
(B) the means of production will be controlled
    by a managerial elite
(C) no one superpower will be able to wage
    war successfully against any other
    superpower
(D) individuals will be diverted from a study
    of past events by the state
(E) only the managerial elite will be permitted
    access to historical records

22. The author's primary concern is to

(A) present his own vision of the future
(B) prove someone else's predictions were
    wrong
(C) critique a political theory
(D) criticize a literary style
(E) compare two competing theories

23. The passage supports which of the following
conclusions about the writings of Yevgeny
Zamyatin?

   I. They are in large part derivative of the
      works of James Burnham.
  II. They describe a future society in
      which the state is all-powerful.
 III. The descriptions they contain are
      based on conditions that existed at the
      time they were written.

(A) I only
(B) II only
(C) I and II only
(D) II and III only
(E) I, II, and III

Items #24–29 are based on the following passage.

Meteorite ALH84001 is a member of a family of meteorites, half of which were found in Antarctica, that are believed to have originated on Mars. Oxygen isotopes, as distinctive as fingerprints, link these meteorites and clearly differentiate them from any Earth rock or other kind of meteorite. Another family member, ETA79001, was discovered to contain gas trapped by the impact that ejected it from Mars. Analysis of the trapped gas shows that it is identical to atmosphere analyzed by the spacecraft that landed on Mars in 1976.

The rock of ALH84001 was formed 4.5 billion years ago, and 3.6 billion years ago, it was invaded by water containing mineral salts precipitated out to form small carbonate globules with intricate chemical zoning. These carbonates are between 1 and 2 billion years old. Sixteen million years ago, an object from space, possibly a small asteroid, impacted Mars and blasted off rocks. One of these rocks traveled in space until it was captured by the Earth's gravity and fell on Antarctica. Carbon-14 dating shows that this rock has been on Earth about 13,000 years.

The carbonate globules contain very small crystals of iron oxide (magnetite) and at least two kinds of iron sulfide (pyrrhotite and another mineral, possibly greigite). Small crystals of these minerals are commonly formed on Earth by bacteria, although inorganic processes can also form them. In addition, manganese is concentrated in the center of each carbonate globule, and most of the larger globules have rims of alternating iron-rich and magnesium-rich carbonates. The compositional variation of these carbonates is not what would be expected from high temperature equilibrium crystallization but is more like low temperature crystallization. It is consistent with formation by non-equilibrium precipitation induced by microorganisms.

There are also unusually high concentrations of PAH-type hydrocarbons. These PAHs are unusually simple compared to most PAHs, including PAHs from the burning of coal, oil, or gasoline or the decay of vegetation. Other meteorites contain PAHs, but the pattern and abundances are different. Of course, PAHs can be formed by strictly inorganic reactions, and abundant PAHs were produced in the early solar system and are preserved on some asteroids and comets. Meteorites from these objects fall to Earth and enable us to analyze the PAHs contained within the parent bodies. While some of these are similar to the PAHs in the Martian meteorite, all show some major differences. One reasonable interpretation of the PAHs is that they are decay products from bacteria.

Also present are unusual, very small forms that could be the remains of microorganisms. These spherical, ovoid, and elongated objects closely resemble the morphology of known bacteria, but many of them are smaller than any known bacteria on Earth. Furthermore, microfossil forms from very old Earth rocks are typically much larger than the forms that we see in the Mars meteorite. The microfossil-like forms may really be minerals and artifacts that superficially resemble small bacteria. Or, perhaps lower gravity and more restricted pore space in rocks promoted the development of smaller forms of microorganisms. Or, maybe such forms exist on Earth in the fossil record but have not yet been found. If the small objects are microfossils, are they from Mars or from Antarctica? Studies so far of the abundant microorganisms found in the rocks, soils, and lakes near the coast of Antarctica do not show PAHs or microorganisms that closely resemble those found in the Martian meteorite.

There is considerable evidence in the Martian meteorite that must be explained by other means if we are to definitely rule out evidence of past Martian life in this meteorite. So far, we have not seen a reasonable explanation by others that can explain all of the data.

24. The main purpose of the passage is to

(A) argue that the available data support the conclusion that life once existed on Mars

(B) examine various facts to determine what thesis about ALH84001 is most strongly supported

(C) answer objections to the contention that Martian meteorites contain evidence of primitive life

(D) pose challenges to scientists who hope to prove that ALH84001 proves that life exists on Mars

(E) explore different scientific theories as to the origin of life on Earth

25. According to the passage, what evidence most strongly establishes that meteorite ALH84001 originated on Mars?

(A) The comparison of trapped gases and the Martian atmosphere
(B) The presence of alternating iron and magnesium carbonates
(C) The evidence of shapes that resemble known bacteria
(D) The pattern of carbonate globules with unusual zoning
(E) The discovery of unusual PAHs in unusual abundances

26. The passage mentions all of the following as tending to prove that ALH84001 may once have contained primitive life EXCEPT

(A) the presence of objects resembling the morphology of known bacteria
(B) extraordinarily high concentrations of unusual PAHs
(C) the presence of iron oxide and iron sulfide crystals
(D) unusual zonings of carbonate globules
(E) distinctive oxygen isotopes trapped in gases

27. According to the passage, the compositional variation of the carbonate deposits and the PAH–type hydrocarbons both

(A) result from chemical processes more likely to occur on Mars than on Earth
(B) might be the product of an organic reaction or the product of an inorganic process
(C) tend to occur at relatively cooler temperatures than other, similar reactions
(D) are evidence of chemical processes that occurred during the formation of the solar system
(E) are byproducts of organic processes and cannot result from inorganic reactions

28. The author mentions lower gravity and restricted pore space (lines 66–67) in order to explain why

(A) bacteria on Mars might be smaller than ones found on Earth
(B) no microfossil record of bacteria has yet been found in Antarctica
(C) the spherical, ovoid, and elongated shapes in ALH84001 cannot be bacteria
(D) restricted pore space in Martian rocks would hinder bacterial growth
(E) non-equilibrium precipitation is probably not the result of an organic reaction

29. With which of the following conclusions about the possibility of life on Mars would the author most likely agree?

(A) The available evidence strongly suggests that conditions on Mars make it impossible for life to have developed there.
(B) The scientific evidence is ambiguous and supports no conclusion about the possibility of life on Mars.
(C) Scientific evidence cannot, in principle, ever demonstrate that life existed on Mars.
(D) Scientific data derived from ALH84001 is consistent with the proposition that life once existed on Mars.
(E) It is as likely that life developed in a hostile environment such as Antarctica as on Mars.

REVIEW

This section contains additional Critical Reading: Passages items further practice. Answers are on page 620.

DIRECTIONS: Each passage below is followed by a set of items based on its content; items following a pair of related passages may also be based on the relationship between the two passages. Answer the items on the basis of what is stated or implied in the corresponding passage(s).

Item #1 is based on the following passage.

What nutrition is to physiological life, education is to social life. As societies become more complex in structure and resources, the need for formal or intentional teaching and learning

5 increases. As formal teaching and training grow in extent, there is the danger of creating an undesirable split between the experience gained in direct associations and what is acquired in school. This danger was never greater than presently, due

10 to the rapid growth of technical modes of skill.

1. In the passage, the author draws an analogy between

   (A) school and family
   (B) teaching and life
   (C) nutrition and education
   (D) experience and ignorance
   (E) intentionality and learning

Items #2–3 are based on the following passage.

Historically, the socialization process in America has been characterized by the interaction of structured groups that share both a sense of mission about the nation's future and codes of

5 behavior rooted in common principles. Communities were bound by religious beliefs, ethnic backgrounds, and strong family relationships. However, this configuration of socializing institutions no longer functions as it

10 once did. Mobility is one factor in the changing picture. One-fifth of Americans change residence each year, but they do not "pack" their culture; they simply move, breaking old community ties. A second factor in the breakdown of the socialization

15 process is depersonalization. Emerson once wrote that an institution is the lengthened shadow of one man. Today's institution is more likely to be the lengthened shadow of itself. By now the process of social decompression may be irreversible.

2. The author cites Emerson (lines 15–17) in order to

   (A) dramatize the power of institutions in our society
   (B) explain the importance of individual freedom
   (C) demonstrate the need for the study of humanities in American schools
   (D) highlight the progress that society has made since Emerson
   (E) argue that all institutions should be run by an individual

3. The tone of the passage can best be described as

   (A) tentative but worried
   (B) scholarly but optimistic
   (C) passionate but controlled
   (D) angry but calm
   (E) analytical but concerned

Items #4–5 are based on the following passage.

It is useful to distinguish between "life events" and "life circumstances" when analyzing depression-inducing factors, as life circumstances and events promote stress in different ways. Stressful life events
5   include the death of a spouse, divorce, or job loss; stressful life circumstances include single parenthood, low income, and poor education. Depression usually includes elements from both categories, though stressful life events most often
10 afflict single mothers. In fact, epidemiological studies show that more women than men exhibit signs of depression. However, the sex difference in rates of depression can also be explained by a condition of learned helplessness, as society encourages women
15 to trust and nurture others rather than to be aggressive and to seek power. Thus, any particular incident of depression in women or men may include a history of learned helplessness as well as an immediate environmental agent of depression.

4. The main purpose of this passage is to

(A) describe the behavior of depressed people
(B) explain the biochemical causes of depression
(C) discuss the factors that contribute to depression
(D) analyze the different rates of depression in men and women
(E) identify the family situations that lead to depression

5. Which of the following best explains the distinction between a life circumstance and a life event?

(A) A life circumstance is a long-term condition, while a life event is a sudden change.
(B) Life circumstances occur less frequently than but are more serious than life events.
(C) A life circumstance is a learned behavior and a life event is caused by an outside agent.
(D) A life circumstance can easily be controlled but a life event cannot be.
(E) A life circumstance is more likely to cause depression in women; a life event is more likely to cause depression in men.

Item #6 is based on the following passage.

A constitution consists of many particulars, and there will be different combinations of opinions on the different points. The majority on one question may be the minority on a second, and a
5   different group altogether may constitute the majority on a third. To establish a constitution, it is necessary to satisfy all parties. But an amendment to a constitution, once established, is a single proposition. There is need to compromise in
10 relation to any other point. The will of the requisite number would at once bring the matter to a decisive issue.

6. The primary purpose of the passage is to

(A) persuade voters that a constitutional amendment is needed
(B) show that a constitutional amendment need not require unanimous consent
(C) explain why it is more difficult to establish than to amend a constitution
(D) illustrate the difficulties inherent in establishing a constitution
(E) compare governments with and without written constitutions.

Items #7–14 are based on the following passage.

A fundamental principle of pharmacology is that all drugs have multiple actions. Actions that are desirable in the treatment of disease are considered therapeutic, while those that are undesirable or
5 pose risks to the patient are called "effects." Adverse drug effects range from the trivial, for example, nausea or dry mouth, to the serious, such as massive gastrointestinal bleeding or thromboembolism; and some drugs can be lethal.
10 Therefore, an effective system for the detection of adverse drug effects is an important component of the healthcare system of any advanced nation. Much of the research conducted on new drugs aims at identifying the conditions of use that maximize
15 beneficial effects and minimize the risk of adverse effects. The intent of drug labeling is to reflect this body of knowledge accurately so that physicians can properly prescribe the drug or, if it is to be sold without prescription, so that consumers can
20 properly use the drug.

The current system of drug investigation in the United States has proved very useful and accurate in identifying the common side effects associated with new prescription drugs. By the time a new drug is
25 approved by the Food and Drug Administration, its side effects are usually well described in the package insert for physicians. The investigational process, however, cannot be counted on to detect all adverse effects because of the relatively small
30 number of patients involved in pre-marketing studies and the relatively short duration of the studies. Animal toxicology studies are, of course, done before marketing in an attempt to identify any potential for toxicity, but negative results do not
35 guarantee the safety of a drug in humans, as evidenced by such well known examples as the birth deformities due to thalidomide.

This recognition prompted the establishment in many countries of programs to which physicians
40 report adverse drug effects. The United States and other countries also send reports to an international program operated by the World Health Organization. These programs, however, are voluntary reporting programs and are intended to
45 serve a limited goal: alerting a government or private agency to adverse drug effects detected by physicians in the course of practice. Other approaches must be used to confirm suspected drug reactions and to estimate incidence rates. These
50 other approaches include conducting retrospective control studies, for example, the studies associating endometrial cancer with estrogen use, and

systematically monitoring hospitalized patients to determine the incidence of acute common side
55 effects, as typified by the Boston Collaborative Drug Surveillance Program.

Thus, the overall drug surveillance system of the United States is composed of a set of information bases, special studies, and monitoring
60 programs, each contributing in its own way to our knowledge about marketed drugs. The system is decentralized among a number of governmental units and is not administered as a coordinated function. Still, it would be inappropriate at this time
65 to attempt to unite all of the disparate elements into a comprehensive surveillance program. Instead, the challenge is to improve each segment of the system and to take advantage of new computer strategies to improve coordination and communication.

7. In line 65, the word "disparate" most nearly means

   (A) useless
   (B) expensive
   (C) temporary
   (D) educational
   (E) unconnected

8. The author's primary concern is to discuss

   (A) methods for testing the effects of new drugs on humans
   (B) the importance of having accurate information about the effects of drugs
   (C) procedures for determining the long-term effects of new drugs
   (D) attempts to curb the abuse of prescription drugs
   (E) the difference between the therapeutic and non-therapeutic actions of drugs

9. The author implies that a drug with adverse side effects

(A) will not be approved for use by consumers without a doctor's prescription
(B) must wait for approval until lengthy studies prove the effects are not permanent
(C) should be used only if its therapeutic value outweighs its adverse effects
(D) should be withdrawn from the marketplace pending a government investigation
(E) could be used in foreign countries even though it is not approved for use in the United States

10. Which of the following can be inferred from the passage?

(A) The decentralization of the overall drug surveillance system results in it being completely ineffective in any attempts to provide information about adverse drug effects.
(B) Drugs with serious adverse side effects are never approved for distribution.
(C) Some adverse drug effects are discovered during testing because they are very rare.
(D) Some adverse drug effects cannot be detected prior to approval because they take a long time to develop.
(E) Animal testing of drugs prior to approval is not required for drugs that are not potentially dangerous.

11. The author introduces the example of thalidomide in the last sentence of the second paragraph to show that some

(A) drugs do not have the same actions in humans that they do in animals
(B) drug testing procedures are ignored by careless laboratory workers
(C) drugs have no therapeutic value for humans
(D) drugs have adverse side effects as well as beneficial actions
(E) physicians prescribe drugs without first reading the manufacturer's recommendations

12. It can be inferred that the estrogen study mentioned in the last sentence of the third paragraph

(A) uncovered long-term side effects of a drug that had already been approved for sale by the Food and Drug Administration
(B) discovered potential side effects of a drug that was still awaiting approval for sale by the Food and Drug Administration
(C) revealed possible new applications of a drug that had previously been approved for a different treatment
(D) is an example of a study that could be more efficiently conducted by a centralized authority than by volunteer reporting
(E) proved that the use of the drug estrogen was not associated with side effects such as thromboembolism

13. The author is most probably leading up to a discussion of some suggestions about how to

(A) centralize authority for drug surveillance in the United States
(B) centralize authority for drug surveillance among international agencies
(C) coordinate better the sharing of information among the drug surveillance agencies
(D) eliminate the availability and sale of certain drugs now on the market
(E) improve drug-testing procedures to detect dangerous effects before drugs are approved

14. The author makes use of which of the following devices in the passage?

(A) Definition of terms
(B) Examples
(C) Analogy
(D) Definition of terms and example
(E) Definition of terms and analogy

Item #15 is based on the following passage.

The day was extremely hot, and we rode without seeing a tree or a bush or a drop of water. Our horses and mules suffered, but at sunset they pricked up their ears and mended their pace. Water
5 was near. We came to a shallow valley with a stream, and along its banks were tents. Troops and wagons were moving over the opposite ridge. In order to find an unoccupied camping ground, we had to pass a quarter mile upstream. In the
10 morning, the country was covered with mist, and we saw through the obscurity that tents were falling and ranks rapidly forming. Almost every day, we met long trains of wagons crawling at a snail's pace toward Santa Fe.

15. The passage states that it was necessary to cross upstream in order to

(A) get a clearer view of the military encampment
(B) find clean water for the horses and mules
(C) join the wagons on the journey to Santa Fe
(D) avoid others who had already made a camp
(E) ford at the shallowest point available

Item #16 is based on the following passage.

If we had to demonstrate for ourselves all the facts that we use every day, the task would never be complete. Life is too short, and we don't have the capacity to test every one of them. Consequently, we
5 trust various opinions that we have neither the time nor the power to verify for ourselves. On this groundwork, we raise the structure of our own thoughts, not by choice, but by the inflexible law of our nature. And it is a good thing too, for society
10 would not otherwise exist. Society presupposes that citizens are held together by common beliefs.

16. The passage implies that if everyone insisted upon testing every proposition for himself or herself

(A) people would eventually reach the same conclusion
(B) citizens would lack the common beliefs necessary for society
(C) only the most intelligent people would possess knowledge
(D) common beliefs would be more firmly founded on truth
(E) factual errors could be eliminated from widely held opinions

Items #17–23 are based on the following passage.

Lightning is an electrical discharge of immense proportions. Some 80 percent of lightning occurs within clouds; about 20 percent is cloud-to-ground lightning; and an extremely small percentage is
5   cloud-to-sky lightning.

Cloud-to-ground lightning begins when complex meteorological processes cause a tremendous electrostatic charge to build up within a cloud. Typically, the bottom of the cloud is
10 negatively charged. When the charge reaches 50 to 100 million volts, air is no longer an effective insulator, and lightning occurs within the cloud itself. Ten to 30 minutes after the onset of intracloud lightning, negative charges called
15 stepped leaders emerge from the bottom of the cloud, moving toward the earth in 50-meter intervals at speeds of 100 to 200 kilometers per second and creating an ionized channel. As the leaders near the Earth, their strong electric field
20 causes streamers of positively charged ions to develop at the tips of pointed objects that are connected directly or indirectly to the ground. These positively charged streamers flow upward.

When the distance, known as the striking
25 distance, between a stepped leader and one of the streamers reaches 30 to 100 meters, the intervening air breaks down completely and the leader is joined to the Earth via the streamer. Now a pulse of current known as a return stroke ranging
30 from thousands to hundreds of thousands of amperes moves at one tenth to one third the speed of light from the Earth through the object from which the streamer emanated and up the ionized channel to the charge center within the cloud. An
35 ionized channel remains in the air and additional negative charges called dart leaders will quickly move down this path resulting in further return strokes. This multiplicity causes the flash to flicker. The entire event typically lasts about one second.
40 The return stroke's extremely high temperature creates the visible lightning and produces thunder by instantly turning moisture into steam. Most direct damage results from the heavy return stroke current because it produces high
45 temperatures in the channel, or from arcing at the point of ground contact. If the lightning current is carried by an enclosed conductor (e.g., within a jacketed cable, through a concrete wall, or beneath a painted surface), entrapped moisture is turned into
50 high-pressure steam that can cause a cable, wall, or painted object to explode. Arcing frequently ignites combustibles.

Lightning causes hundreds of millions of dollars in property losses annually and the majority
55 of forest fires. Lightning is also the leading weather-related killer in the U.S., causing from 100 to 200 deaths each year.

17. In line 14, the word "intracloud" most nearly means

(A) between clouds
(B) within a cloud
(C) from cloud to sky
(D) from ground to cloud
(E) from leader to cloud

18. The selection defines the striking distance as the distance between

(A) the ground and the cloud
(B) a stepped leader and a dart leader
(C) a dart leader and a return stroke
(D) a streamer and a stepped leader
(E) two clouds

19. According to the selection, the flickering appearance of a lightning strike is created by

(A) the stepped movement of leaders
(B) multiple return strokes
(C) water being vaporized
(D) arcing at ground contact
(E) unstable negative leaders

20. What topic might the author logically address in a continuation of the passage?

(A) Precautions to minimize lightning damage
(B) Other weather phenomena that cause injury
(C) Basic principles governing electricity
(D) Identifying different types of clouds
(E) History of scientific theory about lightning

21. According to the passage, which of the following is NOT true of stepped leaders?

(A) They develop 10 to 30 minutes after intracloud lightning.
(B) As they traverse the distance from cloud to ground, they create an ionized channel.
(C) Their powerful positive charge causes streamers to develop in grounded objects.
(D) They emerge from the bottom of the cloud and move downward in intervals of 50 meters.
(E) Their rate of progress is 100 to 200 kilometers per second.

22. The passage answers which of the following questions?

(A) How does lightning produce the associated thunder?
(B) How far above the ground is the bottom of the typical lightning-producing cloud?
(C) How frequently will lightning strike a given object?
(D) How long does it take a cloud to build up an electrostatic charge?
(E) How does intracloud lightning cross from one area of a cloud to another?

23. The author's primary concern is to

(A) warn about the dangers posed by lightning strikes
(B) describe the sequence of events that make up a lightning strike
(C) discuss fundamental scientific laws pertaining to electricity
(D) support the commonly held view that lightning strikes the ground
(E) prove that lightning occurs because of a charge imbalance between a cloud and the ground

Items #24–25 are based on the following passage.

Human beings are the only animals that laugh and weep, for they are the only animals that are struck with the difference between what things are and what they ought to be. We weep at what
5 exceeds our expectations in serious matters; we laugh at what disappoints our expectations in trifles. We shed tears from sympathy with real and necessary distress; we burst into laughter from want of sympathy with that which is unreasonable
10 and unnecessary. Tears are the natural and involuntary response of the mind overcome by some sudden and violent emotions. Laughter is the same sort of convulsive and involuntary movement, occasioned by mere surprise or contrast.

24. According to the passage, tears and laughter have all of the following in common EXCEPT

(A) They are both involuntary reactions.
(B) They are both the result of violent emotions.
(C) They both depend on prior expectations.
(D) They are both natural emotions.
(E) They are both reactions to experiences of the world.

25. The author implies that animals lack the ability to

(A) perceive emotional changes in humans
(B) feel pain or pleasure
(C) evoke sorrow or laughter in humans
(D) respond strongly to external stimuli
(E) imagine things other than as they are seen

Items #26–27 are based on the following passage.

One continuing problem in labor-management relations is the "us/them" mentality. In addition to fiscal constraints, continuing problems with the Fair Labor Standards Act, bad faith negotiations, bad
5 management practices, poor union leadership, and a continued loss of management prerogatives will all combine to produce forces that will cause a significant increase in disruptive job actions in the near future. Neither side is blameless. The tragedy
10 of the situation is that the impact of poor labor-management relations is relatively predictable and is thus avoidable. Since the economic situation will not improve significantly in the next few years, the pressure on the part of union leaders to obtain
15 more benefits for their members will be frustrated, setting the stage for confrontation between labor and management.

26. The author's discussion of labor-management relations can best be described as

(A) extremely pro-labor
(B) mildly pro-labor
(C) neutral
(D) mildly pro-management
(E) extremely pro-management

27. The author implies that if the economic conditions improve

(A) management will lose much of its power
(B) labor leaders will not seek more benefits
(C) labor-management tensions will decline
(D) the Fair Labor Standards Act will be repealed
(E) labor will win a voice in management

Items #28–36 are based on the following passage.

Public general hospitals originated in the almshouse infirmaries established as early as colonial times by local governments to care for the poor. Later, in the late eighteenth and early
5 nineteenth centuries, the infirmary separated from the almshouse and became an independent institution supported by local tax money. At the same time, private charity hospitals began to develop. Both private and public hospitals mainly
10 provided food and shelter for the impoverished sick, since there was little that medicine could actually do to cure illness, and the middle class was treated at home by private physicians.

Late in the nineteenth century, private charity
15 hospitals began trying to attract middle-class patients. Although the depression of 1890 stimulated the growth of charitable institutions and an expanding urban population became dependent on assistance, there was a decline in private
20 contributions to these organizations that forced them to look to local government for financial support. Since private institutions had also lost benefactors, they began to charge patients. In order to attract middle-class patients, private institutions
25 provided services and amenities that distinguished between paying and nonpaying patients, making the hospital a desirable place for private physicians to treat their own patients. As paying patients became more necessary to the survival of the private
30 hospital, the public hospitals slowly became the only place for the poor to get treatment. By the end of the nineteenth century, cities were reimbursing private hospitals for their care of indigent patients and the public hospitals remained dependent on the
35 tax dollars.

The advent of private hospital health insurance, which provided middle-class patients with the purchasing power to pay for private hospital services, guaranteed the private hospital a
40 regular source of income. Private hospitals restricted themselves to revenue-generating patients, leaving the public hospitals to care for the poor. Although public hospitals continued to provide services for patients with communicable
45 diseases and outpatient and emergency services, the Blue Cross plans developed around the needs of the private hospitals and the inpatients they served. Thus, reimbursement for ambulatory care has been minimal under most Blue Cross plans, and provision
50 of outpatient care has not been a major function of the private hospital, in part because private patients can afford to pay for the services of private

physicians. Additionally, since World War II, there
has been a tremendous influx of federal money into
55 private medical schools and the hospitals associated
with them. Further, large private medical centers
with expensive research equipment and programs
have attracted the best administrators, physicians,
and researchers. Because of the greater resources
60 available to the private medical centers, public
hospitals have increasing problems attracting
highly qualified research and medical personnel.
With the mainstream of healthcare firmly
established in the private medical sector, the public
65 hospital has become a "dumping ground."

28. In line 33, the word "indigent" most nearly
means

    (A) without the means to pay
    (B) having emergency medical needs
    (C) lacking health insurance
    (D) reimbursed by the government
    (E) treated by a private doctor

29. According to the passage, the very first private
hospitals

    (A) developed from almshouse infirmaries
    (B) provided better care than public
        infirmaries
    (C) were established mainly to service the
        poor
    (D) were supported by government revenues
    (E) catered primarily to middle-class patients

30. It can be inferred that the author believes the
differences that currently exist between public
and private hospitals are primarily the result of

    (A) political considerations
    (B) economic factors
    (C) ethical concerns
    (D) legislative requirements
    (E) technological developments

31. It can be inferred that the growth of private
health insurance

    (A) relieved local governments of the need to
        fund public hospitals
    (B) guaranteed that the poor would have
        access to medical care
    (C) forced middle-class patients to use public
        hospitals
    (D) prompted the closing of many charitable
        institutions
    (E) reinforced the distinction between public
        and private hospitals

32. Which of the following would be the most
logical topic for the author to introduce in the
next paragraph?

    (A) A plan to improve the quality of public
        hospitals
    (B) An analysis of the profit structure of
        health insurance companies
    (C) A proposal to raise taxes on the middle
        class
    (D) A discussion of recent developments in
        medical technology
    (E) A list of the subjects studied by students in
        medical school

33. The author's primary concern is to

    (A) describe the financial structure of the
        healthcare industry
    (B) demonstrate the importance of
        government support for healthcare
        institutions
    (C) criticize wealthy institutions for refusing
        to provide services to the poor
    (D) identify the historical causes of the
        division between private and public
        hospitals
    (E) praise public hospitals for their
        willingness to provide healthcare for the
        poor

34. The author cites all of the following as factors contributing to the decline of public hospitals EXCEPT

(A) Government money was used to subsidize private medical schools and hospitals to the detriment of public hospitals.
(B) Public hospitals are not able to compete with private institutions for top-flight managers and doctors.
(C) Large private medical centers have better research facilities and more extensive research programs than public hospitals.
(D) Public hospitals accepted the responsibility for treating patients with certain diseases.
(E) Blue Cross insurance coverage does not reimburse subscribers for medical expenses incurred in a public hospital.

35. The author's attitude toward public hospitals can best be described as

(A) contemptuous and prejudiced
(B) apprehensive and distrustful
(C) concerned and understanding
(D) enthusiastic and supportive
(E) unsympathetic and annoyed

36. The author implies that any outpatient care provided by a hospital is

(A) paid for by private insurance
(B) provided in lieu of treatment by a private physician
(C) supplied primarily by private hospitals
(D) a source of revenue for public hospitals
(E) no longer provided by hospitals, public or private

Item #37 is based on the following passage.

A belief in luck is only one element in the psychology of gambling. Betting on contests of speed or strength or skill also includes a desire to heighten the intensity of a win by imposing an
5   additional cost that is proportional to the wager lost. The third element is one that is not put into words nor that is even recognized by the bettor: enhancing the chances of success for the contestant on which the bet is made. At some very primitive
10 level, the bettor feels that the effort expended must somehow matter, like a sacrifice to a god for a bountiful harvest. There is an instinctual feeling that events will inherently favor the side that has offered the sacrifice.

37. The reasoning above presupposes that it is possible for a bettor to

(A) win a wager and yet lose money on a contest of skill
(B) make a gamble fully expecting to lose the wager
(C) place a bet on a contest in which luck is not a factor
(D) lose a gamble yet enjoy the victory of the winning side
(E) act upon motives of which he or she is not aware

Items #38–45 are based on the following passage.

The National Security Act of 1947 created a national military establishment headed by a single Secretary of Defense. The legislation had been a year-and-a-half in the making—beginning when
5 President Truman first recommended that the armed services be reorganized into a single department. During that period, the President's concept of a unified armed service was torn apart and put back together several times; the final
10 measure to emerge from Congress was a compromise. Most of the opposition to the bill came from the Navy and its numerous civilian spokesmen, including Secretary of the Navy James Forrestal. In support of unification (and a separate air force that
15 was part of the unification package) were the Army air forces, the Army, and, most importantly, the President of the United States.

Passage of the bill did not end the bitter interservice disputes. Rather than unify, the act
20 served only to federate the military services. It neither halted the rapid demobilization of the armed forces that followed World War II nor brought to the new national military establishment the loyalties of officers steeped in the traditions of
25 the separate services. At a time when the balance of power in Europe and Asia was rapidly shifting, the services lacked any precise statement of United States foreign policy from the National Security Council on which to base future programs. The
30 services bickered unceasingly over their respective roles and missions, already complicated by the Soviet nuclear capability that, for the first time, made the United States subject to devastating attack. Not even the appointment of Forrestal as the
35 first Secretary of Defense allayed the suspicions of naval officers and their supporters that the role of the U.S. Navy was threatened with permanent eclipse. Before the war of words died down, Forrestal himself was driven to resignation and
40 then suicide.

By 1948, the United States military establishment was forced to make do with a budget approximately 10 percent of what it had been at its wartime peak. Meanwhile, the cost of weapons
45 procurement was rising geometrically as the nation came to put more and more reliance on the atomic bomb and its delivery systems. These two factors inevitably made adversaries of the Navy and the Air Force as the battle between advocates of the B-36
50 and the supercarrier so amply demonstrates. Given severe fiscal restraints on the one hand, and on the other the nation's increasing reliance on strategic nuclear deterrence, the conflict between these two services over roles and missions was essentially a
55 contest over slices of an ever-diminishing pie.

Yet if in the end neither service was the obvious victor, the principle of civilian dominance over the military clearly was. If there had ever been any danger that the United States military
60 establishment might exploit, to the detriment of civilian control, the goodwill it enjoyed as a result of its victories in World War II, that danger disappeared in the interservice animosities engendered by the battle over unification.

38. In line 21, the word "demobilization" most nearly means

(A) shift to a unified military
(B) realignment of allies
(C) change from war to peace
(D) adoption of new technology
(E) adjustment to a renewed threat

39. According to the passage, the interservice strife that followed unification occurred primarily between the

(A) Army and Army air forces
(B) Army and Navy
(C) Army air forces and Navy
(D) Air Force and Army
(E) Air Force and Navy

40. It can be inferred from the passage that Forrestal's appointment as Secretary of Defense was expected to

(A) placate members of the Navy
(B) result in decreased levels of defense spending
(C) outrage advocates of the Army air forces
(D) win Congressional approval of the unification plan
(E) make Forrestal a Presidential candidate against Truman

41. According to the passage, President Truman supported which of the following?

(A) Elimination of the Navy
(B) A unified military service
(C) Establishment of a separate air force
(D) Elimination of the Navy and establishment of a separate air force
(E) A unified military service and establishment of a separate air force

42. With which of the following statements about defense unification would the author most likely agree?

(A) Unification ultimately undermined United States military capability by inciting interservice rivalry.
(B) The unification legislation was necessitated by the drastic decline in appropriations for the military services.
(C) Although the unification was not entirely successful, it had the unexpected result of ensuring civilian control of the military.
(D) In spite of the attempted unification, each service was still able to pursue its own objectives without interference from the other branches.
(E) Unification was in the first place unwarranted, and in the second place ineffective.

43. According to the selection, the political situation following the passage of the National Security Act of 1947 was characterized by all of the following EXCEPT

(A) a shifting balance of power in Europe and in Asia
(B) fierce interservice rivalries
(C) lack of strong leadership by the National Security Council
(D) shrinking postwar military budgets
(E) a lame-duck President who was unable to unify the legislature

44. The author cites the resignation and suicide of Forrestal in order to

(A) underscore the bitterness of the interservice rivalry surrounding the passage of the National Security Act of 1947
(B) demonstrate that the Navy eventually emerged as the dominant branch of service after the passage of the National Security Act of 1947
(C) suggest that the nation would be better served by a unified armed service under a single command
(D) provide an example of a military leader who preferred to serve his country in war rather than in peace
(E) persuade the reader that Forrestal was a victim of political opportunists and an unscrupulous press

45. The author is primarily concerned with

(A) discussing the influence of personalities on political events
(B) describing the administration of a powerful leader
(C) criticizing a piece of legislation
(D) analyzing a political development
(E) suggesting methods for controlling the military

Items #46–47 are based on the following passage.

The Puerto Rican community is an ethnic subgroup with its own unique character. Puerto Rico was "discovered" and colonized by Spanish conquistadors, and the Taino Indians eventually
5 disappeared. Some Indian features are found among Puerto Ricans today, though for all practical purposes their culture was completely destroyed. As the Indian population dwindled, black slaves were transported from Africa in large numbers;
10 these slaves brought elements of their own culture, many of which remain evident in Puerto Rico today. By the nineteenth century, the Puerto Rican had emerged as a distinct personality and could be one of a number of colors: white, black, Indian, or mixed.
15 The pride of the Indian, the "hidalguismo" (flamboyancy and idealism) of the Spaniard, and the fatalism of the African blacks are all aspects of this personality.

46. The passage is primarily concerned with the

(A) evolution of the Puerto Rican character
(B) expeditions of the Spanish conquistadors
(C) African customs that are still practiced in Puerto Rico
(D) disappearance of the Taino Indians
(E) colonization of Puerto Rico

47. Which of the following best explains why the author places the word "discovered" (line 3) in quotation marks?

(A) To show that he is quoting from another source
(B) To show his admiration for Spanish culture
(C) To underscore the fact that the island had been an uninhabited paradise
(D) To acknowledge, ironically, that Puerto Rico was already inhabited
(E) To emphasize the importance of Spanish contributions to Puerto Rican culture

Items #48–55 are based on the following passage.

The founders of the American Republic viewed their revolution primarily in political rather than economic or social terms. Furthermore, they talked about education as essential to the public good—a
5 goal that took precedence over knowledge as occupational training or as a means to self-fulfillment or self-improvement. Over and over again, the Revolutionary generation, both liberal and conservative in outlook, asserted its conviction
10 that the welfare of the Republic rested upon an educated citizenry and that schools, especially free public schools, would be the best means of educating the citizenry in civic values and the obligations required of everyone in a democratic
15 republican society. All agreed that the principal ingredients of a civic education were literacy and the inculcation of patriotic and moral virtues, some others adding the study of history and the study of principles of the republican government itself.
20 The founders, as was the case with almost all their successors, were long on exhortation and rhetoric regarding the value of civic education, but they left it to the textbook writers to distill the essence of those values for schoolchildren. Texts in
25 American history and government appeared as early as the 1790s. The textbook writers turned out to be largely of conservative persuasion, more likely Federalist in outlook than Jeffersonian, and they almost universally agreed that political virtue must
30 rest upon moral and religious precepts. Since most textbook writers were New Englanders, this meant that the texts were infused with Protestant, and above all Puritan, outlooks.
In the first half of the Republic, civic education
35 in the schools emphasized the inculcation of civic values and made little attempt to develop participatory political skills. That was a task left to incipient political parties, town meetings, churches, and the coffee or ale houses where men gathered
40 for conversation. Additionally, as a reading of certain Federalist papers of the period would demonstrate, the press probably did more to disseminate realistic as well as partisan knowledge of government than the schools. The goal of
45 education, however, was to achieve a higher form of *Unum* for the new Republic. In the middle half of the nineteenth century, the political values taught in the public and private schools did not change substantially from those celebrated in the first fifty
50 years of the Republic. In the textbooks of the day, their rosy hues if anything became golden. To the resplendent values of liberty, equality, and a

benevolent Christian morality were now added the middle-class virtues—especially of New England—
55 of hard work, honesty, integrity, the rewards of individual effort, and obedience to parents and legitimate authority. But of all the political values taught in school, patriotism was preeminent; and whenever teachers explained to schoolchildren why
60 they should love their country above all else, the idea of liberty assumed pride of place.

48. In line 5, the phrase "took precedence over" most nearly means

(A) set an example for
(B) formulated a policy of
(C) enlightened someone on
(D) had greater importance than
(E) taught only practical skills

49. The passage deals primarily with the

(A) content of textbooks used in early American schools
(B) role of education in late eighteenth- and early to mid-nineteenth-century America
(C) influence of New England Puritanism on early American values
(D) origin and development of the Protestant work ethic in modern America
(E) establishment of universal, free public education in America

50. According to the passage, the founders of the Republic regarded education primarily as

(A) a religious obligation
(B) a private matter
(C) an unnecessary luxury
(D) a matter of individual choice
(E) a political necessity

51. The author states that textbooks written in the middle part of the nineteenth century

(A) departed radically in tone and style from earlier textbooks
(B) mentioned for the first time the value of liberty
(C) treated traditional civic virtues with even greater reverence
(D) were commissioned by government agencies
(E) contained no reference to conservative ideas

52. Which of the following would LEAST likely have been the subject of an early American textbook?

(A) Basic rules of English grammar
(B) The American Revolution
(C) Patriotism and other civic virtues
(D) Vocational education
(E) Principles of American government

53. The author's attitude toward the educational system discussed in the passage can best be described as

(A) cynical and unpatriotic
(B) realistic and analytical
(C) pragmatic and frustrated
(D) disenchanted and bitter
(E) idealistic and naïve

54. The passage provides information that would be helpful in answering which of the following questions?

(A) Why was a disproportionate share of early American textbooks written by New England authors?
(B) Was the Federalist party primarily a liberal or conservative force in early American politics?
(C) How many years of education did the founders believe were sufficient to instruct young citizens in civic virtue?
(D) What were the names of some of the Puritan authors who wrote early American textbooks?
(E) Did most citizens of the early Republic agree with the founders that public education was essential to the welfare of the Republic?

55. The author implies that an early American Puritan would likely insist that

(A) moral and religious values are the foundation of civic virtue
(B) textbooks should instruct students in political issues of vital concern to the community
(C) textbooks should give greater emphasis to the value of individual liberty than to the duties of patriotism
(D) private schools with a particular religious focus are preferable to public schools with no religious instruction
(E) government and religion are separate institutions and the church should not interfere in political affairs

Item #56 is based on the following passage.

Icing occurs when an aircraft penetrates a cloud of small, supercooled water droplets. When ice accumulates on flying surfaces, the result is loss of control and even loss of lift. One approach to the
5 problem of icing is the use of anti-icing and de-icing systems. This approach requires the installation of complex mechanical or thermal systems. A second approach is to design components in ways that eliminate, or at least minimize, adverse effects of ice
10 accretion. This method requires no external power; systems are less costly to build and to maintain, and there is no chance of failure. While components that are completely unaffected by ice may not be possible, reducing the adverse effects of icing by
15 proper aerodynamic design is feasible.

56. It can be inferred that the author regards anti-icing and de-icing systems as

(A) the preferred approach to the problem of icing
(B) a second best approach to the problem of icing
(C) cost effective when compared to the design approach
(D) more practicable than attempts to design away the problem
(E) safer than design changes intended to minimize the effects of ice

Items #57–58 are based on the following passage.

A sprain is a stretching or a tearing injury to a ligament; a strain is an injury to a muscle or a tendon that is caused by twisting or pulling. The severity of a sprain depends on the extent of injury
5 (whether the tear is partial or complete) and the number of ligaments involved. A strain, depending on the severity of the injury, may be a simple overstretching of the muscle or tendon, or it can result in a partial or complete tear. A sprain usually
10 results from a fall or a sudden twist. Typically, sprains occur when people fall on an outstretched arm, land on the side of the foot, or twist a knee. The usual symptoms include pain, swelling, bruising, and an inability to use the joint. A strain is usually
15 caused by overstressing the muscles. Typically, people with a strain experience pain, muscle spasm, and muscle weakness.

57. The primary purpose of the passage is to

(A) explain how to treat sprains and strains
(B) analyze the common causes of sprains and strains
(C) identify the symptoms of injuries to ligaments, muscles, and tendons
(D) explain how to avoid sprains and strains
(E) distinguish sprains and strains as injuries

58. An injury that results from a sudden twist during a fall and causes a purple swelling and the complete inability to move the joint would most likely be called

(A) acute strain
(B) chronic strain
(C) severe sprain
(D) mild sprain
(E) inflammation

Items #59–60 are based on the following two passages.

Passage 1

An *E. coli* outbreak at a county fair sickened hundreds of people. Epidemiologists concluded that individuals with culture-confirmed cases of *E. coli* infection were exposed on August 28 by consuming
5 beverages sold by vendors supplied with water from Well 6. A dye study performed in late September showed a hydraulic connection between the septic system of a nearby 4-H dormitory and Well 6. Tests of a cattle manure storage area
10 suspected as a possible contamination source did not show a hydraulic connection with Well 6 nor with the presence of the relevant strain of *E. Coli*. Therefore, the outbreak was caused by leakage from the dormitory septic system.

Passage 2

15 Manure runoff from the nearby cattle barn cannot be ruled out as a cause of the outbreak because exact environmental conditions, including drought followed by heavy rain, could not be replicated during the later study. Additionally,
20 manure in the storage area was removed daily. Thus, it can never be known if manure-contaminated water percolated from the manure storage area to Well 6.

59. In line 22, the word "percolated" most nearly means

(A) boiled
(B) infected
(C) tested
(D) was consumed
(E) seeped

60. Which of the following best describes the relationship between the two passages?

(A) The two speakers agree that *E. coli* caused the illnesses but believe that two different strains were involved.

(B) The two speakers agree that *E. coli* caused the illnesses but disagree about the source of the contamination.

(C) The two speakers agree that the same strain of *E. coli* caused the outbreak and agree that the dormitory septic system was the source.

(D) Speaker 1 maintains that *E. coli* was the cause of the outbreak of illness, but Speaker 2 thinks that some other agent might have been involved.

(E) Speaker 2 argues that that several sources contributed to the contamination, while Speaker 1 says that the only source was the dormitory septic system.

STRATEGY SUMMARY

Reading Strategies

Understanding the three levels of reading comprehension and how they relate to the seven Critical Reading: Passages item-types will help you to identify quickly the question that is being asked by a particular item.

Level 1—General Theme

The first level of reading, appreciation of the general theme, is the most basic. Main Idea items test whether you understand the passage at the most general level. The first sentence of a paragraph—often the topic sentence—may provide a summary of the content of that paragraph. Also, the last sentence of a paragraph usually provides concluding material that may also be helpful in understanding the general theme of the passage.

Main Idea items ask about the central theme that unifies the passage(s):

- *Which of the following is the main point of the passage?*
- *The primary purpose of the passage is to....*

Level 2—Specific Points

The second level of reading, understanding of specific points, takes you deeper into the selection. Explicit Detail, Vocabulary, and Development items all test your ability to read carefully. Since this is an "open-book" test, you can always return to the selection. Therefore, if something is highly technical or difficult to understand, do not dwell on it for too long—come back later if necessary.

Explicit Detail items ask about details that are specifically mentioned in the passage. This type of item differs from a Main Idea item in that explicit details are points provided by the author in developing the main idea of the passage. Explicit Detail items provide "locator words" that identify the required information in the passage.

- *The author mentions which of the following?*
- *According to the passage,...?*

Vocabulary items test the understanding of a word or phrase in context. In addition to testing vocabulary, these items incorporate elements that are similar to Critical Reading: Sentence Completion items. The nature of the Vocabulary items indicates two points. First, the correct answer choice will make sense when it is substituted for the referenced word. Second, the correct answer choice may not be the most commonly used meaning of the word; in fact, if it were, then what would be the point of including the item on the test? Thus, the general strategy for this type of item is to favor the less commonly used meaning.

- *The word "-------" in line ## means....*
- *In line ##, what is the best definition of the word "-------"?*

Development items ask about the overall structure of the passage or about the logical role played by a specific part of the passage.

- *The author develops the passage primarily by....*
- *The author mentions...in order to....*

Level 3—Evaluation

The third level of reading, evaluation of the text, takes you even deeper into the selection. Implied Idea, Application, and Voice items ask not just for understanding, but require a judgment or an evaluation of what you have read. This is why these items are usually the most difficult.

Implied Idea items don't ask about what is specifically stated in the passage; rather, Implied Idea items ask about what can be logically inferred from what is stated in the passage. For example, the passage might explain that a certain organism (X) is found only in the presence of another organism (Y). An accompanying Implied Idea item might ask the following question: "If organism Y is not present, what can be inferred?" Since the passage implies that in the absence of Y, X cannot be present, the answer would be "X is not present." Since this type of item generally builds on a specific detail, "locator words" for identifying information in the passage are often provided in the item stem.

- *The passage implies that....*
- *The author uses the phrase "..." to mean....*

Application items are similar to Implied Idea items, but they go one step further: examinees must apply what they have learned from the passage to a new situation.

- *With which of the following statements would the author most likely agree?*
- *The passage is most probably taken from which of the following sources?*

Voice items ask about the author's attitude toward a specific detail or the overall tone of the passage.

- *The tone of the passage can best be described as....*
- *The author regards...as....*

General Strategies

Reading strategies are not an exact science. Practice is essential to mastering the following techniques:

Preview the Passage

Read the first and last sentence of each passage in the test section. After reading the first sentence of each passage, label each passage as either "Easy" or "Hard" based on your initial understanding of the material and your level of interest. Analyze the easier passages first.

Preview Each Paragraph

Read the first and last sentences of the passage. If the selection is more than one paragraph long, begin with a preview of the first and last sentences of each paragraph.

Preview the Item Stems

Code each item stem as one of the following three levels of reading comprehension: GT (Level 1—General Theme); SP (Level 2—Specific Points); or E (Level 3—Evaluation).

Read the Passage

Ask what the author is attempting to describe, especially in the case of Evaluation items. Also, read the first sentence in each paragraph prior to reading the entire selection. This step is optional, depending on the ease of the selection, your personal preference, and the time available. Bracket difficult material, either mentally or with some sort of a mark, and then simply revisit it if necessary or if time permits. Instead of wasting time re-reading, attempt to understand the context in which the author introduces a particular concept.

Code in Groups

Circle the answers to the items in the test booklet and transcribe the answers to all the items for a passage to the answer sheet after finishing each passage. This approach helps increase accuracy and makes checking your work easier and more efficient. For each selection, transcribe the answers to the answer sheet together as a group. Only when the time limit approaches should you transcribe each answer individually.

Additional Practice

To identify items for additional practice, see the Item Index at the back of this book, which offers a breakdown of items by tested concept.

Critical Reading:
Sentence Completions

Course Concept Outline

I. Test Mechanics (p. 127)

  A. Overview (p. 127)

  B. Anatomy (Items #1–5, pp. 128–129)

  C. Pacing (p. 130)

  D. Time Trial (Items #1–6, p. 131)

  E. Game Plan (p. 132)

     1. Quickly Preview the Test Section, but Skip the Directions (p. 132)
     2. Use Your Completion Sense (p. 132)
     3. Get Rid of Excess Baggage (p. 132)
     4. Look for Logical and Grammatical Clues (p. 133)
     5. Use the Process of Elimination (p. 134)
     6. Check Your Answers (p. 134)
     7. Stay on Schedule (p. 134)

II. Lesson (p. 135)

  A. Preliminaries[1]

     1. What Is Tested
     2. Directions
     3. Item Profiles

---

[1] Some concepts in this Course Concept Outline are not illustrated through examples in your student text but may be covered by your instructor in class. They are included here to provide a complete outline of your course.

B. Item-Types

1. Thought Extension
2. Thought Reversal
3. Combined Reasoning

C. Facts about Sentence Completions (p. 135)

1. Sentence Completions Can Be about Almost Any Subject (Item #1, p. 135)
2. Difficulty Range (Items #2–3, p. 135)
3. Wrong Choices Are Wrong for One of Two Reasons (Items #4–5, p. 135)

D. Strategies (p. 135)

1. "Anticipate and Test" (Items #6–8, p. 136)
2. "Simplify Your Life" (Items #9–13, p. 136)
3. Common Logical Patterns (p. 137)
   a) Thought Extension (Item #14, p. 137)
   b) Thought Reversal (Items #15–17, p. 137)
   c) Combined Reasoning
4. Be a Sentence Completions Detective (p. 137)
   a) Coordinate Conjunctions (Items #18–28, pp. 137–138)
   b) Subordinate Conjunctions (Items #29–39, pp. 138–139)
   c) Key Words (Items #40–65, pp. 139–142)
   d) Punctuation Marks (Items #66–76, pp. 142–143)
   e) Explanatory Phrases (Items #77–82, pp. 143–144)
   f) Miscellaneous Elements (Item #83–92, pp. 143–145)
5. Hard Cases (p. 145)
   a) "Go to Pieces" (Items #93–95, p. 145)
   b) Difficult Answers (Items #96–97, p. 145)

III. Quizzes (p. 147)

A. Quiz I (Items #1–16, pp. 147–148)

B. Quiz II (Items #1–16, pp. 149–150)

C. Quiz III (Items #1–16, pp. 151–152)

D. Quiz IV Brain Buster (Items #1–16, pp. 153–155)

IV. Review (Items #1–57, pp. 157–163)

V. Strategy Summary (p. 165)

TEST MECHANICS

Overview

Critical Reading sections include two types of items: Passages and Sentence Completions. A Sentence Completions item consists of a sentence with one or two blanks indicating missing words. Following the sentence are five different substitutions for the blank or blanks. Based on your understanding of the meaning and logic of the sentence, you choose the substitution that best completes the sentence.

The number of Sentence Completions items varies. Five to eight Sentence Completions items in a Critical Reading section is typical. Sentence Completions items are all presented in a group, and they are generally arranged according to order of difficulty, with the easiest first.

Sentence Completions items do not involve a lot of reading—maybe 200 words total, but this does not mean that they are necessarily easy. Some are but others aren't. In many cases, the Sentence Completions items will be about a topic with which you are not familiar. The test-writers sometimes choose unusual topics just to make the item more difficult. The "topic" itself is just window-dressing and not really a part of the question. Some Sentence Completions items are difficult because they test difficult vocabulary words, and others are hard because the logical structure of the sentence to be completed is complicated.

Sentence Completions items do not have a separate time limit, but the Critical Reading sections have a 20- or 25-minute time limit, depending on the number of items. Given that the section as a whole has a time limit, you obviously need to work quickly. Sentence Completions items are not, however, a test of "speed-reading." Even so, you'll probably find that it takes you only 30 to 60 seconds to complete each one.

Anatomy

The directions are simple: fill in the blank(s). You can now safely ignore the directions. Do NOT re-read them on the test.

1. Employees found the charm and warmth of the new department head reassuring, and their initial suspicions of her motives were quickly overcome by her -------.

   (A) spontaneity
   (B) determination
   (C) assertiveness
   (D) liveliness
   (E) sincerity

1. **(E)** *All Sentence Completions items contain verbal clues. You'll study the most important ones in the Sentence Completions Lesson. This sentence says that the initial suspicions were overcome. What would make someone less suspicious? A person's "sincerity," so (E) is the correct choice.*

2. Because Deconstructionists employed their own highly specialized vocabulary and style, their theories were often ------- by other scholars who were unfamiliar with the French tradition of literary criticism.

   (A) imitated
   (B) misinterpreted
   (C) influenced
   (D) captivated
   (E) prefigured

2. **(B)** *Often, Sentence Completions items discuss an unfamiliar topic. Don't worry—you don't need to know anything about the topic to answer the item. This item is not really about "Deconstruction." Instead, it is about something mysterious, with its own jargon, and what kind of reaction would that cause? Puzzlement, confusion, or misunderstanding. So, (B) is the correct choice.*

3. A terribly ineffectual administrator, Alan was -------: even minor matters sat on his desk for weeks awaiting a decision.

   (A) phlegmatic
   (B) opinionated
   (C) penurious
   (D) duplicitous
   (E) spurious

3. **(A)** *Some Sentence Completions items are difficult because they use difficult vocabulary. To answer this one correctly, you need to know that "phlegmatic" means "moving slowly." So, (A) is the correct answer choice.*

4. While the candidate delivered the ------- speech flawlessly, it was when speaking ------- in response to unrehearsed audience questions that her fire and passion were most evident.

   (A) political . . freely
   (B) prematurely . . confidently
   (C) prepared . . spontaneously
   (D) preconceived . . rationally
   (E) practiced . . diligently

4. **(C)** *Some Sentence Completions items have two blanks. These are not necessarily harder than the ones with a single blank. Here, the correct answer, (C), is the one pair of words that are opposites.*

5. Despite the ------- of the situation at the accident scene, it would not have been ------- for the emergency crews to act precipitously.

   (A) seriousness . . unwise
   (B) chaos . . inappropriate
   (C) urgency . . advisable
   (D) turmoil . . predictable
   (E) confusion . . impractical

5. **(C)** *Some Sentence Completions items are difficult because the logic twists and turns. In this item, the words "despite" and "not" keep turning the question on its head, so it's not easy to see that the right answer is (C). But you'll learn techniques to help cut through the tangle.*

Pacing

A good rule of thumb is that you take no longer than 60 seconds per Sentence Completions item. This, of course, means that you should finish the entire group in as many minutes as there are Sentence Completions items, e.g., five Sentence Completions items in five minutes, eight in eight minutes, and six in six minutes.

Within a group, the items get progressively more difficult, so you can't afford to spend an equal amount of time on each. If you spend a full minute answering the first and easiest item in the series, then you're probably not going to have as much time as you'd like for the last and most difficult one. Therefore, you need to use a sliding scale that helps you build up a time reserve for the harder questions toward the end of the series. Of course, this is just a guide. You won't really be keeping track of your time this closely.

CRITICAL READING TEST SECTION FORMAT A (24 items, 25 minutes)			
Type of Item	**Item Number**	**Time on Task**	**Cumulative Time**
Sentence Completions	1	30 seconds	0.5 minutes
	2	45 seconds	1.25 minutes
	3	60 seconds	2.25 minutes
	4	75 seconds	3.5 minutes
	5	90 seconds	5 minutes
Passages	6-24	20 minutes	25 minutes

CRITICAL READING TEST SECTION FORMAT B (24 items, 25 minutes)			
Type of Item	**Item Number**	**Time on Task**	**Cumulative Time**
Sentence Completions	1	30 seconds	0.5 minutes
	2	30 seconds	1 minute
	3	45 seconds	1.75 minutes
	4	45 seconds	2.5 minutes
	5	60 seconds	3.5 minutes
	6	60 seconds	4.5 minutes
	7	90 seconds	6 minutes
	8	120 seconds	8 minutes
Passages	9-24	17 minutes	25 minutes

CRITICAL READING TEST SECTION FORMAT C (19 items, 20 minutes)			
Type of Item	**Item Number**	**Time on Task**	**Cumulative Time**
Sentence Completions	1	30 seconds	0.5 minutes
	2	45 seconds	1.25 minutes
	3	60 seconds	2.25 minutes
	4	60 seconds	3.25 minutes
	5	75 seconds	4.5 minutes
	6	90 seconds	6 minutes
Passages	7-19	14 minutes	20 minutes

Time Trial

(6 Items—6 minutes)

DIRECTIONS: Each item below has one or two blanks; each blank indicates that something has been omitted. Choose the word or pair of words that best fits the meaning of the sentence as a whole when inserted in the sentence.

1. The goal of the archaeological dig is to recover as many artifacts as possible before they are ------- by the construction of the new bridge.

   (A) preserved
   (B) revived
   (C) reproduced
   (D) obliterated
   (E) illustrated

2. The rescue workers' gnawing sense of ------- developed into concern and ultimately despair as they gradually approached the remote site of the car crash.

   (A) resignation
   (B) foreboding
   (C) anticipation
   (D) urgency
   (E) duplicity

3. Although the two students seem to have been longtime friends, in reality they met only -------.

   (A) spontaneously
   (B) ethically
   (C) quietly
   (D) recently
   (E) emotionally

4. Unlike gold, paper money has no ------- value; it is merely a representation of wealth.

   (A) financial
   (B) inveterate
   (C) economic
   (D) intrinsic
   (E) fiscal

5. The statue was so ------- we found it ------- to view.

   (A) repulsive . . amusing
   (B) delightful . . burdensome
   (C) grotesque . . distressing
   (D) warped . . captivating
   (E) precarious . . shocking

6. The treatment of mental illnesses for which there is no cure can only ------- the symptoms, not ------- the disease.

   (A) defend . . eradicate
   (B) disrupt . . deflate
   (C) ameliorate . . eliminate
   (D) confine . . restore
   (E) augment . . delineate

Game Plan

Quickly Preview the Test Section, but Skip the Directions

Last-minute adjustments to the test format are theoretically (but not practically) possible, so check the test section before you start to work, especially the total number of items of each type and the time limit. And yes, the test-writers always tell you to "read the directions carefully." But they don't tell you that you have to read them during the test. Instead, become familiar with them <u>before</u> test day. That way, you won't waste 30 seconds or more (enough time to answer an item) re-reading directions you are already familiar with.

Use Your Completion Sense

Since Sentence Completions items are essentially "fill-in-the-blanks," one or more possible answers may occur to you. Give your "completion sense" a chance to work before you start analyzing the sentence in detail. Read the sentence and try to anticipate a possible answer. Check the answer choices to see if you get a match. This sets up the following basic approach:

Step 1: Read through the sentence for meaning. Read the sentence to yourself at normal speed (as though someone were speaking to you).

Step 2: Formulate a possible completion.

Step 3: Choose the matching answer.

Example:

After his novel was rejected by six publishers, John became embittered and -------, so much so that his friends feared for his sanity.

(A) gentle
(B) wary
(C) morose
(D) pacified
(E) prudent

The correct answer is (C). A reading of the item stem tells you that John was affected negatively and became embittered as well as something else that is like embittered; that is, another negative emotion. Possible completions are words such as "disappointed," "angry," "depressed," or "sullen." The best match is found in (C): "morose."

This basic technique is all you need for many Sentence Completions items, and it should always be your first approach. If your "completion sense" fails you, then you can move on to the more elaborate techniques.

Get Rid of Excess Baggage

Many Sentence Completions items are cluttered up by arcane details. This additional information is not needed to find the correct answer, but it does make things more difficult. A good approach to this "static" is just to tune it out by drawing a line through it.

Example:

By and large, Wittgenstein's treatment of language in *Tractatus Logico-Philosophicus* will be ------- to the lay person, but the more ------- elements will be grasped only by specialists in the philosophy of language.

(A) granted .. general
(B) accessible .. esoteric
(C) concrete .. ingenious
(D) alien .. technical
(E) attractive .. abstract

You don't have to know anything about Wittgenstein to solve this problem, so eliminate the unnecessary detail:

> By and large, ~~Wittgenstein's treatment of language in *Tractatus Logico-Philosophicus*~~ [the book] will be ------- to the lay person, but the more ------- elements will be grasped only by specialists ~~in the philosophy of language.~~

Now, you can see that you need a pair of contrasting words to express the idea that the obvious points are fairly easy to understand but the difficult ones are hard to get. The correct answer is (B).

Look for Logical and Grammatical Clues

If your "completion sense" doesn't get you an answer, then you'll need to analyze the sentence. The test-writers plant a variety of logical and grammatical clues in the sentences for you to find.

Example:

Given the rapidly changing nature of today's technological society, schools should not teach eternal principles, for by tomorrow, today's knowledge is -------.

(A) enriched
(B) reproduced
(C) adequate
(D) precarious
(E) obsolete

The correct answer is (E). The sentence sets up a logical contrast between eternal principles and knowledge that is not eternal. So, you need a word that is the opposite of "eternal," something like "temporary," "outdated," or "transient." (E) provides the best match: "obsolete."

Example:

Retiring by nature and ------- even in private, Eleanor
hardly ever spoke in public.

(A) confident
(B) reticent
(C) preoccupied
(D) untamed
(E) courageous

The correct answer is (B). Here, the clue is a grammatical structure. The introductory phrase "retiring...private" modifies "Eleanor." So, Eleanor was unwilling to speak. Some possible completions are "quiet" and "silent." The best match is "reticent."

Use the Process of Elimination

As you know, the process of elimination is a powerful tool for taking the SAT test. Although there is an adjustment for wrong answers in the Critical Reading sections (minus one-quarter point for each), the odds are in your favor if you can eliminate even one wrong choice. Because Sentence Completions items are in part a test of vocabulary, you may find choices that you know to be wrong as a matter of word meaning and other choices that you can't evaluate because you don't know the word meanings. So, eliminate and guess.

Example:

The ornament was extremely -------, and it broke into
thousands of pieces when it dropped on the floor.

(A) durable
(B) tinfilandulate
(C) prascobituant
(D) wrantofulpact
(E) contagprolistic

In this item, four of the five choices are uncommon words. More precisely, (B) through (E) are made-up words, so you're never going to understand them. Still, you know that (A) has to be wrong because a durable object would not break. And once you have eliminated (A), you have to take a guess—even though you don't know what those other words mean.

Check Your Answers

Once you've found your answer choice, read the sentence a final time with your completion in place. If the result is a smooth-reading sentence that makes sense to you, then the problem yielded the correct answer. Enter your choice and move on to the next item.

Stay on Schedule

You know that it is important to stick to your time schedule, but Sentence Completions items can be a real time trap. You're working on the Sentence Completions items, and they keep getting harder, so you keep spending more and more time. That's the trap. Instead, when the going gets tough, the tough get going—on to the next part of the section.

LESSON

The items in this section accompany the in-class review of the skills and concepts tested by the Sentence Completions part of the SAT Critical Reading test sections. You will work through the items with your instructor in class. Answers are on page 621.

> **DIRECTIONS:** Each item below has one or two blanks; each blank indicates that something has been omitted. Choose the word or pair of words that best fits the meaning of the sentence as a whole when inserted in the sentence.

Facts about Sentence Completions

Sentence Completions Can Be about Almost Any Subject

1. His ------- should not be confused with cowardice; during the war, I saw him on several occasions risk his own life while rescuing members of his unit.

    (A) heroism
    (B) indifference
    (C) caution
    (D) notoriety
    (E) confidence

Difficulty Range

2. Although critics denounced the film as silly and inane, people flocked to the theater to see it, guaranteeing its ------- success.

    (A) scholarly
    (B) hypothetical
    (C) critical
    (D) financial
    (E) eventual

3. Even the most arbitrary and ------- corporation today must be aware of the attitudes of its employees; management may at times be more or less -------, but all must respect the power of an organized workforce.

    (A) influential .. outraged
    (B) prosperous .. precipitous
    (C) flexible .. patronizing
    (D) authoritarian .. responsive
    (E) susceptible .. permanent

Wrong Choices Are Wrong for One of Two Reasons

4. The ease with which the candidate answers difficult questions creates the impression that she has been a public servant for years, but in reality she entered politics only -------.

    (A) securely
    (B) enthusiastically
    (C) frequently
    (D) needfully
    (E) recently

5. Though afflicted by headaches, nausea, and respiratory difficulties, Nietzsche refused to let his ------- problems prevent him from writing.

    (A) imaginary
    (B) financial
    (C) emotional
    (D) theoretical
    (E) physical

Strategies

"Anticipate and Test"

6. The university should ------- the function of the alumni fund so that its importance will be better appreciated by the school's graduates who are asked to contribute to it.

(A) revoke
(B) elucidate
(C) ascertain
(D) prescribe
(E) entice

7. In spite of the ------- of the minister's sermon, when it was finished, most of the congregation was -------.

(A) passion .. fidgety
(B) tedium .. fearful
(C) understanding .. merciful
(D) obtrusiveness .. hurt
(E) veracity .. inspired

8. Because there are so few liberal members in the State Assembly, their influence on legislation is -------.

(A) monumental
(B) insignificant
(C) decisive
(D) undeniable
(E) enhanced

"Simplify Your Life"

9. For Thomas Aquinas, the Scholastic thinker and author of the *Summa Theologica*, the question of angels dancing on a pinhead was not ------- but a ------- issue of vital import to his project of reconciling Aristotelean metaphysics with medieval Church doctrine.

(A) whimsy .. profound
(B) insightful .. complex
(C) comical .. superficial
(D) premeditated .. serious
(E) caprice .. fanciful

10. The rocket scientists had fully expected the thermothrockle to hydrolyze under the intense ionizing radiation, requiring the mission to be aborted, but the astronauts ------- the problem by tekelating the suborbital flexion, and the mission continued.

(A) recreated
(B) transmitted
(C) misjudged
(D) circumvented
(E) proscribed

11. The passage of the mass transit bill over the Governor's veto, despite opposition by key leaders in the legislature, was a devastating ------- for the party machinery and suggests that other, much-needed legislation may receive similar treatment in the future.

(A) victory
(B) optimism
(C) compromise
(D) slap
(E) setback

12. Hiram Maxim, an American who became a British subject and was later knighted by Queen Victoria, was a ------- inventor who held hundreds of patents.

(A) candid
(B) foolish
(C) prolific
(D) naive
(E) modest

13. In *Theory of Justice*, Harvard philosopher John Rawls tries to develop a political theory that will reconcile individual liberty with material equality, a utopian goal that may be as ------- as turning lead into gold.

(A) unattainable
(B) laudable
(C) ironic
(D) tasteful
(E) cautious

Common Logical Patterns

Thought Extension

14. Since the evidence of the manuscript's ------- is -------, its publication will be postponed until a team of scholars has examined it and declared it to be genuine.

    (A) authenticity .. inconclusive
    (B) truthfulness .. tarnished
    (C) veracity .. indubitable
    (D) legitimacy .. infallible
    (E) profundity .. forthcoming

Thought Reversal

15. Although Barbara argues strongly that current policies are unjust, she does not ------- any particular changes.

    (A) reject
    (B) presume
    (C) advocate
    (D) remember
    (E) oppose

16. Despite the fact that they had clinched the divisional title long before the end of regular season play, the team continued to play every game as though it were -------.

    (A) superfluous
    (B) irrational
    (C) lengthy
    (D) hopeless
    (E) vital

17. Although the terms "toad" and "frog" refer to two different animals belonging to different genera, some students ------- the two.

    (A) distinguish
    (B) confuse
    (C) respect
    (D) observe
    (E) mention

Be a Sentence Completions Detective

Coordinate Conjunctions

18. The terms "toad" and "frog" refer to two different animals belonging to different genera, and careful students ------- between the two.

    (A) intermingle
    (B) ignore
    (C) distinguish
    (D) confuse
    (E) dispute

19. The ascent of the mountain is -------, but anyone who makes it to the top is rewarded by a spectacular view.

    (A) helpful
    (B) easy
    (C) unique
    (D) unpleasant
    (E) automatic

20. The term "Indian," introduced by Columbus and ------- by historians, is a misnomer for the Native American.

    (A) eradicated
    (B) arbitrated
    (C) infiltrated
    (D) perpetuated
    (E) coerced

21. The delicate aroma and ------- flavor of this fine wine need a sensitive nose and ------- palate to be appreciated.

    (A) insipid .. educated
    (B) subtle .. discriminating
    (C) pungent .. educated
    (D) adulterated .. cautious
    (E) savory .. untutored

22. He is an ------- student and a ------- to teach.

    (A) intrepid . . hazard
    (B) exceptional . . joy
    (C) exuberant . . power
    (D) insipid . . threat
    (E) ironic . . jubilation

23. The public quite naturally expects that the Picassos and Rembrandts of the museum's painting collection will be on display at all times, but the lack of well-known masterpieces in the photographic collection gives the curator uncommon ------- in deciding which works to exhibit.

    (A) leeway
    (B) guidance
    (C) confidence
    (D) sensitivity
    (E) flair

24. It has been ------- that environment is the ------- factor in the incidence of drug addiction, but recent studies with twins separated at birth indicate that a predisposition to addiction can be inherited.

    (A) proved . . crucial
    (B) demonstrated . . conclusive
    (C) suggested . . predominant
    (D) argued . . logical
    (E) urged . . unimportant

25. The image of the Indian brave on his pinto pony is so common that most people don't realize that horses are not ------- North America but were ------- by the Europeans.

    (A) raised in . . purchased
    (B) indigenous to . . introduced
    (C) native to . . trained
    (D) worshipped in . . bred
    (E) unknown in . . imported

26. She accepted her own misfortune with perfect -------, but was outraged at any abuse or mistreatment of others.

    (A) equanimity
    (B) reluctance
    (C) sincerity
    (D) rabidity
    (E) pulchritude

27. Most sitcoms are -------, but this new one is actually -------.

    (A) banal . . engaging
    (B) vapid . . ordinary
    (C) profound . . solemn
    (D) unsightly . . atrocious
    (E) passionate . . repugnant

28. Laboratory tests which often maim animals and depend solely on observation to determine results are not only ------- but highly ------- since no two people see the same thing.

    (A) safe . . consistent
    (B) patented . . conclusive
    (C) controversial . . valuable
    (D) gratifying . . explosive
    (E) cruel . . unreliable

Subordinate Conjunctions

29. Although there are more female students at the college than male students, the women seem to have a(n) ------- influence on the student government.

    (A) enormous
    (B) negligible
    (C) provocative
    (D) venerable
    (E) active

30. Although his dress is -------, in all other ways he appears to be perfectly normal.

    (A) ordinary
    (B) mellifluous
    (C) eccentric
    (D) nondescript
    (E) recalcitrant

31. Although it may seem a contradiction, psychologists agree that a good marriage is based on the ------- of the partners as well as on their ------- one another.

(A) financial security . . animosity toward
(B) infallibility . . manipulation of
(C) conformity . . denial of
(D) compatibility . . independence from
(E) eccentricity . . perusal of

32. Although all of the guests at the dinner party were -------, the food was so poorly prepared no one ate more than a small portion.

(A) elegant
(B) ravenous
(C) invited
(D) forewarned
(E) surly

33. Although his opponent was much larger, Rocky was ------- as he faced him in the middle of the ring.

(A) intimidated
(B) fearless
(C) cowed
(D) energetic
(E) incompetent

34. Unless we ------- our water resources, there may come a time when our supplies of clean water are completely depleted.

(A) predict
(B) use
(C) conserve
(D) replace
(E) tap

35. If we continue to consume our fossil fuel supply without restraint, then someday it will be -------.

(A) replenished
(B) limited
(C) useless
(D) available
(E) exhausted

36. The critics must have detested the play, for the review was not merely -------, it was -------.

(A) unhappy . . miserable
(B) laudatory . . enthusiastic
(C) sincere . . long
(D) appreciative . . stinging
(E) critical . . scathing

37. Because it preaches total abstinence from almost all of life's pleasures, this fundamental sect finds it difficult to ------- its membership in today's climate of self-indulgence.

(A) admonish
(B) forgive
(C) increase
(D) deride
(E) accept

38. John's parents could not ------- why he was doing so poorly in school since his diagnostic test scores indicated a high degree of ------- which his grades did not reflect.

(A) resolve . . laziness
(B) comprehend . . aptitude
(C) refute . . agility
(D) conclude . . experience
(E) understand . . volition

39. Lars decided to ------- his vacation since he had not yet finished all of the work he had been assigned.

(A) schedule
(B) enjoy
(C) pursue
(D) expand
(E) postpone

Key Words

40. The angry parent ------- the children for their behavior in the restaurant.

(A) scolded
(B) prepared
(C) imitated
(D) delighted
(E) praised

41. The proud parent ------- the children for their behavior in the restaurant.

   (A) scolded
   (B) prepared
   (C) imitated
   (D) delighted
   (E) praised

42. The judge, after ruling that the article had unjustly ------- the reputation of the architect, ordered the magazine to ------- its libelous statements in print.

   (A) praised .. communicate
   (B) injured .. retract
   (C) sullied .. publicize
   (D) damaged .. disseminate
   (E) extolled .. produce

43. Joyce's novel *Finnegans Wake* continues to ------- critics, including those who find it incomprehensible and call it -------.

   (A) appall .. genial
   (B) captivate .. nonsensical
   (C) baffle .. transparent
   (D) bore .. compelling
   (E) entertain .. monotonous

44. Nutritionists have found that certain elements long known to be ------- in large quantities are ------- to life in small amounts.

   (A) lethal .. essential
   (B) deadly .. painful
   (C) healthful .. pleasurable
   (D) fatal .. unbearable
   (E) unfashionable .. important

45. My aunt is so ------- that you cannot have a short conversation with her; she prates on and on until your ears fall asleep.

   (A) garrulous
   (B) engaging
   (C) brusque
   (D) lilting
   (E) impaired

46. We were less impressed by the play's intricate ------- than we were by its difficult -------.

   (A) length .. cast
   (B) theme .. setting
   (C) authorship .. performance
   (D) meaning .. sense
   (E) plot .. language

47. The textbook is a ------- treatment of medieval European history from 800 to 1453 that includes every possible topic.

   (A) dramatic
   (B) sketchy
   (C) inventive
   (D) confused
   (E) comprehensive

48. Paradoxically, this world-renowned performer is sometimes outgoing and at other times -------.

   (A) discourteous
   (B) inventive
   (C) sociable
   (D) reclusive
   (E) passionate

49. In contrast with the early architecture of the Northeast, which was basically utilitarian, the Georgian homes of the early South were far more -------.

   (A) supine
   (B) inconsequential
   (C) grandiose
   (D) acrimonious
   (E) crude

50. Far from the ------- crowds of the city, I find refuge at my ------- cabin on Big Lake.

   (A) pervasive .. dominant
   (B) aggressive .. listless
   (C) petrified .. motivating
   (D) overwhelming .. secluded
   (E) extensive .. scanty

51. It seems ------- to us to dismiss the custodian without a -------.

(A) obligatory .. reason
(B) reactionary .. cause
(C) formidable .. worry
(D) unethical .. hearing
(E) discourteous .. demonstration

52. The novel was long, but the ------- plot kept our interest.

(A) torpid
(B) alien
(C) insipid
(D) labyrinthine
(E) humdrum

53. Anyone who works at home needs to be self-disciplined and -------.

(A) straitlaced
(B) chronic
(C) idiosyncratic
(D) systematic
(E) extremist

54. My dog is a rare breed found ------- in the Arctic.

(A) ultimately
(B) comprehensively
(C) exclusively
(D) vitally
(E) extensively

55. "Great minds think alike": This old ------- is a favorite of mine.

(A) draft
(B) opus
(C) term
(D) maxim
(E) logo

56. My work in the field of ------- takes me to ------- around the world.

(A) spelunking .. homes
(B) geology .. castles
(C) psychiatry .. sanity
(D) ichthyology .. gardens
(E) archaeology .. ruins

57. Tears of the ------- are common in -------.

(A) sorrow .. rulers
(B) cartilage .. competitors
(C) spine .. athletes
(D) helmet .. sports
(E) lesion .. activity

58. Amidst the din at the day-care center, she alone remained -------; it seemed nothing could agitate her.

(A) imperturbable
(B) impermeable
(C) implausible
(D) impassioned
(E) immoderate

59. With little ------- we went about our business, asking only that the ------- leave us alone to work in peace.

(A) ado .. management
(B) fanfare .. regulations
(C) alarm .. community
(D) strain .. effluvium
(E) truth .. overseer

60. Please do not ------- at the man on the corner; he will see you.

(A) trill
(B) gawk
(C) chortle
(D) behold
(E) saunter

61. Although leprosy is not a highly contagious disease, those who have contracted it have always been pariahs who are ------- by others.

(A) ostracized
(B) accepted
(C) sheltered
(D) admonished
(E) lauded

62. Richard is ------- on many topics; he is a true -------.

(A) scholarly . . renaissance
(B) erudite . . prodigy
(C) clever . . intelligentsia
(D) versed . . aficionado
(E) familiar . . aesthete

63. Have you ever ------- the ------- of a macaw?

(A) witnessed . . screech
(B) felt . . hoof
(C) heard . . squawk
(D) remarked . . cry
(E) noticed . . vowels

64. That poor woman—she was ------- by the clever con artists.

(A) curbed
(B) conjoined
(C) deceased
(D) rused
(E) duped

65. We might divert the ------- by building a -------.

(A) snow . . fort
(B) castle . . moat
(C) flowage . . weir
(D) carport . . retaining wall
(E) savannah . . corral

Punctuation Marks

66. People who use their desktop computers for writing can become almost hypnotized by the unbroken succession of letters and text; in such cases, a computer video game can supply a welcome -------.

(A) burden
(B) diversion
(C) handicap
(D) predicament
(E) insight

67. There is no necessary connection between a dollar and what can be purchased for a dollar; the value of money is ------- and can be ------- by supply and demand.

(A) arbitrary . . altered
(B) predetermined . . overruled
(C) conventional . . inspired
(D) lackluster . . improved
(E) optional . . prevented

68. The diva's autobiography was largely -------; when she wasn't saying wonderful things about herself, she ------- her mother, who said them for her.

(A) confidential . . repudiated
(B) anecdotal . . angered
(C) self-congratulatory . . quoted
(D) critical . . rebuked
(E) misunderstood . . flouted

69. The consulting engineer enjoyed the ------- life that she led while visiting projects around the world; she never remained in any one city long enough to get bored.

(A) secretive
(B) mundane
(C) nomadic
(D) rustic
(E) structured

70. Paul is ------- and -------; he volunteers for everything.

(A) saintly . . appreciative
(B) flighty . . moody
(C) unappreciated . . misunderstood
(D) generous . . altruistic
(E) underpaid . . insignificant

71. The speech was -------; it reviewed the main themes of the convention.

(A) holistic
(B) abstract
(C) quantitative
(D) reprisal
(E) summational

72. Since the actor who played the lead was somewhat -------, the property manager had to let out the costumes and have the furniture used in the production reinforced.

(A) winsome
(B) virulent
(C) fragile
(D) corpulent
(E) flirtatious

73. This pamphlet is about -------, the art of ------- spirits.

(A) brewing . . founding
(B) bartending . . manufacturing
(C) sorcery . . imparting
(D) necromancy . . conjuring
(E) juicing . . eliminating

74. The hearing of the white tail deer is remarkably -------, capable of detecting even the slightest rustling of a hunter's clothing.

(A) keen
(B) valid
(C) immune
(D) intact
(E) controlled

75. Prior to the formation of the Central Intelligence Agency, intelligence-gathering functions were ------- with several departments of the executive branch independently engaged in such activities and refusing to share information with each other.

(A) reliable
(B) constricted
(C) fragmented
(D) precarious
(E) indigenous

76. A skillful -------, the dean adopted a posture of patience and ------- toward the protestors, rather than rejecting their demands outright.

(A) administrator . . arrogance
(B) academician . . understanding
(C) negotiator . . compromise
(D) pundit . . tolerance
(E) pedagogue . . obstinacy

Explanatory Phrases

77. Her acceptance speech was -------, eliciting thunderous applause at several points.

(A) tedious
(B) well received
(C) cowardly
(D) uninteresting
(E) poorly written

78. The public debates were often -------, finally deteriorating into mudslinging contests.

(A) informative
(B) bitter
(C) theoretical
(D) inspiring
(E) insightful

79. The star of the show is a ------- performer who acts, sings, and dances with equal facility.

(A) capricious
(B) pretentious
(C) versatile
(D) myopic
(E) quixotic

80. The film was -------, completely lacking in plot, just a series of beautiful images with no particular connection.

(A) incoherent
(B) morbid
(C) moral
(D) romantic
(E) fictitious

81. He views himself as a(n) ------- who has ------- his health for the cause.

(A) martyr . . sacrificed
(B) cherub . . given
(C) victim . . wounded
(D) martinet . . lost
(E) athlete . . aided

82. The conclusion of the program was a modern symphony with chords so ------- that the piece produced a sound similar to the ------- one hears as the individual orchestra members tune their instruments before a concert.

(A) superfluous . . melody
(B) pretentious . . roar
(C) melodious . . applause
(D) versatile . . harmony
(E) discordant . . cacophony

Miscellaneous Elements

83. Elementary school children, who have not yet been repeatedly disappointed by other people, are much more ------- than older and more cynical high school students.

(A) inquisitive
(B) relaxed
(C) enjoyable
(D) trusting
(E) enlightened

84. As a ------- he was a disaster, for his students rarely understood his lectures; yet he was a ------- scholar.

(A) dean . . banal
(B) philosopher . . failed
(C) teacher . . formidable
(D) professor . . second-rate
(E) speaker . . contemptuous

85. Marxist revolution directly challenged the bourgeois order, and Communism explicitly endeavored to destroy traditional religion and to ------- itself as an alternative faith.

(A) repudiate
(B) enshrine
(C) undermine
(D) illuminate
(E) placate

86. Critics are divided in their views on O'Keeffe's art, some admiring her abstractions, others esteeming her figurative works; the first group presents the artist as a progressive while the second places her within the ------- tradition.

(A) conservative
(B) abstract
(C) conciliatory
(D) innovative
(E) victorious

87. Cultural weightlessness is a defining characteristic of Los Angeles, and each new fashion trend or food fad that emanates from its environs causes its ------- to despair of ever hearing Easterners retract their sneering view of the place as nothing more than a disordered set of clogged freeways.

(A) detractors
(B) designers
(C) loyalists
(D) expatriates
(E) imitators

88. The guests invited to meet the famous critic were ------- by a charm that contrasted sharply with the ------- of his writing.

(A) appalled . . inadequacy
(B) frustrated . . wittiness
(C) deceived . . elegance
(D) delighted . . venom
(E) enthralled . . lucidity

89. Portraits painted in Colonial America are quite charming but ------- and demonstrate the isolation of the American painter; they show little or no ------- of the development of painting in Europe.

(A) grotesque . . concern
(B) frivolous . . affirmation
(C) deliberate . . domination
(D) sophisticated . . consideration
(E) primitive . . knowledge

90. In his private life he was quite -------, but he gave large sums of money to charities, so most people thought of him as a -------.

(A) pusillanimous . . charlatan
(B) immodest . . chauvinist
(C) flamboyant . . savant
(D) sinister . . mercenary
(E) miserly . . philanthropist

91. Although the jury thought the defendant had been somewhat less than ------- in his testimony, the ------- summary of the defense attorney finally convinced them of her client's innocence.

(A) interesting . . lackluster
(B) candid . . persuasive
(C) convincing . . inordinate
(D) honest . . confusing
(E) forthright . . irrational

92. Although Mozart's music suggests a composer of great ------- and seriousness, his letters imply that he was naïve and -------.

(A) erudition . . grave
(B) sophistication . . uncouth
(C) fortitude . . macabre
(D) levity . . sanctimonious
(E) fragility . . pensive

Hard Cases

"Go To Pieces"

93. It is highly characteristic of business' ------- attitude that little or no interest was evinced in urban renewal until similar undertakings elsewhere proved that such projects could be -------.

(A) prestigious . . feasible
(B) capitalistic . . rigid
(C) degrading . . completed
(D) mercantile . . insensitive
(E) pragmatic . . profitable

94. George Bernard Shaw expressed his ------- for technological progress when he said that the human race is just interested in finding more ------- ways of exterminating itself.

(A) hope . . impartial
(B) regard . . remote
(C) preference . . violent
(D) support . . effective
(E) contempt . . efficient

95. Although this disease threatens the lives of several thousand people every year, the ------- of supplies and equipment has ------- the progress of medical research for a cure.

(A) discontinuance . . ensured
(B) scarcity . . hampered
(C) rationing . . enhanced
(D) squandering . . facilitated
(E) financing . . neglected

Difficult Answers

96. The committee's report is not as valuable as it might have been because it addresses only the symptoms and not the ------- causes of the problem.

(A) unimpeachable
(B) ephemeral
(C) underlying
(D) incipient
(E) superficial

97. Calvin had long been known for his mendacity, but even those who knew him well were surprised at the ------- explanation he gave for the shortage of funds.

(A) elegant
(B) disingenuous
(C) sincere
(D) dogmatic
(E) bitter

QUIZZES

This section contains three Critical Reading: Sentence Completions quizzes. Complete each quiz under timed conditions. Answers are on page 621.

Quiz I

(16 items; 16 minutes)

> **DIRECTIONS:** Each item below has one or two blanks; each blank indicates that something has been omitted. Choose the word or pair of words that best fits the meaning of the sentence as a whole when inserted in the sentence.

1. Dedicated wildlife photographers willingly travel great distances and gladly endure considerable hardship to share with audiences their ------- for the natural world.

(A) distaste
(B) contempt
(C) preference
(D) expectations
(E) enthusiasm

2. Though the story is set in a small village in a remote area of South America, the novel's themes are so ------- that its events could have occurred anywhere and involved any of us at any time.

(A) mythical
(B) universal
(C) overstated
(D) anguished
(E) complex

3. The football team was ------- by injuries: of the 53 members, only 13 were fit to play.

(A) truncated
(B) decimated
(C) invaded
(D) ostracized
(E) reviled

4. Determinist philosophers have argued that our moral intuitions are ------- rather than learned and that they are dictated by genetic makeup.

(A) transcendental
(B) fortuitous
(C) innate
(D) contingent
(E) empirical

5. The critic thought the film was completely unrealistic; he termed the plot ------- and the acting -------.

(A) contrived .. unbelievable
(B) imaginative .. genuine
(C) ambitious .. courageous
(D) artificial .. unparalleled
(E) absorbing .. uninspiring

6. In Doyle's famous detective stories, Mycroft, the brother of Sherlock Holmes, is described as quite -------, going only from his apartment to his office to his club and back to his apartment.

(A) illustrious
(B) omnivorous
(C) loquacious
(D) spontaneous
(E) sedentary

7. The ------- soldier ------- at the idea that he was to go to battle.

(A) luckless . . rejoiced
(B) youthful . . retired
(C) unwilling . . recoiled
(D) frail . . relapsed
(E) vigorous . . repined

8. A good historian merely makes ------- and accumulates facts; a great historian uses ------- to understand why events occurred the way they did.

(A) statements . . research
(B) references . . evidence
(C) observations . . imagination
(D) arguments . . texts
(E) errors . . sympathy

9. Galileo finally ------- his theories, for it was heresy to ------- the teachings of the Church.

(A) composed . . assuage
(B) recanted . . contradict
(C) invoked . . deploy
(D) demonstrated . . delude
(E) protracted . . ameliorate

10. The experienced ambassador was generally an ------- person who regained her composure quickly even on those ------- occasions when she was close to losing her temper.

(A) articulate . . momentous
(B) imperturbable . . infrequent
(C) unforgiving . . numerous
(D) idealistic . . rare
(E) insistent . . trying

11. The exhibit was a complete -------, thereby confirming the rumors from Paris of the artist's -------.

(A) victory . . malfeasance
(B) triumph . . apathy
(C) disaster . . virtuosity
(D) failure . . geniality
(E) success . . brilliance

12. Conditions in the mine were -------, so the mine workers refused to return to their jobs until the dangers were -------.

(A) hazardous . . eliminated
(B) filthy . . disbanded
(C) deplorable . . collated
(D) conducive . . ameliorated
(E) illegal . . enhanced

13. Karen was ------- in her vindictiveness, frequently feigning disarming warmth while ------- waiting for an opportunity to strike back.

(A) confident . . foolishly
(B) open . . cautiously
(C) withdrawn . . overtly
(D) secure . . immodestly
(E) ruthless . . secretly

14. Despite some bad reviews, Horowitz' stature was not -------, and his fans and critics in Tokyo were unanimous in expressing their ------- his unique talent.

(A) distilled . . kinship with
(B) embellished . . ignorance of
(C) criticized . . disdain for
(D) diminished . . appreciation of
(E) convincing . . concern for

15. ------- the activities of her employees, the director refused to ------- their methods.

(A) Disarming . . condone
(B) Applauding . . question
(C) Repudiating . . punish
(D) Handling . . oversee
(E) Approving . . arrogate

16. His suggestion to amend the club charter was met with -------, if not outright hostility, by the other members who ------- disagreed with him.

(A) gratitude . . allegedly
(B) elation . . tacitly
(C) disapprobation . . vehemently
(D) profusion . . summarily
(E) disdain . . reluctantly

Quiz II

(16 items; 16 minutes)

DIRECTIONS: Each item below has one or two blanks; each blank indicates that something has been omitted. Choose the word or pair of words that best fits the meaning of the sentence as a whole when inserted in the sentence.

1. Carling, a political appointee who was not really able to run the agency, tended to promote others even less ------- than himself who would not question his authority.

   (A) competent
   (B) likable
   (C) honest
   (D) wholesome
   (E) envied

2. It is no longer possible to regard one nation's economy as an ------- system; we are now moving toward becoming a global village with international markets.

   (A) ineffective
   (B) opportunistic
   (C) equitable
   (D) irrational
   (E) isolated

3. Attorneys would be extremely unlikely to boast that no one can hear a word they say, but some doctors seem to be quite proud of their ------- handwriting.

   (A) elegant
   (B) unique
   (C) cultivated
   (D) illegible
   (E) handsome

4. The phrase "physical law" is merely a metaphor, for physical laws do not compel objects to behave in a certain way but simply ------- the way they do behave.

   (A) suggest
   (B) describe
   (C) finish
   (D) become
   (E) condition

5. Because the orchestra's conductor is an intensely private person, he ------- making the appearances at fund-raising functions that are part of the job.

   (A) loathes
   (B) anticipates
   (C) excuses
   (D) prepares
   (E) convenes

6. It is ironic and even tragic that people who have relatively little are generous to those who have even less while the wealthy can be totally -------.

   (A) fortunate
   (B) elite
   (C) selfish
   (D) stylish
   (E) active

7. As science progresses, observations that at one time seemed to conflict with one another can sometimes be ------- by a more advanced theory.

   (A) established
   (B) inferred
   (C) detected
   (D) reconciled
   (E) delimited

8. The ------- treatment of the zoo animals resulted in community-wide -------.

   (A) curious .. apathy
   (B) popular .. neglect
   (C) critical .. distention
   (D) adequate .. revulsion
   (E) inhumane .. criticism

9. Unfortunately, Professor Greentree has the unusual ability to transform a lively discussion on a central issue into a dreadfully boring ------- on a ------- point.

   (A) discourse .. significant
   (B) textbook .. single
   (C) monologue .. tangential
   (D) treatise .. useful
   (E) critique .. stimulating

10. The music was so ------- that we begged for some -------.

   (A) thunderous .. relief
   (B) provocative .. harmony
   (C) noisome .. silence
   (D) lugubrious .. upbeat
   (E) fractious .. tempo

11. Many hours of practice are required of a successful musician, so it is often not so much ------- as ------- which distinguishes the professional from the amateur.

   (A) talent .. discipline
   (B) money .. education
   (C) genius .. understanding
   (D) fortitude .. mediocrity
   (E) technique .. pomposity

12. The Commissioner of Agriculture was so influenced by dairy industry lobbyists that he became a(n) ------- industry goals rather than a ------- of the milk-consuming public.

   (A) apologist for .. believer
   (B) spokesperson for .. practitioner
   (C) opponent of .. defender
   (D) promoter of .. critic
   (E) advocate of .. protector

13. Sally had ------- taste in clothing and always dressed very fashionably, but she was totally ------- her surroundings, and her apartment and office were drab and disorganized.

   (A) impeccable .. indifferent to
   (B) dreadful .. dependent on
   (C) pedestrian .. fascinated by
   (D) bizarre .. suspicious of
   (E) unimaginative .. enamored of

14. The farm consisted of land that was barely ------- with poor soil made ------- by the almost total lack of spring rains.

   (A) cultivated .. productive
   (B) fertile .. rich
   (C) profitable .. consistent
   (D) teeming .. desirable
   (E) arable .. arid

15. His untimely death, at first thought to be due to a ------- fever, was later ------- to poison.

   (A) degenerative .. relegated
   (B) debilitating .. ascribed
   (C) raging .. reduced
   (D) sanguine .. abdicated
   (E) pernicious .. prescribed

16. There is a ------- of verbiage in your writing; try not to be so -------.

   (A) dearth .. pompous
   (B) preponderance .. verbose
   (C) predilection .. long-winded
   (D) element .. prolix
   (E) fraction .. detrimental

Quiz III

(16 items; 16 minutes)

> **DIRECTIONS:** Each item below has one or two blanks; each blank indicates that something has been omitted. Choose the word or pair of words that best fits the meaning of the sentence as a whole when inserted in the sentence.

1. Philosophical differences ------- the unification of the two parties into one.

   (A) delegated
   (B) legislated
   (C) impeded
   (D) enacted
   (E) entrusted

2. When a job becomes too -------, workers get -------, their attention wanders, and they start to make careless errors.

   (A) diverse .. busy
   (B) hectic .. lazy
   (C) tedious .. bored
   (D) fascinating .. interested
   (E) rewarding .. sloppy

3. It is not always easy to ------- one's mistakes, but it is inevitably more ------- to try to hide them.

   (A) cover .. suspect
   (B) confess .. difficult
   (C) cancel .. attractive
   (D) solve .. satisfying
   (E) anticipate .. circumspect

4. The merchant ------- a small neighborhood business into a citywide chain of stores.

   (A) appraised
   (B) transferred
   (C) parlayed
   (D) redeemed
   (E) instilled

5. Since the city cannot ticket their cars, the diplomats can park anywhere with -------.

   (A) penury
   (B) impunity
   (C) precision
   (D) languor
   (E) ignominy

6. Although he wanted to write a lengthy novel of grand proportions, he found himself writing ------- about his carefree childhood in rural America.

   (A) vignettes
   (B) tragedies
   (C) editorials
   (D) epic poetry
   (E) elegies

7. Because of her unpopular opinions, she was unable to ------- broad support among the voters; however, those who did support her were exceptionally -------.

   (A) alienate .. many
   (B) survey .. divided
   (C) cut across .. quiet
   (D) amass .. loyal
   (E) evoke .. languid

8. His ------- of practical experience and his psychological acuity more than ------- his lack of formal academic training.

   (A) claims .. compromise
   (B) background .. repay
   (C) breadth .. account for
   (D) wealth .. compensate for
   (E) fund .. elucidate

9. A professional journalist will attempt to ------- the facts learned in an interview by independent -------.

(A) endorse . . questioning
(B) query . . study
(C) garnish . . sources
(D) verify . . investigation
(E) embellish . . scrutiny

10. If you ------- the charges instead of ------- them, people may conclude that you are guilty.

(A) delegate . . enumerating
(B) preempt . . disclaiming
(C) efface . . disavowing
(D) reduce . . mitigating
(E) ignore . . rebutting

11. Although the novel was generally boring and awkwardly written, there were ------- passages of power and lyricism that hinted at the author's -------.

(A) occasional . . potential
(B) frequent . . malevolence
(C) static . . style
(D) ill-conceived . . superficiality
(E) contrived . . ignorance

12. Although her acting was -------, she looked so good on stage that the audience applauded anyway.

(A) dynamic
(B) laudable
(C) implacable
(D) execrable
(E) intrepid

13. On the narrow and ------- mountain road, the truck skidded when it rounded a curve.

(A) pejorative
(B) salutary
(C) propitious
(D) sedulous
(E) tortuous

14. The press was shocked when they interviewed the famous author, for despite the ------- of his writing, he revealed himself to be a -------.

(A) incomprehensibility . . philanthropist
(B) simplicity . . dolt
(C) power . . scholar
(D) erudition . . philistine
(E) humor . . miser

15. Judging by the ------- of new talent on Broadway and the large number of revivals, we may assume that the era of the American musical is over.

(A) temerity
(B) versatility
(C) laxity
(D) verbosity
(E) paucity

16. Is he -------, or is he merely -------?

(A) amusing . . witty
(B) tranquil . . mannerly
(C) divisive . . voracious
(D) timid . . unruly
(E) uncivil . . reticent

Quiz IV Brain Buster
(16 items; 16 minutes)

DIRECTIONS: Each item below has one or two blanks; each blank indicates that something has been omitted. Choose the word or pair of words that best fits the meaning of the sentence as a whole when inserted in the sentence.

1. The richness and the variety of the instrumentation of *The Flying Dutchman* ------- Wagner's greatness, but the opera itself is a work of promise, not attainment.

   (A) portend
   (B) inspire
   (C) recapitulate
   (D) underscore
   (E) animate

2. The ------- structure of the novel was justified by the author's choice of subject: spies, double spies, and triple spies, all operating for and against various governments and one another.

   (A) torpid
   (B) alien
   (C) insipid
   (D) byzantine
   (E) humdrum

3. Farm products are sold for the most part in highly competitive markets, so prices rise and fall -------, while retail prices of industrial goods hold more nearly to a constant level.

   (A) incrementally
   (B) gradually
   (C) precipitously
   (D) tentatively
   (E) recursively

4. John's parents could not comprehend why he was doing so poorly in school since his diagnostic test scores indicated a high degree of ------- which his grades did not reflect.

   (A) laziness
   (B) aptitude
   (C) agility
   (D) experience
   (E) volition

5. From childhood, Salinger felt a pronounced sense of uniqueness that would later calcify into a complete indifference to other people, rendering the author totally -------.

   (A) misanthropic
   (B) alienated
   (C) solipsistic
   (D) irresolute
   (E) profligate

6. A good mystery writer knows how to lose the reader in a ------- from which there is no easy exit by anticipating and encouraging seemingly plausible theories only to show, at the appropriate juncture, that these are dead ends; to truly enjoy the book, you have to accept this ------- and admire the architecture of the twists and turns and cul-de-sacs.

   (A) chamber . . disorganization
   (B) labyrinth . . manipulation
   (C) confusion . . inequity
   (D) morass . . clarification
   (E) prison . . deception

7. Economic protectionism is seductive, but countries that succumb to its allure soon find that it makes ------- promises; conversely, countries that commit to economic competition ensure a brighter economic future for their citizens.

(A) false
(B) sincere
(C) intrepid
(D) endearing
(E) secret

8. Maxwell moved easily through the corporate structure of the huge company, actually delighting in the ------- of the various organizational complexities that sometimes included intersecting and even inconsistent lines of authority.

(A) certainties
(B) pastimes
(C) intricacies
(D) straightforwardness
(E) shortage

9. The announcement came as no great surprise to anyone familiar with the case, as the details had already been widely -------.

(A) disseminated
(B) disparaged
(C) infiltrated
(D) controverted
(E) consummated

10. If they were indeed more than just friends, theirs was a relationship made in heaven, a blessing rarely offered to ------- lovers.

(A) amiable
(B) collateral
(C) insensitive
(D) sublunary
(E) secretive

11. Matthew enjoys high risk and unorthodox actions and fancies himself a maverick and a buccaneer, someone who ------- convention.

(A) embraces
(B) glorifies
(C) establishes
(D) flouts
(E) adopts

12. Outstanding private collections that have been donated to museums demonstrate that business acumen and great wealth are not incompatible with artistic discrimination and ------- art.

(A) casualness about
(B) munificence toward
(C) indifference to
(D) acceptance by
(E) production of

13. All composers have admirers, but Mahler inspires a fanatical enthusiasm in his veritable army of -------.

(A) resisters
(B) instrumentalists
(C) collaborators
(D) amateurs
(E) critics

14. Heinrich predicted that the end of the Soviet empire would trigger the ------- of art in Russia, but the total lack of any viable new movement proved him dead wrong.

(A) stagnation
(B) efflorescence
(C) stasis
(D) demise
(E) decline

15. As a once generous definition of literature gave way to hierarchies that excluded juvenile and domestic fiction, the male authors were -------, while the female authors were deemed unworthy of serious study.

    (A) criticized
    (B) canonized
    (C) infantilized
    (D) sanitized
    (E) improvised

16. His paintings are unusual in depicting not momentous events but scenes of ------- life, which, in that day, were still unhackneyed.

    (A) quotidian
    (B) reproachable
    (C) iniquitous
    (D) distilled
    (E) ubiquitous

REVIEW

This section contains additional Critical Reading: Sentence Completions items for further practice. Answers are on page 622.

DIRECTIONS: Each item below has one or two blanks; each blank indicates that something has been omitted. Choose the word or pair of words that best fits the meaning of the sentence as a whole when inserted in the sentence.

---

1. The judge shouted to counsel on both sides that he would ------- no argument on the issue and enjoined them to -------.

   (A) hear . . vote
   (B) accept . . speculation
   (C) brook . . silence
   (D) entertain . . toleration
   (E) contrive . . cease

2. In order to ------- the deadline for submitting the research paper, the student tried to ------- additional time from the professor.

   (A) extend . . wheedle
   (B) accelerate . . obtain
   (C) postpone . . forego
   (D) sustain . . imagine
   (E) conceal . . procure

3. Due to the ------- of the materials needed to manufacture the product and the ever-increasing demand for it, it is highly probable that the final cost to the consumer will -------.

   (A) immensity . . evolve
   (B) paucity . . escalate
   (C) scarcity . . relax
   (D) acuity . . stabilize
   (E) certainty . . fluctuate

4. After the ------- journey, the President sent a request to the Prime Minister asking that they ------- their meeting until he had had an opportunity to refresh himself.

   (A) exhilarating . . commence
   (B) lengthy . . defray
   (C) exhausting . . defer
   (D) dilatory . . reschedule
   (E) leisurely . . accelerate

5. Following the aborted Bay of Pigs invasion, Congressional opinion about the CIA shifted from almost universal ------- of the agency as both essential and highly professional to widespread ------- its value as a national policy tool and the integrity of its members.

   (A) endorsement . . skepticism about
   (B) acceptance . . control over
   (C) knowledge . . doubt about
   (D) condemnation . . destruction of
   (E) praise . . victimization of

6. Jazz is an American art form that is now ------- in Europe through the determined efforts of ------- in France, Scandinavia, and Germany.

   (A) foundering . . governments
   (B) diminishing . . musicians
   (C) appreciated . . opponents
   (D) waning . . novices
   (E) flourishing . . expatriates

7. One of the kidnappers, when left alone with the hostage, attempted to persuade him that they were neither ------- nor -------, but only interested in calling international attention to their cause.

    (A) impeccable . . sincere
    (B) redoubtable . . condescending
    (C) antagonistic . . vindictive
    (D) recalcitrant . . clandestine
    (E) intrepid . . compliant

8. Although the comedian was very clever, many of his remarks were ------- and ------- lawsuits against him for slander.

    (A) derogatory . . resulted in
    (B) pithy . . came upon
    (C) protracted . . forestalled
    (D) depraved . . assuaged
    (E) recanted . . sparked

9. Because the disease is relatively rare and doctors know little about it, any treatment prescribed can ------- the pain but cannot ------- the patient.

    (A) alleviate . . infect
    (B) palliate . . cure
    (C) abate . . affect
    (D) minimize . . revive
    (E) intensify . . rejuvenate

10. The ------- customer was ------- by the manager's prompt action and apology.

    (A) pecuniary . . appalled
    (B) weary . . enervated
    (C) sedulous . . consoled
    (D) intrepid . . mortified
    (E) irate . . mollified

11. You must act with ------- if you want to buy your airline ticket before tomorrow's price increase.

    (A) celerity
    (B) clemency
    (C) facility
    (D) lassitude
    (E) laxity

12. The ------- background music hinted of the dangers threatening the movie's heroine.

    (A) trenchant
    (B) ebullient
    (C) sardonic
    (D) portentous
    (E) precocious

13. The junta's promise of free elections was -------, a mere sop to world opinion.

    (A) spurious
    (B) contentious
    (C) unctuous
    (D) lucid
    (E) presumptuous

14. His ------- manner served to hide the fact that he secretly indulged in the very vices he publicly -------.

    (A) sedulous . . dispelled
    (B) sanctimonious . . condemned
    (C) dogmatic . . espoused
    (D) stentorian . . prescribed
    (E) candid . . promulgated

15. The Eighteenth Amendment, often called the Prohibition Act, ------- the sale of alcoholic beverages.

    (A) prolonged
    (B) preempted
    (C) sanctioned
    (D) proscribed
    (E) encouraged

16. The ------- attitudes politicians have today cause them to ------- at the slightest hint of controversy.

(A) dauntless . . recoil
(B) craven . . cower
(C) pusillanimous . . prevail
(D) undaunted . . quail
(E) fractious . . grovel

17. Mrs. Jenkins, upon hearing that her arm was broken, looked ------- at the doctor.

(A) jovially
(B) plaintively
(C) fortuitously
(D) serendipitously
(E) opportunely

18. Even ------- pleasures may leave ------- memories.

(A) ephemeral . . lasting
(B) emphatic . . stalwart
(C) transitory . . fleeting
(D) surreptitious . . secret
(E) enigmatic . . mysterious

19. Unsure of her skills in English, the young girl was ------- when called on to speak in class.

(A) remunerative
(B) transient
(C) reticent
(D) sartorial
(E) resilient

20. Each spring, the ------- tree put out fewer and fewer leaves.

(A) ambient
(B) malignant
(C) desultory
(D) moribund
(E) reclusive

21. The bully's menacing, ------- manner was actually just for show; in reality, it was entirely -------.

(A) imperturbable . . vapid
(B) truculent . . affected
(C) stringent . . credulous
(D) supercilious . . blatant
(E) parsimonious . . contentious

22. A public official must be ------- in all his or her actions to avoid even the appearance of impropriety.

(A) redolent
(B) unctuous
(C) baleful
(D) circumspect
(E) propitious

23. She was ------- as a child, accepting without question everything she was told.

(A) obstreperous
(B) recalcitrant
(C) credulous
(D) truculent
(E) tearful

24. Warned by smoke alarms that a widespread fire was -------, the ushers ------- the theatre immediately.

(A) expected . . filled
(B) ubiquitous . . purged
(C) eminent . . checked
(D) imminent . . evacuated
(E) insidious . . obviated

25. The municipality attracted the country's scientific elite and ------- them, insulating them entirely from the problems of ordinary civilian life.

(A) cajoled
(B) muted
(C) mused
(D) cosseted
(E) impeded

26. Although the bank executive gave the appearance of a(n) ------- businessman, he was really a -------.

   (A) dedicated . . capitalist
   (B) respectable . . reprobate
   (C) depraved . . profligate
   (D) empathetic . . philanthropist
   (E) churlish . . miscreant

27. During a campaign, politicians often engage in ------- debate, attacking each other's proposals in a torrent of ------- words.

   (A) acerbic . . amiable
   (B) acrimonious . . malicious
   (C) intensive . . nebulous
   (D) garrulous . . inarticulate
   (E) impassioned . . vapid

28. ------- by her family, the woman finally agreed to sell the farm.

   (A) Decimated
   (B) Importuned
   (C) Encumbered
   (D) Interpolated
   (E) Designated

29. The ghost of his royal father ------- the young Hamlet to avenge his murder.

   (A) enervates
   (B) parlays
   (C) marauds
   (D) exhorts
   (E) inculcates

30. A life of hardship and poverty has ------- them to petty physical discomforts.

   (A) ascribed
   (B) inured
   (C) remonstrated
   (D) deferred
   (E) impugned

31. Although he was known as a ------- old miser, his anonymous gifts to charity were always -------.

   (A) grasping . . tasteless
   (B) spendthrift . . gracious
   (C) gregarious . . selfish
   (D) penurious . . generous
   (E) stingy . . mangy

32. The composer was ------- enough to praise the work of a musician he detested.

   (A) magnanimous
   (B) loquacious
   (C) munificent
   (D) parsimonious
   (E) surreptitious

33. Though the law's ------- purpose was to curtail false advertising, its actual result was to ------- free speech.

   (A) potential . . preclude
   (B) mendacious . . eschew
   (C) ostensible . . circumscribe
   (D) illicit . . reconcile
   (E) recalcitrant . . repress

34. The royal astrologers were commanded to determine the most ------- date for the king's coronation.

   (A) propitious
   (B) ostensible
   (C) aberrant
   (D) resplendent
   (E) obsequious

35. The poem by the great satirist was dripping with venom and was ------- with scorn.

   (A) contentious
   (B) discordant
   (C) redolent
   (D) sardonic
   (E) vicarious

36. The new regime immediately ------- laws implementing the promised reforms.

(A) vouchsafed
(B) ensconced
(C) augmented
(D) promulgated
(E) parlayed

37. A long illness can ------- even the strongest constitution.

(A) obviate
(B) inculcate
(C) bolster
(D) enervate
(E) disparage

38. The city ------- to the advancing invaders without firing a single shot.

(A) extolled
(B) regressed
(C) equivocated
(D) dissembled
(E) capitulated

39. If you find peeling potatoes to be -------, perhaps you'd prefer to scrub the floors?

(A) felicitous
(B) remunerative
(C) onerous
(D) vilifying
(E) redundant

40. To strengthen her client's case, the lawyer sought to put the ------- of the witness in doubt.

(A) laxity
(B) posterity
(C) probity
(D) onus
(E) sensitivity

41. His ------- CD collection included everything from Bach to rock.

(A) divisive
(B) effusive
(C) eclectic
(D) intrinsic
(E) laconic

42. Her statements were so ------- that we were left in doubt as to her real intentions.

(A) equitable
(B) equivocal
(C) innocuous
(D) dogmatic
(E) incisive

43. Blue whales grow to ------- size and must eat tons of plankton to ------- their huge appetites.

(A) prodigious . . satiate
(B) effusive . . assuage
(C) colossal . . deplete
(D) fortuitous . . exhort
(E) obstreperous . . vanquish

44. Both coffee and tea have beneficial as well as ------- side-effects; while they stimulate the heart and help overcome fatigue, they also ------- insomnia and other nervous disorders.

(A) injurious . . exacerbate
(B) malignant . . interrupt
(C) salutary . . heighten
(D) negligible . . forestall
(E) specious . . prevent

45. The Parks Department claims that there is a ------- of wildlife in the New York City area, and that species that have not lived in the area for most of the century are once again being sighted.

(A) resurgence
(B) paucity
(C) superstructure
(D) prototype
(E) compendium

46. Although he had inherited a substantial amount of money, his ------- soon led to his filing for bankruptcy.

(A) prodigality
(B) volubility
(C) tenacity
(D) fastidiousness
(E) animosity

47. The sonatas of Beethoven represent the ------- of classicism, but they also contain the seeds of its destruction, romanticism, which ------- the sonata form by allowing emotion rather than tradition to shape the music.

(A) denigration .. perpetuates
(B) pinnacle .. shatters
(C) plethora .. heightens
(D) fruition .. restores
(E) ignorance .. encumbers

48. In the Middle Ages, the Benedictine monasteries were often ------- of civilization and a refuge for science in an otherwise ------- and superstitious world.

(A) arbiters .. scholarly
(B) brethren .. sanctimonious
(C) forerunners .. erudite
(D) conservators .. barbarous
(E) advocates .. rarefied

49. Recent studies demonstrate that personal memory is actually quite -------, subject to contamination and reshaping so that aspects of a person's memory are apt to be ------- or erroneous.

(A) implausible .. inaccurate
(B) volatile .. subjective
(C) malleable .. insensitive
(D) inhibited .. recalcitrant
(E) comprehensive .. reflective

50. It is difficult for a modern audience, accustomed to the ------- of film and television, to appreciate opera with its grand spectacle and ------- gestures.

(A) irreverence .. hapless
(B) sophistication .. monotonous
(C) minutiae .. extravagant
(D) plurality .. subtle
(E) flamboyance .. inane

51. Behaviorism was a protest against the ------- psychological tradition that held that the proper data of psychology were -------, which reflected one's consciousness or state of mind.

(A) redoubtable .. superficial
(B) moralistic .. irrelevant
(C) rudimentary .. material
(D) newfangled .. preposterous
(E) orthodox .. mentalistic

52. Psychologists and science fiction writers argue that people persist in believing in extraterrestrial life, even though the federal government ------- all such beliefs, because people need to feel a personal sense of ------- in a godless universe.

(A) decries .. morbidity
(B) endorses .. despair
(C) creates .. guilt
(D) discourages .. spirituality
(E) debunks .. alienation

53. Pollen grains and spores that are 200 million years old are now being extracted from shale and are ------- the theory that the breakup of the continents occurred in stages; in fact, it seems that the breakups occurred almost -------.

(A) refining .. blatantly
(B) reshaping .. simultaneously
(C) countermanding .. imperceptibly
(D) forging .. vicariously
(E) supporting .. haphazardly

54. The period of the fall of the Roman Empire was a dark period for ------- as well as for the other arts, for men had forgotten how to cook; in fact, it seemed as if they had lost all interest in ------- matters.

(A) gastronomy . . culinary
(B) astrology . . sedentary
(C) histrionics . . scientific
(D) numismatics . . cultural
(E) aesthetics . . clandestine

55. Although the manager of the corporation was wrong, his stubborn refusal to ------- or even to compromise ------- an already tense situation.

(A) arbitrate . . thwarted
(B) capitulate . . exacerbated
(C) censure . . rectified
(D) mandate . . violated
(E) scrutinize . . contained

56. The design of the building was magnificent, but its classical lines seemed almost ------- and out of place in the business district that was ------- ultramodern steel and glass skyscrapers.

(A) garish . . beleaguered by
(B) anachronistic . . replete with
(C) untoward . . bereft of
(D) grotesque . . enhanced by
(E) sanguine . . populated by

57. Animal behaviorists theorize that dogs are more ------- than cats because they are pack animals, whereas cats, which are solitary hunters, are more independent and ------- and therefore less likely to try to please their owners.

(A) precocious . . complex
(B) aggressive . . obsequious
(C) tractable . . obdurate
(D) intelligent . . resilient
(E) formidable . . reliable

STRATEGY SUMMARY

General Strategies

There are five main Sentence Completions strategies: "Anticipate and Test," "Simplify Your Life," Logical Pattern Recognition (Thought Extension, Thought Reversal, and Combined Reasoning), Be a Sentence Completions Detective (Coordinate Conjunctions, Subordinate Conjunctions, Key Words, Punctuation Marks, Explanatory Phrases, and Miscellaneous Elements), and Hard Cases ("Go to Pieces" Strategy and Difficult Answers Strategy).

"Anticipate and Test"

Read the sentence through for understanding, trying to imagine what word or words would effectively complete the sentence. Then, look at the answer choices to find the one that comes closest to your initial prediction. Occasionally, you will find the very word or words that you anticipated, but most of the time the answer choices will include words that are similar to those that came to mind when you initially read the sentence. After picking the answer choice that matches your anticipated guesses, insert the selection into the sentence to test it and read the sentence through to make sure that the answer choice reads smoothly and correctly. Upon reading it, you should be convinced that this is the correct answer choice. If that does not work, test the remaining answer choices. The anticipation part of this strategy does not apply when sentences are open-ended, that is, when they allow for multiple possible completion scenarios. In this event, you should directly substitute the various answer choices into the blank(s) and test for validity.

"Simplify Your Life"

The difficulty of Sentence Completions items is based on the number of details that are included. In general, the more details there are in a sentence, the harder the item is to answer. Eliminate unnecessary details to make the item easier.

Logical Pattern Recognition

For more difficult sentences, it may be useful to analyze the underlying logical structure. While a countless number of sentences are possible, logical structure falls into two basic categories that are often signaled via key words or punctuation. One must still be careful to recognize that complex sentences may not contain pure extensions or reversals of thought but may have a mixture of both elements.

- ***Thought Extension:*** An omitted term may serve to extend another thought in the sentence. In this event, look for terminology that continues or reinforces/strengthens the underlying logic. *Key Terms:* "and," "so," "therefore," "since," "because," "as a result," "if/then," "consequently." Also, look for certain punctuation marks that indicate an extension of thought (commas or semicolons).

- ***Thought Reversal:*** An omitted term may serve to reverse another thought in the sentence. In this event, look for terminology that contrasts with or diminishes/weakens the underlying logic. *Key Terms:* "although," "though," "but," "else," "in spite of," "despite," "however," "unless," "large/small."

- ***Combined Reasoning:*** Complex sentences often contain a mixture of extensions and reversals of thought. To correctly answer these items, it is important to first understand the underlying logical structure of the sentence: Identify the ideas and thoughts that are extended and the ideas and thoughts that are reversed.

Be a Sentence Completions Detective

In constructing Sentence Completions items, the test-writers leave clues for you to use. The following are the most important clues:

- **Coordinate Conjunctions:** Conjunctions are words that join together words, phrases, clauses, or sentences. They indicate to the reader how the joined elements are related to each other. In Sentence Completions items, "and" and "but" are the most commonly used coordinate conjunctions.

- **Subordinate Conjunctions:** A subordinate conjunction joins together two ideas in a sentence and indicates that one idea is subordinate to, or dependent upon, the other idea. Since they have to indicate the way in which the subordinate clause depends upon the main clause, subordinate conjunctions will serve as important verbal clues. Examples of subordinate conjunctions include "although," "unless," "if," and "for."

- **Key Words:** In many cases, the elements of the sentence that provide descriptive detail (adjectives and adverbs) are important clues. A key word does not always have to be an adjective or an adverb; some nouns and verbs are unusually descriptive.

- **Punctuation Marks:** Sometimes, a punctuation mark will serve as an important clue. A semicolon or a colon indicates the continuation of a thought.

- **Explanatory Phrases:** A phrase clue consists of any additional information that the test-writers add to make clear what is supposed to go in the blank.

Finally, a single clue may not be sufficient to dispose of an item. In many cases, there are several clues and therefore several different ways of getting the right answer. Combined Reasoning items, for instance, almost always draw upon multiple clues.

Hard Cases

There are Sentence Completions items on the test that are very difficult due to complex logical structures and difficult vocabulary. While the strategies presented above will still be helpful, these items often require a more sophisticated approach. Here are two strategies for handling these "hard cases." The first strategy is for handling sentences with complex logical structures; the second strategy is for handling sentences with difficult vocabulary.

- **"Go to Pieces" Strategy:** When approaching Sentence Completions items with complex logical structures, try to simplify the task by breaking the sentence into pieces and isolating a small part of the sentence that you understand; this part of the sentence must contain an omitted word. Then, test the answer choices, eliminating as many of them as possible. This strategy is useful for items that have two blanks because if either of the two resulting constructions lacks meaning, then you may discard that answer choice. As previously illustrated, an answer choice may be incorrect because it does not create an idiomatic construction.

- **Difficult Answers Strategy:** Remember that difficult items have difficult answers. The more difficult Sentence Completions items tend to be near the end of a group, but they can be anywhere, depending on your vocabulary skills. In fact, you may know all of the words in a more difficult item but not all of the words in an easier item. If forced to guess, do not choose an easy answer choice. Instead, choose the answer choice with the most difficult vocabulary word(s).

Additional Practice

To identify items for additional practice, see the Item Index at the back of this book, which offers a breakdown of items by tested concept.

Math: Multiple-Choice

Course Concept Outline

I. Test Mechanics (p. 171)

    A. Overview (p. 171)

    B. Anatomy (Items #1–4, pp. 172–173)

    C. Pacing (p. 174)

    D. Time Trial (Items #1–4, pp. 175–176)

    E. Game Plan (p. 177)

        1. Quickly Preview the Test Section, but Skip the Directions (p. 177)
        2. Answer the Question That Is Being Asked (p. 177)
          a) Read the Question Carefully (p. 177)
          b) Pay Attention to Units (p. 177)
          c) Pay Attention to Thought Reversers (p. 178)
        3. Use the Answer Choices (p. 178)
          a) Eliminate Answer Choices That Cannot Be Correct (p. 178)
          b) Use the Answer Choices to Check Your Math (p. 179)
        4. Don't Go Calculator Crazy (p. 179)

    F. Calculator Exercise (Items #1–5, pp. 180–181)

II. Lesson (p. 183)

    A. Preliminaries[1]

        1. What Is Tested
        2. Directions
        3. Item Profiles

---

[1] Some concepts in this Course Concept Outline are not illustrated through examples in your student text but may be covered by your instructor in class. They are included here to provide a complete outline of your course.

B. Item-Types (p. 183)

1. Arithmetic (Item #1, p. 183)
2. Algebra (Items #2–6, pp. 183–184)
3. Coordinate Geometry (Item #7, p. 184)
4. Geometry (Items #8–10, pp. 184–185)
5. Data Analysis (Item #11, p. 185)

C. General Strategies (p. 185)

1. A Note about Figures (Items #12–15, pp. 185–186)
2. Important Facts about the Answer Choices (p. 186)
   a) Answer Choices Are Arranged in Order
   b) Wrong Choices Correspond to Conceptual Errors (Item #16, p. 186)
3. "Signal" Words Require Special Attention (Items #17–20, pp. 186–187)
4. Answer the Question Being Asked (Items #21–29, pp. 187–188)
5. Additional Helpful Hints

D. Arithmetic Review and Strategies (p. 188)

1. Simple Manipulation—Just Do It! (Items #30–31, p. 188)
2. Complicated Manipulations—Look for Shortcuts (p. 189)
   a) Simplifying (Item #32, p. 189)
   b) Factoring (Items #33–34, p. 189)
   c) Approximation (Items #35–36, p. 189)
   d) The "Flying-X" Method (Item #37, p. 189)
   e) Decimal-Fraction Equivalents (Item #38, p. 189)
3. Complicated Arithmetic Application Items—Bridge the Gap (Items #39–41, p. 190)
4. Common Arithmetic Items
   a) Properties of Numbers (Items #42–49, pp. 190–191)
   b) Sets: Union, Intersection, and Elements (Items #50–54, pp. 191–192)
   c) Absolute Value (Items #55–57, p. 192)
   d) Percents (Items #58–64, pp. 192–193)
   e) Ratios (Items #65–66, p. 193)
   f) Proportions and Direct-Inverse Variation (Items #67–73, pp. 193–194)
5. Arithmetic Alternative Strategies (p. 194)
   a) "Test-the-Test" (Items #74–80, pp. 194–195)
   b) "Plug-and-Chug" Strategy (Item #81, p. 195)

E. Algebra Review and Strategies (p. 195)

1. Manipulating Algebraic Expressions (p. 195)
   a) Basic Algebraic Manipulations (Items #82–83, p. 195)
   b) Evaluating Expressions (Items #84–87, p. 196)
   c) Manipulating Expressions Involving Exponents (Items #88–89, p. 196)
   d) Factoring Expressions (Items #90–92, pp. 196–197)
   e) Creating Algebraic Expressions (Items #93–94, p. 197)
2. Evaluating Sequences Involving Exponential Growth (Items #95–98, pp. 197–198)
3. Solving Algebraic Equations or Inequalities with One Variable (p. 198)
   a) Simple Equations (Item #99, p. 198)
   b) Simple Inequalities (Item #100, p. 198)
   c) Equations Involving Rational Expressions (Items #101–103, p. 198)
   d) Inequalities Involving Rational Expressions (Item #104, p. 199)
   e) Equations Involving Radical Expressions (Items #105–108, p. 199)
   f) Equations Involving Integer and Rational Exponents (Items #109–112, pp. 199–200)
   g) Equations Involving Absolute Value (Items #113–114, p. 200)
   h) Inequalities Involving Absolute Value (Items #115–117, p. 200)
4. Expressing and Evaluating Algebraic Functions (p. 200)
   a) Function Notation (Items #118–125, pp. 200–201)

       b) Concepts of Domain and Range (Items #126–129, pp. 201–202)
       c) Functions as Models (Item #130, p. 202)
  5. Solving Algebraic Equations with Two Variables (Item #131, p. 202)
  6. Solving Simultaneous Equations (Items #132–135, pp. 202–203)
  7. Solving Quadratic Equations and Relations (Items #136–140, p. 203)
  8. Algebra Alternative Strategies (p. 203)
       a) "Test-the-Test" (Items #141–143, pp. 203–204)
       b) "Plug-and-Chug" (Items #144–150, pp. 204–205)

F. Coordinate Geometry Review and Strategies (p. 205)

  1. The Coordinate System (Items #151–154, pp. 205–206)
  2. Slope of a Line (Items #155–157, pp. 206–207)
  3. Slope-Intercept Form of a Linear Equation (Items #158–159, p. 207)
  4. Distance Formula (Items #160–162, pp. 207–208)
  5. Graphs of Linear Equations (Items #163, p. 208)
  6. Graphs of First-Degree Inequalities (Item #164, p. 209)
  7. Graphs of Quadratic Equations and Relations (Items #165–166, pp. 209–210)
  8. Qualitative Behavior of Graphs of Functions (Items #167–168, p. 210)
  9. Transformations and Their Effects on Graphs of Functions (Items #169–170, p. 211)
  10. Coordinate Geometry Alternative Strategies (p. 212)
       a) "Test-the-Test" (Items #171–173, p. 212)
       b) "Plug-and-Chug" (Item #174, p. 212)

G. Geometry Review and Strategies (p. 212)

  1. Geometric Notation
  2. Lines and Angles (Items #175–179, pp. 212–213)
  3. Triangles
       a) Pythagorean Theorem (Item #180, p. 213)
       b) 45°-45°-90° Triangles (Items #181–182, p. 214)
       c) 30°-60°-90° Triangles (Item #183, p. 214)
       d) Properties of Triangles (Items #184–185, p. 214)
  4. Rectangles and Squares (Items #186–187, p. 215)
  5. Circles (Item #188, p. 215)
  6. Properties of Tangent Lines (Items #189–192, pp. 215–216)
  7. Complex Figures (Items #193–198, pp. 216–217)
  8. Spatial Reasoning (Item #199, p. 217)
  9. Geometry Alternative Strategies
       a) "Test-the-Test" (Item #200, p. 217)
       b) "Plug-and-Chug" (Item #201, p. 217)
       c) "Guesstimate" (Items #202–203, p. 218)
       d) Measure (Items #204–205, p. 218)
       e) "Meastimate" (Items #206–207, p. 219)
       d) Trigonometry as an Alternative Solution Method (Items #208–210, pp. 219–220)

H. Data Analysis Review and Strategies (p. 220)

  1. Data Interpretation (p. 220)
       a) Bar, Cumulative, and Line Graphs (Items #211–215, pp. 220–222)
       b) Pie Charts (Items #216–217, pp. 222–223)
       c) Tables (Matrices) (Item #218, p. 223)
       d) Scatterplots (Item #219, p. 223)
  2. Probability and Statistics
       a) Averages (Items #220–224, pp. 223–224)
       b) Median (Item #225, p. 224)
       c) Mode (Item #226, p. 224)
       d) Arithmetic Probability (Items #227–229, pp. 224–225)
       e) Geometric Probability (Items #230–231, pp. 225–226)

III. Quizzes (p. 227)

    A. Quiz I (Items #1–16, pp. 227–230)

    B. Quiz II (Items #1–20, pp. 231–234)

    C. Quiz III (Items #1–20, pp. 235–239)

    D. Quiz IV Brain Buster (Items #1–15, pp. 240–242)

IV. Review (Items #1–29, pp. 243–248)

V. Strategy Summary (p. 249)

TEST MECHANICS

Overview

The SAT test includes three Math test sections that will be scored. One section has 20 Multiple-Choice items, with a time limit of 25 minutes; another has 16 Multiple-Choice items, with a time limit of 20 minutes; and the third has 8 Multiple-Choice items and 10 Student-Produced Responses items, with a time limit of 25 minutes.

The Math test sections presuppose knowledge of pre-algebra and algebra, intermediate algebra and coordinate geometry, and plane geometry (including basic solids). These are the conceptual building blocks of the Math test sections. While the building blocks are familiar, many of the math items are not what you would expect to see on a high school math exam. Many of them have a special "SAT flavor." If you want to do well on the Math test sections, you will need to learn to appreciate that special feature and learn to control it.

Anatomy

> **DIRECTIONS:** Solve each item and choose the correct answer choice. Use any available space for scratchwork.

Notes:

(1) The use of a calculator is permitted. All numbers used are real numbers.

(2) Figures that accompany problems in this test are intended to provide information useful in solving the problems. They are drawn as accurately as possible EXCEPT when it is stated in a specific problem that the figure is not drawn to scale. All figures lie in a plane unless otherwise indicated.

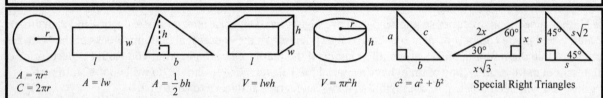

$A = \pi r^2$
$C = 2\pi r$ $A = lw$ $A = \frac{1}{2}bh$ $V = lwh$ $V = \pi r^2 h$ $c^2 = a^2 + b^2$ Special Right Triangles

The number of degrees of arc in a circle is 360.

The sum of the measures in degrees of the angles of a triangle is 180.

You really do not need the directions at all. Problem-solving is your standard-issue Math: Multiple-Choice item. You can use a calculator and figures are not necessarily drawn to scale; these aspects of the test will be addressed in greater detail later during the Math: Multiple-Choice Lesson.

1. $(0.2)(0.005) =$

(A) 0.0001
(B) 0.001
(C) 0.01
(D) 0.1
(E) 1.0

1. **(B)** *This is a simple manipulation item. Manipulation items, as the name implies, test your knowledge of arithmetic or algebraic manipulations. The correct answer is (B). The item tests whether or not you remember how to keep track of the decimal point in multiplication:* $(0.2)(0.005) = 0.001$.

2. If $x + 5 = 8$, then $2x - 1 =$

(A) 25
(B) 12
(C) 5
(D) 4
(E) 0

$x + 5 = 8$
$-8 \quad -8$
$\overline{}$
$x - 3 = 0$

$x = 3$

$2(3) - 1 = 2x - 1$

$2(3) - 1 = 5$

2. **(C)** *This is a manipulation item that tests algebra. The correct answer is (C). Since* $x + 5 = 8$, $x = 3$. *Then, substitute 3 for x in the expression:* $2x - 1 = 2(3) - 1 = 5$.

3. Joe works two part-time jobs. During one week, Joe worked 8 hours at one job, earning $150, and 4.5 hours at the other job, earning $90. What were his average hourly earnings for the week?

(A) $8.00
(B) $9.60
(C) $16.00
(D) $19.20
(E) $32.00

150 + 90 = 240

$$\frac{240}{12.5} = 19.2$$

3. **(D)** *This is a story problem. Story problems go beyond simple manipulations—they require that you use your knowledge of manipulations in practical situations. The correct choice is (D). To find Joe's average hourly earnings, divide the total earnings by the number of hours worked:*

$$\frac{Earnings}{Hours} = \frac{\$150 + \$90}{8 + 4.5} = \frac{\$240}{12.5} = \$19.20$$

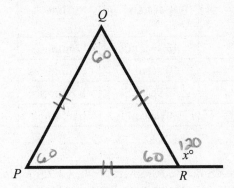

4. In the figure above, $\overline{PQ} = \overline{QR} = \overline{PR}$. What is the value of x?

(A) 120
(B) 308
(C) 458
(D) 608
(E) 908

4. **(A)** *This is obviously a geometry problem. Equally obvious is the fact that geometry problems involve the use of basic principles of geometry. The correct answer is (A). This is an equilateral triangle (one having three equal sides), and equilateral triangles also have three equal angles, each 60 degrees. Then, $\overline{PR}$, as extended, forms a straight line. So, $x + 60 = 180$, and $x = 120$.*

There are three other features of Math: Multiple-Choice items to note:

- *Answer choices are arranged in order.* For most Math: Multiple-Choice items, answer choices are arranged from largest to smallest or vice versa. However, there are some exceptions. Choices that consist entirely of variables do not follow the rule, and items that ask "which of the following is the biggest?" obviously do not follow the rule. That the answer choices are usually arranged in order makes it easier for you to find your choice in the list. It also sets up an important test-taking strategy of starting with the middle choice when applying the "test-the-test" strategy, which you'll learn about later in the Math: Multiple-Choice Lesson.

- *Answer choices are well-defined.* The choices are not created so that you have to do "donkey math." Item #3 above nicely illustrates this point. The correct answer is $19.20, but you are not given choices like $19.19 and $19.21. Instead, the choices usually correspond to errors in thinking—not errors in arithmetic. This feature is important because it is the basis for a couple of time-saving strategies that you'll learn shortly.

- *Items are arranged on a ladder of difficulty.* Of course, you can't tell this from the four examples provided here, but the ladder is an important feature of the math test. Given that the problems become more difficult as you proceed, you're obviously going to have to make some important decisions about speed and skipping items. You'll get more advice on this later in the Math: Multiple-Choice Lesson.

Pacing

The items on the Math test sections are arranged on a ladder of difficulty, so you'll need a pacing plan that helps you move more quickly through the easier items at the beginning of the test and allows you to build up a time reserve for the harder items that are located toward the end. Let's deal first with the two sections that consist entirely of Math: Multiple-Choice items.

MATH TEST SECTION FORMAT A (20 items, 25 minutes)		
Item Number	Time to Spend per Item	Remaining Time
1–4	45 seconds	22 minutes
5–8	60 seconds	18 minutes
9–12	75 seconds	13 minutes
13–17	90 seconds	5.5 minutes
18–20	110 seconds	0 minutes

MATH TEST SECTION FORMAT B (16 items, 20 minutes)		
Item Number	Time to Spend per Item	Remaining Time
1–4	45 seconds	17 minutes
5–8	60 seconds	13 minutes
9–12	75 seconds	8 minutes
13–16	120 seconds	0 minutes

Now, we will look at the Math test section that includes both Multiple-Choice and Student-Produced Responses items. The tricky thing here is that the difficulty level resets when you get to the Student-Produced Responses. So, you'll have to speed up again.

MATH TEST SECTION FORMAT C (18 items, 25 minutes)			
Type of Item	Item Number	Time to Spend per Item	Remaining Time
Multiple-Choice	1–4	60 seconds	21 minutes
	5–8	90 seconds	15 minutes
Student-Produced Responses	9–14	70 seconds	8 minutes
	15–18	120 seconds	0 minutes

Notice that you'll devote more time to Student-Produced Responses than to Multiple-Choice items. There are two reasons for this: first, there are two more Student-Produced Responses items than there are Multiple-Choice items in the section (10 versus 8); second, you have to budget a little extra time for entering your answers on the Student-Produced Responses items. (You will learn more on this in the Math: Student-Produced Responses Lesson.)

Time Trial

(4 Items—5 minutes)

DIRECTIONS: Solve each item and choose the correct answer choice. Use any available space for scratchwork.

Notes:

(1) The use of a calculator is permitted. All numbers used are real numbers.

(2) Figures that accompany problems in this test are intended to provide information useful in solving the problems. They are drawn as accurately as possible EXCEPT when it is stated in a specific problem that the figure is not drawn to scale. All figures lie in a plane unless otherwise indicated.

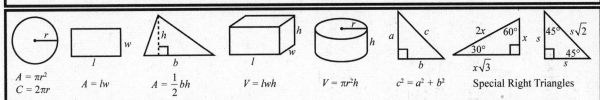

$A = \pi r^2$
$C = 2\pi r$

$A = lw$

$A = \frac{1}{2}bh$

$V = lwh$

$V = \pi r^2 h$

$c^2 = a^2 + b^2$

Special Right Triangles

The number of degrees of arc in a circle is 360.

The sum of the measures in degrees of the angles of a triangle is 180.

---

1. $\dfrac{1}{10^{25}} - \dfrac{1}{10^{26}} =$

(A) $\dfrac{9}{10^{25}}$

(B) $\dfrac{9}{10^{26}}$

(C) $\dfrac{1}{10^{25}}$

(D) $-\dfrac{9}{10^{25}}$

(E) $-\dfrac{1}{10}$

Floor Readings for the Red River				
Time (p.m.)	1:00	2:00	3:00	4:00
Inches above Normal	0.5	1.5	?	13.5

triples

2. The table above shows readings of water levels for the Red River at various times. If readings of the rise of the water level followed a geometric progression, the water level at 3:00 p.m. was how many inches above normal?

(A) 4
(B) 4.5
(C) 4.75
(D) 5
(E) 5.25

$0.5 \times 3 = 1.5$
$1.5 \times 5 = 4.5$
$4.5 \times 3 = 13.5$

3. If s, t, and u are different positive integers and $\dfrac{s}{t}$ and $\dfrac{t}{u}$ are positive integers, which of the following CANNOT be a positive integer?

(A) $\dfrac{s}{u}$

(B) $s \cdot t$

(C) $\dfrac{u}{s}$

(D) $(s+t)u$

(E) $(s-u)t$

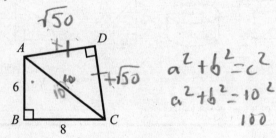

4. In the figure above, $\overline{AD} = \overline{DC}$. What is the value of $\overline{AD} + \overline{DC}$?

(A) $18\sqrt{2}$
(B) 18
(C) $10\sqrt{2}$
(D) 10
(E) $6\sqrt{2}$

Game Plan

Quickly Preview the Test Section, but Skip the Directions

As you get started, take a few seconds to preview the Math test section. It's 99.99% certain that you're going to find everything in place and just as you expected. But a quick overview will guarantee against any unanticipated changes. Do NOT, however, read the directions. Remind yourself of your pacing plan and then get to work.

Answer the Question That Is Being Asked

Read the Question Carefully

Some problems are fairly simple, but others are more complex, particularly practical word problems and more difficult geometry problems. The more complex the question, the easier it is to misread and set off down the wrong track. If the question is very long, then underline the key part of the question.

Example:

If Mark traveled 20 miles in 3 hours and Lester traveled twice as far in half the time, what was Lester's average speed?

(A) $3\frac{1}{3}$ miles per hour

(B) $6\frac{2}{3}$ miles per hour

(C) 12 miles per hour

(D) 26 miles per hour

(E) $26\frac{2}{3}$ miles per hour

The stem states that Lester traveled twice as far as Mark in half the time, or 40 miles in 1.5 hours. Therefore, Lester's average speed was $\dfrac{40 \text{ miles}}{1.5 \text{ hours}} = 26.6\overline{6} = 26\frac{2}{3}$ miles per hour, (E).

Pay Attention to Units

Some items require you to convert units (e.g., feet to inches or hours to minutes). The item stem will tell you what units to use, and if the test-writer senses any possible confusion, the units for the answer choices will be emphasized—underlined or in bold face or capitalized. When you see a word emphasized with any of those signals, circle it and put a star beside it. It is very important.

Example:

A certain copy machine produces 13 copies every 10 seconds. If the machine operates without interruption, how many copies will it produce in an hour?

(A) 780
(B) 4,200
(C) 4,680
(D) 4,800
(E) 5,160

$$\frac{13\ \text{cop}}{10\ \text{s}} \cdot \frac{60\ \text{s}}{1\ \text{min}} \cdot \frac{60\ \text{min}}{1\ \text{hr}} = 4680\ \text{cop/hr}$$

Create an expression that, after cancellation of like units, gives the number of copies produced in an hour:

$$\frac{13\ \text{copies}}{10\ \text{seconds}} \cdot \frac{60\ \text{seconds}}{1\ \text{minute}} \cdot \frac{60\ \text{minutes}}{1\ \text{hour}} = 4{,}680\ \text{copies/hour}.$$ Therefore, the copy machine produces 4,680 copies in an hour, (C).

Pay Attention to Thought-Reversers

A thought-reverser is any word, such as "not," "except," or "but," that turns a question inside out. As shown, below, make sure that you mark the thought-reverser so that it is staring you in the face as you work the problem.

Example:

How many integers in the set of integers from 1 to 144, inclusive, are NOT a square of an integer?

(A)   0
(B)   2
(C)   12
(D) 132
(E) 144

Since 1 is the square of 1, and 144 is the square of 12, there are a total of 12 integers in the set of integers from 1 to 144, inclusive, that are a square of an integer (1^2, 2^2, 3^2, 4^2, 5^2, 6^2, 7^2, 8^2, 9^2, 10^2, 11^2, 12^2). Therefore, there are a total of $144 - 12 = 132$ integers in the set that are NOT a square of an integer, (D).

Use the Answer Choices

In the Math: Multiple-Choice Lesson, you will learn some very powerful test-taking strategies that use the answers. For now, there are two procedural points to consider.

Eliminate Answer Choices That Cannot Be Correct

Sometimes, the array of answers will include choices that, taken at face value, seem to be plausible, but when examined more carefully, must be incorrect.

Example:

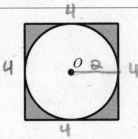

In the figure above, a circle with center O and a radius of 2 is inscribed in a square. What is the area of the shaded portion of the figure?

(A) $2-\pi$
(B) $4-2\pi$
(C) $16-2\pi$
(D) $16-4\pi$
(E) $16-6\pi$

The shaded area is equal to the area of the square minus the area of the circle. Since the radius of the circle is 2, the side of the square is 4 and its area is $4\cdot4=16$. The area of the circle is $\pi(2)^2=4\pi$. Therefore, the shaded area is $16-4\pi$, (D). Notice that without even solving the item, you can eliminate answer choices. Take a closer look at (A), (B), and (E). Since π is approximately 3.14, (A), (B), and (E) are negative. Area, however, cannot be a negative number, so (A), (B), and (E) must be wrong, and you can eliminate them without doing any other work. Now, if you had to, you can make an educated guess from the remaining choices and the odds of guessing correctly are 50 percent.

Use the Answer Choices to Check Your Math

While the SAT test does not test "donkey math," some items do require a calculation or two. One of the fundamental rules of math in school is "check your work." On the SAT test, however, this is a real time-suck. Let's say that you do a calculation (with or without your calculator) and the result is $23.10. If one of the choices is $23.10, pick it, mark your answer sheet, and move on to the next item. Do NOT check your arithmetic. The possibility that you did the arithmetic, made a mistake, and still got a number like 23.10 is just too remote to consider. On the other hand, if you do not find a choice that matches your calculation, then you'd better check both your set-up of the problem and your arithmetic to find the error. In this way, the answer choices function as a feedback loop on the accuracy of your manipulations.

Don't Go Calculator Crazy

Just because you are allowed to use a calculator on the test does not mean that you should try to solve every problem with your calculator. In fact, for most problems, the calculator is the less efficient method of arriving at a solution. Assume, for example, that you have to do the following arithmetic to get your answer: $\left(\dfrac{2}{3}\right)\left(\dfrac{7}{4}\right)\left(\dfrac{1}{6}\right)$.

Since this problem involves single digit multiplication, it's going to be easier to do the arithmetic with a pencil than with a calculator: $\left(\dfrac{2}{3}\right)\left(\dfrac{7}{4}\right)\left(\dfrac{1}{6}\right)=\dfrac{2\cdot7\cdot1}{3\cdot4\cdot6}=\dfrac{14}{72}=\dfrac{7}{36}$. By all means, use the calculator since it will be a definite advantage, but don't automatically assume that every problem requires its use.

Calculator Exercise

This exercise is designed to illustrate when and when not to use your calculator. Make sure that the calculator you bring to the SAT test is one with which you are thoroughly familiar. You may bring any of the following types of calculators: graphing, four-function, or scientific. Although no item requires the use of a calculator, a calculator may be helpful to answer some items. The calculator may be useful for any item that involves complex arithmetic computations, but it cannot take the place of understanding how to set up a mathematical item. The degree to which you can use your calculator will depend on its features. Answers are on page 623.

> **DIRECTIONS:** Label each of the items that follow according to one of the following categories.
>
> Category 1: A calculator would be very useful (saves valuable test time).
> Category 2: A calculator might or might not be useful.
> Category 3: A calculator would be counterproductive (wastes valuable test time).

---

1. What is the average of 8.5, 7.8, and 7.7?

   (A) 8.3
   (B) 8.2
   (C) 8.1
   (D) 8.0
   (E) 7.9

2. If $0 < x < 1$, which of the following is the largest?

   (A) x
   (B) $2x$
   (C) x^2
   (D) x^3
   (E) $x+1$

3. If 4.5 pounds of chocolate cost $10, how many pounds of chocolate can be purchased for $12?

   (A) $4\dfrac{3}{4}$

   (B) $5\dfrac{2}{5}$

   (C) $5\dfrac{1}{2}$

   (D) $5\dfrac{3}{4}$

   (E) 6

4. What is the value of $\dfrac{8}{9} - \dfrac{7}{8}$?

   (A) $\dfrac{1}{72}$

   (B) $\dfrac{15}{72}$

   (C) $\dfrac{1}{7}$

   (D) $\dfrac{1}{8}$

   (E) $\dfrac{15}{7}$

5. Which of the following fractions is the largest?

(A) $\dfrac{111}{221}$ .50

(B) $\dfrac{75}{151}$ .5

(C) $\dfrac{333}{998}$ .33

(D) $\dfrac{113}{225}$ .5

(E) $\dfrac{101}{301}$ .34

LESSON

Answers on pg. 623

The items in this section accompany the in-class review of the skills and concepts tested by the Multiple-Choice part of the SAT Math test sections. You will work through the items with your instructor in class. Answers are on page 623.

DIRECTIONS: Solve each item and choose the correct answer choice. Use any available space for scratchwork.

Notes:

(1) The use of a calculator is permitted. All numbers used are real numbers.

(2) Figures that accompany problems in this test are intended to provide information useful in solving the problems. They are drawn as accurately as possible EXCEPT when it is stated in a specific problem that the figure is not drawn to scale. All figures lie in a plane unless otherwise indicated.

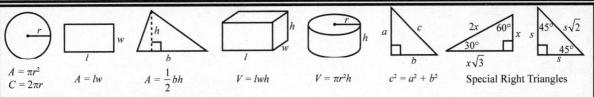

$A = \pi r^2$
$C = 2\pi r$
$A = lw$
$A = \frac{1}{2}bh$
$V = lwh$
$V = \pi r^2 h$
$c^2 = a^2 + b^2$
Special Right Triangles

The number of degrees of arc in a circle is 360.
The sum of the measures in degrees of the angles of a triangle is 180.

Item-Types

Arithmetic

1. If the price of fertilizer has been decreased from 3 pounds for $2 to 5 pounds for $2, how many more pounds of fertilizer can be purchased for $10 than could have been purchased before?

   (A) 2
   (B) 8
   (C) 10
   (D) 12
   (E) 15

Algebra

2. Five students formed a political club to support a candidate for local office. They project that club membership will double every three weeks. Which of the following can be used to find the number of members that the club projects to have after twelve weeks?

   (A) $5\left(2^{\frac{2}{3}}\right)$ 8

   (B) $5\left(2^{\frac{3}{2}}\right)$ 4

   (C) $5\left(2^{\frac{12}{3}}\right)$ 8

   (D) $5\left(2^{\frac{3}{12}}\right)$ 4096

   (E) $5 + 5\left(2^4\right)$
   16

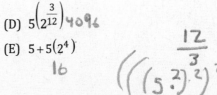

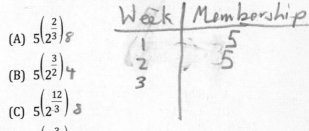

1.53×10^{11}

3. If $\dfrac{2x-5}{3} = -4x$, then $x =$

   (A) −1

   (B) $-\dfrac{5}{14}$

   (C) 0

   (D) $\dfrac{5}{14}$

   (E) 1

4. A hot dog vendor sells h hot dogs every day, each at a cost of d dollars. During a period t days, what is the amount of money in dollars taken in by the hot dog vendor from the sale of hot dogs?

   (A) $\dfrac{100hc}{t}$

   (B) $\dfrac{hct}{100}$

   (C) $\dfrac{th}{c}$

   (D) hct

   (E) $\dfrac{hc}{100t}$

5. If $f(x) = 2x - 3$ and $g(x) = x^2 - 2$, then what does $f(g(3))$ equal?

   (A) 3

   (B) 7

   (C) 11

   (D) 15

   (E) 22

$g(3) = 3^2 - 2$

$g(3) = 7$

$f(7) = 2(7) - 3$

$f(7) = 11$

6. If $|x + 3| = 5$, then $x =$

   (A) −8 or 2

   (B) −2 or 8

   (C) −8

   (D) −2

   (E) 2 or 8

$x + 3 = 5 \qquad x + 3 = -5$

$x = 2 \qquad\quad x = -8$

$\sqrt{}\,2 + 3 = 5 \qquad \sqrt{}\,-8 + 3 = -5$

$5 = 5 \qquad\qquad -5 = -5$

Coordinate Geometry

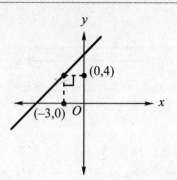

7. In the figure above, the line has a slope of 1. What is the y-intercept of the line?

   (A) −5

   (B) −3

   (C) 0

   (D) 3

   (E) 7

Geometry

8. If a circle has a radius of 1, what is its area?

   (A) $\dfrac{\pi}{2}$

   (B) π

   (C) 2π

   (D) 4π

   (E) π^2

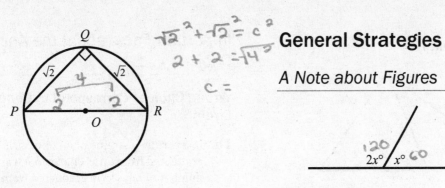

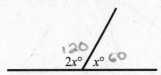

General Strategies

A Note about Figures

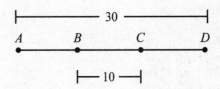

9. In the figure above, $\triangle PQR$ is inscribed in a circle with center O. What is the area of the circle?

(A) $\dfrac{\pi}{2}$

(B) $\dfrac{\pi}{\sqrt{2}}$

(C) π

(D) $\pi\sqrt{2}$

(E) 2π

12. In the figure above, $x =$

(A) 15
(B) 30
(C) 45
(D) 60
(E) 120

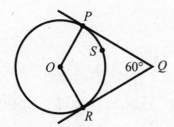

10. In the figure above, $\overline{QP}$ is tangent to circle O at point P, and $\overline{QR}$ is tangent to circle O at point R. What is the degree measure of the minor arc PSR?

(A) 30
(B) 60
(C) 90
(D) 120
(E) 180

13. In the figure above, what is the length of $\overline{AB} + \overline{CD}$?

(A) 5
(B) 10
(C) 15
(D) 20
(E) 40

Data Analysis

11. What is the average of 8.5, 7.8, and 7.7?

(A) 8.3
(B) 8.2
(C) 8.1
(D) 8.0
(E) 7.9

Items #14–15 refer to the following figure:

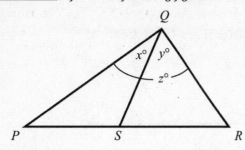

NOTE: Figure not drawn to scale.

14. Which of the following must be true?

 I. $\overline{PS} < \overline{SR}$
 II. $z = 90$
 III. $x > y$

(A) I only
(B) I and II only
(C) I and III only
(D) I, II, and III
(E) Neither I, II, nor III

15. Which of the following must be true?

 I. $\overline{PR} > \overline{PS}$
 II. $z > x$
 III. $x + y = z$

(A) I only
(B) I and II only
(C) I and III only
(D) I, II, and III
(E) Neither I, II, nor III

Important Facts about the Answer Choices

Wrong Choices Correspond to Conceptual Errors

16. In a certain year, the number of girls who graduated from City High School was twice the number of boys who graduated from City High School. If $\frac{3}{4}$ of the girls and $\frac{5}{6}$ of the boys went to college immediately after graduation, what fraction of the graduates that year went to college immediately after graduation?

(A) $\frac{5}{36}$

(B) $\frac{16}{27}$

(C) $\frac{7}{9}$

(D) $\frac{29}{36}$

(E) $\frac{31}{36}$

"Signal" Words Require Special Attention

17. A jar contains black and white marbles. If there are ten marbles in the jar, then which of the following could NOT be the ratio of black to white marbles?

(A) 9:1
(B) 7:3
(C) 1:1
(D) 1:4
(E) 1:10

18. If n is a negative number, which of the following has the <u>smallest</u> value?

(A) $-n$
(B) $n - n$
(C) $n + n$
(D) n^2
(E) n^4

19. If a machine produces 240 thingamabobs per hour, how many <u>minutes</u> are needed for the machine to produce 30 thingamabobs?

(A) 6
(B) 7.5
(C) 8
(D) 12
(E) 12.5

20. Of the 120 people in a room, $\dfrac{3}{5}$ are women. If $\dfrac{2}{3}$ of the people are married, what is the maximum number of women in the room who could be <u>unmarried</u>?

(A) 80
(B) 72
(C) 48
(D) 40
(E) 32

Answer the Question Being Asked

21. Three friends are playing a game in which each person simultaneously displays one of three hand signs: a clenched fist, an open palm, or two extended fingers. How many unique combinations of the signs are possible?

(A) 3
(B) 9
(C) 10
(D) 12
(E) 27

22. If $\dfrac{1}{3}$ of the number of girls in a school equals $\dfrac{1}{5}$ of the total number of students, what is the ratio of girls to boys in the school?

(A) 5:3
(B) 3:2
(C) 2:5
(D) 1:3
(E) 1:5

23. Peter walked from point P to point Q and back again, a total distance of 2 miles. If he averaged 4 miles per hour on the trip from P to Q and 5 miles per hour on the return trip, what was his average walking speed in miles per hour for the entire trip?

(A) $2\dfrac{2}{9}$

(B) 4

(C) $4\dfrac{4}{9}$

(D) $4\dfrac{1}{2}$

(E) 5

24. After a 20 percent decrease in price, the cost of an item is D dollars. What was the price of the item before the decrease?

(A) 0.75D
(B) 0.80D
(C) 1.20D
(D) 1.25D
(E) 1.50D

25. On a certain trip, a motorist drove 10 miles at 30 miles per hour, 10 miles at 40 miles per hour, and 10 miles at 50 miles per hour. What portion of her total driving time was spent driving 50 miles per hour?

(A) $1\dfrac{13}{51}$

(B) $\dfrac{5}{7}$

(C) $\dfrac{5}{12}$

(D) $\dfrac{1}{3}$

(E) $\dfrac{12}{47}$

26. What is the <u>maximum</u> number of non-overlapping sections that can be created when a circle is crossed by three straight lines?

(A) 3
(B) 4
(C) 5
(D) 6
(E) 7

27. At Glenridge High School, 20 percent of the students are seniors. If all of the seniors attended the school play, and 60 percent of all the students attended the play, what percent of the <u>non-seniors</u> attended the play?

(A) 20%   20% = Sen.
(B) 40%   60% = Stu.
(C) 50%
(D) 60%
(E) 100%

Water Usage in Cubic Feet

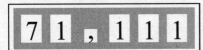

28. The water meter at a factory displays the reading above. What is the <u>minimum</u> number of cubic feet of water that the factory must use before four of the five digits on the meter are again the same?

(A) 10,000
(B) 1,000
(C) 999
(D) 666
(E) 9

29. A telephone call from City *X* to City *Y* costs $1.00 for the first three minutes and $0.25 for each additional minute thereafter. What is the <u>maximum</u> length of time, in minutes, that a caller could talk for $3.00?

(A) 8
(B) 10 $\frac{2}{.25} = 8 + 3 = 11$
(C) 11
(D) 12
(E) 13

Arithmetic Review and Strategies

Simple Manipulation—Just Do It!

30. $\frac{8}{9} - \frac{7}{8} =$

(A) $\frac{1}{72}$

(B) $\frac{1}{8}$

(C) $\frac{1}{7}$

(D) $\frac{15}{72}$

(E) $\frac{15}{7}$

31. $\sqrt{1 - \left(\frac{2}{9} + \frac{1}{36} + \frac{1}{18}\right)} =$

(A) $\frac{1}{5}$

(B) $\sqrt{\frac{2}{3}}$

(C) $\frac{5}{6}$

(D) 1

(E) $\sqrt{3}$

Complicated Manipulations—Look for Shortcuts

Simplifying

32. $\dfrac{1}{2} \cdot \dfrac{2}{3} \cdot \dfrac{3}{4} \cdot \dfrac{4}{5} \cdot \dfrac{5}{6} \cdot \dfrac{6}{7} \cdot \dfrac{7}{8} =$

- (A) $\dfrac{1}{56}$
- (B) $\dfrac{1}{8}$
- (C) $\dfrac{28}{37}$
- (D) $\dfrac{41}{43}$
- (E) $\dfrac{55}{56}$

Factoring

33. $86(37) - 37(85) =$

- (A) 0
- (B) 1
- (C) 37
- (D) 85
- (E) 86

34. Which of the following is a prime factorization of 120?

- (A) (2)(2)(15)
- (B) (2)(3)(4)(5)
- (C) (2)(2)(3)(10)
- (D) (2)(2)(2)(3)(5)
- (E) (2)(2)(3)(3)(5)

Approximation

35. $\dfrac{0.2521 \cdot 8.012}{1.014}$ is approximately equal to which of the following?

- (A) 0.25
- (B) 0.5
- (C) 1.0
- (D) 1.5
- (E) 2.0

36. Which of the following fractions is the largest?

- (A) $\dfrac{111}{221}$ = .50226
- (B) $\dfrac{75}{151}$ = .497
- (C) $\dfrac{333}{998}$ .334
- (D) $\dfrac{113}{225}$ = .50222
- (E) $\dfrac{101}{301}$ = .336

The "Flying-X" Method

37. If $z = \dfrac{x+y}{x}$, $1 - z =$

- (A) $\dfrac{1-x+y}{x}$ $\dfrac{1 - x+y}{x}$
- (B) $\dfrac{x+y-1}{x}$
- (C) $\dfrac{1-x-y}{x}$
- (D) $-\dfrac{y}{x}$
- (E) $1-x-y$

Decimal-Fraction Equivalents

38. $\dfrac{0.111 \cdot 0.666}{0.166 \cdot 0.125}$ is approximately equal to which of the following?

- (A) 6.8
- (B) 4.3
- (C) 3.6
- (D) 1.6
- (E) 0.9

Complicated Arithmetic Application Items—Bridge the Gap

39. If the senior class has 360 students, of whom $\frac{5}{12}$ are women, and the junior class has 350 students, of whom $\frac{4}{7}$ are women, how many more women are there in the junior class than in the senior class?

(A) $(360-350)\left(\frac{4}{7}-\frac{5}{12}\right)$

(B) $\dfrac{(360-350)\left(\frac{4}{7}-\frac{5}{12}\right)}{2}$

(C) $\left(\frac{4}{7}\cdot\frac{5}{12}\right)(360-350)$

(D) $\left(\frac{4}{7}\cdot350\right)-\left(\frac{5}{12}\cdot360\right)$

(E) $\left(\frac{5}{12}\cdot360\right)-\left(\frac{4}{7}\cdot350\right)$

40. If the price of candy increases from 5 pounds for $7 to 3 pounds for $7, how much less candy (in pounds) can be purchased for $3.50 at the new price than at the old price?

(A) $\frac{2}{7}$

(B) 1

(C) $1\frac{17}{35}$

(D) 2

(E) $3\frac{34}{35}$

41. Diana spent $\frac{1}{2}$ of her weekly allowance on a new book and another $3 on lunch. If she still had $\frac{1}{6}$ of her original allowance left, how much is Diana's allowance?

(A) $24
(B) $18
(C) $15
(D) $12
(E) $9

Common Arithmetic Items

Properties of Numbers

42. Which of the following expressions represents the product of two consecutive integers?

(A) $2n+1$

(B) $2n+n$

(C) $2n^2$

(D) n^2+1

(E) n^2+n

43. If n is any integer, which of the following expressions <u>must</u> be even?

    I. $2n$
    II. $2n+n$
    III. $2n \cdot n$

(A) I only
(B) II only
(C) III only
(D) I and II only
(E) I and III only

44. If n is the first number in a series of three consecutive even numbers, which of the following expressions represents the sum of the three numbers?

(A) $n+2$
(B) $n+4$
(C) $n+6$
(D) $3n+6$
(E) $6(3n)$

45. If n is an odd number, which of the following expressions represents the third odd number following n?

(A) $n+3$
(B) $n+4$
(C) $n+6$
(D) $3n+3$
(E) $4n+4$

46. If n is any odd integer, which of the following expressions <u>must</u> also be odd?

    I. $n+n$
    II. $n+n+n$
    III. $n \cdot n \cdot n$

(A) I only
(B) II only
(C) III only
(D) II and III only
(E) I, II, and III

47. If n is a negative number, which of the following expressions <u>must</u> be positive?

    I. $2n$
    II. n^2
    III. n^5

(A) I only
(B) II only
(C) III only
(D) I and II only
(E) II and III only

48. If $0 < x < 1$, which of the following expressions is the largest?

(A) $x = .5$
(B) $2x = 1$
(C) $x^2 \cdot 25$
(D) $x^3 \ .125$
(E) $x+1 \ 1.5$

49. If $-1 < x < 0$, which of the following expressions is the largest?

(A) -1
(B) $x - .5$
(C) $2x - 1$
(D) $x^3 - .25$
(E) $x-1$

Sets: Union, Intersection, and Elements

50. If set $S = \{2, 3, 4\}$ and set P is the set of all products of different elements in set S, then set $P =$

(A) $\{6, 8, 12\}$
(B) $\{6, 8, 18\}$
(C) $\{6, 8, 12, 24\}$
(D) $\{6, 8, 12, 18, 24\}$
(E) $\{6, 8, 12, 18, 24, 36\}$

51. If set X is the set of all integers between 1 and 24, inclusive, that are evenly divisible by 3, and set Y is the set of all integers between 1 and 24, inclusive, that are evenly divisible by 4, what is the set of all elements in both sets X and Y?

(A) $\{12\}$
(B) $\{3, 4\}$
(C) $\{12, 24\}$
(D) $\{4, 12, 24\}$
(E) $\{3, 4, 12, 24\}$

52. If x is an element of set X, in which set X is the set of integers evenly divisible by 3 such that $6 < x < 11$, and y is an element of set Y, where set Y is the set of integers evenly divisible by 4 such that $7 < y < 12$, what is the intersection of sets X and Y?

(A) $\{\}$
(B) $\{8\}$
(C) $\{9\}$
(D) $\{12\}$
(E) $\{8, 12\}$

53. If set S is the set of all positive odd integers and set T is the set of all positive even integers, then the union of sets S and T (the set of all elements that are in either set or both sets) is the set of:

(A) positive integers.
(B) integers.
(C) even integers.
(D) odd integers.
(E) real numbers.

54. In a certain school, each of the 72 music students must participate in the marching band, the orchestra, or both. If only music students participate, 48 students total participate in the marching band, and 54 students total participate in the orchestra, how many students participate in both programs?

(A) 6
(B) 18
(C) 24
(D) 30
(E) 36

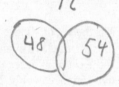

Absolute Value

55. $|-2| + 3 - |-4| =$

(A) −5
(B) −4
(C) −1
(D) 1
(E) 9

56. $|5| - |-5| + |-3| =$

(A) −8
(B) −3
(C) 3
(D) 8
(E) 13

57. $|-3| \cdot |-4| \cdot -5 =$

(A) −60
(B) −30
(C) −7
(D) 20
(E) 60

Percents

58. A jar contains 24 white marbles and 48 black marbles. What percent of the marbles in the jar are black?

(A) 10%
(B) 25%
(C) $33\frac{1}{3}\%$
(D) 60%
(E) $66\frac{2}{3}\%$

59. A group of three friends shared the cost of a tape recorder. If Andy, Barbara, and Donna each paid $12, $30, and $18, respectively, then Donna paid what percent of the cost of the tape recorder?

(A) 10%
(B) 30%
(C) $33\frac{1}{3}\%$
(D) 50%
(E) $66\frac{2}{3}\%$

60. Twenty students attended Professor Rodriguez's class on Monday and 25 students attended on Tuesday. The number of students who attended on Tuesday was what percent of the number of students who attended on Monday?

(A) 5%
(B) 20%
(C) 25%
(D) 80%
(E) 125%

61. If the population of a town was 20,000 in 1997 and 16,000 in 2007, what was the percent decline in the town's population?

(A) 50%
(B) 25%
(C) 20%
(D) 10%
(E) 5%

Items #62–64 refer to the following table:

CAPITOL CITY FIRES	
Year	Number of Fires
2002	100
2003	125
2004	140
2005	150
2006	135

62. The number of fires in 2002 was what percent of the number of fires in 2003?

(A) 25%
(B) $66\frac{2}{3}$%
(C) 80%
(D) 100%
(E) 125%

63. The number of fires in 2006 was what percent of the number of fires in 2005?

(A) 90%
(B) 82%
(C) 50%
(D) 25%
(E) 10%

64. What was the percent decrease in the number of fires from 2005 to 2006?

(A) 10%
(B) 25%
(C) 50%
(D) 82%
(E) 90%

Ratios

65. A groom must divide 12 quarts of oats between two horses. If Dobbin is to receive twice as much as Pegasus, how many quarts of oats should the groom give to Dobbin?

(A) 4
(B) 6
(C) 8
(D) 9
(E) 10

66. If the ratio of John's allowance to Lucy's allowance is $3:2$, and the ratio of Lucy's allowance to Bob's allowance is $3:4$, what is the ratio of John's allowance to Bob's allowance?

(A) 1:6
(B) 2:5
(C) 1:2
(D) 3:4
(E) 9:8

Proportions and Direct-Inverse Variation

67. If 4.5 pounds of chocolate cost $10, how many pounds of chocolate can be purchased for $12?

(A) $4\frac{3}{4}$

(B) $5\frac{2}{5}$

(C) $5\frac{1}{2}$

(D) $5\frac{3}{4}$

(E) 6

68. At Star Lake Middle School, 45 percent of the students bought a yearbook. If 540 students bought yearbooks, how many students did <u>not</u> buy a yearbook?

(A) 243
(B) 540
(C) 575
(D) 660
(E) 957

69. In the equation $y = kx$, k is the constant of variation. If y is equal to 6 when $x = 2.4$, what is the constant of variation?

(A) 0.4
(B) 2.5
(C) 3.4
(D) 3.6
(E) 14.4

70. A train traveling at a constant speed, k, takes 90 minutes to go from point P to point Q, a distance of 45 miles. What is the value of k, in miles per hour?

(A) 20
(B) 30
(C) 45
(D) 60
(E) 75

71. The cost of picture framing depends on the outer perimeter of the frame. If a 15-inch-by-15-inch picture frame costs $35 more than a 10-inch-by-10-inch picture frame, what is the cost of framing, in dollars per inch?

(A) $3.50
(B) $2.75
(C) $2.25
(D) $1.75
(E) $1.50

72. Walking at a constant speed of 4 miles per hour, it took Jill exactly 1 hour to walk home from school. If she walked at a constant speed of 5 miles per hour, how many <u>minutes</u> did the trip take?

(A) 48
(B) 54
(C) 56
(D) 72
(E) 112

73. Ms. Peters drove from her home to the park at an average speed of 30 miles per hour and returned home along the same route at an average speed of 40 miles per hour. If her driving time from home to the park was 20 minutes, how many minutes did it take Ms. Peters to drive from the park to her home?

(A) 7.5
(B) 12
(C) 15
(D) 24
(E) 30

Arithmetic Alternative Strategies

"Test-the-Test"

74. Which of the following is the larger of two numbers, the product of which is 600 and the sum of which is five times the difference between the two?

(A) 10
(B) 15
(C) 20
(D) 30
(E) 50

75. If $\frac{1}{3}$ of a number is 3 more than $\frac{1}{4}$ of the number, then what is the number?

(A) 18
(B) 24
(C) 30
(D) 36
(E) 48

76. If $\frac{3}{5}$ of a number is 4 more than $\frac{1}{2}$ of the number, then what is the number?

(A) 20
(B) 28
(C) 35
(D) 40
(E) 56

77. If both 16 and 9 are divided by n, the remainder is 2. What is n?

(A) 3
(B) 4
(C) 5
(D) 6
(E) 7

78. The sum of the digits of a three-digit number is 16. If the tens digit of the number is 3 times the units digit, and the units digit is $\frac{1}{4}$ of the hundreds digit, then what is the number?

(A) 446
(B) 561
(C) 682
(D) 862
(E) 914

79. If the sum of five consecutive integers is 40, what is the smallest of the five integers?

(A) 4
(B) 5
(C) 6
(D) 7
(E) 8

80. After filling the car's fuel tank, a driver drove from point P to point Q and then to point R. She used $\frac{2}{5}$ of the fuel driving from P to Q. If she used another 7 gallons to drive from Q to R and still had $\frac{1}{4}$ of a tank left, how many gallons does the tank hold?

(A) 12
(B) 18
(C) 20
(D) 21
(E) 35

"Plug-and-Chug"

81. If n is any integer, which of the following is always an odd integer?

(A) $n-1$
(B) $n+1$
(C) $n+2$
(D) $2n+1$
(E) $2n+2$

Algebra Review and Strategies

Manipulating Algebraic Expressions

Basic Algebraic Manipulations

82. If $a^3 + b = 3 + a^3$, then $b = ?$

(A) 3^3
(B) $3\sqrt{3}$
(C) 3
(D) $\sqrt[3]{3}$
(E) $-\sqrt{3}$

83. Which of the following expressions is equivalent to $4a + 3b - (-2a - 3b)$?

(A) $2a$
(B) $12ab$
(C) $2a + 6b$
(D) $6a + 6b$
(E) $8a + 9b$

Evaluating Expressions

84. If $x = 2$, what is the value of $x^2 + 2x - 2$?

(A) -2
(B) 0
(C) 2
(D) 4
(E) 6

85. If $x = 2$, then $\dfrac{1}{x^2} + \dfrac{1}{x} - \dfrac{x}{2} =$

(A) $-\dfrac{3}{4}$

(B) $-\dfrac{1}{4}$

(C) 0

(D) $\dfrac{1}{4}$

(E) $\dfrac{1}{2}$

86. If $\dfrac{1}{3}x = 10$, then $\dfrac{1}{6}x =$

(A) $\dfrac{1}{15}$

(B) $\dfrac{2}{3}$

(C) 2

(D) 5

(E) 30

87. If $p = 1$, $q = 2$, and $r = 3$, what is the value of $\dfrac{(q \cdot r)(r - q)}{(q - p)(p \cdot q)}$?

(A) -3
(B) -1
(C) 0
(D) 3
(E) 6

Manipulating Expressions Involving Exponents

88. $\dfrac{9\left(x^2 y^3\right)^6}{\left(3x^6 y^9\right)^2} =$

(A) 1
(B) 3
(C) $x^2 y^3$
(D) $3x^2 y^3$
(E) $x^{12} y^{12}$

89. $2\left(4^{-\frac{1}{2}}\right) - 2^0 + 2^{\frac{3}{2}} + 2^{-2} = ?$

(A) $-2\sqrt{2} - \dfrac{1}{4}$

(B) $2\sqrt{2} - \dfrac{1}{4}$

(C) $2\sqrt{2}$

(D) $2\sqrt{2} + \dfrac{1}{4}$

(E) $2\sqrt{2} + \dfrac{5}{4}$

Factoring Expressions

90. Which of the following expressions is equivalent to $\dfrac{x^2 - y^2}{x + y}$?

(A) $x^2 - y^2$
(B) $x^2 + y^2$
(C) $x^2 + y$
(D) $x + y^2$
(E) $x - y$

91. Which of the following expressions is equivalent to $\dfrac{x^2 - x - 6}{x + 2}$?

(A) $x^2 - \dfrac{x}{2} - 3$

(B) $x^2 - 2$

(C) $x - 2$

(D) $x - 3$

(E) x

92. Which of the following is the factorization of $6x^2 + 4x - 2$?

(A) $(6x + 1)(x - 3)$

(B) $(6x + 3)(x - 1)$

(C) $(3x - 1)(2x - 2)$

(D) $(2x + 2)(3x - 1)$

(E) $(2x + 4)(3x - 2)$

Creating Algebraic Expressions

93. In a certain game, a player picks an integer between 1 and 10, adds 3 to it, multiplies the sum by 2, and subtracts 5. If x is the number picked by a player, which of the following correctly expresses the final result of the game?

(A) $x + (3)(2) - 5$

(B) $3x + 2 - 5$

(C) $2(x + 3 - 5)$

(D) $2(x + 3) - 5$

(E) $(2)(3)(x) - 5$

94. At 9:00 a.m., when the heat is turned on, the temperature of a room is 55°F. If the room temperature increases by n°F each hour, which of the following can be used to determine the number of hours needed to bring the temperature of the room to 70°F?

(A) $(55 + 70)(n)$

(B) $(55 - 70)(n)$

(C) $\dfrac{(70 - 55)}{n}$

(D) $\dfrac{n}{(70 - 55)}$

(E) $\dfrac{n}{(55 + 70)}$

Evaluating Sequences Involving Exponential Growth

95. In a geometric sequence of positive numbers, the fourth term is 125 and the sixth term is 3,125. What is the second term of the sequence?

(A) 1

(B) 5

(C) 10

(D) 25

(E) 50

96. City University projects that a planned expansion will increase the number of enrolled students every year for the next five years by 50 percent. If 400 students enroll in the first year of the plan, how many students are expected to enroll in the fifth year of the plan?

(A) 200

(B) 600

(C) 675

(D) 1,350

(E) 2,025

97. Jimmy's uncle deposited $1,000 into a college fund account and promised that at the start of each year, he would deposit an amount equal to 10 percent of the account balance. If no other deposits or withdrawals were made and no additional interest accrued, what was the account balance after three additional annual deposits were made by Jimmy's uncle?

(A) $1,030
(B) $1,300
(C) $1,331
(D) $1,500
(E) $1,830

98. A tank with a capacity of 2,400 liters is filled with water. If a valve is opened that drains 25 percent of the contents of the tank every minute, what is the volume of water (in liters) that remains in the tank after 3 minutes?

(A) 1,800
(B) 1,350
(C) 1,012.5
(D) 600
(E) 325.75

Solving Algebraic Equations or Inequalities with One Variable

Simple Equations

99. If $(2+3)(1+x)=25$, then $x=$

5

(A) $\frac{1}{5}$

(B) $\frac{1}{4}$

(C) 1
(D) 4
(E) 5

Simple Inequalities

100. If $2x+3>9$, which of the following can be the value of x?

$2x+3>9$
$\quad -3\ -3$
$\dfrac{2x}{2}>\dfrac{6}{2}$
$x>3$

$2x+3\ <-9$
$\quad -3\ -3$
$\dfrac{2x}{2}=\dfrac{-12}{2}$
$x=-6$

(A) −4
(B) −3
(C) 0
(D) 3
(E) 4

Equations Involving Rational Expressions

101. If $\dfrac{12}{x+1}-1=2$, and $x\neq-1$, then $x=$

(A) 1
(B) 2
(C) 3
(D) 11
(E) 12

102. If $\dfrac{x}{x+2}=\dfrac{3}{4}$, and $x\neq-2$, then $x=$

(A) 6
(B) 4
(C) 3
(D) 2
(E) 1

103. If $\dfrac{x}{x-2}-\dfrac{x+2}{2(x-2)}=8$, and $x\neq2$, which of the following is the complete solution set for x?

(A) {}
(B) {−2}
(C) {2}
(D) {4}
(E) {8}

$\dfrac{x}{x-2}\left(\dfrac{2}{2}\right)-\dfrac{x+2}{2(x-2)}\rightarrow$

$\dfrac{2x}{2(x-2)}-\dfrac{x+2}{2(x-2)}\rightarrow$

$\dfrac{x+2}{2(x-2)}$

Inequalities Involving Rational Expressions

104. If $\dfrac{3}{x-2} > \dfrac{1}{6}$, which of the following defines the possible values for x?

(A) $x < 20$

(B) $x > 0$

(C) $x > 2$

(D) $0 < x < 20$

(E) $2 < x < 20$

Equations Involving Radical Expressions

105. If $\sqrt{2x+1} - 1 = 4$, then $x =$

(A) -5

(B) -1

(C) 1

(D) 12

(E) 24

106. Which of the following is the complete solution set for $\sqrt{3x-2} - 3 = -4$?

(A) $\{\}$

(B) $\{-1\}$

(C) $\{1\}$

(D) $\{-1, 1\}$

(E) $\{1, 2\}$

107. If $\sqrt{2x-5} = 2\sqrt{5-2x}$, then $x =$

(A) 1

(B) 2

(C) $\dfrac{5}{2}$

(D) 10

(E) 15

108. Which of the following is the complete solution set for $\sqrt{x^2+9} = 5$?

(A) $\{-4, 4\}$

(B) $\{-4\}$

(C) $\{0\}$

(D) $\{4\}$

(E) $\{\}$

Equations Involving Integer and Rational Exponents

109. If $4^{x+2} = 64$, then $x =$

(A) 1

(B) 2

(C) 3

(D) 4

(E) 5

110. If $8^x = 2^{x+3}$, then $x =$

(A) 0

(B) 1

(C) $\dfrac{2}{3}$

(D) 3

(E) $\dfrac{3}{2}$

111. If $3^{2x} = \dfrac{1}{81}$, then $x =$

(A) -2

(B) $-\dfrac{3}{2}$

(C) $-\dfrac{2}{3}$

(D) $\dfrac{2}{3}$

(E) $\dfrac{3}{2}$

112. If $5^3 = \left(\sqrt{5}\right)^{-2x}$, then $5^x =$

    (A) $\dfrac{1}{125}$

    (B) $\dfrac{1}{25}$

    (C) $\dfrac{1}{5}$

    (D) 5

    (E) 25

Equations Involving Absolute Value

113. Which of the following is the complete solution set for $\left|\dfrac{2x+1}{3}\right| = 5$?

    (A) $\{-8, -7\}$

    (B) $\{-8, 7\}$

    (C) $\{-7, 8\}$

    (D) $\{7\}$

    (E) $\{8\}$

Handwritten work:
$2x + 1 = 15$
$-1 \quad -1$
$\dfrac{2x}{2} = \dfrac{14}{2}$
$x = 7$

$2x + 1 = -15$
$-1 \quad -1$
$\dfrac{2x}{2} = \dfrac{-16}{2}$
$x = -8$

114. Which of the following is the complete solution set for $|x+6| = 3x$?

    (A) $\left\{-3, \dfrac{3}{2}\right\}$

    (B) $\left\{-\dfrac{3}{2}, 3\right\}$

    (C) $\left\{\dfrac{3}{2}, 3\right\}$

    (D) $\{3\}$

    (E) $\{\}$

Handwritten work:
$x + 6 = 3x$
$-x \qquad -x$
$\dfrac{6}{2} = \dfrac{2x}{2}$
$3 = x$

$x + 6 = -3x$
$-x \qquad -x$
$\dfrac{6}{4} = \dfrac{4x}{4}$
$\dfrac{3}{2} = x$

Inequalities Involving Absolute Value

115. Which of the following is the complete solution set for $|2x - 1| > 3$?

    (A) All real numbers
    (B) The null set
    (C) All real numbers less than -1 or greater than 2
    (D) All real numbers less than -2 or greater than 1
    (E) All real numbers less than -3

116. If $|3x - 6| > 9$, then which of the following must be true?

    (A) $-3 < x < 2$
    (B) $-2 < x < 3$
    (C) $x < -3$ or $x > 2$
    (D) $x < -1$ or $x > 5$
    (E) $x < -1$ or $x > 9$

Handwritten work:
$3x - 6 > 9$
$+6 \quad +6$
$\dfrac{3x}{3} > \dfrac{15}{3}$
$x > 5$

$3x - 6 < -9$
$+6 \quad +6$
$\dfrac{3x}{3} < \dfrac{-3}{3}$
$x < -1$

117. Which of the following identifies exactly those values of x that satisfy $|-2x + 4| < 4$?

    (A) $x > -4$
    (B) $x < 4$
    (C) $x > 0$
    (D) $0 < x < 4$
    (E) $-4 < x < 0$

Handwritten work:
$-2x + 4 < 4$
$-4 \quad -4$
$\dfrac{-2x}{-2} < \dfrac{0}{-2}$
$x < 0$

$-2x + 4 > -4$
$-4 \quad -4$
$\dfrac{-2x}{-2} > \dfrac{-8}{-2}$
$x > 4$

Expressing and Evaluating Algebraic Functions

Function Notation

118. If $f(x) = x^2 + x$, what is the value of $f(-2)$?

    (A) -8
    (B) -2
    (C) 2
    (D) 8
    (E) 12

Handwritten work: $f(-2) = (-2)^2 + (-2)$

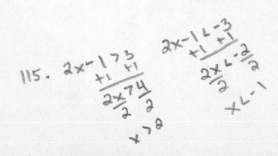

Handwritten work:
$115. \quad 2x - 1 > 3$
$+1 \quad +1$
$\dfrac{2x}{2} > \dfrac{4}{2}$
$x > 2$

$2x - 1 < -3$
$+1 \quad +1$
$\dfrac{2x}{2} < \dfrac{-2}{2}$
$x < -1$

119. If $y = f(x) = \left(\dfrac{6x^2 - 2^{-x}}{|x|} \right)^{-\frac{1}{2}}$ for all integers and

$x = -1$, what is the value of y?

(A) 2

(B) $\dfrac{1}{2}$

(C) $\dfrac{1}{4}$

(D) $-\dfrac{1}{2}$

(E) -2

120. If $f(x) = x + 3$ and $g(x) = 2x - 5$, what is the value of $f(g(2))$?

(A) -2
(B) 0
(C) 2
(D) 4
(E) 10

$g(2) = 2(2) - 5$
$g(2) = -1$
$f(-1) = -1 + 3$
$f(-1) = 2$

121. If $f(x) = 3x + 2$ and $g(x) = x^2 + x$, what is the value of $g(f(-2))$?

(A) 15
(B) 12
(C)   6
(D)   3
(E) -2

$f(-2) = 3(-2) + 2$
$f(-2) = -4$
$g(-4) = (-4)^2 + (-4)$
$g(-4) = 12$

122. If $f(x) = 2x^2 + x$ and $g(x) = f(f(x))$, what is the value of $g(1)$?

(A)   3
(B) 18
(C) 21
(D) 39
(E) 55

$g(1) = f(f(1))$
$f(1) = 2(1)^2 + 1$
$f(1) = 3$
$f(3) = 2(3)^2 + 3$
$f(3) = 21$

123. If $f(x) = 3x + 4$ and $g(x) = 2x - 1$, for what value of x does $f(x) = g(x)$?

(A) -5
(B) -2
(C) 0
(D) 3
(E) 7

124. If $\boxed{x} = x^2 - x$ for all integers, then $\boxed{-2} =$

(A) -6
(B) -2
(C) 0
(D) 4
(E) 6

125. If $\boxed{x} = x^2 - x$ for all integers, then $\boxed{\boxed{3}} =$

(A) 27
(B) 30
(C) 58
(D) 72
(E) 121

Concepts of Domain and Range

126. If $f(x) = 3x - 2$ and $-5 < x < 5$, which of the following defines the range of $f(x)$?

(A) $-17 < f(x) < 13$
(B) $-13 < f(x) < 17$
(C) $-5 < f(x) < 12$
(D) $0 < f(x) < 17$
(E) $3 < f(x) < 13$

127. If $f(x) = \dfrac{x+2}{x-1}$, for which of the following values of x is $f(x)$ undefined?

(A) -2
(B) -1
(C) $\dfrac{1}{2}$
(D) 1
(E) 2

128. If $f(x) = \dfrac{2 - 2x}{x}$, which of the following defines the range of $f(x)$?

(A) All real numbers
(B) All real numbers except -2
(C) All real numbers except 0
(D) All real numbers except 2
(E) All real numbers greater than 2

129. If $|4x - 8| < 12$, which of the following defines the possible values of x?

(A) $-8 < x < -4$
(B) $-4 < x < 8$
(C) $-1 < x < 5$
(D) $1 < x < 5$
(E) $4 < x < 8$

Functions as Models

130. The cost of making a call using a phone-card is $0.15 for dialing and $0.04 per minute of connection time. Which of the following equations could be used to find the cost, y, of a call x minutes long?

(A) $y = x(0.04 + 0.15)$
(B) $y = 0.04x + 0.15$
(C) $y = 0.04 + 0.15x$
(D) $y = 0.15 - 0.04x$
(E) $y = 0.04 - 0.15x$

Solving Algebraic Equations with Two Variables

131. If $x + y = 3$, then $2x + 2y =$

(A) $-\dfrac{2}{3}$

(B) $\dfrac{1}{2}$

(C) $\dfrac{2}{3}$

(D) 6

(E) 8

Solving Simultaneous Equations

132. If $7x = 2$ and $3y - 7x = 10$, then $y =$

(A) 2
(B) 3
(C) 4
(D) 5
(E) 6

133. If $2x + y = 8$ and $x - y = 1$, what is the value of $x + y$?

(A) -1
(B) 1
(C) 2
(D) 3
(E) 5

134. If $4x + 5y = 12$ and $3x + 4y = 5$, what is the value of $7(x + y)$?

(A) 7
(B) 14
(C) 49
(D) 77
(E) 91

x	-2	-1	0	1	2
y	$\dfrac{10}{3}$	$\dfrac{8}{3}$	2	$\dfrac{4}{3}$	$\dfrac{2}{3}$

135. Which of the equations that follow correctly describes the relationship between the values shown for x and y in the table above?

    (A) $3x + 2y = 6$
    (B) $3x - 2y = 3$
    (C) $3x + 3y = -6$
    (D) $6x + 4y = 7$
    (E) $2x + 3y = 6$

Solving Quadratic Equations and Relations

136. Which of the following is the solution set for $2x^2 - 2x = 12$?

    (A) $\{-3, -2\}$
    (B) $\{-2, 3\}$
    (C) $\left\{\dfrac{2}{3}, 3\right\}$
    (D) $\left\{\dfrac{3}{2}, 2\right\}$
    (E) $\{2, 3\}$

137. If $x^2 - 3x = 4$, then which of the following shows all possible values of x?

    (A) $\{4, 1\}$
    (B) $\{4, -1\}$
    (C) $\{-4, 1\}$
    (D) $\{-4, -1\}$
    (E) $\{-4, 1, 4\}$

138. If $x^2 - y^2 = 0$ and $x + y = 1$, then $x - y = ?$

    (A) -1
    (B) 0
    (C) 1
    (D) 2
    (E) 4

139. Which of the following is the solution set for $3x^2 + 3x = 6$?

    (A) $\{1, -2\}$
    (B) $\{1, 2\}$
    (C) $\left\{\dfrac{1}{2}, 1\right\}$
    (D) $\left\{\dfrac{1}{2}, \dfrac{1}{3}\right\}$
    (E) $\{-1, -2\}$

140. Which of the following is the solution set for $2x^2 - 3x = 2$?

    (A) $\left\{\dfrac{1}{2}, 2\right\}$
    (B) $\left\{-\dfrac{1}{2}, 2\right\}$
    (C) $\left\{-\dfrac{1}{2}, -2\right\}$
    (D) $\{2, -2\}$
    (E) $\{2, 4\}$

Algebra Alternative Strategies

"Test-the-Test"

141. In a certain game, a player had five successful turns in a row, and after each one, the number of points added to his total score was double what was added the preceding turn. If the player scored a total of 465 points, how many points did he score on the first play?

    (A) 15
    (B) 31
    (C) 93
    (D) 155
    (E) 270

142. Harold is twice as old as Jack, who is three years older than Dan. If Harold's age is five times Dan's age, how old (in years) is Jack?

(A) 2
(B) 4
(C) 5
(D) 8
(E) 10

143. On a playground, there are x seesaws. If 50 children are all riding on seesaws, two to a seesaw, and five seesaws are <u>not</u> in use, what is the value of x?

(A) 15
(B) 20
(C) 25
(D) 30
(E) 35

"Plug-and-Chug"

144. At a certain firm, d gallons of fuel are needed per day for each truck. At this rate, g gallons of fuel will supply t trucks for how many days?

(A) $\dfrac{dt}{g}$

(B) $\dfrac{gt}{d}$

(C) dgt

(D) $\dfrac{t}{dg}$

(E) $\dfrac{g}{dt}$

145. Y years ago, Paul was twice as old as Bob. If Bob is now 18 years old, how old is Paul today in terms of Y?

(A) $36+Y$
(B) $18+Y$
(C) $18-Y$
(D) $36-Y$
(E) $36-2Y$

146. If pencils cost x cents each, how many pencils can be purchased for y dollars?

(A) $\dfrac{100}{xy}$

(B) $\dfrac{xy}{100}$

(C) $\dfrac{100y}{x}$

(D) $\dfrac{y}{100x}$

(E) $100xy$

147. A tank with capacity t gallons is empty. If water flows into the tank from Pipe X at the rate of x gallons per minute, and water is pumped out by Pipe Y at the rate of y gallons per minute, and x is greater than y, in how many <u>minutes</u> will the tank be filled?

(A) $\dfrac{t}{y-x}$

(B) $\dfrac{t}{x-y}$

(C) $\dfrac{t-x}{y}$

(D) $\dfrac{x-y}{60t}$

(E) $\dfrac{60t}{xy}$

148. If a train travels m miles in h hours and 45 minutes, what is its average speed in miles per hour?

(A) $\dfrac{m}{h+\dfrac{3}{4}}$

(B) $\dfrac{m}{1\dfrac{3}{4}h}$

(C) $m\left(h+\dfrac{3}{4}\right)$

(D) $\dfrac{m+45}{h}$

(E) $\dfrac{h}{m+45}$

149. A merchant increased the original price of an item by 10 percent. If she then reduces the new price by 10 percent, the final price, in terms of the original price, is equal to which of the following?

(A) a decrease of 11 percent
(B) a decrease of 1 percent
(C) no net change
(D) an increase of 1 percent
(E) an increase of 11 percent

150. Machine X produces w widgets in five minutes. Machine X and Machine Y, working at the same time, produce w widgets in two minutes. How long will it take Machine Y working alone to produce w widgets?

(A) 2 minutes, 30 seconds
(B) 2 minutes, 40 seconds
(C) 3 minutes, 20 seconds
(D) 3 minutes, 30 seconds
(E) 3 minutes, 40 seconds

Coordinate Geometry Review and Strategies

The Coordinate System

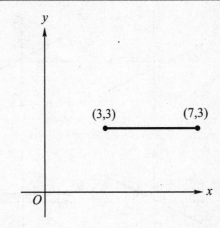

151. In the figure above, the line segment joining points (3,3) and (7,3) forms one side of a square. Which of the following CANNOT be the coordinates of another vertex of the square?

(A) (3,−1)
(B) (3,7)
(C) (7,−3)
(D) (7,−1)
(E) (7,7)

152. Which of the following is a graph of the line that passes through the points $(-5,3)$, $(-1,1)$, and $(3,-1)$?

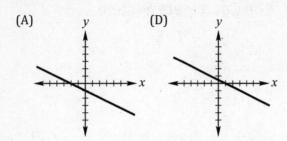

(A)

(D)

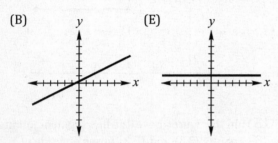

(B)

(E)

(C)

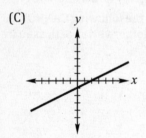

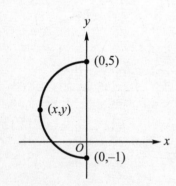

153. In the figure above, what are the coordinates, (x,y), of the point on the semicircle that is farthest from the y-axis?

(A) $(-4,-4)$

(B) $(-3,-3)$

(C) $(-2,-3)$

(D) $(-3,2)$

(E) $(3,2)$

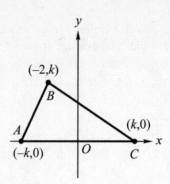

154. In the figure above, the area of $\triangle ABC$ is 8. What is the value of k?

(A) 2

(B) $2\sqrt{2}$

(C) 4

(D) $4\sqrt{2}$

(E) 8

Slope of a Line

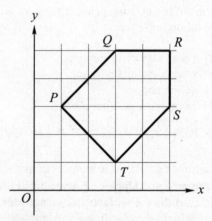

155. In the figure above, which two sides of polygon $PQRST$ have the same slope?

(A) $\overline{PQ}$ and $\overline{QR}$

(B) $\overline{PQ}$ and $\overline{RS}$

(C) $\overline{PQ}$ and $\overline{ST}$

(D) $\overline{QR}$ and $\overline{RS}$

(E) $\overline{RS}$ and $\overline{ST}$

156. Line *l* is the graph of the equation $y = \dfrac{3x}{2} + 2$.

The graph of which of the following equations is perpendicular to line *l* at (0,2)?

(A) $y = \dfrac{3x}{2} - 2$

(B) $y = \dfrac{2x}{3} - 2$

(C) $y = -\dfrac{2x}{3} + 2$

(D) $y = -\dfrac{3x}{2} + 3$

(E) $y = -3x + 4$

157. If set $A = \{(-2,3), (-1,1), (-4,-5)\}$, and set $B = \{(3,4), (4,3), (2,-1)\}$, how many lines can be drawn with a positive slope that include exactly one point from set *A* and one point from set *B*?

(A) 2
(B) 3
(C) 4
(D) 5
(E) 6

Slope-Intercept Form of a Linear Equation

158. If the graph of a line in the coordinate plane includes the points (2,4) and (8,7), what is the *y*-intercept of the line?

(A)   6
(B)   4
(C)   3
(D) −1
(E) −3

159. If the slope and *y*-intercept of a line are −2 and 3, respectively, then the line passes through which of the following points?

(A) (−5,−10)
(B) (−5,10)
(C) (−2,3)
(D) (3,4)
(E) (4,−5)

Distance Formula

160. What is the distance between the points (−3,−2) and (3,3)?

(A) $\sqrt{3}$
(B) $2\sqrt{3}$
(C) 5
(D) $\sqrt{29}$
(E) $\sqrt{61}$

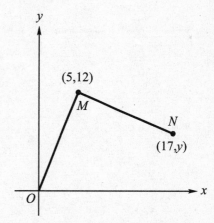

161. In the coordinate plane above, $\overline{MO} \cong \overline{MN}$ and $\overline{MO} \perp \overline{MN}$. What is the value of *y*?

(A)   5
(B)   7
(C) 12
(D) 13
(E) 17

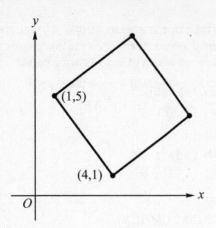

162. In the figure above, what is the area of the square region?

(A) 4
(B) 8
(C) $8\sqrt{2}$
(D) 16
(E) 25

Graphs of Linear Equations

163. A school rented a hotel ballroom for a dance. The cost of the rental is $1500 plus $5.00 per person who attends. Each person who attends will pay an admission charge of $12.50. If x represents the number of people who attend, which of the graphs can be used to determine how many people must attend for the admission charges to cover exactly the cost of renting the ballroom?

(A)

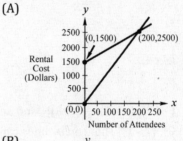

(B)

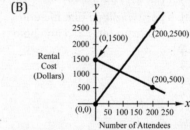

(C)

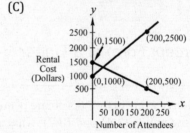

(D)

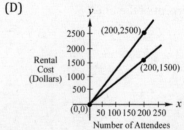

(E)

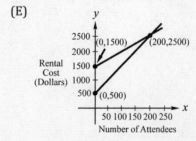

Graphs of First-Degree Inequalities

164. Which of the following is the graph of the inequality $y \geq 2x$?

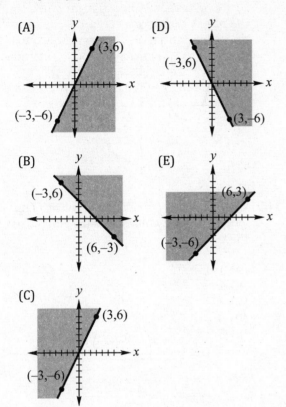

Graphs of Quadratic Equations and Relations

165. Which of the following is the graph of the equation $(x-1)^2 + y^2 = 4$?

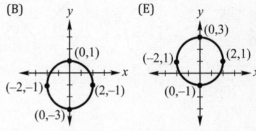

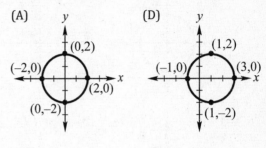

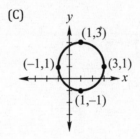

166. Which of the following is the graph of the

equation $\dfrac{x^2}{9} + \dfrac{y^2}{16} = 1$?

Qualitative Behavior of Graphs of Functions

(A)

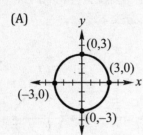

(D)

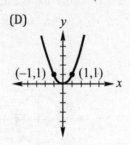

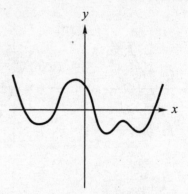

(B)

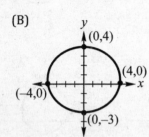

(E)

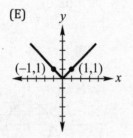

167. The figure above shows the graph of a function $g(x)$. How many times does the graph cross the x-axis?

(A) 1
(B) 2
(C) 3
(D) 4
(E) 5

(C)

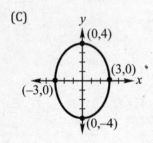

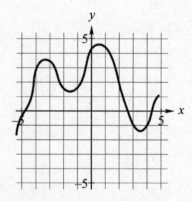

168. The figure above shows the graph of $f(x)$ in the coordinate plane. For the portion of the graph shown, for how many values of x is $f(x) = 3$?

(A) 0
(B) 1
(C) 2
(D) 3
(E) 4

Transformations and Their Effects on Graphs of Functions

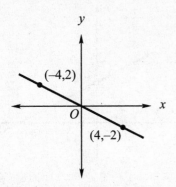

169. The figure above represents the graph of $y = f(x)$ in the coordinate plane. Which of the graphs that follow is the graph of $y' = f(x-1)$?

(A)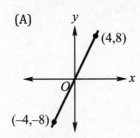

(D)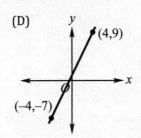

(B)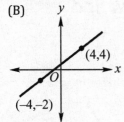

(E)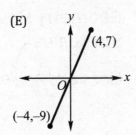

(C)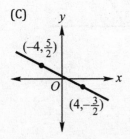

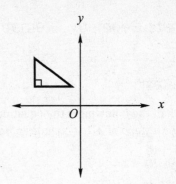

170. If the triangle in the figure above is reflected across the y-axis and then reflected across the x-axis, which of the graphs that follow shows the resulting position of the triangle?

(A)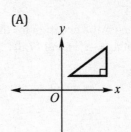

(D)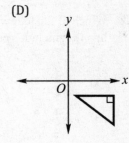

(B)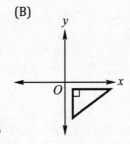

(E)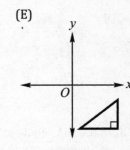

(C)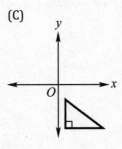

Coordinate Geometry Alternative Strategies

"Test-the-Test"

171. Which of the following is the equation for the line with slope of 2 that includes point (0,2)?

(A) $y = x - 1$
(B) $y = 2x - 1$
(C) $y = 2x - 2$
(D) $y = 2x + 2$
(E) $y = x + 1$

172. Which of the following is the equation for the line that includes points (−1,1) and (7,5)?

(A) $y = \dfrac{x}{2} + 2$

(B) $y = \dfrac{x}{2} + \dfrac{3}{2}$

(C) $y = \dfrac{x}{2} + \dfrac{2}{3}$

(D) $y \doteq 2x + \dfrac{3}{2}$

(E) $y = 2x + 2$

173. In the coordinate plane, what is the midpoint of the line segment with endpoints (−3,−5) and (5,7)?

(A) (1,1)
(B) (1,6)
(C) $\left(3, \dfrac{7}{2}\right)$
(D) (4,6)
(E) (8,12)

"Plug-and-Chug"

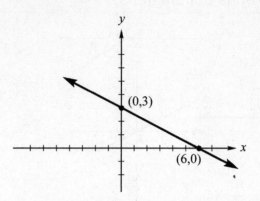

174. The figure above is the graph of which of the following equations?

(A) $x + 2y = 6$
(B) $2x + y = 6$
(C) $x + \dfrac{y}{2} = 6$
(D) $\dfrac{x}{2} + y = 2$
(E) $x - 3y = 2$

Geometry Review and Strategies

Lines and Angles

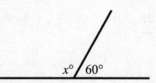

175. In the figure above, $x =$

(A) 45
(B) 60
(C) 75
(D) 90
(E) 120

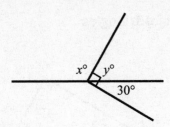

176. In the figure above, $x =$

(A)   45
(B)   60
(C)   90
(D) 105
(E) 120

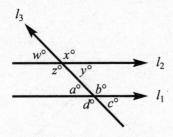

177. In the figure above, l_1 is parallel to l_2. Which of the following <u>must</u> be true?

    I. $w = a$
    II. $y + b = 180$
    III. $x + d = 180$

(A) I only
(B) II only
(C) I and II only
(D) II and III only
(E) I, II, and III

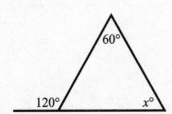

178. In the figure above, $x =$

(A) 30
(B) 45
(C) 60
(D) 75
(E) 90

179. In the figure above, what is the sum of the indicated angles?

(A)   540
(B)   720
(C)   900
(D) 1,080
(E) 1,260

Triangles

Pythagorean Theorem

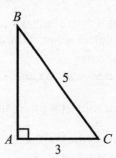

180. In the figure above, what is the length of $\overline{AB}$?

(A) 2
(B) $2\sqrt{3}$
(C) 4
(D) $4\sqrt{2}$
(E) 8

45°-45°-90° Triangles

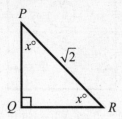

181. In the figure above, what is the length of $\overline{PQ}$?

(A) 1
(B) $\sqrt{2}$
(C) $2\sqrt{2}$
(D) 4
(E) 5

182. In a right isosceles triangle, the hypotenuse is equal to which of the following?

(A) Half the length of either of the other sides
(B) The length of either of the other sides multiplied by $\sqrt{2}$
(C) Twice the length of either of the other sides
(D) The sum of the lengths of the other two sides
(E) The sum of the lengths of the other two sides multiplied by $\sqrt{2}$

30°-60°-90° Triangles

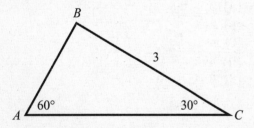

183. In the triangle above, what is the length of $\overline{AC}$?

(A) 2
(B) $\sqrt{3}$
(C) $2\sqrt{3}$
(D) $3\sqrt{3}$
(E) 6

Properties of Triangles

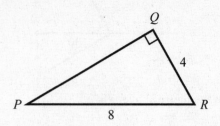

184. In the figure above, the perimeter of $\triangle PQR =$

(A) $12+\sqrt{3}$
(B) $12+2\sqrt{3}$
(C) $12+4\sqrt{3}$
(D) 28
(E) 56

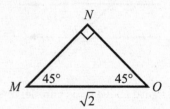

185. In the figure above, what is the area of $\triangle MNO$?

(A) $\dfrac{1}{2}$
(B) $\dfrac{\sqrt{2}}{2}$
(C) 1
(D) $\sqrt{2}$
(E) 2

Rectangles and Squares

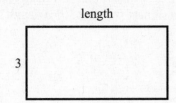

length

3

186. If the area of the rectangle above is 18, what is the perimeter?

(A) 9
(B) 12
(C) 18
(D) 24
(E) 30

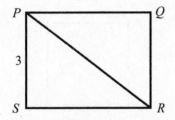

P   Q

3

S   R

187. In the figure above, *PQRS* is a rectangle. If $\overline{PR} =$ 5 centimeters, what is the area, in square centimeters, of the rectangle?

(A) 2
(B) 3
(C) 4
(D) 8
(E) 12

Circles

188. If the area of a circle is equal to 9π, which of the following is (are) true?

　I.　The radius is 3.
　II.　The diameter is 6.
　III.　The circumference is 6π.

(A) I only
(B) II only
(C) III only
(D) I and II only
(E) I, II, and III

Properties of Tangent Lines

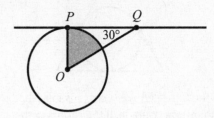

P   Q
30°
O

189. In the figure above, *O* is the center of the circle, and $\overline{PQ}$ is tangent to the circle at *P*. If the radius of circle *O* has a length of 6, what is the area of the shaded portion of the figure?

(A) 　π
(B) 　3π
(C) 　6π
(D) 　9π
(E) 12π

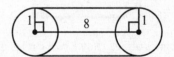

1   8   1

NOTE: Figure not drawn to scale.

190. The figure above shows two pulleys connected by a belt. If the centers of the pulleys are 8 feet apart and the pulleys each have a radius of 1 foot, what is the length, in feet, of the belt?

(A) 4π
(B) 8π
(C) $8+\pi$
(D) $16+\pi$
(E) $16+2\pi$

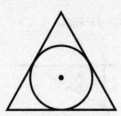

191. In the figure above, a circle is inscribed in an equilateral triangle. If the radius of the circle is 1, what is the perimeter of the triangle?

(A) $\sqrt{3}$
(B) $2\sqrt{3}$
(C) $3\sqrt{3}$
(D) 6
(E) $6\sqrt{3}$

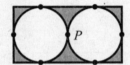

192. The figure above shows two circles of diameter 2 that are tangent to each other at point P. The line segments form a rectangle and are tangent to the circles at the points shown. What is the area of the shaded portion of the figure?

(A) $8-2\pi$
(B) $8-\pi$
(C) $4-2\pi$
(D) $4-\pi$
(E) 2π

Complex Figures

193. If a circle of radius 1 foot is inscribed in a square, what is the area, in square feet, of the square?

(A) $\dfrac{\sqrt{2}}{2}$
(B) 1
(C) $\sqrt{2}$
(D) 2
(E) 4

194. An isosceles right triangle is inscribed in a semicircle with a radius of 1 inch. What is the area, in square inches, of the triangle?

(A) $\dfrac{\sqrt{2}}{3}$
(B) $\dfrac{1}{2}$
(C) 1
(D) $\sqrt{2}$
(E) $2\sqrt{2}$

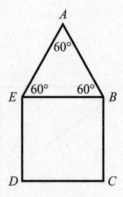

195. In the figure above, $BCDE$ is a square with an area of 4. What is the perimeter of $\triangle ABE$?

(A) 3
(B) 4
(C) 6
(D) 8
(E) 12

196. In the figure above, if $QRST$ is a square and the length of $\overline{PQ}$ is $\sqrt{2}$, what is the length of $\overline{RU}$?

(A) $\sqrt{2}$
(B) $2\sqrt{2}$
(C) $\sqrt{6}$
(D) 4
(E) $4\sqrt{3}$

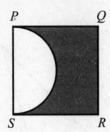

197. In the figure above, *PQRS* is a square, and $\overline{PS}$ is the diameter of a semicircle. If the length of $\overline{PQ}$ is 2, what is the area of the shaded portion of the diagram?

(A) $4-2\pi$

(B) $4-\pi$

(C) $4-\dfrac{\pi}{2}$

(D) $8-\pi$

(E) $8-\dfrac{\pi}{2}$

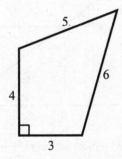

198. If the lengths of the sides, in inches, are as marked on the figure above, what is the area, in square inches, of the quadrilateral?

(A) 6

(B) $6+\sqrt{3}$

(C) 12

(D) 18

(E) 24

Spatial Reasoning

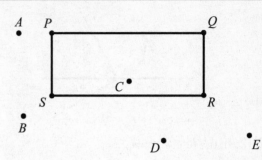

199. In the figure above, *PQRS* is a rectangle such that $\overline{PQ}=3\overline{QR}$. If the figure is folded along diagonal $\overline{PR}$, then point Q would coincide with which of the following points?

(A) *A*

(B) *B*

(C) *C*

(D) *D*

(E) *E*

Geometry Alternative Strategies

"Test-the-Test"

200. What is the width of a rectangle with an area of $48x^2$ and a length of $24x$?

(A) 2

(B) $2x$

(C) $24x$

(D) $2x^2$

(E) $2x^3$

"Plug-and-Chug"

201. If the width of a rectangle is increased by 10 percent and the length of the rectangle is increased by 20 percent, by what percent does the area of the rectangle <u>increase</u>?

(A) 2%

(B) 10%

(C) 15%

(D) 32%

(E) 36%

"Guesstimate"

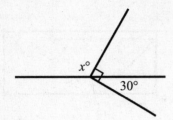

202. In the figure above, *x* =

(A) 30
(B) 65
(C) 120
(D) 150
(E) 170

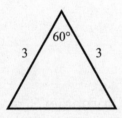

203. What is the perimeter of the triangle shown above?

(A) $3\sqrt{2}$
(B) 6
(C) 7.5
(D) 9
(E) 15

Measure

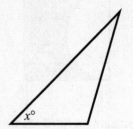

204. In the figure above, *x* =

(A) 30
(B) 45
(C) 60
(D) 75
(E) 90

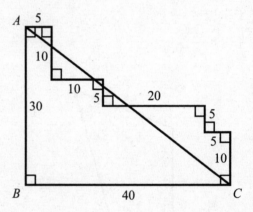

205. In the figure above, what is the length of $\overline{AC}$?

(A) $30\sqrt{2}$
(B)   50
(C)   75
(D) $60\sqrt{2}$
(E)   100

"Meastimate"

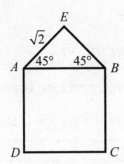

206. In the figure above, what is the area of square *ABCD*?

(A) 2
(B) $2\sqrt{2}$
(C) 4
(D) $4\sqrt{2}$
(E) 8

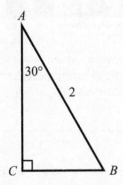

207. In the triangle above, the measure of $\angle BAC$ is 30° and the length of $\overline{AB}$ is 2. Which of the following best approximates the length of $\overline{AC}$?

(A) 0.8
(B) 1.0
(C) 1.7
(D) 1.9
(E) 2.3

Trigonometry as an Alternative Solution Method

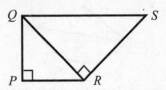

208. In the figure above, $\triangle PQR$ and $\triangle QRS$ are isosceles right triangles. If $\overline{QP} = 3$, what is the length of $\overline{QS}$? $\left(\sin 45° = \dfrac{\sqrt{2}}{2} \right)$

(A) $\sqrt{2}$
(B) $2\sqrt{2}$
(C) 4
(D) 6
(E) 8

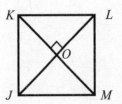

209. If the area of the square *JKLM* in the figure above is 4, what is the sum of the lengths of the diagonals $\overline{JL}$ and $\overline{KM}$? $\left(\sin 45° = \dfrac{\sqrt{2}}{2} \right)$

(A) $\dfrac{\sqrt{2}}{2}$

(B) $2 + \dfrac{\sqrt{2}}{2}$

(C) $4\sqrt{2}$

(D) $4 + 4\sqrt{2}$

(E) $8\sqrt{2}$

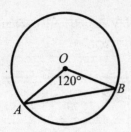

210. In the figure above, O is the center of the circle with radius 10. What is the area of $\triangle AOB$?

$$\left(\sin 30° = \frac{1}{2} \ ; \ \sin 60° = \frac{\sqrt{3}}{2} \right)$$

(A) $10\sqrt{3}$
(B) 10
(C) 25
(D) $25\sqrt{3}$
(E) 50

Data Analysis Review and Strategies

Data Interpretation

Bar, Cumulative, and Line Graphs

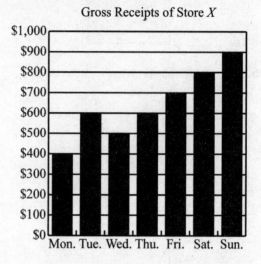

211. During the week shown in the graph above, what was the greatest increase in sales from one day to the next?

(A) $50
(B) $100
(C) $150
(D) $200
(E) $250

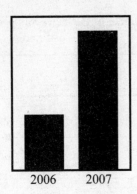

2006   2007

212. If the graph above represents expenditures by Corporation *X* in two different years, what was the approximate ratio of expenditures in 2006 to those in 2007?

(A) $\dfrac{1}{5}$

(B) $\dfrac{2}{5}$

(C) $\dfrac{1}{2}$

(D) $\dfrac{2}{3}$

(E) 2

Number of Corporation *X* Employees

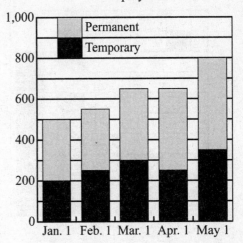

213. Based on the data presented above, what was the difference, if any, between the number of permanent workers employed by Corporation *X* on March 1st and the number of permanent workers employed by Corporation *X* on April 1st?

(A)   0
(B)   50
(C) 100
(D) 150
(E) 200

Company *T* Domestic Sales
(in millions of dollars)

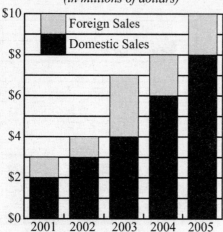

Number of Packages Shipped Monthly
by PostExpress

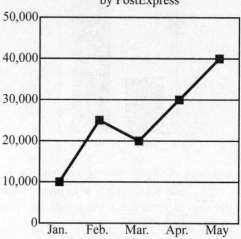

214. Based on the data presented above, what was the difference in the value of foreign sales by Company *T* between 2003 and 2005?

(A) $1,000,000
(B) $2,000,000
(C) $3,000,000
(D) $5,000,000
(E) $6,000,000

215. Based on the data presented above, what was the approximate total number of packages shipped by Post Express for the months January, February, and March, inclusive?

(A) 40,000
(B) 55,000
(C) 60,000
(D) 70,000
(E) 85,000

Pie Charts

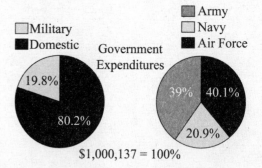

$1,000,137 = 100\%$

216. Based on the data presented above, approximately how much money was spent on the Air Force?

(A) $39,704
(B) $79,409
(C) $96,123
(D) $198,027
(E) $401,054

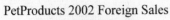

PetProducts 2002 Foreign Sales
(Total = $2,000,000)

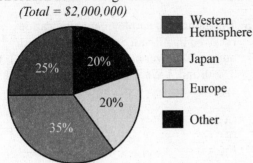

217. Based on the data presented above, what was the dollar value of foreign sales to Europe by Pet Products in 2002?

(A) $200,000
(B) $400,000
(C) $1,200,000
(D) $1,600,000
(E) $2,000,000

Tables (Matrices)

T-Shirt Prices			
	Blue	**Red**	**White**
Small	$5.00	$6.00	$7.00
Large	$5.75	$6.50	$7.25
Extra Large	$6.50	$7.25	$8.00

218. Based on the data presented above, what is the total cost of 5 large blue t-shirts, 8 small red t-shirts, and 4 extra-large white t-shirts?

(A) $56.00
(B) $88.25
(C) $105.50
(D) $108.75
(E) $135.00

Scatterplots

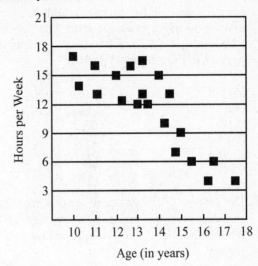

Age (in years)

219. The above scatterplot shows the video-game playing habits of 20 students. The graph most strongly supports the conclusion that the number of hours per week spent playing video-games

(A) is constant from age 10 to age 18
(B) increases as age increases from 10 to 18
(C) decreases as age increases from 10 to 18
(D) is constant for ages 10 through 14 and then decreases
(E) is constant for ages 10 through 14 and then increases

Probability and Statistics

Averages

220. If the average of 35, 38, 41, 43, and *x* is 37, what is *x*?

(A) 28
(B) 30
(C) 31
(D) 34
(E) 36

221. The average weight of 6 packages is 50 pounds per package. Another package is added, making the average weight of the 7 packages 52 pounds per package. What is the weight, in pounds, of the additional package?

(A) 2
(B) 7
(C) 52
(D) 62
(E) 64

222. The average of 10 test scores is 80. If the high and low scores are dropped, the average is 81. What is the average of the high and low scores?

(A) 76
(B) 78
(C) 80
(D) 81
(E) 82

223. In Latin 101, the final exam grade is weighted two times as heavily as the mid-term grade. If Leo received a score of 84 on his final exam and 90 on his mid-term, what was his course average?

(A) 88
(B) 87.5
(C) 86.5
(D) 86
(E) 85

224. In a group of children, three children are 10 years old and two children are 5 years old. What is the average age, in years, of the children in the group?

(A) 6
(B) 6.5
(C) 7
(D) 7.5
(E) 8

Median

225. The number of employment applications received by All-Star Staffing each month during 2002 was as follows: 8, 3, 5, 3, 4, 3, 1, 0, 3, 4, 0, and 7. What was the median number of applications received per month in 2002?

(A) 3
(B) 4
(C) 5
(D) 6
(E) 7

Mode

226. William's monthly electric bills for last year were as follows: $40, 38, 36, 38, 34, 34, 30, 32, 34, 37, 39, and 40. What is the mode of the bills?

(A) $33
(B) $34
(C) $35
(D) $36
(E) $37

Arithmetic Probability

227. If set $A = \{1, 2, 3, 4, 5, 6\}$ and set $B = \{1, 2, 3, 4, 5, 6\}$, what is the probability that the sum of one number from set A and one number from set B will total 7?

(A) $\dfrac{1}{12}$

(B) $\dfrac{5}{36}$

(C) $\dfrac{1}{6}$

(D) $\dfrac{1}{5}$

(E) $\dfrac{1}{3}$

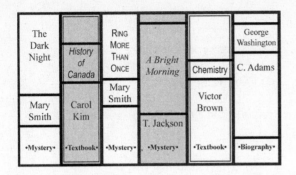

Geometric Probability

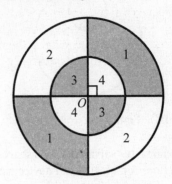

228. If a book is selected at random from the six-book collection shown above, which of the following has the greatest probability of being selected?

(A) A book by Mary Smith
(B) A textbook
(C) A mystery
(D) A book written by either Carol Kim or Victor Brown
(E) A biography

229. If a jar contains r red marbles, b blue marbles, and g green marbles, which of the following expresses the probability that a marble drawn at random will NOT be red?

(A) $\dfrac{-r}{r+b+g}$

(B) $\dfrac{r}{r+b+g}$

(C) $\dfrac{b+g-r}{b+g+r}$

(D) $\dfrac{r}{b+g}$

(E) $\dfrac{b+g}{b+g+r}$

230. The figure above shows a dartboard consisting of two concentric circles with center O. The radius of the larger circle is equal to the diameter of the smaller circle. What is the probability that a randomly thrown dart striking the board will score a 3?

(A) $\dfrac{1}{16}$

(B) $\dfrac{1}{8}$

(C) $\dfrac{1}{4}$

(D) $\dfrac{1}{2}$

(E) $\dfrac{3}{4}$

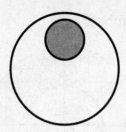

NOTE: Figure not drawn to scale.

231. An underwater salvage team is searching the ocean floor for a lost signal device using a large circular search pattern and a smaller circular search pattern with a radius equal to one-third that of the larger pattern. If the device is known to be inside the boundary of the larger search area, what is the probability that it is NOT located in the shaded portion of the figure?

(A) $\dfrac{1}{9}$

(B) $\dfrac{1}{6}$

(C) $\dfrac{1}{3}$

(D) $\dfrac{1}{2}$

(E) $\dfrac{8}{9}$

QUIZZES

This section contains three Math: Multiple-Choice quizzes. Complete each quiz under timed conditions. Use any available space in the section for scratch work. Answers are on page 624.

Quiz I

(16 items; 20 minutes)

> **DIRECTIONS:** Solve each item and choose the correct answer choice. Use any available space for scratchwork.

Notes:

(1) The use of a calculator is permitted. All numbers used are real numbers.

(2) Figures that accompany problems in this test are intended to provide information useful in solving the problems. They are drawn as accurately as possible EXCEPT when it is stated in a specific problem that the figure is not drawn to scale. All figures lie in a plane unless otherwise indicated.

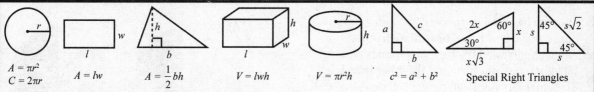

$A = \pi r^2$
$C = 2\pi r$

$A = lw$

$A = \frac{1}{2}bh$

$V = lwh$

$V = \pi r^2 h$

$c^2 = a^2 + b^2$

Special Right Triangles

The number of degrees of arc in a circle is 360.
The sum of the measures in degrees of the angles of a triangle is 180.

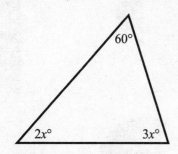

1. In the triangle above, $x =$

(A) 24
(B) 20
(C) 16
(D) 12
(E) 10

2. A normal dozen contains 12 items, and a baker's dozen contains 13 items. If x is the number of items that could be measured either in a whole number of normal dozens or in a whole number of baker's dozens, what is the <u>minimum</u> value of x?

(A)   1
(B)   12
(C)   13
(D)   25
(E)   156

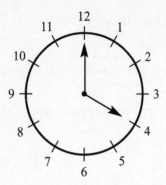

3. In the figure above, what is the degree measure of the <u>smaller</u> of the two angles formed by the hour and minute hands of the clock?

(A)   45
(B)   60
(C)   90
(D) 120
(E) 240

4. Starting from points that are 200 kilometers apart, two trains travel toward each other along two parallel tracks. If one train travels at 70 kilometers per hour and the other travels at 80 kilometers per hour, how much time, in hours, will elapse before the trains pass each other?

(A) $\dfrac{3}{4}$

(B) 1

(C) $\dfrac{4}{3}$

(D) $\dfrac{3}{2}$

(E) 2

5. A student begins heating a certain substance with a temperature of 50°C over a Bunsen burner. If the temperature of the substance will rise 20°C for every 24 minutes it remains over the burner, what will be the temperature, in degrees Celsius, of the substance after 18 minutes?

(A) 52
(B) 56
(C) 60
(D) 65
(E) 72

Team Expenses		
Transportation	$240	■
Lodging	$360	▨
Meals	$120	□

6. Which of the following pie charts represents the data shown above?

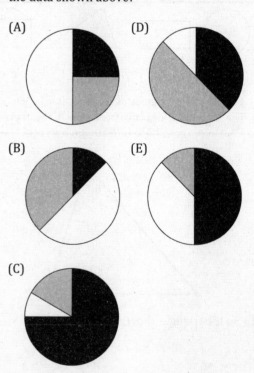

7. If the ratio of apples to oranges in a salad is 8 to 7, what fractional part of the salad is oranges?

(A) $\dfrac{1}{56}$

(B) $\dfrac{1}{15}$

(C) $\dfrac{1}{7}$

(D) $\dfrac{7}{15}$

(E) $\dfrac{8}{7}$

8. The object of a popular board game is to use clues to identify a suspect and the weapon used to commit a crime. If there are 3 suspects and 6 weapons, how many different solutions to the game are possible?

(A) 2
(B) 3
(C) 9
(D) 12
(E) 18

9. The average weight of three boxes is $25\dfrac{1}{3}$ pounds. If each box weighs at least 24 pounds, what is the greatest possible weight, in pounds, of any one of the boxes?

(A) 25
(B) 26
(C) 27
(D) 28
(E) 29

10. If n subtracted from $\dfrac{13}{2}$ is equal to n divided by $\dfrac{2}{13}$, what is the value of n?

(A) $\dfrac{2}{3}$

(B) $\dfrac{13}{15}$

(C) 1

(D) $\dfrac{13}{11}$

(E) 26

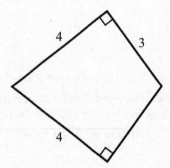

11. In the figure above, what is the area of the quadrilateral?

(A) 18
(B) 15
(C) 12
(D) 9
(E) 8

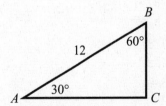

12. In the figure above, what is the length of $\overline{BC}$?
$$\left(\sin 30° = \dfrac{1}{2}\right)$$

(A) 2
(B) 3
(C) $3\sqrt{3}$
(D) 6
(E) $6\sqrt{3}$

13. After being dropped from a height of h meters, a ball bounces 3 meters high on the third bounce and $\frac{4}{3}$ meters high on the fifth bounce. What is the value, in meters, of h?

(A) $\dfrac{27}{8}$

(B) $\dfrac{9}{2}$

(C) $\dfrac{27}{4}$

(D) $\dfrac{81}{8}$

(E) $\dfrac{27}{2}$

14. Set $A = \{-2, -1, 0\}$, and set $B = \{-1, 0, 1\}$. If a is an element of set A and b is an element of set B, for how many pairs (a, b) is the product ab a member of both set A and set B?

(A) 0
(B) 2
(C) 4
(D) 6
(E) 9

15. Which of the following is the complete solution set for $|2x + 4| = 12$?

(A) $\{-8, 4\}$
(B) $\{-4, 8\}$
(C) $\{0, 8\}$
(D) $\{4, 8\}$
(E) $\{6, 8\}$

16. If $f(x) = \dfrac{(x-1)^2}{(-2-x)}$, for what value of x is $f(x)$ undefined?

(A) -2
(B) -1
(C) 0
(D) 1
(E) 2

Quiz II

(20 items; 25 minutes)

DIRECTIONS: Solve each item and choose the correct answer choice. Use any available space for scratchwork.

Notes:

(1) The use of a calculator is permitted. All numbers used are real numbers.

(2) Figures that accompany problems in this test are intended to provide information useful in solving the problems. They are drawn as accurately as possible EXCEPT when it is stated in a specific problem that the figure is not drawn to scale. All figures lie in a plane unless otherwise indicated.

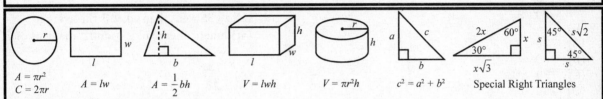

$A = \pi r^2$
$C = 2\pi r$

$A = lw$

$A = \dfrac{1}{2}bh$

$V = lwh$

$V = \pi r^2 h$

$c^2 = a^2 + b^2$

Special Right Triangles

The number of degrees of arc in a circle is 360.
The sum of the measures in degrees of the angles of a triangle is 180.

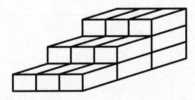

1. The figure above is a plan that shows a solid set of steps to be constructed from concrete blocks of equal size. How many blocks are needed to construct the steps?

(A) 12
(B) 15
(C) 18
(D) 21
(E) 24

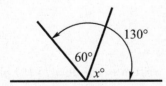

2. In the figure above, what is the value of *x*?

(A) 70
(B) 60
(C) 50
(D) 40
(E) 30

3. If $2^{x+1} = 4^{x-1}$, what is the value of *x*?

(A) 1
(B) 2
(C) 3
(D) 4
(E) 5

4. Of the actors in a certain play, five actors are in Act I, 12 actors are in Act II, and 13 actors are in Act III. If 10 of the actors are in exactly two of the three acts and all of the other actors are in just one act, how many actors are in the play?

(A) 17
(B) 20
(C) 24
(D) 30
(E) 38

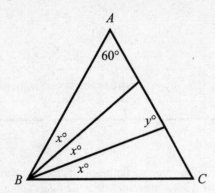

5. In the figure above, $\overline{AB} \cong \overline{BC} \cong \overline{CA}$. What is the value of y?

    (A)   20
    (B)   60
    (C)   80
    (D) 100
    (E) 120

6. Under certain conditions, a bicycle traveling k meters per second requires $\dfrac{k^2}{20} + k$ meters to stop. If $k = 10$, how many <u>meters</u> does the bicycle need to stop?

    (A) 10
    (B) 12
    (C) 15
    (D) 20
    (E) 30

7. What is the slope of a line that passes through the origin and $(-3, -2)$?

    (A) $\dfrac{3}{2}$

    (B) $\dfrac{2}{3}$

    (C) 0

    (D) $-\dfrac{2}{3}$

    (E) $-\dfrac{3}{2}$

8. An album contains x black-and-white photographs and y color photographs. If the album contains 24 photographs, then which of the following CANNOT be true?

    (A) $x = y$
    (B) $x = 2y$
    (C) $x = 3y$
    (D) $x = 4y$
    (E) $x = 5y$

9. If $2a = 3b = 4c$, then what is the average (arithmetic mean) of a, b, and c, in terms of a?

    (A) $\dfrac{13a}{18}$

    (B) $\dfrac{13a}{9}$

    (C) $\dfrac{8a}{3}$

    (D) $\dfrac{4a}{3}$

    (E) $2a$

10. If $x = 6 + y$ and $4x = 3 - 2y$, what is the value of x?

    (A) 4

    (B) $\dfrac{11}{3}$

    (C) $\dfrac{5}{2}$

    (D) $-\dfrac{2}{3}$

    (E) $-\dfrac{7}{2}$

11. If $\dfrac{2}{3}$ is written as a decimal to 101 places, what is the sum of the first 100 digits to the right of the decimal point?

    (A) 66
    (B) 595
    (C) 599
    (D) 600
    (E) 601

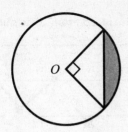

12. In the figure above, O is the center of the circle with radius 1. What is the area of the shaded region?

(A) $\dfrac{3\pi}{4}+\dfrac{1}{2}$

(B) $\dfrac{3\pi}{4}-\dfrac{1}{2}$

(C) $\dfrac{\pi}{4}+\dfrac{1}{2}$

(D) $\dfrac{\pi}{4}-\dfrac{1}{2}$

(E) $\pi-1$

13. If $f(3)=5$ and $f(7)=7$, what is the slope of the graph of $f(x)$ in the coordinate plane?

(A) -2

(B) $-\dfrac{1}{2}$

(C) 1

(D) $\dfrac{1}{2}$

(E) 2

14. In a list of the first 100 positive integers, the digit 9 appears how many times?

(A) 9
(B) 10
(C) 11
(D) 19
(E) 20

15. If $\dfrac{x}{x+3}=\dfrac{3}{4}$, and $x\neq-3$, then $x=$

(A) 3
(B) 4
(C) 5
(D) 7
(E) 9

16. Which of the following is the complete solution set for $\sqrt{2x+3}+2=5$?

(A) $\{\}$
(B) $\{-1\}$
(C) $\{3\}$
(D) $\{-1, 3\}$
(E) $\{1, 2\}$

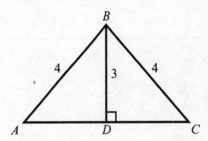

17. In the figure above, what is the length of $\overline{AC}$?
$$\left(\sin\angle ABD=\frac{\sqrt{7}}{4}\right)$$

(A) 5
(B) $2\sqrt{7}$
(C) $4\sqrt{3}$
(D) 7
(E) $3\sqrt{7}$

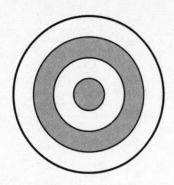

18. A dartboard has four concentric circles with the center as indicated in the figure above. If the diameter of each circle except for the smallest is twice that of the next smaller circle, what is the probability that a randomly thrown dart will strike the shaded portion of the figure?

(A) $\dfrac{3}{16}$

(B) $\dfrac{1}{4}$

(C) $\dfrac{13}{64}$

(D) $\dfrac{17}{64}$

(E) $\dfrac{1}{2}$

19. If $f(3)=4$ and $f(-3)=1$, what is the y-intercept of the graph of $f(x)$ in the coordinate plane?

(A) $-\dfrac{5}{2}$

(B) $-\dfrac{2}{5}$

(C) 0

(D) $\dfrac{2}{5}$

(E) $\dfrac{5}{2}$

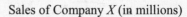

Sales of Company X (in millions)

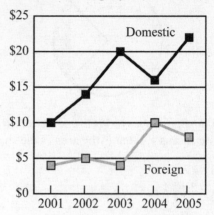

20. The above graph shows the data for domestic and foreign sales for Company X over five years. Which of the following pie graphs best represents the division of total sales between foreign and domestic sales for 2004?

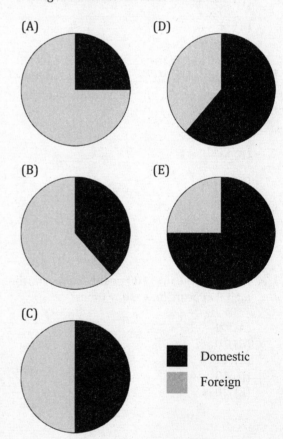

Quiz III

(20 items; 25 minutes)

DIRECTIONS: Solve each item and choose the correct answer choice. Use any available space for scratchwork.

Notes:

(1) The use of a calculator is permitted. All numbers used are real numbers.

(2) Figures that accompany problems in this test are intended to provide information useful in solving the problems. They are drawn as accurately as possible EXCEPT when it is stated in a specific problem that the figure is not drawn to scale. All figures lie in a plane unless otherwise indicated.

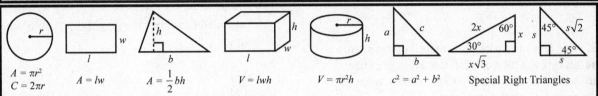

$A = \pi r^2$
$C = 2\pi r$

$A = lw$

$A = \frac{1}{2}bh$

$V = lwh$

$V = \pi r^2 h$

$c^2 = a^2 + b^2$

Special Right Triangles

The number of degrees of arc in a circle is 360.

The sum of the measures in degrees of the angles of a triangle is 180.

---

1. What is the average (arithmetic mean) of all integers 6 through 15 (including 6 and 15)?

(A) 6
(B) 9
(C) 10.5
(D) 11
(E) 21

2. Which of the following numbers is the largest?

(A) 0.08
(B) 0.17
(C) 0.171
(D) 0.1077
(E) 0.10771

3. If the rectangle above has an area of 72, then $x = ?$

(A) 3
(B) 4
(C) 6
(D) 8
(E) 9

4. Machine X produces 15 units per minute, and Machine Y produces 12 units per minute. In one hour, Machine X will produce how many more units than Machine Y?

(A) 90
(B) 180
(C) 240
(D) 270
(E) 360

5. On the first day after being given an assignment, a student read $\frac{1}{2}$ the number of pages assigned, and on the second day, the student read 3 more pages. If the student still has 6 additional pages to read, how many pages were assigned?

(A) 15
(B) 18
(C) 24
(D) 30
(E) 36

6. The average (arithmetic mean) of Pat's scores on three tests was 80. If the average of her scores on the first two tests was 78, what was her score on the third test?

(A) 82
(B) 84
(C) 86
(D) 88
(E) 90

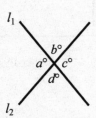

7. In the figure above, $a + c - b$ is equal to which of the following?

(A) $2a - d$
(B) $2a + d$
(C) $2d - a$
(D) $2a$
(E) 180

8. If $3a + 6b = 12$, then $a + 2b = ?$

(A) 1
(B) 2
(C) 3
(D) 4
(E) 6

$$\frac{3a+6b}{3} = \frac{12}{3}$$

$$a + 2b = 4$$

9. Two circles with radii r and $r + 3$ have areas that differ by 15π. What is the radius of the <u>smaller</u> circle?

(A) 4
(B) 3
(C) 2
(D) 1
(E) $\frac{1}{2}$

10. If x, y, and z are integers, $x > y > z > 1$, and $xyz = 144$, what is the <u>greatest</u> possible value of x?

(A) 8
(B) 12
(C) 16
(D) 24
(E) 36

11. For all integers, $x \, \Phi \, y = 2x + 3y$. Which of the following must be true?

    I. $3 \, \Phi \, 2 = 12$
    II. $x \, \Phi \, y = y \, \Phi \, x$
    III. $0 \, \Phi \, (1 \, \Phi \, 2) = (0 \, \Phi \, 1) \, \Phi \, 2$

(A) I only
(B) I and II only
(C) I and III only
(D) II and III only
(E) I, II, and III

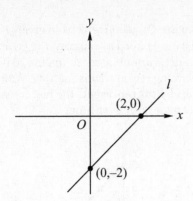

(2,0)

(0,−2)

12. In the figure above, what is the slope of line *l*?

(A)   1

(B) $\frac{1}{2}$

(C)   0

(D) $-\frac{1}{2}$

(E)   −1

$\frac{\Delta y}{\Delta x}$ $\frac{0--2}{0-2} = \frac{2}{-2} = -1$

13. If Yuriko is now twice as old as Lisa was 10 years ago, how old is Lisa today if Yuriko is now *n* years old?

$x = L$
$2x = Y$

(A) $\frac{n}{2}+10$

(B) $\frac{n}{2}-10$

(C) $n-10$

(D) $2n+10$

(E) $2n-10$

14. In the figure above, *ABCD* is a rectangle with sides $\overline{AB}$, $\overline{BC}$, and $\overline{CD}$ touching the circle with center *O*. If the radius of the circle is 2, what is the area of the shaded region?

(A) $\frac{3\pi}{2}$

(B) $\frac{3\pi}{4}$

(C) $8-2\pi$

(D) $2-\pi$

(E) $\pi-1$

15. The sum of two positive consecutive integers is *n*. In terms of *n*, what is the value of the larger of the two integers?

(A) $\frac{n-1}{2}$

(B) $\frac{n+1}{2}$

(C) $\frac{n}{2}+1$

(D) $\frac{n}{2}-1$

(E) $\frac{n}{2}$

	Old Scale	New Scale
Minimum Score	0	120
Minimum Passing Score	60	?
Maximum Score	100	180

16. The table above shows a teacher how to convert scores for a test from the Old Scale to the New Scale. What is the Minimum Passing Score on the New Scale?

(A) 108
(B) 136
(C) 156
(D) 164
(E) 208

17. If a polygon with all equal sides is inscribed in a circle, then the measure in degrees of the minor arc created by adjacent vertices of the polygon could be all of the following EXCEPT

(A) 30
(B) 25
(C) 24
(D) 20
(E) 15

18. A jar contains 5 blue marbles, 25 green marbles, and x red marbles. If the probability of drawing a red marble at random is $\frac{1}{4}$, what is the value of x?

(A) 25
(B) 20
(C) 15
(D) 12
(E) 10

19. When the 10-gallon tank of an emergency generator is filled to capacity, the generator operates without interruption for 20 hours, consuming fuel at a constant rate. Which of the graphs below represents the fuel consumption of the generator over time?

(A)

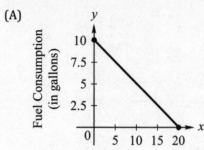

(B)

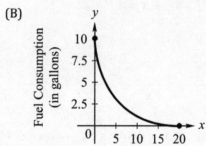

(C)

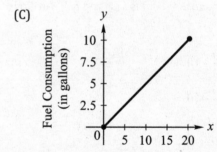

(D)

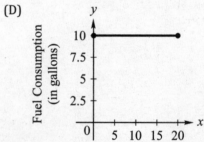

(E)

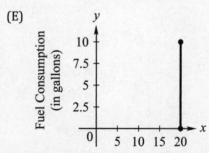

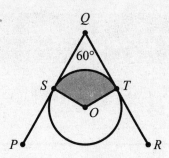

20. In the figure above, $\overline{PQ}$ is tangent to circle O at point S and $\overline{QR}$ is tangent to circle O at point T. If the radius of circle O is 2, what is the area of the shaded portion of the figure?

(A) $\dfrac{\pi}{3}$

(B) $\dfrac{2\pi}{3}$

(C) π

(D) $\dfrac{4\pi}{3}$

(E) 2π

Quiz IV Brain Buster
(15 items; 20 minutes)

DIRECTIONS: Solve each item and choose the correct answer choice. Calculator use is permitted; however, some items are best solved without the use of a calculator.

Notes:

(1) The use of a calculator is permitted. All numbers used are real numbers.

(2) Figures that accompany problems in this test are intended to provide information useful in solving the problems. They are drawn as accurately as possible EXCEPT when it is stated in a specific problem that the figure is not drawn to scale. All figures lie in a plane unless otherwise indicated.

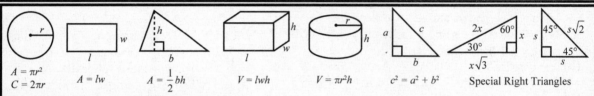

$A = \pi r^2$
$C = 2\pi r$

$A = lw$

$A = \dfrac{1}{2}bh$

$V = lwh$

$V = \pi r^2 h$

$c^2 = a^2 + b^2$

Special Right Triangles

The number of degrees of arc in a circle is 360.
The sum of the measures in degrees of the angles of a triangle is 180.

1. Maggie has to inventory her employer's collection of books. There are three categories of books. Historical novels account for one-fourth of the books. Classics comprise half of the remaining books and there are 30 travel books. How many books does she have to inventory?

   (A)   50
   (B)   70
   (C)   80
   (D) 100
   (E) 120

2. The local university's enrollment figures for a six-year period are detailed in the table below. Between which two consecutive years did the university experience the greatest percent of increase in student enrollment?

UNIVERSITY ENROLLMENT					
2006	**2007**	**2008**	**2009**	**2010**	**2011**
14,000	15,100	15,900	16,500	17,600	17,400

   (A) 2006–2007
   (B) 2007–2008
   (C) 2008–2009
   (D) 2009–2010
   (E) 2010–2011

3. The local modeling agency is looking for some new models for a specific job. The job requires that the model's height be within 2 inches of 70 inches. Which of the following absolute value inequalities describe this condition, where x is the model's height?

(A) $|x+2| \le 70$
(B) $|x-2| < 70$
(C) $|x+70| < 2$
(D) $|x-70| < 2$
(E) $|x+70| \le 2$

4. Tommy has blue, green, and red marbles. The number of blue marbles and green marbles combined total 25. The number of blue and red marbles combined total 30. There are twice as many red marbles as green marbles. How many green marbles does Tommy have?

(A) 5
(B) 10
(C) 15
(D) 20
(E) 25

5. Amanda has to arrange the five shapes below in a row. How many arrangements can Amanda make if the circle cannot be placed at the beginning or end of the row?

(A) 5
(B) 24
(C) 36
(D) 72
(E) 120

6. If $x = a^2 - b^2$ and $y = a^2 + 2ab + b^2$, then $\dfrac{x}{y} = ?$

(A) $2a^2 + 2ab$
(B) $\dfrac{a^2 - b^2}{a^2 + b^2}$
(C) $\dfrac{a+b}{a-b}$
(D) $\dfrac{-1}{2ab}$
(E) $\dfrac{a-b}{a+b}$

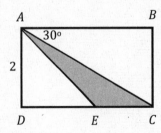

7. A 13-foot ladder is leaning against a building and the bottom of the ladder is 5 feet from the wall. The ladder begins to slide down the building. When the bottom of the ladder is 8 feet from the wall, about how far has the top of the ladder slipped down?

(A) less than 1 foot
(B) exactly 1 foot
(C) between 1 foot and 2 feet
(D) exactly 2 feet
(E) more than 2 feet

8. In rectangle $ABCD$ below, $\overline{AD} = \overline{DE}$, $\overline{AD} = 2$, and $\angle BAC = 30°$. What is the area of the shaded portion of the figure?

(A) $2\sqrt{3} - 2$
(B) $4 - 2\sqrt{3}$
(C) $2\sqrt{2}$
(D) $2\sqrt{2} - 3$
(E) $2\sqrt{3}$

9. In the figure below, $\overset{\frown}{DE}$ is the arc of a circle with center C. If the length of $\overset{\frown}{DE}$ is 2π, what is the area of sector CDE?

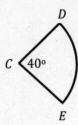

(A) 4π
(B) 9π
(C) 12π
(D) 18π
(E) 24π

10. If a is the greatest prime factor of 24 and b is the greatest prime factor of 80, what is ab?

(A) 4
(B) 6
(C) 10
(D) 15
(E) 16

11. If the average (arithmetic mean) of a, b, and c is z, which of the following is the average of a, b, c and d?

(A) $\dfrac{z+d}{3}$

(B) $\dfrac{z+d}{4}$

(C) $\dfrac{3z+d}{3}$

(D) $\dfrac{3z+d}{4}$

(E) $\dfrac{3(z+d)}{4}$

12. When 21 is divided by a positive integer d, the remainder is 5. For how many different values of d is this true?

(A) One
(B) Two
(C) Three
(D) Four
(E) Five

13. In a rectangular coordinate system, the center of a circle has coordinates $(3,-10)$. The circle touches the y-axis only once. What is the diameter of the circle?

(A) 3
(B) 6
(C) 9
(D) 10
(E) 20

14. If $x^2 + 3x - 18 = 0$ and $2m = x$, which of the following could be a value of m?

(A) −3
(B) 1
(C) 3
(D) 6
(E) 9

15. Which of the following coordinate points lie completely inside the circle whose equation is $x^2 + y^2 = 36$?

(A) $(6,0)$
(B) $(0,-6)$
(C) $(-4,5)$
(D) $(2,7)$
(E) $(4,4)$

REVIEW

This section contains additional Math: Multiple-Choice items for further practice. Answers are on page 624.

DIRECTIONS: Solve each item and choose the correct answer choice. Use any available space for scratchwork.

Notes:

(1) The use of a calculator is permitted. All numbers used are real numbers.

(2) Figures that accompany problems in this test are intended to provide information useful in solving the problems. They are drawn as accurately as possible EXCEPT when it is stated in a specific problem that the figure is not drawn to scale. All figures lie in a plane unless otherwise indicated.

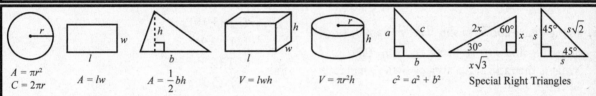

$A = \pi r^2$
$C = 2\pi r$

$A = lw$

$A = \frac{1}{2}bh$

$V = lwh$

$V = \pi r^2 h$

$c^2 = a^2 + b^2$

Special Right Triangles

The number of degrees of arc in a circle is 360.
The sum of the measures in degrees of the angles of a triangle is 180.

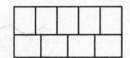

1. Nine playing cards from the same deck are placed as shown in the figure above to form a large rectangle of area 180 sq. in. How many inches are there in the perimeter of this large rectangle?

(A) 29
(B) 58
(C) 64
(D) 116
(E) 210

2. If each of the dimensions of a rectangle is increased by 100 percent, by what percent is the area increased?

(A) 100%
(B) 200%
(C) 300%
(D) 400%
(E) 500%

3. What is 10 percent of $\frac{x}{3}$ if $\frac{2x}{3}$ is 10 percent of 60?

(A) 0.1
(B) 0.2
(C) 0.3
(D) 0.4
(E) 0.5

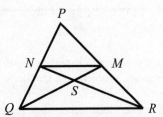

4. In the figure above, M and N are midpoints of sides $\overline{PR}$ and $\overline{PQ}$, respectively, of $\triangle PQR$. What is the ratio of the area of $\triangle MNS$ to that of $\triangle PQR$?

(A) 2:5
(B) 2:9
(C) 1:4
(D) 1:8
(E) 1:12

5. A cube has an edge that is 4 inches long. If the edge is increased by 25 percent, which of the following is the best approximation of the percent increase in the volume of the cube?

(A) 25%
(B) 48%
(C) 73%
(D) 95%
(E) 122%

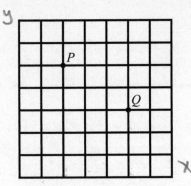

6. In the figure above is a portion of the (x, y) coordinate plane. If each small square has an area of 1 and the coordinates of point P are $(3,7)$, what are the (x, y) coordinates of point Q?

(A) (5,6)
(B) (1,10)
(C) (6,9)
(D) (6,5)
(E) (5,10)

7. The average of 8 numbers is 6; the average of 6 other numbers is 8. What is the average of all 14 numbers?

(A) 6
(B) $6\frac{6}{7}$
(C) 7
(D) $7\frac{2}{7}$
(E) $8\frac{1}{7}$

8. The front wheels of a wagon are 7 feet in circumference and the back wheels are 9 feet in circumference. When the front wheels have made 10 more revolutions than the back wheels, what distance, in feet, has the wagon gone?

(A) 126
(B) 180
(C) 189
(D) 315
(E) 630

9. Doreen can wash her car in 15 minutes, while her younger brother Dave takes twice as long to do the same job. If they work together, how many minutes will the job take them?

(A) 5

(B) $7\frac{1}{2}$

(C) 10

(D) $22\frac{1}{2}$

(E) 30

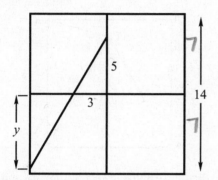

10. In the figure above, the sides of the large square are each 14 inches long. Joining the midpoints of each opposite side forms 4 smaller squares. What is the value of y, in inches?

(A) 5
(B) 6

(C) $6\frac{5}{8}$

(D) $6\frac{2}{3}$

(E) 6.8

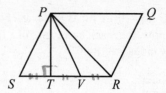

NOTE: Figure not drawn to scale.

11. In the figure above, $PQRS$ is a parallelogram, and $\overline{ST} = \overline{TV} = \overline{VR}$. If $\angle PTS = 90°$, what is the ratio of the area of $\triangle SPT$ to the area of the parallelogram?

(A) $\frac{1}{6}$

(B) $\frac{1}{5}$

(C) $\frac{2}{7}$

(D) $2\frac{1}{3}$

(E) $2\frac{2}{7}$

12. If $p > q$ and $r < 0$, which of the following is (are) true?

  I. $pr < qr$
  II. $p + r > q + r$
  III. $p - r < q - r$

(A) I only
(B) II only
(C) I and III only
(D) I and II only
(E) I, II, and III

13. A pound of water is evaporated from 6 pounds of seawater that is 4 percent salt. What is the percentage of salt in the remaining solution?

(A) 3.6%
(B) 4%
(C) 4.8%
(D) 5.2%
(E) 6%

14. John is now three times Pat's age. Four years from now, John will be x years old. In terms of x, how old is Pat now?

(A) $\dfrac{x+4}{3}$

(B) $3x$

(C) $x+4$

(D) $x-4$

(E) $\dfrac{x-4}{3}$

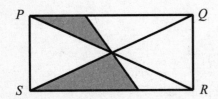

15. In the figure above, what percent of the area of rectangle $PQRS$ is shaded?

(A) 20%
(B) 25%
(C) 30%
(D) $33\dfrac{1}{3}$%
(E) 35%

16. A cylindrical container has a diameter of 14 inches and a height of 6 inches. Since one gallon equals 231 cubic inches, what is the approximate capacity, in gallons, of the tank?

(A) $\dfrac{2}{3}$

(B) $1\dfrac{1}{7}$

(C) $2\dfrac{2}{7}$

(D) $2\dfrac{2}{3}$

(E) 4

17. A train running between two towns arrives at its destination 10 minutes late when it travels at a constant rate of 40 miles per hour and 16 minutes late when it travels at a constant rate of 30 miles per hour. What is the distance, in miles, between the two towns?

(A) $8\dfrac{6}{7}$

(B) 12
(C) 192
(D) 560
(E) 720

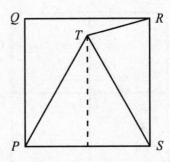

18. In the figure above, $PQRS$ is a square and PTS is an equilateral triangle. What is the degree measure of $\angle TRS$?

(A) 60
(B) 75
(C) 80
(D) 90
(E) 120

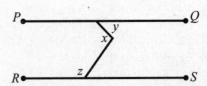

19. In the figure above, $\overline{PQ}$ is parallel to $\overline{RS}$, $y = 60°$, and $z = 130°$. What is the degree measure of $\angle x$?

(A) 90
(B) 100
(C) 110
(D) 120
(E) 130

20. Paul can paint a fence in 2 hours and Fred can paint the same fence in 3 hours. If Paul and Fred work together, how many hours will it take them to paint the fence?

(A) 5

(B) $2\frac{1}{2}$

(C) $1\frac{1}{5}$

(D) 1

(E) $\frac{5}{6}$

21. A motorist drives 60 miles to her destination at an average speed of 40 miles per hour and makes the return trip at an average speed of 30 miles per hour. What is her average speed, in miles per hour, for the entire trip?

(A) 17

(B) $34\frac{2}{7}$

(C) 35

(D) $43\frac{1}{3}$

(E) 70

22. An ice cream truck drives down Willy Street 4 times a week. The truck carries 5 different flavors of ice cream bars, each of which comes in 2 different designs. If the truck runs Monday through Thursday, and Monday was the first day of the month, by what day of the month could Zachary, buying 1 ice cream bar each time the truck drives down the street, purchase all of the different varieties of ice cream bars?

(A) the 11ᵗʰ day
(B) the 16ᵗʰ day
(C) the 21ˢᵗ day
(D) the 24ᵗʰ day
(E) the 30ᵗʰ day

23. If $N! = N(N-1)(N-2)\ldots[N-(N-1)]$, what does $\dfrac{N!}{(N-2)!}$ equal?

(A) $N^2 - N$

(B) $N^5 + N^3 - N^2 + \dfrac{N}{N^2}$

(C) $N + 1$
(D) 1
(E) 6

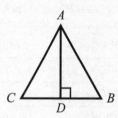

24. In the figure above, ABC is an equilateral triangle with a perpendicular line drawn from point A to point D. If the triangle is "folded over" on the perpendicular line so that points B and C meet, the perimeter of the new triangle is approximately what percent of the perimeter of the triangle before the fold?

(A) 100%
(B) 78%
(C) 50%
(D) 32%
(E) 25%

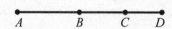

NOTE: Figure not drawn to scale.

25. In the figure above, $\overline{AB}$ is three times longer than $\overline{BC}$, and $\overline{CD}$ is two times longer than $\overline{BC}$. If $\overline{BC}$ is removed from the line and the other two segments are joined to form one line, what is the ratio of the original length of $\overline{AD}$ to the new length of $\overline{AD}$?

(A) 3:2
(B) 6:5
(C) 5:4
(D) 7:6
(E) 11:10

26. If $(x+1)(x-2)$ is positive, then which of the following statements is true?

(A) $x < -1$ or $x > 2$
(B) $x > -1$ or $x < 2$
(C) $-1 < x < 2$
(D) $-2 < x < 1$
(E) $x = -1$ or $x = 2$

ABC SOUND STORES	
Annual Sale of Compact Discs	
Year	Number Sold
2002	7,000
2003	9,000
2004	12,000
2005	16,000
2006	20,000
2007	24,000

27. In the table above, which yearly period had the smallest percent increase in sales?

(A) 2002–2003
(B) 2003–2004
(C) 2004–2005
(D) 2005–2006
(E) 2006–2007

Items #28–29 refer to the following table:

ANNUAL EXPENDITURES FOR THE JONES FAMILY *(percent of disposable income)*		
Category	2006	2007
Rent	23.0%	19.3%
Food	17.6%	18.2%
Clothing	14.2%	15.1%
Automobile	11.3%	12.3%
Utilities	10.9%	10.2%
Savings	6.2%	5.1%
Entertainment	5.2%	5.3%
Medical and Dental Care	4.0%	3.7%
Charitable Contributions	3.2%	3.9%
Household Furnishings	2.9%	3.1%
Other	1.5%	3.8%
Total	100.0%	100.0%
Total Expenditures	$34,987.00	$40,012.00

28. Approximately how much money did the Jones family spend on medical and dental care in 2006?

(A) $1,200
(B) $1,400
(C) $1,520
(D) $2,250
(E) $4,000

29. If the categories in the table are rank ordered from one to eleven in each year, for how many categories would the rank ordering change from 2006 to 2007?

(A) 2
(B) 3
(C) 4
(D) 5
(E) 6

STRATEGY SUMMARY

General Strategies

When approaching a Math: Multiple-Choice item, you should pay careful attention to several things:

Figures

Unless otherwise specifically noted, the figures included as illustrations are drawn to scale.

Answer Choices

Most answer choices are arranged in order of ascending or descending value and many incorrect answer choices correspond to conceptual errors.

"Signal" Words

Typically, "signal" words are capitalized (e.g., thought-reversers, such as "NOT," "CANNOT," and "EXCEPT"); however, they may sometimes be underlined or italicized (e.g., specified units). While the specific formatting of these words may vary, they are critical to correctly understanding the item. Pay careful attention to thought-reversers, as they reverse the apparent meaning of an item.

Ladder of Difficulty

For each group of Multiple-Choice items in a Math test section, the difficulty level increases as the item number increases. Therefore, allot less time for earlier items. When solving items that are high on the ladder of difficulty, do NOT expect obvious answers or easy solutions. It is unlikely that answers corresponding to easy solutions or to numbers in the item stem will be the correct choice. Remember to pace yourself—difficult, time-consuming items have the same value as the easy items.

Preview Item Stems

Read the item stem first. Only then should you read the details of the item, keeping this item stem in mind.

Confirm Solutions

Double-check the solution by confirming that it answers the particular question that is being asked. When applicable, this confirmation includes verifying that the solution is given in the units specified by the item stem.

If you are unable to either find an elegant (quick) solution or solve the item directly based on subject knowledge, the following alternative solutions strategies can be extremely helpful:

"Test-the-Test" Strategy

The correct answer to any item is always one of five given choices. Sometimes, the easiest and quickest way to solve an item is to test each of the answer choices. The "test-the-test" strategy can mean plugging answer choices back into the item—starting with (C)—to test the validity of an expression, or it can mean checking each answer choice against any stated conditions. The "test-the-test" strategy is typically useful for items with numerical solutions or variables and values that meet stated conditions.

"Plug-and-Chug" Strategy

This strategy is similar to the "test-the-test" strategy because the item stem and answer choices (rather than direct mathematical solution strategies) are used to isolate the correct answer. The difference is that rather than testing the validity of each answer choice against the item stem conditions, the item stem and/or answer choices are evaluated by plugging in chosen numbers: "plug-and-chug." This strategy is especially helpful when solving Algebra items.

"Eliminate-and-Guess" Strategy

If unable to determine the correct answer directly by using mathematical methods or indirectly by using either the "test-the-test" or "plug-and-chug" strategy, eliminate as many answer choices as possible and then guess from the remaining answer choices. For difficult mathematics items, eliminate answer choices that can be reached either by a single step or by copying a number from the item.

Checklist of Skills and Concepts

Arithmetic

___ Simplifying: Fractions, Collecting Terms

___ Factoring

___ Approximation

___ The "Flying-X" Method

___ Decimal/Fraction Equivalents

___ Properties of Numbers (Odd, Even, Negative, Positive, Consecutive)

___ Sets (Union, Intersection, Elements)

___ Absolute Value

___ Percents (Change, Original Amount, Price Increase)

___ Ratios (Two-Part, Three-Part, Weighted)

___ Proportions (Direct, Indirect)

Algebra

___ Evaluation of Expressions (Rational, Radical)

___ Exponents (Integer, Rational, Negative)

___ Factoring

___ Sequence

___ Solving Single Variable Equations and Inequalities

___ Absolute Value

___ Function Math

___ Domain and Range

___ Solving Equations (Multi-Variable, Linear, Quadratic, Simultaneous)

___ Story Problems: Work (Joint Effort), Averages

Coordinate Geometry

___ Coordinate Plane

___ Slope of a Line

___ Slope-Intercept Form of a Linear Equation

___ Distance Formula

___ Graphing Linear Equations

___ Graphing First-Degree Inequalities

___ Graphing Quadratic Equations

___ Permutations of Equations and Graphs

Geometry

___ Lines and Angles (Perpendicular, Parallel, Intersecting, Big Angle/Little Angle Theorem)

___ Triangles (Equilateral, Isosceles, Acute, Obtuse, Perimeter, Area, Altitudes, Angles, Bisectors, Pythagorean Theorem)

___ Quadrilaterals (Squares, Rectangles, Rhombuses, Parallelograms, Trapezoids, Perimeter, Area)

___ Polygons (Sum of Interior Angles)

___ Circles (Chords, Tangents, Radius, Diameter, Circumference, Area)

___ Solids (Cubes, Cylinders, Spheres, Volumes, Surface Areas)

___ Complex Figures

Data Analysis

___ Graphs (Bar, Cumulative, Line)

___ Pie Charts

___ Tables (Matrices)

___ Scatterplots

___ Averages (Simple, Weighted), Median, and Mode

___ Arithmetic Probability

___ Geometric Probability

Additional Practice

To identify items for additional practice, see the Item Index at the back of this book, which offers a breakdown of items by tested concept.

Math: Student-Produced Responses

Course Concept Outline

I. Test Mechanics (p. 255)

    A. Overview (p. 255)

    B. Anatomy (Items #1–5, pp. 256–259)

    C. Pacing (p. 260)

    D. Time Trial (Items #1–5, pp. 261–262)

    E. Game Plan (p. 263)

        1. Quickly Preview the Test Section, but Skip the Directions (p. 263)
        2. Answer the Question That Is Being Asked (p. 263)
            a) Read the Question Carefully (p. 263)
            b) Pay Attention to Units (p. 263)
            c) Pay Attention to Thought-Reversers (p. 263)
        3. Code Your Answers Carefully (p. 263)
        4. Guess If You Want To (p. 263)
        5. Don't Go Calculator Crazy (p. 263)

    F. Calculator Exercise (Items #1–5, pp. 265–266)

II. Lesson (p. 267)

    A. Preliminaries[1]

        1. What Is Tested

---

[1] Some concepts in this Course Concept Outline are not illustrated through examples in your student text but may be covered by your instructor in class. They are included here to provide a complete outline of your course.

2. Directions
3. Item Profiles

B. Answer Situations Illustrated (p. 268)

1. Answer Grid Guidelines
2. Answer Is a Whole Number (Item #1, p. 268)
3. Answer Is a Decimal (Item #2, p. 268)
4. Answer Is a Fraction (Item #3, p. 268)
5. More Than One Answer Form
   a) Reduce Fractions to Lowest Terms
   b) Omit Unnecessary Zeros
   c) Watch the Units of Measure

C. Math: Student-Produced Responses Items Illustrated (Items #4–32, pp. 269–274)

III. Quizzes (p. 275)

A. Quiz I (Items #1–10, pp. 275–277)

B. Quiz II (Items #1–10, pp. 278–281)

C. Quiz III (Items #1–10, pp. 282–284)

D. Quiz IV Brain Buster (Items #1–5, pp. 285–286)

IV. Review (Items #1–13, pp. 287–291)

V. Strategy Summary (p. 293)

TEST MECHANICS

Overview

The SAT test includes three Math test sections that will be scored. One section has 20 Multiple-Choice items, with a time limit of 25 minutes; another has 16 Multiple-Choice items, with a time limit of 20 minutes; and the third has 8 Multiple-Choice items and 10 Student-Produced Responses items, or SPRs, with a time limit of 25 minutes. The SPRs are NOT multiple-choice items. Instead, you need to arrive at a numerical solution to the problem and then enter your answer by coding it on the answer sheet. (This procedure will be described later in the Math: Student-Produced Responses Lesson.)

Like the Math: Multiple-Choice items, SPRs presuppose a knowledge of pre-algebra and algebra, intermediate algebra and coordinate geometry, and plane geometry (including basic solids). These are the conceptual building blocks of the Math test sections, whether the items are Math: Multiple-Choice items or SPRs.

In most ways, SPRs are really Multiple-Choice items that are simply stripped of the answer choices. The following example is the same item stem that appears in the Math: Multiple-Choice "Basics" feature, but as an SPR it lacks the five corresponding lettered answer choices.

Example:

How many integers in the set of integers from 1 to 144, inclusive, are NOT a square of an integer?

Of course, the numerical solution is the same as when the item is presented in multiple-choice format. Since 1 is the square of 1, and 144 is the square of 12, there are a total of 12 integers in the set of integers from 1 to 144, inclusive, that are a square of an integer (1^2, 2^2, 3^2, 4^2, 5^2, 6^2, 7^2, 8^2, 9^2, 10^2, 11^2, 12^2). Therefore, there are a total of $144 - 12 = 132$ integers in the set that are NOT a square of an integer. But in this case, you must code the number "132" on the answer grid according to procedures that will be discussed later in the Math: Student-Produced Responses lesson.

Anatomy

DIRECTIONS: Solve each item. Use any available space for scratchwork.

Notes:

(1) The use of a calculator is permitted. All numbers used are real numbers.

(2) Figures that accompany problems in this test are intended to provide information useful in solving the problems. They are drawn as accurately as possible EXCEPT when it is stated in a specific problem that the figure is not drawn to scale. All figures lie in a plane unless otherwise indicated.

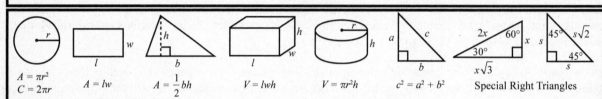

The number of degrees of arc in a circle is 360.

The sum of the measures in degrees of the angles of a triangle is 180.

Each item requires you to solve an item and mark your answer on a special answer grid. For each item, you should write your answer in the boxes at the top of each column and then fill in the ovals beneath each part of the answer you write. Here are some examples:

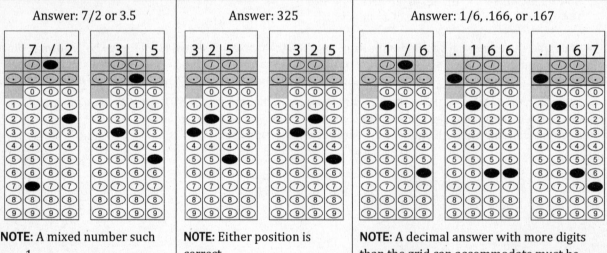

NOTE: A mixed number such as $3\frac{1}{2}$ must be gridded as 7/2 or as 3.5. If gridded as "31/2," it will be read as "thirty-one halves."

NOTE: Either position is correct.

NOTE: A decimal answer with more digits than the grid can accommodate must be truncated. A decimal such as $0.16\overline{6}$ must be gridded as .166 or .167. A less accurate value such as .16 or .17 will be scored as incorrect.

1. An hour-long class included <u>40 minutes of instruction</u>. What fraction of the hour-long class was NOT instructional?

$$\frac{20}{60} = \frac{1}{3}$$

1. *This is an arithmetic item with the thought-reverser "NOT." If 40 minutes of the 60 minutes were devoted to instruction, then 20 minutes were not instructional. Therefore, the fraction of the hour-long class that was NOT instructional is:* $\dfrac{20}{60} = \dfrac{1}{3}$.

2. Test Car *A* travels 80 miles and averages 20 miles per gallon of fuel used. If Test Car *B* travels 30 miles for each gallon of fuel used, how many miles does Test Car *B* travel on the same amount of fuel used by Test Car *A* to travel 80 miles?

$$\frac{80 \text{ miles}}{20 \text{ miles/gallon}} = 4 \text{ gallons}$$

$$4 \text{ gallons} \cdot \frac{30 \text{ miles}}{\text{gallon}} = 120$$

2. *This is a story problem that basically tests the concept of proportions. If Test Car A goes 80 miles and averages 20 miles per gallon, then it would use:*

$$\frac{80 \text{ miles}}{20 \text{ miles/gallon}} = 4 \text{ gallons}$$

Therefore, if Test Car B gets 30 miles per gallon, on 4 gallons it would travel:

$$4 \text{ gallons} \cdot \frac{30 \text{ miles}}{\text{gallon}} = 120 \text{ miles}$$

3. If $2(x-y)(x+y)=24$ and $x-y=3$, then what is the value of $x+y$?

$$2(3)(x+y)=24$$

$$\frac{6(x+y)}{6}=\frac{24}{6}$$

$$\boxed{x+y=4}$$

3. *This is an algebra item with variables, but the answer will still be a number. Since $x-y=3$, substitute 3 for $x-y$ in the given expression and solve for $x+y$:*

$$2(x-y)(x+y)=24$$
$$2(3)(x+y)=24$$
$$x+y=4$$

4. In a rectangular coordinate system, the center of a circle has coordinates $(3,4)$, and the circle touches the *x*-axis at only one point. What is the radius of the circle?

4. *This item tests coordinate geometry. Since the center has coordinates $(3,4)$ and rests on the x-axis, we have:*

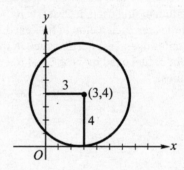

Therefore, $r=4$.

HAPPY RIDE AMUSEMENT PARK VISITORS	
Day	**Number of Visitors**
Monday	2,534
Tuesday	2,899
Wednesday	w
Thursday	2,219
Friday	2,733

5. The table above shows the number of visitors at the Happy Ride Amusement Park from Monday through Friday. If the median number of visitors for the week was 2,534, and no two days had the same number of visitors, what is the greatest possible value for w?

2533

5. *This item tests the statistical concept of median. Arrange the four known values from least to greatest: 2,219; **2,534**; 2,733; 2,899. For 2,534 to be the median, w must be less than 2,534. It doesn't have to be the smallest of the five values; it just has to be smaller than 2,534. And the greatest integer less than 2,534 is 2,533. (The value coded on the answer grid will not include the comma: 2533. But again, the coding procedure will be described later in the Math: Student-Produced Responses Lesson.)*

Pacing

When you think about pacing for the SPRs, you have to do so in the context of the Math test section that contains both Multiple-Choice items and SPRs. This section will have 8 Multiple-Choice items and 10 SPR items, with a total time limit of 25 minutes.

MATH TEST SECTION with SPRs (8 Multiple-Choice items, 10 SPRs; 25 minutes)			
Type of Item	**Item Number**	**Time to Spend per Item**	**Remaining Time**
Multiple-Choice	1–4	60 seconds	21 minutes
	5–8	60 seconds	15 minutes
Student-Produced Responses	9–14	70 seconds	8 minutes
	15–18	120 seconds	0 minutes

As the pacing table shows, you'll spend more time on SPRs than on the Multiple-Choice items. One reason for this is that there are two more SPRs than there are Multiple-Choice items. Another reason is that it takes longer to code in the answer to an SPR item than it does to code in the one circle for a Multiple-Choice item. With an SPR item, you need to write down your answer, making sure to include a decimal or a slash if required. Then, you have to code the whole sequence of numbers and symbols. A third reason that you will spend more time on SPRs than on Multiple-Choice items is that you will not be able to use some of the quicker strategies like the "plug and chug" method. You will have to work from the start instead of taking a shortcut. So, it takes a little longer, and the times suggested in the chart take that into account.

Time Trial

(5 Items; 6 minutes)

DIRECTIONS: Solve each item. Use any available space for scratchwork.

Notes:

(1) The use of a calculator is permitted. All numbers used are real numbers.

(2) Figures that accompany problems in this test are intended to provide information useful in solving the problems. They are drawn as accurately as possible EXCEPT when it is stated in a specific problem that the figure is not drawn to scale. All figures lie in a plane unless otherwise indicated.

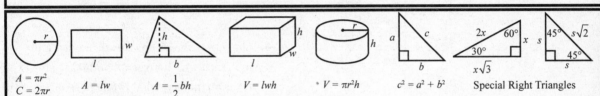

$A = \pi r^2$
$C = 2\pi r$ $A = lw$ $A = \frac{1}{2}bh$ $V = lwh$ $V = \pi r^2 h$ $c^2 = a^2 + b^2$ Special Right Triangles

The number of degrees of arc in a circle is 360.

The sum of the measures in degrees of the angles of a triangle is 180.

Each item requires you to solve an item and mark your answer on a special answer grid. For each item, you should write your answer in the boxes at the top of each column and then fill in the ovals beneath each part of the answer you write. Here are some examples:

Answer: 7/2 or 3.5	Answer: 325	Answer: 1/6, .166, or .167

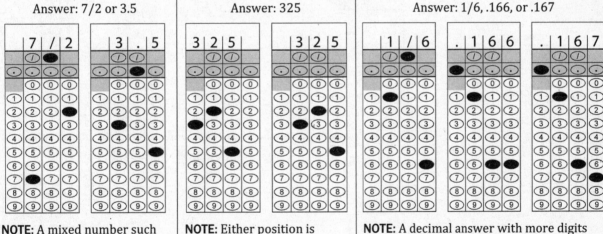

NOTE: A mixed number such as $3\frac{1}{2}$ must be gridded as 7/2 or as 3.5. If gridded as "31/2," it will be read as "thirty-one halves."

NOTE: Either position is correct.

NOTE: A decimal answer with more digits than the grid can accommodate must be truncated. A decimal such as $0.16\overline{6}$ must be gridded as .166 or .167. A less accurate value such as .16 or .17 will be scored as incorrect.

1. A recipe for spaghetti sauce uses 4 gallons of tomatoes to make 32 servings. At this rate, how many gallons of tomatoes are needed to make 144 servings of spaghetti sauce?

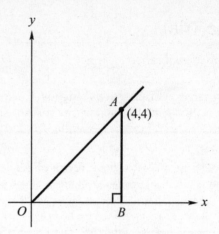

4. Line *l* (not shown) passes through *O* and intersects $\overline{AB}$ between *A* and *B* at point (x, y). If *y* is an integer, what is one possible value of the slope of line *l*?

2. The perimeter of a rectangular garden is 280 feet. If the length of one side of the garden is 60 feet, what is the area of the garden, in square feet?

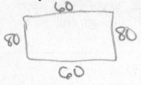

$A = lw$

$A = (60)(80)$

$A = 4800$

5. If $f(x) = x^2 + 32$, what is the positive number *n* such that $2[f(n)] = f(2n)$?

3. If $2^{3x} = 4^{x+1}$, what is the value of *x*?

Game Plan

Quickly Preview the Test Section, but Skip the Directions

As you get started, take a few seconds to preview the Math test section. It's 99.99% certain that you're going to find everything in place and just as you expected. But a quick overview will guarantee against any unanticipated changes. Do NOT, however, read the directions. Remind yourself of your pacing plan and then get to work.

Answer the Question That Is Being Asked

Read the Question Carefully

Some problems are fairly simple, but others are more complex, particularly practical word problems and more difficult geometry problems. The more complex the question, the easier it is to misread and set off down the wrong track. If the question is very long, then underline the key part of the question.

Pay Attention to Units

Some items require you to convert units (e.g., feet to inches or hours to minutes). The item stem will tell you what units to use, and if the test-writer senses any possible confusion, the units for the answer choices will be emphasized—underlined or in boldface or capitalized. When you see a word emphasized with any of those signals, circle it and put a star beside it. It is very important.

Pay Attention to Thought-Reversers

A thought-reverser is any word, such as "not," "except," or "but," that turns a question inside out. Make sure that you mark the thought-reverser so that it is staring you in the face as you work the problem.

Code Your Answers Carefully

With the Math: Multiple-Choice items, coding choices is a fairly simple process: locate the circle and fill it in. Here, however, you must enter your answer in the answer grids provided, and then code each element—number and "slash" or decimal, if required—in the corresponding circles. Later in the Math: Student-Produced Responses Lesson, you'll review all of the detailed rules for entering the information. For now, just remember to obey those rules, or you won't receive credit for your response.

Guess If You Want To

As with other sections of the test, if you are unsure of an answer, you should make an educated guess and move on. When applying this strategy to SPRs, consider the following:

- First, there is no penalty for a wrong answer to an SPR item, so a wrong answer will not hurt your score.

- Second, if you have worked on a problem but are not sure of your method or your answer, it's still worth taking the time to make a guess.

- However, if you literally have no idea about the item, it's a waste of time to code in an answer when this time could be more profitably spent working on another item.

Don't Go Calculator Crazy

Just because you are allowed to use a calculator on the test does not mean that you should try to solve every problem with your calculator. In fact, for most problems, the calculator is the less efficient method of arriving at a solution. Assume, for example, that you have to do the following arithmetic to get your answer: $\left(\frac{2}{3}\right)\left(\frac{7}{4}\right)\left(\frac{1}{6}\right)$.

Since this problem involves single digit multiplication, it's going to be easier to do the arithmetic with a pencil than with a calculator: $\left(\frac{2}{3}\right)\left(\frac{7}{4}\right)\left(\frac{1}{6}\right)=\frac{2\cdot7\cdot1}{3\cdot4\cdot6}=\frac{14}{72}=\frac{7}{36}$. By all means, use the calculator when necessary since it will be a definite advantage, but don't automatically assume that every problem requires its use.

Calculator Exercise

This exercise is designed to illustrate when and when not to use your calculator. Make sure that the calculator you bring to the SAT test is one with which you are thoroughly familiar. You may bring any of the following types of calculators: graphing, four-function, or scientific. Although no item requires the use of a calculator, a calculator may be helpful to answer some items. The calculator may be useful for any item that involves complex arithmetic computations, but it cannot take the place of understanding how to set up a mathematical item. The degree to which you can use your calculator will depend on its features. Answers are on page 625.

DIRECTIONS: Label each of the items that follow according to one of the following categories.

Category 1: A calculator would be very useful (saves valuable test time).

Category 2: A calculator might or might not be useful.

Category 3: A calculator would be counterproductive (wastes valuable test time).

---

1. If $2m + 4n$ is equal to 175 percent of $4n$, what is the value of $\dfrac{m}{n}$?

2. A company distributes samplers that include 1 jar of jam and 2 jars of jelly. If the company makes 4 different jams and 4 different jellies, how many different samplers are possible?

3. Lyle played in 5 basketball games and scored at least 1 point in each game. If Lyle scored an average of 8 points for the 5 games, what is the greatest possible number of points he could have scored in any one game?

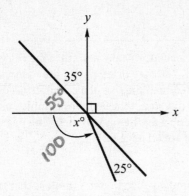

NOTE: Figure not drawn to scale.

4. In the figure above, what is the value of x?

5. Let the function $g(x)$ be defined by

$g(x) = 12 + \dfrac{x^2}{9}$. If $g(3n) = 7n$, what is one

possible value of n?

LESSON

The items in this section accompany the in-class review of the skills and concepts tested by the Student-Produced Responses part of the SAT Math test sections. You will work through the items with your instructor in class. Answers are on page 625.

DIRECTIONS: Solve each item. Use any available space for scratchwork.

Notes:

(1) The use of a calculator is permitted. All numbers used are real numbers.

(2) Figures that accompany problems in this test are intended to provide information useful in solving the problems. They are drawn as accurately as possible EXCEPT when it is stated in a specific problem that the figure is not drawn to scale. All figures lie in a plane unless otherwise indicated.

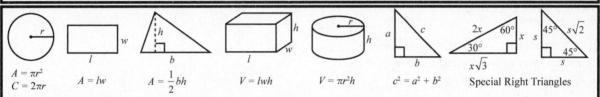

$A = \pi r^2$
$C = 2\pi r$

$A = lw$

$A = \frac{1}{2}bh$

$V = lwh$

$V = \pi r^2 h$

$c^2 = a^2 + b^2$

Special Right Triangles

The number of degrees of arc in a circle is 360.
The sum of the measures in degrees of the angles of a triangle is 180.

Each item requires you to solve an item and mark your answer on a special answer grid. For each item, you should write your answer in the boxes at the top of each column and then fill in the ovals beneath each part of the answer you write. Here are some examples:

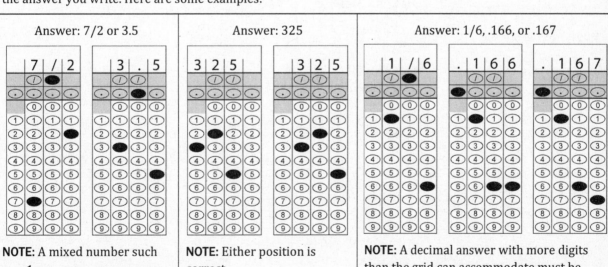

Answer: 7/2 or 3.5	Answer: 325	Answer: 1/6, .166, or .167

NOTE: A mixed number such as $3\frac{1}{2}$ must be gridded as 7/2 or as 3.5. If gridded as "31/2," it will be read as "thirty-one halves."

NOTE: Either position is correct.

NOTE: A decimal answer with more digits than the grid can accommodate must be truncated. A decimal such as $0.16\overline{6}$ must be gridded as .166 or .167. A less accurate value such as .16 or .17 will be scored as incorrect.

Answer Is a Whole Number

1. What number increased by 25 equals twice the number?

Answer Is a Decimal

2. A fence runs along the entire perimeter of a rectangular area 2.8 yards by 4 yards. What is the length, in yards, of the fence?

Answer Is a Fraction

3. At State College, one-fourth of the students are from abroad. Of those from abroad, one-eighth are from China. What fraction of the student body is from China?

Math: Student-Produced Responses Items Illustrated

4. What is the value of $\dfrac{2}{3} - \dfrac{5}{8}$?

5. What is the value of $65(1) + 65(2) + 65(3) + 65(4)$?

650

6. A jar contains 15 pennies and 25 nickels. Expressed in lowest terms, what fraction of the coins are pennies?

$\dfrac{15}{25}$

3 / 5

7. Matinee ticket prices are $1.50 for children and $3.50 for adults. Regular ticket prices are $4.50 for children and $6.50 for adults. If 3 adults and 1 child attend a matinee, what percentage of the regular price will they pay?

8. If the average of 8, 10, 15, 20, and x is 11, what is x?

$$8+10+15+20 = 53$$
$$+\ 2$$
$$55$$

$$55 \div 5 = 11$$

2

9. If $x = 14$, what is the value of $2x - (2 + x)$?

1 2

10. If $3x + y = 33$ and $x + y = 17$, then what is the value of *x*?

$\dfrac{3x}{3} + y = \dfrac{33}{3}$

$y = 11$

$x + 11 = 17$
$-11 \quad -11$
$\overline{}$
$x = 6$

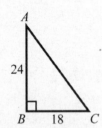

11. In the figure above, what is the length of $\overline{AC}$?

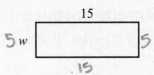

12. In the figure above, if the perimeter of the rectangle is 40, what is the area of the rectangle?

13. If a circle with radius 0.25 is inscribed in a square, what is the area of the square?

14. If the price of a book increases from $10.00 to $12.50, what is the percent increase in price?

15. Boys and girls belong to the chess club. There are 36 people in the club, 15 of whom are girls. In lowest terms, what fraction of the club are boys?

$$\frac{21}{36} \rightarrow \frac{7}{12}$$

16. Jason built a fence around the perimeter of his rectangular garden. The width of the garden is 2.8 yards, and the length is twice the width. How many yards of fencing did Jason use?

$$w = 2.8 \text{ yds}$$
$$2w = \text{length}$$
$$5.6 \text{ yds} = \text{length}$$

$$5.6 + 5.6 + 2.8 + 2.8 =$$
$$16.8 \text{ yds}$$

17. If $x = 9$, what is the value of $x^2 + 2x - 9$?

18. For all numbers, $x \blacktriangle y = 2xy$. What is $1.5 \blacktriangle 2.5$?

19. If $x = 3y - 1$ and $x + y = 15$, what is the value of x?

$$3y - 1 + y = 15$$
$$4y - 1 = 15$$
$$\underline{+1 \quad +1}$$
$$\frac{4y}{4} = \frac{16}{4}$$
$$y = 4$$
$$x = 3(4) - 1$$
$$x = 11$$

20. Jane and Hector have the same birthday. When Hector was 36, Jane was 30. How old was Jane when Hector was twice her age?

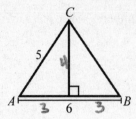

21. In the figure above, what is the area of isosceles △*ABC*?

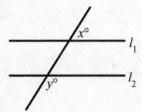

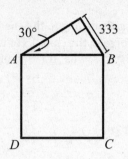

23. In the figure above, what is the perimeter of square *ABCD*?

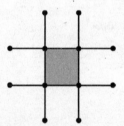

22. In the figure above, if l_1 and l_2 are parallel, what is $x + y$?

24. In the figure above, equally spaced points are joined by line segments that intersect each other at 90 degrees. If the total length of the four largest line segments in the figure is 24, what is the area of the shaded part?

25. Su Li made $45 working as a mother's helper. She spent $\frac{1}{5}$ of the money, deposited $\frac{1}{3}$ of the remainder in the bank, and kept the rest for expenses. What fraction of the original $45 did she keep?

Day	Sales
Monday	$40
Tuesday	$60
Wednesday	$80
Thursday	$20
Friday	$50

27. What is the average (arithmetic mean) daily sales in dollars for the five days shown in the table above?

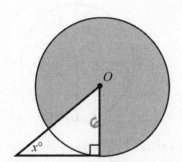

NOTE: Figure not drawn to scale.

26. In the figure above, the circle with center O has a radius of 6. If the area of the shaded region is 30π, what is the value of x?

28. If the sum of two consecutive integers is 29, what is the least of these integers?

29. If a jar of 300 black and white marbles contains 156 white marbles, what percent of the marbles is black?

$$\frac{144}{300}$$

30. Mr. Wahl spends $\frac{1}{3}$ of his day in meetings, $\frac{1}{6}$ of his day on the phone, and $\frac{1}{8}$ of his day answering questions. What fraction of his day can be devoted to other things?

31. Line l, with a slope of $\frac{1}{2}$, passes through the points $\left(0, \frac{1}{4}\right)$ and $(2, y)$. What is the value of y?

Smith 30%
120
Jones 45%
180
Undecided 25%
100

32. A total of 400 voters responded to the survey represented by the pie chart above. How many more respondents were in favor of Jones than Smith?

180
120
100

QUIZZES

This section contains four Math: Student-Produced Responses quizzes. Complete each quiz under timed conditions. Use any available space in the section for scratch work. Answers are on page 625.

Quiz I

(10 items; 15 minutes)

> **DIRECTIONS:** Solve each item. Use any available space for scratchwork.

Notes:

(1) The use of a calculator is permitted. All numbers used are real numbers.

(2) Figures that accompany problems in this test are intended to provide information useful in solving the problems. They are drawn as accurately as possible EXCEPT when it is stated in a specific problem that the figure is not drawn to scale. All figures lie in a plane unless otherwise indicated.

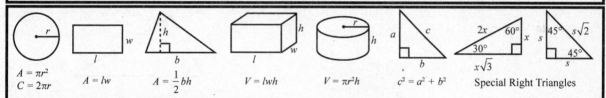

$A = \pi r^2$
$C = 2\pi r$ 　　　$A = lw$ 　　　$A = \frac{1}{2}bh$ 　　　$V = lwh$ 　　　$V = \pi r^2 h$ 　　　$c^2 = a^2 + b^2$ 　　　Special Right Triangles

The number of degrees of arc in a circle is 360.
The sum of the measures in degrees of the angles of a triangle is 180.

Each item requires you to solve an item and mark your answer on a special answer grid. For each item, you should write your answer in the boxes at the top of each column and then fill in the ovals beneath each part of the answer you write. Here are some examples:

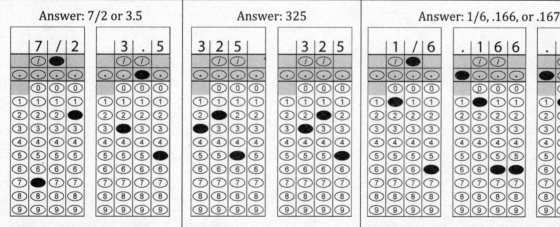

Answer: 7/2 or 3.5	Answer: 325	Answer: 1/6, .166, or .167

NOTE: A mixed number such as $3\frac{1}{2}$ must be gridded as 7/2 or as 3.5. If gridded as "31/2," it will be read as "thirty-one halves."

NOTE: Either position is correct.

NOTE: A decimal answer with more digits than the grid can accommodate must be truncated. A decimal such as $0.16\overline{6}$ must be gridded as .166 or .167. A less accurate value such as .16 or .17 will be scored as incorrect.

1. The difference between x and $3x$ is greater than 7 but less than 11. If x is an integer, what is one possible value of x?

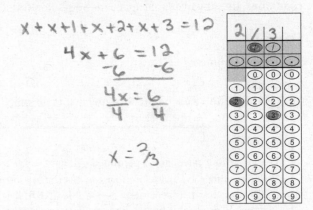

3. In the figure above, if $\overline{PT}$ has a length of 12, then what is the value of x?

$$x + x + 1 + x + 2 + x + 3 = 12$$
$$4x + 6 = 12$$
$$ -6 \quad -6$$
$$\frac{4x}{4} = \frac{6}{4}$$
$$x = \frac{2}{3}$$

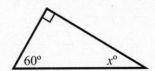

2. If p and q are integers such that $p > q > 0$ and $p + q = 12$, what is the least possible value of $p - q$?

4. In the figure above, what is the value of x?

5. As part of an orienteering exercise, a hiker walks due north from point P for 3 miles to point Q and then due east for 4 miles to point R. What is the straight-line distance (in miles) from point R to point P?

6. If 0.129914 is rounded off to the nearest hundredth, what is the value of the hundredths digit?

7. The average of 4, 5, x, and y is 6, and the average of x, z, 8, and 9 is 8. What is the value of $z - y$?

8. Copy Machine X produces 20 copies per minute, and Copy Machine Y produces 30 copies per minute. If Y is started 1 minute after X, how many minutes after X is started will Y have produced the same number of copies as X?

9. A triangle has sides of x, 4, and 5. If x is an integer, what is the maximum value of x?

10. Ray is now 10 years older than Cindy. In 8 years, Ray will be twice as old as Cindy is then. How old is Cindy now?

Quiz II

(10 items; 15 minutes)

DIRECTIONS: Solve each item. Use any available space for scratchwork.

Notes:

(1) The use of a calculator is permitted. All numbers used are real numbers.

(2) Figures that accompany problems in this test are intended to provide information useful in solving the problems. They are drawn as accurately as possible EXCEPT when it is stated in a specific problem that the figure is not drawn to scale. All figures lie in a plane unless otherwise indicated.

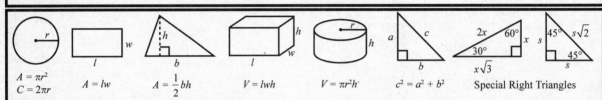

$A = \pi r^2$
$C = 2\pi r$ $A = lw$ $A = \frac{1}{2}bh$ $V = lwh$ $V = \pi r^2 h$ $c^2 = a^2 + b^2$ Special Right Triangles

The number of degrees of arc in a circle is 360.

The sum of the measures in degrees of the angles of a triangle is 180.

Each item requires you to solve an item and mark your answer on a special answer grid. For each item, you should write your answer in the boxes at the top of each column and then fill in the ovals beneath each part of the answer you write. Here are some examples:

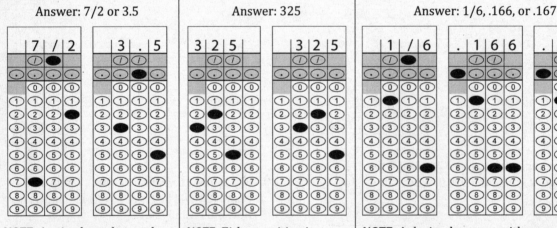

Answer: 7/2 or 3.5   Answer: 325   Answer: 1/6, .166, or .167

NOTE: A mixed number such as $3\frac{1}{2}$ must be gridded as 7/2 or as 3.5. If gridded as "31/2," it will be read as "thirty-one halves."

NOTE: Either position is correct.

NOTE: A decimal answer with more digits than the grid can accommodate must be truncated. A decimal such as $0.16\overline{6}$ must be gridded as .166 or .167. A less accurate value such as .16 or .17 will be scored as incorrect.

1. In the figure above, what is the maximum number of different diagonals that can be drawn in the pentagon?

2. If $4x = 2(2+x)$ and $6y = 3(2+y)$, then what is the value of $2x + 3y$?

3. Let the "JOSH" of a number be defined as 3 less than 3 times the number. What number is equal to its "JOSH"?

4. Machine A produces flue covers at a uniform rate of 2,000 per hour. Machine B produces flue covers at a uniform rate of 5,000 in $2\frac{1}{2}$ hours. After $7\frac{1}{4}$ hours, Machine A has produced how many more flue covers than Machine B?

5. $\frac{1}{100}$ is the ratio of 0.1 to what number?

6. In the figure above, $\overline{AB} \parallel \overline{ED}$ and $\overline{AC} = \overline{BC}$. If $\angle BED$ is 50°, then what is the value of x?

7. At NJL High School, $\frac{1}{4}$ of the student population are seniors, $\frac{1}{5}$ are juniors, and $\frac{1}{3}$ are sophomores. If the rest of NJL High School's student population consists of 390 freshmen, what is the total student population of NJL High School?

8. From the town of Williston Park to Albertson, there are 3 different roads. From the town of Albertson to Mineola, there are 5 roads. How many different road paths are there to go from Willistown Park to Mineola through Albertson?

9. If 12 candies cost $1.70, how many of these candies can be bought for $10.20?

10. Two roads intersect at right angles. A pole is 30 meters from one road and 40 meters from the other road. How far (in meters) is the pole from the point where the roads intersect?

Quiz III

(10 items; 15 minutes)

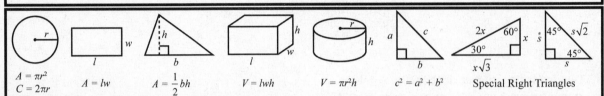

DIRECTIONS: Solve each item. Use any available space for scratchwork.

Notes:

(1) The use of a calculator is permitted. All numbers used are real numbers.

(2) Figures that accompany problems in this test are intended to provide information useful in solving the problems. They are drawn as accurately as possible EXCEPT when it is stated in a specific problem that the figure is not drawn to scale. All figures lie in a plane unless otherwise indicated.

$$A = \pi r^2 \qquad A = lw \qquad A = \frac{1}{2}bh \qquad V = lwh \qquad V = \pi r^2 h \qquad c^2 = a^2 + b^2$$
$$C = 2\pi r$$

Special Right Triangles

The number of degrees of arc in a circle is 360.

The sum of the measures in degrees of the angles of a triangle is 180.

Each item requires you to solve an item and mark your answer on a special answer grid. For each item, you should write your answer in the boxes at the top of each column and then fill in the ovals beneath each part of the answer you write. Here are some examples:

Answer: 7/2 and 3.5	Answer: 325	Answer: 1/6, .166, or .167

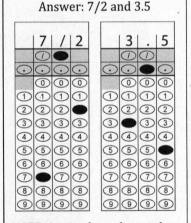

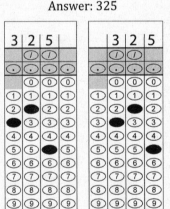

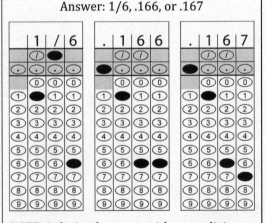

NOTE: A mixed number such as $3\frac{1}{2}$ must be gridded as 7/2 or as 3.5. If gridded as "31/2," it will be read as "thirty-one halves."

NOTE: Either position is correct.

NOTE: A decimal answer with more digits than the grid can accommodate must be truncated. A decimal such as $0.16\overline{6}$ must be gridded as .166 or .167. A less accurate value such as .16 or .17 will be scored as incorrect.

1. What is the value of $\left(2a^2 - a^3\right)^2$ when $a = -1$?

2. A jar contains 2 red marbles, 3 green marbles, and 4 orange marbles. If a marble is picked at random, what is the probability that the marble is not orange?

3. In the country of Glup, 1 glop is 3 glips, and 4 glips are 5 globs. How many globs are 2 glops?

4. If $\dfrac{k}{3} + \dfrac{k}{4} = 1$, then what is the value of k?

5. If the area of a square with side x is 5, what is the area of a square with side $3x$?

6. If $2x + 2y = 6$ and $3x - 3y = 9$, what is the value of $x^2 - y^2$?

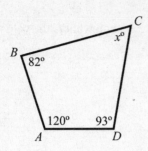

7. In the figure above, *ABCD* is a quadrilateral. If the measure of $\angle A$ is 120°, the measure of $\angle B$ is 82°, and the measure of $\angle D$ is 93°, what is the value of *x*?

9. If $\dfrac{4}{5}$ is subtracted from its reciprocal, then what value is the result?

10. If the ratio of $a:b$ is $1:5$ and the ratio of $b:c$ is $3:2$, then the ratio of $(2a+c):c$ can expressed as $8:w$. What is the value of *w*?

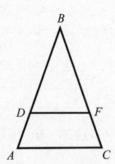

8. In the figure above, $\triangle ABC$ is similar to $\triangle DBF$. If $\overline{DF}=3$, $\overline{BD}=\overline{BF}=6$, and $\overline{AC}=4$, what is the perimeter of $\triangle ABC$?

Quiz IV Brain Buster
(5 items; 9 minutes)

DIRECTIONS: Solve each item. Use any available space for scratchwork.

Notes:

(1) The use of a calculator is permitted. All numbers used are real numbers.

(2) Figures that accompany problems in this test are intended to provide information useful in solving the problems. They are drawn as accurately as possible EXCEPT when it is stated in a specific problem that the figure is not drawn to scale. All figures lie in a plane unless otherwise indicated.

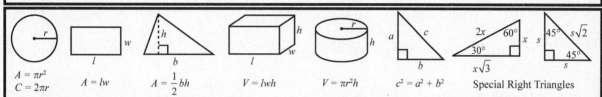

$A = \pi r^2$
$C = 2\pi r$ $A = lw$ $A = \frac{1}{2}bh$ $V = lwh$ $V = \pi r^2 h$ $c^2 = a^2 + b^2$ Special Right Triangles

The number of degrees of arc in a circle is 360.
The sum of the measures in degrees of the angles of a triangle is 180.

Each item requires you to solve an item and mark your answer on a special answer grid. For each item, you should write your answer in the boxes at the top of each column and then fill in the ovals beneath each part of the answer you write. Here are some examples:

Answer: 7/2 and 3.5	Answer: 325	Answer: 1/6, .166, or .167

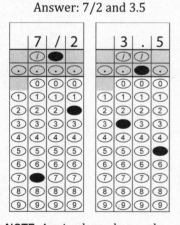   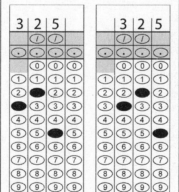

NOTE: A mixed number such as $3\frac{1}{2}$ must be gridded as 7/2 or as 3.5. If gridded as "31/2," it will be read as "thirty-one halves."

NOTE: Either position is correct.

NOTE: A decimal answer with more digits than the grid can accommodate must be truncated. A decimal such as $0.16\overline{6}$ must be gridded as .166 or .167. A less accurate value such as .16 or .17 will be scored as incorrect.

1. If $f(x) = \dfrac{x^2 + x}{x - 1}$ and $g(x) = 2x + 3$, then

$g(f(-2)) = ?$

2. Set A contains all the positive factors of 24. Set B contains all the prime numbers less than 20. How many numbers are elements in both set A and set B?

3. If $x - y = 7$ and $x^2 - y^2 = 35$, what is $x + y$?

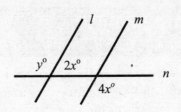

4. In the figure above, line l is parallel to line m. What is the value of x?

5. Let the operation $\odot$ be defined by $x \odot y = xy + y$ for all numbers x and y. If $2 \odot 3 = z \odot 1$, what is the value of z?

REVIEW

This section contains additional Math: Student-Produced Responses items for further practice. Answers are on page 626.

DIRECTIONS: Solve each item. Use any available space for scratchwork.

Notes:

(1) The use of a calculator is permitted. All numbers used are real numbers.

(2) Figures that accompany problems in this test are intended to provide information useful in solving the problems. They are drawn as accurately as possible EXCEPT when it is stated in a specific problem that the figure is not drawn to scale. All figures lie in a plane unless otherwise indicated.

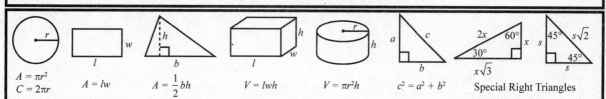

$$A = \pi r^2$$
$$C = 2\pi r$$

$$A = lw$$

$$A = \frac{1}{2}bh$$

$$V = lwh$$

$$V = \pi r^2 h$$

$$c^2 = a^2 + b^2$$

Special Right Triangles

The number of degrees of arc in a circle is 360.

The sum of the measures in degrees of the angles of a triangle is 180.

Each item requires you to solve an item and mark your answer on a special answer grid. For each item, you should write your answer in the boxes at the top of each column and then fill in the ovals beneath each part of the answer you write. Here are some examples:

Answer: 7/2 or 3.5	Answer: 325	Answer: 1/6, .166, or .167

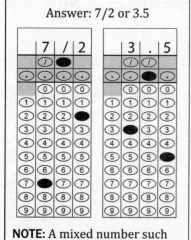

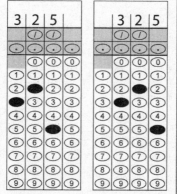

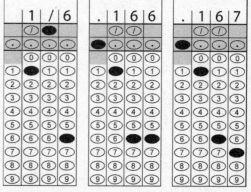

NOTE: A mixed number such as $3\frac{1}{2}$ must be gridded as 7/2 or as 3.5. If gridded as "31/2," it will be read as "thirty-one halves."

NOTE: Either position is correct.

NOTE: A decimal answer with more digits than the grid can accommodate must be truncated. A decimal such as $0.16\overline{6}$ must be gridded as .166 or .167. A less accurate value such as .16 or .17 will be scored as incorrect.

1. In a three-hour examination of 350 questions, there are 50 mathematical problems. If twice as much time should be allowed for each mathematical problem as for each of the other questions, how many minutes should be spent on the mathematical problems?

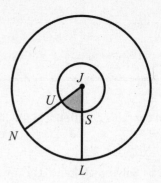

3. Given the circles above, if radius $\overline{JN}$ is 3 times the length of $\overline{JU}$, then the ratio of the shaded area to the area of sector *NJL* is $1:b$. What is the value of *b*?

2. In a pantry, there are 28 cans of vegetables of which 8 have labels with white lettering, 18 have labels with green lettering, and 8 have labels with neither white nor green lettering. How many cans have both white and green lettering?

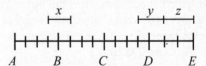

4. In the figure above, points *B*, *C*, and *D* divide $\overline{AE}$ into 4 equal parts. $\overline{AB}$, $\overline{BC}$, and $\overline{CD}$ are divided into 4 equal parts as shown above. $\overline{DE}$ is divided into 3 equal parts as shown. What does $\dfrac{x+z}{y}$ equal?

5. The shortest distance from the center of a circle to a chord is 5. If the length of the chord is 24, what is the length of the radius of the circle?

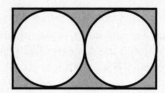

7. In the figure above, two circles are tangent to each other and each is tangent to 3 sides of the rectangle. If the radius of each circle is 3, then the area of the shaded portion is $a - 18\pi$. What is the value of a?

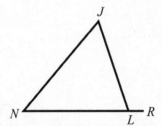

6. In the figure above, $\angle N = (9x - 40)°$, $\angle J = (4x + 30)°$, and $\angle JLR = (8x + 40)°$. What is the measure of $\angle J$? (Do not grid the degree symbol.)

8. The length of the line segment with end points that are $(3, -2)$ and $(-4, 5)$ is $b\sqrt{2}$. What is the value of b?

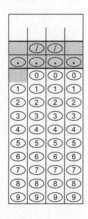

9. A car travels from Town A to Town B, a distance of 360 miles, in 9 hours. How many hours would the same trip have taken had the car traveled 5 mph faster?

10. The area of a circle that is inscribed in a square with a diagonal of 8 is $a\pi$. What is the value of a?

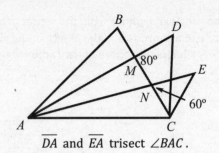

$\overline{DA}$ and $\overline{EA}$ trisect $\angle BAC$.

11. In the figure above, $\angle DMC = 80°$ and $\angle ENC = 60°$. How many degrees is $\angle BAC$? (Do not grid the degree symbol.)

12. Mrs. Smith has a total of x dollars to donate to various charities. If Mrs. Smith gives $73 to each charity, she will be $4 short; if she gives $70 to each charity, she will have $56 left over. What is the value of x?

13. $a - b = b - c = c - a$. What is the value of $\dfrac{2a + 3b}{c}$?

STRATEGY SUMMARY

General Strategies:

1. Remember the following details about the grid:

    - grid answers are no more than four digits in length;

    - grid answers, if decimals (non-zero digits to the right of the decimal point), are between .001 and 99.9;

    - grid answers, if fractions, are between 1/99 and 99/1; and

    - grid answers are always positive.

2. Write answers so that the final digit is on the right.

3. Make sure to fill in the circles corresponding to the answer.

4. A decimal point fills one whole space, and therefore it counts as one of the four digits.

5. A fraction bar fills one whole space, and therefore it counts as one of the four digits.

6. Reduce fractions to lowest terms when necessary.

7. Omit unnecessary zeros.

8. Watch the units of measure.

Pay attention to thought-reversers (in all capital letters) and underlined words. Items are arranged according to a ladder of difficulty. The material tested is the same as that for the Math: Multiple-Choice items—strategies and concepts are also the same.

Additional Practice

To identify items for additional practice, see the Item Index at the back of this book, which offers a breakdown of items by tested concept.

Writing

Course Concept Outline

I. Test Mechanics (p. 299)

  A. Overview (Multiple-Choice) (p. 299)

  B. Anatomy (Multiple-Choice) (Items #1–3, pp. 300–301)

  C. Pacing (Multiple-Choice) (p. 302)

  D. Time Trial (Multiple-Choice) (Items #1–6, pp. 303–304)

  E. Game Plan (Multiple-Choice) (p. 305)

    1. Improving Sentences (p. 305)
      a) Don't Read the Directions (p. 305)
      b) Read the Sentence, Looking for Errors (p. 305)
      c) Don't Read Choice (A) (p. 305)
      d) Look for Multiple Errors (p. 305)
      e) Work Backwards from the Answer Choices (p. 305)
      f) Don't Look for Spelling or Capitalization Errors (p. 305)
      g) Make Educated Guesses (p. 305)
      h) Don't Be Afraid to Pick Choice (A) (p. 305)
    2. Identifying Sentence Errors (p. 306)
      a) Don't Read the Directions (p. 306)
      b) Read the Sentence, Looking for an Error (p. 306)
      c) Don't Look for Multiple Errors (p. 306)
      d) Work Backward from the Underlined Parts (p. 306)
      e) Don't Look for Spelling or Capitalization Errors (p. 306)
      f) Make Educated Guesses (p. 306)
      g) Don't Be Afraid to Pick Choice (E) (p. 306)
    3. Improving Paragraphs (p. 307)
      a) Don't Read the Directions (p. 307)
      b) Read the Passage First (p. 307)
      c) Compare and Contrast Answer Choices (p. 307)
      d) Make Educated Guesses (p. 307)

e) Don't Be Afraid to Pick Choice (A) (p. 307)

F. Writing Exercise (Multiple-Choice)

G. Overview (Essay) (p. 308)

H. Anatomy (Essay) (p. 309)

I. Pacing (Essay) (p. 310)

J. Time Trial (Essay) (p. 311)

K. Game Plan (Essay) (p. 313)

1. Respond to the Specific Prompt (p. 313)
2. Write Legibly (p. 313)
3. Don't Copy the Prompt (p. 313)
4. Don't Skip Lines (p. 313)
5. Use a Pencil (p. 313)
6. Be Specific (p. 313)

II. Lesson (p. 315)

A. Preliminaries[1]

1. What Is Tested
2. Directions
    a) Identifying Sentence Errors
    b) Improving Sentences
    c) Improving Paragraphs
    d) Essay
3. Item Profiles

B. Identifying Sentence Errors and Improving Sentences (p. 315)

1. Grammar (p. 315)
    a) Fragments (Items #1–3, pp. 315–316)
    b) Subject-Verb Agreement (Item #4, p. 316)
        (1) Material Inserted Between Subject and Verb (Items #5–10, p. 316)
        (2) Inverted Sentence Structure (Items #11–12, pp. 316–317)
        (3) Compound Subjects (Items #13–15, p. 317)
    c) Pronoun Usage (p. 317)
        (1) Pronouns Must Have Antecedents (Items #16–17, p. 317)
        (2) Antecedents Must Be Clear (Item #18, p. 317)
        (3) Pronoun-Antecedent Agreement (Items #19–22, pp. 317–318)
        (4) Pronouns Must Have Proper Case (Items #23–24, p. 318)
    d) Adjectives and Adverbs (p. 318)
        (1) Adjectives Modify Nouns; Adverbs Modify Verbs, Adjectives, and Other Adverbs (Items #25–26, p. 318)
        (2) Linking Verbs (Items #27–28, p. 318)
        (3) Watch for Adjectives Posing as Adverbs (Items #29–30, p. 318)
    e) Double Negatives (Items #31–32, pp. 318–319)
    f) Nouns and Noun Clauses (Items #33–37, p. 319)
2. Sentence Structure (p. 319)
    a) Run-on Sentences (Item #38, p. 319)
    b) Problems of Coordination and Subordination (Items #39–42, pp. 319–320)
    c) Faulty Parallelism (Items #43–45, p. 320)

---

[1] Some concepts in this Course Concept Outline are not illustrated through examples in your student text but may be covered by your instructor in class. They are included here to provide a complete outline of your course.

d) Incomplete Split Constructions (Items #46–47, p. 320)

     e) Verb Tense (p. 320)

       (1) Principal Parts of Verbs (Item #48, p. 320)

       (2) When to Use the Perfect Tenses (Item #49, p. 320)

       (3) The Subjunctive Mood (Item #50, p. 320)

  3. Logical Expression (p. 321)

     a) Faulty Comparisons (Items #51–56, p. 321)

     b) Illogical Tense Sequence (Items #57–60, pp. 321–322)

     c) Unintended Meanings (Item #61, p. 322)

     d) Directness (Items #62–69, pp. 322–323)

     e) Misplaced Modifiers (Items #70–72, p. 323)

  4. Clarity of Expression (p. 323)

     a) Diction and Idioms (p. 323)

       (1) Wrong Word Choice (Items #73–74, pp. 323–324)

       (2) Wrong Preposition (Items #75–76, p. 324)

       (3) Gerund versus Infinitive (Items #77–78, p. 324)

     b) Ambiguity in Scope (Item #79, p. 324)

     c) Low-Level Usage (Item #80, p. 324)

  5. Punctuation (p. 324)

     a) Commas (Items #81–97, pp. 324–326)

     b) Semicolons (Items #98–101, p. 327)

     c) Colons (Items #102–103, p. 327)

     d) End-Stop Punctuation (Item #104, p. 327)

     e) Dashes (Item #105, p. 328)

     f) Hyphens (Item #106, p. 328)

     g) Quotation Marks (Item #107, p. 328)

     h) Punctuating for Clarity (Item #108, p. 328)

  6. Identifying Sentence Errors and Improving Sentences Strategies

C. Improving Paragraphs (p. 326)

  1. How Much Emphasis to Put on Improving Paragraphs

  2. Format of Improving Paragraphs Items

     a) Ignore the Directions

     b) Typical Passage Length

     c) Types of Passage Topics

     d) Revisions Must Be In Context

  3. Strategies for Reading Passages

     a) Read the Entire Passage First

     b) Pay Attention to Relationships Between and Among Sentences

     c) Pay Attention to Development and Organization

  4. Strategies for Answering Improving Paragraphs Items

     a) Sentence Elements

     b) Paragraph Structure

     c) Passage Development

  5. Illustrative Improving Paragraphs Items (Items #109–120, pp. 329–331)

  6. Improving Paragraphs Pre-Assessment Examples

D. The SAT Essay (p. 332)

  1. Essay Scoring Guide

  2. Composing the Essay

     a) Pre-Writing

     b) Beginning the Writing Process

     c) The Introduction

     d) The Body

     e) The Conclusion

     f) Revision

3. Essay Writing Strategies
   a) Begin with the Prompt
   b) Write Only on the Assigned Topic
   c) Do Not Try to Do Too Much
   d) Outline the Essay
   e) Organize Ideas into Paragraphs
   f) Write Grammatically
   g) Punctuate and Spell Correctly
   h) Write Clearly, Concisely, and Legibly
   i) Proofread the Essay

III. Quizzes (p. 333)

A. Quiz I (Items #1–16, pp. 333–336)

B. Quiz II (Items #1–16, pp. 337–340)

C. Quiz III (Items #1–16, pp. 341–343)

D. Quiz IV Brain Buster (Items #1–16, pp. 344–347)

E. Quiz V (1 Essay, p. 348)

IV. Review (Items #1–37, pp. 351–357; 1 Essay, p. 358)

V. Strategy Summary (p. 361)

TEST MECHANICS

Overview (Multiple-Choice)

The Writing tests sections are a test of your understanding of the rules of grammar, and that announcement should be enough to strike dread into the hearts of most students: "You mean like '*i* before *e* except after *c*'?" No, that's a rule of spelling, not grammar, and the exam does not test spelling. Actually, the exam doesn't really test your knowledge of the rules of grammar either, though it does test your ability to write using those rules.

You might be asked to spot an error in a sentence.

Example:

The <u>recently</u> created wildlife <u>refuge, which</u> includes
    A   B

nearly 30 small ponds for migrating geese and ducks,

<u>were</u> made possible by substantial gifts <u>by</u> an
 C   D

anonymous donor to the Wildlife Protection Fund.

<u>No error</u>
  E

For this example, (C) is the correct answer.

Or, you might be asked to correct the error, as in the following example.

Example:

The recently created wildlife refuge, which includes
nearly 30 small ponds for migrating geese and ducks,
<u>were</u> made possible by substantial gifts by an
anonymous donor to the Wildlife Protection Fund.

(A) were
(B) was
(C) have been
(D) being
(E) have to be

For this example, the correct answer is (B) because the sentence should read "refuge...was," not "refuge...were." But you would not be asked to state the grammatical rule that explains the error or how to correct it: *a verb must agree in both number and person with its subject.*

You also will be required to edit sentences in the context of a brief passage. There are some additional issues with regard to this type of Writing item, such as ensuring consistency throughout the text and using appropriate transition phrases, but, again, you don't need to know the rules of formal grammar to do well on this type either.

Anatomy (Multiple-Choice)

> **DIRECTIONS (IMPROVING SENTENCES):**
> Improving Sentences items test correct, effective expression. Each sentence contains an underlined portion, or the entire sentence may be underlined. Following each sentence are five ways of phrasing the underlined portion. Choice (A) repeats the original; the other four choices are different. If you think the original is better than any of the other choices, choose (A); otherwise, choose one of the other choices.
>
> In choosing answers, follow the requirements of standard written English; that is, pay attention to grammar, word choice, sentence construction, and punctuation. Your choice should produce the most effective sentence—clear and precise, without awkwardness or ambiguity.

There are only two points mentioned in the directions that are worth remembering. First, of the five alternatives, the first always repeats the original. Sometimes the first choice (the original) is correct, so you don't need to make a change. Second, pick the best way of writing the sentence. The directions mention several factors like "clear" and "exact," and those will be covered in the Writing Lesson later.

1. No one in the school is <u>more happier than me</u> that we won the basketball championship.

    (A) more happier than me
    (B) as happy as me
    (C) happier than I
    (D) as happy like me
    (E) happier except me

1. (C) *The sentence contains two errors. First, "more happier" should be simply "happier." (The comparative of an adjective is usually formed by adding "-er" or "-ier" or using "more"; however, they cannot both be used together.) Second, "me" is supposed to introduce an elliptical sentence: "than me am happy." But "me" cannot be used as the subject of a sentence. For that, you need "I." (Subjects use the nominative case pronouns.)*

> **DIRECTIONS (IDENTIFYING SENTENCE ERRORS):**
> Identifying Sentence Errors items test your knowledge of grammar, usage, diction (choice of words), and idiom. Each sentence contains either no error or a single error. If there is an error, it is underlined and lettered. If the sentence contains an error, choose the one underlined portion that must be changed to produce a correct sentence. If there is no error, choose answer choice (E). In choosing answers, follow the conventions of standard written English.

Like the directions for Improving Sentences, there are only two points to remember here. First, choice (E) is always "No error," and this is the right answer when the sentence is correct as written. Second, if there is an error, choose the underlined part of the sentence that includes it. There's nothing more to the directions than those two points.

2. If I am reading the directions <u>correct</u>, we should
   A   B

   <u>have mounted</u> the thermothrockle to the housing
        C

   <u>before</u> we secured the hypotorsion. <u>No error</u>
     D   E

2. (B) *"Correct" is used to describe "reading," a verb, so it should have the characteristic adverb ending "-ly": "correctly."*

DIRECTIONS (IMPROVING PARAGRAPHS):
Improving Paragraphs items are based on passages that are early drafts of essays. Some portions of the passages need to be revised.

Read each passage and answer the items that follow. Items may be about particular sentences or parts of sentences, asking you to improve the word choice or sentence structure. Other items may refer to parts of the essay or the entire essay, asking you to consider organization or development. In making your decisions, follow the conventions of standard written English.

The directions really don't add much to the layout of Improving Paragraphs items, which is fairly self-explanatory. Basically, you read the passage and then answer the items that follow.

(1) A few years ago, when I was a small child, nearly two hundred people at the county fair got sick from *E. coli* bacteria. **(2)** A few even died. **(3)** The source of the outbreak was a Mr. Freezie that made its frozen treats from what should have been pure well water. **(4)** Unusually heavy rains the week before the fair, however, washed animal waste from the barns into the ground where it contaminated the drinking water. **(5)** The incident was one of those things that never happens, except in this case it did.

3. In the context, which of the following is the best version of sentence 2 (reproduced below)?

A few even died.

(A) (As it is now.)
(B) A few definitely died.
(C) A few even were dying.
(D) Even though a few died.
(E) While a few died.

3. (A) *Yes, a "no change" answer choice for a Writing item can be correct. In fact, it is likely to be correct about one-fifth of the time, which is just what you'd expect given that there are five choices. In this case, "As it is now" is correct because the short, concise sentence accentuates the author's point that people died.*

Pacing (Multiple-Choice)

The SAT has two multiple-choice Writing test sections. The first Writing section has a 25-minute time limit and 35 items consisting of the three types of Writing: Multiple-Choice items. This makes pacing a little tricky as you have to make sure that you don't become bogged down in the more difficult items near the beginning and therefore not get a look at the easier questions that are waiting later in the section. Here is a general guide to the pacing for this section:

MIXED WRITING TEST SECTION (35 items, 25 minutes)			
Type of Item	Item Number	Time to Spend per Item	Remaining Time
Improving Sentences	1–4	30 seconds	23 minutes
	5–8	45 seconds	20 minutes
	9–11	60 seconds	17 minutes
Identifying Sentence Errors	12–29	30 seconds	8 minutes
Improving Paragraphs	30–35	80* seconds	0 minutes

*Allocates approximate time for reading the passage across all six items.

You'll notice that all of the Identifying Sentence Errors items will take about the same time. This is because the structure of those items is so simple—there are no extra choices to read. And Improving Paragraphs items will take whatever time remains. You'll probably devote just under a minute and a half to each of those questions because they often require you to return to the passage.

The other Writing section has a 10-minute time limit and consists of 14 Improving Sentences items. You will probably find that the items become more difficult as you work through this section, so you'll need to allocate your time accordingly.

IMPROVING SENTENCES ITEMS-ONLY WRITING TEST SECTION (14 items, 10 minutes)			
Type of Item	Item Number	Time to Spend per Item	Remaining Time
Improving Sentences	1–4	30 seconds	8 minutes
	5–7	40 seconds	6 minutes
	8–11	45 seconds	3 minutes
	12–14	60 seconds	0 minutes

The tricky thing about the 10-minute Writing test section is that it is very unforgiving of timing mistakes. In the 25-minute section, if you get off track and waste time on an item, you still have time remaining to recover. In this section, however, if you spend two minutes on a problem that you've allocated 30 seconds for, then you've wasted 15 percent of your time. So, in this section, more than any other on the test, you have to pay attention to your pacing.

Time Trial (Multiple-Choice)

(*6 Items—5 minutes*)

1. The track meet begins at 10:00 a.m., so the team needs to depart from the school <u>at a reasonable early hour</u>.

   (A) at a reasonable early hour
   (B) at a reasonably early hour
   (C) during a reasonable early hour
   (D) while a reasonably early hour
   (E) at a reasonably hour that is early

2. After the broken glass and other debris were cleaned up, we realized that the thief <u>had took</u> not only the necklace but a valuable ring as well.

   (A) had took
   (B) had taken
   (C) was took
   (D) was taken
   (E) were took

3. The company <u>offers</u> a plastic key card
             A

   so that employees <u>can carry</u> it in <u>their</u> <u>wallet</u>.
                B   C   D

   <u>No error</u>
    E

4. <u>By the middle of June,</u> the foliage on the trees
       A

   and the underbrush <u>was</u> lush and green and so
               B

   thick <u>that</u> it was impossible to see <u>very far, into</u>
      C   D

   the woods. <u>No error</u>
           E

DIRECTIONS : _Items #5–6:_ The following passage is an early draft of an essay. Some portions of the passage needs to be revised.

Read the passage and answer the items that follow. Items may be about particular sentences or parts of sentences, asking you to improve the word choice or sentence structure. Other items may refer to parts of the essay or the entire essay, asking you to consider organization or development. In making your decisions, follow the conventions of standard written English.

(1) On my vacation to Alaska, I took a trip to Porcupine. (2) In 1905, Porcupine was a thriving town of 2,000 people, retail stores, and a post office. (3) Hardly any of the town remains today, but there is still gold there, and our guide showed us how to pan for gold. (4) It's easy to learn how, and anyone can do it.

(5) The technique of panning depends on the weight of gold. (6) It's about 20 times heavier than water, so the gold stays at the bottom of a stream and gets caught in the sand in slow flowing water around bends and along the edge of the stream. (7) It can also get stuck in small crevices of rock and even wedged into pieces of wood.

(8) You need to find where the gold is. (9) Then concentrate on those areas that are most likely to trap the little bits of gold. (10) To start panning, put a few handfuls of material into your gold pan and submerge the pan in the water of the stream. (11) Hold the pan under the surface and move it in a circular motion so that the lighter material sloshes over the edge. (12) Keep moving the pan until about half the original material has been carried away. (13) Lift the pan out of the water, tilt it toward the side with the riffles (the small ridges), and swirl until the water is gone. (14) Repeat this process until nearly all the material is gone. (15) Finally, use a small stream of water suction pipette to sort the gold from the remaining debris.

5. Which of the following sentences inserted following sentence 4 at the end of the first paragraph would best introduce the remaining paragraphs of the essay?

   (A) Gold is one of the most valuable substances on earth.
   (B) Just follow these simple instructions.
   (C) I try to do a lot of different things on my vacations.
   (D) Did you even know that there was a gold rush in Alaska?
   (E) Porcupine, the town, was named for the small quilled animal.

6. The best placement for the final sentence in Paragraph 2 would be:

   (A) where it is now.
   (B) as the first sentence of Paragraph 2.
   (C) in Paragraph 2, following the sentence ending "...weight of gold."
   (D) as the first sentence of Paragraph 3.
   (E) as the last sentence of Paragraph 3.

Game Plan (Multiple-Choice)

Improving Sentences

In the mixed Writing section, you'll do the types of items in the order presented, and in the Improving Sentences-only section, you'll obviously do only Improving Sentences items. Either way, you'll be working with these items first.

Don't Read the Directions

By the time you get to the test, you'll know what to do when you see the Writing sections. Some of the items have underlined parts with different choices for writing those parts—these are the Improving Sentences items. Do a quick preview and let the appearance of the items on the page be all the direction you need, and then get started immediately.

Read the Sentence, Looking for Errors

Begin by reading the sentence, looking for an error or errors. If you can spot an error, then you're more than halfway home. Grammar principles that will be covered are provided in the Writing Course Concept Outline on pages 295-298. You can treat this outline as a checklist of important things to look for in Improving Sentences items.

Don't Read Choice (A)

Choice (A) always repeats the original, underlined part of the sentence. There is absolutely no reason to re-read that part, so skip choice (A).

Look for Multiple Errors

Some Improving Sentences items contain multiple errors. If you can correct even one error, you can eliminate answer choices on the basis that they fail to correct the original.

Work Backward from the Answer Choices

If you are having difficulty locating the right answer, use the answer choices to help you. Compare each answer choice with the original, and explain to yourself what the important difference is between the two of them. This can help you see an error that you may have overlooked. Additionally, you can compare choices to each other, asking yourself, in what way is this choice better or worse than the other one? Again, this technique can help you uncover a hidden error and make the right choice.

Don't Look for Spelling or Capitalization Errors

These topics are not tested, so don't waste your time looking for errors of this sort. Even if you think you've found a spelling mistake (and you're almost certain to be wrong anyway), there is nothing you can do with the information. The correct response is correct because it "follows the requirements of standard written English."

Make Educated Guesses

You should be able to eliminate some of the Improving Sentences answer choices because they introduce new errors that are not found in the original. Or, a choice may fail to correct an error that you know to be in the underlined part of the sentence. If you are able to eliminate even one answer choice, for any reason whatsoever, then you must guess—because you are making an educated guess.

Don't Be Afraid to Pick Choice (A)

Choose (A) if you think that the original is correct as written. Many students automatically refuse to pick (A) because they figure that there must be something wrong with the original—even if they are unable to say what. But this reasoning is faulty. Choice (A) is statistically as likely to be correct as is (B), (C), (D), or (E). About one-fifth of the answers to Improving Sentences items are (A), which means that about one-fifth of the originals are correct.

Identifying Sentence Errors

Identifying Sentence Errors are short and sweet. There is much less reading to do with this type than there is with the other two Writing types, and there are no answer choices, except for the underlined parts of the sentence. Plus, you don't have to correct anything—just spot where the error is.

Don't Read the Directions
By the time you get to the test, you'll know what to do when you see the Writing section. Some of the questions have underlined parts with no answer choices except for the letters underneath the underlined parts—these are the Identifying Sentence Errors items. Do a quick preview and let the appearance of the questions on the page be all the direction you need, and then get started immediately.

Read the Sentence, Looking for an Error
Begin by reading the sentence, looking for an error. If you can spot an error, then the game is over. Mark your answer and move on. As noted earlier, later in the Writing Lesson, you'll cover the important principles of writing and grammar that are tested by this section, and there is a list of them provided in the Writing Course Concept Outline. You can treat this outline as a checklist of important things to look for in Identifying Sentence Errors items.

Don't Look for Multiple Errors
An Identifying Sentence Errors item contains at most one error. So, when you find one, it's game over. Mark your choice and move on.

Work Backward from the Underlined Parts
If you are having difficulty locating the right answer, use the underlined parts to help you. Ask yourself what grammatical function the word or phrase plays in the sentence and whether it is used correctly. For example, if the underlined word is a pronoun, make sure that it has an antecedent (the word it refers to) and that it agrees with its antecedent (e.g., both are plural or both are singular). Or, if the underlined word is an adjective, does it modify a noun? If not, does it modify a verb, adjective, or other adverb and therefore need to be changed to an adverb?

Don't Look for Spelling or Capitalization Errors
To repeat a point made above, these topics are not tested, so don't waste your time looking for errors of this sort.

Make Educated Guesses
You should be able to eliminate some answers to an Identifying Sentence Errors item because you know for certain that those underlined parts are correct. Eliminate all parts that you are confident are correct (and therefore cannot be the right answer), and make your guess from among the others. This is an educated guess, not a random guess. And the odds are in your favor.

Don't Be Afraid to Pick Choice (E)
Choose (E) if you think that the sentence is correct as written. Many students automatically refuse to pick (E) because they figure that there must be something wrong with the sentence—even if they are unable to say what. But this reasoning is faulty. Choice (E) is statistically as likely to be correct as is (A), (B), (C), or (D). About one-fifth of the answers to Identifying Sentence Errors items are (E), which means that about one-fifth of the originals are correct.

Improving Paragraphs

Improving Paragraphs is the "bear" of the Writing section. You have to read a passage before you can answer the items. A few of the items are like Improving Sentences items, but some of them are like Critical Reading: Passages items, such as Main Idea and Development.

Don't Read the Directions

By the time you get to the test, you'll know what to do when you see the Writing section. Some of the items have a passage followed by items—these are the Improving Paragraphs items. So, don't even think about reading the directions.

Read the Passage First

Start by reading the passage. You're not specifically looking for errors during this read. Even if you notice a couple of errors, they may not be useful because they may not show up in any of the items. There are only six or so items, so the test-writer cannot ask something about every angle of the little passage.

Instead, read the passage in the same way that you would a passage in the Critical Reading: Passages section. Try to identify the main point; note the important transitions in the development; determine what's being discussed in each paragraph. These are the kinds of points that are likely to be the basis for questions: What is the main point? What is the purpose of the second paragraph? Where does sentence 3 belong?

Compare and Contrast Answer Choices

This is a technique that is very helpful in the Critical Reading section, so it is not surprising that it would also be useful here. If you are asked to rewrite a sentence and cannot say for certain which is the best version, then point your finger at each choice, and ask yourself how it differs from the one above it and the one below it and whether it is better.

Make Educated Guesses

You should be able to eliminate some answers to every Improving Paragraphs item. For example, with a question that asks for the best place to locate sentence 4, you may know that it doesn't belong at the beginning or at the end of the passage, and this information would allow you to eliminate one or two choices. Or, you may know that two or even three of the choices are not good descriptions of the author's main point and would therefore not be good answers to a Main Idea question. So, eliminate those and make an educated guess. With some conscientious effort, you should be able to eliminate one or two (or maybe more) answers for each and every Improving Paragraphs item, thereby leaving no blanks in this series.

Don't Be Afraid to Pick Choice (A)

A couple of your Improving Paragraphs items (though probably not many) may contain a choice (A) that reads "(As it is now.)" Choose (A) for Improving Paragraphs items if you think that the sentence should remain "as it is now," or is correct as written. Many students automatically refuse to pick this choice because they figure that there must be something wrong somewhere, but this choice, when it appears, is statistically as likely to be correct as is (B), (C), (D), or (E).

Overview (Essay)

The Writing: Essay test section will assess in broad terms your ability to develop and express ideas in writing. It is not intended to evaluate if you'd be a good novelist or how well you'd write if given time to do research, writing several drafts before submitting a final version. In short, you will produce an on-demand piece of writing that will likely be of rough draft quality.

The Writing: Essay test section is also not intended to test your mastery of any body of knowledge. The topic will be sufficiently broad so that arguments and explanations can be drawn from personal experience; for example, the topic might ask you to express your opinions about sports, music, psychology, current events, or even modern technology.

The essay topic will be described as a "prompt." The word "prompt" was chosen because it indicates that the topic is really just an *excuse* or *opportunity* for you to write something. The test could just as easily say, "During the next 25 minutes, write an essay on anything of interest to you." However, the readers would then have to deal with essays on an unwieldy number of topics; the prompt keeps everyone more or less on the same page.

Essays are scored *holistically*, which means they are given a grade based on the overall impression created. Bonus points are not awarded for a well-turned phrase, and specific points are not deducted for specific grammatical mistakes (though consistently poor grammar that interferes with meaning will affect the essay score). All essays are read by two readers, and each reader assigns a score of "1" to "6" (an essay will receive a "0" if it is off-topic, illegible, or does not respond to the prompt). The two scores are combined to produce a final score between "2" and "12." The final score is also combined with your Writing score on the multiple-choice test sections to produce the 200 to 800 score for the Writing part of the test.

Anatomy (Essay)

DIRECTIONS: The essay tests your ability to express ideas, develop a point of view, present ideas in a clear and logical fashion, and use language precisely.

Write your essay on the lines provided on your answer sheet—you will receive no other paper on which to write. Do not write your essay in your test book. You will receive credit only for what appears on your answer sheet. Write legibly, and remember that graders must be able to read your handwriting.

You have 25 minutes to plan and write an essay on the topic assigned below. Do not write on any other topic. An essay on another topic is not acceptable.

Think carefully about the issue presented in the following excerpt and the assignment below.

> Some people are perfectionists. They want a perfect plan and a perfect outcome and are willing to spend whatever time and effort is necessary to achieve it. But in an imperfect world with deadlines, budgets, and unanticipated consequences, it is rarely if ever possible to achieve the perfect result. Trade-offs are always necessary.

Assignment: In your opinion, is it always necessary to sacrifice perfection because of time, money, or other considerations? Plan and write an essay in which you develop your point of view on this issue. Support your position with reasoning and examples taken from your reading, studies, experience, and observations.

Notice that the prompt does not test a specific body of knowledge. For example, it does not ask "What were the causes of World War II?" or "What is the best recipe for chocolate cake?" Also, notice that the prompt is constructed so you can provide a very successful response based simply on your own personal experience. Finally, notice that the prompt provides you with encouragement and points you in the right direction. It asks you a question, and all you need to do is respond to the question and meet the requirements outlined above. These requirements will be discussed in more detail later in the Writing Lesson.

Pacing (Essay)

There is one essay prompt, and there is a 25-minute time limit. During the 25 minutes, you must read the prompt, formulate a position, outline your argument or analysis, write your essay, and proofread your essay. Here is a suggested breakdown for those tasks:

TASK	TIME TO SPEND ON TASK	TIME REMAINING
Read the prompt	1 minute	24 minutes
Formulate your position	1 minute	23 minutes
Outline your essay	2 minutes	21 minutes
Write the introduction	1 minute	20 minutes
Write the first paragraph	5–6 minutes	14-15 minutes
Write the second paragraph	5-6 minutes	8-10 minutes
Write the third paragraph	5–6 minutes	2-5 minutes
Write the conclusion	1 minutes	1-4 minutes
Proofread your essay	1-4 minutes	0 minutes

If you follow this approximate schedule, it is likely your essay will score at least a "4" from each reader. After all, your essay will include an introduction, three paragraphs of development, and a brief conclusion. Obviously, if your essay is also expressed in clear and precise language, and if it does not include any major grammatical errors, you will likely receive an even higher score.

Time Trial (Essay)

(1 Essay—10 minutes)

DIRECTIONS: Read the following topic, and write a brief response.

Think carefully about the issue presented in the following excerpt and the assignment below.

Someone once said that there are no new stories—only different ways of handling them. In thousands of years of human civilization, this must certainly be proved true. After all, every existing story must have been told at least once before.

Assignment: In your opinion, are there no new stories to be told? Plan and write an essay in which you develop your point of view on this issue. Support your position with reasoning and examples taken from your reading, studies, experience, and observations.

_____

_____

_____

_____

_____

_____

_____

_____

_____

_____

_____

_____

_____

_____

_____

_____

_____

_____

_____

_____

_____

Game Plan (Essay)

Respond to the Specific Prompt

Write on the topic that is presented. If you write an essay that is off-topic, your essay will automatically receive a "0" because it will be considered "not responsive."

Write Legibly

Write clearly and legibly. If you write an essay that is illegible, your essay will automatically receive a "0." Readers cannot give a grade to what they cannot read. So, if your handwriting is hard to read, take a little extra time and try printing.

Don't Copy the Prompt

Do not copy the prompt onto the lined paper. The readers know the topic, and it is already written on the page. If you copy the prompt onto the lined paper, it looks like you're simply trying to fill up space.

Don't Skip Lines

Do not skip lines when writing your essay on the lined paper. You should be able to make your essay legible without skipping lines. If you skip lines, it looks like you're trying to "pad" your essay to make it look longer.

Use a Pencil

Write your essay in pencil. Do not use a pen. Any essay written in pen will automatically receive a "0."

Be Specific

When writing your essay, be specific. Avoid vague generalizations. For example, here are a few sentences that are weak because they are too vague:

> *Perfection in house painting is very time-consuming and requires a lot of hard work. You just can't do it in a short time; you've got to invest a lot of effort.*

If you include specific details, the same point can be made much more persuasively. For example, here is the same argument about house painting but made with specific details:

> *House painting requires attention to details. You have to prepare the surface by scraping away all old and loose paint and carefully washing it. You have to put down hundreds of strips of masking tape to protect those areas that should not receive paint, like glass panes, trim to be painted a second color, and fixtures. You have to apply a primer, then a base coat, and then the finish coat. Finally, you have to apply the second color and clean up all the mistakes. A perfect paint job would take 6 months or longer, and the cost would be prohibitive. That is why when you look closely you will always see imperfections.*

As you can see, the response is much more compelling because the point of view is supported by specific details. Specific details are frequently the difference between an essay that receives a reader's score of "2" or "3" and an essay that receives a reader's score of "4" or "5."

LESSON

The items in this section accompany the in-class review of the skills and concepts tested by the SAT Writing test sections. You will work through the items with your instructor in class. Answers are on page 627.

DIRECTIONS (IDENTIFYING SENTENCE ERRORS):
Identifying Sentence Errors items test your knowledge of grammar, usage, diction (choice of words), and idiom. Each sentence contains either no error or a single error. If there is an error, it is underlined and lettered. If the sentence contains an error, choose the one underlined portion that must be changed to produce a correct sentence. If there is no error, choose answer choice (E). In choosing answers, follow the conventions of standard written English.

DIRECTIONS (IMPROVING SENTENCES):
Improving Sentences items test correct, effective expression. Each sentence contains an underlined portion, or the entire sentence may be underlined. Following each sentence are five ways of phrasing the underlined portion. Choice (A) repeats the original; the other four choices are different. If you think the original is better than any of the other choices, choose (A); otherwise, choose one of the other choices.

In choosing answers, follow the conventions of standard written English. Make sure to consider issues of grammar, word choice, sentence construction, and punctuation. Your choice should produce the most effective sentence. It should be clear, precise, and free of ambiguity or awkwardness.

Identifying Sentence Errors and Improving Sentences

Grammar

Fragments

1. With an insurmountable lead over the next closest competitor, the highly-experienced runner <u>slowing in order to conserve</u> energy for the remaining track and field events.

   (A) slowing in order to conserve
   (B) slowing, in order to conserve
   (C) slowing and conserving
   (D) slowed in order to conserve
   (E) slowed in order that conserving

2. Lake George in the Adirondack Mountains of New York, <u>visited in 1646 by the French missionary Isaac Jogues who named</u> it *Le Lac du Saint-Sacrement*.

   (A) visited in 1646 by the French missionary Isaac Jogues who named
   (B) visited in 1646 by the French missionary Isaac Jogues and named
   (C) visiting in 1646 by the French missionary Isaac Jogues and naming
   (D) was visited in 1646 by the French missionary Isaac Jogues, who named
   (E) was visited in 1646 by the French missionary Isaac Jogues named

3. The announcement of the final <u>results, delayed</u> <u>for nearly an hour because</u> one of the contestants had filed an objection alleging interference at the start of the race.

(A) results, delayed for nearly an hour because
(B) results, delayed for nearly an hour and
(C) results, delayed when
(D) results were delayed for nearly an hour because
(E) results was delayed for nearly an hour because

Subject-Verb Agreement

4. The professor <u>were traveling</u> in Europe <u>when</u> she
              A   B

<u>received</u> notice of <u>her</u> promotion. <u>No error</u>
  C   D   E

Material Inserted Between Subject and Verb

5. The professor <u>voted Teacher of the Year</u> by the
                    A

students <u>were traveling</u> in Europe <u>when</u> she
            B   C

received notice of <u>her</u> promotion. <u>No error</u>
           D   E

6. Most teachers, unless <u>they have</u> an appointment
                     A

to a prestigious university, <u>earns</u> relatively
                  B

<u>less as</u> a teacher <u>than they might</u> in business.
  C   D

<u>No error</u>
  E

7. Many nutritionists now <u>believe</u> <u>that</u> a balanced
                  A   B

diet and not large doses of vitamins <u>are</u> the <u>best</u>
                            C   D

guarantee of health. <u>No error</u>
            E

8. Television comedies <u>in which</u> <u>there is</u> at least
                     A   B

one <u>really detestable</u> character <u>captures</u> the
          C   D

interest of viewers. <u>No error</u>
            E

9. The opposition to smoking in public places <u>are</u> <u>prompting many state legislatures to consider</u> banning smoking in such locations.

(A) are prompting many state legislatures to consider
(B) is prompting many state legislatures to consider
(C) are prompting many state legislatures considering
(D) is prompting many state legislatures considering
(E) is prompting many state legislatures' consider

10. Diplomats sent to an unstable region or a genuinely hostile territory usually <u>is assigned an aide or chauffeur who function</u> also as a bodyguard.

(A) is assigned an aide or chauffeur who function
(B) are assigned an aide or chauffeur who function
(C) are assigned an aide or chauffeur who functions
(D) is assigned an aide or chauffeur that function
(E) are assigned an aide or chauffeur which functions

Inverted Sentence Structure

11. <u>Though</u> this is the wealthiest country in the
    A

world, within a <u>few</u> blocks of the White House
               B

<u>there is</u> scores of homeless people <u>who live</u> on
  C   D

the streets. <u>No error</u>
        E

12. Just a few miles from the factories and
A

skyscrapers stand a medieval castle which looks
B   C

exactly as it did in the twelfth century. No error
D   E

Compound Subjects

13. John, his wife, and the rest of his family plans
A

to attend the award dinner to be given by the
B   C

company for the employees with the most
D

seniority. No error
E

14. Either the governor or one of his close aides

prefer not to have the Senator seated at the head
A   B   C

table where he would be conspicuous. No error
D   E

15. Surrounded by layers of excelsior, none of the
A

crystal goblets were broken when the workers
B   C

dropped the crate. No error
D   E

Pronoun Usage

Pronouns Must Have Antecedents

16. During her rise to fame, she betrayed many of
her friends, and because of it, very few people
trust her.

(A) and because of it
(B) and in spite of it
(C) and because of her friends
(D) and even though
(E) and because of her behavior

17. In New York City, they are brusque and even
A

rude but quick to come to one another's
B   C

assistance in a time of crisis. No error
D   E

Antecedents Must Be Clear

18. Ten years ago, the United States imported ten
A

times as much French wine as Italian wine, but
B

today Americans are drinking more of it.
C   D

No error
E

Pronoun-Antecedent Agreement

19. Although a police officer used to be a symbol of
A

authority, today they receive little respect
B   C

from most people. No error
D   E

20. The Abbot was an effective administrator
A

who attempted to assign each monk a task
B

particularly suited to their talents and training.
C   D

No error
E

21. After three years of college education, a person

should be allowed to apply to graduate school,
A

because by that time you are ready to choose a
B   C   D

profession. No error
E

22. If one wishes <u>to apply for</u> a scholarship, <u>you</u>
    A   B   C

must submit a <u>completed</u> application by March 1.
                D

<u>No error</u>
  E

Pronouns Must Have Proper Case

23. The judges <u>were</u> unable to make a final decision
              A

on a single winner, so <u>they</u> divided the first prize
                         B

<u>between</u> John and <u>he</u>. <u>No error</u>
  C   D   E

24. Although Peter <u>had been looking</u> <u>forward to</u> the
                  A   B

debate for weeks, a sore throat <u>prevented him</u>
                            C

taking <u>part</u>. <u>No error</u>
      D   E

Adjectives and Adverbs

Adjectives Modify Nouns; Adverbs Modify Verbs, Adjectives, and Other Adverbs

25. The company's mission statement took into consideration the <u>significant changes</u> that were made in the field of technology.

(A) significant changes
(B) significantly changes
(C) significant changed
(D) significantly changed
(E) significantly to change

26. When asked about the chance that the defenders might concentrate their forces at the beachhead, the general responded <u>tart that he was fully</u> aware of all the possibilities.

(A) tart that he was fully
(B) tartly that he was full
(C) tart that he was full
(D) tart that he fully was
(E) tartly that he was fully

Linking Verbs

27. When the door burst open, Kevin <u>looked up angry</u> from his desk.

(A) looked up angry
(B) was looking up angry
(C) looked up angrily
(D) looks up angrily
(E) looked angry up

28. The director explained that the scene required Edmund <u>to look distraughtly</u> on hearing the news of his sister's death.

(A) to look distraughtly
(B) looking distraughtly
(C) to have looked distraughtly
(D) to have looked distraught
(E) to look distraught

Watch for Adjectives Posing as Adverbs

29. Some psychologists maintain that a child <u>who</u>
                                      A

<u>has seen</u> violence on television <u>is</u> more likely to
  B   C

react <u>violent</u> in situations of stress. <u>No error</u>
      D   E

30. The <u>recent created</u> commission <u>has done</u> nothing
        A   B

to address the problem <u>except to approve</u> the
                        C

color of <u>the commission's</u> stationery. <u>No error</u>
            D   E

Double Negatives

31. <u>Not hardly</u> a sound <u>could be heard</u> in the
    A   B

auditorium <u>when</u> the speaker <u>approached</u> the dais
            C   D

to announce the result of the contest. <u>No error</u>
                            E

32. Although she <u>had been hired</u> by the magazine
                        A

<u>to write</u> book reviews, <u>she knew</u> <u>scarcely nothing</u>
  B   C   D

about current fiction. <u>No error</u>
                   E

Nouns and Noun Clauses

33. The reason Harriet <u>fired</u> her secretary is <u>because</u>
                 A   B

he <u>was</u> <u>frequently</u> late and spent too much time
  C   D

on personal phone calls. <u>No error</u>
                     E

34. <u>The reason the manager changed catchers was because</u> he hoped that the opposing side would put in a left-handed pitcher.

(A) The reason the manager changed catchers was because
(B) The reason that catchers were changed by the manager was because
(C) The reason the manager changed catchers which
(D) The manager changed catchers because
(E) The manager changed catchers, the reason being

35. I read in a magazine <u>where</u> scientists <u>believe</u> that
                      A   B

<u>they</u> <u>have discovered</u> a new subatomic particle.
 C   D

<u>No error</u>
  E

36. <u>According to</u> the job posting, officers who want
     A

to be <u>a detective</u> <u>should</u> register <u>to take</u> the next
      B   C   D

examination. <u>No error</u>
              E

37. <u>Relatively</u> few of the high school athletes <u>who</u> go
     A   B

on to participate in college football <u>will have</u> the
                               C

opportunity to become <u>a professional player</u>.
                          D

<u>No error</u>
  E

Sentence Structure

Run-on Sentences

38. From the perspective of an artist, the Impressionist school is viewed as the natural successor to the painters of the Ecole des Beaux <u>Art, to</u> the historian, however, it was a guerilla movement that aimed at bringing down a powerful political institution supported by state funds.

(A) Art, to
(B) Art, but to
(C) Art and to
(D) Art for
(E) Art, as to

Problems of Coordination and Subordination

39. Carlos telephoned to say that weather had delayed his <u>plane, but he will</u> not be able to attend the meeting.

(A) plane, but he will
(B) plane, so he will
(C) plane, but he was
(D) plane when he will
(E) plane because he could

40. By the fifth inning, Cindy was showing signs of fatigue and walked three consecutive <u>batters, so</u> the coach refused to take her out of the game.

(A) batters, so
(B) batters, when
(C) batters, moreover
(D) batters during
(E) batters, but

41. Because the wetlands were protected by federal law, the owners were not able to build the shopping center that they had planned.

(A) Because
(B) In fact
(C) However
(D) Moreover
(E) So that

42. Victoria was nominated to the office of club president, or it is doubtful that she would serve even if elected.

(A) president, or
(B) president so
(C) president, though
(D) president, in that
(E) president, even

Faulty Parallelism

43. To abandon their homes, leave behind their
A

families, and traveling across the ocean required
B   C

great courage on the part of the immigrants

who moved to America. No error
D   E

44. The review praised the wit, charm, and
A

interpreting of the recitalist but never once
B   C

mentioned her voice. No error
D   E

45. To acknowledge that one has something to learn
A   B

is taking the first step on the road to true
C   D

wisdom. No error
E

Incomplete Split Constructions

46. The students are critical of the dean because he is
A   B

either unfamiliar or doesn't care about the urgent
C

need for new student housing on campus.
D

No error
E

47. Baseball has and probably always will be the
A

sport that symbolizes for people in other
B   C   D

countries the American way of life. No error
E

Verb Tense

Principal Parts of Verbs

48. The winter was so severe that several of Hillary's
A   B

prize rose bushes had sustained serious damage
C   D

from the frost. No error
E

When to Use the Perfect Tenses

49. John, having took his seat at the head of the
A

table, announced that the dinner would feature
B   C   D

specialties from Thailand. No error
E

The Subjunctive Mood

50. It is almost certain that Hamilton's plan will have
A

resulted in Pickney's election to the presidency if
A   B   C

sectional pride in New England had not been as
D

powerful as that in the south. No error
D   E

Logical Expression

Faulty Comparisons

51. The great pianist Vladimir Horowitz <u>played</u> the
                                          A

music <u>of</u> the Romantic Era <u>better than</u> <u>any pianist</u>
     B   C   D

in history. <u>No error</u>
            E

52. <u>Like Neil Simon, many of Tennessee Williams'</u>
<u>plays</u> reflect a culture familiar to the
playwright.

  (A) Like Neil Simon, many of Tennessee
      Williams' plays
  (B) Many of Tennessee Williams' plays, like
      Neil Simon's,
  (C) Many of Tennessee Williams' plays, like
      Neil Simon,
  (D) Many of Neil Simon and Tennessee
      Williams' plays
  (E) As with the plays of Neil Simon, many of
      Tennessee Williams' plays

53. Educators <u>are</u> now expressing <u>their</u> concern that
           A   B

American school children <u>prefer</u> watching
                        C

television <u>to books</u>. <u>No error</u>
         D   E

54. The novels of Nathaniel Hawthorne <u>contain</u>
                               A

characters who <u>are</u> every bit <u>as</u> sinister and
           B   C

frightening <u>as the master</u> of cinematic suspense,
            D

Alfred Hitchcock. <u>No error</u>
               E

55. A Japanese firm <u>has developed</u> a computer so
                  A

small that users <u>can carry</u> it in <u>their</u> <u>briefcase</u>.
             B   C   D

<u>No error</u>
 E

56. Mary Lou was awarded the gold medal
because she scored <u>more points than any child</u>
<u>participating</u> in the field day.

  (A) more points than any child participating
  (B) more points than any other child
      participating
  (C) most points than any child participating
  (D) more points than any child who had
      participated
  (E) more points as any child participating

Illogical Tense Sequence

57. The teacher had begun <u>to discuss</u> the homework
                      A

assignment <u>when</u> he <u>will be</u> interrupted <u>by</u> the
           B   C   D

sound of the fire alarm. <u>No error</u>
                 E

58. The conductor <u>announced</u> that the concert would
              A

resume <u>as soon as</u> the soloist <u>replaces</u> the broken
       B   C

string on <u>her</u> violin. <u>No error</u>
        D   E

59. <u>Many</u> patients begin <u>to show</u> symptoms again
    A   B

after <u>they</u> <u>stopped</u> taking the drug. <u>No error</u>
     C   D   E

60. The sheriff called off the search for the escaped convict because he doubted that <u>the convict can successfully cross the river because the current was so swift</u>.

(A) the convict can successfully cross the river because the current was so swift
(B) the convict successfully crossed the river because the current was so swift
(C) the convict successfully crossed the river being that the current was so swift
(D) the convict would have been successful in crossing the river, the current being so swift
(E) a successful attempt to cross the river was made by the convict because the current was so swift

Unintended Meanings

61. <u>Appearing</u> in his first American tour, the British singer's album rose to the top of the charts.

(A) Appearing
(B) While appearing
(C) While he was appearing
(D) When appearing
(E) Upon appearing

Directness

62. Angela is hoping to save enough for a trip to Europe, during which <u>the small village where her grandparents were born will be visited</u>.

(A) the small village where her grandparents were born will be visited
(B) the small village where her grandparents had been born will be visited
(C) she will visit the small village where her grandparents were born
(D) there will be a visit to the small village where her grandparents were born
(E) a visit to the small village where her grandparents were born will be included

63. <u>Finally and at long last</u> the old dog opened his eyes and noticed the intruder.

(A) Finally and at long last
(B) Finally
(C) So finally
(D) Yet at long last
(E) Finally and long lastingly

64. The speaker declared that <u>alternative ways of utilizing</u> waterfront land ought to be explored.

(A) alternative ways of utilizing
(B) alternatives of use for
(C) alternative utilizations of
(D) alternative ways of utilization of
(E) alternate uses of

65. After months of separation, Gauguin finally joined Van Gogh <u>in Arles in October of 1888, Gauguin left a few weeks later</u>.

(A) in Arles in October of 1888, Gauguin left a few weeks later
(B) in Arles; Gauguin, however, leaving a few weeks later
(C) in Arles, while Gauguin left a few weeks later
(D) in Arles, it was three weeks later when Gauguin was gone
(E) in Arles, in October of 1888, but left a few weeks later

66. The nineteenth-century composers Wagner and Mahler did more than just write <u>music, they conducted</u> their own works.

(A) music, they conducted
(B) music, in that they conducted
(C) music; they conducted
(D) music, with their conducting of
(E) music; as conductors, they did

67. <u>Since only</u> the ruling party <u>is allowed to</u> vote, <u>its</u>
    A   B   C

members are able to maintain the <u>existing</u> status
                                                D

quo. <u>No error</u>
     E

68. Each year, the geese <u>make</u> their <u>annual</u> <u>migration</u>
$$ABC$$

from Northern Canada to <u>their winter habitats</u> in
$$D$$

the United States. <u>No error</u>
$$E$$

69. <u>Although</u> the committee met for over two weeks
$$A$$

and issued a 50-page report, <u>its findings</u> were
$$B$$

<u>of little</u> <u>importance or</u> consequence. <u>No error</u>
$$CDE$$

Misplaced Modifiers

70. <u>Letters were received by the editor of the newspaper that complained of its editorial policy.</u>

(A) Letters were received by the editor of the newspaper that complained of its editorial policy.
(B) Letters were received by the editor of the newspaper having complained of its editorial policy.
(C) The editor of the newspaper received letters complaining of the newspaper's editorial policy.
(D) Letters were received by the editor in which there were complaints to the editor of the newspaper about its editorial policy.
(E) Letters were received by the editor complaining of the newspaper's editorial policy by the editor.

71. Riding in a carriage and wearing the crown jewels, <u>the crowd cheered the royal couple who waved</u>.

(A) the crowd cheered the royal couple who waved
(B) cheering for the royal couple who waved was done by the crowd
(C) the royal couple waved to the cheering crowd
(D) the waving royal couple's cheering was done by the crowd
(E) the royal couple, who waved and was being cheered by crowd

72. <u>Wrapped in several thicknesses of newspaper, packed carefully in a strong cardboard carton, and bound securely with tape, the worker made sure that the fragile figurines would not be broken.</u>

(A) Wrapped in several thicknesses of newspaper, packed carefully in a strong cardboard carton, and bound securely with tape, the worker made sure that the fragile figurines would not be broken.
(B) Wrapped in several thicknesses of newspaper, packed carefully in a strong cardboard carton, and then binding the carton securely with tape, the worker made sure that the fragile figurines would not be broken.
(C) The figurines, having been securely wrapped in several thicknesses of newspaper, packed carefully in a strong cardboard carton which was then securely bound with tape, the worker made sure would not be broken.
(D) The worker, wrapping the figurines in several thicknesses of newspaper, packing them carefully in a strong cardboard carton, and securely binding the carton with tape, made sure that they would not be broken.
(E) To make sure that the figurines would not be broken, the worker wrapped them in several thicknesses of newspaper, packed them carefully in a strong cardboard carton, and securely bound the carton with tape.

Clarity of Expression

Diction and Idioms

Wrong Word Choice

73. By midnight the guests still <u>had not been served</u>
$$A$$

anything <u>to eat</u>, so <u>they</u> were <u>ravishing</u>. <u>No error</u>
$$BCDE$$

74. The <u>raise</u> in the number of accidents <u>attributable</u>
     A   B

to drunk drivers <u>has prompted</u> a call for <u>stiffer</u>
                  C   D

penalties for driving while intoxicated. <u>No error</u>
                                           E

Wrong Preposition

75. <u>In contrast of</u> the prevailing opinion, the
     A

editorial <u>lays</u> the blame <u>for</u> the strike on the
            B   C

workers and <u>their</u> representatives. <u>No error</u>
                D   E

76. Although ballet and modern dance are both

<u>concerned in</u> movement in space to musical
   A

accompaniment, the training for ballet <u>is more</u>
                                   B C

rigorous <u>than that</u> for modern dance. <u>No error</u>
          D   E

Gerund versus Infinitive

77. The idea of trying <u>completing</u> the term paper <u>by</u>
                        A   B

Friday <u>caused</u> Ken <u>to cancel</u> his plans for the
        C   D

weekend. <u>No error</u>
           E

78. Psychologists <u>think</u> that many people eat
             A

<u>satisfying</u> <u>a need</u> for affection that is not
   B   C

otherwise <u>fulfilled</u>. <u>No error</u>
          D   E

Ambiguity in Scope

79. <u>Along with an end to featherbedding and no-show jobs,</u> the new head of the Transit Authority has eliminated many other inefficient employment practices.

(A) Along with an end to featherbedding and no-show jobs,
(B) In addition to eliminating featherbedding and no-show jobs,
(C) Not only did he end featherbedding and no-shows jobs,
(D) Besides featherbedding and no-show jobs coming to an end,
(E) Together with the ending of featherbedding and no-show jobs,

Low-Level Usage

80. <u>Being that</u> the hour <u>was</u> late, we <u>agreed</u> to
     A   B   C

adjourn the meeting and <u>reconvene</u> at nine
                         D

o'clock the following morning. <u>No error</u>
                            E

Punctuation

Commas

81. I think that Doré's illustrations of Dante's *Divine Comedy* <u>are excellent; but my favorite drawing is "Don Quixote in His Library."</u>

(A) are excellent; but my favorite drawing is "Don Quixote in His Library."
(B) are excellent, but my favorite drawing is "Don Quixote in His Library."
(C) are excellent and my favorite drawing is "Don Quixote in His Library."
(D) are excellent in that my favorite drawing is "Don Quixote in His Library."
(E) are excellent even though "Don Quixote in His Library" is my favorite drawing.

82. <u>Practically</u> all nitrates are crystalline and <u>readily</u>
    A   B

    <u>soluble, and</u> they are characterized by marked
       C

    decrepitation <u>when</u> heated on charcoals by a
                     D

    blowpipe. <u>No error</u>
             E

83. The door <u>was</u> <u>ajar,</u> and the house <u>had been</u>
            A   B   C

    <u>ransacked</u>. <u>No error</u>
      D   E

84. Since many diseases and insects cause serious

    damage to <u>crops,</u> special national legislation has
              A

    been passed to provide for the quarantine of

    imported <u>plants;</u> and under provisions of various
            B

    <u>acts,</u> inspectors are placed at ports of entry to
     C

    prevent smugglers from bringing in plants

    <u>that might be</u> dangerous. <u>No error</u>
        D   E

85. <u>A full train crew consists of a motorman, a</u>
    <u>brakeman, a conductor, and two ticket takers.</u>

    (A) A full train crew consists of a motorman, a
         brakeman, a conductor, and two ticket
         takers.
    (B) A full train crew consists of a motorman,
         brakeman, a conductor and two ticket
         takers.
    (C) A full train crew consists of a motorman,
         brakeman, conductor, and two ticket
         takers.
    (D) A full train crew consists of, a motorman, a
         brakeman, a conductor, and two ticket
         takers.
    (E) A full train crew consists of a motorman a
         brakeman a conductor and two ticket
         takers.

86. The procedure requires that you open the outer

    cover <u>plate,</u> remove the <u>thermostat,</u> replace the
         A   B

    broken <u>switch,</u> <u>and then</u> replace the thermostat.
          C   D

    <u>No error</u>
     E

87. <u>After</u> Peter finished painting the bird <u>feeder</u> he
    A   B

    and Jack <u>hung it</u> from a limb of the oak tree.
    C   D

    <u>No error</u>
     E

88. <u>When</u> Pat explained to his mother that ten was
    A

    the highest mark <u>given</u> on the entrance <u>test</u> she
                B   C

    <u>breathed</u> a sigh of relief. <u>No error</u>
      D   E

89. <u>Tim hopes to score well on the exam because</u>
    <u>he plans to go to an Ivy League school.</u>

    (A) Tim hopes to score well on the exam
         because he plans to go to an Ivy League
         school.
    (B) Tim hopes to score well on the exam and
         he plans to go to an Ivy League school.
    (C) Tim hopes to score well on the exam,
         because he plans to go to an Ivy League
         school.
    (D) Tim hopes to score well on the exam, and
         he plans to go to an Ivy League school.
    (E) Tim hopes to score well on the exam he
         plans to go to an Ivy League school.

90. <u>In this impoverished region with its arid soil a</u>
<u>typical diet may contain only 800 calories per</u>
<u>day.</u>

(A) In this impoverished region with its arid
soil a typical diet may contain only 800
calories per day.
(B) In this impoverished region with its arid
soil; a typical diet may contain only 800
calories per day.
(C) In this impoverished region, with its arid
soil, a typical diet may contain only 800
calories per day.
(D) In this impoverished region with its arid
soil, a typical diet may contain only 800
calories per day.
(E) In this impoverished region with its arid
soil: a typical diet may contain only 800
calories per day.

91. <u>Begun</u> in 1981 and completed in <u>1985</u> the bridge
   A   B

<u>provided</u> the first link <u>between</u> the island and the
  C   D

mainland. <u>No error</u>
         E

92. <u>To slow the bleeding Van tied a pressure</u>
<u>bandage around the lower portion of the leg.</u>

(A) To slow the bleeding Van tied a pressure
bandage around the lower portion of the
leg.
(B) To slow the bleeding—Van tied a pressure
bandage around the lower portion of the
leg.
(C) To slow the bleeding, Van tied a pressure
bandage around the lower portion of the
leg.
(D) To slow the bleeding, Van tied a pressure
bandage, around the lower portion of the
leg.
(E) Van tied a pressure bandage, to slow the
bleeding, around the lower portion of the
leg.

93. <u>Niagara Falls,</u> <u>which</u> forms part of the border
   A   B

between the United States and <u>Canada,</u> was the
                           C

site of a saw mill <u>built by the French in 1725</u>.
                      D

<u>No error</u>
 E

94. Secretary of State <u>Acheson,</u> <u>however,</u> made a
                 A   B

<u>reasoned</u> defense <u>of</u> the treaty. <u>No error</u>
 C   D   E

95. Until the end of the eighteenth <u>century,</u> the only
                       A

musicians in <u>Norway,</u> were simple,
         B

unsophisticated peasants <u>who</u> traveled <u>about</u>
                C   D

the countryside. <u>No error</u>
         E

96. Prizes <u>will be</u> awarded in each <u>event,</u> and the
     A   B

<u>participant, who compiles the greatest overall</u>
               C

<u>total, will receive</u> a special prize. <u>No error</u>
 C   D   E

97. Since learning of the dangers of <u>caffeine,</u> <u>neither</u>
                        A   B

my wife <u>nor</u> I have consumed any <u>beverage,</u>
      C   D

containing caffeine. <u>No error</u>
            E

Semicolons

98. He grew up on a farm in Nebraska; he is now the captain of a Navy ship.

   (A) He grew up on a farm in Nebraska; he is now the captain of a Navy ship.
   (B) He grew up on a farm in Nebraska, he is now the captain of a Navy ship.
   (C) He grew up on a farm in Nebraska he is now the captain of a Navy ship.
   (D) He grew up on a farm; in Nebraska he is now the captain of a Navy ship.
   (E) He grew up on a farm in Nebraska but he is now the captain of a Navy ship.

99. The Smithtown players cheered the referee's decision; the Stonybrook players booed it.

   (A) The Smithtown players cheered the referee's decision; the Stonybrook players booed it.
   (B) The Smithtown players cheered the referee's decision the Stonybrook players booed it.
   (C) The Smithtown players cheered the referee's decision, the Stonybrook players booed it.
   (D) The Smithtown players cheered the referee's decision: the Stonybrook players booed it.
   (E) The Smithtown players cheered the referee's decision but the Stonybrook players booed it.

100. When John entered the room; everyone stood up.
     A   B   C   D

   No error
    E

101. Clem announced that the prize would be donated
         A   B   C

   to Harbus House; a well-known charity. No error
          D   E

Colons

102. The seemingly tranquil lane has been the scene of
         A

   many crimes including: two assaults, three
               B   C

   robberies, and one murder. No error
    D   E

103. In addition to test scores, college admissions
                  A

   officers take into consideration many other

   factors such as: grades, extracurricular activities,
           B   C   D

   and letters of recommendation. No error
   D   E

End-Stop Punctuation

104. Peter notified Elaine. The guidance counselor, that he had been accepted.

   (A) Peter notified Elaine. The guidance counselor, that he had been accepted.
   (B) Peter notified Elaine the guidance counselor, that he had been accepted.
   (C) Peter notified Elaine, the guidance counselor that he had been accepted.
   (D) Peter notified Elaine, the guidance counselor, that he had been accepted.
   (E) Peter notified Elaine that the guidance counselor had been accepted.

Dashes

105. <u>Peanuts—blanched or lightly roasted, add an</u>
<u>interesting texture and taste to garden salads.</u>

   (A) Peanuts—blanched or lightly roasted, add
      an interesting texture and taste to garden
      salads.

   (B) Peanuts—blanched or lightly roasted—
      add an interesting texture and taste to
      garden salads.

   (C) Peanuts: blanched or lightly roasted, add
      an interesting texture and taste to garden
      salads.

   (D) Peanuts, blanched or lightly roasted—add
      an interesting texture and taste to garden
      salads.

   (E) Peanuts blanched or lightly roasted; add
      an interesting texture and taste to garden
      salads.

Hyphens

106. The optimist <u>feels that</u> his glass is <u>one-half</u> <u>full;</u>
                A   B   C

the pessimist feels that his glass is one-half

<u>empty.</u> <u>No error</u>
  D   E

Quotation Marks

107. <u>The first chapter of *The Scarlet Letter* is "The</u>
<u>Custom House."</u>

   (A) The first chapter of *The Scarlet Letter* is
      "The Custom House."

   (B) The first chapter of *The Scarlet Letter* is
      "The Custom House".

   (C) The first chapter of *The Scarlet Letter* is
      The Custom House.

   (D) The first chapter of *The Scarlet Letter* is
      The Custom House.

   (E) The first chapter of *"The Scarlet Letter"* is
      "The Custom House."

Punctuating for Clarity

> **DIRECTIONS:** Punctuate the following paragraph.

108. On Monday Mark received a letter of
acceptance from State College He
immediately called his mother herself a
graduate of State College to tell her about
his acceptance When he told her he had
also been awarded a scholarship she was
very excited After hanging up Mark's
mother decided to throw a surprise party
for Mark She telephoned his brother his
sister and several of his friends Because the
party was supposed to be a surprise she
made them all promise not to say anything
to Mark Mark however had a similar idea a
party for his mother to celebrate his
acceptance at her alma mater He
telephoned his brother his sister and
several of his parents' friends to invite
them to a party at his house on Saturday
night and he made them all promise to say
nothing to his mother On Saturday night
both Mark and his mother were surprised

Improving Paragraphs

Illustrative Improving Paragraphs Items

> **DIRECTIONS (IMPROVING PARAGRAPHS):**
> Improving Paragraphs items are based on passages that are early drafts of essays. Some portions of the passages need to be revised.
>
> Read each passage and answer the items that follow. Items may be about particular sentences or parts of sentences, asking you to improve the word choice or sentence structure. Other items may refer to parts of the essay or the entire essay, asking you to consider organization or development. In making your decisions, follow the conventions of standard written English.

Items #109–114 are based on the following passage.

(1) Each year, my family plants a vegetable garden. **(2)** Both my parents work, and with this, it is the job of the children to tend the garden.

(3) Work starts several weeks before the growing season actually begins. **(4)** We put little pots of soil containing seeds that must sprout before they are planted outdoors on the sun porch. **(5)** Then, my father prepares the ground with a rototiller. **(6)** The danger of frost is past, it is time to plant.

(7) For the first few weeks, we water the seed beds regularly and pull weeds by hand. **(8)** Once the plants are established, the leaves of the good plants block the sunlight so weeds can't grow. **(9)** There are other jobs such as staking tomatoes and tending to running vines.

(10) Then the blossoms appear and are pollinated by bees and other insects. **(11)** As small vegetables appear, the blossoms drop off. **(12)** They continue to grow and later in the summer begin to ripen. **(13)** Up to this point, tending the garden has been a chore, but now it becomes a pleasure. **(14)** Each afternoon, we pick the ripe ones and wash them so that they are ready for cooking. **(15)** I suppose that I feel proud that I have helped to feed my family. **(16)** I have to admit that my greatest enjoyment is the taste of the freshly picked vegetables.

109. Which of the following is the best way to revise the underlined portion of sentence 2 (reproduced below)?

Both my parents work, <u>and with this, it is</u> the job of the children to tend the garden.

(A) a situation that makes it
(B) because it is
(C) in that it is
(D) so it is
(E) unless it is

110. In context, which of the following is the best way to revise sentence 6 (reproduced below)?

The danger of frost is past, it is time to plant.

(A) When the danger of frost is past, it is time to plant.
(B) The danger of frost is past, when it is time to plant.
(C) The danger of frost being past, it is time to plant.
(D) Planting begins, and the danger of frost passes.
(E) The time to plant is when the danger of frost is passing.

111. In context, which of the following would be best to insert at the beginning of sentence 9?

(A) However,
(B) Further,
(C) Actually,
(D) Because
(E) Since

112. In sentence 14, the word "ones" refers to

(A) blossoms
(B) bees
(C) gardens
(D) chores
(E) vegetables

113. Which of the following is the best way to combine sentences 15 and 16 (reproduced below)?

I suppose that I feel proud that I have helped to feed my family. I have to admit that my greatest enjoyment is the taste of the freshly picked vegetables.

(A) Feeling proud that I have helped to feed my family, I have to admit that my greatest enjoyment is the taste of the freshly picked vegetables.

(B) I suppose that I feel proud that I have helped to feed my family, but I have to admit that my greatest enjoyment is the taste of the freshly picked vegetables.

(C) Supposing that I feel proud that I have helped to feed my family, I have to admit that my greatest enjoyment is the taste of the freshly picked vegetables.

(D) I have to admit that my greatest enjoyment is the taste of the freshly picked vegetables, so I suppose that I feel proud that I have helped to feed my family.

(E) Helping to feed my family makes me supposedly feel proud as well as admitting that my greatest enjoyment is the taste of the freshly picked vegetables.

114. Which of the following best describes the overall organization of the passage?

(A) Chronological development
(B) Explanation of two sides of an issue
(C) Generalization of a statement with illustrations
(D) Posing a question and then answering it
(E) Citing an authority and then drawing a conclusion

Items #115–120 are based on the following passage.

(1) In my mind, one of the most pressing issues facing America today is healthcare. **(2)** One aspect of the problem is going to the doctor. **(3)** Many people just cannot afford to pay for a visit to a doctor. **(4)** They avoid going to the doctor until they are really sick. **(5)** If they were treated in the first place, they wouldn't get so sick. **(6)** This practice not only causes human suffering but is wasteful. **(7)** Health insurance for surgery is also an issue. **(8)** Many people do not get adequate health insurance with their jobs and cannot afford to pay for it. **(9)** This also creates an unfair distribution of health care in America.

(10) An even more important aspect of the healthcare problem in America is the choices that people make for themselves. **(11)** Take smoking for example. **(12)** Scientific evidence proves that smoking causes lung cancer and other diseases. **(13)** Yet, many people continue to smoke, and young people continue to start smoking. **(14)** There are other health problems such as overweight and drugs that may also come from private choices.

(15) Some government assistance is needed for those who cannot afford medical care or health insurance. **(16)** The most important thing is for people to be concerned with their own health. **(17)** If we take care of ourselves by eating better, exercising more, and avoiding destructive choices, we will all live longer, healthier, and happier lives.

115. In context, which of the following is the best way of revising the underlined portion of sentence 2 (reproduced below)?

One aspect of the problem is <u>going to the doctor</u>.

(A) going to the doctor
(B) medicine
(C) doctors and patients
(D) getting to go to the doctor
(E) lack of access to a doctor

116. Which of the following is the best way to combine sentences 3 and 4 (reproduced below)?

Many people just cannot afford to pay for a visit to a doctor. They avoid going to the doctor until they are really sick.

(A) Because many people just cannot afford to pay for a visit to a doctor, and they avoid going until they are really sick.
(B) Because many people just cannot afford to pay for a visit to a doctor, they avoid going until they are really sick.
(C) In that many people avoid going to a doctor until they are really sick, they cannot afford to pay for a visit.
(D) When many people cannot afford to pay for a visit to a doctor, they avoid going until they are all really sick.
(E) People just cannot afford to pay for a visit to a doctor if they avoid going until they are really sick.

117. Which of the following would be the best substitute for "this" in sentence 9?

(A) Medical care and health insurance
(B) The fact that health insurance doesn't exist
(C) Health insurance
(D) The availability of health insurance
(E) The inability to pay for health insurance

118. In context, which of the following is the best way of wording sentence 11 (reproduced below)?

Take smoking for example.

(A) Take smoking, for example.
(B) Smoking to take an example.
(C) An example of smoking.
(D) To smoke is an example.
(E) Taking smoking as an example.

119. Which of the following is the best way to revise the underlined portion of sentence 14 (reproduced below)?

There are other health problems <u>such as overweight and drugs that may also come from private choices</u>.

(A) such as being overweight and using drugs that may also come from private choices
(B) such as overweightness and drug usage that may also come from private choices
(C) like overweight and drugs that may also come from private choices
(D) that may also come from private choices such as overweight and drugs
(E) that may also come from private choices including overweight and drugs

120. In context, which of the following best describes the purpose of the final paragraph?

(A) To expose faulty reasoning
(B) To evaluate a theory set forth earlier
(C) To provide specific illustrations
(D) To propose a solution to a problem
(E) To persuade the reader to change an opinion

The SAT Essay

DIRECTIONS: Read the following essay prompt and assignment. Then, instead of writing an entire essay (as directed by the assignment), use the space provided below to create an <u>outline</u> for an essay that responds to the assignment. Include a thesis, as well as a topic sentence and a list of several examples for each part of your essay. A sample essay outline is on page 627.

Think carefully about the issue presented in the following excerpt and the assignment below.

> Human beings are often cruel, but they also have the capacity for kindness and compassion. In my opinion, an example that demonstrates this capacity is ----.

Assignment: Complete the statement above with an example from current affairs, history, literature, or your own personal experience. Then write a well-organized essay explaining why you regard that event favorably. Support your position with reasoning and examples taken from your reading, studies, experience, and observations.

Essay Outline

QUIZZES

This section contains four Writing: Multiple-Choice quizzes and one Writing: Essay quiz. Complete each quiz under timed conditions. Answers are on page 628.

Quiz I

(16 items; 12 minutes)

> **DIRECTIONS:** *Items #1–6:* The following sentences test your knowledge of grammar, usage, diction (choice of words), and idiom. Each sentence contains either no error or a single error. If there is an error, it is underlined and lettered. If the sentence contains an error, choose the one underlined portion that must be changed to produce a correct sentence. If there is no error, choose answer choice (E). In choosing answers, follow the conventions of standard written English.

1. <u>During</u> the televised meeting of the Senate, the
     A

   first issue <u>to be discussed</u> <u>were</u> Federal grants and
           B   C

   loans <u>for</u> higher education. <u>No error</u>
       D   E

2. Men in the Navy <u>spend</u> more time <u>away from</u>
             A   B

   home <u>than</u> <u>any other branch</u> of the service.
        C   D

   <u>No error</u>
    E

3. Illiteracy is a <u>widespread</u> problem in the United
            A

   States; many mistakes <u>are made</u> in the workplace
             B

   by people <u>who</u> do not know how <u>to read</u>.
        C   D

   <u>No error</u>
    E

4. The <u>earliest</u> Americans originated in Northeast
       A

   Asia and <u>have migrated</u> <u>across</u> a land bridge
            B   C

   sometime <u>during</u> the Pleistocene era. <u>No error</u>
          D   E

5. The comedian <u>found</u> that capturing the <u>audience's</u>
           A   B

   attention <u>was</u> easy, but <u>to maintain</u> it was
         C   D

   difficult. <u>No error</u>
         E

6. <u>Because</u> the project <u>had been</u> a team effort,
     A   B

   <u>we divided</u> the bonus equally <u>between</u> the five of
      C   D

   us. <u>No error</u>
      E

DIRECTIONS: _Items #7–10:_ The following sentences test correct, effective expression. Each sentence contains an underlined portion, or the entire sentence may be underlined. Following each sentence are five ways of phrasing the underlined portion. Choice (A) repeats the original; the other four choices are different. If you think the original is better than any of the other choices, choose (A); otherwise, choose one of the other choices.

In choosing answers, follow the conventions of standard written English. Make sure to consider issues of grammar, word choice, sentence construction, and punctuation. Your choice should produce the most effective sentence. It should be clear, precise, and free of ambiguity or awkwardness.

7. The most important food-energy source <u>of three-fourths of the world's population are grains</u>.

   (A) of three-fourths of the world's population are grains
   (B) for three-fourths of the world's population are grains
   (C) for three-fourths of the world's population is grains
   (D) for three-fourths of the worlds' population is grains
   (E) for three-fourths of the world's population is grain

8. Fluoride helps protect a child's teeth while the teeth grow, <u>but it is unharmful to their bodies</u>.

   (A) but it is unharmful to their bodies
   (B) and it is unharmful to their bodies
   (C) and it is not harmful to their bodies
   (D) and it is not harmful to the bodies
   (E) and it is not harmful to the body

9. <u>Greek fire, a gelatinous, incendiary mixture, was used in warfare before gunpowder was invented.</u>

   (A) Greek fire, a gelatinous, incendiary mixture, was used in warfare before gunpowder was invented.
   (B) Greek fire, a gelatinous, incendiary mixture, was used during warfare before the invention of gunpowder.
   (C) Greek fire, a gelatinous, incendiary mixture before the invention of gunpowder, was used in warfare.
   (D) A gelatinous, incendiary mixture, warfare involved the use of Greek fire before the invention of gunpowder.
   (E) Gelatinous and incendiary, Greek fire was a mixture that was used in warfare before the invention of gunpowder.

10. <u>After having had Anne Boleyn beheaded, the next day King Henry VIII was betrothed to Jane Seymour.</u>

    (A) After having had Anne Boleyn beheaded, the next day King Henry VIII was betrothed to Jane Seymour.
    (B) After having had Anne Boleyn beheaded, King Henry VIII was betrothed to Jane Seymour the next day.
    (C) Having had Anne Boleyn beheaded, King Henry VIII was betrothed to Jane Seymour the next day.
    (D) On the day after he had Anne Boleyn beheaded, King Henry VIII was betrothed to Jane Seymour.
    (E) On the day after having had Anne Boleyn beheaded, King Henry VIII was betrothed to Jane Seymour.

DIRECTIONS: _Items #11–16:_ The following passage is an early draft of an essay. Some portions of the passage need to be revised.

Read the passage and answer the items that follow. Items may be about particular sentences or parts of sentences, asking you to improve the word choice or sentence structure. Other items may refer to parts of the essay or the entire essay, asking you to consider organization or development. In making your decisions, follow the conventions of standard written English.

(1) I now live in the country, but when I was younger, my family lived in Brooklyn, New York. **(2)** You might think of Brooklyn as nothing but high-rise buildings. **(3)** However, in my old neighborhood, most people lived in two- or three-family houses that were attached to each other. **(4)** They call these row houses. **(5)** Row houses have small front yards, usually covered with concrete, and somewhat larger backyards. **(6)** People who live in Brooklyn do many of the same things that we do in the country, only slightly differently. **(7)** Cookouts are a favorite summer pastime. **(8)** People who do not have a backyard take their grills to the park. **(9)** Row houses do not have garages, but they do have front steps that are called stoops. **(10)** So instead of garage sales, they have stoop sales. **(11)** Families put used clothing and other articles for sale on their stoop, and people stop by to look and maybe buy just like at a garage sale.

(12) There is no county fair in the city, but there are feasts and festivals. **(13)** A street is closed down for a day or even a week. **(14)** Both sides are lined with stands. **(15)** Some stands have traditional fair games such as throwing darts at balloons. **(16)** Like the county fair, you can win a stuffed animal if you are lucky. **(17)** There are also stands serving Italian sausages and peppers, Vietnamese spring rolls, Mexican tacos, or Chinese noodles. **(18)** So in a different cultural setting, a county fair becomes a world's fair.

11. Which of the following is the best way to revise the underlined portion of sentence 4 (reproduced below)?

They call these row houses.

(A) They call these
(B) They call them
(C) Called
(D) These are called
(E) Defined as

12. In context, which of the following is the best way of combining sentences 7 and 8 (reproduced below)?

Cookouts are a favorite summer pastime. People who do not have a backyard take their grills to the park.

(A) Cookouts are a favorite summer pastime, and people who not have a backyard take their grills to the park.
(B) Cookouts, a favorite summer pastime, are had by people in the park who do not have backyards.
(C) A favorite summer pastime, cookouts are enjoyed by people who do not have a backyard in the park.
(D) A favorite summer pastime, people with and without backyards enjoy cookouts, but some in the park.
(E) People have cookouts as a favorite summer pastime, and those without backyards do it in the park.

13. In context, which of the following is the best way to revise sentence 10 (reproduced below)?

So instead of garage sales, they have stoop sales.

(A) (As it is now)
(B) So instead of garage sales, stoop sales are held.
(C) So instead of garage sales, people have stoops sales.
(D) They have stoop sales instead of garage sales.
(E) They have stoop sales, but they do not have garage sales.

14. In context, which of the following is the best way of revising sentence 16 (reproduced below)?

Like the county fair, you can win a stuffed animal if you are lucky.

(A) As the county fair, you can win a stuffed animal if you are lucky.

(B) As at the county fair, you can win a stuffed animal if you are lucky.

(C) You can win a stuffed animal at the county fair if you are lucky.

(D) If you are lucky, like the county fair, you can win a stuffed animal.

(E) If you are lucky, as the county fair, you can win a stuffed animal.

15. The passage makes use of all of the following techniques EXCEPT

(A) defining a term for the reader

(B) comparing different situations

(C) contrasting different situations

(D) providing examples for the reader

(E) relying on a noted authority

16. Which of the following would be an appropriate discussion if this passage were continued?

(A) Techniques used in the construction of row houses

(B) Fire department regulations for grilling in the park

(C) Aspects of holiday celebrations that are unique to the city

(D) Methods for cooking various types of the dishes mentioned

(E) More details on the types of games played at county fairs

Quiz II

(16 items; 12 minutes)

> **DIRECTIONS:** *Items #1–6:* The following sentences test your knowledge of grammar, usage, diction (choice of words), and idiom. Each sentence contains either no error or a single error. If there is an error, it is underlined and lettered. If the sentence contains an error, choose the one underlined portion that must be changed to produce a correct sentence. If there is no error, choose answer choice (E). In choosing answers, follow the conventions of standard written English.

1. Although the script <u>is interesting</u> and well
　　　　　　　　　　　A

written, <u>it</u> will <u>have to be</u> <u>adopted</u> for television.
　　　　　B　　　　　C　　　　D

<u>No error</u>
　E

2. The differences in climate <u>accounts</u> for the
　　　　　　　　　　　　　　　A

<u>marked</u> distinction <u>between</u> the north and south
　B　　　　　　　　C

<u>of</u> some countries. <u>No error</u>
　D　　　　　　　　E

3. The conductor <u>would like to have been</u> a
　　　　　　　　　　A

composer <u>but</u> after years of <u>unsuccessful</u>
　　　　　B　　　　　　　　　C

attempts, he <u>has given</u> it up. <u>No error</u>
　　　　　　D　　　　　　E

4. The judge <u>sentenced</u> the president of the
　　　　　　　A

corporation to 10 years in prison <u>for embezzling</u>
　　　　　　　　　　　　　　　B

funds, but he <u>gave</u> the president's partner <u>less</u>
　　　　　　C　　　　　　　　　　D

<u>of a</u> sentence.　<u>No error</u>
　D　　　　　　　E

5. <u>You taking</u> the <u>initiative</u> in the negotiations
　　A　　　　　　B

<u>will profit</u> the company to a <u>great degree</u>.
　C　　　　　　　　　　D

<u>No error</u>
　E

6. The princess, <u>along with</u> her entourage, <u>travel</u> by
　　　　　　　A　　　　　　　　B

ship because <u>she is</u> afraid <u>to fly</u>. <u>No error</u>
　　　　　C　　　　　D　　　E

---

7. The possibility of massive earthquakes <u>are regarded by most area residents with</u> a mixture of skepticism and caution.

   (A) are regarded by most area residents with
   (B) is regarded by most area residents with
   (C) is regarded by most area residents as
   (D) is mostly regarded by area residents with
   (E) by most area residents is regarded with

8. Certain infections are <u>made up by both viral and bacterial elements which makes</u> treatment of these infections difficult.

   (A) made up by both viral and bacterial elements which makes
   (B) composed by viral as well as bacterial elements and they make
   (C) composed of both viral and bacterial elements which make
   (D) composed of both viral and bacterial elements; this combination makes
   (E) including both viral as well as bacterial elements that make

9. <u>When it rains outside, most parents prefer small children to play indoors.</u>

   (A) When it rains outside, most parents prefer small children to play indoors.
   (B) Most parents prefer the indoors for their children's play when it rains.
   (C) Most parents prefer that small children play indoors when it rains.
   (D) When raining outside, most parents prefer small children to play indoors.
   (E) When raining, most parents prefer small children to play indoors.

10. <u>Opening the door to the street, the heat waves distorted the lamppost causing it to shimmer like a mirage.</u>

   (A) Opening the door to the street, the heat waves distorted the lamppost causing it to shimmer like a mirage.
   (B) The heat waves distorted the lamppost causing it to shimmer like a mirage through the open door to the street.
   (C) Through the open door to the street, one could see the lamppost, distorted by the heat waves, shimmering like a mirage.
   (D) Through the door which opened to the street, one could see the lamppost shimmering, distorted by the heat waves.
   (E) The heat waves distorted the lamppost, causing it to shimmer through the door like a mirage which opened to the street.

(1) The country that I would most like to visit is France. (2) I have taken two years of French in school. (3) I would like to practice what I have learned.

(4) Like everyone else, I want to visit Paris. (5) Many movies have been made about that city, such as the classic "An American in Paris," and it seems very glamorous. (6) I would walk along the Seine River, and then stop into a sidewalk cafe for a "limonade" (lemonade). (7) I would see historical places such as the site where the Bastille once stood and the Tomb of Napoleon as well as other points of interest such as Montmartre and the Eiffel Tower. (8) The Eiffel Tower was designed by Gustav Eiffel for the Exposition of 1889.

(9) Most of all, however, I would like to visit the beaches of Normandy, where allied troops landed in 1944. (10) My grandfather, who lived with my family when I was growing up, was a soldier at Normandy on D-Day. (11) As his only granddaughter, we were very close. (12) He used to tell me about the landing and where the army went as they moved inland. (13) I know he won medals, but he always talked about how brave the others were. (14) He never talked about war, but he talked a lot about how happy the French were when the Allied forces arrived. (15) Before he died, he gave me the diary he kept during that time. (16) I want to start at the beach and following the route that he took.

11. Which of the following is the best way to revise the underlined portions of sentences 2 and 3 (reproduced below) in order to combine the two sentences?

I have taken two years of French in <u>school. I would like to</u> practice what I have learned.

(A) school, but I would like to
(B) school, and I would like to
(C) school, being able to
(D) school, so I
(E) school, while I

12. In context, which of the following is the best way of revising sentence 5 (reproduced below)?

Many movies have been made about that city, such as the classic "An American in Paris," and it seems very glamorous.

(A) (As it is now)
(B) Many classic movies, such as "An American in Paris," have been made about that city, and it seems very glamorous.
(C) "An American in Paris," a classic movie, was made about that city, and it seems very glamorous.
(D) Many classic movies have been made about that city, such as "An American in Paris," and it seems very glamorous.
(E) Many movies, such as the classic "An American in Paris," have been made about that city, and they seem very glamorous.

13. In context, the most appropriate revision of sentence 8 is to

(A) make it the first sentence of paragraph 2
(B) make it the first sentence of paragraph 3
(C) make it the last sentence of the passage
(D) place it in parentheses
(E) delete it entirely

14. In context, which of the following is the best revision of sentence 11 (reproduced below)?

As his only granddaughter, we were very close.

(A) His only granddaughter was very close to him.
(B) I was his only granddaughter, so we were very close.
(C) We were very close, being his only granddaughter.
(D) We were very close, and I was his only granddaughter.
(E) Being an only granddaughter, we were very close.

15. In context, which of the following is the best revision of sentence 16 (reproduced below)?

I want to start at the beach and following the route that he took.

(A) I want to start at the beach and follow the route that he took.
(B) Starting at the beach and following the route that he took.
(C) In order to start at the beach, I want to follow the route that he took.
(D) Following the route that he took, I want to start at the beach.
(E) The route that he took I want to follow starting at the beach.

16. Which of the following best describes the structure of the essay?

(A) An answer to a question with two reasons
(B) An answer to a question with three reasons
(C) Two answers to a single question
(D) Three answers to a single question
(E) Two theories about a single event

Quiz III

(16 items; 12 minutes)

DIRECTIONS: *Items #1–6:* The following sentences test your knowledge of grammar, usage, diction (choice of words), and idiom. Each sentence contains either no error or a single error. If there is an error, it is underlined and lettered. If the sentence contains an error, choose the one underlined portion that must be changed to produce a correct sentence. If there is no error, choose answer choice (E). In choosing answers, follow the conventions of standard written English.

---

1. Alfred Stieglitz <u>launched</u> the career of Georgia

                A

   O'Keeffe, <u>who</u> he later married, <u>by exhibiting</u> her

       B   C

   paintings <u>in</u> his gallery. <u>No error</u>

         D   E

2. A recent study <u>indicates</u> that the average person

               A

   <u>ignores</u> most commercial advertising and <u>does</u>

  B   C

   <u>not buy</u> products because of <u>them</u>. <u>No error</u>

  C   D   E

3. The dean <u>lectured</u> <u>us students</u> <u>on</u> the privilege

          A   B   C

   and responsibility <u>of attending</u> the university.

                  D

   <u>No error</u>

  E

4. Only one of the animals in the zoo <u>is</u> in <u>their</u>

                      A   B

   natural <u>habitat</u>, but there are plans <u>to remedy</u> the

       C   D

   situation. <u>No error</u>

       E

5. <u>Feeling guilty about raising his voice, Webster</u>

         A   B

   <u>sought out</u> his friend in the local tavern and <u>tried</u>

  B   C

   <u>to assuage</u> his friend's bitterness <u>by offering him</u>

  C   D

   a glass of port. <u>No error</u>

           E

6. Eleanor <u>was</u> undecided <u>whether to go</u> to the

        A   B

   authorities with the money or <u>if she should keep</u>

                           C

   <u>it</u>; but finally <u>greed got</u> the better of her. <u>No error</u>

  C   D   E

DIRECTIONS: *Items #7–10:* The following sentences test correct, effective expression. Each sentence contains an underlined portion, or the entire sentence may be underlined. Following each sentence are five ways of phrasing the underlined portion. Choice (A) repeats the original; the other four choices are different. If you think the original is better than any of the other choices, choose (A); otherwise, choose one of the other choices.

In choosing answers, follow the conventions of standard written English. Make sure to consider issues of grammar, word choice, sentence construction, and punctuation. Your choice should produce the most effective sentence. It should be clear, precise, and free of ambiguity or awkwardness.

---

7. All of the students except George and <u>she intends on ordering</u> the newest edition of the textbook.

   (A) she intends on ordering
   (B) her intends on ordering
   (C) her intends to order
   (D) her intend to order
   (E) she intends to order

8. <u>According to tradition</u>, Vishnu appeared as Krishna to rid the world of a tyrannical king named Kamsa, the son of a demon.

(A) According to tradition
(B) Due to tradition
(C) Because of tradition
(D) Tradition has it that
(E) Traditionally

9. Scholars recognized immediately after <u>publication that the language experiments in *Finnegan's Wake* are different than</u> any other novel.

(A) publication that the language experiments in *Finnegan's Wake* are different than
(B) publication that the language experiments in *Finnegan's Wake* are different from
(C) publication that the language experiments in *Finnegan's Wake* are different from those of
(D) its publication that the language experiments in *Finnegan's Wake* differ from
(E) its publication that the language experiments in *Finnegan's Wake* are different from those of

10. <u>He had few redeeming virtues and those were obscured by his acerbic personality, and</u> I was extremely fond of him.

(A) He had few redeeming virtues and those were obscured by his acerbic personality, and
(B) He had few redeeming virtues, which were obscured by his acerbic personality, and
(C) Although he had few redeeming virtues and those were obscured by his acerbic personality,
(D) Although he had few redeeming virtues, which were obscured by his acerbic personality,
(E) Although he had few redeeming virtues, and those obscured by his acerbic personality,

DIRECTIONS: *Items #11–16:* The following passage is an early draft of an essay. Some portions of the passage need to be revised.

Read the passage and answer the items that follow. Items may be about particular sentences or parts of sentences, asking you to improve the word choice or sentence structure. Other items may refer to parts of the essay or the entire essay, asking you to consider organization or development. In making your decisions, follow the conventions of standard written English.

(1) Human beings are using more and more energy. (2) One reason is that the world's population is growing, so there is more demand for energy. (3) Another is that people, especially those whose standard of living is beginning to improve, want to consume more and more energy. (4) However, it is creating new threats to the environment.

(5) Nuclear power plants produce electricity for people to use. (6) What should be done with the spent reactor fuel? (7) Some experts say to put it deep into abandoned salt mines, but other experts say to store it temporarily until a better solution is found. (8) Additionally, it has been known for over 30 years that smog caused by cars is a health hazard. (9) We haven't been able to solve the problem. (10) Some experts say we have come a long way, but others say that we haven't even begun. (11) Some scientists say that global warming will cause the polar ice caps to melt, with the result of massive flooding. (12) Other scientists say this will not happen.

(13) I am not a scientist, so I cannot say who is right. (14) However, I would argue more attention needs to be paid to the common cause of all these problems. (15) Perhaps then, an overall solution would be arrived at by the experts.

11. In context, the word "it" in sentence 4 refers to

(A) A higher standard of living
(B) The increase in the world's population
(C) The demand for energy
(D) The increased consumption of energy
(E) New environmental problems

12. Which of the following is the most effective way to combine sentences 5 and 6 (reproduced below)?

Nuclear power plants produce electricity for people to use. What should be done with the spent reactor fuel?

(A) Nuclear power plants produce electricity, so what should be done with the spent reactor fuel?
(B) Nuclear power plants produce electricity, but what should be done with the spent reactor fuel?
(C) What should be done with the spent reactor fuel because nuclear power plants produce electricity?
(D) How should the spent reactor fuel from the nuclear power plants producing electricity be disposed of?
(E) What should be done with the spent reactor fuel as it produces electricity as a nuclear power plant?

13. In context, which of the following would be the most effective word to introduce sentence 8?

(A) Because
(B) Now,
(C) Still,
(D) Also,
(E) Fortunately,

14. In context, which of the following would be the best revision of the underlined portion of sentence 11 (reproduced below)?

Some scientists say that global warming will cause the polar ice caps <u>to melt, with the result of massive flooding</u>.

(A) to melt, resulting in massive flooding
(B) to melt, to result in massive flooding
(C) melting, with the result of massive flooding
(D) to melt and to flood massively
(E) to melt and resulting with massive floods

15. In context, which of the following is the best revision of sentence 15 (reproduced below)?

Perhaps then, an overall solution would be arrived at by the experts.

(A) Perhaps then, an overall solution would be arrived at by the experts.
(B) Perhaps then, an overall solution will be arrived at by the experts.
(C) Perhaps then, the experts would arrive at an overall solution.
(D) The experts, perhaps then, would arrive at an overall solution.
(E) An overall solution would, then, perhaps be arrived at by the experts.

16. The author develops the essay primarily by

(A) posing a question and answering it
(B) citing statistics
(C) criticizing experts and scientists
(D) discussing a complicated problem
(E) contrasting expert opinions

Quiz IV Brain Buster
(16 items; 12 minutes)

NOTE: Unlike previous quizzes, which showcase the variety of Writing: Multiple-Choice items you will see on the SAT, Quiz IV focuses on the item-type that lends itself to the most difficult item.

DIRECTIONS: The following sentences test correct, effective expression. Each sentence contains an underlined portion, or the entire sentence may be underlined. Following each sentence are five ways of phrasing the underlined portion. Choice A repeats the original; the other four choices are different. If you think the original is better than any of the other choices, choose (A); otherwise, choose one of the other choices.

In choosing answers, follow the conventions of standard written English. Make sure to consider issues of grammar, word choice, sentence construction, and punctuation. Your choice should produce the most effective sentence. It should be clear, precise, and free of ambiguity or awkwardness.

1. Although the Battle of Fort Ann is rarely mentioned in history texts, it <u>may have been the most significant engagement of the Revolutionary War because it led</u> ultimately to General Burgoyne's defeat at Saratoga.

   (A) may have been the most significant engagement of the Revolutionary War because it led
   (B) could have been the most significant engagement of the Revolutionary War because it led
   (C) could have been the most significant engagement of the Revolutionary War if it led
   (D) might have been the most significant engagement of the Revolutionary War leading
   (E) might have been the more significant engagement of the Revolutionary War that led

2. The paintings of Gustav Klimt are different <u>from the painters he inspired who were more interested in exploring the unconscious than him</u>.

   (A) from the painters he inspired who were more interested in exploring the unconscious than him
   (B) from those of the painters he inspired being more interested in the exploration of the unconscious than he
   (C) than those of the painters he inspired who were more interested in the exploration of the unconscious than he
   (D) than the painters he inspired because they were more interested in exploring the unconscious than he was
   (E) from those of the painters he inspired who were more interested in exploring the unconscious than he

3. <u>To protest their being underpaid in comparison to other city agencies, a strike was called by the sanitation workers.</u>

   (A) To protest their being underpaid in comparison to other city agencies, a strike was called by the sanitation workers.
   (B) To protest them being underpaid in comparison with other city agencies, the sanitation workers called a strike.
   (C) To protest their being comparatively underpaid with other city agencies, a strike was called by the sanitation workers.
   (D) To protest their being underpaid in comparison with workers of other city agencies, the sanitation workers called a strike.
   (E) The sanitation workers called a strike to protest them being underpaid in comparison with other city workers.

4. <u>The Bichon Frisé is a breed of non-sporting dog, descending from the water spaniel and originating</u> in ancient times in the Mediterranean area.

(A) The Bichon Frisé is a breed of non-sporting dog, descending from the water spaniel and originating

(B) The Bichon Frisé, which is a breed of non-sporting dog descending from the water spaniel, originated

(C) The Bichon Frisé, a breed of non-sporting dog descended from the water spaniel, originated

(D) The Bichon Frisé, a breed of non-sporting dog, descended from the water spaniel which originated

(E) A Bichon Frisé is a breed of non-sporting dog, descended from the water spaniel, and has its origin

5. During the card game, the defense found the only lead that was likely to defeat the contract, the declarer <u>ruffed in, sloughed her losing club on dummy's ace of diamonds,</u> after drawing trumps, was able to score six spade tricks to make the grand slam.

(A) ruffed in, sloughed her losing club on dummy's ace of diamonds,

(B) ruffed in and sloughed her losing club on dummy's ace of diamonds

(C) ruffing in, sloughed her losing club on dummy's ace of diamonds

(D) ruffed in, sloughed her losing club on dummy's ace of diamonds, and

(E) ruffed in, sloughing her losing club on dummy's ace of diamonds,

6. <u>Lincoln, discovering in young manhood the secret that the Yankee peddler has learned before him, knew</u> how to use a good story to generate good will.

(A) Lincoln, discovering in young manhood the secret that the Yankee peddler has learned before him, knew

(B) Discovering in young manhood the secret that the Yankee peddler has learned before him, Lincoln knew

(C) Lincoln, discovering the secret that the Yankee peddler had learned in young manhood before him, knew

(D) In young manhood Lincoln discovered the secret that the Yankee peddler had learned before him:

(E) Lincoln, discovered in young manhood the secret that the Yankee peddler had learned before him, knew

7. The portfolio, which was apparently <u>left inadvertent on the bus, contained three completed watercolors, including several uncompleted sketches</u>.

(A) left inadvertent on the bus, contained three completed watercolors, including several uncompleted sketches

(B) left inadvertently on the bus, contained three completed watercolors, including several uncompleted sketches

(C) inadvertently left on the bus containing three completed watercolors, including several uncompleted sketches

(D) inadvertently left on the bus, contained three completed watercolors and several uncompleted sketches

(E) left inadvertently on the bus with three completed watercolors and several uncompleted sketches

8. Recent tests on a variety of herbal supplements designed to reduce cholesterol found that half did not contain the listed <u>ingredients, were so poorly manufactured that the active ingredients, when present,</u> could not be absorbed.

(A) ingredients, were so poorly manufactured that the active ingredients, when present,
(B) ingredients, which were so poorly manufactured that the active ingredients, when present,
(C) ingredients or were so poorly manufactured that the active ingredients, when present,
(D) ingredients were so poorly manufactured that the present active ingredients,
(E) ingredients, were so poorly manufactured, and that the active ingredients, when present,

9. Both Samuel Beckett and Joseph Conrad were brought up speaking one language <u>and they wrote in another language when they wrote novels</u>.

(A) and they wrote in another language when they wrote novels
(B) having written novels in another language altogether
(C) but wrote their novels in another language
(D) yet when they wrote novels, they wrote them in another language
(E) with their novels being written in a different language

10. <u>The relationship of smoking and lung cancer have been firmly established, yet people continue to ignore warnings, jeopardizing their health and that of others.</u>

(A) The relationship of smoking and lung cancer have been firmly established, yet people continue to ignore warnings, jeopardizing their health and that of others.
(B) The relationship of smoking to lung cancer has been firmly established, yet people continue to ignore the warnings, jeopardizing their health and that of others.
(C) The relationship of smoking to lung cancer has been firmly established, yet people continually ignore the warnings that jeopardize their own health and that of others.
(D) The relationship between smoking and lung cancer has been firmly established, yet people continue to ignore warnings, jeopardizing their own health and that of others.
(E) The relationship of smoking with lung cancer has been firmly established, with people continuing to ignore the warnings and jeopardizing their own health and others.

11. More than just a movie star, Audrey Hepburn was celebrated for her luminous beauty, for her acclaimed acting ability, <u>and everyone knew of her humanitarian work with organizations</u> such as UNICEF.

(A) and everyone knew of her humanitarian work with organizations
(B) and everyone knew of her humanitarian organizations work
(C) and for her humanitarian work with organizations
(D) and her humanitarian work with organizations
(E) along with her humanitarian work with organizations

12. The driving snow made the roadway slippery and reduced visibility to no more than a few feet, <u>and fortunately there were no</u> accidents despite the heavy volume of traffic.

(A) and fortunately there were no
(B) but fortunately there were no
(C) and fortunately there were some
(D) while fortunately there were no
(E) so fortunately there were no

13. India's movie industry <u>may not be as well known as the United States, but it is much bigger because</u> film is the principal storytelling vehicle in a country where more than 40 percent of the population is illiterate and the cheapest ticket costs no more than a quarter.

(A) may not be as well known as the United States, but it is much bigger because
(B) may not be as well known as that of the United States, but it is much bigger because
(C) might not be as well known as that of the United States, but it is much bigger on account of
(D) could not be as well known as the United States, but they are much bigger because
(E) may not be as well known as that of the United States and bigger because

14. <u>Although the American relay team did not qualify for the finals, the</u> anchor runner dropped the baton shortly after the hand-off.

(A) Although the American relay team did not qualify for the finals, the
(B) When the American relay team did not qualify for the finals, the
(C) The American relay team did not qualify for the finals, and the
(D) The American relay team did not qualify for the finals because the
(E) Not qualifying for the finals, the American relay team's

15. The <u>newly released worm is especially dangerous because</u> it directs infected computers to launch a distributed denial of service attack on the very web sites that offer instructions for combating the worm.

(A) newly released worm is especially dangerous because
(B) released new worm is especially dangerous because
(C) released new worm is dangerous especially because
(D) newly released worm is especially dangerous on account of
(E) new released worm is dangerous especially as it

16. Many geologists believe that the likelihood of a devastating earthquake of magnitude 8 or higher <u>is as great or greater in the eastern part of the United States than</u> in California.

(A) is as great or greater in the eastern part of the United States than
(B) may be at least as great or greater in the eastern part of the United States than
(C) is so great or greater in the eastern part of the United States than
(D) is at least as great in the eastern part of the United States as
(E) can be at least so great in the eastern part of the United States as

Quiz V

(1 essay; 25 minutes)

DIRECTIONS: The essay tests your ability to express ideas, develop a point of view, present ideas in a clear and logical fashion, and use language precisely.

Write your essay on the lines provided on your answer sheet—you will receive no other paper on which to write. Do not write your essay in your test book. You will receive credit only for what appears on your answer sheet. Write legibly, and remember that graders must be able to read your handwriting.

You have 25 minutes to plan and write an essay on the topic assigned below. Do not write on any other topic. An essay on another topic is not acceptable. Sample essays begin on page 628.

Think carefully about the issue presented in the following excerpts and the assignment below.

1. Actors and athletes, or anyone in the public eye, should not be surprised that the public is interested in their private lives. Having a public profession, and all the rewards that come with that occupation, means that public figures must contend with diminished privacy.

2. Just because someone works in a so-called public profession does not necessarily mean that he or she should not expect a degree of privacy. Signing a contract to play professional sports, seeking fame as an actor or actress, or having a high-profile job is not giving away the right to a private life. Being famous does not mean that a person should have to contend with intrusive fans and media members.

Assignment: Should anyone with a profession that puts them in the public eye expect to live a private life? Plan and write an essay in which you develop your point of view on this issue. Support your position with reasoning and examples taken from your reading, studies, experience, or observations.

Essay Outline

REVIEW

This section contains additional Writing: Multiple-Choice items and one Writing: Essay for further practice. Answers are on page 629.

> **DIRECTIONS:** _Items #1–19:_ The following sentences test your knowledge of grammar, usage, diction (choice of words), and idiom. Each sentence contains either no error or a single error. If there is an error, it is underlined and lettered. If the sentence contains an error, choose the one underlined portion that must be changed to produce a correct sentence. If there is no error, choose answer choice (E). In choosing answers, follow the conventions of standard written English.

1. If Mary Outerbridge <u>would not have seen</u> English
                          A

   officers <u>playing</u> tennis in Bermuda <u>where</u> she
          B   C

   <u>was vacationing</u> at the time, she would not have
      D

   introduced the game to America. <u>No error</u>
                             E

2. <u>When we consider</u> the miracles of modern
      A

   science, we find it hard to imagine <u>that</u> in 1349
                           B

   the Black Death <u>killed</u> one-third of <u>England's</u>
            C   D

   population. <u>No error</u>
           E

3. <u>When</u> the critics <u>wrote</u> negative reviews of the
    A   B

   Broadway <u>opening</u> of the rock star's new
            C

   musical, neither the producer nor the director

   <u>were</u> available for an interview. <u>No error</u>
    D   E

4. Those <u>who are successful in business</u> often
                  A

   discover <u>that</u> wealth and fame <u>do not guarantee</u>
           B   C

   happiness and <u>learning</u> that peace of mind is
               D

   important. <u>No error</u>
           E

5. About 3,500 B.C., ancient Egypt made great

   progress in agriculture after <u>they</u> adopted several
                        A

   new techniques of cultivation <u>among which</u>
                     B

   <u>were</u> <u>raking, plowing, and spreading manure.</u>
    C   D

   <u>No error</u>
    E

6. In the southwest corner of the cemetery, where
A

the honeysuckle vines have all but covered the
B

grave markers, lays the body of the county's
C

greatest war hero. No error
D   E

7. The final number of the musical, a duet, was
A

written by Sue and is sung by she and Reginald,
A   B

the male lead, as the other members of the cast
C

take their bows. No error
D   E

8. The owner of the property, who had farmed the
A

land for more than 40 years, listened to the
B   C

company's offer but said that he could not answer

definite without further consideration. No error
D   E

9. Immediately after the legislators freezed the level
A

of benefits, citizens groups began contacting their
B   C

members to encourage them to write letters of

protest to their representatives in Congress.
D

No error
E

10. Since the treasurer and him had already discussed
A   B

the details of the financial report, Robert felt that

it was not necessary for him to attend the budget
C   D

meeting. No error
E

11. The history of the ancient Egyptians, as recorded

by graphic drawings called hieroglyphics,
A   B

describe in great detail the burial of King
C   D

Tutankhamen's body in a sarcophagus of wood

and gold. No error
E

12. The conditions of the subway system having been
A   B

improved dramatically over the past three years,
B   C

but much work still remains to be done. No error
D   E

13. Introduced at the last moment by the Scholastic
A

Council was a demand that the college allocate
B   C

funds for a day-care center and a demand that the

college hire more minority faculty members.
D

No error
E

14. <u>Summarily rejecting</u> the demands of the students
     A

for a greater voice in determining <u>university</u>
                                  B

policy, the dean now worries <u>that</u> her decision
                           C

<u>might result</u> in new student demonstrations.
   D

<u>No error</u>
  E

15. The dog <u>has been replaced</u> by the cat as the pet of
         A

choice for Americans <u>because</u> cats <u>are</u> more
               B   C

independent and require less care <u>than</u> dogs.
                          D

<u>No error</u>
  E

16. Because many modern actors <u>study</u> method
                  A

acting, <u>a system devised</u> by Stanislavsky, <u>their</u>
        B   C

interpretations of the role of Hamlet differ <u>from</u>
                                D

<u>Shakespeare's time</u>. <u>No error</u>
    D   E

17. <u>During</u> the second half of the nineteenth century,
  A

waves of immigration <u>in</u> the United States
                  B

<u>brought</u> hundreds of thousands of foreigners to
  C

America's cities <u>and created</u> the condition termed
                  D

the "melting pot." <u>No error</u>
               E

18. The governor's oratorical skill, <u>which</u> has helped
                        A

him <u>to win</u> several elections, <u>comes</u> either from
     B   C

his college debating experience <u>and</u> from an in-
                          D

depth knowledge of the issues. <u>No error</u>
                    E

19. The decade of the 1920s was <u>an important one</u>
                          A

for English literature, for during that time a large

<u>amount</u> of works now considered classics were
  B

written <u>by</u> great writers <u>such as</u> Ezra Pound,
       C   D

D. H. Lawrence, and T. S. Eliot. <u>No error</u>
                      E

DIRECTIONS: _Items #20–33:_ The following sentences test correct, effective expression. Each sentence contains an underlined portion, or the entire sentence may be underlined. Following each sentence are five ways of phrasing the underlined portion. Choice (A) repeats the original; the other four choices are different. If you think the original is better than any of the other choices, choose (A); otherwise, choose one of the other choices.

In choosing answers, follow the conventions of standard written English. Make sure to consider issues of grammar, word choice, sentence construction, and punctuation. Your choice should produce the most effective sentence. It should be clear, precise, and free of ambiguity or awkwardness.

20. Unemployed laborers ignored the picket lines set up by striking workers at the factory's only <u>entrance, and they thereby rendered it</u> ineffective.

   (A) entrance, and they thereby rendered it
   (B) entrance and therefore rendered it
   (C) entrance, by which the strike was rendered
   (D) entrance, thereby this rendered the strike
   (E) entrance, thereby rendering the strike

21. <u>Ignoring a projected decline in births over the next decade,</u> the school board allocated funds for a new elementary school based upon an increase in the infant population last year.

   (A) Ignoring a projected decline in births over the next decade,
   (B) By ignoring a projected decline in births over the next decade,
   (C) To ignore a projected decline in births over the next decade,
   (D) The next decade's projected decline in births having been ignored,
   (E) A projected decline in births over the next decade is ignored when

22. The supporters of the volunteer ambulance corps were assured <u>as to the deductibility of their donations on their tax returns</u>.

   (A) as to the deductibility of their donations on their tax returns
   (B) as to their donations being deductible on their tax returns
   (C) that their, the supporters', donations are deductible on their tax returns
   (D) that in regards to their tax returns the donations are deductible
   (E) that their donations are deductible on their tax returns

23. <u>A million dollars before his twenty-fifth birthday having been made</u>, the young entrepreneur decided to write a book instructing others in the techniques of his success.

   (A) A million dollars before his twenty-fifth birthday having been made
   (B) A million dollars before his twenty-fifth birthday made
   (C) By twenty-five, when he made a million dollars
   (D) When he made a million dollars by his twenty-fifth birthday
   (E) Having made a million dollars by his twenty-fifth birthday

24. The most frequently advanced justifications for rising physicians' fees <u>is they pay increasing malpractice insurance premiums and invest</u> in costly equipment.

   (A) is they pay increasing malpractice insurance premiums and invest
   (B) are they pay increasing malpractice insurance premiums and invest
   (C) are that physicians pay increasing malpractice insurance premiums and that they invest
   (D) is increasing malpractice insurance premiums and investing
   (E) are increasing malpractice insurance premiums and the need to invest

25. Visiting Europe as a tourist ten years after the end of the war, <u>the rapid pace of the postwar reconstruction amazed the former soldier</u>.

    (A) the rapid pace of the postwar reconstruction amazed the former soldier
    (B) the postwar reconstruction that had taken place at a rapid pace amazed the former soldier
    (C) the former soldier was amazed at the rapid pace of the postwar reconstruction
    (D) the former soldier who was amazed at the rapid pace of the postwar reconstruction
    (E) the former soldier was amazed at how rapid the postwar reconstruction was

26. Although Janice has expressed a desire to become a couture designer, <u>she lacks the necessary sewing skills and has no</u> interest in detail work.

    (A) she lacks the necessary sewing skills and has no
    (B) lacking the necessary sewing skills, she has no
    (C) she is without the necessary sewing skills and
    (D) she does not have the necessary sewing skills nor the
    (E) she is lacking in the necessary sewing skills and

27. It is distressing to many would-be teachers that the Board of Examiners in New York City has the sole power to decide <u>about licensing teachers</u>.

    (A) about licensing teachers
    (B) whether or not a teacher should be licensed
    (C) whether or not teachers' licensing
    (D) as to whether or not a teacher should be licensed
    (E) the licensing of teachers, if they so choose

28. A person's decision to pursue a career in law sometimes results <u>from a lack of any true direction rather than from</u> any commitment to the principles of justice.

    (A) from a lack of any true direction rather than from
    (B) from a lack of any true direction as from
    (C) As a lack of any true direction as much as from
    (D) from a lack of any true direction and
    (E) from a lack of any true direction but

29. Left to his own devices, a curious four-year-old can learn much from computerized <u>toys, the problem being that the learning experience</u> is devoid of any social element.

    (A) toys, the problem being that the learning experience
    (B) toys, but the problem is that using computerized toys to learn
    (C) toys; in learning from toys, one
    (D) toys, but that learning experience
    (E) toys; the problem is that in learning from them, it

30. Since some vegetables, such as tomatoes, peppers, and eggplants, are difficult to grow from seed, <u>seedlings will</u> improve your chances of a rich harvest.

    (A) seedlings will
    (B) seedlings
    (C) the use of seedlings will
    (D) to use seedlings will
    (E) using seedlings to

31. Because Ian had been wounded in the European <u>Campaign, so he was asked</u> to serve as Grand Marshal of the Memorial Day Parade.

    (A) Campaign, so he was asked
    (B) Campaign, he was asked
    (C) Campaign, they asked him
    (D) Campaign, so they asked him
    (E) Campaign, that he was asked

32. The present administration <u>has always and will continue to be</u> committed to a policy of guaranteeing a good education to every child in the district.

    (A) has always and will continue to be
    (B) has always and continues to be
    (C) has always been and will continue
    (D) has always been and will continue to be
    (E) always has been and continues

33. The gift certificate for a hot-air balloon ride gives the recipient the option <u>that you may exchange the certificate</u> for cash.

    (A) that you may exchange the certificate
    (B) that the certificate may be exchanged
    (C) of exchanging the certificate
    (D) of your exchanging the certificate
    (E) to exchange the certificate

DIRECTIONS: *Items #34–36:* The following passage is an early draft of an essay. Some portions of the passage need to be revised.

Read the passage and answer the items that follow. Items may be about particular sentences or parts of sentences, asking you to improve the word choice or sentence structure. Other items may refer to parts of the essay or the entire essay, asking you to consider organization or development. In making your decisions, follow the conventions of standard written English.

(1) Today, planners are looking for renewable energy sources to satisfy the growing demand for energy. (2) One idea that gets much attention in the press is generating electricity from wind power. (3) Articles in newspapers and magazines are often written as though wind power is a new idea, but it is really one of the oldest energy sources used by human beings.

(4) No records of the earliest wind machines survive, but they may have been built in China more than three thousand years ago or perhaps on the windy plains of Afghanistan. (5) Some sources hint that Egyptians during the time of the Pharaohs used wind power for drawing water for agricultural purposes. (6) Around 2,000 B.C., Hammurabi may have taken time out from developing his legal code to sponsor development of some sort of wind machine.

(7) The earliest confirmed wind machines were located in Persia. (8) Persian writers described gardens irrigated by wind-driven water lifts. (9) The Persian machines were horizontal devices, carousel-like contraptions that revolved around a center pole and that caught the wind with bundles of reeds. (10) Indeed, there is a certain engineering advantage to the carousel: it doesn't matter from which direction the wind is blowing.

(11) From the Middle East, wind machine technology may have been carried to Europe by returning Crusaders, for soon after the Crusades windmills appeared in Northern Europe and on the British Isles. (12) Windmills flourished for a while in Europe but gave way to steam power.

(13) Those engaged in research and development on wind power now face the same problem that caused the shift from wind to steam power: how to handle the extremes of wind velocity. (14) Wind, after all, is real iffy. (15) It can fail to blow just when it is needed, or it can blow a gale right when it isn't needed.

34. Which of the following best explains why sentence 7 should begin a new paragraph?

    (A) The writer begins to discuss wind power in Persia rather than in China, Afghanistan, or Egypt.
    (B) The writer shifts to a discussion of historical records rather than speculation.
    (C) The Persian wind machines were horizontal wheels rather than vertical ones.
    (D) It is not certain that wind machine technology was brought to Europe from the Middle East.
    (E) The Persians were the first to successfully harness the power of the wind.

35. Which of the following is the LEAST appropriate revision of the underlined part of sentence 11?

From the Middle East, wind machine technology may have been carried to Europe by returning Crusaders, for soon after the Crusades windmills appeared in Northern Europe and on the British Isles.

(A) since windmills appeared in Northern Europe and on the British Isles soon after the Crusades

(B) inasmuch as windmills appeared soon after the Crusades in Northern Europe and on the British Isles

(C) because windmills appeared in Northern Europe and on the British Isles soon after the Crusades

(D) given that windmills appeared soon after the Crusades in Northern Europe and on the British Isles

(E) therefore windmills appeared in Northern Europe and on the British Isles soon after the Crusades

36. Which of the following revisions is most needed?

(A) Substitute "increasing" for "growing" in sentence 1.

(B) Substitute "exist" for "survive" in sentence 4.

(C) Substitute "built" for "located" in sentence 7.

(D) Substitute "yielded" for "gave way" in sentence 12.

(E) Substitute "very variable" for "real iffy" in sentence 14.

37. Which of the following is the best order for paragraphs 2, 3, and 4?

(A) 2, 3, 4

(B) 2, 4, 3

(C) 3, 2, 4

(D) 3, 4, 2

(E) 4, 2, 3

DIRECTIONS: The essay tests your ability to express ideas, develop a point of view, present ideas in a clear and logical fashion, and use language precisely.

Write your essay on the lines provided on your answer sheet—you will receive no other paper on which to write. Do not write your essay in your test book. You will receive credit only for what appears on your answer sheet. Write legibly, and remember that graders must be able to read your handwriting.

You have 25 minutes to plan and write an essay on the topic assigned below. Do not write on any other topic. An essay on another topic is not acceptable. Sample essays begin on page 629.

Think carefully about the issue presented in the following excerpts and the assignment below.

1. Many people rightfully reminisce about "the good old days," insisting that the quality of life was much better thirty or forty years ago. The problems of the modern world were less then. Environmental issues were of no concern, overcrowding was less of a problem, and life was simpler.

2. While conditions have definitely changed since "the good old days," the quality of life today is considerably improved over that of thirty or forty years ago. Modernization has brought many positive changes in the world including increased food production, faster transportation, and greatly improved global communication.

Assignment: Which do you find more compelling, the belief that the quality of life was better thirty or forty years ago or that it is better today? Plan and write an essay in which you develop your point of view on this issue. Support your position with reasoning and examples taken from your reading, studies, experience, or observations.

Essay Outline

STRATEGY SUMMARY

General Strategies

After you memorize the directions, they can be safely ignored; therefore, do not waste valuable test time by re-reading instructions. The Writing: Multiple-Choice items should be answered according to difficulty level—from easiest to hardest. The Identifying Sentence Errors items are generally the easiest of the three types, followed by the Improving Sentences items, and lastly the Improving Paragraphs items. Each Writing item-type counts the same towards the Writing score.

Strategy for Identifying Sentence Error Items

1. Read the entire sentence once quickly. Look for obvious errors.

2. Take a closer look at the underlined parts of the sentence. Remember that answer choice (E) is always "No error." Look for obvious errors in the underlined parts.

3. Look for errors in usage—when an underlined part of the sentence is not properly connected to another part of the sentence that is not underlined.

4. Do not be afraid to choose answer choice (E). Approximately one-fifth of the correct answer choices will be (E).

5. The "Checklist for Possible Writing Errors" on the following page summarizes the types of writing errors for which to search.

Strategy for Improving Sentences Items

1. Read the entire sentence for comprehension of the overall meaning. Look for possible errors. Mentally note how to correct possible errors.

2. Study the answer choices, looking for one that matches your anticipated answer. Do not read answer choice (A) because it is always the same as the underlined part of the original sentence.

3. Compare answer choices. What makes them different? Is the difference good or bad?

4. Do not choose answer choices that introduce new errors or change the meaning of the sentence.

5. Do not be afraid to choose answer choice (A). Approximately one-fifth of the correct answer choices will be (A).

6. The "Checklist for Possible Writing Errors" on the following page summarizes the types of writing errors for which to search and to avoid when revising sentences.

Strategy for Improving Paragraphs Items

1. Do not ignore the essay prompt—it may provide valuable information about the overall point of the essay.

2. Remember that all revisions must be made in context—changes to the original sentences and structure of the essay cannot change the original meaning.

3. Read the entire essay first. Develop a mental picture of the main point, development, and organization.

4. Pay attention to the development and organization—the relationships between and among sentences.

5. The "Checklist for Possible Writing Errors" on the following page summarizes the types of writing errors for which to search and to avoid when revising sentences.

6. When revising sentences, be sure that the new sentence structure follows all rules for standard written English and maintains consistency in the verb tense, pronoun case, tone, etc. with the overall essay.

7. When revising the essay, make sure that the new revisions maintain the logical development and organization of the essay. Make sure that the revised paragraphs refer to only one main topic.

Checklist for Possible Writing Errors

1. *Verbs:* Does the sentence have a main verb? Do all verbs agree with their subjects? Are they in the correct tense?

2. *Pronouns:* Do all pronouns have clearly identifiable referents? Do they agree with their referents? Are they in the proper case?

3. *Adjectives and Adverbs:* Do all adjectives or adverbs correctly modify nouns, verbs, or other adjectives? Is the use of a specific adjective or adverb appropriate?

4. *Prepositions:* Are all prepositions used idiomatically?

5. *Conjunctions:* Are all conjunctions consistent with the logic of the sentence?

6. *Modifier:* If the sentence has a modifier, is it close to what it modifies? Is the idea clearly and logically presented?

7. *Comparisons:* If the sentence makes a comparison, are like things being compared? Is the idea clearly and logically presented?

8. *Parallelism:* If the sentence includes a series of ideas, are the ideas presented in the same form?

9. *Diction:* Do the words mean what the sentence intends for them to mean?

10. *Conciseness:* Does the sentence use more words than necessary? For Improving Sentences and Improving Paragraphs items, does the proposed answer choice eliminate unnecessary wordiness without introducing additional errors?

11. *Directness:* Can the sentence be worded more directly? For Improving Sentences and Improving Paragraphs items, does the proposed answer choice eliminate unnecessary indirectness without introducing additional errors?

Strategy for the Essay

1. Begin with the prompt.

2. Write only on the assigned topic. Writing on any other topic will result in a score of 0.

3. Do not try to do too much. Try to mentally limit the scope of your topic.

4. Organize your thoughts and write an outline before beginning the essay. Do not spend more than two minutes writing the outline.

    a) Familiarize yourself with the essay prompt and assignment.

    b) Develop a point of view.

    c) Develop a thesis.

    d) Identify two to four important points.

    e) Decide on the order of presentation of the major points.

5. Organize your ideas into paragraphs.

    a) Introduction

    b) Two to four body paragraphs

    c) Conclusion

6. Write grammatically.

7. Write clearly, concisely, and legibly.

8. Punctuate and spell correctly.

9. Spend a few minutes proofreading your essay.

Additional Practice

To identify items for additional practice, see the Item Index at the back of this book, which offers a breakdown of items by tested concept.

Practice Test Reinforcement

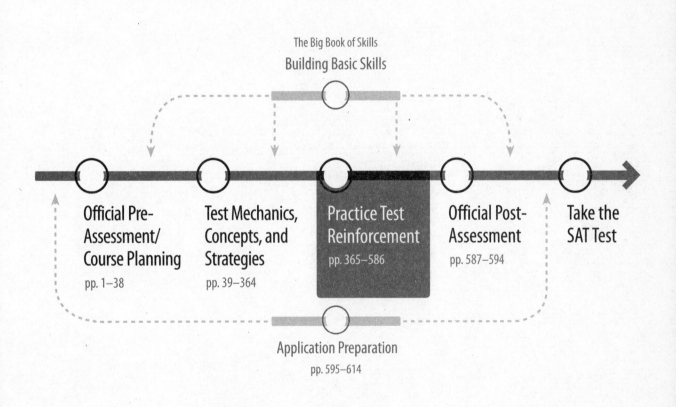

The Big Book of Skills
Building Basic Skills

Official Pre-Assessment/ Course Planning
pp. 1–38

Test Mechanics, Concepts, and Strategies
pp. 39–364

Practice Test Reinforcement
pp. 365–586

Official Post-Assessment
pp. 587–594

Take the SAT Test

Application Preparation
pp. 595–614

CAMBRIDGE
VICTORY FOR THE
SAT TEST

Directed Study Practice Test

Outline

I. **Section 1:** Writing (pp. 369–371)

II. **Section 2:** Math (pp. 372–381)

III. **Section 3:** Writing (pp. 382–396)

IV. **Section 4:** Critical Reading (pp. 397–407)

V. **Section 5:** Math (pp. 408–415)

VI. **Section 6:** Critical Reading (pp. 416–428)

VII. **Section 8:** Math (pp. 429–435)

VIII. **Section 9:** Critical Reading (pp. 436–446)

IX. **Section 10:** Writing (pp. 447–453)

Directed Study Practice Test

SECTION 1—WRITING
1 Essay

DIRECTIONS: The essay tests your ability to express ideas, develop a point of view, present ideas in a clear and logical fashion, and use language precisely.

Plan and write an essay on the topic assigned below. Do not write on any other topic. An essay on another topic is not acceptable.

Think carefully about the issue presented in the following excerpt and the assignment below.

> The image of America as a "melting pot" is false and outdated. The United States absorbed millions of immigrants at the turn of the last century who, over time, lost their cultural heritage to become "American." This melting away of cultures into one larger "American" culture that took on some specific cultural influences of its new citizens can largely be attributed to the fact that many of these new immigrants were of European descent and could physically "fit in" with their neighbors. Today, immigrants from all corners of the globe tend to hold onto their cultural legacy, making modern American society closer to a "salad bowl" than a "melting pot."

Assignment: In your opinion, is the United States more of a cultural "Melting Pot" or "Salad Bowl"? Plan and write an essay in which you develop your point of view on this issue. Support your position with reasoning and examples taken from your reading, studies, experience, and observations.

Above Average Essay Response

Is the image of America as a "Melting Pot" false and outdated, or is it alive and vital? People of many cultures and backgrounds populated the country from the beginning. Thus, the term the great "Melting Pot" for America. I feel that the people who have arrived in recent years have not assimilated, and have made our country more of a "Salad Bowl." The separateness is especially seen in recent immigrant commercial and business areas, and in their media. Other major evidence of the "Salad Bowl" effect is seen in the public school system.

In our major cities, there are areas of services, restaurants, grocery stores and clubs completely oriented to particular immigrant populations and their language and customs. As these areas expand, the immigrants have little need to adapt their language or life activities to the larger "American" culture. This is in contrast to earlier immigrant influxes, where they were immersed in the life of the cities with varied cultures and interests.

Thousands of immigrants from a particular country have settled in some rural cities in the Midwest areas of the USA, such as where my Grandparents live. Here again their culture, language and traditions are imported with them, and they live in these small towns as separate islands. The public schools are especially challenged to educate in the face of varied language backgrounds, clothing requirements, and expectations of male/female differences.

The widespread availability of hundreds of channels of television on cable and satellite has increased the "Salad Bowl" effect. The major networks were watched by most Americans in the recent past, and this helped assimilate them into a set of common ideas and norms. With a channel for every major national group or language, the media can be viewed as encouraging the lack of assimilation.

A contrary view to the "Salad Bowl" idea can be expressed. The contention is that as the children of immigrants grow up in America, they will help bring their families and communities into the mainstream. This has occurred with many immigrant populations in the past, including the Irish, the Italians and people from the Middle East. However, I feel that the "Salad Bowl" prevails over the "Melting Pot" now because of the issues detailed above.

Writing skill and position on issue: This essay shows good facility with written English and clear organization. The writer takes a clear stance on the topic with a strong thesis statement. The writer introduces the topic clearly and effectively, and each of the following paragraphs elaborates upon the writer's main points and builds on the idea of cultural separateness in America ("Salad Bowl").

Development of ideas and organization of essay: A strong position on the issue is presented. Overall, the writer adheres to the organizational scheme that is introduced in the first paragraph. The only discrepancy occurs in the third and fourth paragraphs. In the thesis statement, the writer refers to the "media" before the "public school system"; and, in the body, he or she refers to the "public school system" in the third paragraph and the "media" in the fourth paragraph. However, this alteration does not detract from the overall development of the essay. In the last paragraph, the writer cleverly presents the opposing argument (America as a "Melting Pot"), only to explicitly refute its claims by referring to the points presented in the body paragraphs of the essay.

Structure of essay, paragraphs, and transitions: The initial paragraph expresses strong ideas, and introduces the topics of the supporting paragraphs. The supporting paragraphs are appropriate, and each deals with an argument or position of the writer. The writer elaborates on the ideas presented but fails in most cases to provide specific examples. Such examples would make the argument more difficult to refute.

Language usage, sentence structure, and punctuation: Sophisticated vocabulary (e.g., "assimilated," "oriented," and "contention") and the effective use of metaphor (e.g., "small towns as separate islands") strengthen the essay. Some lengthy sentences might slow the reader slightly, but they communicate the argument effectively. The few minor punctuation errors will not distract the reader from understanding the essay and are likely the result of the time restrictions placed on the writer.

Summary and conclusions: The writer uses vivid examples that pertain to his or her position and to the subject matter in general. Personal experience and historical experience are both cited effectively. The essay would likely receive a reader's score of average to above average (5–6).

Below Average Essay Response

I feel America continues to be a "Melting Pot" for immigrants coming to America. People come here with their own language and ideas. But they come here for the benefits of our country. They want free speech, and the choice of where they live and what they do in life. Sure some immigrants keep to their own stores and business services such as lawyers and doctors. And they watch television for news and events in their former countries. But most want what they came here for, a better life for them and their kids. You can see evidence of the "Melting Pot" idea versus the "Salad Bowl" in the schools and in the daily newspaper.

I have seen students from many backgrounds playing well on our schools athletic teams. Immigrant students I know work very hard to improve their language skills. We all listen to some of the same tunes, and like popular bands. Their parents get on them to study harder just as mine do. The common experience we share is trying to do OK in school and get out afterwards to succeed in America.

The community newspaper has ads for many of the businesses owned by recent immigrants. They have to compete hard against more traditional businesses to make money. So over time established businesses will have to appeal to the new immigrants, and the new immigrant businesses will have to appeal to more of us. Over time we will become more alike.

The "Melting Pot" will continue to simmer in America, and with time immigrants will adapt and become more like immigrants have in the past, that is "Americans."

Writing skill and position on issue: The essay illustrates some developing skills. The writer's position is presented clearly but ineffectively. The introductory paragraph is not structured in any logical fashion; it rambles on about the reasons why people immigrate to America without relating these reasons to the topic of America as a "Melting Pot." Additionally, this paragraph raises the opposing point of view (America as a "Salad Bowl") without first establishing the writer's thesis statement. The opposing argument would be better positioned in one of the later body paragraphs, with an organized and structured refutation of every one of its points. An explication of the difference between a "Melting Pot" and a "Salad Bowl" would also be helpful in order to clarify the use of these metaphors.

Development of ideas and organization of essay: The organization of the introduction lacks a clear structure. The introductory paragraph tries to address too many varied points when it should only introduce the topic and present the writer's position and thesis statement. Although the writer does present some interesting examples throughout the essay, these examples are not fully developed and supported. For example, the second paragraph does not explain how these certain common experiences lead to a "Melting Pot" society in which the constituents lose their cultural identity. The third paragraph is better at explaining this connection, but the paragraph would be improved if it made explicit the connection between becoming "more alike" and losing cultural identity.

Structure of essay, paragraphs, and transitions: The writer simply and clearly sets up the structure of the essay. The essay is rather short, and could have been more effective with further expansion of some of the arguments. There is no use of transitions throughout the essay, and the third paragraph lacks a topic sentence. The concluding paragraph is brief, but the metaphor of the "Melting Pot" is nicely reinforced.

Language usage, sentence structure, and punctuation: Low-level language usage and some language errors distract from the presentation. Starting a sentence with "Sure some immigrants..." is low-level usage. The term "OK" should not be used in an essay such as this one. There are minor punctuation errors.

Summary and conclusions: Additional information on the ideas listed would more ably support the writer's position. The essay would likely receive a reader's score of below average to average (3–4).

Directed Study Practice Test

SECTION 2—MATH

18 Items

DIRECTIONS: In this section, solve each item, and choose the correct answer choice. Use any available space for scratchwork.

Notes:

(1) The use of a calculator is permitted. All numbers used are real numbers.

(2) Figures that accompany problems in this test are intended to provide information useful in solving the problems. They are drawn as accurately as possible EXCEPT when it is stated in a specific problem that the figure is not drawn to scale. All figures lie in a plane unless otherwise indicated.

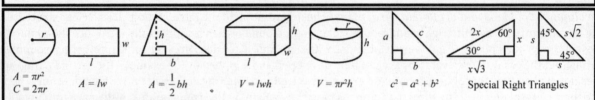

$A = \pi r^2$
$C = 2\pi r$ $\quad A = lw \quad A = \dfrac{1}{2}bh \quad V = lwh \quad V = \pi r^2 h \quad c^2 = a^2 + b^2 \quad$ Special Right Triangles

The number of degrees of arc in a circle is 360.
The sum of the measures in degrees of the angles of a triangle is 180.

---

1. If $x^3 > x^2$, then which of the following could be the value of x?

(A) -2

(B) $-\dfrac{1}{2}$

(C) $\dfrac{1}{2}$

(D) 1

(E) $\dfrac{3}{2}$

$\left(\dfrac{3}{2}\right)^3 = 1.14$

$\dfrac{3}{2} = .75$ →

1. **(E)** *Math: Multiple-Choice/Algebra/Solving Algebraic Equations or Inequalities with One Variable/Manipulating Expressions Involving Exponents*

Solve this problem by reasoning abstractly about the properties of the terms used. A negative number cubed is negative, but squared it is positive. Thus, x is not less than 0. A positive fraction grows smaller each time it is multiplied by itself. For example: $\left(\dfrac{1}{2}\right)^2 = \dfrac{1}{4} \Rightarrow \left(\dfrac{1}{4}\right)^2 = \dfrac{1}{16}$.

Thus, the fewer times it is multiplied by itself, the larger it is. Therefore, x cannot be a positive number less than 1. Finally, x cannot be 1, because $x^3 > x^2 \Rightarrow \left(1^3\right) > \left(1^2\right) \Rightarrow 1 > 1$, which is false. Only (E) remains.

2. A researcher has determined the following about the ages of three individuals:

The sum of Tom and Herb's age is 22.
The sum of Herb and Bob's age is 17.
The sum of Bob and Tom's age is 15.

How old is Herb?

(A) 5
(B) 7
(C) 10
(D) 12
(E) 15

$$|x-2| = 6$$
$$|y+8| = 10$$

3. If $x < 0$ and $y < 0$, what is the value of $x - y$?

(A) 3
(B) 6
(C) 9
(D) 10
(E) 14

4. The sum of three consecutive even integers is 156. If n is the least of the three integers, which one of the following equations represents the information given in the statement above?

(A) $n + 3 = 156$
(B) $3n + 2 = 156$
(C) $3n + 3 = 156$
(D) $3n + 4 = 156$
(E) $3n + 6 = 156$

2. (D) *Math: Multiple-Choice/Algebra/Solving Simultaneous Equations*

Set up a system of equations to solve this problem: $T + H = 22$; $H + B = 17$; and $B + T = 15$. Using the first two equations:

$$\begin{aligned} T + H &= 22 \\ -(H + B &= 17) \\ \hline T - B &= 5 \end{aligned}$$

Couple the result with the third equation:

$$\begin{aligned} T - B &= 5 \\ +(B + T &= 15) \\ \hline 2T = 20 &\Rightarrow T = 10 \end{aligned}$$

Since $T + H = 22$, and Tom is 10, Herb must be 12.

3. (E) *Math: Multiple-Choice/Algebra/Solving Algebraic Equations or Inequalities with One Variable/Equations Involving Absolute Value*

Solve using absolute value conventions. $|x - 2| = 6$, so either $x - 2 = 6$ or $x - 2 = -6$. So, $x = 8$ or $x = -4$ -4. And $|y + 8| = 10$, so either $y + 8 = 10$ or $y + 8 = -10$. Thus, $y = 2$ or $y = -18$. So, since x and y are both negative, $x - y = -4 - (-18) = 14$.

4. (E) *Math: Multiple-Choice/Arithmetic/Common Arithmetic Items/Properties of Numbers*

If n is the least of the three integers, then the other two can be represented as $n + 2$ and $n + 4$, so the sum of the three integers must be:

$$n + (n + 2) + (n + 4) = 156$$
$$3n + 6 = 156$$

5. The figure above shows nine tiles with single-digit numbers painted on them. If xy is the product of the value of any two tiles selected at random, how many different possible values for xy are there?

(A) 4
(B) 7
(C) 10
(D) 12
(E) 16

5. **(B)** *Math: Multiple-Choice/Arithmetic/Common Arithmetic Items/Properties of Numbers*

The best way to solve the problem is to test for the different values. The seven possibilities are 0, 2, 3, 4, 6, 8, and 12.

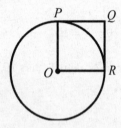

6. In the figure above, if the area of the square $OPQR$ is 2, what is the area of the circle with center O?

(A) $\dfrac{\pi}{4}$

(B) $\pi\sqrt{2}$

(C) 2π

(D) $2\sqrt{2\pi}$

(E) 4π

6. **(C)** *Math: Multiple-Choice/Geometry/Complex Figures*

This item includes a composite figure. The side of the square is also the radius of the circle. Since the square has an area of 2, its side is:

$$s \cdot s = 2$$
$$s^2 = 2$$
$$s = \sqrt{2}$$

And $\sqrt{2}$ is the radius of the circle. So, the area of the circle is $\pi r^2 = \pi\left(\sqrt{2}\right)^2 = 2\pi$.

7. How many positive integers less than 30 are equal to 3 times an odd integer?

(A) 10
(B) 7
(C) 5
(D) 4
(E) 3

7. **(C)** *Math: Multiple-Choice/Arithmetic/Common Arithmetic Items/Properties of Numbers*

You can solve this problem mathematically by reasoning that the eligible integers must meet two requirements. They must be between 0 and 30, and they must equal 3 times an odd integer. So, the eligible numbers are 3 multiplied by the sequence of odd numbers, whose product is less than 30.

But why reason that way? Instead, simply start counting. The first such number is 3 $(3 \cdot 1)$. The next eligible number is 9 $(3 \cdot 3)$. The next number is 15 $(3 \cdot 5)$. The next number is 21 $(3 \cdot 7)$. Finally, the last number is 27 $(3 \cdot 9)$. So, there are 5 of them.

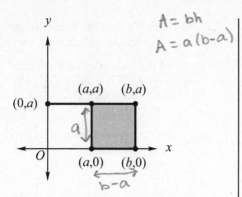

$A = bh$
$A = a(b-a)$

8. In the figure above, what is the area of the shaded portion, expressed in terms of a and b?

(A) $a(b-a)$

(B) $a(a-b)$

(C) $b(a-b)$

(D) $b(b-a)$

(E) ab

8. (A) *Math: Multiple-Choice/Coordinate Geometry/ The Coordinate System* **and** *Algebra/Manipulating Algebraic Expressions/Creating Algebraic Expressions*

The coordinates establish that this figure is a rectangle. The width of the rectangle is a, and the length is $b-a$. So, the area is $a(b-a)$.

Alternatively, you can assume values and get the same result. Assume that $a=2$ and $b=4$. The rectangle has a width of 2, a length of $4-2=2$, and an area of $2 \cdot 2 = 4$. Substitute 2 for a and 4 for b into the formulas in the answer choices and the correct formula will yield 4.

Each item requires you to solve an item and mark your answer on a special answer grid. For each item, you should write your answer in the boxes at the top of each column and then fill in the ovals beneath each part of the answer you write. Here are some examples:

Answer: 7/2 or 3.5	Answer: 325	Answer: 1/6, .166, or .167

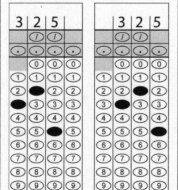

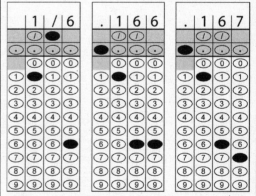

<u>Note:</u> A mixed number such as $3\frac{1}{2}$ must be gridded as 7/2 or as 3.5. If gridded as "31/2," it will be read as "thirty-one halves."

<u>Note:</u> Either position is correct.

<u>Note:</u> A decimal answer with more digits than the grid can accommodate must be truncated. A decimal such as $.16\overline{6}$ must be gridded as .166 or .167. A less accurate value such as .16 or .17 will be scored as incorrect.

9. $\sqrt{(43-7)(29+7)} =$ $\sqrt{(36)(36)} = \sqrt{1296} =$

$\boxed{36}$

9. (36) *Math: Student-Produced Responses/*
Arithmetic/Simple Manipulations

Perform the indicated operations:
$\sqrt{(43-7)(29+7)} = \sqrt{(36)(36)} = 36.$

10. A certain concrete mixture uses 4 cubic yards of cement for every 20 cubic yards of grit. If a contractor orders 50 cubic yards of cement, how much grit (in cubic yards) should he order if he plans to use all of the cement?

10. (250) *Math: Student-Produced Responses/*
Arithmetic/Common Arithmetic Items/
Proportions and Direct-Inverse Variation

Set up a direct proportion and solve for the missing value:

$$\frac{\text{Cement X}}{\text{Cement Y}} = \frac{\text{Grit X}}{\text{Grit Y}}$$

$$\frac{4}{50} = \frac{20}{x}$$

$$4x = (20)(50)$$

$$x = \frac{(20)(50)}{4} = 250$$

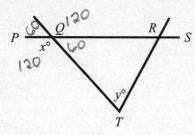

11. In the figure above, $\overline{QT} = \overline{QR}$. If $x = 120$, then $y =$

$$y = 60$$

$$180 - 60 = \frac{120}{2} = 60$$

11. (60) *Math: Student-Produced Responses/ Geometry/Lines and Angles*

Label the other two angles in the triangle:

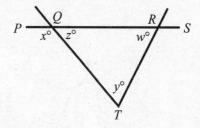

$$x + z = 180$$
$$120 + z = 180$$
$$z = 60$$

Next: $z + w + y = 180$. And since $\overline{QT} = \overline{QR}$, $y = w$. Therefore:

$$60 + y + y = 180$$
$$2y = 120$$
$$y = 60$$

12. If $\dfrac{x}{y} = -1$, then $x + y = $ 0

12. (0) *Math: Student-Produced Responses/Algebra/ Solving Algebraic Equations with Two Variables*

You have only one equation but two variables, so you cannot solve for x and y individually. Instead, look for a way to rewrite the first equation in terms of $x + y$:

$$\frac{x}{y} = -1$$
$$x = -y$$
$$x + y = 0$$

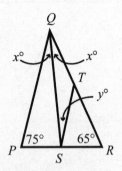

Note: Figure not drawn to scale.

13. In $\triangle PQR$ above, if $\overline{PQ} \parallel \overline{ST}$, then $y =$

13. (20) *Math: Student-Produced Responses/ Geometry/Triangles/Working with Triangles*

Since $\overline{PQ} \parallel \overline{ST}$, $x = y$ because the alternate interior angles of parallel lines are equal. Furthermore, since the sum of angles in $\triangle PRQ$ is 180°:

$$75 + 65 + x + x = 180$$
$$2x + 140 = 180$$
$$2x = 40$$
$$x = 20 \Rightarrow y = 20$$

14. The average of seven different positive integers is 12. What is the greatest that any one of the integers could be?

14. (63) *Math: Student-Produced Responses/Data Analysis/Probability and Statistics/Averages*

Use the method for finding the missing element of an average. The smallest possible sum for six different positive integers is $1+2+3+4+5+6 = 21$. The sum of all seven integers is $7 \cdot 12 = 84$. So, with the average of the seven numbers still being 12, the largest the seventh number could be is $84 - 21 = 63$.

15. A drawer contains 4 green socks, 6 blue socks, and 10 white socks. If socks are pulled out of the drawer at random and not replaced, what is the minimum number of socks that must be pulled out to guarantee that 2 of every color have been selected?

15. (18) *Math: Student-Produced Responses/Data Analysis/Probability and Statistics*

This item is a little tricky, but it doesn't require any advanced mathematics. If the room were dark and you were in a hurry to make sure that you got at least one pair of each color, how many socks would you need to pull from the drawer? Well, what's the worst thing that might happen? You might pull all 10 white socks on the first 10 tries, then all 6 blue socks on the next 6 tries. So far, you have only white socks and blue socks, and you have pulled 16 socks. Now, there is nothing left in the drawer but green socks. Two more picks and you'd have 2 green socks. So, on the worst assumption, 18 picks will guarantee you a pair of each color.

16. On a trip, a motorist drove 10 miles at 20 miles per hour, 10 miles at 30 miles per hour, and 10 miles at 60 miles per hour. What fraction of her total driving time was spent driving 60 miles per hour?

16. **(1/6, .166, or .167)** *Math: Student-Produced Responses/Arithmetic/Solving Complicated Arithmetic Application Items*

Time = distance/rate . So, in this case,

time $= \dfrac{10}{20} + \dfrac{10}{30} + \dfrac{10}{60}$. Giving the fractions a

common denominator, time $= \dfrac{3}{6} + \dfrac{2}{6} + \dfrac{1}{6}$, or $\dfrac{6}{6}$. She

spent $\dfrac{1}{6}$ of $\dfrac{6}{6}$ time driving 60 miles per hour, so

$\dfrac{1}{6}$ of her total driving time was spent at that rate.

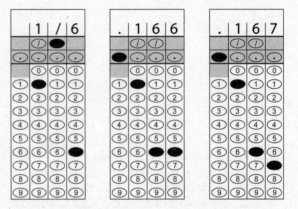

17. In Company *A*, 50 percent of the employees are women. In Company *B*, 40 percent of the employees are women. If Company *A* has 800 employees, and Company *B* has half that number, how many more women are employed at Company *A* than at Company *B*?

17. **(240)** *Math: Student-Produced Responses/Arithmetic/Common Arithmetic Items/Percents*

This is a simple problem with multiple steps. You know that Company *A* has 800 employees, and Company *B* has half that, or 400 employees. Of those at Company *A*, 50 percent are women. At Company *B*, 40 percent are women. Therefore:

Company *A*: 0.50(800) = 400 women

Company *B*: 0.40(400) = 160 women

And, 400 − 160 = 240.

18. In the country of Zzyzyyx, $\dfrac{2}{5}$ of the population has blue eyes. How many people would you have to look at to find 50 with blue eyes, assuming that your sample has blue-eyed people in the same ratio as the general population?

18. **(125)** *Math: Student-Produced Responses/ Arithmetic/Common Arithmetic Items/ Proportions and Direct-Inverse Variation*

Set up a direct proportion and solve for the missing value:

$$\frac{2}{5} = \frac{50}{x}$$
$$2x = 250$$
$$x = 125$$

Directed Study Practice Test

SECTION 3—WRITING
35 Items

DIRECTIONS: In this section, solve each item, and choose the correct answer choice.

Items #1–5: The following sentences test correct, effective expression. Each sentence contains an underlined portion, or the entire sentence may be underlined. Following each sentence are five ways of phrasing the underlined portion. Choice (A) repeats the original; the other four choices are different. If you think the original is better than any of the other choices, choose (A); otherwise, choose one of the other choices.

In choosing answers, follow the conventions of standard written English. Make sure to consider issues of grammar, word choice, sentence construction, and punctuation. Your choice should produce the most effective sentence. It should be clear, precise, and free of ambiguity or awkwardness.

Example:

Allen <u>visiting</u> his cousin in France last summer.

(A) visiting
(B) visited
(C) does visit
(D) a visit
(E) is visiting

---

1. Surprised by the enemy, <u>the general's pursuit of total victory was abruptly halted</u>.

   (A) the general's pursuit of total victory was abruptly halted
   (B) the pursuit of total victory by the general was abruptly halted
   (C) the pursuit of the general of total victory was halted abruptly
   (D) the general abruptly halted his pursuit of total victory
   (E) then the general's pursuit of total victory halted abruptly

1. (D) *Writing/Improving Sentences/Logical Expression/Misplaced Modifiers*

Since it is the general who was surprised by the enemy, "general" should be placed as close to the modifying phrase as possible. Since the modifying phrase is the introductory part of the sentence, this means making "general" the subject of the sentence. The original implies that the pursuit was surprised by the enemy. (B) is incorrect because it does not correct the modifier placement. (C) not only fails to correct the original error but introduces a new error. The use of "of" changes the meaning of the original. Finally, in addition to not correcting the original error, (E) is wrong because it introduces a gratuitous "then."

2. Larkspur High is only the tenth largest school in the district in terms of student enrollment <u>but wins</u> regional championships in many sports year after year.

   (A) but wins
   (B) though wins
   (C) while wins
   (D) still winning
   (E) yet a winner of

2. (A) *Writing/Improving Sentences/No Error*

The original is correct. In this context, "but" is the appropriate conjunction because it joins two verbs ("is" and "wins"), thereby creating the necessary contrasting structure (the school is *this* but does *that*). (B) and (C) are wrong because they incorrectly introduce subordinate conjunctions ("though" and "while," respectively). A subordinate conjunction is used to introduce a clause with a subject; however, the second clause in this sentence lacks a subject. (D) is wrong because "winning" is a participle that does not clearly modify a noun. Finally, (E) is wrong because it eliminates the verb in the second clause.

3. Rene Descartes, the seventeenth-century French thinker, <u>who is as famous as</u> the mathematician who introduced Cartesian geometry.

   (A) who is as famous as
   (B) who is as famous than
   (C) is as famous as
   (D) being as famous as
   (E) as famous as

3. (C) *Writing/Improving Sentences/Grammar/Fragments*

The problem with the original is that it is a fragment rather than a complete sentence because it lacks a main verb. The relative pronoun "who" should be eliminated to fix the problem. (C) is the correct answer choice because it eliminates the relative pronoun. As a result, "is" becomes the main verb of the sentence, with "Rene Descartes" as its subject. (B) fails to solve the problem of the original, and it introduces a new problem; "as famous than" is not an idiomatic expression. Finally, (D) and (E) are wrong because they do not solve the problem of the original; in each case, the resulting sentence lacks a main verb.

4. The new findings on the genetic causes of various diseases provide at once answers for researchers who have gone before <u>and pose</u> questions for future generations of thinkers who must use this information for the good of humanity.

   (A) and pose
   (B) but pose
   (C) and posing
   (D) while posed
   (E) and posed

4. (A) *Writing/Improving Sentences/No Error*

The original is correct. The phrase "at once" indicates that the findings simultaneously possess two qualities. In the underlined portion, the use of the conjunction "and" creates a structure that appropriately demonstrates this simultaneity (the findings provide something *and* pose something else). In addition, the verb "pose" correctly parallels the verb "provide." (B) is wrong because the conjunction "but" distorts the intended meaning of the original—that the findings simultaneously possess two qualities. Finally, (C), (D), and (E) are wrong because they destroy the parallelism between the two verbs.

5. If one compares the number of SUVs sold annually in this country with the compact car, we see clearly how much Americans admire large, ungainly vehicles.

(A) If one compares the number of SUVs sold annually in this country with the compact car
(B) If we compare the number of SUVs sold annually in this country with the compact car
(C) Upon comparing the number of SUVs sold annually in this country with the compact car
(D) When we compare the number of SUVs sold annually in this country with the number of compact cars
(E) Comparing the number of SUVs sold annually in this country and the compact car

---

Items #6–25: The following sentences test your knowledge of grammar, usage, diction (choice of words), and idiom. Each sentence contains either no error or a single error. If there is an error, it is underlined and lettered. If the sentence contains an error, choose the one underlined portion that must be changed to produce a correct sentence. If there is no error, choose answer choice (E). In choosing answers, follow the conventions of standard written English.

Example:

The principal <u>asked</u> five of <u>we</u> students
        A

<u>to enter</u> the <u>public speaking</u> contest.
  C   D

No error
  E

---

6. <u>Her</u> and <u>the other</u> members of the team <u>spoke</u> to
  A   B   C

the press after <u>their</u> final victory. <u>No error</u>
          D   E

---

5. **(D)** *Writing/Improving Sentences/Grammar/Pronoun Usage* and *Logical Expression/Faulty Comparisons*

There are two problems with the original sentence. First, it suffers from a shifting point of view. The underlined portion is written from the third person point of view ("one"). However, the second part of the sentence arbitrarily shifts to the first person point of view ("we"). Remember that point of view must always remain consistent. Second, the original suffers from a faulty comparison; it attempts to make a comparison between the number of SUVs sold and the actual concept of a compact car. However, the sentence intends to make a comparison between the number of SUVs sold and the number of compact cars sold. (D) is the only answer choice that corrects both of these problems. (B), (C), and (E) fail to address the faulty comparison.

6. **(A)** *Writing/Identifying Sentence Errors/Grammar/Pronoun Usage*

"Her" is an objective case pronoun. It cannot function as the subject of a sentence. The sentence should read "She and...."

(B) "The other" correctly and logically modifies "members."
(C) "Spoke" is a logical verb tense in this context

7. Andre Breton <u>started</u> the Surrealist movement
                A

<u>with</u> a manifesto <u>that</u> included the theories of
B   C

Freud <u>as well as</u> his own. <u>No error</u>
      D   E

8. In early America <u>there</u> <u>has been</u> very little <u>to read</u>
                 A   B   C

<u>except</u> for the books sent from Europe. <u>No error</u>
D   E

9. After <u>having took</u> the entrance exam, she <u>was</u>
         A   B

<u>absolutely</u> sure that she <u>would be admitted</u> to the
C   D

college. <u>No error</u>
      E

---

and indicates that the action is in the past.

(D) "Their" correctly agrees with the plural subject.

7. **(E)** *Writing/Identifying Sentence Errors/No Error*

The sentence is correct as written.

(A) The verb correctly indicates a past action.
(B) The phrase "started...with a..." is an acceptable English idiom.
(C) "That" is a correctly used relative pronoun that refers to "manifesto."
(D) "As well as" is an acceptable English construction that is used to connect two ideas of equal importance.

8. **(B)** *Writing/Identifying Sentence Errors/Logical Expression/Illogical Tense Sequence*

The verb "has been" is used when an action that started in the past continues into the present. But the action in the sentence is already completed and is entirely in the past. A correct sentence might use the verb "was" instead.

(A) "There" is correctly used to connect "In America" with the rest of the sentence.
(C) "To read" should be used here rather than any other noun form of the verb. It would be incorrect, for example, to use the construction "was very little reading."
(D) "Except" is a logical choice of preposition for the content of the sentence.

9. **(A)** *Writing/Identifying Sentence Errors/Sentence Structure/Verb Tense*

"Took" is the past tense of the verb "to take." The construction "having..." requires the past participle of the verb, "having taken."

(B) "Was" is a logical choice of verb tense to indicate that the action belongs to the past, and the verb correctly agrees with its subject, "she."
(C) "Absolutely" correctly modifies the adjective "sure." It would be incorrect to use the adjective form "absolute sure."
(D) "Would be admitted" is the correct choice of verb to show speculation or a contrary-to-fact condition. The verb "would" indicates that admission to the school either has not yet occurred or did not occur.

10. <u>Although</u> the average person <u>watches</u> a news
     A   B

program every day, <u>they do</u> not always
                 C

<u>understand</u> the issues discussed. <u>No error</u>
   D   E

10. **(C)** *Writing/Identifying Sentence Errors/ Grammar/Pronoun Usage*

"They" is a plural pronoun, but its antecedent, "person," is singular. So, the correct choice of pronouns is "he," "she," or "he or she." Notice that the verb "do" is underlined as well. This is because the verb must be changed to conform to the correct choice of pronoun: "he or she does."

(A) The "although" is a conjunction that is correctly used to join the subordinate idea that is expressed in the first clause with the more important idea that is expressed in the main clause.
(B) "Watches" is a correct choice of verb. It agrees with its singular subject, "person," and its tense is consistent with the tenses of the other verbs in the sentence.
(D) "Understand" is the correct form of the verb to complete the construction "do...understand."

11. <u>Being that</u> black bears <u>are</u> large and powerful,
     A   B

many people fear <u>them</u> <u>even though</u> the bears are
               C   D

really quite shy. <u>No error</u>
               E

11. **(A)** *Writing/Identifying Sentence Errors/Clarity of Expression/Low-Level Usage*

"Being that" is low-level usage and is not acceptable in standard written English. The sentence could be corrected by substituting "since" for "being that."

(B) "Are" is a correctly used verb. Its tense is consistent with the tense of the other verbs in the sentence, and it agrees with its plural subject, "bears."
(C) "Them" is a correctly used pronoun. It is the object of the verb "fear," and it correctly agrees in number with its plural antecedent, "bears."
(D) "Even though" is a conjunction that is correctly used to introduce an idea that is less important than the idea in the main clause.

12. The review of the concert <u>mentioned</u> <u>that</u> the
                          A   B

soloist was a very <u>promising</u> talent and that the
                 C

orchestra played <u>capable</u>. <u>No error</u>
               D   E

12. **(D)** *Writing/Identifying Sentence Errors/ Grammar/Adjectives and Adverbs*

"Capable" is an adjective and cannot be used to modify the verb "played." The correct choice is the adverb "capably."

(A) "Mentioned" correctly describes an action that was completed in the past.
(B) "That" is correctly used to introduce the noun clause that is the object of the verb "mentioned."

13. The point of the <u>coach's</u> remarks <u>were</u> clearly
                 A   B

<u>to encourage</u> the team and to restore <u>its</u>
   C   D

competitive spirit. <u>No error</u>
                 E

14. The professor <u>deals</u> harshly with students <u>who are</u>
              A   B

not prepared, and he is even <u>more severe</u> with
                           C

<u>those who</u> plagiarize. <u>No error</u>
  D   E

15. When Mozart <u>wrote</u> "The Marriage of Figaro,"
             A

the Emperor was <u>shocked</u> by <u>him using</u> mere
                B   C

servants <u>in</u> important roles. <u>No error</u>
       D   E

(C) The use of "promising" to modify "talent" is idiomatic.

13. (B) *Writing/Identifying Sentence Errors/ Grammar/Subject-Verb Agreement*

The subject of the sentence is "point," not "remarks," Therefore, the singular verb, "was," is needed for agreement.

(A) "Coach's" is a possessive form of the noun "coach," which correctly modifies "remarks" to establish the source of the remarks.
(C) "To encourage" is the proper and idiomatic choice of verb form.
(D) "Its" is a possessive pronoun that modifies "spirit." The antecedent of "its" is "team," and "team" can be either singular or plural depending on the intent of the speaker. In this case, the speaker refers to the team as a whole, which is singular.

14. (E) *Writing/Identifying Sentence Errors/No Error*

The sentence is correct as written.

(A) The use of the present tense verb, "deals," is consistent with the other verbs in the sentence, and the verb agrees with its subject, "professor."
(B) "Who" is the correct choice of pronoun to refer to people ("students"), and "are" correctly reflects the fact that "who" refers to a plural noun.
(C) "More severe" is the comparative form of "severe." And it is correct to use an adjective, because it is the pronoun "he" ("professor") that is modified.
(D) Again, "who" is the correct pronoun to refer to people. And "those" is a pronoun that can be used instead of the construction "those people."

15. (C) *Writing/Identifying Sentence Errors/ Grammar/Pronoun Usage*

"Him" is an objective case pronoun. It cannot be used to modify the "-ing" form (gerund) of a verb. The correct choice of pronoun is "his."

(A) The verb "wrote" correctly describes an action that was completed in the past. And it is consistent with the other verb in the sentence, "was shocked," which is also in the past.

(B) "Was shocked" is consistent with the other verb in the sentence. And "was" correctly agrees with its subject, "Emperor," which is singular.

(D) "In" is an acceptable choice of preposition for the sentence.

16. For a young woman who is ready to join the
　　　A　　　　　　　　　　　　　　　B

work force, there now exists many more
　　　　　　　　　　　　C

opportunities than existed for her mother.
　　　　　　　D

No error
　E

16. (C) *Writing/Identifying Sentence Errors/ Grammar/Subject-Verb Agreement*

The sentence has an inverted structure; that is, the subject follows the verb. The subject of the sentence is "opportunities," which is plural. The verb should be "exist."

(A) "For" is an acceptable choice of preposition.

(B) "To join" is the correct verb form. It would be incorrect to use the "-ing" form: "... ready in joining...."

(D) "Than existed" correctly sets up a comparison between two like situations: "than existed for her mother." ("Opportunities" is understood.)

17. If he had known how difficult law school
　　　　　A　　　　　B

would be, he would of chosen a different
　C　　　　　D

profession. No error
　　　　　　E

17. (D) *Writing/Identifying Sentence Errors/Clarity of Expression/Low-Level Usage*

"Would of chosen" is low-level usage. "Of" is a preposition rather than an auxiliary verb, and so it cannot be included in the construction of a verb phrase. The correct construction is "would have chosen."

(A) "Had known" correctly indicates an action that was completed in the past and placed in time before some other action ("would have chosen").

(B) "Difficult" is an adjective that is correctly used to modify "law school."

(C) "Would be" is a correct choice of verb to indicate that the difficulty did not become manifest until after the person was already in law school.

18. The museum required that all people with an
　　　　　　　　A　　　　　　　　B

umbrella leave them at the door before entering the
　B　　　　　C　　　　　　　　　D

exhibit. No error
　　　　　E

18. (B) *Writing/Identifying Sentence Errors/ Grammar/Pronoun Usage*

There is no agreement between the subject, the object, and the object's pronoun; they should all be plural: "people," "umbrellas," "them." The sentence intends to refer to several people, each with an umbrella. As written, however, it implies that several people jointly possess a single umbrella. The sentence can be corrected by changing "an umbrella" to "umbrellas."

(A) The verb "required" correctly describes an action that was completed in the past.

(C) "Them" is a correctly chosen pronoun. It will agree with the corrected version of underlined part (B).

(D) "Entering" is correctly used as the object of the preposition "before."

19. Americans <u>used to go</u> to the movies <u>as often as</u>
              A   B

they watched television; but now that <u>they can</u>
                                           C

<u>watch</u> movies in their homes, they <u>are doing less of</u>
 C   D

<u>it.</u> <u>No error</u>
 D   E

19. **(D)** *Writing/Identifying Sentence Errors/ Grammar/Pronoun Usage*

The pronoun "it" lacks a clear antecedent. It wants to refer to something like "movie-going," but there is no such expression in the sentence. The sentence can be corrected by replacing "it" with "are going to the movies less frequently."

(A) "Used to go" is correctly used to show repeated past actions extending over a period of time.

(B) "As often as" correctly sets up a comparison of the frequency of two actions.

(C) "They can watch" is correct. "They" agrees in number with its antecedent, "Americans," and "can watch" provides the needed contrast between what used to be the case and what is now the case.

20. When automobiles <u>get designed</u> and manufactured,
                            A

corporations <u>are</u> often <u>more concerned</u> about cost
               B   C

<u>than</u> safety. <u>No error</u>
 D   E

20. **(A)** *Writing/Identifying Sentence Errors/Clarity of Expression/Low-Level Usage*

"Get designed" is low-level usage. The sentence should read "are designed."

(B) "Are" is the correct choice. Its tense conveys the idea that the problem described is ongoing, and it agrees in number with its subject, "corporations."

(C) "More concerned" is the correct way to make a comparison here.

(D) The comparison is correctly completed by "than": "…more concerned with this than that."

21. Most people <u>do not realize</u> that some white
                A

wines <u>are</u> <u>actually</u> <u>made from</u> red grapes.
     B   C   D

<u>No error</u>
  E

21. **(E)** *Writing/Identifying Sentence Errors/No Error*

The sentence is correct as written.

(A) The verb "do not realize" is correctly used to describe a present and ongoing state of affairs, and it agrees in number with its plural subject, "people."

(B) The use of the "-ing" form of the verb "to include" is idiomatic.

(C) "Are" is consistent in tense with the other

verb in the sentence ("do not realize"), and it correctly agrees with its subject, "wines."

(D) "From" is the correct choice of preposition here.

---

22. <u>Travel</u> to countries with <u>less than</u> ideal sanitary
    A   B

conditions <u>increases</u> the <u>amount</u> of victims of
             C   D

hepatitis. <u>No error</u>
          E

22. **(D)** *Writing/Identifying Sentence Errors/Clarity of Expression/Diction and Idioms*

"Amount" is the wrong choice of word in this context. When used correctly, it describes bulk quantities, like air, water, and sand, that are not measured out in units. Here, the correct word is "number," because each victim is a separate entity.

(A) "Travel" is a noun with a meaning that is appropriate in this context.
(B) "Less than" correctly sets up a comparison between those countries that have ideal conditions and those that do not.
(C) "Increases" describes an action that is present and ongoing, and it agrees in number with the subject, "travel."

---

23. Movie fans <u>claim</u> there is <u>no greater</u> director than
           A   B

<u>him</u>, although most critics <u>would cite</u> Bergman or
C   D

Kurosawa. <u>No error</u>
        E

23. **(C)** *Writing/Identifying Sentence Errors/ Grammar/Pronoun Usage*

"Him" is the wrong choice of pronoun. The construction "no greater...than" means "no greater...than he is." The "is" is understood, and the correct choice of pronouns is a subject (not object) pronoun. The sentence should read "than he."

(A) The verb "claim" correctly describes action in the present, and it agrees with its subject, "fans."
(B) "No greater" correctly sets up a comparison between one director and the other two directors.
(D) The use of "would" correctly indicates a conditional event. The critics would, if given a chance, mention the names of the others. And the word "cite" is correctly chosen because it means "to mention."

24. Economists <u>have established</u> a <u>correlation</u>—<u>albeit</u>
                   A   B   C

an indirect one—<u>between</u> the sale of oil and the
                   D

number of traffic accidents. <u>No error</u>
                               E

24. (E) *Writing/Identifying Sentence Errors/No Error*

The sentence is correct as written.

(A) The verb "have established" refers to action in the past, and "have correctly" agrees with its subject, "economists."
(B) "Correlation" has an appropriate meaning in this context.
(C) "Albeit" has an appropriate meaning in this context.
(D) "Between" is a correct choice of preposition to show the needed connection.

25. The duckbill platypus, unlike other <u>mammal,</u>
                                      A

<u>does</u> not bear live young but instead <u>reproduces</u> by
 B   C

<u>laying</u> eggs. <u>No error</u>
 D   E

25. (A) *Writing/Identifying Sentence Errors/Grammar*

The word "other" implies more than one, so the singular "mammal" should be replaced with the plural "mammals."

(B) The singular verb "does" agrees with the singular subject "platypus."
(C) The singular verb "reproduces" agrees with the singular subject "platypus."
(D) The gerund, or "-ing" form, is correctly used in this context to convey the sense of an ongoing action: "by laying."

Items #26–35: The following passages are early drafts of essays. Some portions of the passages need to be revised.

Read each passage and answer the items that follow. Items may be about particular sentences or parts of sentences, asking you to improve the word choice or sentence structure. Other items may refer to parts of the essay or the entire essay, asking you to consider organization or development. In making your decisions, follow the conventions of standard written English.

Items #26–31 refer to the following passage.

(1) My first real job was working at the Burger Barn. (2) Before that, I did odd jobs for neighbors such as mowing lawns and shoveling snow and was paid by them. (3) The Burger Barn is a typical fast food restaurant. (4) It serves food such as hamburgers and french fries. (5) The only experience that most people have with a fast food restaurant is as a customer. (6) They order and pay for it and then either sit down or go home to eat. (7) A lot more goes on behind the counter.

(8) There are rules for everything. (9) The oil for the french fries must be exactly 375 degrees, and the fries must cook until the timer sounds. (10) The patties must be cooked until they are well-done. (11) All counters, floors, and utensils must be cleaned and disinfected every evening.

(12) There must be so many orders of fries under the warming lamp and a certain number of burgers on the grill. (13) Paper products and condiments must be restocked every half hour, and employees receive five-minute breaks every two hours with 20 minutes for lunch during a six-hour shift. (14) To outsiders, these rules may seem silly. (15) They are necessary to make sure that the food we serve is safe to eat and that during evening rush we can serve as many as 150 people. (16) The evening rush is from 5:30 p.m. to 7:00 p.m.

26. In context, which is the best version of the underlined portion of sentence 2 (reproduced below)?

Before that, I did odd jobs for neighbors such as mowing lawns and shoveling snow and was paid by them.

(A) (As it is now.)
(B) did odd jobs for neighbors such as mowing lawns and shoveling snow who paid me for them
(C) was paid by neighbors for doing odd jobs such as mowing lawns and shoveling snow
(D) received pay by neighbors for odd jobs such as mowing lawns and shoveling snow
(E) mowed lawns and shoveled snow and did odd jobs for neighbors who paid me for them

27. In context, which is the best way to revise and combine the underlined portions of sentences 3 and 4 (reproduced below)?

The Burger Barn is a typical fast food restaurant. It serves food such as hamburgers and french fries.

(A) The Burger Barn is a typical fast food restaurant, serving
(B) The Burger Barn is a typical fast food restaurant in that it serves
(C) Typically, a fast food restaurant such as the Burger Barn serves
(D) A fast food restaurant such as your typical Burger Barn serves
(E) At the Burger Barn, the food that is typically served is

28. Which of the following is the most logical replacement for the word "it" in sentence 6?

(A) experience
(B) restaurant
(C) food
(D) people
(E) Burger Barn

26. (C) *Writing/Improving Paragraphs/Sentence Elements*

The original sentence is incorrect––the pronoun "them" does not have a clear antecedent. (C) corrects this error by clarifying who did the paying: "Before that, I was paid by neighbors for doing odd jobs such as mowing lawns and shoveling snow." (B) and (E) fail to correct this error. (D) is not correct because "received pay by" is not idiomatic English. The correct usage is "received pay from."

27. (A) *Writing/Improving Paragraphs/Sentence Elements*

This item asks you to combine two related sentences. (A) is the correct answer: "The Burger Barn is a typical fast food restaurant, serving food such as hamburgers and french fries." (B) and (E) are needlessly wordy; (C) and (D) change the intended meaning of the original sentences.

28. (C) *Writing/Improving Paragraphs/Sentence Elements*

The item asks you to replace "it" in sentence 6. Since the Burger Barn serves food and "they" in sentence 6 refers to Burger Barn customers, the logical choice is (C), "food."

29. In context, which of the following would be the best phrase to insert at the beginning of sentence 13?

(A) However,
(B) In addition,
(C) Therefore,
(D) Perhaps,
(E) For example,

29. (B) *Writing/Improving Paragraphs/Paragraph Structure*

The last paragraph of this essay gives several examples of rules that the Burger Barn employees must follow in order to ensure adequate amounts of safe food. Sentence 12 states that "there must be so many orders of fries under the warming lamp and a certain number of burgers on the grill." Sentence 13 continues to give additional rules. Therefore, the best answer is choice (B): "In addition, paper products and condiments must be restocked every half hour...." None of the remaining choices are logical in the context of the paragraph.

30. In context, which is the best version of the underlined portions of sentences 14 and 15 (reproduced below)?

To outsiders, these rules may seem silly. They are necessary to make sure that the food we serve is safe to eat and that during evening rush we can serve as many as 150 people.

(A) may seem silly, but they are necessary to make sure
(B) may seem silly, since they are necessary to make sure
(C) are necessary to make sure, even though they may seem silly,
(D) are necessary, even though they may seem silly, and make sure
(E) could be silly except that they are necessary to make sure

30. (A) *Writing/Improving Paragraphs/Sentence Elements*

This item asks you to combine two related sentences. Sentences 14 and 15 represent a thought-reverser—while the "rules may seem silly" to outsiders, there are reasons for these rules. (B) uses the conjunction "since" which fails to reverse the thought. (C) and (D) present the thought-reverser but are structurally awkward. (E), likewise, is awkward, and "could be silly" is not an idiomatic expression in this context. (A) is the best answer: "To outsiders, these rules may seem silly, but they are necessary to make sure...."

31. In context, which of the following would be the most appropriate revision of sentence 16?

(A) Delete it because it does not contribute to the development of the essay.
(B) Delete it because definitions are not appropriate in an essay.
(C) Place it in quotation marks because it is a definition.
(D) Move it to the beginning of the final paragraph.
(E) Place it between sentences 5 and 6.

31. (A) *Writing/Improving Paragraphs/Passage Development*

This item asks you for the best revision of sentence 16. (B) and (C) are nonsensical: definitions are appropriate if they contribute to the essay's development, and definitions need not be in quotation marks. Moving the sentence, as in (D) and (E), does nothing to further the essay development. The best choice is (A), to delete the sentence, because it does not contribute to the development of the essay.

Items #32–35 refer to the following passage.

(1) In the past several years, lawyers have increasingly been in the negative public spotlight. (2) A group of students hires a lawyer to sue their school because they don't like the mascot. (3) A driver sues a take-out restaurant because he was scalded by the hot coffee he spilled while driving. (4) A prison inmate goes all the way to the Supreme Court because the jail uses the wrong kind of peanut butter.

(5) All of these examples make lawyers seems like publicity-hungry, money-grubbing parasites. (6) Seemingly outrageous cases, are often incorrectly reported by the media.

(7) Take the famous "peanut butter case" as an example. (8) Since inmates aren't permitted to have cash, they have accounts with the prison commissary where they buy items like soap, stationery, and snacks. (9) An inmate ordered a jar of crunchy-style peanut butter but got creamy-style instead. (10) Then the commissary repeatedly refused to fix the mistake. (11) The inmate properly returned the merchandise, but the commissary didn't credit his account. (12) So the inmate sued the commissary for the price of the peanut butter. (13) The inmate won, so the prison appealed and lost.

(14) When you hear the actual facts of the "peanut butter case," you can see that the inmate had a legitimate beef. (15) This is true of most of the other cases you hear about as well.

32. Which of the following would be the most suitable sentence to insert immediately after sentence 1?

(A) Lawyers go to school for an additional three years after graduating from college.
(B) Every night, the news has stories of how people have been hurt or injured that day.
(C) I have often thought about becoming a lawyer after I graduate from college.
(D) It seems as though every day we hear of another frivolous lawsuit.
(E) Of course, not all lawyers are bad; a few are morally responsible.

32. (D) *Writing/Improving Paragraphs/Passage Development*

In order for a sentence to be inserted, it must not only be generally relevant to the topic, but it needs to make sense when inserted at the particular point. In this case, the writer has started off by saying generally that lawyers get bad press and then has followed up with three specific examples. Therefore, a sentence that provides a transition would be appropriate, and (D) does this by introducing the three examples that follow. (A) introduces a topic that is out of place in the overall essay. (A) would be appropriate if the author were talking about education requirements, but it does not fit into the passage as written. (B) is somewhat like (D), but the point of the focus of the passage is not injuries but the behavior of lawyers. (C) is irrelevant to the topic of the passage, even though it mentions lawyers. As for (E), it is consistent with the idea of the passage (those horror stories are not necessarily true), but (E) doesn't fit in between (1) and (2).

33. To best connect the second paragraph with the rest of the essay, which is the best word or phrase to insert after the underlined portion of sentence 6 (reproduced below)?

Seemingly outrageous cases, are often incorrectly reported by the media.

(A) certainly,
(B) more or less,
(C) however,
(D) fortunately,
(E) in a word,

34. Which of the following changes in the organization of the third paragraph is most needed?

(A) (As it is now.)
(B) Start a new paragraph with sentence 9.
(C) Put sentence 10 after sentence 11.
(D) Start a new paragraph with sentence 12.
(E) Put sentence 12 after sentence 13.

35. Which of the following would be most appropriate for the writer to do in a fifth paragraph to be added to the essay?

(A) Explain why the media gets the facts of cases wrong.
(B) Analyze the legal arguments in the "peanut butter case."
(C) Refute the contention that prison inmates have legal rights.
(D) Present cases where people falsely claimed to be seriously injured.
(E) Encourage the reader to consult with a lawyer.

33. (C) _Writing/Improving Paragraphs/Passage Development_

The item asks you to choose a word or phrase that will integrate the second paragraph into the overall development. Sentence 6 is intended to signal a shift from the discussion of the three initial examples, which seem outrageous, to a more careful examination of one of the examples to show that the case was not as crazy as reported. "However" is a good word to signal this shift. (A) and (D) don't signal a change of direction. (B) and (D) do not have appropriate meanings in this context.

34. (C) _Writing/Improving Paragraphs/Paragraph Structure_

The third paragraph tells the story of the "peanut butter case." As written, sentences 10 and 11 are out of order. In the sequence of events, the commissary's failure to credit the account comes before its repeated refusal to fix the mistake. (C) makes the needed change. As for (E), the other sentences are presented in the right order. And as for (B) and (D), the third paragraph properly functions as a paragraph because it discusses a single topic.

35. (A) _Writing/Improving Paragraphs/Passage Development_

Thus far, the author has shown that the crazy cases you hear about in the news may not be so crazy after all. At least, that's what the peanut butter case is supposed to show. And in the fourth paragraph, the writer says that "this is true of most other cases as well." The writer needs to back up that claim, and a good approach would be to explain how the media manages to get this so wrong—as (A) suggests. (B) is incorrect because the legal arguments would be technical and beyond the scope of the essay. As for (C), the writer seems to think that inmates have some legal rights, as demonstrated by the peanut butter case. As for (D), the essay is going in the wrong direction for this choice. The writer doesn't want to discuss those cases where people made false claims but cases where legitimate claims were ridiculed by the press. Finally, as for (E), while the writer wants to show that lawyers have been given a bad rap (those silly cases really aren't so silly), (E) goes too far. Nothing in the passage suggests that the writer believes that everyone should go see a lawyer.

Directed Study Practice Test

SECTION 4—CRITICAL READING
24 Items

DIRECTIONS: In this section, solve each item, and choose the correct answer choice.

Items #1–9: Each item below has one or two blanks, each blank indicating that something has been omitted. Beneath the sentence are five lettered words or sets of words. Choose the word or set of words that best fits the meaning of the sentence as a whole.

Example:

Although its publicity has been -------, the film itself is intelligent, well acted, handsomely produced, and altogether -------.

(A) tasteless . . respectable
(B) extensive . . moderate
(C) sophisticated . . amateur
(D) risqué . . crude
(E) perfect . . spectacular

---

1. Although for centuries literature was considered something that would instruct as well as entertain, many modern readers have little patience with ------- works and seek only to be -------.

(A) epic . . demoralized
(B) didactic . . distracted
(C) bawdy . . absorbed
(D) superficial . . enlightened
(E) ambiguous . . misled

1. (B) *Critical Reading: Sentence Completions/ Thought Reversal/Subordinate Conjunctions*

The logical key to this item is a double reversal of thought. The subordinate conjunction "although" seems to indicate that the positive overtones of the description in the first clause will contrast with those of the description in the second clause. However, the second clause contains the key phrase "little patience," which functions as a negative. This double reversal of thought implies that the blanks will actually extend the thought that is expressed in the first clause. The first blank extends the concept of literature that instructs as well as entertains, so you should look for an adjective that describes this type of literature. All of the first choices might describe literature, so unless you know that "didactic" means "instructive," you have to look at the second blank. "Only" sets up a contrast between the second blank and the first. You are now looking for something that is more or less opposite to "instructive." Again, all of the second elements make some sense when substituted into the blanks, but only one reverses the idea of "instructive," and that is "distracted," meaning pleasure or entertainment. Only (B) offers a synonym for "instructive," so you can quickly eliminate (A), (C), and (D).

2. Because the poet was restless and uneasy in society, he sought a ------- existence and a life of -------.

   (A) stable . . pleasure
   (B) claustrophobic . . frivolity
   (C) materialistic . . urbanity
   (D) conservative . . squalor
   (E) nomadic . . solitude

2. **(E)** *Critical Reading: Sentence Completions/ Thought Extension/Subordinate Conjunctions*

In this sentence, the subordinate conjunction "because" sets up an extension of thought. The blanks are further indications of the poet's restlessness and uneasiness in society. Also, the coordinate conjunction "and" indicates that the two blanks will parallel each other. You can eliminate (B) on the grounds of usage, because it makes no sense to say that someone seeks a claustrophobic existence. You can eliminate (C) because someone who is uneasy in society would hardly seek a life of urbanity. Although (A) and (D) create meaningful sentences, they do not extend the logic of the first part of the sentence. The poet would not seek a conservative or a stable existence as a result of his restlessness, nor would he seek a life of pleasure or squalor as a result of his uneasiness in society. (E) is the only choice that logically completes the idea: the poet became nomadic because he felt restless.

3. Because he was ------- and the life of the party, his friends thought that he was happy; but his wife was ------- and shy and was thought to be unhappy.

   (A) melancholy . . sympathetic
   (B) philanthropic . . conciliatory
   (C) vitriolic . . sophomoric
   (D) garrulous . . taciturn
   (E) inimical . . gregarious

3. **(D)** *Critical Reading: Sentence Completions/ Combined Reasoning/Coordinate Conjunctions* and *Subordinate Conjunctions*

This sentence contains both an extension of thought, as indicated by the coordinate conjunction "and," and a reversal of thought, as indicated by the subordinate conjunction "although," as its logical keys. The first blank must parallel the idea that someone was the life of the party. Immediately eliminate (A), because someone who is melancholy is not likely to be the life of a party. (B) makes no logical sense. Eliminate (C) and (E) on the same grounds. This is largely a matter of vocabulary since you must know that "garrulous" means "talkative," "inimical" means "hostile," and "vitriolic" means "nasty." Only (D) makes any sense. His wife must be the opposite of "the life of the party." The second element of (D), "taciturn," which means "silent," works very nicely.

4. His offhand, rather ------- remarks ------- a
character that was really rather serious and not at
all superficial.

    (A) flippant . . masked
    (B) pernicious . . betrayed
    (C) bellicose . . belied
    (D) controversial . . revealed
    (E) shallow . . enlivened

4. (A) *Critical Reading: Sentence Completions/
Combined Reasoning/Key Words*

This sentence begins with an extension of
thought, indicating that the first blank needs an
adjective that is related to the key word "offhand"
that could also be applied to "remarks." So, this
becomes a matter of vocabulary because you
must know the meanings of all five of the first
elements. All five answers make some sense, so it
is a matter of substituting each pair to make sure
that the logic of the sentence is maintained. If you
know that "flippant" means lacking seriousness,
you don't have to look any further: "He was
flippant, but this attitude masked a serious
nature." This nicely maintains the underlying
reversal of thought: "He seemed one way but was
really the opposite."

5. Although the faculty did not always agree with the
chairperson of the department, they ------- her ideas
mostly in ------- her seniority and out of respect for
her previous achievements.

    (A) scoffed at . . fear of
    (B) harbored . . defense of
    (C) implemented . . deference to
    (D) marveled at . . lieu of
    (E) ignored . . honor of

5. (C) *Critical Reading: Sentence Completions/
Combined Reasoning/Subordinate Conjunctions*
and *Coordinate Conjunctions*

This sentence contains both a reversal of thought,
as indicated by the subordinate conjunction
"although," and an extension of thought, as
indicated by the coordinate conjunction "and," as
its logical keys. The subordinate conjunction
"although" signals that the second part of the
sentence should reverse the idea of the first part
of the sentence. (A) does not reverse the idea. The
same is true of (D) and (E). (B) and (C) remain
possibilities, so test the second elements. The
coordinate conjunction "and" signals that the
second blank must parallel the idea of "respect."
The faculty might harbor her ideas, but they can't
be doing it in defense of her seniority. That makes
no sense. (C) works well. Because they respect
her seniority, the faculty implements her ideas
although they do not always agree with her. This
makes a perfectly logical and idiomatic sentence.

6. Although his work was often ------- and ------- he
was promoted anyway, simply because he had been
with the company longer than anyone else.

    (A) forceful . . extraneous
    (B) negligent . . creative
    (C) incomplete . . imprecise
    (D) predictable . . careful
    (E) expeditious . . concise

6. (C) *Critical Reading: Sentence Completions/
Combined Reasoning/Subordinate Conjunctions*
and *Coordinate Conjunctions*

First, the subordinate conjunction "although" sets
up a contrast between the idea of a promotion
and the quality of the person's work: the work
must be bad, even though the person was
promoted. Second, the two blanks must
themselves be parallel since both describe the
poor quality of the work and are connected with a
coordinate conjunction "and." Only (C) includes
the pair of negatives needed to complete the idea.

7. Shopping malls account for 60 percent of the retail business in the United States because they are controlled environments, which ------- concerns about the weather.

(A) eliminate
(B) necessitate
(C) foster
(D) justify
(E) maintain

7. (A) Critical Reading: Sentence Completions/ Thought Extension/Subordinate Conjunctions

In this sentence, the subordinate conjunction "because" indicates an extension of thought. So, the blank explains the result of a controlled environment. The result of a controlled environment would be that you do not have to worry about the weather. Only (A) logically completes the thought.

8. An oppressive -------, and not the festive mood one might have expected, characterized the gathering.

(A) senility
(B) capriciousness
(C) inanity
(D) solemnity
(E) hysteria

8. (D) Critical Reading: Sentence Completions/ Thought Reversal/Key Words

The adverb "not" indicates a reversal of thought. The blank requires a word that means the opposite of a "festive mood" (key phrase). Also, the key adjective "oppressive" clues students to try "solemnity," which is a good fit. Neither "capriciousness" nor "hysteria" can be logically modified by "oppressive," so (B) and (E) are incorrect. "Senility" and "inanity" have similar meanings; since both cannot be correct, (A) and (C) are wrong. Furthermore, (A) and (C) can be eliminated because "loss of sanity" has no logical relationship to the meaning of the sentence.

9. In order to ------- museums and legitimate investors, and to facilitate the ------- of pilfered artifacts, art magazines often publish photographs of stolen archaeological treasures.

(A) perpetuate . . return
(B) protect . . recovery
(C) encourage . . excavation
(D) undermine . . discovery
(E) confuse . . repossession

9. (B) Critical Reading: Sentence Completions/ Thought Extension/Coordinate Conjunctions

The overall logical structure of this sentence is defined by an extension of thought. The information that comes before the comma must explain why art magazines publish photos of stolen property. Additionally, the two blanks must create a parallel because of the coordinate conjunction "and." Publishing the photos must do roughly the same thing for museums and "legitimate investors" (key phrase) that is done for stolen property. In this case, the result must be good. The museums and investors are protected and the stolen property is recovered. Only (B) logically completes this thought.

Items #10–24: Each passage below is followed by one or more items based on its content. Answer the items following each passage on the basis of what is stated or implied in the passage.

Items #10–17 are based on the following passage.

The following selection is an excerpt from a history text. It talks about athletic games in ancient Greece.

Perhaps the best-known of the ancient Greek religious festivals are the Panhellenic gatherings at Olympia, in honor of Zeus, where the Olympics originated in 776 B.C. These and other festivals in
5 honor of Zeus were called "crown festivals" because the winning athletes were crowned with wreaths, such as the olive wreaths of Olympia. Yet, in ancient Greece there were at least 300 public, state-run religious festivals that were celebrated at more than 250
10 locations in honor of some 400 deities. Most of these were held in the cities, in contrast to the crown festivals, which were held in rural sanctuaries. In Athens, for example, four annual festivals honored Athena, the city's divine protectress, in addition to
15 those for other gods. In all, some 120 days were devoted annually to festivals.

By far, the largest event of the Athenian religious calendar, rivaling the crown gatherings in prestige, was the Great Panathenaic festival. The development of the
20 Panathenaic festival—the ritual embodiment of the cult of Athena—evolved from a purely local religious event into a civic and Panhellenic one. This transformation, and that of the image of Athena from an aggressively martial goddess to a more humane figure of victory,
25 parallels the great political change that occurred in Athens from 560 B.C. to 430 B.C., as it evolved from a tyranny to a democracy.

Athenian reverence for Athena originated in a myth that recounts a quarrel between Poseidon and
30 Athena over possession of Attica. In a contest arranged by Zeus, Athena was judged the winner and made the patron goddess of Athens, to which she gave her name. The origin of the Panathenaia, however, is shrouded in mystery. Perhaps it was founded by Erichthonius, a
35 prehistoric king of Athens. According to legend, after having been reared by Athena on the Acropolis, he held games for his foster mother and competed in the chariot race, which he reputedly invented. The first archaeological evidence for the festival is a
40 Panathenaic prize vase from 560 B.C. depicting a horse race, so scholars infer that equestrian events were part of the festival.

Much more is known about the Panathenaia after 566 B.C., when the festival was reorganized under the
45 tyrant Peisistaros. At that time, the festival, in addition to its annual celebration, was heightened every fourth year into the Great Panathenaia, which attracted top athletes from all over the region to compete for valuable prizes—such as 140 vases of olive oil for
50 winning the chariot race—rather than for honorific wreaths.

Every four years, some 1,300 painted amphorae were commissioned and filled with olive oil to be used as prizes. The accouterments of Athena—helmet,
55 spear, and shield—figured prominently in the iconic representations of the goddess on these vases, and served to identify the stylized figure and to associate the festival with the goddess. So far as is known, none of the crown games commissioned any art for their
60 festivals. From the mid-sixth century B.C. until the end of antiquity when the Christian emperors suppressed the pagan religions, the high point of Athenian religious life was the Great Panathenaia, held at a time that falls in our month of July.

10. The selection is mainly concerned with

(A) identifying the origins of the modern Olympic games
(B) describing the development of athletic games at Athens
(C) contrasting religious practices in honor of Zeus and Athena
(D) tracing the growth of democracy in ancient Greece
(E) presenting a picture of the pageantry and art of ancient Greece

10. (B) *Critical Reading: Passages/Social Studies/ Main Idea*

This item has the unmistakable identifying feature of a Main Idea item: "mainly concerned." The correct answer will summarize the development of the passage. (A) is too narrow because the modern Olympic games go back to the crown festivals—a different set of games than the Panathenaic games. (C) is too broad because the passage focuses almost exclusively on games, not on religious practices in general. (D) must be wrong since there is only a passing mention of democracy. Finally, (E) is incorrect since the discussion of art is incidental to the main topic: the development of the games.

11. Which of the following is NOT mentioned as a characteristic of the games at Olympia?

(A) The games were held in honor of Zeus.
(B) Winners were crowned with wreaths.
(C) The games originated in 776 B.C.
(D) The games were held in or near cities.
(E) Winners did not receive valuable prizes.

11. (D) *Critical Reading: Passages/Social Studies/ Explicit Detail*

The word "mentioned" tags this as an Explicit Detail item, and it has a thought-reverser: NOT. Four of the five choices are mentioned in the selection. The one idea that is not mentioned is the right answer. (D) is the correct answer because the author does not mention this idea. In fact, the author says that the crown games were *rural* festivals. The other ideas are mentioned in the selection as characteristics of the crown games.

12. The author regards the suggestions that the Panathenaia originated under Erichthonius as

(A) conclusively proved
(B) a theoretical possibility
(C) historically impossible
(D) a hoax perpetrated by Athenians
(E) a simple myth of ancient times

12. (B) *Critical Reading: Passages/Social Studies/ Voice*

The author says that the origin of the Panathenaia is "shrouded in mystery," so nothing is definite. But the author also says that the identification of the games with the prehistoric king Erichthonius is "perhaps" correct. Only (B) describes this attitude.

13. The word "equestrian" (line 41) refers to

(A) weapons
(B) gods
(C) horses
(D) tyrants
(E) slaves

13. (C) *Critical Reading: Passages/Social Studies/ Vocabulary*

The reference to chariots and horse races makes it clear that "equestrian" must relate to horses. In fact, that is the primary definition of the word. When you have a word that is unusual, the correct answer is usually the primary meaning. It's only when the word is a common one that the Vocabulary item refers to an uncommon meaning.

14. Which of the following is NOT mentioned as a characteristic of the Great Panathenaia?

(A) It was held every four years.
(B) It inspired the modern Olympic games.
(C) It began at the time of Peisistaros.
(D) It was held during our month of July.
(E) It died out under the Christian emperors.

15. What word has most nearly the same meaning as "amphorae" (line 52)?

(A) vases
(B) wreaths
(C) representations
(D) games
(E) crowns

16. "Iconic" (line 55) most nearly means

(A) stylized depiction
(B) religious statue
(C) religious festival
(D) assorted weapons
(E) legendary figures

14. **(B)** *Critical Reading: Passages/Social Studies/ Explicit Detail*

Since the item contains the thought-reverser "NOT," the correct answer is the only one of the five choices that is NOT in the passage. The author does not say that the Great Panathenaia inspired the modern games. Rather, the author says that the games at Olympia in honor of Zeus inspired the modern games.

15. **(A)** *Critical Reading: Passages/Social Studies/ Vocabulary*

"Amphorae" is an unusual word, so the correct answer will likely be the standard meaning, vase. If you know in advance the meaning of amphorae, then this is an easy item. Even if you do not know the meaning before reading the paragraph, you can infer the meaning from the context. The author is talking about vases filled with olive oil as prizes and refers to decorated amphorae filled with oil, so, you can infer that amphorae means vase.

16. **(A)** *Critical Reading: Passages/Social Studies/ Vocabulary*

You may have seen the word "icon" before in connection with the graphical interface of a computer: click on the icon to do something. That is not the meaning intended here, but it is related. The iconic representations are stylized representations with features that enable the viewer to associate the icon with a concept, in this case, with the goddess Athena. (C), (D), and (E) are incorrect because they are not representations. A "religious statue" is a representation, but it would not be on a vase, so (B) is also wrong.

17. With which of the following statements would the author probably agree about any new evidence that art was commissioned for some crowned games?

(A) The evidence disproves the theory that the crown games were held in honor of Zeus.
(B) The evidence tends to show that Athena and Zeus were actually the same ancient Greek deity.
(C) The evidence suggests that some crown games offered prizes but does not require a major reevaluation of current theories.
(D) The evidence is irrelevant to what is known about ancient games because the most important were the Panathenaia and not the crown games.
(E) The evidence reinforces the distinction between the crown games as amateur games and the Panathenaia as a contest for professional athletes.

17. (C) *Critical Reading: Passages/Social Studies/ Application*

The phrase "probably agree" is the clue that this is an Application item. So, the question is: what would new evidence do to the author's analysis? Not much. Remember that the author draws a distinction between the rural, crown, and Panathenaic games. One of the minor points in the analysis is that the rural games did not offer grand prizes. If it turned out that a couple did, that wouldn't really require a complete revision of the analysis.

Items #18–24 are based on the following passage.

The following is an excerpt from a report that was prepared by an engineering firm on the feasibility of electric cars. The excerpt focuses on the uses of electromechanical batteries as a power source.

Except that their output is alternating current rather than direct current, electromechanical batteries, or EMBs, would power an electric car in the same way as a bank of electrochemical batteries. The modular
5 device contains a flywheel that is stabilized by nearly frictionless magnetic bearings integrated with a special ironless generator motor and housed in a sealed vacuum enclosure. The EMB is "charged" by spinning its rotor to maximum speed with an integral
10 generator/motor in its "motor mode." It is "discharged" by slowing the rotor of the same generator/motor to draw out the kinetically stored energy in its "generator mode." Initial research focused on the possibility of using one or two relatively large EMBs, but subsequent
15 findings point in a different direction.

Compared to stationary EMB applications such as with wind turbines, vehicular applications pose two special problems. Gyroscopic forces come into play whenever a vehicle departs from a straight-line course,
20 as in turning. The effects can be minimized by vertically orienting the axis of rotation, and the designer can mount the module in limited-excursion gimbals to resist torque. By operating the EMB modules in pairs—one spinning clockwise and the

25 other counterclockwise—the net gyroscopic effect on the car would be nearly zero.

The other problem associated with EMBs for vehicles is failure containment. Any spinning rotor has an upper speed limit that is determined by the tensile
30 strength of the material from which it is made. On the other hand, at a given rotation speed, the amount of kinetic energy stored is determined by the mass of the flywheel. It was originally thought that high-density materials such as metals were optimal for flywheel
35 rotors, and a metal flywheel does store more energy than an equivalent-size flywheel made of low-density material and rotating at the same speed. However, a low-density wheel can be spun up to a higher speed until it reaches the same internal tensile stresses as the
40 metal one, where it stores the same amount of kinetic energy at a much lower weight. Lightweight graphite fiber, for example, is more than 10 times more effective per unit mass for kinetic energy storage than steel. Plus, tests show that a well-designed rotor made
45 of graphite fibers that fails turns into an amorphous mass of broken fibers. This failure is far more benign than that of metal flywheels, which typically break into shrapnel-like pieces that are difficult to contain.

Not only is the uncontrolled energy that can be
50 released by each unit reduced, but the danger posed by a failed rotor is very small compared to that of rotors just two or three times larger. Thus, an array of small EMB modules offers major advantages over one or two large units.

18. The author's primary concern is to

(A) describe technological advances that make possible containment of uncontrolled kinetic energy discharge due to cataclysmic rotor failure

(B) report on new technologies that will make electric cars competitive with vehicles employing conventional internal combustion engines

(C) argue that an array of small EMB modules mounted in an electric car is more energy efficient than a single large EMB

(D) construct field tests that will prove whether or not mobile EMBs can be arranged so as to minimize unwanted torque

(E) demonstrate how a group of small EMB modules for use in an electric car can avoid technological problems that are associated with a single large EMB

19. It can be inferred that a non-metallic, low-density flywheel that has stored kinetic energy equivalent to that of a metallic, high-density flywheel is

(A) operating in its "motor mode" and discharging energy as it spins

(B) oriented vertically to the axis of rotation of the metallic flywheel

(C) spinning in the opposite direction of the metallic flywheel

(D) rotating at a higher speed than the metallic flywheel

(E) made of graphite fibers that disintegrate into harmless fragments upon failure

18. **(E)** *Critical Reading: Passages/Natural Sciences/ Main Idea*

The first and last sentences of the selection effectively provide the answer that you are looking for. (A) is too narrowly drafted because the author does not only discuss the containment issue (the second issue). (B) goes beyond the explicit scope of the selection because "competitiveness" is not mentioned. (C) likewise is wide of the mark. The author focuses on physical forces, not energy efficiency. And finally, (D) is incorrect because the author does not suggest any new experiments.

19. **(D)** *Critical Reading: Passages/Natural Sciences/ Implied Idea*

In the third paragraph, the author explains that the energy stored by a flywheel is a function of its weight and speed and that a lightweight flywheel would have to spin faster in order to store the same energy as a heavier one. So, you can infer that if the weights are different but the stored energy is the same, the lighter wheel is spinning faster—and that's choice (D). (A) is a confused reading of the first paragraph, and that information doesn't help answer the question that is asked. Similarly, (B) and (C) come out of the second paragraph and aren't relevant here. Finally, (E) bears on the issue of safety, not on the physics by which energy is stored.

20. With which of the following statements would the author of the passage LEAST likely agree?

   (A) Gyroscopic forces in applications such as wind turbines are not relevant factors because wind turbines remain in one place.

   (B) Lightweight non-metallic flywheels made of materials such as graphite fiber are less likely to fail at maximum stress than non-metallic flywheels.

   (C) An array of small EMB modules can provide the same amount of energy to the system of an electric car as one or two relatively large EMBs.

   (D) The amount of kinetic energy that can be stored by a flywheel is a function of the weight of its constituent materials and its maximum rotational speed.

   (E) Technological innovations such as frictionless bearings can help to make electromechanical batteries sufficiently efficient for use in electric cars.

20. (B) *Critical Reading: Passages/Natural Sciences/ Application*

The author says that lightweight flywheels cause less damage when they fail but does not say that they are less likely to fail. In fact, in the third paragraph, the author talks of spinning a lightweight wheel until it "reaches the same internal tensile stresses" as the heavier one. At this point it is just as likely to break; the consequences are just not so horrendous. The author would probably agree with (A) since windmills are stationary. And the author would probably agree with (C) since the opening sentence says that EMBs would power an electric car. (D) is based upon the third paragraph. (E) finds adequate support in the first paragraph.

21. In line 46, the phrase "more benign" means

   (A) less dangerous
   (B) more reliable
   (C) equally stable
   (D) less expensive
   (E) less efficient

21. (A) *Critical Reading: Passages/Natural Sciences/ Vocabulary*

If you know in advance that the meaning of "benign" is "nonthreatening" or "not dangerous," (A) is the obvious choice. The correct answer can also be found within the context of the third paragraph. The author is discussing what happens when one of these rapidly spinning wheels breaks up. If it's made of heavy metal, the result is a lot of shrapnel flying everywhere. But if it's made of graphite fiber, then the result is a tangled bunch of threads—much less dangerous than the alternative.

22. The author regards the new EMB technology as

   (A) overrated
   (B) unattainable
   (C) promising
   (D) untested
   (E) impractical

22. (C) *Critical Reading: Passages/Natural Sciences/ Voice*

Remember that you can often arrange the attitudes on a scale from negative to positive. The author's attitude in this case is positive. So, you can eliminate every choice but (C).

23. The author states that the gyroscopic effect of EMB modules operating in pairs can be minimized if they are

(A) constructed of high-density metal
(B) rotated in opposite directions
(C) operating in their "motor" mode
(D) stabilized by frictionless bearings
(E) spinning at high speeds

23. (B) *Critical Reading: Passages/Natural Sciences/ Explicit Detail*

Because this is an Explicit Detail item, the correct answer must satisfy two criteria: be explicitly stated (though perhaps not in the same words) in the passage and respond to the question that is asked. The answer to this item is specifically given in the second paragraph: the net effect is zero when they are spinning in opposite directions, (B).

24. Which of the following best describes the logical development of the selection?

(A) It mentions some technological challenges and describes some possible solutions.
(B) It identifies some technological problems and dismisses attempts to solve them.
(C) It outlines technological demands of an engineering application and minimizes their significance.
(D) It presents a history of a technological question but offers no answers.
(E) It examines some new approaches to an engineering problem and rejects them.

24. (A) *Critical Reading: Passages/Natural Sciences/ Development*

The author introduces the idea of EMBs for use in cars and describes generally how they would work. Then, in the second paragraph, the author states that they pose "two special problems." The author describes those problems and explains how they are minimized by using different technological solutions, (A). The other choices simply do not fit the logical development of the passage.

Directed Study Practice Test

SECTION 5—MATH

20 Items

DIRECTIONS: In this section, solve each item, and choose the correct answer choice. Use any available space for scratchwork.

Notes:

(1) The use of a calculator is permitted. All numbers used are real numbers.

(2) Figures that accompany problems in this test are intended to provide information useful in solving the problems. They are drawn as accurately as possible EXCEPT when it is stated in a specific problem that the figure is not drawn to scale. All figures lie in a plane unless otherwise indicated.

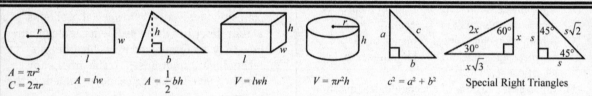

$A = \pi r^2$
$C = 2\pi r$ $A = lw$ $A = \frac{1}{2}bh$ $V = lwh$ $V = \pi r^2 h$ $c^2 = a^2 + b^2$ Special Right Triangles

The number of degrees of arc in a circle is 360.

The sum of the measures in degrees of the angles of a triangle is 180.

---

1. A barrel contained 5.75 liters of water and 4.5 liters evaporated. How many liters of water remain in the barrel?

   (A)   0.75
   (B)   1.25
   (C)   1.75
   (D)   2.25
   (E)   13.25

1. (B) *Math: Multiple-Choice/Arithmetic/Simple Manipulations*

Perform the indicated operation:
$5.75 - 4.5 = 1.25$.

2. The expression "3 less than the product of 4 times x" can be written as

   (A) $4x - 3$
   (B) $3x - 4$
   (C) $4(x - 3)$
   (D) $3(4x)$
   (E) $\dfrac{4x}{3}$

2. (A) *Math: Multiple-Choice/Algebra/Manipulating Algebraic Expressions/Evaluating Expressions*

Translate the expression into "algebrese." The product of 4 times x is written as $4x$, and 3 less than that would be $4x - 3$.

3. If $\frac{3}{4}$ of x is 36, then $\frac{1}{3}$ of x is

    (A) 9
    (B) 12
    (C) 16
    (D) 24
    (E) 42

3. **(C)** *Math: Multiple-Choice/Algebra/Solving Algebraic Equations or Inequalities with One Variable*

If $\frac{3}{4}$ of x is 36, then:

$$\frac{3}{4}(x)=36$$

$$x=36\left(\frac{4}{3}\right)=48$$

And $\frac{1}{3}$ of 48 is 16.

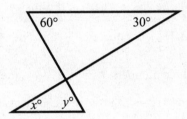

4. In the figure above, what is the value of $x+y$?

    (A) 45
    (B) 60
    (C) 75
    (D) 90
    (E) 120

4. **(D)** *Math: Multiple-Choice/Geometry/Lines and Angles*

The measure of the unlabeled angle in the triangle on the top is 90°. The angle vertically opposite it in the triangle on the bottom is therefore also equal to 90°. Thus:

$$x+y+90=180$$
$$x+y=90$$

5. If n is a multiple of 3, which of the following is also a multiple of 3?

    (A) $2+n$
    (B) $2-n$
    (C) $2n-1$
    (D) $2n+1$
    (E) $2n+3$

5. **(E)** *Math: Multiple-Choice/Arithmetic/Common Arithmetic Items/Properties of Numbers*

There are two ways to attack this item. One is to reason that:

(A) $2+n$ cannot be a multiple of 3. Since n is a multiple of 3, when $2+n$ is divided by 3, there will be a remainder of 2;

(B) $2-n$ cannot be a multiple of 3 for the same reason that $2+n$ cannot be a multiple of 3;

(C) $2n-1$ cannot be a multiple of 3. Since n is a multiple of 3, $2n$ will also be a multiple of 3, and so $2n-1$ cannot be a multiple of 3;

(D) $2n+1$ cannot be a multiple of 3 for the same reason that $2n-1$ cannot be a multiple of 3; and finally,

(E) $2n+3$ is a multiple of 3. $2n$ is a multiple of 3; 3 is a multiple of 3; so, $2n+3$ is a multiple of 3.

Alternatively, you can reach the same conclusion by substituting an assumed value that is a multiple of 3 into the choices. Assume $n = 3$:

(A) $2 + n = 2 + 3 = 5$, not a multiple of 3. ✗
(B) $2 - n = 2 - 3 = -1$, not a multiple of 3. ✗
(C) $2n - 1 = 2(3) - 1 = 6 - 1 = 5$, not a multiple of 3. ✗
(D) $2n + 1 = 2(3) + 1 = 6 + 1 = 7$, not a multiple of 3. ✗
(E) $2n + 3 = 2(3) + 3 = 6 + 3 = 9$, a multiple of 3. ✓

6. Which of the following is NOT equal to the ratio of two whole numbers?

(A) $\left(\dfrac{1}{5}\right)^2$

(B) $\dfrac{1}{5}$

(C) 0.20

(D) 5%

(E) $\sqrt{\dfrac{5}{1}}$

6. (E) *Math: Multiple-Choice/Arithmetic/Common Arithmetic Items/Properties of Numbers* and *Ratios*

Remember that a ratio is another way of writing a fraction. So, inspect each of the answer choices. As for (A), $\left(\dfrac{1}{5}\right)^2$ is equal to $\dfrac{1}{25}$, and both 1 and 25 are whole numbers. As for (B), $\dfrac{1}{5}$ is the ratio of 1 to 5, so (B) is not the correct choice. As for (C), 0.20 is equal to $\dfrac{1}{5}$, the ratio of two whole numbers. And 5% can be written as $\dfrac{5}{100}$, or $\dfrac{1}{20}$.

Finally, $\sqrt{5}$ is not a whole number, so the expression in (E) is not the ratio of two whole numbers.

7. If the area of a square is 16, what is the perimeter?

(A) 2
(B) 4
(C) 8
(D) 16
(E) 32

7. (D) *Math: Multiple-Choice/Geometry/Rectangles and Squares*

If you know the area of a square, you can find its perimeter, and vice versa:

$$\text{area}_{\text{square}} = \text{side} \cdot \text{side} = 16$$

$$s^2 = 16 \Rightarrow s = 4 \ (\text{distances are positive})$$

So, the perimeter is equal to $4s$, or $4 \cdot 4 = 16$.

8. If $12 + x = 36 - y$, then $x + y =$

(A) −48
(B) −24
(C) 3
(D) 24
(E) 48

8. (D) *Math: Multiple-Choice/Algebra/Manipulating Algebraic Expressions/Basic Algebraic Manipulations*

Here, you have one equation with two variables. It's not possible to solve for x or y individually, but you don't need to. Instead, simply rewrite the equation so that you have it in the form $x + y$:

$$12 + x = 36 - y$$
$$x + y = 36 - 12 = 24$$

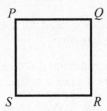

9. Two security guards, Jane and Ed, patrol the perimeter of the square area shown above. Starting at corner P at 8:00 p.m., Jane walks around the outside of the fence in a clockwise direction while Ed walks around the inside in a counterclockwise direction. If it takes exactly 10 minutes for each guard to walk from one corner to the next, where will they be two hours later, at 10 p.m.?

(A) Both at corner P
(B) Both at corner R
(C) Jane at corner P and Ed at corner R
(D) Ed at corner P and Jane at corner Q
(E) Ed at corner P and Jane at corner R

10. Depending on the value of k, the expression $3k + 4k + 5k + 6k + 7k$ may or may not be divisible by 7. Which of the terms, when eliminated from the expression, guarantees that the resulting expression is divisible by 7 for every positive integer k?

(A) $3k$
(B) $4k$
(C) $5k$
(D) $6k$
(E) $7k$

9. (A) *Math: Multiple-Choice/Geometry/Spatial Reasoning*

One way of analyzing this item is to reason that the square has four sides and each guard requires 10 minutes to walk the distance of a side. In 2 hours, or 120 minutes, each guard will walk $120 \div 10 = 12$ sides. So, each guard will make three complete trips around the lot ($12 \div 4 = 3$), bringing each back to his or her original starting point.

That's a big explanation for something that is not really that complicated. Why not let your fingers do the walking? Trace the route that each guard will follow. At 8:10, Jane is at point Q; at 8:20, she is at point R; at 8:30, she is at point S; and so on. Not very elegant, but effective.

10. (B) *Math: Multiple-Choice/Arithmetic/Common Arithmetic Items/Properties of Numbers* and *Algebra/Manipulating Algebraic Expressions/ Evaluating Expressions*

Analyze the problem as follows. The sum of $3k$, $4k$, $5k$, $6k$, and $7k$ is $25k$, a number that will be divisible by 7 only if k is divisible by 7. If, however, the coefficient of k were divisible by 7, then that number would be divisible by 7 regardless of the value of k. If the term $4k$ were dropped from the group, the sum of the remaining terms is $21k$. Since 21 is divisible by 7, $21k$ will be divisible by 7 regardless of the value of k.

Alternatively, assume a value for k, say $k = 1$. Then, the total of the five terms is $3 + 4 + 5 + 6 + 7 = 25$. Getting rid of which one will yield a number divisible by 7? The answer is to get rid of the 4, because 21 is divisible by 7.

11. If $\frac{1}{3} < x < \frac{3}{8}$, which of the following is a possible value of x?

(A) $\frac{1}{2}$

(B) $\frac{3}{16}$

(C) $\frac{17}{48}$

(D) $\frac{9}{24}$

(E) $\frac{5}{12}$

11. **(C) Math: Multiple-Choice/Arithmetic/Complicated Manipulations/Simplifying**

It would be a mistake to try to convert each of these fractions to decimals to find the value that lies between $\frac{1}{3}$ and $\frac{3}{8}$. Instead, find an escape route. Use a benchmark, approximate, or do whatever else is available. First, eliminate (A), because $\frac{1}{2}$ is more than $\frac{3}{8}$. Next, eliminate (B). $\frac{3}{15}$ is equal to $\frac{1}{3}$, so $\frac{3}{16}$ is smaller than $\frac{1}{3}$ (a larger denominator makes for a smaller fraction, given the same numerator). (C) is close to and slightly less than $\frac{18}{48}$, which is $\frac{3}{8}$. So, (C) is the correct choice. But let's finish the line of reasoning. As for (D), $\frac{9}{24}$ is equal to $\frac{3}{8}$, not less than $\frac{3}{8}$. Finally, $\frac{5}{12}$ is equal to $\frac{10}{24}$, and $\frac{3}{8}$ is equal to $\frac{9}{24}$.

12. If $x^2 - y^2 = 3$ and $x - y = 3$, then $x + y =$

(A) 0
(B) 1
(C) 2
(D) 3
(E) 9

12. **(B) Math: Multiple-Choice/Algebra/Manipulating Algebraic Expressions/Factoring Expressions**

By this point in your study, you should automatically factor the expression $x^2 - y^2$ into $(x + y)(x - y)$. Since $x - y = 3$, $(x + y)(3) = 3$, so $x + y = 1$.

13. If n is a positive integer, which of the following must be an even integer?

(A) $n + 1$
(B) $3n + 1$
(C) $3n + 2$
(D) $n^2 + 1$
(E) $n^2 + n$

13. **(E) Math: Multiple-Choice/Arithmetic/Common Arithmetic Items/Properties of Numbers**

As for (A), whether $n + 1$ is odd or even will depend on whether n is odd or even. The same is true for (B) and (C), because whether $3n$ is odd or even will depend on whether n is odd or even. As for (D), n^2 could be odd or even. If n^2 is even, then the expression $n^2 + 1$ is equal to an odd number. And if n^2 is odd, the expression is equal to an even number. Therefore, every choice has been eliminated except (E), so (E) must be the correct answer.

Alternatively, you can assume some numbers.

14. If the area of a square inscribed in a circle is 16, what is the area of the circle?

(A) 2π
(B) 4π
(C) 8π
(D) 16π
(E) 32π

14. (C) *Math: Multiple-Choice/Geometry/Complex Figures* and *Circles* and *Rectangles and Squares*

No figure is provided, so sketch one:

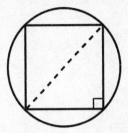

Since the square has an area of 16, it has a side of 4 and a diagonal of $4\sqrt{2}$ (the diagonal forms the hypotenuse of a 45°-45°-90° triangle—refer to the formula summary available at the start of the test section). The diagonal of the square is also the diameter of the circle. So, the circle has a diameter of $4\sqrt{2}$ and a radius of $2\sqrt{2}$. Finally, a circle with a radius of length $2\sqrt{2}$ has an area of

$$\pi\left(2\sqrt{2}\right)^2 = \pi(8) = 8\pi.$$

15. In a certain group of 36 people, only 18 people are wearing hats and only 24 people are wearing sweaters. If 6 people are wearing neither a hat nor a sweater, how many people are wearing both a hat and a sweater?

(A) 30
(B) 22
(C) 12
(D) 8
(E) 6

15. (C) *Math: Multiple-Choice/Arithmetic/Solving Complicated Arithmetic Application Items*

This item can be solved using a Venn diagram:

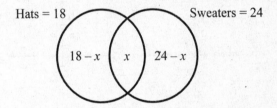

The twist here is that the diagram is not intended to represent all 36 people in the group. 6 of the 36 are wearing neither a hat nor a sweater. So, the total represented by the diagram is $36-6=30$.

$$18-x+x+24-x=30$$
$$-x+x-x+18+24=30$$
$$-x+42=30$$
$$-x=-12$$
$$x=12$$

16. $\left|-3\right| \cdot \left|2\right| \cdot \left|\dfrac{1}{2}\right| + (-4) =$

    (A)   −1
    (B)   0
    (C)   1
    (D) $\dfrac{3}{2}$
    (E)   4

16. **(A)** *Math: Multiple-Choice/Arithmetic/Simple Manipulations*

Simply do the indicated calculation. Since $\left|-3\right| = 3$:

$$\left|-3\right| \cdot \left|2\right| \cdot \left|\dfrac{1}{2}\right| + (-4) = 3 \cdot 2 \cdot \dfrac{1}{2} - 4 = 3 - 4 = -1$$

17. What are the values for which $\dfrac{x(x+3)}{(x-1)(x+2)}$ is undefined?

    (A)   −3 only
    (B)   −2 only
    (C)   1 only
    (D)   −2 and 1 only
    (E)   −3, −2, and 1

17. **(D)** *Math: Multiple-Choice/Algebra/Manipulating Algebraic Expressions/Evaluating Expressions*

When $x = 1$, $x - 1 = 0$, so the entire expression is undefined. Similarly, when $x = -2$, $x + 2$ is 0, and the expression is undefined. When $x = -3$, then $x + 3$ is equal to 0, so the value of the expression is 0 and that is perfectly allowable.

18. Which of the following graphs in the standard (x, y) coordinate plane correctly shows the points on the graph of $y = \left|x^2 - 3\right|$ for $x = -1$, 0, and 1?

    (A)   (D)

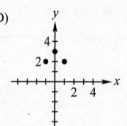

    (B)   (E)

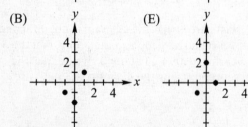

    (C)

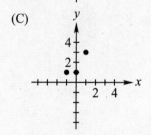

18. **(D)** *Math: Multiple-Choice/Coordinate Geometry/ Graphs of Quadratic Equations and Relations*

Find the corresponding values for y:

$$y = \left|(-1)^2 - 3\right| = \left|1 - 3\right| = \left|-2\right| = 2$$

$$y = \left|(0)^2 - 3\right| = \left|-3\right| = 3$$

$$y = \left|(1)^2 - 3\right| = \left|1 - 3\right| = \left|-2\right| = 2$$

(D) is the correct plotting of the points $(-1, 2)$, $(0, 3)$, and $(1, 2)$.

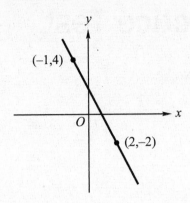

19. The figure above is a graph of which of the following equations?

(A) $y = 3x + 5$

(B) $y = 2x + 2$

(C) $y = -\dfrac{3}{2}x - 2$

(D) $y = \dfrac{2}{3}x + 3$

(E) $y = x + 2$

19. (B) *Math: Multiple-Choice/Coordinate Geometry/ Graphs of Linear Equations*

Create an equation of the form $y = mx + b$, in which m is the slope of the line and b is the y-intercept. Begin by calculating the slope:

$$m = \frac{(-2) + (-4)}{(2) - (-1)} = \frac{-6}{3} = -2$$

Therefore: $y = -2x + b$.

Now, use one of the pairs of coordinates provided in the graph:

$$4 = -2(-1) + b$$
$$4 = 2 + b$$
$$b = 2$$

20. The relation defined by the set of ordered pairs $\{(0,3),\ (2,1),\ (3,0),\ (-1,2),\ (0,5),\ \text{and}\ (-2,5)\}$ is NOT a function. Deleting which of the ordered pairs will make the resulting set a function?

(A) $(0,3)$

(B) $(2,1)$

(C) $(3,0)$

(D) $(-1,2)$

(E) $(-2,5)$

20. (A) *Math: Multiple-Choice/Algebra/Expressing and Evaluating Algebraic Functions/Concepts of Domain and Range*

To be a function, a relation can have only one output for each input. In other words, for all ordered pairs (x, y), for any value x there can be only one y. Inspecting the relation defined by the given set, either $(0,3)$ or $(0,5)$ must be eliminated to make the relation a function. Only $(0,3)$ is given as a possible answer.

Directed Study Practice Test

SECTION 6—CRITICAL READING
24 Items

DIRECTIONS: In this section, solve each item, and choose the correct answer choice.

Items #1–8: Each item below has one or two blanks, each blank indicating that something has been omitted. Beneath the sentence are five lettered words or sets of words. Choose the word or set of words that best fits the meaning of the sentence as a whole.

Example:

Although its publicity has been -------, the film itself is intelligent, well acted, handsomely produced, and altogether -------.

(A) tasteless . . respectable
(B) extensive . . moderate
(C) sophisticated . . amateur
(D) risqué . . crude
(E) perfect . . spectacular

---

1. Despite the millions of dollars that are spent on improvements, the telephone system in India remains ------- and continues to ------- the citizens who depend on it.

   (A) primitive . . inconvenience
   (B) bombastic . . upset
   (C) suspicious . . connect
   (D) outdated . . elate
   (E) impartial . . vex

1. **(A)** *Critical Reading: Sentence Completions/ Combined Reasoning/Subordinate Conjunctions* and *Explanatory Phrases*

This sentence contains both a reversal of thought and an extension of thought as its logical keys. First, the subordinate conjunction "despite" indicates that the correct choice will describe something unexpected given the amount of money that is invested. Second, the second blank will be a logical continuation of the first blank, as the phrase "continues to" indicates. Immediately eliminate (B), (C), and (E) because they do not create meaningful phrases when substituted into the first blank. (A) and (D) are possibilities because a phone system can be both primitive and outdated. Next, eliminate (D) because an outdated phone system would hardly elate those who depend on it. (A) creates a logical sentence: the system is primitive, despite the money spent on it, and it continues to inconvenience those who use it.

2. Contrary to popular opinion, bats are not generally aggressive and rabid; most are shy and -------.

(A) turgid
(B) disfigured
(C) punctual
(D) innocuous
(E) depraved

3. The ballet company demonstrated its ------- by putting both classical and modern works in the repertoire.

(A) versatility
(B) mollification
(C) treachery
(D) dignity
(E) obtrusiveness

4. Unlike the images in symbolist poetry, which are often vague and ------- the images of surrealist poetry are startlingly ------- and bold.

(A) extraneous . . furtive
(B) trivial . . inadvertent
(C) obscure . . concrete
(D) spectacular . . pallid
(E) symmetrical . . virulent

2. **(D)** *Critical Reading: Sentence Completions/ Combined Reasoning/Explanatory Phrases* and *Coordinate Conjunctions*

This sentence contains both a reversal of thought and an extension of thought as its logical keys. First, the phrase clue "contrary to popular opinion" indicates a reversal of thought; therefore, bats are going to be something that is the opposite of "aggressive" and "rabid." Second, the blank would have to be filled with a word that parallels "shy," as indicated by the coordinate conjunction "and." Eliminate (A), (B), and (C) because they are not things one would say about bats and are not opposites for "aggressive" and "rabid." Also eliminate (E) because a bat would probably not be described as "depraved." (D), "innocuous," which means "harmless," is the opposite of "aggressive" and goes nicely with "shy."

3. **(A)** *Critical Reading: Sentence Completions/ Thought Extension/Explanatory Phrases*

This is basically a matter of vocabulary. You need to know what noun means "the ability to do more than one thing well," as indicated by the key phrase, "both classical and modern works." Only "versatility" completes the sentence. (B), (C), (D), and (E) create meaningless sentences.

4. **(C)** *Critical Reading: Sentence Completions/ Combined Reasoning/Coordinate Conjunctions* and *Key Words*

This sentence contains both an extension of thought and a reversal of thought as its logical keys. The first blank needs a word that continues the idea of "vagueness," as indicated by the coordinate conjunction "and." The second blank is "unlike" the first and must therefore be something close to an opposite. Also, the second blank should be close to "bold" because of the coordinate conjunction "and." All of the choices make sense since they can all be used to describe images, but only one parallels "vague," and that is "obscure." The second element of (C), "concrete," is an opposite of "obscure" and completes the sentence nicely. The second elements of (A), (B), (D), and (E) are not fitting descriptors of images and make no sense when substituted in the sentence.

5. A good trial lawyer will argue only what is central to an issue, eliminating ------- information or anything else that might ------- the client.

    (A) seminal . . amuse
    (B) extraneous . . jeopardize
    (C) erratic . . enhance
    (D) prodigious . . extol
    (E) reprehensible . . initiate

6. When the real estate agent finally suggested a property that the young couple could -------, they were shocked to see a ------- house that seemed as though it was on the verge of collapse.

    (A) renovate . . modern
    (B) purchase . . galling
    (C) afford . . ramshackle
    (D) diversify . . dilapidated
    (E) envision . . reserved

7. Psychologists agree that human beings have a strong need to ------- their time; having too much idle time can be as stressful as having none at all.

    (A) threaten
    (B) annihilate
    (C) structure
    (D) punctuate
    (E) remand

5. **(B)** *Critical Reading: Sentence Completions/ Combined Reasoning/Explanatory Phrases*

This sentence contains both a reversal of thought and an extension of thought as its logical keys. The sentence says that the lawyer argues only what is central, eliminating something. For the first blank, students should focus on the key word "eliminating," which indicates the reversal of thought. Logically, when something is eliminated, it is not central to the issue, so you should look for a word that means "not central." (A) and (B) are both possibilities. Eliminate (C), (D), and (E) because they do not make sense in this context. The second element is the deciding factor here. The phrase "anything else" indicates that the second blank is an extension of the first blank. The lawyer would not want to jeopardize her client by arguing extraneous information; therefore, (B) is the best answer. It makes no sense to say that the lawyer would not want to amuse her client.

6. **(C)** *Critical Reading: Sentence Completions/ Thought Extension/Explanatory Phrases*

This item is a matter of vocabulary. By focusing on the second blank and the key phrase "on the verge of collapse," it is clear that the only two possible answers are (C) or (D). Eliminate (D) on the basis of usage because one does not diversify a house. The second element of (A) disqualifies that answer. A modern house would not look as if it were about to collapse. A house can be neither galling nor reserved, so that eliminates (B) and (E). "Ramshackle," the second word of choice in (C), means "broken down or about to collapse" and completes the sentence perfectly.

7. **(C)** *Critical Reading: Sentence Completions/ Combined Reasoning/Key Words* and *Punctuation Marks*

This sentence contains both a reversal of thought and an extension of thought as its logical keys. Before looking at the choices, you already know that you need a word that describes something you can do with time so that it is *not* idle, which is reinforced by the extending nature of the semicolon. Eliminate all choices except (C) because they not only say nothing useful about time, but they create meaningless sentences.

8. While scientists continue to make advances in the field of -------, some members of the clergy continue to oppose the research arguing that it is ------- for human beings to tamper with life.

(A) psychology . . imperative
(B) astronomy . . fallacious
(C) genetics . . immoral
(D) geology . . erroneous
(E) botany . . unethical

8. **(C)** *Critical Reading: Sentence Completions/ Combined Reasoning/Subordinate Conjunctions* and *Explanatory Phrases*

You cannot eliminate any of the choices on the grounds of usage, since each, when substituted into the sentence, will create a meaningful idiomatic phrase. So, be a Sentence Completions detective, and look to the clues in the sentence. This sentence contains both a reversal of thought, the subordinate conjunction "while," and an extension of thought, the phrase "tamper with life," as its logical keys. The field of study that completes the first blank must be a science that not only studies but directs the course of life, as indicated by the phrase "tamper with life." This eliminates (B), (D), and (E). Although one might say that psychology tampers with life, it makes no sense to say that some members of the clergy oppose it and think that it is imperative. This process of elimination leaves only (C).

Items #9–24: Each passage below is followed by one or more items based on its content. Answer the items following each passage on the basis of what is stated or implied in the passage.

Items #9–10 are based on the following passage.

Some scientists have theorized that the initial explosion of the dying star generates the high energy particles observed in supernova remnants, but these particles would quickly lose their energy as they cool
5 in the expanding cloud or escape from the remnant altogether. Instead, the acceleration of particles to high energies must be associated with the shockwave produced by the supernova explosion. The particles are accelerated to very high energies through collisions
10 with fragments in a process analogous to that of a ping-pong ball bouncing through a collection of randomly moving bowling balls. Over the course of many collisions, the ping-pong ball would be accelerated to a very high speed. It is too soon to say definitely that the
15 size and number of fragments associated with the shockwave are adequate to generate the high-energy electrons but a preliminary analysis looks promising.

9. The author regards the conclusion stated in the final sentence as

(A) unproved but likely
(B) unsubstantiated and doubtful
(C) conclusively demonstrated
(D) true by definition
(E) unfounded speculation

9. (A) *Critical Reading: Passages/Natural Sciences/ Voice*

The words "unproved but likely" do not appear specifically in the passage, but you can infer that this is the author's attitude. The author says that it is "too soon" to say definitely that the theory is correct but adds that it "looks promising." (B) is incorrect because the author does not regard the theory as "doubtful." (C) overstates the case in the other direction: "promising" does not mean "conclusively demonstrated." (D) is simply a bad description of the passage: the author is not defining terms. (E) is incorrect because the author believes that there is evidence for the theory.

10. The author develops the passage primarily by

(A) raising an issue and discussing both pros and cons
(B) logically deducing conclusions from a premise
(C) explaining a known sequence of events
(D) providing a list of examples to illustrate a principle
(E) criticizing one theory and offering an alternative explanation

10. (E) *Critical Reading: Passages/Natural Sciences/ Development*

The author first cites one theory (the particles come from the initial explosion). Then, the author says this theory cannot be right (the particles would run out of energy). Finally, the author offers a different explanation (the particles are bounced around by fragments in the shockwave.) (A) is a distracter since it recognizes that the author seems to debate, but the author doesn't discuss pros and cons of an issue; the author compares two theories. (B) is incorrect because there is no logical deduction. (C) is incorrect because there is no sequence outlined. (D) is incorrect because there is no list of examples.

<u>Item #11</u> is based on the following passage.

Chicory is a perennial wildflower, two to three feet high, with a taproot like the Dandelion. The flowers are somewhat like those of the Dandelion though they have a delicate tint of blue. You'll find it
5 growing throughout the summer along roadsides. Chicory, or Cichorium, is a word of Egyptian origin, and the Arab physicians called it "Chicourey." Cichorium is mentioned by Theophrastus as it was used amongst the ancient Greeks, and the names by
10 which the wild plant is known in all the languages of modern Europe are merely corruptions of the original Greek word. The root is roasted and ground for blending with coffee, though Chicory itself is totally lacking in caffeine.

11. The author assumes that

(A) readers are familiar with the Dandelion
(B) Chicory originated in the Middle East
(C) modern European languages derive mainly from Greek
(D) ancient Greeks preferred caffeine-free beverages
(E) dandelions do not grow along roadsides

11. (A) *Critical Reading: Passages/Natural Sciences/ Implied Idea*

In the first two sentences, the author describes the appearance of chicory by comparing it to dandelions, but this assumes that the reader is familiar with dandelions. As for (B), the fact that the plant was known in the Middle East does not mean that it originated there. In addition, the fact that there are Greek words in modern European languages doesn't mean that Greek is the main influence, so (C) is incorrect. As for (D), the fact that the Greeks knew of chicory does not mean that they brewed it nor that they knew it lacked caffeine. And finally, (E) at least has the merit of mentioning dandelions, but there is nothing in the passage to support the suggestion that dandelions do not grow on roadsides.

Item #12 is based on the following passage.

To one unaccustomed to it, there is something inexpressibly lonely in the solitude of a prairie. The loneliness of a forest seems nothing compared to it. In a forest, the view is shut in by trees, and the
5 imagination is left free to picture a livelier scene beyond. However, in the case of a prairie, there is an immense extent of landscape without signs of human existence; one is struck by the feeling of being far beyond the bounds of human habitation. It is a lonely
10 waste bounded by undulating swells of land, naked and uniform, and due to the deficiency of landmarks and distinct features, an inexperienced traveler may become lost as readily as upon the wastes of the ocean.

12. The author states that the prairie seems lonelier than the forest because

(A) it is possible for a traveler to become lost more easily on the prairie
(B) the forest is marked by paths that show routes to various destinations
(C) the prairie is larger and more open than the ocean itself
(D) trees of the forest resemble people who keep a traveler from feeling alone
(E) the unobstructed view on the prairie shows the absence of other people

12. (E) *Critical Reading: Passages/Humanities/ Explicit Detail*

The author states that the prairie seems lonelier than the forest because the lines of sight are longer, making it clear that there is no one else around. At least with the forest, according to the author, one can always imagine that just around the next group of trees there might be others; but on the prairie, one can see that there is no one else. (E) summarizes this notion. (A) is incorrect because the idea of getting lost is found in the comparison of the prairie to the ocean; this question is asking about the feeling of loneliness that is caused by the lack of other people. (B) is incorrect because the author never mentions any paths. (C) is incorrect because the comparison of ocean and prairie is not used to explain the feeling of loneliness. (D) has no support in the passage.

Item #13 is based on the following passage.

Every 10 years, the federal government conducts a comprehensive census of the entire population, and the data gathered are published by the Bureau of Census. By studying census data, demographers are
5 able to identify counties and communities throughout the country with populations that have specific characteristics, for example: high or low median age, large numbers of families with children, a high percentage of two-career couples, or particularly
10 affluent households. Characteristics such as these are often associated with particular viewpoints on important political issues.

13. The author is most likely leading up to a proposal to

(A) require the census to be conducted more frequently
(B) use census data to advise candidates on political issues
(C) expand the scope of the census to gather more detailed data
(D) maintain the confidentiality of census records
(E) discontinue the practice of conducting the census

13. (B) *Critical Reading: Passages/Social Studies/ Application*

The author states that the census data are useful in identifying certain characteristics that seem to determine thinking about some political issues. It seems likely that the author would elaborate on this statement by discussing exactly how the data could be used: in choosing candidates or advising candidates in light of what the voters likely believe, (B). (A) is incorrect because "10 years" is simply a bit of background. The remainder of the passage does not refer to the frequency of the census. As for (C), while a political advisor might like to have more detailed data, no such proposal is suggested by the passage. It is not that (C) is impossible; rather, it is simply that (B) is a much easier conclusion to reach. You should always prefer the easier or safer conclusion for a problem like this. (D) is incorrect because confidentiality is never mentioned. Finally, (E) is incorrect because it goes well beyond the passage. There is absolutely nothing to suggest that the author opposes the census. Again, (B) is a much easier conclusion to reach.

Item #14 is based on the following passage.

"Locks," says the old saw, "are installed to keep out honest people." In fact, most locks do not present much of a challenge to lock pickers, whether amateur or professional. The one on your front door probably
5 consists of a cylinder held in place by a series of spring-loaded pins. When you insert the serrated key, the sharp edges of the key push the pins out of the way allowing you to turn the cylinder with the key, thereby operating the bolt. The same result can be
10 accomplished by inserting a pick and wrench, both small wire-like tools, and manipulating them in the right way. Gently turn the wrench to keep a constant rotational force on the cylinder while using the pick to push the pins out of the way one at a time. When the
15 last pin is cleared, the wrench will naturally turn the cylinder and the lock will open for you. After a little practice, anyone with larceny in the heart can open your front door in less than 30 seconds.

14. Which of the following best describes the relationship between the last sentence of the passage and the first sentence?

(A) The first sentence states a hypothesis that is disproved by the passage and summarized by the last sentence.
(B) The first sentence makes a generalization that is then illustrated by examples referenced by the last sentence.
(C) The last sentence summarizes the development of the passage and notes that the first sentence makes a false statement.
(D) The last sentence shows that the development of the passage proves the point made in the first sentence.
(E) The last sentence uses details from the passage to contradict the assertion of the first sentence.

14. (D) *Critical Reading: Passages/Humanities/ Development*

The author begins by saying that locks only keep out honest people and then goes on to talk about how easy it is to pick a lock. The last sentence is a reiteration: "...anyone with larceny in the heart can open your front door...." So, the last sentence is a summary of the development of the passage (the instructions on how to pick a lock), and this development shows that locks are not much use against anyone but an honest person. Since the last sentence ties the passage together in a consistent whole, (A), (C), and (E) have to be incorrect. (B) is incorrect because it misses the point that the examples are supposed to prove: crooks are not deterred by locks.

Items #15–24 are based on the following passage.

Is the Constitution of the United States a mechanism or an organism? Does it furnish for the American community a structure or a process? The Constitution is Newtonian in that it establishes a set of
5 forces and counter-forces. These confer power and impose limitations on power, and one of the great virtues of the Newtonian model is that correctives can be self-generated. They do not have to be imposed from without. The homely illustration is the cutting of
10 a pie into two pieces so that brother and sister will have equal shares. Rather than setting up a system of judicial review under an equal-protection clause—a device that might not work until the pie has become stale—you simply let one sibling cut the pie and the other choose a
15 piece.

The Newtonian system assumes that each branch has a capacity to act that is commensurate with its authority to act and to improve its ability to discharge its constitutional responsibilities. For example, on the
20 Congressional side, this means a rationalizing of the legislative process to improve its capability to formulate and carry through a legislative program that is coherent in policies and technically proficient. The goal involves better access to disinterested information
25 through better research staffs and facilities, as well as the selection of committee chairs most likely on a basis other than simple seniority. Other devices might alleviate the overburdened executive branch: a strengthened Cabinet, with a smaller, executive
30 Cabinet of respected statesmen to serve as a link between the White House and the departments, and between the President and the Congress. No constitutional impediment stands in the way of any of the structural changes on either the legislative or the
35 executive side.

In a Newtonian constitution, extraordinary force in one direction is likely to produce extraordinary, and sometimes excessive, force in another direction. In the early years of the New Deal, the Supreme Court,
40 generally over the dissent of its most respected members, engaged in a series of judicial vetoes that reflected a non-judicial approach to the function of judging. The President, on his part, countered with the Court reorganization plan, which seriously threatened
45 the independence of the judiciary. A Newtonian system demands constitutional morality. It would be possible, by excessive use of legal power, to bring the system to a standstill. Congress might refuse to appropriate for executive departments. The President might ignore
50 Supreme Court decisions. The Court might declare unconstitutional all laws that a majority of its members

would not have voted for. Without constitutional morality, the system breaks down.

The constitution is also Darwinian and stresses
55 process and adaptation. Justice Holmes remarked that "the provisions of the Constitution are not mathematical formulas having their essence in their form; they are organic living institutions." Growth and adaptation, to be sure, have sometimes been seen as
60 mutations, threatening the constitutional order. Chief Justice Marshall, near the close of his life, viewing with despair the developments of the Jacksonian era, confided to Justice Story, "The Union has been preserved thus far by miracles. I fear they cannot
65 continue."

It must be admitted that we have all too readily assigned responsibility for the Darwinian constitutional evolution to the Supreme Court. Congress has too often either neglected its opportunities and responsibilities or
70 has acted tentatively. When Congress does legislate, it is apt to regard its own constitutional judgment as only provisional, to await as a matter of course a submission to the Supreme Court. A striking example is the recent campaign finance law. But in the final analysis, is the
75 Constitution a mechanism or an organism? If light can be viewed as both wave and particles, depending on which analysis is the more serviceable for a given problem, why cannot the Constitution be seen as both a mechanism and an organism, a structure and a process?

15. The main purpose of the selection is to

    (A) discuss two models of constitutional law
    (B) criticize Congress and the executive branch for inaction
    (C) suggest a new role for the Supreme Court
    (D) challenge the validity of Supreme Court rulings
    (E) call for a revised Constitution

16. In the first paragraph, the author makes use of

    (A) circular reasoning
    (B) authority
    (C) analogy
    (D) generalization
    (E) ambiguity

17. The author mentions the possibility of better research staffs for Congress (line 25) as a method of

    (A) weakening the executive branch of government
    (B) improving the ability of the legislature to act
    (C) encouraging the judiciary to be independent
    (D) illegally increasing the workload of Congress
    (E) curtailing the power of the government

18. It can be inferred that the author's attitude toward the Supreme Court's decisions during the early years of the New Deal is one of

    (A) reflection
    (B) acceptance
    (C) support
    (D) indifference
    (E) disapproval

---

15. (A) *Critical Reading: Passages/Social Studies/ Main Idea*

The author begins by asking which of two models better describes the Constitution. The selection then examines both models. The author ends by creating an analogy between constitutional theory and physics that suggests that both models are useful. (A) provides the best description of this development. (B) is too narrow to be a correct description of the main idea of the selection. The author also criticizes the judiciary, and the main emphasis of the passage is theoretical. (C) is also too narrow. The author suggests obliquely that the Supreme Court has perhaps taken too much responsibility for evolving constitutional doctrine, but that is not the main point of the passage. Finally, (E) is surely wrong because the author is concerned about how to interpret the existing Constitution.

16. (C) *Critical Reading: Passages/Social Studies/ Development*

In the first paragraph, the author likens a certain view of the Constitution to dividing a pie between two siblings. The best description of this technique is "analogy," (C). The author does not make use of any of the other answer choices in the first paragraph.

17. (B) *Critical Reading: Passages/Social Studies/ Explicit Detail*

In the second paragraph, the author mentions a couple of ways to strengthen the ability of Congress to act, and one of these is getting better information. This change would presumably make Congress more efficient and therefore would not simply increase the workload, so (D) is incorrect. Since the suggestion is aimed specifically at the legislature, (A), (C), and (E) are incorrect.

18. (E) *Critical Reading: Passages/Social Studies/ Voice*

There are two very strong clues to answer this item: "respected" and "unjudicial." According to the author, the Supreme Court overrode its most respected members and acted unjudicially. So, the author disapproves strongly of those decisions. Since the other choices are at worst neutral, all of the other choices are incorrect.

19. The author regards the President's attempt to reorganize the Supreme Court as

(A) understandable but wrong
(B) ineffective but correct
(C) impractical but well-intentioned
(D) necessary but misguided
(E) half-hearted but moral

20. The author means for the word "Darwinian" (line 54) to echo the meaning of

(A) self-generated (line 8)
(B) homely (line 9)
(C) proficient (line 23)
(D) unjudicial (line 42)
(E) organic (line 58)

21. With which of the following statements would the author most likely agree?

(A) The Darwinian model and the Newtonian model produce almost identical interpretations of the Constitution.
(B) A constitutionally permissible action might still be constitutionally immoral.
(C) One branch of government is morally obligated not to criticize the actions of another.
(D) The Newtonian model of the Constitution is superior to the Darwinian model.
(E) The Supreme Court should have primary responsibility for evolving a Darwinian model of government.

19. **(A)** *Critical Reading: Passages/Social Studies/ Voice*

In the third paragraph, the author notes that in a Newtonian model, extraordinary action may trigger excessive reaction. And the author uses the Court reorganization plan as an example. Since the plan was an excessive reaction, the author would condemn it. Further, the author uses terms such as "unjudicial" and "seriously threatened." (A) provides the best description of this attitude: the author understands why the President acted as he did but disagrees with the policy. The remaining choices are incorrect because the author thinks the policy was wrong.

20. **(E)** *Critical Reading: Passages/Social Studies/ Vocabulary*

This item works a little like a Development item, since you are supposed to connect the word "Darwinian" back to something earlier in the passage. In the first sentence, the author distinguishes between two views of the Constitution: mechanistic and organic. The discussion of the Newtonian view analyzes the Constitution in terms of mechanisms; e.g., force, counterforce, etc. Then, the fourth paragraph marks a shift: the Constitution is also Darwinian—this would be the organic view. The other choices must be incorrect because they don't preserve the parallelism: "Newton is to Darwin as mechanistic is to organic."

21. **(B)** *Critical Reading: Passages/Social Studies/ Application*

In the third paragraph, the author states that a Newtonian system requires "constitutional morality" or restraint. He explains that a branch of government might well have the legal authority to do acts that would interfere with the proper functioning of government. Thus, the author would likely agree with statement (B). Conversely, the author would almost surely reject (A). In the final paragraph, the analogy between constitutional theory and physics implies that both models are useful—one has advantages that the other lacks and vice versa. (C) represents a misreading of the phrase "constitutional morality." The "morality" that is called for in the third paragraph is restraint, but not restraint from criticism. "Constitutional morality" is restraint from legal but counterproductive actions. (D) makes the same type of mistake that

(A) makes. The author states that both models have their advantages and that both should be used. Finally, (E) is directly contradicted by the first sentence of the final paragraph; the author states that it is unfortunate that the Court has had so much responsibility for the Darwinian model.

22. In the final sentence, the author

(A) poses a question for future research
(B) introduces a new problem of constitutional theory
(C) rejects the Darwinian model
(D) suggests ways for improving governmental efficiency
(E) asks a rhetorical question

22. (E) *Critical Reading: Passages/Social Studies/ Development*

In the final paragraph, having discussed the merits of the two models, the author draws an analogy between physics and constitutional theory. A physicist might, suggests the author, use either of two models to understand light depending on the need. With the analogy, the author implies that the same is true of constitutional theory. So, the author asks a question in the final sentence that he believes has already been answered. (A) is wrong because the author apparently believes the analogy disposes of the problem introduced in the first paragraph. (B) is wrong because the problem that is addressed by the selection was introduced in the first paragraph. (C) is wrong because the author regards both models as useful. And (D) is a description of some of the other paragraphs in the selection—but not of the final sentence.

23. The passage implies that

(A) Congress is more important than either the executive or the judiciary
(B) branches of government may have more constitutional authority than they use
(C) the earliest Supreme Court justices were more sincere than today's justices
(D) the Constitution sets up a very simple system for governmental decisions
(E) constitutionally created hurdles block needed improvements in governmental efficiency

23. (B) *Critical Reading: Passages/Social Studies/ Implied Idea*

In the second paragraph, the author suggests some things that the executive and legislative branches might do to make government better— things that are constitutionally permissible. Thus, it is inferable that the branches of government may have more authority than they are using. (A) is incorrect because the author seems to regard all three branches as equally important. (That is part of the Newtonian model.) (C) is wrong because the only part of the passage that even hints that judges might be "insincere" is the discussion about the New Deal decisions—and that compares members of the same Court. (D) must be incorrect because the author implies that the constitutional process is sufficiently complex that it cannot be explained by a single model. Finally, analysis of the correct choice shows that (E) is wrong; the author believes that govern-mental efficiency can be improved by taking constitutionally permissible action.

24. The author is primarily concerned with

    (A) creating a dilemma
    (B) evading a question
    (C) answering a question
    (D) pointing out a contradiction
    (E) reporting on a development

24. **(C)** *Critical Reading: Passages/Social Studies/Main Idea*

Our analysis for the previous items shows that the author's main purpose is to answer the questions posed at the beginning of the selection. As for (A), a dilemma occurs when a person finds herself in an "either/or" situation and neither alternative is particularly attractive. Here, rather than creating a dilemma, the author avoids one by arguing that it is not necessary to embrace one model to the exclusion of the other: you can use both models. As for (B), the author does not explicitly answer the question that is posed in the last sentence because it is rhetorical. This is not because the author wishes to evade the question; the author does not answer because she thinks that the answer is obvious. As for (D), the author discusses two different models but does not examine points of inconsistency between them. Finally, as for (E), though the author does state that the Darwinian model talks of "process," it would be incorrect to say that the author is reporting on a development.

Directed Study Practice Test

SECTION 8—MATH

16 Items

DIRECTIONS: In this section, solve each item, and choose the correct answer choice. Use any available space for scratchwork.

Notes:

(1) The use of a calculator is permitted. All numbers used are real numbers.

(2) Figures that accompany problems in this test are intended to provide information useful in solving the problems. They are drawn as accurately as possible EXCEPT when it is stated in a specific problem that the figure is not drawn to scale. All figures lie in a plane unless otherwise indicated.

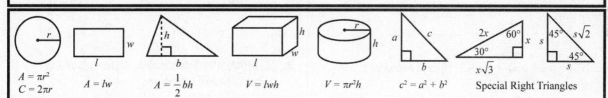

$A = \pi r^2$
$C = 2\pi r$

$A = lw$

$A = \frac{1}{2}bh$

$V = lwh$

$V = \pi r^2 h$

$c^2 = a^2 + b^2$

Special Right Triangles

The number of degrees of arc in a circle is 360.

The sum of the measures in degrees of the angles of a triangle is 180.

Fabric	Cost
A	3 yards for $8
B	2 yards for $6
C	4 yards for $9
D	5 yards for $7
E	8 yards for $10

1. According to the table above, which fabric costs the <u>least</u> per square yard?

   (A) A
   (B) B
   (C) C
   (D) D
   (E) E

1. (E) *Math: Multiple-Choice/Data Analysis/Data Interpretation/Tables (Matrices)* and *Arithmetic/ Common Arithmetic Items/Proportions and Direct-Inverse Variation*

   Do not do lengthy calculations. Set up the cost of each fabric as a fraction and compare the fraction directly, using a benchmark:

   (A) $\frac{8}{3} = 2\frac{2}{3}$

   (B) $\frac{6}{2} = 3$

   (C) $\frac{9}{4} = 2\frac{1}{4}$

(D) $\dfrac{7}{5}=1\dfrac{2}{5}$

(E) $\dfrac{10}{8}=\dfrac{5}{4}=1\dfrac{1}{4}$

(E) is the smallest.

2. $\dfrac{10^3\left(10^5+10^5\right)}{10^4}=$

(A) 10^4

(B) 10^6

(C) $2\left(10^2\right)$

(D) $2\left(10^4\right)$

(E) $2\left(10^9\right)$

2. (D) *Math: Multiple Choice/Arithmetic/ Complicated Manipulations/Factoring*

Obviously, you cannot do the calculation, so look for an escape route. Cancel and factor:

$$\dfrac{10^3\left(10^5+10^5\right)}{10^4}=\dfrac{10^3\left[2\left(10^5\right)\right]}{10^4}=\dfrac{2\left(10^8\right)}{10^4}=2\left(10^4\right).$$

3. If $x=b+4$ and $y=b-3$, then in terms of x and y, $b=$

(A) $x+y-1$

(B) $x+y+1$

(C) $x-y-1$

(D) $\dfrac{x+y+1}{2}$

(E) $\dfrac{x+y-1}{2}$

3. (E) *Math: Multiple-Choice/Algebra/Solving Simultaneous Equations*

To find b in terms of x and y, you will first need to set b equal to x and equal to y:

$$\begin{array}{ll} x=b+4 & y=b-3 \\ b=x-4 & \text{and} \quad b=y+3 \end{array}$$

Now, combine the two equations by adding:

$$\begin{array}{r} b=x-4 \\ +\,(b=y+3) \\ \hline 2b=x+y-1 \\ b=\dfrac{(x+y-1)}{2} \end{array}$$

Alternatively, you can arrive at the same conclusion by substituting some numbers. Let $b=1$. Then, $x=1+4=5$, and $y=1-3=-2$. Substitute 5 for x and -2 for y into the answer choices. The correct choice will yield the value 1.

4. If $5x = 3y = z$, and x, y, and z are positive integers, all of the following must be integers EXCEPT

(A) $\dfrac{z}{xy}$

(B) $\dfrac{z}{5}$

(C) $\dfrac{z}{3}$

(D) $\dfrac{z}{15}$

(E) $\dfrac{x}{3}$

5. What is the width of a rectangle with an area of $48x^2$ and a length of $24x$?

(A) 2
(B) $2x$
(C) $24x$
(D) $2x^2$
(E) $2x^3$

6. If $x = \dfrac{1}{y+1}$ and $y \neq 1$, then $y =$

(A) $x+1$
(B) x
(C) $\dfrac{x+1}{x}$
(D) $\dfrac{x-1}{x}$
(E) $\dfrac{1-x}{x}$

4. **(A)** *Math: Multiple-Choice/Algebra/Manipulating Algebraic Expressions/Basic Algebraic Manipulations*

Since $z = 5x = 3y$, and x, y, and z are integers, z is a multiple of both 3 and 5, so z is evenly divisible by 5, 3, and 15. And z is divisible by both x and y individually, but z is not necessarily divisible by the product of x and y. Finally, since $5x = 3y$, and x and y are integers, x is a multiple of 3 (and evenly divisible by 3).

Alternatively, you can reach the same conclusion by substituting some numbers. The most natural assumption is to let $z = 15$, so $x = 3$ and $y = 5$. But on that assumption, every answer choice is an integer. So, try the next multiple of 15. Let $z = 30$, so $x = 6$ and $y = 10$. Now, (A) is no longer an integer: $30 \div (6)(10)$.

5. **(B)** *Math: Multiple-Choice/Geometry/Rectangles and Squares*

You can solve the problem by using the formula for finding the area of a rectangle:

$$\text{Area}_{\text{rectangle}} = \text{width} \cdot \text{length}$$
$$48x^2 = w(24x)$$
$$w = \frac{48x^2}{24x} = 2x$$

Alternatively, you can reach the same conclusion by substituting numbers. If $x = 2$, the area of the rectangle is $48(2^2) = 48(4) = 192$, and the length is 48. So, 48 times the width is equal to 192, and the width is $192 \div 48 = 4$. So, if $x = 2$, the correct choice will yield the value 4. Only choice (B) works.

6. **(E)** *Math: Multiple-Choice/Algebra/Manipulating Algebraic Expressions/Basic Algebraic Manipulations*

Rewrite the equation: $x = \dfrac{1}{y+1} \Rightarrow x(y+1) =$

$1 \Rightarrow y+1 = \dfrac{1}{x} \Rightarrow y = \dfrac{1}{x} - 1 \Rightarrow y = \dfrac{1-x}{x}$.

Alternatively, assume some numbers. If $y = 1$,

$x = \dfrac{1}{2}$. Substitute $\dfrac{1}{2}$ for x in the answer choices; the correct choice will yield the value 1.

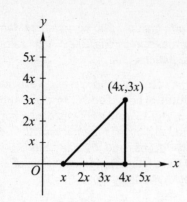

7. In the figure above, if the area of the triangle is 54, then $x =$

(A) $3\sqrt{3}$
(B) 3
(C) $2\sqrt{3}$
(D) 2
(E) $\sqrt{3}$

7. **(C)** *Math: Multiple-Choice/Coordinate Geometry/ The Coordinate System*

The length of the base of the triangle is $4x - x = 3x$, and the length of the altitude is $3x - 0 = 3x$ (the difference in the y-coordinate). Use the formula for finding the area of a triangle to determine x:

$$\frac{1}{2}(3x)(3x) = 54$$
$$(3x)(3x) = 108$$
$$9x^2 = 108$$
$$x^2 = 12$$
$$x = \sqrt{12} = 2\sqrt{3} \ \text{(distance must be positive)}$$

8. If $\Delta(x) = x + 1$ and $\nabla(x) = x - 1$, then which of the following is equal to $\Delta(3) \cdot \nabla(5)$?

(A) $\Delta(8)$
(B) $\Delta(12)$
(C) $\Delta(14)$
(D) $\nabla(17)$
(E) $\nabla(20)$

8. **(D)** *Math: Multiple-Choice/Algebra/Expressing and Evaluating Algebraic Functions/Function Notation*

This item a "picture math" or defined function item. First, do "Δ" to 3 and "∇" to 5:
$\Delta(3) = 3 + 1 = 4$ and $\nabla(5) = 5 - 1 = 4$. So, $\Delta(3) \cdot \nabla(5) = 16$. Now, evaluate each answer choice to find the one that equals 16:

(A) $\Delta(8) = 8 + 1 = 9$ ✗
(B) $\Delta(12) = 12 + 1 = 13$ ✗
(C) $\Delta(14) = 14 + 1 = 15$ ✗
(D) $\nabla(17) = 17 - 1 = 16$ ✓
(E) $\nabla(20) = 20 - 1 = 19$ ✗

9. If $x + y = 14$, then $\dfrac{x}{2} + \dfrac{y}{2} =$

(A) 4
(B) 5
(C) 6
(D) 7
(E) $\dfrac{y}{2}$

9. **(D)** *Math: Multiple-Choice/Algebra/Manipulating Algebraic Expressions/Basic Algebraic Manipulations*

You may be able to figure this out without doing any arithmetic by thinking $\dfrac{1}{2}x + \dfrac{1}{2}y = \dfrac{1}{2}(14)$.

Alternatively, try any numbers that fit in place of x

10. If the average of 10 numbers—1, 2, 3, 4, 5, 6, 7, 8, 9, and x—is 6, what is x?

(A) 5
(B) 6
(C) 10
(D) 12
(E) 15

11. A certain mixture of gravel and sand consists of 2.5 kilograms of gravel and 12.5 kilograms of sand. What percent of the mixture, by weight, is gravel?

(A) 10%
(B) $16\frac{2}{3}$%
(C) 20%
(D) 25%
(E) $33\frac{1}{3}$%

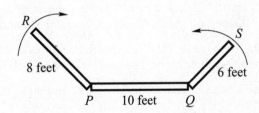

12. The figure above is the top view of a folding room divider, hinged at P and Q. If sections PR and QS are moved as shown until R and S meet, what will be the area, in square feet, enclosed? (Ignore the thickness of the hinges and the screen's sections.)

(A) 6
(B) 12
(C) 6π
(D) 24
(E) 12π

and y:

$$4+10=14 \qquad\qquad 6+8=14$$
$$\frac{1}{2}(4)+\frac{1}{2}(10)=7 \quad \text{and} \quad \frac{1}{2}(6)+\frac{1}{2}(8)=7$$

10. (E) *Math: Multiple-Choice/Data Analysis/ Probability and Statistics/Averages*

If the average of 10 numbers is 6, then the total of the 10 numbers must be 60 since $60\div10=6$. The total of the first 9 numbers is: $1+2+3+4+5+6+7+8+9=45$. The difference is $60-45=15$, so x must be equal to 15.

11. (B) *Math: Multiple-Choice/Arithmetic/Common Arithmetic Items/Percents*

Use the "is-over-of" equation. The "of," which is the denominator of the fraction, is the mixture. How much of the mixture is there? $2.5+12.5=15$. The word "is," which is the numerator of the fraction, is the 2.5 kilograms of gravel. Thus:

$$\frac{\text{is}}{\text{of}}=\frac{\text{gravel}}{\text{mixture}}=\frac{2.5}{15}=\frac{1}{6}$$

Remember that $\frac{1}{6}=0.1\overline{6}=16\frac{2}{3}$%.

12. (D) *Math: Multiple-Choice/Geometry/Triangles/ Working with Triangles*

Complete the sketch:

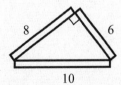

The triangle has sides of 6, 8, and 10, which you should recognize as multiples of 3, 4, and 5. So, the triangle is a right triangle. The sides of 6 and 8 form the right angle, so they can be used as altitude and base for finding the area:

$$\text{area}=\frac{1}{2}\cdot\text{altitude}\cdot\text{base}=\frac{1}{2}\cdot6\cdot8=24.$$

13. Motorcycle A averages 40 kilometers per liter of gasoline while Motorcycle B averages 50 kilometers per liter. If the cost of gasoline is $2 per liter, what will be the difference in the cost of operating the two motorcycles for 300 kilometers?

(A) $3
(B) $6
(C) $12
(D) $15
(E) $20

13. **(A)** *Math: Multiple-Choice/Arithmetic/Common Arithmetic Items/Proportions and Direct-Inverse Variation*

Proportions make this calculation easy. First, complete the calculation for Motorcycle A:

$$\frac{\text{Fuel Used } X}{\text{Fuel Used } Y} = \frac{\text{Miles Driven } X}{\text{Miles Driven } Y}$$

$$\frac{1}{x} = \frac{40}{300}$$

$$40x = 300$$

$$x = 7.5$$

Thus, Motorcycle A uses 7.5 liters of fuel for the 300-mile trip. Now, do the same for Motorcycle B:

$$\frac{1}{x} = \frac{50}{300}$$

$$50x = 300$$

$$x = 6$$

Therefore, Motorcycle B uses 6 liters of fuel for the trip. Since Motorcycle A uses $7.5 - 6 = 1.5$ liters more than Motorcycle B, the fuel for Motorcycle A costs $1.5 \cdot \$2 = \$3$ more.

14. For all positive integers, $[n] = \dfrac{n}{2}$ if n is even, and $[n] = n + 1$ if n is odd. $[2] \cdot [7] =$

(A) 4
(B) 5
(C) 6
(D) 7
(E) 8

14. **(E)** *Math: Multiple-Choice/Algebra/Expressing and Evaluating Algebraic Functions/Function Notation*

This item is a defined function item. Simply do the indicated operations. The first function is used for $n = 2$ because 2 is even: $[2] = \dfrac{2}{2} = 1$. And the second function is used for $n = 7$ because 7 is odd: $[7] = 7 + 1 = 8$. Finally, $1 \cdot 8 = 8$.

15. For a positive integer k, which of the following equals $6k + 3$?

(A) $\dfrac{k+1}{2}$

(B) $\dfrac{1}{k} + 4$

(C) $2k + 1$

(D) $3(k + 1)$

(E) $3(2k + 1)$

15. **(E)** *Math: Multiple-Choice/Algebra/Manipulating Algebraic Expressions/Factoring Expressions*

Factor $6k + 3$: $6k + 3 = 3(2k + 1)$.

Alternatively, substitute 1 for k in the given expression: $6k + 3 = 6(1) + 3 = 6 + 3 = 9$. The correct answer choice will also return the value 9 for $k = 1$. Only (E) works: $3(2k + 1) = 3[2(1) + 1] = 3(3) = 9$.

16. To mail a letter costs x cents for the first ounce and y cents for every additional ounce or fraction of an ounce. Which of the following equations can be used to determine the cost, C, in cents to mail a letter that weighs a whole number of ounces, w?

(A) $C = w(x+y)$

(B) $C = x(w-y)$

(C) $C = x(w-1)+y(w-1)$

(D) $C = x+wy$

(E) $C = x+y(w-1)$

16. **(E)** *Math: Multiple-Choice/Algebra/Manipulating Algebraic Expressions/Creating Algebraic Expressions*

Devise the formula as follows. The formula will be x, the cost for the first ounce, plus some expression to represent the additional postage for each additional ounce over the first ounce. The postage for the additional weight is y cents per ounce, and the additional weight is w minus the first ounce, or $w-1$. Therefore, the additional postage is $y(w-1)$, and the total postage is $x+y(w-1)$.

Alternatively, assume some numbers. For ease of calculations, assume that the first ounce costs 1 cent and every additional ounce is 2 cents. If $x=1$ and $y=2$, then a letter, of say, 3 ounces ($w=3$) will cost $1+2(2)=5$ cents. Substitute these values for x, y, and w into the answer choices and the correct choice will return the value 5:

(A) $w(x+y)=3(1+2)=3(3)=9$ ✗

(B) $x(w-y)=1(3-2)=1(1)=1$ ✗

(C) $x(x-1)+y(w-1)=1(1-1)+2(3-1)$
$\qquad =1(0)+2(2)=4$ ✗

(D) $x+wy=1+3(2)=7$ ✗

(E) $x+y(w-1)=1+2(3-1)=1+2(2)=5$ ✓

Directed Study Practice Test

SECTION 9—CRITICAL READING
19 Items

DIRECTIONS: In this section, solve each item, and choose the correct answer choice.

Items #1–5: Each item below has one or two blanks, each blank indicating that something has been omitted. Beneath the sentence are five lettered words or sets of words. Choose the word or set of words that best fits the meaning of the sentence as a whole.

Example:

Although its publicity has been -------, the film itself is intelligent, well acted, handsomely produced, and altogether -------.

(A) tasteless . . respectable
(B) extensive . . moderate
(C) sophisticated . . amateur
(D) risqué . . crude
(E) perfect . . spectacular

---

1. Large corporations use advertising not to liberate consumers with information about freedom of choice but to ------- them, holding them captive to the company's particular brand.

   (A) enslave
   (B) attract
   (C) enlighten
   (D) aid
   (E) secure

1. (A) *Critical Reading: Sentence Completions/ Combined Reasoning/Key Words* and *Explanatory Phrases*

The logical structure of this sentence provides two context clues. First, the "*not* this but that" structure in the first part of the sentence indicates that the blank must be filled in with a word that means the opposite of "liberate." So, (C), (D), and (E) can safely be eliminated. Second, the clause that follows the comma is a further explanation of the missing word, so the blank must be filled in with a word that has the same meaning as "holding...captive." (B) is wrong because it is a "distracter" answer choice; you should not confuse "holding...captive" with "captivate," and you should also recognize that "attract" does not mean the opposite of "liberate." Therefore, (A) is the correct answer choice.

2. Hoping to impress his professor, Eugene did the work required for the course with -------, submitting all of the assignments on or before their due dates.

(A) reluctance
(B) alacrity
(C) insouciance
(D) fortitude
(E) lassitude

3. John was bright but lazy and because of his ------- was never promoted to senior partner.

(A) novelty
(B) perjury
(C) zeal
(D) indemnity
(E) indolence

4. The film was completely devoid of plot or character development: It was merely a ------- of striking images.

(A) renouncement
(B) montage
(C) calumny
(D) carnage
(E) premonition

5. Though the concert had been enjoyable, it was overly ------- and the three encores seemed -------.

(A) extensive . . curtailed
(B) protracted . . gratuitous
(C) inaudible . . superfluous
(D) sublime . . fortuitous
(E) contracted . . lengthy

2. (B) *Critical Reading: Sentence Completions/ Thought Extension/Explanatory Phrases*

This item primarily focuses on vocabulary. The clause that follows the comma is a further explanation of the missing word, so the blank must be filled in with a word that describes speed and efficiency. (B) is the only answer choice that satisfies this meaning; "alacrity" means "speed or quickness."

3. (E) *Critical Reading: Sentence Completions/ Thought Extension/Key Words*

This is a straightforward vocabulary question. The word substituted in the blank must extend the idea of "lazy," as indicated by the subordinate conjunction "because." In fact, since the blank refers to "lazy," the substituted word will be a synonym. Only (E), which means "slothfulness" or "laziness," does the job.

4. (B) *Critical Reading: Sentence Completions/ Thought Extension/Punctuation Marks*

As with the previous item, this item is also primarily a vocabulary question. The colon signals that the second clause extends the thought in the first clause. You can eliminate (A), (C), (D), and (E) since they are not things that could be said of images and therefore fail on the grounds of usage. This leaves you with the correct answer, (B). A montage is a series of rapid images in film.

5. (B) *Critical Reading: Sentence Completions/ Combined Reasoning/Subordinate Conjunctions* and *Coordinate Conjunctions*

The subordinate conjunction "though" indicates a reversal of thought. The concert was enjoyable, but it suffers from some defect. Eliminate (D) since to be sublime is not to have a defect. Additionally, the two blanks themselves are parallel since they complete similar thoughts and are joined by the coordinate conjunction "and," which indicates an extension of thought. (A) and (E) contain words that are opposite in meaning, so they must be wrong. Finally, the words in (C) are unrelated, so they cannot provide the needed contrast.

Items #6–9: Each passage below is followed by one or more items based on its content. Answer the items following each passage on the basis of what is stated or implied in the passage.

Items #6–7 are based on the following passage.

On one of those sober and melancholy days in the latter part of autumn, when the shadows of morning and evening almost mingle together and throw a gloom over the decline of the year, I passed several hours
5 rambling about Westminster Abbey. It seems as if the awful nature of the place presses down upon the soul, and hushes the beholder into noiseless reverence. We are surrounded by the congregated bones of great men of past times, who have filled history with their deeds,
10 and the earth with their renown.* Yet, it provokes a smile at the vanity of human ambition to see how they are crowded together and jostled in the dust; what parsimony is observed in doling out a scanty nook, a gloomy corner, and a little portion of earth, to those,
15 whom, when alive, kingdoms could not satisfy. I passed some time in Poet's Corner, which occupies an end of one of the transepts or cross aisles of the abbey. The monuments are generally simple; for the lives of literary men afford no striking themes for the sculptor.
20 Shakespeare and Addison have statues erected to their memories; but the greater part have busts, medallions, and sometimes mere inscriptions.

*Over 3,000 famous people are buried in Westminster Abbey.

6. As used in this context, the word "awful" (line 6) means

    (A) frightening
    (B) impressive
    (C) terrible
    (D) unlit
    (E) dilapidated

6. **(B)** *Critical Reading: Passages/Humanities/ Vocabulary*

Because this is a Vocabulary item, you should stay away from the most common meanings of the word such as those suggested by (A) and (C). A good clue to the author's use is "reverence" (line 7); in fact, the word means "awe-ful," or full of awe. (D) and (E) are ideas found in the passage but not in connection with "awful."

7. The author finds it amusing that

(A) people would be buried inside a structure like Westminster Abbey
(B) only Shakespeare and Addison have statues erected to them
(C) famous people are buried in relatively modest circumstances
(D) even the powerful and famous eventually die
(E) writers are buried in a remote part of the building

7. (C) *Critical Reading: Passages/Humanities/Explicit Detail*

The only mention of anything amusing is the reference to the observation that the bones of famous and powerful people are jammed together into small corners and plots—as (C) indicates. As for (A), while you might find this fact amusing, the author does not say that he finds it amusing, so (A) cannot be correct. As for (B), while the author does point out that Shakespeare and Addis have statues erected to them, he does not say that *only* Shakespeare and Addis have statues, so (B) cannot be correct. Finally, (D) and (E) seem to be true, according to the author, but these ideas do not respond to the question that is asked.

Item #8 is based on the following passage.

By the 1870s, several manufacturers were offering for sale prefabricated houses and other structures using a variety of building systems. Prefabricated units were used extensively as army
5 barracks, field hospitals, railway stations, storehouses, fruit stands, and summer cottages. When the Klondike gold rush began, a New York company immediately began loading a vessel to carry houses to Seattle via Cape Horn, all of them ready-made in sections so that
10 they could be carried easily in boats up the Yukon or packed on sleds. However, these early experiments with prefabricated houses did not revolutionize the building industry. Carpenters and builders organized to resist the adoption of a method that threatened to
15 deprive many of their jobs. Architects, who had the weight and prestige of tradition behind them, also quietly did all that they could to discourage people from buying mass-produced products that threatened the integrity of their craft.

20 **8.** The author states that the main reason that prefabricated building did not succeed was

(A) shipping cost of transporting components to remote building sites
(B) organized opposition by important sectors of the building trade
(C) limited number of applications for prefabricated structures
(D) reluctance of large buyers to purchase prefabricated units
(E) lack of sufficiently precise manufacturing processes

8. (B) *Critical Reading: Passages/Social Studies/ Explicit Detail*

The author explicitly says the reason that prefabricated building did not succeed was opposition by carpenters, builders, and architects, (B). As for (A), the author mentions that the components had to be shipped to building sites but does not indicate that the cost was prohibitive. As for (C), the author seems to think that there were quite a few uses for the units. (D) must be incorrect since railroads and the army, both large organizations, bought such units. Finally, the author does not mention (E).

<u>Item #9</u> is based on the following passage.

The beginning of the United States was characterized by two competing philosophies: the humanitarian philosophy of the French Enlightenment and the French philosophy of laissez-faire. The
5 humanitarian strain espoused the notion of human perfectibility and had as its goal an equalitarian democracy in which the state would promote the welfare of all. The laissez-faire variation stressed the needs of an abstract "economic man" and saw the
10 state's main function as ensuring free markets. The first of these antagonistic philosophies was accepted by the agrarian leaders and came to be associated with Jefferson; the second came to dominate the thinking of the mercantile, capitalistic America and took form in
15 Hamiltonian Federalism.

9. The word "antagonistic" in line 11 means

   (A) incompatible
   (B) abstract
   (C) formal
   (D) uncivil
   (E) irreverent

9. **(A)** *Critical Reading: Passages/Social Studies/ Vocabulary*

As a matter of test-taking strategy you should be ready to eliminate any choices that have overly negative overtones, so eliminate (D) and (E). The correct choice is (A). The organizing principle of the passage is the division between the two philosophies: humanitarianism and laissez-faire economics. These philosophies are built on different assumptions and reach drastically different conclusions. Hence, they are incompatible with each other. As for "abstract" and "formal," philosophy can be both of those things, but that is not the meaning of "antagonistic" in this context.

Items #10–19: The two passages below are followed by items based on their content and the relationship between the two passages. Answer the items on the basis of what is stated or implied in the passages and in any introductory material that may be provided.

Passage 1

In 1893, Frederick Jackson Turner presented a paper to a group of historians convening in Chicago during the Columbian Exposition. Entitled "The Significance of the American Frontier in History," Turner's paper drew little immediate reaction. Yet, no theory of history has had a greater influence on the direction and methodology of inquiry and the issues of debate in American history. Later historians took issue with some of Turner's interpretations; even some of his own students were among those whose research proved some of his views to be wrong. Yet, these debates merely serve to illustrate the importance of Turner's hypothesis.

Turner's argument was a grand hypothesis about how the settlement of the frontier had shaped the American experience and character. As with all general hypotheses in any field of study, it gave a coherent interpretation to many facts that had been largely ignored by historians up to that time.

Turner used statistical evidence from the 1880 census as the basis for a startling conclusion: Prior to 1880 there had been a frontier to be settled. By 1890, Turner pointed out, there was no longer any area of wilderness completely untouched by settlements. The frontier had disappeared. The passing of the frontier, Turner concluded, was a historic moment.

Turner further claimed that the frontier experience had produced a distinctively American character, which was not explainable simply as the predictable behavioral traits molded by English political institutions. Frontier settlers developed inquisitiveness, inventiveness, energy, and a great passion for freedom. These attributes defined a new American character—one evidenced in nationalism, independence, and democracy. This new sense of national identity derived from the fact that people from every section of the country mixed at the Western frontier. Economic independence could be traced to the fact that the settlers no longer depended on England for goods but had become self-sufficient. In addition, the frontier settlers, whose basic social unit was the family, enjoyed freedom from direct governmental interference. Frontier life thus reinforced the fundamental ideals of populist democracy.

In addition, Turner argued that the frontier fostered democracy in the cities of the East. The availability of free land at the frontier provided a "safety-valve" against possible social unrest: those discontented with social inequities and economic injustice could strike out and settle the free land that was available in frontier territories.

Turner's thesis was thus original in both what it said and in the methodology that Turner used in formulating it. Up to the time of Turner's essay, history had been essentially the history of politics. A Midwesterner, Turner challenged this traditional approach of Eastern historians by incorporating techniques of the social sciences, showing how factors of geography, economics, climate, and society influenced the development of the American West. Although now common among historians, at the time this interdisciplinary approach was novel.

Passage 2

Three years before Turner put forth the frontier thesis, the U.S. Census Bureau had announced the disappearance of a contiguous frontier line. For Turner, the significance of the frontier was its effect on the American character. According to Turner, uniquely American traits were developed by the frontier culture, including a can-do problem-solving attitude, a nervous energy, and rugged individualism.

Turner's essay reached triumphant heights in his belief that the promotion of individualistic democracy was the most important consequence of the frontier. Individuals, forced to rely on their own wits and strength, were necessarily skeptical of hierarchies and fearful of centralized authority.

Turner's thesis that the frontier is the key to American history as a whole has rightfully been abandoned. There is too much evidence for the critical influence of factors like slavery and the Civil War, immigration, and the development of industrial capitalism. But even as an account of the West and frontier, Turner's thesis was lacking.

Turner's formulation of "free land" ignored the presence of the numerous Indian peoples whose subjugation was required by the nation's westward march. The many Indian wars started by American expansion belie Turner's argument that the American frontier, in sharp contrast to European borders between nation-states, was "free land."

More fundamentally, the very concept of a frontier is dubious, because it applies to too many disparate places and times to be useful. How much do

Puritan New England and the California of the
95 transcontinental railroad really have in common? Many
such critics have sought to replace the idea of a moving
frontier with the idea of the West as a distinctive
region, much like the American South.

Additionally, cooperation and communities of
100 various sorts, not isolated individuals, made possible
the absorption of the West into the United States. Most
migrant wagon trains, for example, were composed of
extended kinship networks. Moreover, the role of the
federal government and large corporations grew
105 increasingly important. Corporate investors built the
railroads; government troops defeated Indian nations;
even cowboys, enshrined in popular myth as rugged
loners, were generally low-level employees of cattle
corporations.

10. According to Passage 1, Turner's methodology was
original in its

(A) reliance on the history of politics to explain the
American experience
(B) use of an interdisciplinary approach to study a
historical question
(C) reliance on a presentation at a professional
conference to announce a theory
(D) suggestion that key terms like "frontier" have
to be more clearly defined
(E) insistence that historical theories be supported
by statistical evidence

10. **(B)** *Critical Reading: Passages/Social Studies/*
Explicit Detail

In the last paragraph, and the last sentence in
particular, the author of the first passage states
that the interdisciplinary approach used by
Turner was a new technique. (B) best captures
this idea. As for (A), the same paragraph states
specifically that the reliance on political history
was characteristic of history prior to Turner. As
for (C), although Turner made the original
presentation at a conference, the passage does not
say that presenting was a technique of study.
While Turner used the opportunity to present his
new theory, he could equally well have published
an article or made an informal presentation to
colleagues. As for (D), the first passage doesn't
enter into such a debate, though you will find
some mention of this in the second passage. But
because the information appears in the second
passage, it cannot be an answer to this Explicit
Detail item about the first passage. Finally, as for
(E), while Turner did use statistics from the
Census, the author does not say that Turner
insisted that everything be supported by
statistics.

11. The phrase "even some of his own students" (lines 9–10) implies that students are

(A) not necessarily familiar with the most recent scholarly work
(B) ordinarily sympathetic to the views of one of their professors
(C) not likely to accept a theory until it has been studied for some time
(D) disposed to propose new theories that have little merit
(E) inclined to accept a new theory just because of its novelty

11. **(B)** *Critical Reading: Passages/Social Studies/ Implied Idea*

The first passage notes even some students of Turner demonstrated that some of his points were wrong. There would have been no reason to use "even" unless one would ordinarily expect for students to support the work of a professor. And in the development of the passage, the author is pointing out that even though Turner's thesis was criticized by some scholars who might otherwise have been supporters, the thesis still remains important. As for (A), the passage implies that the students did scholarly work on the thesis, not that they were ignorant of it. As for (D), there is no support for this conclusion in the text. (C) and (E) are wrong because there is nothing to support these conclusions. While students might be inclined to embrace the work of a professor, that is not equivalent to accepting a new theory just because it is new.

12. The attitude of the author of Passage 1 toward Turner's work can best be described as

(A) suspicious
(B) condescending
(C) undecided
(D) approving
(E) irreverent

12. **(D)** *Critical Reading: Passages/Social Studies/ Voice*

The author of Passage 1 evidently approves of Turner's work. The passage says that it had great influence, that it was original, and that it used a novel approach. That's a pretty good review. As for (A), while the author allows that Turner's thesis was not immune to debate or even criticism, this does not mean that the author was "suspicious" of the work itself. After all, it could turn out to be that Turner's conclusions are ultimately false; but the groundbreaking approach and radical theory would still have value. As for (B) and (E), the thesis is not treated negatively, so neither "condescending" nor "irreverent" can be used to express the author's attitude. Finally, as for (C), the author takes a pretty strong position, so "undecided" is not a good description.

13. In this context, "grand" (line 14) means

(A) incorrect
(B) comprehensive
(C) lavish
(D) tentative
(E) formal

13. **(B)** *Critical Reading: Passages/Social Studies/ Vocabulary*

Because "grand" is a word with some common meanings, you can pretty much discount any choices that use these more common synonyms. That would certainly eliminate (C) and (E). Instead, the author is using the word "grand" in a derivative sense to mean large or great or overall. Turner's thesis did try to be comprehensive, accounting for the uniquely American character. As for (A), though the author allows that Turner's thesis was not perfect, line 15 is not where that discussion occurs. And (D) must be wrong since Turner's thesis was not tentative.

14. The author of Passage 2 lists the "factors" in lines 80–82 in order to show that

(A) Turner's thesis did not adequately explain the history of the frontier
(B) historians prior to Turner had tended to focus on only a single explanatory factor
(C) the frontier was only one of many important factors in American history
(D) different regions of America had different experiences of the frontier
(E) westward expansion occurred contemporaneously with other important historical events

14. **(C)** *Critical Reading: Passages/Social Studies/ Development*

The author of Passage 2 discusses the limitations of Turner's theory, and one of the most important of these is its attempt to explain everything American in terms of the frontier. At the referenced lines, the author lists some other very important historical factors in order to show that the frontier could not have been the entire story. As for (A), this is the topic introduced at the end of that paragraph and developed in the following paragraphs, but it is not an answer to this question. As for (B), even granting that this statement is correct, it is not an answer to this question. For example, the author mentions the Civil War in order to show that Turner's thesis was too limited, not that traditional histories were too limited. As for (D), this is a point that is raised in the fifth paragraph, so it is not an answer to the question asked about the third paragraph. As for (E), while this statement is true (Westward expansion lasted for years during which time other important events took place.), it doesn't give the reason that the author has in mind. The author doesn't intend to show that these events occurred but that the events were important.

15. The author of Passage 2 mentions wagon trains (line 102) in order to show that

(A) frontier land had previously been inhabited by indigenous peoples
(B) groups were as important in the westward expansion as individuals
(C) government army troops were needed to secure the safety of settlers
(D) groups from different regions came into contact at the frontier
(E) the frontier constituted a permanent region rather than moving line

15. **(B)** *Critical Reading: Passages/Social Studies/ Development*

At the end of the third paragraph, the author of Passage 2 states that Turner's thesis, in addition to failing as a comprehensive theory of American history, does not do an adequate job of explaining the frontier. The next three paragraphs are the specific points to support this argument: (i) land wasn't free, (ii) frontier is a dubious concept, and (iii) groups as well as individuals were important. The information about wagon trains supports this last point: it was groups, not loners, who moved into the westward regions and stayed. As for (A), (C), (D), and (E), these are ideas that are mentioned, but they do not explain the significance of the wagon trains.

16. It can be inferred that the author of Passage 2 believes that Turner's thesis

    (A) is still generally valid
    (B) had very limited usefulness
    (C) was intellectually dishonest
    (D) intentionally ignored evidence
    (E) was not serious scholarship

17. In context, "belie" (line 88) means

    (A) tell an untruth about
    (B) conceal a flaw in
    (C) prove to be false
    (D) retract a point
    (E) support strongly

18. Both passages mention all of the following as elements of Turner's view regarding the American character EXCEPT

    (A) practical inventiveness
    (B) pro-democracy attitude
    (C) skepticism toward authority
    (D) nationalistic feelings
    (E) energetic lifestyle

16. **(B)** *Critical Reading: Passages/Social Studies/ Voice*

The author of Passage 2 is critical of the frontier thesis, but you'll notice that the criticisms all deal with Turner's ideas. For example, Turner thought that the frontier offered free land, but the author of Passage 2 argues that he was wrong because the land was already used by indigenous peoples. So, while the passage criticizes Turner's idea, it doesn't criticize Turner himself. Thus, (C), (D), and (E) are wrong, and (B) is correct. As for (A), the author says that the thesis has "rightfully" been abandoned because of its weaknesses.

17. **(C)** *Critical Reading: Passages/Social Studies/ Vocabulary*

You get the information you need to answer the question from the discussion about the significance of the Indian Wars. Turner claimed that the land was free, but in reality, it was necessary to pursue a policy of military aggression to secure the land. So, when the author writes that the wars "belie" the free land theory, the author means "prove false." (A) is a distracting choice, but don't be misled by the superficial connection between "lie" and "untruth." In this context, the phrase is "prove to be false," not "lie about." As for (B), (C), and (E), while these are phrases that relate generally to the idea of debating the merits of a theory, they don't focus on the connection between the wars and the free land thesis.

18. **(D)** *Critical Reading: Passages/Social Studies/ Explicit Detail*

The key word other than "EXCEPT" in this item is "both;" therefore, the correct answer choice is the only one that is *not* mentioned in *both* passages. Both authors mention (A), (B), (C), and (E). However, "nationalism" is only mentioned in the first passage.

19. The evidence that frontier land was not free (lines 84–90) most undermines what aspect of Turner's thesis as explained in Passage 1?

(A) safety-valve theory
(B) census data of 1880
(C) claim of self-sufficiency
(D) mixing at the frontier
(E) influence of English institutions

19. (A) *Critical Reading: Passages/Social Studies/ Application*

To a certain extent, any weakening of Turner's theory would have implications for all aspects of the theory. So, you might argue that the referenced evidence, in some way, tends to show that people from different regions did not mix at the frontier because the frontier was not quite as well-defined as Turner thought. But that's a pretty feeble point, and so (D) is wrong. You can apply similar reasoning to (B), (C), and (E). The best answer here is (A). The "safety valve" point, as explained in Passage 1, maintained that people who were dissatisfied with life in the urban areas could simply pack up and move to the country because there was land for the claiming. If the "free land" thesis is false, then the "safety valve" thesis must also be false.

Directed Study Practice Test

SECTION 10—WRITING

14 Items

DIRECTIONS: In this section, solve each item, and choose the correct answer choice.

Items #1–14: The following sentences test correct, effective expression. Each sentence contains an underlined portion, or the entire sentence may be underlined. Following each sentence are five ways of phrasing the underlined portion. Choice (A) repeats the original; the other four choices are different. If you think the original is better than any of the other choices, choose (A); otherwise, choose one of the other choices.

In choosing answers, follow the conventions of standard written English. Make sure to consider issues of grammar, word choice, sentence construction, and punctuation. Your choice should produce the most effective sentence. It should be clear, precise, and free of ambiguity or awkwardness.

Example:

Allen <u>visiting</u> his cousin in France last summer.

(A) visiting
(B) visited
(C) does visit
(D) a visit
(E) is visiting

---

1. The paintings by Frederic Remington <u>depict and romanticized the American West</u>.

   (A) depict and romanticized the American West
   (B) was depicting the American West and also romanticizing it
   (C) depict and romanticize the American West
   (D) having depicted the American West also romanticized it
   (E) depicts and romanticizes the American West

1. **(C)** *Writing/Improving Sentences/Sentence Structure/Faulty Parallelism*

   (C) corrects the error in the original sentence: the present tense "romanticize" is needed to parallel the present tense "depict."

   (A) The underlined portion is characterized by an illogical choice of verbs. "Depict," which shows present action, clashes with "romanticized," which shows past action.
   (B) This choice introduces a new error. "Was" does not agree with the subject, "paintings," and the verb tense is not improved. "Was depicting" shows an ongoing action in the

past, a verb tense which is not appropriate here.

(D) This choice does not reflect the logic of the sentence. The artist's paintings accomplish both a depiction and a romanticization at the same time. The verb tenses here suggest that the effects were separate in time.

(E) This choice is almost correct, but the verbs do not agree with their plural subject, "paintings."

2. To succeed in business dealings <u>you must have a thorough knowledge of the market, be aggressive, and also the will to win.</u>

(A) you must have a thorough knowledge of the market, be aggressive, and also the will to win

(B) one must have a thorough knowledge of the market, you must be aggressive, and have the will to win

(C) you must have a thorough knowledge of the market, the willingness to win and be aggressive

(D) requires being aggressive, knowing the market, and to have the will to win

(E) requires that you have a thorough knowledge of the market, be aggressive, and have the will to win

2. (E) *Writing/Improving Sentences/Sentence Structure/Faulty Parallelism*

(E) provides the needed parallelism. Three verbs follow the subject "you": "must have," "be," and "have."

(A) The original sentence is characterized by a lack of parallelism. The elements in the series "knowledge," "be aggressive," and "also the will" must have parallel forms.

(B) This choice does not correct the faulty parallelism and introduces the additional error of shifting subjects ("One...you.").

(C) This choice does not correct the faulty parallelism. "Be aggressive" is a verb, but the other two similar elements are nouns ("knowledge" and "willingness").

(D) "To have" is not parallel with "being" and "knowing."

3. There is new evidence to suggest that a child's personality is <u>developed more by everyday interactions rather than by</u> traumatic events.

(A) developed more by everyday interactions rather than by

(B) developed more by everyday interactions than by

(C) developed more by everyday interactions and not by

(D) being developed more by everyday interactions instead of

(E) developing more by everyday interactions than by

3. (B) *Writing/Improving Sentences/Clarity of Expression/Diction and Idioms*

(B) uses the correct construction "more...than."

(A) The construction "more...rather than" is not idiomatic.

(C) This choice makes an error in logic. The construction "more...and not by" is illogical. The "more" shows that something has what the other thing has, just more so. But the "not" indicates that something completely lacks what the other thing has.

(D) This choice makes two errors. First, it makes the same kind of logical mistake that (C) makes. Additionally, the phrase "is being developed" changes the logic of the sentence. As changed, the sentence seems to describe the development of a single child.

(E) This choice also changes the meaning of the sentence. The original sentence (which uses the passive voice) states that the child's personality is being acted upon by outside forces. This choice makes the child's personality the source of the action.

4. Hopelessly addicted to alcohol, the writings of Edgar Allan Poe are often about death and the supernatural.

(A) Hopelessly addicted to alcohol, the writings of Edgar Allan Poe are often
(B) Edgar Allan Poe's being hopelessly addicted to alcohol and he often wrote
(C) Hopelessly addicted to alcohol, Edgar Allan Poe often wrote
(D) In that he was hopelessly addicted to alcohol, Edgar Allan Poe often wrote
(E) The writings of Edgar Allan Poe, with his hopeless addiction to alcohol, are often

4. **(C)** *Writing/Improving Sentences/Logical Expression/Misplaced Modifiers*

(C) solves the problem of the misplaced modifier and clearly renders the meaning of the sentence.

(A) The original sentence commits the error of the misplaced or dangling modifier. As written, the sentence implies that the writings (of Poe) have the bad habit.
(B) This choice avoids the problem of the misplaced modifier but introduces two new errors. First, the construction "Poe's being" turns a verb phrase into a noun phrase where one is not appropriate. Second, the sentence lacks a clear division between the ideas of addiction and writing (and is a run-on sentence).
(D) "In that" is low-level usage and is not acceptable in standard written English.
(E) The phrase "with his...alcohol" should not be used here. If a phrase is set off like this following the subject, it is usually intended to modify the subject, for example, "The writings of Poe, with their vivid descriptions, ..." To refer to Poe himself at this point in the sentence requires a clause: "Poe, who was hopelessly addicted to alcohol, often wrote, ..."

5. With the writing of *Huckleberry Finn,* it marked the first time that the American vernacular was used in a novel.

(A) With the writing of Huckleberry Finn it marked the first time that the American Vernacular was used in a novel.
(B) Marking the first time that the American vernacular was used in a novel was the writing of Huckleberry Finn.
(C) The writing of Huckleberry Finn was the first time that the American vernacular was used in a novel.
(D) The writing of Huckleberry Finn marked the first time that the American vernacular was used in a novel.
(E) For the first time the American vernacular was used in a novel was *Huckleberry Finn.*

5. **(D)** *Writing/Improving Sentences/Clarity of Expression/Diction and Idioms* and *Grammar/ Pronoun Usage*

(D) corrects both the errors in the original sentence.

(A) The original sentence is characterized by two problems. The "with" construction is not idiomatic, and the "it" has no antecedent.
(B) This choice does not have enough subjects for its verbs. If you read "was" as having "marking" for its subject, then the other verb, "was used," has no subject, and vice versa.
(C) This choice introduces a logic error. The sentence means to say that the novel was the first one in which the American vernacular was used. This choice asserts, however, that it was the author's act of writing that was the first time the vernacular was used.
(E) This choice has the same problem as (B): not enough subjects for its verbs. If you read "was

used" to have the subject "first time," then the other verb "was" has no subject, and vice versa.

6. Parents and civic leaders are concerned about <u>protecting the children and the drugs that are available</u>.

  (A) protecting the children and the drugs that are available
  (B) the protection of the children and the drugs that are available
  (C) protecting the children and about the drugs that are available
  (D) protecting the children and the availability of drugs to them
  (E) protecting the children and the availability of drugs

6. (C) *Writing/Improving Sentences/Logical Expression/Unintended Meanings*

(C) eliminates the ambiguity by defining the scope of the "about protecting."

  (A) The original sentence contains an ambiguity. The scope of the phrase "about protecting" is not clearly defined. As originally written, the sentence implies that the parents and civic leaders are protecting the drugs.
  (B) This choice does not eliminate the error and introduces the awkward construction "concerned about the protection."
  (D) This choice introduces an additional error. The phrase "to them," tacked on to the end of this choice, is not necessary or idiomatic.
  (E) This choice has the same problem as (A): the scope of the "about protecting" is still not clearly defined. This choice implies that people wish to protect the availability of drugs.

7. Before this century, young girls were not expected to participate in <u>sports, so</u> they were never seriously trained to be athletes.

  (A) sports, so
  (B) sports that
  (C) sports and so
  (D) sports and
  (E) sports, and so consequently

7. (A) *Writing/Improving Sentences/No Error*

The original sentence is correct. The "so" shows the logical connection between the first idea and the second. The second idea is a consequence of the first. Additionally, the underlined portion is correctly punctuated. You need a comma to keep the two ideas from running together.

  (B) This choice obscures the connection between the two ideas.
  (C) This choice is incorrectly punctuated. You can't use "and" to do the job of a comma here.
  (D) This choice is incorrect because a comma is needed before the coordinating conjunction, "and." Additionally, the connection between the ideas that are clearly stated in the original sentence are obscured.
  (E) This choice is correctly punctuated, but it is packed with unnecessary conjunctions. You don't need "and," "so," and "consequently."

8. Teachers of the old Italian school taught nothing but breathing, <u>believing that the better the breath support, the more beautiful the tone</u>.

(A) believing that the better the breath support, the more beautiful the tone
(B) believing it to be the case that the better the breath support would result in a more beautiful tone
(C) in the belief that better breath support would result in that the tone would be more beautiful
(D) believing the better breath support to be resulting in more beautiful tones
(E) believing there to be a relationship between breath support and the more beautiful tone

9. In European countries where socialism is a dominant force, <u>they often strike for political rather than for economic reasons</u>.

(A) they often strike for political rather than for economic reasons
(B) they often strike on account of political rather than for economic reasons
(C) strikes are often called for political reasons rather than for economics
(D) strikes are called by them for political reasons rather than for economic ones
(E) strikes are often called for political rather than for economic reasons

10. James Fenimore Cooper was the first author <u>who writes</u> about truly American themes.

(A) who writes
(B) having written
(C) to write
(D) who had been writing
(E) who has written

8. **(A)** *Writing/Improving Sentences/No Error*

The sentence as originally written is correct.

(B) This choice puts the phrase "it to be the case that" where it isn't needed, disrupting the logic of the sentence.
(C) This choice begins correctly, but the inclusion of the second "that" disrupts the logic of the sentence.
(D) This is a variation of (B) and (C). The result is an awkward rendering of the idea in the original sentence.
(E) This choice makes the same sort of mistake that (D) makes. It begins correctly, but then the use of "more beautiful" distorts the meaning of the sentence.

9. **(E)** *Writing/Improving Sentences/Grammar/ Pronoun Usage*

(E) succeeds where (C) fails. It corrects the error in the original sentence, and the thought is properly completed: "political reasons rather than for economic reasons."

(A) The original sentence commits the error of using the "ubiquitous they." "They" doesn't have a clear antecedent.
(B) This choice fails to eliminate the "ubiquitous they" and introduces another error: "on account" is low-level usage.
(C) This choice almost succeeds. It corrects the error in the original sentence, but the phrase is never completed.
(D) This choice, too, almost succeeds, but it substitutes a "ubiquitous them" for the "ubiquitous they."

10. **(C)** *Writing/Improving Sentences/Logical Expression/Illogical Tense Sequence*

(C) corrects the original problem by using the infinitive. Since the infinitive doesn't show time (past, present, or future), it doesn't conflict with the other verb.

(A) The original sentence contains an illogical choice of verb tense. Cooper was the first author to do something (an action completed in the past). If there is to be a second main verb in the other clause, it must also show a completed past action.
(B) "Having written" indicates past action, but it is not a verb form that can be the main verb in a clause.

(D) "Had been writing" indicates an action that was completed in the past, but it implies an action that ended before another action in the past, for example, "Cooper had been writing at his desk when the butler announced dinner."

(E) "Has written" does not indicate a completed past action, but implies that the action continues into the present. For example, "Cooper, who will be here tomorrow, has written ...."

11. To be a successful musician requires extensive training, practice, and <u>you should also love performing</u>.

    (A) you should also love performing .
    (B) loving to perform
    (C) one should love to perform
    (D) to love to perform
    (E) a love of performing

11. **(E)** *Writing/Improving Sentences/Sentence Structure/Faulty Parallelism*

(E) provides the necessary parallelism. The noun "love" is parallel to the other two nouns: "training" and "practice."

(A) The original sentence suffers from faulty parallelism. "Training" and "practice" are nouns, so the third element in the series should also be a noun.

(B) This choice attempts to introduce a noun, but the noun form of the verb (the "-ing" form) is not idiomatic here. The sentence now reads "requires...loving to perform."

(C) This choice merely repeats the error with a different subject.

(D) This choice makes the same kind of mistake made by (B). The noun form of the verb (this time, the "to" form) does not create an idiomatic phrase. The choice now reads "requires...to love to perform."

12. After the American Revolution, most of <u>those who had been loyal to the crown having gone</u> to Canada, where they settled.

    (A) those who had been loyal to the crown having gone
    (B) those who had been loyal to the crown have gone
    (C) them who have been loyal to the crown went
    (D) them having been loyal to the crown went
    (E) those who had been loyal to the crown went

12. **(E)** *Writing/Improving Sentences/Logical Expression/Illogical Tense Sequence*

(E) corrects the problem of tense. The "had been" signals an action that took place in the past before another action took place in the past. Then, "went" refers to the other past action.

(A) The verb tense in the original is incorrect. The logic of the sentence shows a sequence of events. People were loyal to the crown; the loyalist side was defeated; the loyalists went to Canada. The "having gone" implies that the flight to Canada came before the defeat.

(B) This choice changes the incorrect tense, but "have gone" is also incorrect. "Have gone" is used to show past action in reference to the present. But the other action in the sentence is a completed past action.

(C) This choice incorrectly changes "had been" to

"have been" which does not reflect that the action is a completed past action. Additionally, the phrase "them who" is low-level usage.

(D) This choice combines the weakest aspects of (B) and (C).

13. Although it is cost effective to make perfumes from synthetic ingredients, in France <u>they used to make the classic fragrances using only flowers and natural essences</u>.

(A) they used to make the classic fragrances using only flowers and natural essences
(B) the classic fragrances used to be made by them using only flowers and natural essences
(C) the classic fragrances used to be made using only flowers and natural essences
(D) it used to be that the classic fragrances were made only with flowers and natural essences
(E) the classic fragrances used to be made with flowers and natural essences only

13. (C) *Writing/Improving Sentences/Grammar/Pronoun Usage*

(C) corrects the problem in the original sentence, and it does not introduce any new errors. This may not be the absolutely best way of rendering the thought, but it is the best of the five answer choices.

(A) Here is another example of the "ubiquitous they."
(B) This choice substitutes the "ubiquitous them" for the "ubiquitous they," a substitution which does not improve the sentence.
(D) This choice is difficult to eliminate. It contains no glaring grammatical error, but it is awkward; "it used to be that" is unnecessarily wordy.
(E) This is the second best choice. What the sentence means to state is that the fragrances were made "from" or "using" natural ingredients, not "with" natural ingredients. "Only" is moved to the end of the sentence and becomes a dangling modifier. It is unclear exactly what "only" modifies.

14. Although the stock market seems to offer the possibility of great personal gain, you must understand that to invest in stocks <u>is accepting the risk of financial ruin as well</u>.

(A) is accepting the risk of financial ruin as well
(B) is to accept the risk of financial ruin as well
(C) is to accept the risk as well of financial ruin
(D) are accepting the risk of financial ruin as well
(E) are to accept the risk of financial ruin as well

14. (B) *Writing/Improving Sentences/Sentence Structure/Faulty Parallelism*

The original sentence suffers from faulty parallelism: "to invest...is accepting...." (B) makes the necessary correction: "to invest is to accept."

(A) "To invest...is accepting" lacks parallelism.
(C) The faulty parallelism is corrected with "to invest... is to accept," but this choice changes the meaning of the original sentence and includes the phrase "as well of financial ruin," which is not idiomatic.
(D) The problem of faulty parallelism remains, and a new agreement error, "to invest...are," is introduced.
(E) This choice does correct the faulty parallelism but includes the same agreement error as (D).

Practice Test I

Outline

I. **Section 1:** Writing (p. 457)

II. **Section 2:** Critical Reading (pp. 458–464)

III. **Section 3:** Math (pp. 466–469)

IV. **Section 5:** Critical Reading (pp. 470–475)

V. **Section 6:** Math (pp. 476–479)

VI. **Section 7:** Writing (pp. 480–485)

VII. **Section 8:** Critical Reading (pp. 486–490)

VIII. **Section 9:** Math (pp. 492–495)

IX. **Section 10:** Writing (pp. 496–498)

Practice Test I

SECTION 1—WRITING
Time—25 Minutes
1 Essay

DIRECTIONS: The essay tests your ability to express ideas, develop a point of view, present ideas in a clear and logical fashion, and use language precisely.

Write your essay on the lines provided on your answer sheet—you will receive no other paper on which to write. Do not write your essay in your test book. You will receive credit only for what appears on your answer sheet. Write legibly, and remember that graders must be able to read your handwriting.

You have 25 minutes to plan and write an essay on the topic assigned below. Do not write on any other topic. An essay on another topic is not acceptable. Sample essays and analyses begin on page 633.

Think carefully about the issue presented in the following excerpt and the assignment below.

> A 98-year-old farmer was recently asked what he thought was the greatest technological advancement of the past 125 years. He responded: "electricity, since it made so many chores much easier and faster." A 35-year-old executive was asked the same question, and she responded: "computers, since they made so many chores much easier and faster."

Assignment: In your opinion, what has been the greatest technological advancement of the past 125 years? Plan and write an essay in which you develop your point of view on this issue. Support your position with reasoning and examples taken from your reading, studies, experience, and observations.

S T O P

**IF YOU FINISH BEFORE TIME IS CALLED, YOU MAY CHECK YOUR WORK ON THIS SECTION
ONLY. DO NOT TURN TO ANY OTHER SECTION IN THE TEST.**

Practice Test I

SECTION 2—CRITICAL READING

Time—25 Minutes

24 Items

DIRECTIONS: In this section, solve each item, and choose the correct answer choice. Fill in the corresponding oval on the answer sheet. Answers are on page 636.

Items #1–8: Each item below has one or two blanks, each blank indicating that something has been omitted. Beneath the sentence are five lettered words or sets of words. Choose the word or set of words that best fits the meaning of the sentence as a whole.

Example:

Although its publicity has been -------, the film itself is intelligent, well acted, handsomely produced, and altogether -------.

(A) tasteless . . respectable
(B) extensive . . moderate
(C) sophisticated . . amateur
(D) risqué . . crude
(E) perfect . . spectacular

---

1. All attempts to keep the cabin warm were ------- due to the frigid weather and the fact that the cabin was -------.

    (A) delegated . . well-constructed
    (B) futile . . poorly insulated
    (C) successful . . well-appointed
    (D) punctual . . well-situated
    (E) profitable . . extremely spacious

2. Although the candidate is ------- and a popular media figure, her platform is not ------- the general populace, and she will probably lose the election.

    (A) reclusive . . accessible to
    (B) distressed . . opposed by
    (C) personable . . supported by
    (D) diminutive . . injurious to
    (E) rabid . . relevant to

3. Traditionally, clubs with ------- membership are ------- admit new members without a thorough investigation of their backgrounds.

    (A) a raucous . . anxious to
    (B) an elite . . reluctant to
    (C) a turgid . . fearful to
    (D) a sensible . . urged to
    (E) a disruptive . . elated to

4. The ability to compose music depends on a solid background in theory, but the musical talent is essentially ------- and cannot be taught.

    (A) destroyed
    (B) experienced
    (C) innate
    (D) forgotten
    (E) assured

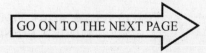
GO ON TO THE NEXT PAGE

5. Although the professor had ------- support from the faculty who were either indifferent or downright hostile, he continued to teach using his ------- methods.

   (A) adequate . . similar
   (B) minimal . . idiosyncratic
   (C) resounding . . archaic
   (D) adverse . . popular
   (E) bracing . . suspicious

6. Van Gogh's shapes and colors are so ------- that some art historians have attributed his view of the world to illness or to madness.

   (A) inaccessible
   (B) startling
   (C) intermediate
   (D) corrupt
   (E) trivial

7. Although he was usually -------, he ------- the hostess and was never invited back.

   (A) tidy . . flattered
   (B) disinterested . . suspected
   (C) forgetful . . enchanted
   (D) tactful . . insulted
   (E) careful . . concealed

8. The will was ------- according to the law because there was ------- evidence that the deceased had been mentally incompetent.

   (A) sanctimonious . . chronological
   (B) invalid . . overwhelming
   (C) punitive . . subsequent
   (D) signed . . irrefutable
   (E) suspect . . inadequate

Items #9–24: Each passage below is followed by one or more items based on its content. Answer the items following each passage on the basis of what is stated or implied in the passage.

Item #9 is based on the following passage.

Art, like words, is a form of communication. Words—spoken and written—make available to each new generation the knowledge discovered through the experience and reflection of preceding generations. Art
5 makes available to each new generation the feelings and emotions of preceding generations. Just as the evolution of knowledge proceeds by dislodging and replacing mistaken beliefs, so too the evolution of feeling proceeds through art. Feelings that are not
10 beneficial to humankind are replaced by others that aid human well-being. This is the purpose of art.

9. The author of the passage would most likely agree with which of the following statements about words and art?

   (A) The function of both art and words is to depict the world as accurately as possible.
   (B) Art and words—in their respective spheres— are both cumulative and progressive.
   (C) As an activity, art is more important for improving the human condition than communication.
   (D) Art is less necessary to the advancement of human ideals than word communication.
   (E) Art is dependent on word communication since ultimately words must be used to explain the significance of art.

GO ON TO THE NEXT PAGE

Item #10 is based on the following passage.

The omnipresent television set is the American's personal sensory deprivation kit. It deprives the viewer of stereoscopic sight, fully dimensional sounds, and the taste, smell, and feel of the action. Furthermore, there
5 is no personal involvement in the content presented. Reality TV, were it truly a depiction of reality, would use a camera to film the back of a television viewer's upper body and head. Over the viewer's shoulder would be a television showing the same scene. Thus,
10 the experience of the viewer would be identical to that of the "viewer": the same visually flat and thin auditory experiences and completely lacking any experiences of taste, smell, or feel.

10. The author's primary purpose is to

(A) suggest ways in which television programming might be improved
(B) describe the differences between reality and television programming
(C) demonstrate that television cannot convey a sense of reality
(D) illustrate the harmful effects of television on society at large
(E) propose rules to regulate the content of television programming

Items #11–12 are based on the following passage.

In the presidential election of 1792, George Washington received the unanimous vote of Federalist and Republican electors alike. However, Southern planters, who in 1789 were ready to cooperate with the
5 moneyed men of the North, parted with them when they realized that policies designed to benefit the Northern merchants and bankers brought no profit to the Southern planters. While willing to support Washington in 1792, they would not accept Vice
10 President John Adams, as he represented the commerce, shipbuilding, fisheries, and banking institutions of New England and the North. Appealing to shopkeepers, artisans, laboring men, and farmers of the North because of their sympathy with the French
15 Revolution and to Southern landowners with their agrarian bias, the Republicans waged a gallant but losing campaign to have their leader, Thomas Jefferson, elected Vice President. Then, in 1793, England declared war on republican France over the
20 guillotining of Louis XVI. The following year, John Jay authored a treaty that was suggestive of a sympathetic policy toward monarchical and conservative England over republican, liberty-loving France. The treaty intensified the Republicans' spirit
25 and gave the party—originally known by the uninspiring term Anti-Federalists—a unified sense of mission for the 1796 election: the Republican lovers of liberty against the Monocrats.

11. It can be inferred from the passage that the term "Monocrats" (line 28) was

(A) used by John Jay in his treaty to refer to France's King Louis XVI
(B) invented by the Federalists to refer to the landowners of the South
(C) coined by Republicans to disparage the Federalists' support of England
(D) employed by Republicans to describe their leader, Thomas Jefferson
(E) suggested by the Federalists as an appropriate description of John Adams

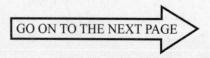 GO ON TO THE NEXT PAGE

12. The primary purpose of the passage is to

    (A) discuss the origins of Jefferson's Republican party

    (B) describe Jefferson's defeat in the 1792 election

    (C) theorize about the effects of wealth on political parties

    (D) criticize England's foreign policy toward France in the 1790s

    (E) correct a misunderstanding about political debate in the 1790s

Item #13 is based on the following passage.

In 1969, the United States landed astronauts on the moon, and television and newspapers showed images of the astronauts on the barren moonscape. The following week, a storyteller in rural northwest
5 Tanzania interpreted the event for a gathering of Hayan elders. The storyteller sang of Kisha Lishno, who enticed a vain monarch to invade a nearby "land without a ruler." The glory-hungry king set out with his army. When they arrived, the army, tired and bleary-
10 eyed from a forced march, did not realize the newfound territory was a lake. The army marched into the lake and nearly everyone drowned. The few men that escaped returned to a homeland ruled by a new king: Kisha Lishno.

13. The main point of the storyteller's moon landing interpretation is that

    (A) the United States did not really land astronauts on the moon

    (B) it would be unwise for Tanzania to fund a space program

    (C) Kisha Lishno assumed control as the result of a power vacuum

    (D) the moon landing was a wasteful undertaking inspired by vanity

    (E) the military of the United States is a significant threat

Item #14 is based on the following passage.

Throughout history, successful organizations have recognized people as their most important institutional resource. Thus, religious organizations, educational institutions, and even businesses have
5 worked to recruit and train highly qualified people, who in serving the purposes of their employment have contributed more or less directly to the solutions of more significant problems. Organizations such as the Jesuit order, Oxford University, and the Hudson Bay
10 Company provide outstanding examples. These groups have created management atmospheres that foster the growth of people by allowing them the freedom to apply their mental talents to larger problems. By doing so, the emergence of new intellectual and social
15 paradigms is possible.

14. It can be inferred that the author regards the Hudson Bay Company as a

    (A) successful business that developed sound management practices

    (B) wealthy corporation unable to develop strong leadership talent

    (C) short-lived institution with little historical significance

    (D) profitable enterprise founded upon religious principles

    (E) typical corporation following accepted business practices

GO ON TO THE NEXT PAGE

Items #15–24 are based on the following passage.

Traditional strategies for controlling insect-pests tend to rely on the use of nonselective insecticides that cause extensive ecological disruption. The alternative sterile insect technique, in which members of the target
5 species are irradiated to cause sterility, has enjoyed some modest success. When released into an infested area, the sterile insects mate with normal insects but produce no offspring. Unfortunately, the irradiation weakens the insects, making it less likely that they will
10 mate; and, in any event, sterile insects do not search selectively for non-sterile mates. A third, newly developed strategy is based on parasite release.

Pest hosts and their associated parasites have evolved biological and behavioral characteristics that
15 virtually ensure that the relative numbers of hosts and parasites in the ecosystem they inhabit remain within relatively narrow limits—even though coexisting populations may fluctuate up to 100-fold during a single season. The close numerical relationships are
20 entirely consistent with nature's balancing mechanisms, which permit closely associated organisms to live together in harmony. Thus, in natural populations, the ratios of parasites to hosts are not high enough to result in dependable control. However, it is
25 possible to mass-rear parasites so that they can be released at strategic times and in numbers that result in parasite-to-host ratios sufficient to control host populations.

Biosteres tryoni, for example, has a strong
30 affinity for medfly larvae. Let us assume that a new medfly infestation is discovered. It is likely to have originated from a single female and, even in an area with a good surveillance program, to be in the third reproductive cycle. The rate of population increase is
35 tenfold per generation; so at the time the infestation comes to light, about 1,000 males and 1,000 females are emerging and will produce a total of approximately 80,000 larvae. Reproduction will be concentrated in an area of about one square mile, but scattered
40 reproduction will occur anywhere within a 25-square-mile area. At first glance, the odds of controlling the infestation by parasite release seem low; but with new techniques for mass-producing parasites, it is possible to release one million males and one million females
45 into the infested area. This would mean an average of 62 females per acre, and the average female parasitizes about 30 host larvae during its lifetime. Additionally, the parasites actively search for host habitats by using the kairomone signals emanating from infested fruit.
50 Even assuming that only 10 percent of the released females are successful and, further, that they parasitize an average of only 10 larvae, they could still parasitize one million larvae. Only 80,000 larvae are available, however; so the actual ratio would be 12.5:1. A ratio
55 as low as 5:1 results in 99 percent parasitism.

This method of pest eradication presents no health or environmental problems and is actually cheaper. The cost of mass-rearing and distributing *B. tryoni* is about $2,000 per million. So even if six
60 million parasites of both sexes are released during a period corresponding to three medfly reproductive cycles, the total cost of the treatment would be $12,000—compared to $25,000 for a single insecticide spray application to the same 25-square mile area.

15. The author implies that the sterile insect release strategy is not completely effective because

(A) some sterile insects mate with other sterile insects
(B) weakened sterile insects refuse to mate with healthy insects
(C) the cost of producing a sufficient number of sterile insects is prohibitive
(D) sterile insects are incapable of producing offspring
(E) irradiation leaves a radioactive residue offensive to healthy insects

16. Which of the following words, when substituted for "strategic" in line 26, would best preserve the meaning of the original sentence?

(A) military
(B) random
(C) critical
(D) ill-advised
(E) frequent

GO ON TO THE NEXT PAGE

17. According to the passage, *Biosteres tryoni* is effective in controlling medfly infestations because

(A) female *B. tryoni* feed on adult medflies
(B) male and female *B. tryoni* parasitize medfly larvae
(C) male and female *B. tryoni* mate with medflies
(D) male *B. tryoni* prevent male medflies from mating
(E) female *B. tryoni* parasitize medfly larvae

18. It can be inferred that if *B. tryoni* were not attracted by kairomone signals from medfly-infested fruit that the parasite release strategy would be

(A) less effective because some *B. tryoni* would remain in areas not infested
(B) less effective because none of the *B. tryoni* would parasitize medfly larvae
(C) equally as effective because *B. tryoni* do not damage fruit crops
(D) more effective because some *B. tryoni* would fail to reproduce
(E) more effective because the *B. tryoni* would remain more widely dispersed

19. In the development of the passage, the author

(A) explains a scientific theory and then offers evidence to refute it
(B) cites statistics to compare the relative effectiveness of different strategies
(C) speculates on the probable course of scientific developments
(D) states a general principle and then provides an example of its application
(E) poses a question and then provides a detailed answer to it

20. Which of the following statements about medfly reproduction can be inferred from the passage?

(A) The medfly is capable of reproducing asexually.
(B) A typical generation contains 10 times as many females as males.
(C) A new generation of medfly is produced once a year.
(D) A medfly colony will reproduce for only three generations.
(E) Only about 25 percent of larvae reach adulthood.

21. It can be inferred that an insecticide application for the hypothetical infestation would treat a 25-square mile area because

(A) the cost for a single spray application to the area is $25,000
(B) *B. tryoni* would tend to concentrate themselves in infested areas
(C) medfly reproduction might occur anywhere within that region
(D) the spray would repel medflies from fruit not already infested
(E) medflies from another, yet undiscovered infestation might be in the area

22. In the final paragraph, the phrase "even if" (line 59) indicates that the author is

(A) making an unproved assumption about the effectiveness of parasite pest control programs
(B) providing evidence of the ecological harm done by indiscriminate use of pesticides
(C) responding to a point about program cost that was specifically developed in the previous paragraph
(D) offering proof that parasite-release programs actually destroy the host pest insects
(E) considering the strongest possible objection against the cost of the parasite release strategy

GO ON TO THE NEXT PAGE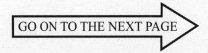

23. The author is primarily concerned with

    (A) criticizing the use of nonselective
        insecticides
    (B) defending the use of parasite release
        programs
    (C) explaining the workings of a new pest-
        control method
    (D) refuting the suggestion that parasite release is
        costly
    (E) analyzing the reproductive habits of the
        medfly

24. It can be inferred that the author regards the
    release of parasites to control pests as

    (A) reasonably effective
    (B) prohibitively expensive
    (C) environmentally reckless
    (D) highly experimental
    (E) unnecessarily complex

STOP

**IF YOU FINISH BEFORE TIME IS CALLED, YOU MAY CHECK YOUR WORK ON THIS SECTION
ONLY. DO NOT TURN TO ANY OTHER SECTION IN THE TEST.**

NO TEST MATERIAL ON THIS PAGE

Practice Test I

SECTION 3—MATH
Time—25 Minutes
20 Items

DIRECTIONS: In this section, solve each item, and choose the correct answer choice. Fill in the corresponding oval on the answer sheet. Use any available space for scratchwork. Answers are on page 636.

Notes:

(1) The use of a calculator is permitted. All numbers used are real numbers.

(2) Figures that accompany problems in this test are intended to provide information useful in solving the problems. They are drawn as accurately as possible EXCEPT when it is stated in a specific problem that the figure is not drawn to scale. All figures lie in a plane unless otherwise indicated.

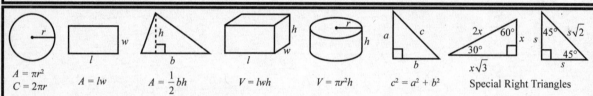

$A = \pi r^2$
$C = 2\pi r$ $\qquad$ $A = lw$ $\qquad$ $A = \frac{1}{2}bh$ $\qquad$ $V = lwh$ $\qquad$ $V = \pi r^2 h$ $\qquad$ $c^2 = a^2 + b^2$ $\qquad$ Special Right Triangles

The number of degrees of arc in a circle is 360.
The sum of the measures in degrees of the angles of a triangle is 180.

1. If $\dfrac{1}{2N} + \dfrac{1}{2N} = \dfrac{1}{4}$, then $N =$

(A) 4
(B) 2
(C) 1
(D) $\dfrac{1}{2}$
(E) $\dfrac{1}{4}$

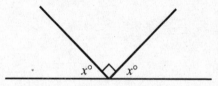

2. In the figure above, $x =$

(A) 30
(B) 45
(C) 60
(D) 75
(E) 90

GO ON TO THE NEXT PAGE

3. In a certain game, a person's age is multiplied by 2 and then the product is divided by 3. If the result of performing the operations on John's age is 12, what is John's age?

(A) 2
(B) 8
(C) 12
(D) 18
(E) 36

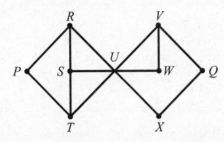

4. The figure above is a map showing the stations and connecting subway lines for a city's subway system. If a man wishes to travel by subway from station P to station Q without passing through any station more than once, which of the following MUST be true?

(A) If he passes through T, he must next pass through S.
(B) If he passes through S, he must next pass through U.
(C) If he passes through U, he must next pass through V.
(D) If he passes through R, he cannot later pass through T.
(E) If he passes through V, he cannot later pass through W.

5. A helper must load 38 bricks onto a truck. Given that she can carry at most 4 bricks at a time, what is the fewest number of trips that she must make to move all of the bricks from the brick pile onto the truck?

(A) 9
(B) 9.5
(C) 10
(D) 10.5
(E) 12

6. For all numbers, $(a-b)(b-c)-(b-a)(c-b) =$

(A) -2
(B) -1
(C) 0
(D) $ab-ac-bc$
(E) $2ab-2ac-2bc$

7. n is a positive integer. If n is a multiple of both 6 and 9, what is the least possible value of n?

(A) 12
(B) 18
(C) 27
(D) 36
(E) 54

8. If $f(x) = x^2 - x$, what is the value of $f(f(2))$?

(A) 0
(B) 1
(C) 2
(D) 4
(E) 8

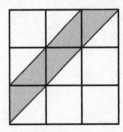

9. The figure above shows a square piece of land that is divided into 9 smaller square lots. The shaded portion is a railroad right-of-way. If the area of the shaded portion of the figure is 5 square miles, what is the area, in square miles, of the entire piece of land?

(A) 9
(B) 10
(C) 13
(D) 18
(E) 36

GO ON TO THE NEXT PAGE

10.

Set $X = \{1, 2, 3, 4\}$
Set $Y = \{1, 2, 3, 4\}$

For how many different ordered pairs (a, b) in which a is an element of set X and b is an element of set Y is $a - b > 0$?

(A) 24
(B) 18
(C) 15
(D) 12
(E) 6

11. If x and y are negative integers, and $x > y$, which of the following is the greatest?

(A) $-(xy)^2$

(B) x^2y

(C) xy

(D) $x + y$

(E) $y - x$

12. A student receives an average of 75 on three exams that are scored on a scale from 0 to 100. If one of her test scores was 75, what is the lowest possible score that she could have received on any of the three tests?

(A) 0
(B) 1
(C) 25
(D) 40
(E) 50

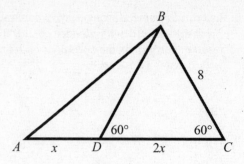

13. In $\triangle ABC$ above, what is the length of side $\overline{AC}$?

(A) 4
(B) 8
(C) 12
(D) 18
(E) 22

14. During a certain shift, a quality control inspector inspects 6 out of every 30 items produced. What was the ratio of inspected items to uninspected items during that shift?

(A) $1:4$
(B) $1:5$
(C) $1:6$
(D) $5:1$
(E) $6:1$

GO ON TO THE NEXT PAGE

15. For which of the following pairs of numbers is it true that their sum is 9 times their product?

    (A) $1, \frac{1}{19}$

    (B) $1, \frac{1}{9}$

    (C) $1, \frac{1}{8}$

    (D) 1, 8

    (E) 1, 9

16. $\frac{1}{2^{-3}} \cdot \frac{1}{3^{-2}} =$

    (A) −36
    (B) −6
    (C) 2
    (D) 9
    (E) 72

17. What is the solution set for $\left| \frac{x-2}{3} \right| = 4$?

    (A) {14, −10}
    (B) {14, 10}
    (C) {10, −14}
    (D) {10, 10}
    (E) {10, −10}

18. If $f(-1) = 1$ and $f(2) = 7$, what is the slope of the graph of $f(x)$ in the coordinate system?

    (A) −3

    (B) $-\frac{1}{2}$

    (C) $\frac{1}{2}$

    (D) 2

    (E) $\frac{5}{2}$

Student Population at School X			
	Juniors	Seniors	Total
Women	124		
Men			280
Total			880

19. The table above shows the student population at School X according to gender and class standing. Which of the following quantities is NOT, in and of itself, sufficient to complete the matrix?

    (A) The number of women who are seniors
    (B) The number of men who are seniors
    (C) The number of juniors who are men
    (D) The number of juniors
    (E) The number of seniors

20. The cost of a taxi ride is $1.50 for hiring the cab and $0.40 per mile or any part of a mile of distance traveled. Which of the following equations can be used to find the cost, y, of a ride of exactly x miles, in which x is an integer?

    (A) $y = x(0.4 + 1.5)$
    (B) $y = 0.4x + 1.5$
    (C) $y = 0.4 + 1.5x$
    (D) $y = 1.5 - 0.4x$
    (E) $y = 0.4 - 1.5x$

STOP

IF YOU FINISH BEFORE TIME IS CALLED, YOU MAY CHECK YOUR WORK ON THIS SECTION ONLY. DO NOT TURN TO ANY OTHER SECTION IN THE TEST.

Practice Test I

SECTION 5—CRITICAL READING
Time—25 Minutes
24 Items

DIRECTIONS: In this section, solve each item, and choose the correct answer choice. Fill in the corresponding oval on the answer sheet. Answers are on page 636.

Items #1–8: Each item below has one or two blanks, each blank indicating that something has been omitted. Beneath the sentence are five lettered words or sets of words. Choose the word or set of words that best fits the meaning of the sentence as a whole.

Example:

Although its publicity has been -------, the film itself is intelligent, well acted, handsomely produced, and altogether -------.

(A) tasteless . . respectable
(B) extensive . . moderate
(C) sophisticated . . amateur
(D) risqué . . crude
(E) perfect . . spectacular

---

1. The manuscripts of Thomas Wolfe were so ------- that the publisher was forced to ------- them in order to make them coherent and concise.

   (A) obscure . . expand
   (B) lengthy . . edit
   (C) unpopular . . recall
   (D) interesting . . organize
   (E) depressing . . inspire

2. The changes in the organization were so gradual that they seemed almost -------.

   (A) hasty
   (B) spontaneous
   (C) imperceptible
   (D) distorted
   (E) omitted

3. Although it is difficult to be ------- the plight of one's adversary, it is not necessary to be ------- or cruel.

   (A) sympathetic to . . callous
   (B) excited about . . capricious
   (C) pessimistic about . . dilatory
   (D) jealous of . . rigorous
   (E) ignorant of . . esoteric

4. Professor Gray's translation of the work is so ------- that it completely ------- the material and renders it incomprehensible.

   (A) thematic . . retards
   (B) grandiose . . obviates
   (C) accurate . . obscures
   (D) ubiquitous . . transforms
   (E) idiosyncratic . . distorts

5. The customers were so incensed at the obvious ------- of the waiter that they could not be ------- and refused to pay their check.

(A) exigence . . disconcerted
(B) volubility . . condoned
(C) ineptitude . . assuaged
(D) lassitude . . thwarted
(E) fortitude . . mollified

6. The poetry of Mallarmé, like the poetry of most of the symbolists, is not clear and easily accessible but rather vague and -------.

(A) opaque
(B) redundant
(C) lucid
(D) straightforward
(E) concrete

7. Mary was very annoyed that her secretary did not meet her deadlines, and she warned her that her laziness and ------- could result in her dismissal.

(A) procrastination
(B) ambition
(C) zeal
(D) veracity
(E) fortitude

8. Although a solemn tone was appropriate to the seriousness of the occasion, the speaker lapsed into -------, which was depressing rather than moving.

(A) reverence
(B) frankness
(C) loquaciousness
(D) levity
(E) morbidity

Items #9–24: Each passage below is followed by one or more items based on its content. Answer the items following each passage on the basis of what is stated or implied in the passage.

Item #9 is based on the following passage.

Biologists have discovered a new species of fairy shrimp that live in the dry lakebeds of Idaho's desert. Though these shrimp look delicate enough to indicate their name, their eggs are hard enough to survive for
5 years in the baking heat of summer and the frozen cold of winter until enough rain falls to create the pools of water in which the shrimp live. A few weeks after hatching, the shrimp mate, leaving behind tiny cyst-like offspring, and then die.

9. According to the passage, the fairy shrimp spends the active phase of its life in

(A) frozen ground
(B) standing water
(C) dry sand
(D) running streams
(E) underground niches

GO ON TO THE NEXT PAGE

Item #10 is based on the following passage.

The prospect of an avian flu pandemic reminds us all that the forces of nature can be far more lethal than anything created by humans. While the U.S. is not on the brink of such an epidemic, experts agree that it is
5 only a matter of time before some new, virulent strain of influenza will threaten the world. The government is already testing the first doses of an experimental vaccine and closely monitoring a variety of disease indicators.

10. The tone of the passage can best be described as

(A) alarmed
(B) concerned
(C) dismissive
(D) irreverent
(E) optimistic

Items #11–12 are based on the following passage.

Having grown up in the liberal culture of King Henry VIII's court, Elizabeth was a bold horsewoman, an expert shot, a graceful dancer, a skilled musician, and an accomplished scholar. She spoke Italian and
5 French as fluently as English and read Greek. From her father, Henry VIII, Elizabeth inherited her frank and hardy address, her courage, and her self-confidence. Her sensuous and self-indulgent nature she inherited from her mother, Ann Boleyn. She loved gaiety,
10 laughter, and wit, but her vanity and caprice played no part in the affairs of state. No nobler group of ministers ever gathered round the council-board than those of Queen Elizabeth, but she was the instrument of none. Her policy, founded on good common sense, was her
15 own.

11. The primary purpose of the passage is to

(A) describe an interesting personality
(B) discuss important historical events
(C) appraise the policies of a leader
(D) criticize monarchy as a type of government
(E) provide a family history

12. In line 7, "address" most nearly means

(A) geographical location
(B) artistic talent
(C) title of honor
(D) manner of speaking
(E) physical prowess

GO ON TO THE NEXT PAGE

Items #13–14 are based on the following passage.

Some botanists believe that maize evolved independently in Asia and in the Americas. However, it is more likely that maize originated first in the Americas: Columbus brought maize back to Spain
5 following his 1492 voyage. It was then distributed throughout Europe and carried along trade routes, ultimately reaching China within 60 years. This rapid spread of cultivation from west to east was the result of maize being particularly well-suited to the climates of
10 those regions in Eurasia where it was introduced. The Bahamas encompass the same latitudes as Egypt, Saudi Arabia, Pakistan, Nepal, Bangladesh, and Yunnan in southwestern China. This model for the geographical evolution of maize follows a pattern similar to the well-
15 established spread of wheat and barley several thousand years earlier from the Middle East to Ireland in the west and to Japan in the east.

13. The author introduces the examples of wheat and barley in order to

   (A) demonstrate that wheat and barley are more important foods than maize
   (B) support the thesis that maize appeared independently in both China and the Americas
   (C) prove that wheat and barley also originated in the Americas and then spread to Europe and Asia
   (D) refute the claim that new plant species generally propagate in a west to east direction
   (E) illustrate that maize could also have spread across the various regions as argued

14. The author's list of regions through which the cultivation of maize spread assumes that

   (A) maize could have originated exclusively in Asia
   (B) regions at the same latitudes have similar climates
   (C) maize is a hardier crop than either wheat or barley
   (D) maize was introduced to Spain no later than 1493
   (E) Columbus visited no islands other than the Bahamas

Items #15–24 are based on the following passage.

The following passage discusses certain aspects of the evolution of stars.

The theory of stellar evolution predicts that when the core of a star has used up its nuclear fuel, the core will collapse. If the star is about the size of the Sun, it will turn into a degenerate dwarf star. If it is somewhat
5 larger, it may undergo a supernova explosion that leaves behind a neutron star. However, if the stellar core has a mass greater than about three solar masses, gravitational forces overwhelm nuclear forces and the core will collapse. Since nuclear forces are the strongest
10 repulsive forces known, nothing can stop the continued collapse of the star. A black hole in space is formed.
   Because of the intense gravitational forces near the black hole, nothing can escape from it, not even light. If we were to send a probe toward an isolated
15 black hole, the probe would detect no radiation from the black hole. Yet, it would sense a gravitational field like the one that would be produced by a normal star of the same mass. As the probe approached the black hole, the gravitational forces would increase
20 inexorably. At a distance of a few thousand kilometers, the gravitational forces would be so great that the side of the probe closest to the black hole would literally be torn away from the side furthest away from the black hole. Eventually, at a distance of a few kilometers from
25 the black hole, the particles that made up the probe would be lost forever down the black hole. This point of no return is called the gravitational radius of the black hole.
   Given this, how can we hope to observe such an
30 object? Nature, herself, could conceivably provide us with a "probe" of a black hole: a binary star system in which one of the stars has become a black hole and is absorbing the mass of its companion star. As the matter of the companion star falls into the black hole, it would
35 accelerate. This increased energy of motion would be changed into heat energy. Near the gravitational radius the matter would move at speeds close to the speed of light, and temperatures would range from tens of millions of degrees to perhaps as much as a billion
40 degrees. At these temperatures, X- and gamma radiation are produced. Further, since the matter near the gravitational radius would be orbiting the black hole about once every millisecond, the X-radiation should show erratic, short-term variability unlike the
45 regular or periodic variability associated with neutron stars and degenerate dwarfs.

GO ON TO THE NEXT PAGE

The X-ray source Cygnus X-1 fulfills these "experimental" conditions. It is part of a binary star system, in which a blue supergiant star is orbiting an
50 invisible companion star. This invisible companion has a mass greater than about nine times the mass of the Sun, and it is a strong X-ray source with rapid variations in the intensity of its X-ray flux. Most astronomers believe that Cygnus X-1 is a black hole;
55 but this belief is tempered with a dose of caution. The idea of a black hole is still difficult to swallow, but theorists can think of no other object that could explain the phenomenon of Cygnus X-1. For this reason, in most scientific papers, Cygnus X-1 is referred to
60 simply as a black hole "candidate."

15. The primary concern of the passage is to

(A) present a theory and describe the kind of evidence that would prove it correct
(B) outline a widely accepted theory and offer evidence that refutes that theory
(C) describe a phenomenon and present a theory to explain the phenomenon
(D) advance a theory and then supply a specific example as proof of the theory
(E) describe the result of an experiment that was conducted to prove a theory

16. The passage indicates that a neutron star (line 6) originated as a

(A) degenerate dwarf star of any size
(B) normal star with a mass less than one-third that of our sun
(C) normal star with a mass greater than that of our sun but less than three times that of our sun
(D) normal star with a mass at least three times greater than that of our sun
(E) supernova with a mass at least three times greater than that of our sun

17. In line 10, the word "repulsive" most nearly means

(A) forbidding
(B) disgusting
(C) offensive
(D) disagreeable
(E) repellent

18. The passage suggests that the mass of a black hole would be

(A) negligible
(B) about one-third that of the normal star from which it was formed
(C) approximately the same mass as the normal star from which it was formed
(D) approximately equal to the mass of two binary stars
(E) just about equal to the mass of our star

19. The passage defines the "gravitational radius" of a black hole as the

(A) orbital distance separating a visible star from a black hole in a binary star system
(B) distance at which matter is irreversibly drawn into the black hole by gravitational forces
(C) distance from the black hole at which an approaching rocket would first start to disintegrate
(D) radius of the massive star that created the black hole when it collapsed in upon itself
(E) scale for measuring the short-term variability of X-radiation emitted by a black hole

20. In line 55, the word "tempered" most nearly means

(A) moderated
(B) hardened
(C) kneaded
(D) cooled
(E) proved

GO ON TO THE NEXT PAGE

21. The passage indicates that a black hole would be

  (A) most likely to develop in a binary star system
  (B) a source of large quantities of X- and gamma rays
  (C) observable through a powerful telescope
  (D) formed from a degenerate dwarf star
  (E) invisible even at close range

22. In line 60, the word "candidate" most nearly means

  (A) pretender
  (B) possibility
  (C) official
  (D) office-seeker
  (E) scientist

23. Which of the following is NOT mentioned by the author as evidence to suggest that the Cygnus X-1 source might be a black hole?

  (A) Cygnus X-1 is a source of powerful X-ray radiation.
  (B) The companion star of Cygnus X-1 has a mass sufficiently large enough to create a black hole.
  (C) The intensity of the X-rays emanating from Cygnus X-1 exhibits short-term variability.
  (D) The star around which the visible star of Cygnus X-1 is orbiting is not itself visible.
  (E) The visible star of the Cygnus X-1 system is a blue supergiant.

24. The author regards the existence of black holes as

  (A) unprovable in principle
  (B) theoretically possible
  (C) extremely unlikely
  (D) experimentally confirmed
  (E) a logical contradiction

STOP

IF YOU FINISH BEFORE TIME IS CALLED, YOU MAY CHECK YOUR WORK ON THIS SECTION ONLY. DO NOT TURN TO ANY OTHER SECTION IN THE TEST.

Practice Test I

SECTION 6—MATH
Time—25 Minutes
18 Items

DIRECTIONS: In this section, solve each item, and choose the correct answer choice. Fill in the corresponding oval on the answer sheet. Use any available space for scratchwork. Answers are on page 636.

Notes:

(1) The use of a calculator is permitted. All numbers used are real numbers.

(2) Figures that accompany problems in this test are intended to provide information useful in solving the problems. They are drawn as accurately as possible EXCEPT when it is stated in a specific problem that the figure is not drawn to scale. All figures lie in a plane unless otherwise indicated.

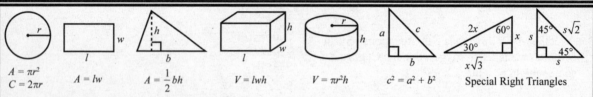

$A = \pi r^2$
$C = 2\pi r$

$A = lw$

$A = \frac{1}{2}bh$

$V = lwh$

$V = \pi r^2 h$

$c^2 = a^2 + b^2$

Special Right Triangles

The number of degrees of arc in a circle is 360.
The sum of the measures in degrees of the angles of a triangle is 180.

August Book Sales

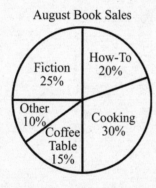

1. The graph above shows all of the books, categorized by type, that were sold by a store in the month of August. If the store sold 150 Fiction books, how many books did it sell for the entire month?

   (A) 25
   (B) 300
   (C) 450
   (D) 600
   (E) 750

2. In the xy-coordinate system, $(m, 0)$ is one of the points of intersection of the graphs of $y = x^2 - 4$ and $y = -x^2 + 4$. If $m > 0$, what is the value of m?

   (A) 2
   (B) 4
   (C) 8
   (D) 16
   (E) 32

GO ON TO THE NEXT PAGE

Entries for the Dog Show

Number of Dogs	Number of Owners
1	3
2	4
3	X
4	1

3. The table above shows the number of dogs entered per owner and the number of owners that entered that number of dogs. If the average (arithmetic mean) number of dogs entered by each owner is 2, what is the value of X?

(A) 1
(B) 2
(C) 3
(D) 4
(E) 5

4. After the first term of a series, each term in the sequence is $\frac{1}{2}$ the sum of the preceding term and 4. If n is the first term of the sequence and $n \neq 0$, what is the ratio of the first term to the second term?

(A) $\dfrac{2}{n+4}$

(B) $\dfrac{2}{n+2}$

(C) $\dfrac{2n}{n+4}$

(D) $\dfrac{2n}{n+2}$

(E) $\dfrac{2}{4-n}$

5. If the radius of circle O is 20 percent less than the radius of circle P, the area of circle O is what percent of the area of circle P?

(A) 60%
(B) 64%
(C) 72%
(D) 80%
(E) 120%

6. If the average (arithmetic mean) of 20, 23, 24, x, and y is 26, and $\dfrac{x}{y} = \dfrac{3}{4}$, then $x =$

(A) 25
(B) 27
(C) 36
(D) 41
(E) 63

7. The price of 5 boxes of candy is d dollars. If each box contains 30 pieces of candy, what is the price, in *cents*, of 12 pieces of candy?

(A) $8d$
(B) $12d$
(C) $\dfrac{25d}{2}$
(D) $50d$
(E) $72d$

8. If a cube has a side of length 2, what is the distance from any vertex to the center of the cube?

(A) $\dfrac{\sqrt{2}}{2}$
(B) $\sqrt{3}$
(C) $2\sqrt{2}$
(D) $2\sqrt{3}$
(E) $\dfrac{3}{2}$

GO ON TO THE NEXT PAGE

Each item requires you to solve an item and mark your answer on a special answer grid. For each item, you should write your answer in the boxes at the top of each column and then fill in the ovals beneath each part of the answer you write. Here are some examples:

Answer: 7/2 or 3.5

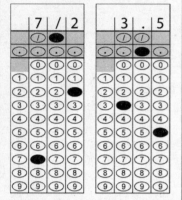

Note: A mixed number such as $3\frac{1}{2}$ must be gridded as 7/2 or as 3.5. If gridded as "31/2," it will be read as "thirty-one halves."

Answer: 325

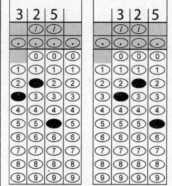

Note: Either position is correct.

Answer: 1/6, .166, or .167

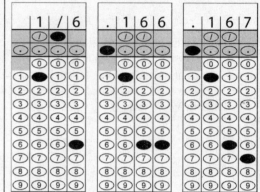

Note: A decimal answer with more digits than the grid can accommodate must be truncated. A decimal such as $.16\overline{6}$ must be gridded as .166 or .167. A less accurate value such as .16 or .17 will be scored as incorrect.

9. If $x + 1 + 2x + 2 + 3x + 3 = 6$, then $x =$

10. If a horse gallops at an average speed of 40 feet per second, how many seconds will it take for the horse to gallop 500 feet?

11. If n is a positive integer greater than 6, and if the remainder is the same when 13 and 21 are divided by n, then $n =$

12. If $\dfrac{64}{x} - 6 = 2$, then $x =$

GO ON TO THE NEXT PAGE

13. If x, y, and z are consecutive integers, and $x > y > z$, then $(x-y)(x-z)(y-z) =$

14. If x is a positive odd number less than 10, and y is a positive even number less than 10, what is the greatest number that xy can equal?

15. Cyrus worked 8 hours on Monday. On each successive day, he worked half as long as he did on the previous day. How many total hours had he worked by the end of the day on Friday?

16. Imagine a right triangle ABC with $\overline{AB}$ congruent to $\overline{BC}$. What is the measure, in degrees, of $\angle BAC$?

17. At Auburn Mills High, 80 percent of the graduating seniors go on to college. Of those college-bound seniors, 75 percent will attend school in-state. If there are 150 graduating seniors in all, how many will attend college out-of-state?

18. Danielle sliced a pizza into sixths. She then sliced each slice into thirds. She served 4 of the small slices to Pete. In lowest terms, what fraction of the whole pizza did Pete have?

STOP

IF YOU FINISH BEFORE TIME IS CALLED, YOU MAY CHECK YOUR WORK ON THIS SECTION ONLY. DO NOT TURN TO ANY OTHER SECTION IN THE TEST.

Practice Test I

SECTION 7—WRITING
Time—25 Minutes
35 Items

DIRECTIONS: In this section, solve each item, and choose the correct answer choice. Fill in the corresponding oval on the answer sheet. Answers are on page 636.

Items #1–5: The following sentences test correct, effective expression. Each sentence contains an underlined portion, or the entire sentence may be underlined. Following each sentence are five ways of phrasing the underlined portion. Choice (A) repeats the original; the other four choices are different. If you think the original is better than any of the other choices, choose (A); otherwise, choose one of the other choices.

In choosing answers, follow the conventions of standard written English. Make sure to consider issues of grammar, word choice, sentence construction, and punctuation. Your choice should produce the most effective sentence. It should be clear, precise, and free of ambiguity or awkwardness.

Example:

Allen <u>visiting</u> his cousin in France last summer.

(A) visiting
(B) visited
(C) does visit
(D) a visit
(E) is visiting

1. The average starting salary of a lawyer in a firm in New York City is about 25 percent higher <u>than a lawyer</u> in a firm in Chicago.

   (A) than a lawyer
   (B) than that of a lawyer
   (C) than lawyers
   (D) than that of lawyers
   (E) as a lawyer

2. A horse's chance of winning a race depends not so much on the final times of previous races <u>but instead</u> on class, a measurable factor that is the horse's determination to win.

   (A) but instead
   (B) rather than
   (C) so much as
   (D) than
   (E) as

3. People in show business say that you should be careful how you treat people on your way up <u>because one meets</u> the same people on the way back down.

   (A) because one meets
   (B) being that one meets
   (C) because you meet
   (D) because we meet
   (E) for you to meet

GO ON TO THE NEXT PAGE ⇒

4. Trying to make the streets safer, many neighborhood committees have asked the police to install surveillance cameras on light <u>posts, for it will record</u> any criminal activities.

    (A) posts, for it will record
    (B) posts, in that it will record
    (C) posts in order to record
    (D) posts for the recording of
    (E) posts to be able to record

5. Of all of the introductory courses offered by the biology department, <u>only Professor Collins devotes</u> several class periods to the effects of Global Warming on the extinction of species in the rain forest.

    (A) only Professor Collins devotes
    (B) Professor Collins only devotes
    (C) Professor Collins devotes only
    (D) only Professor Collins is the teacher who devotes
    (E) only that taught by Professors Collins devotes

<u>Items #6–25:</u> The following sentences test your knowledge of grammar, usage, diction (choice of words), and idiom. Each sentence contains either no error or a single error. If there is an error, it is underlined and lettered. If the sentence contains an error, choose the one underlined portion that must be changed to produce a correct sentence. If there is no error, choose answer choice (E). In choosing answers, follow the conventions of standard written English.

Example:

The principal <u>asked</u> five of <u>we</u> students
          A   B

<u>to enter</u> the <u>public speaking</u> contest.
  C   D

<u>No error</u>
 E   

---

6. The Everglades, located on the <u>southern</u> tip of
                     A

Florida, is a soggy, low-lying <u>tropical</u> area of
                     B

<u>solidly</u> packed muck, saw grass, and <u>having</u>
 C   D

<u>marshy knolls</u>. <u>No error</u>
   D   E

7. Sir Edward Elgar was an English composer <u>who</u>
                          A

lived from 1857 to 1934 and is best known for <u>his</u>
                             B

Pomp and Circumstance marches that <u>are</u> most
                         C

often associated <u>with</u> graduation ceremonies.
          D

<u>No error</u>
 E

8. An electrolyte <u>is</u> any electrical conductor <u>such as</u>
        A   B

a solution of salt in water <u>where</u> the current is
                  C

carried by ions <u>instead of</u> free electrons. <u>No error</u>
         D   E

9. <u>During</u> World War II, over 300,000 Allied troops
 A

were stranded at Dunkirk and cut off from <u>land</u>
                           B

<u>retreat</u> by the Germans; <u>however</u>, a fleet of British
 B   C

ships and boats <u>will rescue</u> most of them. <u>No error</u>
         D   E

GO ON TO THE NEXT PAGE

10. Though dragonflies have elongated bodies that
       A   B

    today reach five inches, during the Permian

    period, one species it had a wingspan of more
                  C   D

    than two feet. No error
      D   E

11. The eagle, a large, predatory bird, is solitude; but
                                  A   B

    when it mates, it mates for life. No error
         C   D   E

12. The Embargo Act of 1807, which was in force
                       A

    until 1809, prohibits international shipping to and
            B   C   D

    from all United States ports. No error
      D   E

13. The Chunnel, consisting of a central service tube
                 A   B

    and two railway tubes, run beneath the English
                     C   D

    Channel between England and France. No error
                          E

14. Calling Aurora by the Romans, Eos was the
      A   B   C

    Greek goddess of dawn and the mother of the

    winds. No error
      D   E

15. Enzymes are proteins that accelerate chemical
           A   B   C

    reactions in a cell that would otherwise proceed

    imperceptible or not at all. No error
      D   E

16. Since ancient times, days have arbitrarily been
      A   B

    inserted into calendars because the solar year not
      C   D

    being evenly divisible into months and days.
      D

    No error
      E

17. The Hopi, a people of the Southwest United
                  A

    States, they resisted European influence more
           B   C

    successfully than other Pueblo tribes. No error
              D   E

18. Hokusai was a Japanese painter and wood
           A

    engraver whose prodigious output included book
            B   C

    illustrations, printed cards, and landscapes in a
                          D

    variety of styles. No error
              E

19. Dramatic theater developed in ancient Greece
                A

    from religious rituals in which the actors were
                  B   C

    believed to participate directly in the events that
      C

    were depicted and not merely represent characters
          D

    in the action. No error
            E

GO ON TO THE NEXT PAGE

20. Although <u>both are</u> elected to national office,
　　　　　　　A

members of the House of Representatives are
　B

typically more attentive to local issues than
　C

the Senate. No error
　D　　　　E

21. The Dean stressed that the university depends

upon donations by <u>their</u> graduates <u>to help</u> students
　　　　　　　　　A　　　　　　　B

<u>who</u> might <u>otherwise</u> not be able to afford the
　C　　　　　D

tuition. No error
　　　　E

22. The New England aster, which <u>has</u> a long straight
　　　　　　　　　　　　　　A

stalk and rayed flowers that <u>varies</u> in color from
　　　　　　　　　　　　B

deep purple to pale pink, normally <u>grows</u> along
　　　　　　　　　　　　　C

roadsides and drainage ditches <u>and</u> blooms in the
　　　　　　　　　　　　　D

early autumn. No error
　　　　　　E

23. <u>Calling it</u> the "Gateway to the West," the city of
　　A

St. Louis <u>was</u> the starting point for <u>many</u> of the
　　　　　B　　　　　　　　　　C

important trails that were <u>used</u> during the great
　　　　　　　　　　　D

westward migration. No error
　　　　　　　E

24. <u>Most</u> recreational hot air ballooning is restricted
　　A

to short day trips over terrain that <u>has been</u>
　　　　　　　　　　　　　B

<u>mapped</u> out ahead of time, so there <u>is hardly no</u>
　C　　　　　　　　　　　　　D

need for navigational instruments. No error
　　　　　　　　　　　　E

25. The company's most valuable asset is <u>its</u>
　　　　　　　　　　　　A

engineers for <u>he or she</u> is willing to work long
　　　　　　B

hours for no additional pay <u>just</u> for the intellectual
　　　　　　　　　　C

reward <u>of solving</u> a difficult problem. No error
　　　　D　　　　　　　　　　E

Items #26–35: The following passages are early drafts of essays. Some portions of the passages need to be revised.

Read each passage and answer the items that follow. Items may be about particular sentences or parts of sentences, asking you to improve the word choice or sentence structure. Other items may refer to parts of the essay or the entire essay, asking you to consider organization or development. In making your decisions, follow the conventions of standard written English.

Items #26–30 refer to the following passage.

(1) I have been an amateur astronomer for years. (2) My first telescope was a gift from my uncle. (3) He taught astronomy at the local college. (4) I was only nine years old.
(5) One of the advantages of astronomy as a hobby is that you did not have to be an expert to enjoy it. (6) With even an inexpensive telescope, you can step outside on a clear night and see thousands of stars.
(7) How many are there?
(8) We know that our solar system is part of a much larger system of hundreds of billions of stars.

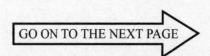
GO ON TO THE NEXT PAGE

(9) As such, this system is the Milky Way Galaxy, a huge disk of stars and gas.

(10) We also know that ours is not the only galaxy in the universe. **(11)** As far as the largest telescopes in the world can see, there are galaxies in every direction. **(12)** The nearest large galaxy to the Milky Way is the Andromeda Galaxy, which is about two million light years away. **(13)** Andromeda is a giant spiral galaxy, much like our own in size, shape, and number and type of stars. **(14)** This nearby sister galaxy provides us an opportunity to get a good view of a galaxy much like our own.

26. What is the best way to deal with sentence 3?

   (A) (As it is now.)
   (B) Connect it to sentence 2 with the word "who."
   (C) Place it before sentence 2.
   (D) Connect it to sentence 2 with the word "and."
   (E) Delete it.

27. In the context, which is the best version of "that you did not have to be" in sentence 5?

   (A) (As it is now.)
   (B) that you do not have to be
   (C) that you not being
   (D) which you did not have to be
   (E) your not being

28. Which is the best way to deal with the phrase "as such" in sentence 9?

   (A) (As it is now.)
   (B) Move it to the end of the sentence.
   (C) Replace it with "actually."
   (D) Replace it with "as a matter of fact."
   (E) Delete it.

29. The writer wishes to add the following parenthetical sentence to the last paragraph:

   (A light year is the distance traveled by light in a year, almost 10 million, million kilometers.)

   The sentence would best fit the context if inserted

   (A) before sentence 10
   (B) between sentences 10 and 11
   (C) between sentences 11 and 12
   (D) between sentences 12 and 13
   (E) between sentences 13 and 14

30. Which of the following, if placed after sentence 14, would be the most effective concluding sentence for the essay?

   (A) However, astronomy may not be suitable for very young children.
   (B) Finally, you can learn more about galaxies by becoming an amateur astronomer yourself.
   (C) Therefore, think about the Andromeda Galaxy the next time you look at the night sky.
   (D) The Mellagenic Clouds are my favorite galaxies, but they are seen only in the southern skies.
   (E) In effect, we get to see ourselves as others would see us.

Items #31–35 refer to the following passage.

(1) My favorite American artist is Georgia O'Keeffe. **(2)** Her parents were dairy farmers, but Georgia knew she was going to be an artist from early on. **(3)** She studied and taught art in Chicago, Virginia, Texas, and South Carolina.

(4) After years of teaching, Georgia did a series of abstract charcoals. **(5)** She sent the drawings to a friend who in turn showed them to Alfred Stieglitz, a well-known photographer and gallery owner in New York. **(6)** Stieglitz exhibited the drawings without first consulting Georgia. **(7)** This angered her, and she went to New York with the intention of removing the drawings. **(8)** After meeting Stieglitz, she agreed to let him show her work.

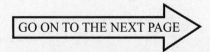
GO ON TO THE NEXT PAGE

(9) This began a relationship that was to result in their marrying. **(10)** Georgia painted cityscapes inspired by the spectacular view from their 30th floor apartment. **(11)** Stieglitz and O'Keeffe also spent a lot of time in the Adirondack Mountains, where she created many paintings of the Lake George area. **(12)** After 12 years, Georgia had had enough of the city as a subject and felt the need to travel again and took a trip to New Mexico. **(13)** She was inspired by the mountains and deserts of the region and the mysterious aura of the place. **(14)** She referred to landscape as "the faraway" and would travel dusty roads in a Model A Ford to find scenes to paint. **(15)** After Stieglitz's death in 1946, Georgia established permanent residence in New Mexico, so she could paint her famous images of sun-bleached skulls.

(16) With eyesight failing, she spent her final years in Santa Fe. **(17)** She died on March 6, 1986, at the age of 98, and her ashes were scattered over her "faraway."

31. Which of the following would be the most suitable sentence to insert immediately after sentence 1?

    (A) Georgia graduated from the Chatham Episcopal Institute in 1905.
    (B) In 1985, she was awarded the National Medal of Arts.
    (C) She was born in Wisconsin in 1887.
    (D) My favorite European artist is Vincent Van Gogh.
    (E) Her family moved from the dairy farm to Virginia.

32. To best connect sentence 8 with the rest of the second paragraph, which is the best word or phrase to insert following the underlined portion of sentence 8 (reproduced below)?

    After meeting Stieglitz, she agreed to let him show her work.

    (A) however,
    (B) naturally,
    (C) you see,
    (D) certainly,
    (E) for that reason,

33. In context, sentence 9 could be made more precise by adding which of the following words after "this"?

    (A) teaching
    (B) trip
    (C) incident
    (D) example
    (E) friend

34. Which of the following versions of the underlined portion of sentence 15 (reproduced below) best suits the context?

    After Stieglitz's death in 1946, Georgia established permanent residence in New Mexico, so she could paint her famous images of sun-bleached skulls.

    (A) (As it is now.)
    (B) so she could be painting
    (C) and she painted
    (D) though she painted
    (E) where she painted

35. The author uses the phrase "faraway" in sentence 17 to

    (A) set up a contrast between the discussion of O'Keeffe's landscapes and her cityscapes
    (B) reinforce the idea that O'Keeffe felt a strong personal connection to New Mexico
    (C) show the tragedy of O'Keeffe's death after a lengthy career as an artist
    (D) remind the reader that O'Keeffe knew from an early age that she wanted to be an artist
    (E) plant doubts in the reader's mind about the mysterious circumstances of O'Keeffe's death

STOP

IF YOU FINISH BEFORE TIME IS CALLED, YOU MAY CHECK YOUR WORK ON THIS SECTION ONLY. DO NOT TURN TO ANY OTHER SECTION IN THE TEST.

Practice Test I

SECTION 8—CRITICAL READING

Time—20 Minutes

19 Items

DIRECTIONS: In this section, solve each item, and choose the correct answer choice. Fill in the corresponding oval on the answer sheet. Answers are on page 637.

Items #1–4: Each item below has one or two blanks, each blank indicating that something has been omitted. Beneath the sentence are five lettered words or sets of words. Choose the word or set of words that best fits the meaning of the sentence as a whole.

Example:

Although its publicity has been -------, the film itself is intelligent, well acted, handsomely produced, and altogether -------.

(A) tasteless . . respectable
(B) extensive . . moderate
(C) sophisticated . . amateur
(D) risqué . . crude
(E) perfect . . spectacular

---

1. The treatment of the mental illnesses for which there is no cure can only ------- the symptoms, not ------- the disease.

   (A) defend . . eradicate
   (B) disrupt . . deflate
   (C) ameliorate . . eliminate
   (D) confine . . restore
   (E) augment . . delineate

2. Although Senator Jones had the ------- needed to run for office, it was his ------- that the party considered his greatest asset.

   (A) credentials . . charisma
   (B) experience . . apathy
   (C) esteem . . wrongdoing
   (D) greed . . altruism
   (E) serenity . . haughtiness

3. Due to the ------- of the materials needed to manufacture the product and the ever-increasing demand for it, it is highly probable that the final cost to the consumer will -------.

   (A) immensity . . evolve
   (B) paucity . . escalate
   (C) scarcity . . relax
   (D) acuity . . stabilize
   (E) certainty . . fluctuate

4. Although the comedian was very clever, many of his remarks were ------- and ------- lawsuits against him for slander.

   (A) derogatory . . resulted in
   (B) pithy . . came upon
   (C) protracted . . forestalled
   (D) depraved . . assuaged
   (E) recanted . . sparked

GO ON TO THE NEXT PAGE

Items #5–19: The two passages below are followed by items based on their content and the relationship between the two passages. Answer the items on the basis of what is stated or implied in the passages and in any introductory material that may be provided.

The following passages are excerpts from two different sources that discuss particular approaches to history.

Passage 1

As Carl Hempel demonstrates in his seminal essay "The Function of General Laws in History," a general law plays the same role in both history and the natural sciences. According to Hempel's deductive-
5   nomological model, proper scientific explanation—whether for history or the natural sciences—includes three sorts of statements:
(A) A set of statements about conditions (that can be designated as C1, C2, and so on) that are true at a
10 particular place and time.
(B) A set of universal hypotheses connecting events of type C with events of type E.
(C) A statement asserting that E is logically deducible from the statements of A and B.
15 The "C" events are, of course, causes, while the "E" events are effects. Given a sufficiently precise description of background conditions by Set A and an adequately articulated set of empirical laws in Set B, a conclusion such as "A popular uprising overthrew the
20 government" can be logically deduced with as much certainty as that of a syllogism.*
The notion that a historian cannot study past events in the same way that a chemist studies reactions or a physicist studies falling objects is due to a
25 misunderstanding. Historical explanations intentionally omit from Set A statements about human nature that are well-known to the sciences of psychology and sociology because they are too numerous to mention. Further, many of the general laws used by historians do
30 not seem susceptible to easy confirmation in the way that laboratory experiments are. It is difficult to find a sufficiently large number of revolutions to assess the validity of the assertion that a drop of a certain magnitude in a population's standard of living will
35 inevitably be followed by revolution.

Thus, we should more accurately speak not of scientific explanations of historical events but of "sketches" of history. This terminology would call attention to the incompleteness and the imprecision in
40 historical explanation, while at the same time reminding us that the form of explanation is the same as that of the natural sciences.

*A syllogism is a form of reasoning in which a conclusion is drawn from two statements:

> Major Premise: All ruminants are quadrupeds.
> Minor Premise: All cows are ruminants.
> Conclusion: Therefore, all cows are quadrupeds.

Passage 2

The obvious distinction between history and the natural sciences is that history is concerned with
45 human actions. The historian makes a distinction between what may be called the outside and the inside of an event. The outside of the event is everything belonging to it that can be described in terms of bodies and their movements: the passage of Caesar across a
50 river called the Rubicon on a certain date or the spilling of Caesar's blood on the senate-house floor on another. The inside of the event can only be described in terms of thought: Caesar's defiance of Republican law or the clash of constitutional policy between Caesar and
55 Caesar's assassins. The historian is not investigating mere events (a mere event is one that has only an outside and no inside) but actions, and an action is the unity of the outside and inside of an event.
The task of the historian is thus distinguished
60 from that of the natural scientist in two ways. On the one hand, the historian must undertake an additional investigation that is neither needed by nor available to the natural scientist. The historian must inquire after the "why" of an event, that is, the thought behind it. On
65 the other hand, the task of the historian is somewhat simpler than that of the natural scientist because once that question has been answered there is no further question to be raised. There is no reason to look behind the thought associated with the event for a supervening
70 general law.
Since the questions that the historian asks are different from those posed by the natural scientist, the historian will employ a different method. The historian penetrates to the inner aspect of the event by the
75 technique of *Verstehen*.* To be sure, the historian will study whatever documents and other physical evidence are available, but these are important only insofar as

GO ON TO THE NEXT PAGE →

they provide an access to the inside of the event.

    A purely physical event can only be understood
80 as a particular occurrence governed by a universal or
general law, but the inside of an event is a thought—
unique, and as such, not subject to a law-like
explanation. Nor is this reason for disappointment. It is
not the case that there are historical laws but the
85 techniques just do not yet exist to find them. Rather,
the laws just do not exist to be found. To expect to find
causal explanation in history and to demand of history
predictions about the course of future events is an
illegitimate expectation conceived and fostered by the
90 false analogy of history to the natural sciences and the
incorrect assumption that the natural sciences are the
paradigm for all human knowledge.

    The positivist will object that this means that
history is, in principle, less rigorous than natural
95 science, but this objection ignores the point that there
simply are no historical laws to be discovered. In fact,
because an historical event has both an inside and an
outside, it is the events of natural science that are, in a
sense, deficient. As R. G. Collingwood wrote so boldly
100 in the concluding section of *The Idea of History*,
"Natural science…depends on historical thought for its
existence." In history, there are no general scientific
laws to be uncovered, and the search for them is the
foolish pursuit of a will-o'-the-wisp that exists only in
105 the fables of positivist literature.

    *Verstehen is the German word for "understanding."

5. As used in line 5, the word "nomological" most
nearly means

  (A) law-like
  (B) historical
  (C) accurate
  (D) logical
  (E) scientific

6. In line 18, the phrase "adequately articulated"
means

  (A) verbally presented
  (B) only preliminary
  (C) confidently denoted
  (D) precisely defined
  (E) sufficiently detailed

7. In the second paragraph of Passage 1, the author
suggests that a series of historical events could
serve the same scientific function as

  (A) eyewitness accounts
  (B) general laws
  (C) laboratory experiments
  (D) historical sketches
  (E) syllogisms

8. According to the author of Passage 1, it is
difficult to formulate a general historical law
about revolution because

  (A) revolutions, by definition, involve the
overthrow of an existing government
  (B) too few revolutions are available for study to
yield valid conclusions
  (C) details about a revolution are generally only
known to a few key participants
  (D) historical events ordinarily involve a large
number of unidentified actors
  (E) the intentions of the leaders of a revolution
cannot be determined

9. The attitude of the author of Passage 1 toward
psychology and sociology is one of

  (A) skepticism
  (B) indifference
  (C) confidence
  (D) outrage
  (E) disappointment

10. Passage 1 is primarily an argument against the
position that

  (A) revolutions are caused by factors that can be
identified
  (B) history is not a science like physics or
chemistry
  (C) science is an undertaking requiring the use of
logic
  (D) history is more important than the physical
sciences
  (E) laboratory experiments produce conclusions
that are scientifically reliable

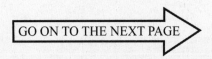

GO ON TO THE NEXT PAGE

11. Passage 2 explains that the technique of *Verstehen* is used to enable the historian to study

   (A) the outside of historical events
   (B) motives and intentions of historical actors
   (C) psychology and sociology
   (D) historical laws
   (E) natural events in a historical context

12. According to Passage 2, any "disappointment" at the failure of general laws to explain historical events (line 83) is due to

   (A) failure to correctly apply the deductive-nomological model
   (B) the inability to make meaningful statements about historical events
   (C) the complexity of historical events when compared to natural occurrences
   (D) inadequate facts to support a legitimate conclusion about the events
   (E) an unreasonable expectation about the universality of natural sciences

13. In line 92, the word "paradigm" most nearly means

   (A) logic
   (B) understanding
   (C) foundation
   (D) model
   (E) goal

14. Which of the following would most likely be a "positivist," as that term is used in line 93?

   (A) the author of Passage 1
   (B) the author of Passage 2
   (C) any natural scientist
   (D) any historical figure
   (E) R. G. Collingwood

15. According to Passage 2, what is the main difference between history and the natural sciences?

   (A) History explains events that have occurred in the past, while natural sciences predict the future.
   (B) The natural sciences produce true knowledge of actual events, while history consists of subjective opinions.
   (C) The natural sciences require the use of logic, while history depends solely upon *Verstehen*.
   (D) Natural sciences depend upon experimental data, while history relies solely upon recollection.
   (E) The natural sciences study purely physical events, while history is concerned with reasons for human actions.

16. In line 105, the word "fables" most nearly means

   (A) ancient folklore
   (B) moral stories
   (C) fictitious narratives
   (D) plot lines
   (E) misconceptions

GO ON TO THE NEXT PAGE

17. The author of Passage 1 and the author of Passage 2 would be most likely to agree with which of the following statements?

(A) Psychology and sociology use the same methodology as the natural sciences.
(B) Scientific historians should construct their explanations in the same way that the physicist does.
(C) The inability of historians to conduct laboratory testing shows that history is not a science.
(D) Syllogistic reasoning is an important tool for historical research.
(E) Events that have no element of thought are governed by law-like regularities.

18. Which statement best expresses the objection that the Passage 2 author would be most likely to make to Hempel's theory of history?

(A) It is incomplete because it fails to include information from disciplines such as psychology and sociology.
(B) It is misguided because it ignores the fact that human actions have a mental as well as a physical component.
(C) It is weak because historians are not able to use experiments to test the validity of their theories.
(D) It is not particularly useful because historical events are too complex to be predicted successfully.
(E) It is incorrect because it relies upon the syllogism, an outmoded form of reasoning.

19. In order to account for what Passage 2 calls the "inside" of a historical event, the author of Passage 1 would most likely refer to

(A) various principles of psychology and sociology
(B) well-known laws of physical science
(C) experiments conducted in a laboratory
(D) documents written by a key actor
(E) authoritative historical writings

STOP

IF YOU FINISH BEFORE TIME IS CALLED, YOU MAY CHECK YOUR WORK ON THIS SECTION ONLY. DO NOT TURN TO ANY OTHER SECTION IN THE TEST.

NO TEST MATERIAL ON THIS PAGE

Practice Test I

SECTION 9—MATH
Time—20 Minutes
16 Items

DIRECTIONS: In this section, solve each item, and choose the correct answer choice. Fill in the corresponding oval on the answer sheet. Use any available space for scratchwork. Answers are on page 637.

Notes:

(1) The use of a calculator is permitted. All numbers used are real numbers.

(2) Figures that accompany problems in this test are intended to provide information useful in solving the problems. They are drawn as accurately as possible EXCEPT when it is stated in a specific problem that the figure is not drawn to scale. All figures lie in a plane unless otherwise indicated.

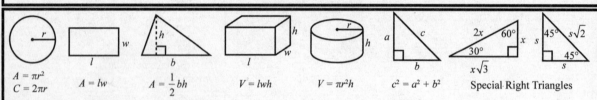

$A = \pi r^2$
$C = 2\pi r$
$A = lw$
$A = \frac{1}{2}bh$
$V = lwh$
$V = \pi r^2 h$
$c^2 = a^2 + b^2$
Special Right Triangles

The number of degrees of arc in a circle is 360.
The sum of the measures in degrees of the angles of a triangle is 180.

---

1. If 1 mil = 0.1 cents, how many mils are there in $3.13?

   (A)   0.313
   (B)   3.13
   (C)   31.3
   (D)   313
   (E) 3,130

2. Which of the following is a pair of numbers that are not equal?

   (A) $\dfrac{63}{6}$, $\dfrac{21}{2}$

   (B) 0.3%, 0.003

   (C) $\dfrac{44}{77}$, $\dfrac{4}{7}$

   (D) $\dfrac{3}{8}$, 0.375

   (E) $\sqrt{3^2}$, 9

GO ON TO THE NEXT PAGE

3. If x and y are different positive integers and $\dfrac{x}{y}$ is an integer, then which of the following must be true?

   I. $x > y$
  II. $xy > 0$
 III. $y - x < 0$

(A) I only
(B) II only
(C) III only
(D) I and II only
(E) I, II, and III

Items #4–5 refer to the following information.

For all positive integers n:

$$[n] = 2n \text{ if } n \text{ is even.}$$
$$[n] = 3n \text{ if } n \text{ is odd.}$$

4. If n is a prime number greater than 2, then $[n-1] =$

(A) $3n$
(B) $2n$
(C) $3n - 3$
(D) $2n - 2$
(E) n

5. $[3] \cdot [4] =$

(A) $[6]$
(B) $[7]$
(C) $[12]$
(D) $[18]$
(E) $[36]$

6. Which of the following is the equation for the line that includes points $(-1,1)$ and $(7,5)$?

(A) $y = \dfrac{x}{2} + 2$

(B) $y = \dfrac{x}{2} + \dfrac{2}{3}$

(C) $y = \dfrac{x}{2} + \dfrac{3}{2}$

(D) $y = 2x + \dfrac{3}{2}$

(E) $y = 2x + 2$

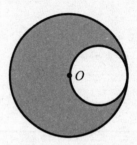

7. In the figure above, O is the center of the circle. What is the ratio of the shaded area in the figure to the unshaded area in the figure?

(A) $\dfrac{4}{1}$

(B) $\dfrac{\pi}{1}$

(C) $\dfrac{3}{1}$

(D) $\dfrac{5}{2}$

(E) $\dfrac{2}{1}$

8. If a cube has a surface area of $54x^2$, what is its volume?

(A) $3x$
(B) $3x^2$
(C) $3x^3$
(D) $9x^3$
(E) $27x^3$

GO ON TO THE NEXT PAGE

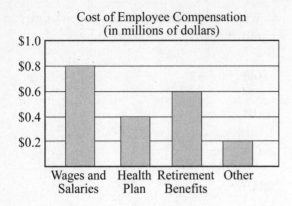

Cost of Employee Compensation
(in millions of dollars)

9. In the graph above, Wages and Salaries account for what percent of employee compensation?

(A) 40%
(B) 25%
(C) $12\frac{1}{2}$%
(D) 10%
(E) 8%

10. If x is an integer that is a multiple of both 9 and 5, which of the following must be true?

   I. x is equal to 45.
  II. x is a multiple of 15.
 III. x is odd.

(A) I only
(B) II only
(C) III only
(D) II and III only
(E) I, II, and III

11. Initially, 24 people apply for jobs with a firm, and $\frac{1}{3}$ of those people are turned down without being given an interview. If $\frac{1}{4}$ of the remaining applicants are hired, how many applicants are given jobs?

(A) 2
(B) 4
(C) 6
(D) 8
(E) 12

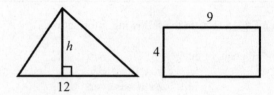

12. In the figures above, if the area of the rectangle is equal to the area of the triangle, then $h =$

(A) 2
(B) 3
(C) 4
(D) 6
(E) 9

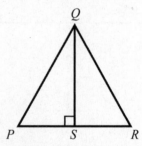

13. In the figure above, $\overline{PQ} = \overline{QR} = \overline{PR}$. If $\overline{PS} = 3$, what is the area of $\triangle PQR$? ($\cos 30° = \frac{\sqrt{3}}{2}$)

(A) 3
(B) $3\sqrt{3}$ (approximately 5.2)
(C) 6
(D) $6\sqrt{3}$ (approximately 10.39)
(E) $9\sqrt{3}$ (approximately 15.59)

GO ON TO THE NEXT PAGE

14. The price of a book, after it was reduced by $\frac{1}{3}$, is B dollars. What was the price of the book, in dollars, before the reduction?

   (A) $\frac{2B}{3}$

   (B) $\frac{3B}{4}$

   (C) $\frac{6B}{5}$

   (D) $\frac{4B}{3}$

   (E) $\frac{3B}{2}$

15. Y years ago, Tom was three times as old as Julie was at the time. If Julie is now 20 years old, how old is Tom in terms of Y?

   (A) $60 + 2Y$
   (B) $30 + 2Y$
   (C) $30 - 2Y$
   (D) $60 - 2Y$
   (E) $60 - 3Y$

16. If S is the sum of x consecutive integers, then S must be even if x is a multiple of

   (A) 6
   (B) 5
   (C) 4
   (D) 3
   (E) 2

STOP

IF YOU FINISH BEFORE TIME IS CALLED, YOU MAY CHECK YOUR WORK ON THIS SECTION ONLY. DO NOT TURN TO ANY OTHER SECTION IN THE TEST.

Practice Test I

SECTION 10—WRITING

Time—10 Minutes

14 Items

DIRECTIONS: In this section, solve each item, and choose the correct answer choice. Fill in the corresponding oval on the answer sheet. Answers are on page 637.

Items #1–14: The following sentences test correct, effective expression. Each sentence contains an underlined portion, or the entire sentence may be underlined. Following each sentence are five ways of phrasing the underlined portion. Choice (A) repeats the original; the other four choices are different. If you think the original is better than any of the other choices, choose (A); otherwise, choose one of the other choices.

In choosing answers, follow the conventions of standard written English. Make sure to consider issues of grammar, word choice, sentence construction, and punctuation. Your choice should produce the most effective sentence. It should be clear, precise, and free of ambiguity or awkwardness.

Example:

Allen <u>visiting</u> his cousin in France last summer.

(A) visiting
(B) visited
(C) does visit
(D) a visit
(E) is visiting   

---

1. Three hundred years ago, famine was a periodic experience that came so <u>regular that people accepted periods of extreme hunger as normal</u>.

   (A) regular that people accepted periods of extreme hunger as normal
   (B) regularly that people accepted periods of extreme hunger as normal
   (C) regularly that people normally accepted periods of extreme hunger
   (D) regularly as people accepted periods of extreme hunger as normal
   (E) regularly since people accepted periods of extreme hunger as normal

2. The Puritan was composed of two different persons: <u>the one all self-abasement and penitence;</u> the other, proud and inflexible.

   (A) the one all self-abasement and penitence
   (B) one of them all self-abasement and penitence
   (C) the one self-abasing and penitent
   (D) the one self-abasement and penitence
   (E) self-abasing and penitent

3. <u>In 1896, when she began studying the effects of radium,</u> Marie Curie was building on the work of Roentgen and Becquerel.

   (A) In 1896, when she began studying the effects of radium
   (B) In 1896, beginning to study the effects of radium
   (C) Beginning to study the effects of radium in 1896
   (D) Since she began to study the effects of radium in 1896
   (E) In order to begin to study the effects of radium in 1896

GO ON TO THE NEXT PAGE

4. <u>Having been forbidden by Church law to marry, it was not unusual for priests during the Middle Ages to sire families.</u>

(A) Having been forbidden by Church law to marry, it was not unusual for priests during the Middle Ages to sire a families.
(B) Forbidden by Church law to marry, it was not unusual for a priest during the Middle Ages to sire a family.
(C) Although they were forbidden by Church law to marry, it was not unusual for a priest during the Middle Ages to sire a family.
(D) Although a priest was forbidden by Church law to marry, it was not unusual for him during the Middle Ages to sire families.
(E) Although they were forbidden by Church law to marry, it was not unusual for priests during the Middle Ages to sire families.

5. The singing teachers of the old Italian school taught <u>little more but</u> breath control because they believed that with proper breath control, all other technical problems could be easily solved.

(A) little more but
(B) little more than
(C) little more as
(D) more than a little
(E) rather than

6. These extensive forest reserves must be defended from the acquisitive hands of those whose ruthless axes <u>would destroy the trees and</u> expose the land to the ravages of sun and rain.

(A) would destroy the trees and
(B) will destroy the trees and
(C) would destroy the trees to
(D) would destroy the trees which would
(E) would destroy the trees that could

7. In the early stages of the development of the common law, <u>equitable remedies were available only in the courts of the Chancery and not in the courts of law, such as injunctions</u>.

(A) equitable remedies were available only in the courts of the Chancery and not in the courts of law, such as injunctions
(B) equitable remedies, such as injunctions, were available only in the courts of the Chancery and not in the courts of law
(C) only equitable remedies, such as injunctions, were available in the courts of Chancery and not in the courts of law
(D) the availability of equitable remedies, such as injunctions, was restricted to the courts of Chancery and not to the courts of law
(E) equitable remedies, such as injunctions, were not available in the courts of law but only in the courts of Chancery

8. Good American English is simply good English; that of London and Sydney <u>differ no more from</u> Boston and Chicago than the types of houses in which people live.

(A) differ no more from
(B) differs no more from
(C) differ no more than
(D) differs no more from that of
(E) differ no more from those of

9. Concrete is an artificial engineering material made from a mixture of portland cement, water, fine and coarse aggregates, <u>having a small</u> amount of air.

(A) having a small
(B) having added a small
(C) adding a small
(D) and a little
(E) and a small

GO ON TO THE NEXT PAGE

10. During the Middle Ages, literacy was defined as <u>one who could read and write</u> Latin.

(A) one who could read and write
(B) one who would read and write
(C) reading and writing
(D) those who could read and write
(E) the ability to read and write

11. Ballet dancers warm up before each performance by doing a series of pliés and stretching <u>exercises, and it reduces</u> the chance of injury.

(A) exercises, and it reduces
(B) exercises, which reduces
(C) exercises, reducing
(D) exercises; the routine reduces
(E) exercises, so the routine reduces

12. An airline may overbook a flight <u>to ensure a full passenger load, but it is required to pay compensation to</u> any passenger who cannot be accommodated on that flight.

(A) to ensure a full passenger load, but it is required to pay compensation to
(B) ensuring a full passenger load, but it is required to pay compensation to
(C) to ensure a full passenger load, since compensation is required to
(D) to ensure a full passenger load, which is required to pay compensation to
(E) to ensure a full passenger load and pay compensation

13. It is typical of the high soprano voice, <u>like</u> the highest voices within each vocal range, to be lighter in weight and more flexible.

(A) like
(B) as
(C) like it is of
(D) as it is of
(E) similar to

14. After her admission to the bar, <u>Margaret, herself a childless attorney's only daughter</u>, specialized in adoption and family law.

(A) Margaret, herself a childless attorney's only daughter
(B) Margaret herself, a childless attorney's only daughter
(C) Margaret, herself the childless and only daughter of an attorney
(D) Margaret, only a childless attorney's daughter herself
(E) Margaret herself, only a daughter of a childless attorney

STOP

IF YOU FINISH BEFORE TIME IS CALLED, YOU MAY CHECK YOUR WORK ON THIS SECTION ONLY. DO NOT TURN TO ANY OTHER SECTION IN THE TEST.

Practice Test II

Outline

I. **Section 1:** Writing (p. 501)

II. **Section 2:** Math (pp. 502–505)

III. **Section 3:** Critical Reading (pp. 506–512)

IV. **Section 4:** Math (pp. 514–517)

V. **Section 6:** Writing (pp. 518–523)

VI. **Section 7:** Critical Reading (pp. 524–529)

VII. **Section 8:** Math (pp. 530–533)

VIII. **Section 9:** Critical Reading (pp. 534–539)

IX. **Section 10:** Writing (pp. 540–542)

Practice Test II

SECTION 1—WRITING
Time—25 Minutes
1 Essay

DIRECTIONS: The essay tests your ability to express ideas, develop a point of view, present ideas in a clear and logical fashion, and use language precisely.

Write your essay on the lines provided on your answer sheet—you will receive no other paper on which to write. Do not write your essay in your test book. You will receive credit only for what appears on your answer sheet. Write legibly, and remember that graders must be able to read your handwriting.

You have 25 minutes to plan and write an essay on the topic assigned below. Do not write on any other topic. An essay on another topic is not acceptable. Sample essays and analyses begin on page 665.

Think carefully about the issue presented in the following excerpt and the assignment below.

Stockbrokers in New York can trade on the London Stock Exchange as easily as they can on Wall Street. Scrap metal from an alley in Chicago is helping fuel a boom in China. The world is shrinking because of advances in transportation and communication. This allows for increased trade, stronger world and local economies, and less poverty on a global scale—all extremely positive effects of a global economy.

Globalization has some positive benefits, but the negatives far outweigh these. For one, globalization has led to a loss of native and indigenous cultures. Tribes in Brazil's Amazon rain forest are being forced out of their ancestral lands because of the world's insatiable demand for building materials and land for crops or livestock. Keeping up with a world market has bankrupted countries that cannot keep up leading to famine and political unrest.

Assignment: Have globalization's positive or negative effects been dominant? Plan and write an essay in which you develop your point of view on this issue. Support your position with reasoning and examples taken from your reading, studies, experience, and observations.

STOP

IF YOU FINISH BEFORE TIME IS CALLED, YOU MAY CHECK YOUR WORK ON THIS SECTION ONLY. DO NOT TURN TO ANY OTHER SECTION IN THE TEST.

Practice Test II.

SECTION 2—MATH

Time—25 Minutes

20 Items

DIRECTIONS: In this section, solve each item, and choose the correct answer choice. Fill in the corresponding oval on the answer sheet. Use any available space for scratchwork. Answers are on page 668.

Notes:

(1) The use of a calculator is permitted. All numbers used are real numbers.

(2) Figures that accompany problems in this test are intended to provide information useful in solving the problems. They are drawn as accurately as possible EXCEPT when it is stated in a specific problem that the figure is not drawn to scale. All figures lie in a plane unless otherwise indicated.

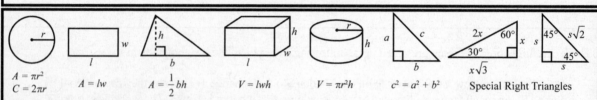

$A = \pi r^2$
$C = 2\pi r$ $A = lw$ $A = \frac{1}{2}bh$ $V = lwh$ $V = \pi r^2 h$ $c^2 = a^2 + b^2$ Special Right Triangles

The number of degrees of arc in a circle is 360.

The sum of the measures in degrees of the angles of a triangle is 180.

---

1. If $x + 2 = 7$ and $x + y = 11$, then $y =$

   (A) 2
   (B) 4
   (C) 6
   (D) 7
   (E) 9

2. In the figure above, if $y + z = 150$, then $x =$

   (A) 30
   (B) 45
   (C) 75
   (D) 90
   (E) 120

GO ON TO THE NEXT PAGE

> The product of x and 5 is equal to one-half of the sum of $3x$ and 3.

3. Which of the following equations correctly expresses the relationship described above?

(A) $5x = \dfrac{9x}{2}$

(B) $5x = 2(3x + 3)$

(C) $5x = \dfrac{(3x + 3)}{2}$

(D) $\dfrac{x}{5} = 2(3x + 3)$

(E) $\dfrac{x}{5} = \dfrac{(3x + 3)}{2}$

4. If $f(x) = -2x^2 + 2$, then $f(3) =$

(A) 16
(B) 4
(C) 0
(D) −4
(E) −16

5. During a sale, 3 of a certain item can be purchased for the usual cost of 2 of the items. If John buys 36 of the items at the sale price, how many of the items could he have bought at the regular price?

(A) 18
(B) 24
(C) 30
(D) 48
(E) 72

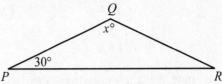

Note: Figure not drawn to scale.

6. In $\triangle PQR$ above, if $\overline{PQ} \cong \overline{QR}$, then $x =$

(A) 30
(B) 60
(C) 90
(D) 120
(E) 150

7. If $px + 2 = 8$ and $qx + 3 = 10$, what is the value of $\dfrac{p}{q}$?

(A) $\dfrac{3}{5}$

(B) $\dfrac{8}{15}$

(C) $\dfrac{10}{13}$

(D) $\dfrac{6}{7}$

(E) $\dfrac{16}{13}$

8. If $2^x = 16$ and $x = \dfrac{y}{2}$, then $y =$

(A) 2
(B) 3
(C) 4
(D) 6
(E) 8

GO ON TO THE NEXT PAGE

$$\begin{array}{r} 8\bullet \\ +\ \bullet 2 \\ \hline 1\blacklozenge 6 \end{array}$$

9. The figure above shows a correctly performed addition problem. The symbols ● and ◆ each represent a single digit which may or may not be the same digit. What is the value of ◆ ?

(A) 2
(B) 4
(C) 6
(D) 8
(E) 9

10. If $\sqrt{5x}+4=9$, $x=$

(A) −5
(B) −3
(C) 0
(D) 3
(E) 5

11. If a triangle has a height of $\dfrac{1}{x}$ and an area of 2, what is the length of the base of the triangle?

(A) $4x$
(B) x
(C) $\dfrac{1}{2x}$
(D) $\dfrac{1}{4x}$
(E) x^2

12. If the sum of three numbers is $4x$ and the sum of four other numbers is $3x$, then the average (arithmetic mean) of all seven numbers is

(A) $7x$
(B) x
(C) $\dfrac{x}{7}$
(D) 7
(E) 1

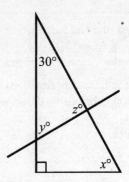

13. In the figure above, if $x = y$, then $z =$

(A) 30
(B) 45
(C) 60
(D) 75
(E) 90

14. If $6 \le x \le 30$, $3 \le y \le 12$, and $2 \le z \le 10$, then what is the least possible value of $\dfrac{x+y}{z}$?

(A) $\dfrac{9}{10}$
(B) $\dfrac{9}{5}$
(C) $\dfrac{21}{5}$
(D) $\dfrac{9}{2}$
(E) 21

15. $(-3x)^3 \left(\dfrac{-3x^{-3}}{27} \right) =$

(A) −1
(B) 3
(C) 9
(D) 27
(E) $27x^3$

GO ON TO THE NEXT PAGE

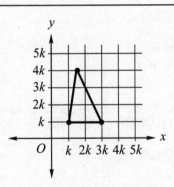

16. The figure above shows a rectangular piece of cardboard with sides of 10 centimeters and 12 centimeters. From each of the four corners, a 1 centimeter by 1 centimeter square is cut out. If an open rectangular box is then formed by folding along the dotted lines, what is the volume of the box in cubic centimeters?

(A)   80
(B)   96
(C)   99
(D)   120
(E)   168

17. If the area of the triangle in the figure above is 12, then $k =$

(A) 1
(B) 2
(C) 3
(D) 4
(E) 6

18. For the numbers a, b, c, and d, the average (arithmetic mean) is twice the median. If $a < b < c < d$, $a = -2c$, $b = 0$, and $d = nc$, what is the value of n?

(A)   −5
(B)   −3
(C)   0
(D)   3
(E)   5

19. If x and y are two different positive integers and $x^3 y^2 = 200$, then $xy =$

(A)   5
(B)   6
(C)   10
(D)   25
(E)   40

20. After trimming, a sapling has $\dfrac{9}{10}$ of its original height. If it must grow $\dfrac{9}{10}$ of a foot to regain its original height, what was its original height?

(A)   8
(B)   9
(C)   10
(D)   16
(E)   18

STOP

IF YOU FINISH BEFORE TIME IS CALLED, YOU MAY CHECK YOUR WORK ON THIS SECTION ONLY. DO NOT TURN TO ANY OTHER SECTION IN THE TEST.

Practice Test II

SECTION 3—CRITICAL READING

Time—25 Minutes

24 Items

DIRECTIONS: In this section, solve each item, and choose the correct answer choice. Fill in the corresponding oval on the answer sheet. Answers are on page 668.

Items #1–8: Each item below has one or two blanks, each blank indicating that something has been omitted. Beneath the sentence are five lettered words or sets of words. Choose the word or set of words that best fits the meaning of the sentence as a whole.

Example:

Although its publicity has been -------, the film itself is intelligent, well acted, handsomely produced, and altogether -------.

(A) tasteless . . respectable
(B) extensive . . moderate
(C) sophisticated . . amateur
(D) risqué . . crude
(E) perfect . . spectacular

---

1. Since there are so few conservative thinkers on the committee, their influence on its recommendations is -------.

 (A) monumental
 (B) negligible
 (C) discriminatory
 (D) impractical
 (E) cathartic

2. Laboratory tests that often maim animals and depend solely upon observation to determine results are not only ------- but highly ------- since no two people see the same thing.

 (A) safe . . consistent
 (B) patented . . conclusive
 (C) controversial . . valuable
 (D) gratifying . . explosive
 (E) cruel . . unreliable

3. Execution by lethal injection, although horrifying, is certainly more civilized than the ------- penalty of death by torture or dismemberment.

 (A) pervasive
 (B) viler
 (C) humane
 (D) prolific
 (E) complacent

4. Although vitamins are helpful for maintaining good health, alcohol, caffeine, and other drugs severely ------- their effectiveness, leaving the body's defenses -------.

 (A) augment . . weakened
 (B) reduce . . indelible
 (C) inhibit . . impaired
 (D) confuse . . allied
 (E) duplicate . . activated

GO ON TO THE NEXT PAGE

5. To understand a work of art, it is necessary to place it in ------- context to capture its ------- significance as well as its present meaning.

   (A) a specious . . referential
   (B) a random . . cumulative
   (C) an inventive . . partial
   (D) a historical . . original
   (E) a sophisticated . . international

6. The victim confronted his attacker in the courtroom calmly, with ------- and without apparent ------- although he had been severely traumatized by the incident.

   (A) woe . . composure
   (B) ineptitude . . obstinacy
   (C) tempering . . philanthropy
   (D) equanimity . . rancor
   (E) scorn . . malingering

7. The politician hungered for power; as a result of his -------, he succeeded in winning the election but ------- his closest friends and supporters.

   (A) furtiveness . . dissuaded
   (B) winsomeness . . disgruntled
   (C) malevolence . . mesmerized
   (D) acerbity . . seduced
   (E) cupidity . . alienated

8. With the evidence ------- from numerous X-ray studies, scientists are beginning to form a picture of the atomic structure of the cell.

   (A) remanded
   (B) gleaned
   (C) pilfered
   (D) atrophied
   (E) implored

Items #9–24: Each passage below is followed by one or more items based on its content. Answer the items following each passage on the basis of what is stated or implied in the passage.

Item #9 is based on the following passage.

Technology has the potential to help public television better fulfill its mission to provide programming that emphasizes education, innovation, diversity, and local relevance. Multicasting will make
5 available additional channels for thematically linked program series that are designed for specific segments of the population. For example, a channel for Hispanic families will include local, regional, and national programs and services in Spanish as well as English. A
10 discrete children's service will feature an expanded line-up of Ready-to-Learn programs. With enhanced television, viewers with interactive keypads or remote controls will be able to navigate seamlessly through program elements for additional resources, text,
15 graphics, animation, or audio clips. The possibilities are infinite—limited only by producer and educator imaginations.

9. The author's attitude toward the possibility of using technology to improve public television programming is

   (A) untrusting and skeptical
   (B) indifferent and unsupportive
   (C) cautious and noncommittal
   (D) concerned and wary
   (E) optimistic and enthusiastic

GO ON TO THE NEXT PAGE

Item #10 is based on the following passage.

Mayors, though usually nowhere nearly as powerful, are more important to local residents than either a governor or the President. A mayor works in closer physical proximity to citizens than either the
5 governor or the President. City Hall is no farther from home than the grocery store or place of employment, and it is still possible to reach a mayor or at least a staff member by telephone. Moreover, most citizens have seen and even spoken to the mayor, who spends a lot of
10 time in public; and local newspapers often report on the activities of the mayor, nearly all of which take place in the community and concern local residents. The President may be the Commander-in-Chief, but the mayor is the person who makes sure that the garbage is
15 picked up every week.

10. The author refers to garbage collection in the final sentence in order to

(A) minimize the importance of a mayor's role in international affairs
(B) remind readers that government should serve the needs of the citizens
(C) underscore the importance of the mayor's role as a local official
(D) express skepticism about the ability of local government to function effectively
(E) clarify the distinction among local, state, and national levels of government

Item #11 is based on the following passage.

About 190 million acres of federal forest and rangeland in the lower forty-eight states face a high risk of large-scale insect or disease epidemics and catastrophic fire due to deteriorating ecosystem health
5 and drought. While some experts blame the increased risk of catastrophic wildland fire on long-term drought or on expansion of the wildland-urban interface in the Western United States, the underlying cause is the buildup of forest fuel and changes in vegetation
10 composition over the last century. Unnaturally dense stands competing for limited water and nutrients are at increased risk of unnaturally intense wildland fires and insect or disease epidemic.

11. It can be inferred that the author of the passage disagrees with other experts over the

(A) extent of forest and rangeland that is at risk
(B) threat posed to forest and rangeland by fire, insects, and disease
(C) source of the danger to threatened forest and rangeland
(D) advisability of avoiding insects and disease and unnecessary fires
(E) cost of implementing a program to save threatened forests and rangeland

 GO ON TO THE NEXT PAGE

Item #12 is based on the following passage.

Historical records contain relatively few accounts of ship-whale collisions before 1950. It seems unlikely that collisions were ignored, as the few such incidents that were reported were treated as great curiosities. For
5 example, a whale carried into Baltimore harbor by a tanker in 1940 attracted a crowd of 10,000. The low number of collisions recorded before 1950 might be due to three factors: the depleted whale populations caused by commercial overexploitation; limited traffic
10 in areas frequented by whales; and the small number of ships that were large enough to seriously injure or kill an animal the size of a whale. Additionally, historical records suggest that ship strikes fatal to whales only first occurred late in the 1800s as ships began to reach
15 speeds of 13 to 15 knots. These strikes remained infrequent until about 1950 and then became more frequent through the 1970s as the speed of ships increased.

12. The author believes that all of the following have contributed to the increased number of ship-whale collisions in modern times EXCEPT

(A) faster speeds at which modern ships operate
(B) an increase in the number of ships in whale habitats
(C) a greater number of large ships
(D) a resurgence in the population of whales
(E) a lack of accurate record keeping about collisions

Items #13–14 are based on the following passage.

While the potential benefits of genetic research may seem obvious to the scientific community, it is important to realize that non-scientists may not be aware of these benefits. By being open with
5 communities about the goals and process of their research before it is conducted, scientists can better design studies to yield meaningful data while working within distinct social and cultural contexts. By sharing results with a community after a study has been
10 completed, research participants are more likely to know what to do to seek treatment or how to implement preventive measures to improve their health. In general, well-informed communities that have a window into the research process are likely to
15 maintain a more positive attitude about scientific research—not only about how research is conducted but about what great benefits science can offer humankind.

13. The primary purpose of the passage is to

(A) suggest some ideas to make genetic research more acceptable to the public
(B) describe the public health advantages of engaging in genetic research
(C) outline the negative consequences of invading the privacy of patients
(D) encourage members of the public to participate in scientific research
(E) familiarize laypersons with the design of important scientific studies

14. In lines 8–13, the author implies that research participants who are unfamiliar with the results of a scientific study will be

(A) more likely to work closely with the scientists
(B) less likely to enjoy health benefits from the study
(C) better able to participate in the scientific inquiry
(D) reluctant to volunteer information about personal identity
(E) adequately prepared to make healthcare decisions for others

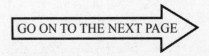
GO ON TO THE NEXT PAGE

Items #15–24 are based on the following passage.

There has been considerable debate on the issue of violence in television and in motion pictures. The following passage explores the question of whether violence in television commercials directed at children is a serious problem.

The violence employed in television commercials directed specifically at children usually appears in the context of fantasy. The impact of the violent portrayals varies according to the number of fantasy cues present in the portrayal. Cartoon violence generally has three such cues (animation, humor, and a remote setting); make-believe violence generally has two cues (humor and a remote setting) and realistic, acted violence generally has only one cue (the viewer's knowledge that the portrayal is fictional).

Most children as young as four years can distinguish these three contexts; however, about one-quarter of four- to eight-year-olds define cartoon violence as a depiction of violence *per se*; about half also perceive make-believe violence in this way; and over half see realistic (acted) violence as violence. Children appear to make these distinctions solely on the basis of the physical fantasy cues. There is no support for the idea that children, especially young children, can differentiate types of violence on a cognitive or rational basis—for example, by justification of the motives for the violent behavior or the goodness of its consequences.

Still, there is very little evidence of direct imitation of television violence by children, though there is evidence that fantasy violence, as well as portrayals of real-life violence, can energize previously learned aggressive responses such as a physical attack on another child during play. It is by no means clear, however, that the violence in a portrayal is solely responsible for this energizing effect. Rather, the evidence suggests that any exciting material triggers subsequent aggressive behavior and that it is the effect of violence that instigates or energizes any subsequent violent behavior.

Moreover, this type of "violent" behavior demonstrated in experiments with children is more likely to reflect either novel play activities or, more typically, a lowering of previously learned play inhibitions, than an increase in socially threatening aggression. In short, cold imitation of violence by children is extremely rare, and the very occasional evidence of direct, imitative associations between television violence and aggressive behavior has been limited to extremely novel and violent acts by teenagers or adults with already established patterns of deviant behavior.

The instigational effect means, in the short term, that exposure to violent portrayals could be dangerous to a child if shortly after the exposure (within 15 to 20 minutes) the child happens to be in a situation that calls for interpersonal aggression as an appropriate response, e.g., an argument between siblings or among peers. This same instigational effect, however, could be produced by other exciting but non-violent television content or by any other excitational source, including, ironically enough, television failure or a parent's turning off the set.

So, there is no convincing causal evidence of any cumulative instigational effects such as more aggressive or violent dispositions in children. In fact, passivity is a more likely long-term result of heavy viewing of television violence. Any instigation of deviant behavior by children seems to be confined to short-term circumstantial effects.

All of this implies that an indictment of fantasy violence in children's programming must rest mainly on a very slight risk that the violent portrayal may be imitated and a somewhat greater risk that the violence may have a short-term instigational effect when circumstances suggest aggression as an appropriate response. The evidence does not warrant the strong conclusions advanced by many critics who tend to use television violence as a scapegoat to draw public attention away from the real causes of violence—causes like abusive spouses and parents and a culture that celebrates violence generally. The violent acts depicted in these television commercials are rarely imitable and the duration of the violence is much too short to have an instigational effect.

15. The primary purpose of the passage is to

(A) correct a popular misconception
(B) outline the history of a phenomenon
(C) propose a solution to a social problem
(D) criticize the work of earlier researchers
(E) offer a theory of criminal behavior

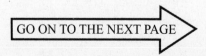 GO ON TO THE NEXT PAGE

16. The passage suggests that which of the following would deter a child from regarding an incident of television violence as real?

   I. Including easily recognized cartoon characters
  II. Setting the action far into the future or past
 III. Having characters laugh at their misfortunes

  (A) I only
  (B) II only
  (C) I and II only
  (D) II and III only
  (E) I, II, and III

17. In line 41, "cold" most nearly means

  (A) chilling
  (B) wrongful
  (C) dangerous
  (D) exact
  (E) crafty

18. In line 52, "appropriate" most nearly means

  (A) acceptable
  (B) desirable
  (C) normal
  (D) learned
  (E) violent

19. It can be inferred that a child who has an argument with a sibling two to three hours after watching fantasy violence on television would

  (A) almost surely be more aggressive than usual
  (B) tend to act out the fantasy violence on the sibling
  (C) probably not be unusually violent or aggressive
  (D) likely lapse into a state of total passivity
  (E) generally, but not always, be more violent

20. The information provided in the second paragraph most strongly supports which of the following conclusions?

  (A) Children judge the morality of an action according to the motives of the actor.
  (B) Realistic, acted violence is more likely than fantasy to trigger violent behavior.
  (C) People are born with a sense of right and wrong but later learn to be violent.
  (D) Children who are unable to distinguish fantasy from reality are more likely to be aggressive.
  (E) Some children are not always able to distinguish between fantasy and reality.

21. In line 57, the author uses the word "ironically" to indicate that

  (A) the outcome of an action may be the opposite of what might be expected
  (B) the moral consequences of an action do not depend on its effects on others
  (C) personal expectations about someone's personality may be wrong
  (D) it is not possible to predict reliably how children will behave
  (E) different theories of child behavior reach contradictory conclusions

22. Which of the following best describes the author's attitude about critics who say that television is an important cause of violent behavior in children?

  (A) qualified endorsement
  (B) contemptuous dismissal
  (C) enthusiastic acceptance
  (D) moderate skepticism
  (E) cautious criticism

GO ON TO THE NEXT PAGE

23. The discussion in lines 11–16 implies that children are more likely to perceive realistic violence than make-believe violence as violence *per se* because of

   (A) a predisposition to react violently to more violent situations
   (B) an inability to recognize the significance of cartoon figures
   (C) the lack of contextual clues accompanying realistic violence
   (D) the failure to appreciate the importance of humor
   (E) a natural inclination to feel a sense of identity with victims

24. In line 60, "cumulative" means

   (A) short-term
   (B) added together
   (C) concealed
   (D) predetermined
   (E) inventive

STOP

IF YOU FINISH BEFORE TIME IS CALLED, YOU MAY CHECK YOUR WORK ON THIS SECTION ONLY. DO NOT TURN TO ANY OTHER SECTION IN THE TEST.

NO TEST MATERIAL ON THIS PAGE

Practice Test II

SECTION 4—MATH
Time—25 Minutes
18 Items

DIRECTIONS: In this section, solve each item, and choose the correct answer choice. Fill in the corresponding oval on the answer sheet. Use any available space for scratchwork. Answers are on page 668.

Notes:

(1) The use of a calculator is permitted. All numbers used are real numbers.

(2) Figures that accompany problems in this test are intended to provide information useful in solving the problems. They are drawn as accurately as possible EXCEPT when it is stated in a specific problem that the figure is not drawn to scale. All figures lie in a plane unless otherwise indicated.

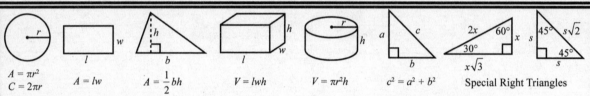

$A = \pi r^2$
$C = 2\pi r$

$A = lw$

$A = \dfrac{1}{2}bh$

$V = lwh$

$V = \pi r^2 h$

$c^2 = a^2 + b^2$

Special Right Triangles

The number of degrees of arc in a circle is 360.

The sum of the measures in degrees of the angles of a triangle is 180.

---

1. If the average (arithmetic mean) of 5, 5, 10, 12, and x is equal to x, what is the value of x?

   (A) 6
   (B) 8
   (C) 10
   (D) 12
   (E) 16

2. If $(3x + 3)(3x + 3) = 0$, what are all the possible values of x?

   (A) -1 only

   (B) $\dfrac{1}{3}$ only

   (C) -1 and 1 only

   (D) 3 only

   (E) -3 and 3 only

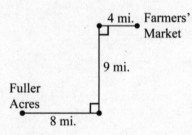

3. The figure above shows the roads that connect Fuller Acres with Farmers' Market. If there existed a direct and straight path from Fuller Acres to Farmers' Market, how much shorter, in miles, would the trip be from Fuller Acres to Farmers' Market?

   (A) 1
   (B) 3
   (C) 4
   (D) 6
   (E) 8

GO ON TO THE NEXT PAGE

4. Let $[x]$ be defined as $[x]=x^2+x$ for all values of x. If $[n]=[n+2]$, what is the value of n?

(A) $-\dfrac{3}{2}$

(B) $-\dfrac{2}{3}$

(C) $\dfrac{2}{3}$

(D) 2

(E) 3

5. If $\dfrac{13t}{7}$ is an integer, then t could be any of the following EXCEPT

(A) −91
(B) −7
(C) 3
(D) 70
(E) 91

6. If $\dfrac{(x+y)}{x}=4$ and $\dfrac{(y+z)}{z}=5$, what is the value of $\dfrac{x}{z}$?

(A) $\dfrac{1}{4}$

(B) $\dfrac{1}{3}$

(C) $\dfrac{3}{4}$

(D) $\dfrac{4}{3}$

(E) $\dfrac{3}{1}$

7. On Monday, Juan withdraws $\dfrac{1}{2}$ of the money in his savings account. On Tuesday, he withdraws another $60, leaving $\dfrac{1}{5}$ of the original amount in the account. How much money was originally in Juan's savings account?

(A) $600
(B) $300
(C) $200
(D) $150
(E) $120

8. A painter is planning to paint a row of three houses, using the colors red, gray, and white. If each house is to be painted a single color, and if the painter must use each of the three colors, how many different ways are there of painting the three houses?

(A) 1
(B) 2
(C) 3
(D) 6
(E) 9

GO ON TO THE NEXT PAGE

Each item requires you to solve an item and mark your answer on a special answer grid. For each item, you should write your answer in the boxes at the top of each column and then fill in the ovals beneath each part of the answer you write. Here are some examples:

Answer: 7/2 or 3.5

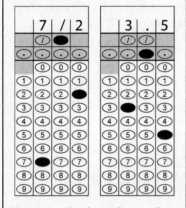

Note: A mixed number such as $3\frac{1}{2}$ must be gridded as 7/2 or as 3.5. If gridded as "31/2," it will be read as "thirty-one halves."

Answer: 325

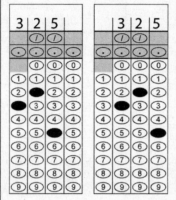

Note: Either position is correct.

Answer: 1/6, .166, or .167

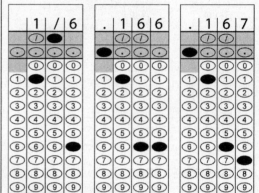

Note: A decimal answer with more digits than the grid can accommodate must be truncated. A decimal such as $.16\overline{6}$ must be gridded as .166 or .167. A less accurate value such as .16 or .17 will be scored as incorrect.

9. If $x = 2$, then $x^2 - 2x =$

10. If 2 pounds of coffee make exactly 7 pots of coffee, how many pots of coffee can be made from a 10-pound bag of coffee?

11. If roses cost $1.00 each and carnations cost $0.50 each, how many more carnations than roses can be purchased for $10.00?

12. If $(x + y)^2 = (x - y)^2 + 4$, then $xy =$

GO ON TO THE NEXT PAGE

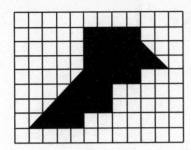

13. In the figure above, each of the small squares has a side of length 1. What is the area of the shaded region?

Estimated Time of Cleaning		
Room	*Number*	*Time per Room*
Bedroom	4	20 minutes
Bathroom	2	30 minutes
Kitchen	1	45 minutes
Living Area	4	25 minutes
Garage	1	75 minutes

16. The table above shows the estimated time by area needed to clean a house. How many <u>hours</u> will it take to clean the whole house?

14. If the points $(-3,-3)$, $(-2,2)$, and $(3,-3)$ are the vertices of a triangle, what is the area of the triangle?

17. If $f(x) = 2x - 5$ and $g(x) = x - 2$, for what value of x does $f(x) = g(x)$?

15. What is the smallest of 5 consecutive integers if the sum of the integers is 55?

18. If the slope of the line that passes through the points $(x, 0)$ and $(3, -4)$ is 2, what is the value of x?

STOP

IF YOU FINISH BEFORE TIME IS CALLED, YOU MAY CHECK YOUR WORK ON THIS SECTION ONLY. DO NOT TURN TO ANY OTHER SECTION IN THE TEST.

Practice Test II

SECTION 6—WRITING
Time—25 Minutes
35 Items

DIRECTIONS: In this section, solve each item, and choose the correct answer choice. Fill in the corresponding oval on the answer sheet. Answers are on page 668.

Items #1–5: The following sentences test correct, effective expression. Each sentence contains an underlined portion, or the entire sentence may be underlined. Following each sentence are five ways of phrasing the underlined portion. Choice (A) repeats the original; the other four choices are different. If you think the original is better than any of the other choices, choose (A); otherwise, choose one of the other choices.

In, choosing answers, follow the conventions of standard written English. Make sure to consider issues of grammar, word choice, sentence construction, and punctuation. Your choice should produce the most effective sentence. It should be clear, precise, and free of ambiguity or awkwardness.

Example:

Allen <u>visiting</u> his cousin in France last summer.

(A) visiting
(B) visited
(C) does visit
(D) a visit
(E) is visiting   

1. Personal style depends not so much on the actual clothing you wear <u>but one's choice of</u> items such as jewelry and make-up.

   (A) but one's choice of
   (B) but one's choosing
   (C) but your choice of
   (D) as your choice of
   (E) as your choosing

2. Kevin has been accepted by the nation's top engineering school, but <u>the tuition cannot be afforded by his family</u>.

   (A) the tuition cannot be afforded by his family
   (B) his family cannot afford to do so
   (C) his family cannot afford to pay the tuition
   (D) his family cannot afford to do it
   (E) affording the tuition is something his family cannot do

3. In Irish step dancing, the peculiar juxtaposition of the rigid torso and arms with rapidly tapping feet <u>is attributed to</u> the concern of parish priests about overly sensual displays.

   (A) is attributed to
   (B) are attributed to
   (C) is attributable for
   (D) attributed to
   (E) attribute

GO ON TO THE NEXT PAGE

4. One of the thrills of bird-watching is catching a fleeting glimpse of <u>a very rare specimen including the Northern Bobwhite or</u> the Red-shouldered Hawk.

(A) a very rare specimen including the Northern Bobwhite or

(B) a very rare specimen such as the Northern Bobwhite or

(C) a very rare specimen such as the Northern Bobwhite and

(D) very rare specimens including the Northern Bobwhite or

(E) very rare specimens such as the Northern Bobwhite or

5. The cause of the declining number of frogs in the swamp is <u>unknown, nor is it known</u> why amphibians in the area exhibit congenital malformations.

(A) unknown, nor is it known

(B) unknown, neither do they know

(C) not known, nor do they know

(D) not known, unknown too is

(E) not known, neither do they

Items #6–25: The following sentences test your knowledge of grammar, usage, diction (choice of words), and idiom. Each sentence contains either no error or a single error. If there is an error, it is underlined and lettered. If the sentence contains an error, choose the one underlined portion that must be changed to produce a correct sentence. If there is no error, choose answer choice (E). In choosing answers, follow the conventions of standard written English.

Example:

The principal <u>asked</u> five of <u>we</u> students
           A   B

<u>to enter</u> the <u>public speaking</u> contest.
   C   D

<u>No error</u>
E

---

6. <u>Being called</u> etymology, the study of word
   A
<u>origins</u> can provide archaeologists with
  B
information <u>about</u> the migration of <u>ancient</u>
         C   D
populations. <u>No error</u>
          E

7. The <u>most important</u> of <u>all</u> economic indicators of
      A   B
prosperity and growth <u>in</u> a given region <u>are</u> new
               C   D
construction. <u>No error</u>
           E

8. The <u>development</u> of new software tools <u>made</u> it
      A   B
possible to communicate <u>easy</u> over the internet,
                   C
and now virtually everyone <u>is</u> connected to the
                     D
web. <u>No error</u>
    E

9. Of the many environmental problems <u>threatening</u>
                           A
animals and plants on various endangered species
<u>lists</u>, destruction of habitat by humans <u>is</u> usually
 B   C
the <u>greatest</u>. <u>No error</u>
    D   E

10. <u>By studying</u> the observed color shift of light
   A
emitted by stars, astronomers <u>can determine</u> the
                       B
speed <u>at which</u> a galaxy <u>is</u> traveling. <u>No error</u>
      C   D   E

GO ON TO THE NEXT PAGE

11. Large-scale withdrawal of savings from banks

    occur when interest rates offered by banks are not
    A   B   C

    competitive with financial returns on other
                                        D

    investments and savers look for higher returns
    D

    elsewhere. No error
              E

12. The runners from the Downtown Athletic Club

    who competed in Monday's track meet were not
    A   B

    only faster but better conditioned than the Greater
              C   D

    City Track Club. No error
    D   E

13. The Democrats and the Republicans now

    dominate the political landscape of America, but
    A   B

    European democracies have numerous smaller
                          C

    ones. No error
    D   E

14. Ceremonial versions of the flag of the United
    A

    States are trimmed with a decorative fringe
          B   C

    resembling some oriental rugs. No error
    D   E

15. A subsidiary of a large corporation that becomes
                                        A

    an independent company may initially be less
                                        B

    profitable because it must cover expenses
                        C

    formally paid by the parent corporation. No error
    D   E

16. In order to be effective as a team, both oxen in a
    A   B

    yoke must pull in the same direction with
         C

    approximate equal force. No error
    D   E

17. Not only is the Granny Smith apple among the
    A   B

    most versatile apples produced today, but they are
                                          C

    also among the most widely cultivated. No error
    D   E

18. An olive, when picked from the trees, is not
                                 A   B

    edible and must first be cured in brine or lye
                          C

    before it can be eaten. No error
            D   E

19. Abraham Lincoln, largely on the strength of their
                    A   B

    performance in the famous Lincoln-Douglas

    debates, became known as one of the greatest
            C

    orators in American history. No error
           D   E

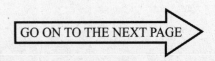

GO ON TO THE NEXT PAGE

20. Monkfish is sometimes <u>called</u> the "poor man's
　　　　　　　　　　　　 A

lobster" <u>because</u> the texture and taste of the fish
　　　　　　　B

<u>resemble</u> the <u>more expensive crustacean.</u>
　　C　　　　　　D

<u>No error</u>
　E

21. After <u>everyone</u> had been eliminated from the
　　　　　　 A

contest except <u>Jim and I</u>, the judge <u>announced</u> a
　　　　　　　　　 B　　　　　　　　 C

10-minute break <u>before the final round</u> would
　　　　　　　　　　 D

begin. <u>No error</u>
　　　　 E

22. After <u>decisively</u> winning several crucial battles
　　　　　 A

during the early part of the war, the general

<u>was appointed</u> commander of the entire combined
　B

armed forces, but he <u>was</u> less successful as a
　　　　　　　　　　 C

commanding general <u>than his earlier campaigns.</u>
　　　　　　　　　　　　 D

<u>No error</u>
　E

23. In 1970, the United States <u>passed</u> a law <u>required</u>
　　　　　　　　　　　　　　　 A　　　　　 B

all men eighteen years <u>or older</u> <u>to register</u> with
　　　　　　　　　　 C　　　　 D

the Selective Service System. <u>No error</u>
　　　　　　　　　　　　　　　 E

24. <u>During</u> the Golden Age of the City College of
　　　 A

New York, when the school <u>produced</u> <u>several</u>
　　　　　　　　　　　　　　 B　　　　 C

<u>Nobel Prize winners</u>, seven out of every 10
　　　　 C

students enrolled at the school <u>had been born</u>
　　　　　　　　　　　　　　　　　 D

outside the United States. <u>No error</u>
　　　　　　　　　　　　　 E

25. George Gershwin <u>composed</u> the soundtracks for
　　　　　　　　　　 A

several <u>films</u>, <u>including</u> *Shall We Dance*, <u>which</u>
　　　 B　　　 C　　　　　　　　　　　 D

his brother, Ira, wrote the lyrics. <u>No error</u>
　　　　　　　　　　　　　　　 E

Items #26–35: The following passages are early
drafts of essays. Some portions of the passages
need to be revised.

Read each passage and answer the items that
follow. Items may be about particular sentences
or parts of sentences, asking you to improve the
word choice or sentence structure. Other items
may refer to parts of the essay or the entire essay,
asking you to consider organization or development. In making your decisions, follow the
conventions of standard written English.

Items #26–30 refer to the following passage.

　　(1) Uranus is a strange planet. **(2)** It lies tipped
over on its side. **(3)** Instead of spinning like a top, it
rolls like a ball along the path of its orbit. **(4)** The
geographic poles are located on either side, one
pointing toward the Sun and the other pointing away.
(5) The clouds in the Uranian atmosphere move in the
same direction that the planet rotates.
　　(6) The moons of Uranus are equally as strange.
(7) Miranda, the one closest to the planet, has huge
markings where terrains of totally different types
appear to have been jammed together. **(8)** On Ariel, the

GO ON TO THE NEXT PAGE

next moon out, the landscape has huge faults; however, there is no evidence of any geologic activity on Ariel. **(9)** Umbriel, the third moon, seems to be painted with a dark substance. **(10)** On one side is the "doughnut," it being a bright, round indentation caused by the impact of a large object. **(11)** Between the orbit of Miranda and the planet's surface are up to one hundred charcoal-colored rings, ringlets, and bands of dust.

(12) Like the clouds in the planet's atmosphere, they circle Uranus in the same direction as the planet rotates. **(13)** That is, they orbit over the top and bottom of the planet rather than around the sides, as the Earth's atmosphere does.

(14) Scientists are confident that they will discover additional planets in our Solar System. **(15)** Until they do it, Uranus will remain the strangest of all.

26. The sentence that best states the main idea of the passage is

    (A) sentence 1
    (B) sentence 5
    (C) sentence 6
    (D) sentence 8
    (E) sentence 14

27. In context, which of the following is the best version of sentence 4 (reproduced below)?

The geographic poles are located on either side, one pointing toward the Sun and the other pointing away.

    (A) (As it is now.)
    (B) Located on either side, the geographic poles are pointing, one toward the Sun and the other away.
    (C) On either side, the geographic poles are located pointing toward the Sun or away.
    (D) The geographic poles are pointing toward and away from the Sun with one being on each side.
    (E) Pointing toward the Sun and away from it are the geographic poles located on either side.

28. In the context of the second paragraph, which revision is most needed in sentence 10?

    (A) Insert "nevertheless" at the beginning.
    (B) Omit the phrase "the impact of."
    (C) Omit the words "it being."
    (D) Change the first comma to a semicolon.
    (E) Insert "was" before the word "caused."

29. Which of the following revisions would most improve the organization of paragraphs two and three?

    (A) Make a new paragraph following sentence 7.
    (B) Make a new paragraph following sentence 9.
    (C) Make sentence 11 the first sentence of paragraph three.
    (D) Make sentence 12 the last sentence of paragraph two.
    (E) Combine paragraphs two and three.

30. Which of the following is the best version of the underlined portion of sentence 15 (reproduced below)?

Until they do it, Uranus will remain the strangest of all.

    (A) (As it is now.)
    (B) Until the discovery, Uranus
    (C) Until others are discovered, Uranus
    (D) Regardless of it, Uranus
    (E) Regardless of that, Uranus

Items #31–35 refer to the following passage.

(1) Do you like music, art, sports or some similar activity? **(2)** Then you would enjoy stamp collecting. **(3)** Stamps offer a look at the major cultural trends that shape our world. **(4)** Plus they honor individual artists, musicians, athletes, and others whose have made important contributions to their fields.

(5) It's easy to start a stamp collection. **(6)** Simply save stamps from letters, packages and postcards, and ask friends and family to save stamps from their mail. **(7)** Neighborhood businesses that get a lot of mail might save their envelopes for you, too.

GO ON TO THE NEXT PAGE

(8) At some point in your collecting, you'll find an old stamp and wonder whether it might be valuable. **(9)** That depends on how rare the stamp is and what condition it is in.

(10) Then, as to condition, a cancelled stamp is one which has been through the postal system and bears a postmark. **(11)** Cancelled stamps are usually the least valuable. **(12)** An unused stamp has no cancellation but may not have any gum on the back. **(13)** A stamp in mint condition is the same as it was when purchased from the post office. **(14)** Mint stamps are usually worth more than unused stamps.

(15) You probably will not find a rare stamp on an envelope that has just been through the mail, but you might find one in the attic or garage in a box with old records and papers. **(16)** Even if you don't find a stamp that is worth a lot of money, you are sure to have a good time looking for them.

31. The function of sentence 1 is to

    (A) ask a rhetorical question to get the reader's attention
    (B) tell the reader the order in which topics will appear
    (C) inform the reader what position the author will take
    (D) show puzzlement about various cultural activities
    (E) assure the reader that the topic is a suitable one

32. In context, sentence 9 could be made more precise by changing

    (A) "that" to "which"
    (B) "that" to "value"
    (C) "that" to "collecting"
    (D) "it" to "they"
    (E) "it" to "them"

33. Which of the following would be the most suitable sentence to insert immediately after sentence 9?

    (A) The value of items such as paintings and books as well as stamps depends on how rare they are.
    (B) Commemorative stamps are issued by the Post Office to celebrate a particular event such as the first moon landing.
    (C) You can get an idea of how rare the stamp is by consulting a buyer's guide at your local library.
    (D) The most valuable stamps are usually sold at auction to wealthy collectors.
    (E) The first postage stamp issued by the United States was a five cent stamp showing Benjamin Franklin.

34. Of the following, which is the best version of sentence 11 (reproduced below)?

    Cancelled stamps are usually the least valuable.

    (A) (As it is now.)
    (B) Cancelled stamps are usually the less valuable.
    (C) Cancelled stamps are usually less valuable than the others.
    (D) Of other stamps, cancelled ones are usually less valuable.
    (E) Of all stamps, cancelled ones are usually less valuable.

35. In the context of the final paragraph, which revision is most needed in sentence 16?

    (A) Change "them" to "one."
    (B) Change "them" to "it."
    (C) Change "if" to "though."
    (D) Change "sure" to "surely."
    (E) Omit "even."

STOP

IF YOU FINISH BEFORE TIME IS CALLED, YOU MAY CHECK YOUR WORK ON THIS SECTION ONLY. DO NOT TURN TO ANY OTHER SECTION IN THE TEST.

Practice Test II

SECTION 7—CRITICAL READING

Time—25 Minutes

24 Items

DIRECTIONS: In this section, solve each item, and choose the correct answer choice. Fill in the corresponding oval on the answer sheet. Answers are on page 668.

Items #1–8: Each item below has one or two blanks, each blank indicating that something has been omitted. Beneath the sentence are five lettered words or sets of words. Choose the word or set of words that best fits the meaning of the sentence as a whole.

Example:

Although its publicity has been -------, the film itself is intelligent, well acted, handsomely produced, and altogether -------.

(A) tasteless . . respectable
(B) extensive . . moderate
(C) sophisticated . . amateur
(D) risqué . . crude
(E) perfect . . spectacular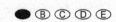

---

1. His seemingly casual and ------- tone ------- a serious concern for the welfare of his clients.

    (A) flippant . . belied
    (B) worried . . displayed
    (C) effective . . disputed
    (D) callous . . betrayed
    (E) contentious . . minimized

2. The actress owed her reputation to her ------- public and not to the ------- reviews that bordered on being cruel.

    (A) diffident . . approbatory
    (B) congenial . . simpering
    (C) trusting . . didactic
    (D) adoring . . scathing
    (E) innocent . . deferential

3. Treason is punishable by death because ------- constitutes a threat to the very ------- of the state.

    (A) perfidy . . survival
    (B) grief . . existence
    (C) veracity . . foundation
    (D) pacifism . . dismantling
    (E) patriotism . . well-being

4. Although scientists have sought to measure time, only writers and poets have truly ------- its quality and our ------- experience of it.

    (A) neglected . . uniform
    (B) understood . . benign
    (C) captured . . ephemeral
    (D) belied . . credulous
    (E) devised . . fractious

5. Although a gala performance, the conducting was -------, and the orchestra less than enthusiastic, but the audience seemed ------- the defects and was enthralled.

    (A) auspicious . . sensitive to
    (B) perfunctory . . oblivious to
    (C) decimated . . mindful of
    (D) voracious . . excited by
    (E) animated . . impaired by

GO ON TO THE NEXT PAGE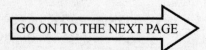

6. Although the language was ------- and considered to be inferior to standard English, Robert Burns wrote his love poetry in the dialect of the Scots.

   (A) interpreted
   (B) belittled
   (C) distinguished
   (D) appreciated
   (E) elevated

7. Given the Secretary of State's ------- the President's foreign policies, he has no choice but to resign.

   (A) reliance upon
   (B) antipathy toward
   (C) pretense of
   (D) support for
   (E) concurrence with

8. In order to ------- the deadline for submitting the research paper, the student tried to ------- additional time from the professor.

   (A) extend . . wheedle
   (B) accelerate . . obtain
   (C) postpone . . forego
   (D) sustain . . imagine
   (E) conceal . . procure

   Items #9–24: Each passage below is followed by one or more items based on its content. Answer the items following each passage on the basis of what is stated or implied in the passage.

Item #9 is based on the following passage.

The Constitutional Convention of 1787 kept its proceedings secret in order to avoid any premature public disclosure of its deliberations. Many historians view that secrecy was the key to the convention's success. Often, we reflexively insist that government should be completely transparent; however, U.S. democracy, the most successful government in all of history, was born behind closed doors.

9. In this context, "transparent" (line 6) means

   (A) simplistic
   (B) uncontroversial
   (C) civilian
   (D) perfect
   (E) open to public view

Item #10 is based on the following passage.

You can tell a lot about a neighborhood by looking at its sidewalks. My sidewalk is not in bad shape, but its lifespan probably caught a huge break this past winter when the jet stream developed a kink and sent much of our usual northwest precipitation south to California.

Concrete is often a symbol of permanence, but rain and ice have an amazing capacity to erode and eventually destroy any kind of mineral-based slab. The ground has a tendency to settle. Trees that are planted too closely to pavement will cause the pavement to shift or snap as the roots grow. Recently, I decided to clean my sidewalk using a power washer. The sidewalk is definitely cleaner, but the high-pressure spray also blasted grit and dirt from every nook and cranny, which makes obvious even the smallest cracks. As the old saying goes: "No good deed goes unpunished."

10. The author of the passage would most likely apply the "old saying" (lines 16–17) to which of the following?

   (A) Purchasing a new washing machine that makes laundry cleaner and brighter
   (B) Depositing money into a savings account that pays a fixed rate of interest each year
   (C) Lowering the value of an antique table by stripping and refinishing the piece
   (D) Substituting milk in a recipe that calls for cream, thereby lowering the fat content
   (E) Redesigning a roadway so that traffic will flow more smoothly

GO ON TO THE NEXT PAGE

Items #11 is based on the following passage.

The Africanized honeybee, popularly known as the "killer bee," is moving into the southern United States. Scientists are not certain how far north the bee will spread, but they do know that it will cause
5 problems wherever it resides in large numbers. This insect, which has been migrating from South America since the 1950s, looks just like a domestic honeybee, but the Africanized bee is a wild bee that is not comfortable being around people or animals. Any
10 colony of bees will defend its hive, but Africanized bees are more likely to sense a threat at greater distances, become more upset with less reason, and sting in much greater numbers.

11. The author implies that the most important difference between the Africanized honeybee and the domestic honeybee is the Africanized bee's

(A) migratory habits
(B) natural range
(C) aggressiveness
(D) ability to sting
(E) reproductive rate

Item #12 is based on the following passage.

Protecting solar access is not a new concept. The Roman Empire had solar access laws, and the Doctrine of Lights protected landowners' rights to light in nineteenth-century Britain. Some U.S. communities
5 adopted solar access regulations in response to the 1970s energy crisis, and many others are now considering solar access protection. The definition of solar access varies slightly from one jurisdiction to another. In San Jose, for instance, solar access is
10 defined as the unobstructed availability of direct sunlight at solar noon on December 21st. In Boulder, Colorado, sunlight must not be obstructed between 10 a.m. and 2 p.m. on December 21st. Other laws specify the percentage of wall area, glazing, or roof that can be
15 shaded by buildings or mature vegetation, and some guidelines even allow for "solar friendly vegetation," such as deciduous trees with branching patterns that allow a maximum amount of winter sunlight to reach the building.

12. The discussion in lines 1–7 is intended primarily to

(A) demonstrate the importance of national leadership on environmental issues
(B) provide the reader with historical background on solar access
(C) point out limitations to proposals that use solar energy devices
(D) correct a common misunderstanding about the distribution of sunlight
(E) start a debate over the need to conserve scarce energy resources

GO ON TO THE NEXT PAGE

Items #13–14 are based on the following passage.

Amphibian malformations have been reported in 44 states since 1996. These deformities include extra legs, extra eyes, misshapen or incompletely formed limbs, limb formation in anatomically inappropriate
5 places, missing limbs, and missing eyes. While anatomical deformities are a natural phenomenon within virtually all species, the widespread occurrence of these deformities and the relatively high frequency of malformations within local populations concern
10 wildlife biologists. Most agree that the rates of deformities far exceed what can be considered natural, and these biologists are currently investigating several factors—including parasites, contaminants, and UV radiation—which may be causing the deformities. It is
15 important to keep in mind that the cause of deformities in one region may, or may not, be responsible for those in another area. Alternatively, a combination of factors may be the cause of malformation occurrences across the country.

13. The author regards the research on the causes of amphibian malformations as

(A) haphazard
(B) exhaustive
(C) contradictory
(D) unreliable
(E) inconclusive

14. Which of the following words, when substituted for "natural" in line 11, best preserves the meaning of the original?

(A) elevated
(B) uncontrived
(C) normal
(D) insignificant
(E) frequent

Items #15–24 are based on the following passage.

The following passage discusses the effects of microwave radiation on the body temperature of an organism.

Behavior is one of two general responses available to endothermic (warm-blooded) species for the regulation of body temperature, the other being innate mechanisms of heat production and heat loss.
5 Human beings rely primarily on the first to provide a hospitable thermal microclimate for themselves in which the transfer of heat between the body and the environment is accomplished with minimal involvement of innate mechanisms of heat production
10 and loss. Thermoregulatory behavior *anticipates* hyperthermia, and the organism adjusts its behavior to avoid becoming hyperthermic: it removes layers of clothing, it goes for a cool swim, etc. The organism can also respond to changes in the temperature of the body
15 core, as is the case during exercise; but such responses result from the direct stimulation of thermoreceptors distributed widely within the central nervous system, and the ability of these mechanisms to help the organism adjust to gross changes in its environment is
20 limited.

Until recently, it was assumed that organisms respond to microwave radiation in the same way that they respond to temperature changes that are caused by other forms of radiation. After all, the argument runs,
25 microwaves are radiation and heat body tissues. This theory ignores the fact that the stimulus to a behavioral response is normally a temperature change that occurs at the surface of the organism. The thermoreceptors that prompt behavioral changes are located within the
30 first millimeter of the skin's surface, but the energy of a microwave field may be selectively deposited in deep tissues, effectively bypassing these thermoreceptors, particularly if the field is at near-resonant frequencies. The resulting temperature profile may well be a kind of
35 reverse thermal gradient in which the deep tissues are warmed more than those of the surface. Since the heat is not conducted outward to the surface to stimulate the appropriate receptors, the organism does not appreciate this stimulation in the same way that it does heating
40 and cooling of the skin. In theory, the internal organs of a human being or an animal could be quite literally cooked well-done before the animal even realizes that the balance of its thermomicroclimate has been disturbed.

GO ON TO THE NEXT PAGE

45   Until a few years ago, microwave irradiations at equivalent plane-wave power densities of about 100 mW/cm^2 were considered unequivocally to produce "thermal" effects; irradiations within the range of 10 to 100 mW/cm^2 might or might not produce "thermal"
50 effects; while effects observed at power densities below 10 mW/cm^2 were assumed to be "nonthermal" in nature. Experiments have shown this to be an oversimplification, and a recent report suggests that fields as weak as 1mW/cm^2 can be thermogenic. When
55 the heat generated in the tissues by an imposed radio frequency (plus the heat generated by metabolism) exceeds the heat-loss capabilities of the organism, the thermoregulatory system has been compromised. Yet, surprisingly, not long ago, an increase in the internal
60 body temperature was regarded merely as "evidence" of a thermal effect.

15. The author is primarily concerned with

(A) showing that behavior is a more effective way of controlling bodily temperature than innate mechanisms

(B) criticizing researchers who will not discard their theories about the effects of microwave radiation on organisms

(C) demonstrating that effects of microwave radiation are different from those of other forms of radiation

(D) analyzing the mechanism by which an organism maintains its bodily temperature in a changing thermal environment

(E) discussing the importance of thermoreceptors in the control of the internal temperature of an organism

16. In line 4, the word "innate" most nearly means

(A) natural
(B) voluntary
(C) reflexive
(D) acquired
(E) reproductive

17. The author makes which of the following points about innate mechanisms for heat production?

 I. They are governed by thermoreceptors inside the body of the organism rather than at the surface.
 II. They are a less effective means of compensating for gross changes in temperature than behavioral strategies.
 III. They are not affected by microwave radiation.

(A) I only
(B) I and II only
(C) I and III only
(D) II and III only
(E) I, II, and III

18. The author suggests that the proponents of the theory that microwave radiation acts on organisms in the same way as other forms of radiation based their conclusions primarily on

(A) laboratory research
(B) unfounded assumption
(C) control group surveys
(D) deductive reasoning
(E) causal investigation

19. In line 38, the word "appreciate" most nearly means

(A) esteem
(B) prefer
(C) enjoy
(D) notice
(E) regard

GO ON TO THE NEXT PAGE

20. The author's strategy in lines 40–44 is to

(A) introduce a hypothetical example to
dramatize a point
(B) propose an experiment to test a scientific
hypothesis
(C) cite a case study to illustrate a general
contention
(D) produce a counterexample to disprove an
opponent's theory
(E) speculate about the probable consequences of
a scientific phenomenon

21. In line 58, the word "compromised" most nearly
means

(A) agreed
(B) permitted
(C) endangered
(D) settled
(E) adjusted

22. The tone of the passage can best be described as

(A) genial and conversational
(B) alarmed and disparaging
(C) facetious and cynical
(D) scholarly and noncommittal
(E) analytical and concerned

23. The author is primarily concerned with

(A) pointing out weaknesses in a popular
scientific theory
(B) developing a hypothesis to explain a
scientific phenomenon
(C) reporting on new research on the effects of
microwave radiation
(D) criticizing the research methods of earlier
investigators
(E) clarifying ambiguities in the terminology
used to describe a phenomenon

24. Which of the following would be the most logical
topic for the author to take up in the paragraph
following the final paragraph of the selection?

(A) A suggestion for new research to be done on
the effects of microwaves on animals and
human beings
(B) An analysis of the differences between
microwave radiation and other forms of
radiation
(C) A proposal that the use of microwave
radiation be prohibited because it is
dangerous
(D) A survey of the literature on the effects of
microwave radiation on human beings
(E) A discussion of the strategies used by various
species to control hyperthermia.

STOP

**IF YOU FINISH BEFORE TIME IS CALLED, YOU MAY CHECK YOUR WORK ON THIS SECTION
ONLY. DO NOT TURN TO ANY OTHER SECTION IN THE TEST.**

Practice Test II

SECTION 8—MATH
Time—20 Minutes
16 Items

DIRECTIONS: In this section, solve each item, and choose the correct answer choice. Fill in the corresponding oval on the answer sheet. Use any available space for scratchwork. Answers are on page 669.

Notes:

(1) The use of a calculator is permitted. All numbers used are real numbers.

(2) Figures that accompany problems in this test are intended to provide information useful in solving the problems. They are drawn as accurately as possible EXCEPT when it is stated in a specific problem that the figure is not drawn to scale. All figures lie in a plane unless otherwise indicated.

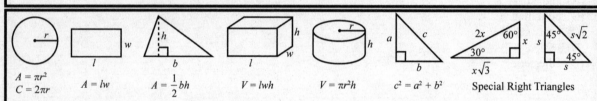

$A = \pi r^2$
$C = 2\pi r$
$A = lw$
$A = \frac{1}{2}bh$
$V = lwh$
$V = \pi r^2 h$
$c^2 = a^2 + b^2$
Special Right Triangles

The number of degrees of arc in a circle is 360.
The sum of the measures in degrees of the angles of a triangle is 180.

Box	Dimensions
A	$2 \times 3 \times 4$
B	$2 \times 3 \times 3$
C	$3 \times 4 \times 5$
D	$5 \times 4 \times 2$
E	$4 \times 4 \times 2$

1. According to the table above, which box has the greatest volume?

(A) A
(B) B
(C) C
(D) D
(E) E

2. The product of an even positive number and an odd negative number is

(A) negative and even
(B) negative and odd
(C) negative and either even or odd
(D) positive and odd
(E) positive and even

3. If w, x, y, and z are positive numbers, each of the following expressions equals $w(x + y + z)$ EXCEPT

(A) $wx + wy + wz$
(B) $wx + w(y + z)$
(C) $w(x + y) + wz$
(D) $w(x + z) + wy$
(E) $w(xy) + w(yz)$

GO ON TO THE NEXT PAGE

4. Originally, a group of 11 students was supposed to equally share a cash prize. If 1 more student is added to the group and the 12 students share the prize equally, then each new share is worth what fraction of each original share?

(A) $\dfrac{1}{12}$

(B) $\dfrac{1}{11}$

(C) $\dfrac{1}{10}$

(D) $\dfrac{10}{11}$

(E) $\dfrac{11}{12}$

Having X and Y	10
Having X but not Y	30
Having Y but not X	40
Having neither X nor Y	20

6. The table above gives the distribution of two genetic characteristics, X and Y, in a population of 100 subjects. What is the ratio of the number of people having characteristic X to the number of people having characteristic Y?

(A) $1:3$
(B) $1:2$
(C) $2:3$
(D) $4:5$
(E) $3:2$

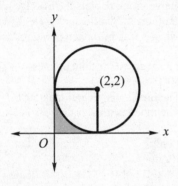

5. In the figure above, the center of the circle has coordinates $(2,2)$. What is the area of the shaded portion of the figure?

(A) $2-\pi$
(B) $4-\pi$
(C) $8-2\pi$
(D) $8-\pi$
(E) $16-4\pi$

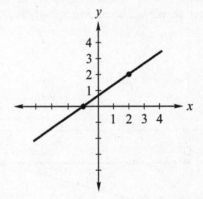

7. What is the linear equation for the line through points $(-1,0)$ and $(2,2)$ in the coordinate graph above?

(A) $y=\dfrac{2x}{3}-\dfrac{2}{3}$

(B) $y=\dfrac{2x}{3}-3$

(C) $y=\dfrac{2x}{3}+\dfrac{2}{3}$

(D) $y=x+\dfrac{2}{3}$

(E) $y=3x+2$

GO ON TO THE NEXT PAGE

8. A 10,000 bushel shipping compartment is being filled with grain by a pipe at a constant rate. After 20 minutes, the container is filled to 40 percent of its capacity. After another 15 minutes, the container will be filled to what percent of its capacity?

(A) 55%
(B) 60%
(C) $66\frac{2}{3}$%
(D) 70%
(E) 75%

9. A bowling team has 5 members, 40 percent of whom averaged over 230 this fall. Of those team members who averaged more than 230, 50 percent had scores averaging 250 or better. How many people had scores averaging below 250?

(A) 1
(B) 2
(C) 3
(D) 4
(E) 5

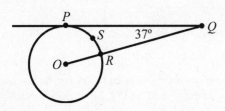

10. In the figure above, with O as the center of the circle, what is the degree measure of minor $\overarc{PSR}$?

(A) 30°
(B) 43°
(C) 53°
(D) 86°
(E) 90°

Average Noon Temperatures
in Seattle During 1994

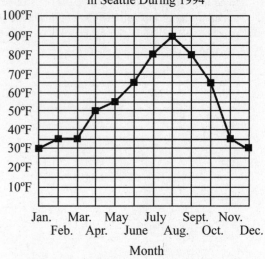

Month

11. The above graph depicts the average monthly temperatures in Seattle during 1994. Which of the following is true of the temperatures?

  I. The average (arithmetic mean) is greater than 50°F.
  II. The median is greater than 50°F.
  III. The mode is greater than 50°F.

(A) I only
(B) II only
(C) I and II only
(D) II and III only
(E) I, II, and III

12. What is the solution set for k in the equation $\left| k - \frac{1}{8} \right| = \left| \frac{1}{3} - \frac{1}{2} \right|$?

(A) $\left\{ -\frac{1}{24}, \frac{7}{24} \right\}$

(B) $\left\{ -\frac{1}{24}, \frac{1}{8} \right\}$

(C) $\left\{ \frac{1}{8}, \frac{1}{24} \right\}$

(D) $\left\{ \frac{7}{24}, \frac{1}{24} \right\}$

(E) $\left\{ \frac{1}{3}, \frac{1}{7} \right\}$

GO ON TO THE NEXT PAGE

Age Difference for Children in Five Families				
Family	*Oldest*	*Age*	*Youngest*	*Age*
LaTours	Joan	15	Ed	12
Pickett	Harold	17	Claire	8
Thibault	Rene	16	Henri	3
Barber	Fred	9	Gloria	7
Newcomb	Danny	12	Syd	8

13. The table above shows the ages for the oldest and youngest children in five different families. If "Difference" is defined as the age of the oldest child minus the age of the youngest child, then what is the median of the "Difference" for the five families?

    (A)   1
    (B)   3
    (C)   4
    (D)   9
    (E) 13

14. If $x^{\frac{1}{4}} = 20$, then $x =$

    (A) $\sqrt[4]{20}$
    (B) 5
    (C) 80
    (D) 2,000
    (E) 160,000

15. In the coordinate plane, the graph of which of the following lines is perpendicular to the graph of line $y = \frac{3}{2}x + 1$?

    (A) $y = \frac{3}{2}x - 1$

    (B) $y = \frac{3}{4}x + 1$

    (C) $y = \frac{3}{4}x - 1$

    (D) $y = -\frac{2}{3}x + 2$

    (E) $y = -\frac{3}{2}x - 1$

16. A tank contains g gallons of water. Water flows into the tank by one pipe at the rate of m gallons per minute, and water flows out by another pipe at the rate of n gallons per minute. If $n > m$, how many minutes will it take to empty the tank?

    (A) $\dfrac{(g - m)}{n}$

    (B) $\dfrac{g}{(m - n)}$

    (C) $\dfrac{(n - g)}{m}$

    (D) $\dfrac{(n - m)}{g}$

    (E) $\dfrac{g}{(n - m)}$

STOP

IF YOU FINISH BEFORE TIME IS CALLED, YOU MAY CHECK YOUR WORK ON THIS SECTION ONLY. DO NOT TURN TO ANY OTHER SECTION IN THE TEST.

Practice Test II

SECTION 9—CRITICAL READING

Time—20 Minutes

19 Items

DIRECTIONS: In this section, solve each item, and choose the correct answer choice. Fill in the corresponding oval on the answer sheet. Answers are on page 669.

<u>Items #1–4:</u> Each item below has one or two blanks, each blank indicating that something has been omitted. Beneath the sentence are five lettered words or sets of words. Choose the word or set of words that best fits the meaning of the sentence as a whole.

Example:

Although its publicity has been -------, the film itself is intelligent, well acted, handsomely produced, and altogether -------.

(A) tasteless . . respectable
(B) extensive . . moderate
(C) sophisticated . . amateur
(D) risqué . . crude
(E) perfect . . spectacular   ●Ⓑ Ⓒ Ⓓ Ⓔ

---

1. According to recent studies, prices in supermarkets are considerably higher in the inner city, thus ------- the poor who receive assistance to buy the food.

   (A) reprimanding
   (B) intimidating
   (C) alleviating
   (D) assuaging
   (E) exploiting

2. Legislation to stop smoking in public places has been ------- by some as a move to save lives, while it is ------- by the tobacco industry, which calls the action "alarmist."

   (A) heralded . . condemned
   (B) thwarted . . buffered
   (C) initiated . . condoned
   (D) prejudiced . . supported
   (E) extolled . . elicited

3. Joyce's novel *Finnegans Wake* continues to ------- critics, including those who find it incomprehensible and call it -------.

   (A) appall . . genial
   (B) enthrall . . nonsensical
   (C) baffle . . transparent
   (D) bore . . compelling
   (E) entertain . . monotonous

4. Jazz is an American art form that is now ------- in Europe through the determined efforts of ------- in France, Scandinavia, and Germany.

   (A) foundering . . governments
   (B) diminishing . . musicians
   (C) appreciated . . opponents
   (D) waning . . novices
   (E) flourishing . . expatriates

GO ON TO THE NEXT PAGE ⟹

Items #5–19: The two passages below are followed by items based on their content and the relationship between the two passages. Answer the items on the basis of what is stated or implied in the passages and in any introductory material that may be provided.

The passages are adapted from remarks by college professors and experts in the Tibetan language and culture made during a roundtable discussion on the political, linguistic, and cultural challenges faced by Tibet.

Passage 1

There is a real threat of extinction to the Tibetan language and the Tibetan culture within two or, at the most, three generations. Languages convey very specific social and cultural behaviors and ways of
5 thinking. As a result, the extinction of the Tibetan language would have tremendous consequences for the Tibetan culture. The culture cannot be preserved without it.

Why is it important to preserve the language and
10 its culture? Tibetan language and culture are original. Alongside Sanskrit, Chinese, and Japanese literatures, Tibetan literature is one of the oldest, most original, and greatest in volume. Language is also important for the economic survival of Tibetans. Many rural
15 Tibetans, whether nomads or peasants, are almost like foreigners in their own country; they do not have the linguistic ability to find jobs. When they come to the cities, their culture is marginalized and devalued. This leads also to the marginalization and devaluation of the
20 people themselves. The language and culture are also extremely important for the secularization and modernization of Tibetan society. Right now, many young Tibetans go to monasteries because that is one of the few places left for traditional study. If they could
25 study their own culture in middle school, a lot of them would prefer to study in lay schools.

Think about 5 million Tibetan people surrounded by more than 1.5 billion Chinese-speaking people, and you will understand the nature of the threat. Right now,
30 the Tibetan people are not really allowed to have meetings in Tibetan. Even when 20 or more Tibetans are meeting together, they speak in Chinese. All middle school education is in Chinese. Even though Tibetan books and manuals exist for mathematics, physics, and
35 chemistry, teachers will not use them. The Chinese government is not unaware of this situation and has enacted regulations protecting the Tibetan language, a so-called "minority language," within the People's Republic of China. This is encouraging, but at the same
40 time, it shows that the need to act is urgent.

The goal is to promote the Tibetan language and culture in the educational system and to establish a real Tibetan-Chinese bilingual society, not as it is now: a monolingual Chinese society. This goal implies a need
45 for advertising the new Chinese law and exerting pressure so that it is really implemented. Promoting standard, spoken Tibetan is also extremely important because there is a high rate of unemployment and an incredible level of illiteracy. It is important to promote
50 standard, spoken Tibetan by funding projects that will publish classical texts in the vernacular. There are some very concrete ways in which people from Western countries can contribute to the promotion of the Tibetan language and culture. For example,
55 universities and arts foundations should sponsor literary prizes and awards for Tibetan writers. Artists and writers who live in Western countries should travel to Tibet, interacting with the people and organizing cultural festivals. Other ways to promote Tibetan
60 language and culture include: donating to public radio stations and encouraging stations to broadcast the classics of Tibetan and foreign literature; paying Tibetan teachers to compile tapes of traditional music and folk tales that have not yet been recorded; and
65 developing calligraphy and Tibetan spelling competitions. These are all very concrete steps that will encourage Tibetans to believe that their language and culture are not only alive but thriving.

Passage 2

In the first place, it is important to understand that
70 Tibetan is not a language in the way that modern English is a language, with a range of dialects so that speakers easily understand each other in accordance with common vocabulary, grammar, and so forth. There is no standard Tibetan. There is, however, an
75 emergent proto-standard Tibetan that is spoken widely in the diasporic community.* This language derives from the Lhasa language, a good basis for a standard Tibetan that could be used across Tibet in addition to regional dialects.

80 Second, literary Tibetan, typically referred to as classical Tibetan, has a long and distinguished tradition going back at least to the seventh century. Classical

 GO ON TO THE NEXT PAGE

Tibetan is remarkably conservative in terms of spelling, grammar usage, and vocabulary. Someone
85 who is conversant in modern classical Tibetan can actually pick up tenth-century texts and read them fluently, something which is not at all true of English. Unfortunately, most Tibetan dialects are not equally conservative in pronunciation and vocabulary. As a
90 result, classical Tibetan is dramatically divergent from spoken Tibetan, which makes classical Tibetan unnecessarily difficult to learn. Also, many standard colloquial spoken terms have no standardized spelling or use in literary Tibetan. A modern literary Tibetan
95 language has begun to emerge in creative writing, newspapers, and the like, but this modern literary Tibetan has yet to become a fully transregional vernacular: a literary Tibetan that can be easily understood, easily learned, and used for daily
100 communications.

   Third, Tibetans who are fluent in spoken Tibetan often lack specific colloquial competencies not because they are pressured to switch over to Chinese, but because often they are actually unable to use Tibetan in
105 specific professional or intellectual environments. They do not know the vocabulary. When speaking of computer science, mathematics, biology, or certain governmental activities, they literally do not know how to talk. Thus, it is important to promote the use of
110 Tibetan equivalents to Chinese terms in these professional areas.

   Consequently, why do the Tibetans not give up Tibetan altogether and simply speak Chinese? Everyone could become, in two or three generations,
115 native speakers of Chinese. This shift to Chinese would be damaging because it would create a traumatic rift between the way of life for modern Tibetans and their 1,300-year literary and cultural history. A people's sense of identity, place, and time is inextricably bound
120 up with its language. By losing the Tibetan language, the specifically Tibetan identity and world, with its culture, insights, values and behaviors, is essentially consigned to the past.

   Within two or three decades, it is possible that the
125 Tibetan language will be all but extinct, surviving only as the province of a few isolated monasteries. There is, however, another possibility in which standard Tibetan could become widely spoken and again become a medium for educational and commercial context. A
130 newly generated vernacular Tibetan could become one that is meaningful in educational and personal context.

*A diasporic community refers to Tibetans and their descendants living outside of Tibet.

5. The author develops Passage 1 primarily by

   (A) asking a question and then exploring several possible answers
   (B) posing a dilemma and then showing that one of its assumptions is false
   (C) outlining a problem and then revealing that it is worse than thought
   (D) proposing a plan of action and then criticizing the plan
   (E) describing a situation and its causes and suggesting some solutions

6. According to Passage 1, many rural Tibetans have difficulty finding jobs because

   (A) the unemployment rate in the cities is higher than in the rural areas
   (B) they lack any skills that would make them employable
   (C) they are not able to speak a language that is understood by employers
   (D) they insist on preserving traditional Tibetan values
   (E) employers are primarily interested in hiring Chinese workers

7. It can be inferred from the comparison of lay middle schools and monasteries as educational centers (lines 22–26) that

   (A) monasteries are better equipped to provide students with valuable job skills than are lay schools
   (B) the preference of many students for monastery schools retards the secularization of Tibetan society
   (C) monasteries in Tibet are doing a better job than lay schools at teaching mathematics and physical sciences
   (D) monasteries are a powerful force in Tibet for the secularization and modernization of the country
   (E) lay schools have become less popular as monasteries have strengthened their cultural studies programs

GO ON TO THE NEXT PAGE

8. The author of Passage 1 thinks that the regulations passed by the Chinese government to protect the Tibetan language

    (A) are unlikely to be effective in encouraging the use of Tibetan rather than Chinese
    (B) will almost certainly prevent Chinese from replacing Tibetan as the dominant culture
    (C) were secretly intended to undermine the use of Tibetan in public discourse
    (D) could help preserve Tibetan culture if aggressively implemented
    (E) should be repealed in favor of laws intended to promote a monolingual society

9. In line 51, the word "vernacular" means

    (A) bilingualism
    (B) classical text
    (C) ordinary language
    (D) unpublished works
    (E) handwritten documents

10. The suggestions by the author of Passage 1 for moving toward a bilingual society in Tibet include all of the following EXCEPT

    (A) programs to lower the unemployment rate
    (B) awards for Tibetan writers
    (C) paying teachers to preserve folk culture
    (D) competitions centered on Tibetan language
    (E) organizing cultural festivals

11. In line 75, the word "emergent" most nearly means

    (A) uniform
    (B) widespread
    (C) modern
    (D) developing
    (E) flexible

12. In Passage 2, the comparison of English and Tibetan suggests that written English

    (A) is a more difficult language to learn than classical Tibetan
    (B) consists of fewer distinct dialects than modern Tibetan
    (C) displays greater variation of regional form than proto-Tibetan
    (D) has changed more over the centuries than classical Tibetan
    (E) is not directly related to modern culture in English speaking regions

13. As used in this context, the word "conservative" (line 83) means

    (A) illiterate
    (B) limited
    (C) subordinate
    (D) collective
    (E) stable

14. The author of Passage 2 develops the first three paragraphs by

    (A) listing the advantages of classical Tibetan over more modern versions
    (B) describing a series of problems that affect Tibetan and possible solutions to each
    (C) discussing various attempts to restore Tibetan to the status it enjoyed in classical times
    (D) providing examples of features of the Tibetan language that make its mastery difficult
    (E) challenging members of the diasporic Tibetan community to modernize Tibetan

GO ON TO THE NEXT PAGE

15. The author of Passage 2 poses the question at the beginning of the fourth paragraph to

    (A) suggest that the problems outlined earlier are less pressing than they might otherwise seem
    (B) show the similar roles played by Chinese and Tibetan in Tibetan society
    (C) introduce a discussion of what could happen to Tibetan culture if the language is simply abandoned
    (D) shift the discussion from Tibetan language to Tibetan culture
    (E) signal a shift from a discussion of abstract concerns to specific problems

16. It can be inferred that both authors agree that

    (A) the classical form of a language is more important than its modern version
    (B) it is possible to study language without learning about culture
    (C) language is essential to the survival of a culture
    (D) Tibetan and Chinese express similar social and cultural norms
    (E) certain languages are better suited to modern discourse than others

17. The attitude of the two authors toward the possibility of the continued survival of Tibetan is best summarized by which of the following?

    (A) Both believe that Tibetan and its culture are most likely to disappear entirely within a relatively few years.
    (B) Both believe that Tibetan and its culture are threatened but could survive if steps are taken to preserve them.
    (C) The author of Passage 1 believes that Tibetan language and culture cannot survive while the author of Passage 2 believes that they can.
    (D) The author of Passage 2 believes that Tibetan language and culture cannot survive while the author of Passage 1 believes that they can.
    (E) The authors agree that Tibetan language and culture are still vital and will continue as they have for centuries regardless of other events.

18. Both authors provide information to help answer each of the following questions EXCEPT

    (A) What would be the consequences of Tibetans abandoning their language?
    (B) What is the significance of Tibetan language and culture?
    (C) What events or actions might help preserve Tibetan as a language?
    (D) How long is Tibetan likely to survive as a viable language?
    (E) How does the Tibetan language compare in various ways with English?

 GO ON TO THE NEXT PAGE

19. Which of the following best describes the relationship between the analyses of Tibetan presented by the two authors?

   (A) The author of Passage 1 emphasizes the political problems facing Tibetan while the author of Passage 2 focuses on features of the language itself.

   (B) The author of Passage 1 highlights the strengths of classical Tibetan while the author of Passage 2 describes the advantages of modern Tibetan.

   (C) The author of Passage 1 writes about the development of written Tibetan while the author of Passage 2 is primarily concerned with the spoken version of the language.

   (D) The author of Passage 1 treats language as a manifestation of culture while the author of Passage 2 regards language as existing independently of culture.

   (E) The author of Passage 1 identifies several misunderstandings about the Tibetan language while the author of Passage 2 advocates specific plans to improve Tibetan.

STOP

IF YOU FINISH BEFORE TIME IS CALLED, YOU MAY CHECK YOUR WORK ON THIS SECTION ONLY. DO NOT TURN TO ANY OTHER SECTION IN THE TEST.

Practice Test II

SECTION 10—WRITING
Time—10 Minutes
14 Items

DIRECTIONS: In this section, solve each item, and choose the correct answer choice. Fill in the corresponding oval on the answer sheet. Answers are on page 669.

Items #1–14: The following sentences test correct, effective expression. Each sentence contains an underlined portion, or the entire sentence may be underlined. Following each sentence are five ways of phrasing the underlined portion. Choice (A) repeats the original; the other four choices are different. If you think the original is better than any of the other choices, choose (A); otherwise, choose one of the other choices.

In choosing answers, follow the conventions of standard written English. Make sure to consider issues of grammar, word choice, sentence construction, and punctuation. Your choice should produce the most effective sentence. It should be clear, precise, and free of ambiguity or awkwardness.

Example:

Allen <u>visiting</u> his cousin in France last summer.

(A) visiting
(B) visited
(C) does visit
(D) a visit
(E) is visiting

---

1. More and more fashion-conscious dressers are asking themselves <u>if it is</u> moral to wear clothing made from the skin of an animal.

    (A) if it is
    (B) about if it is
    (C) whether it is
    (D) as to whether or not it is
    (E) about whether it is

2. <u>When used together, the cosmetic company claims that its products enhance the appearance of the skin by preventing blemishes and reducing signs of aging.</u>

    (A) When used together, the cosmetic company claims that its products enhance the appearance of the skin by preventing blemishes and reducing signs of aging.
    (B) The cosmetic company claims that, when used together, the appearance of the skin will be enhanced by the products by their preventing blemishes and reducing signs of aging.
    (C) When used together, the products will enhance the appearance of the skin, also preventing blemishes and reducing signs of aging, or so the company claims.
    (D) According to the cosmetic company, when its products are used together, they will enhance the appearance of the skin, prevent blemishes, and reduce signs of aging.
    (E) According to the cosmetic company, when its products are used together, the appearance of the skin will be enhanced and blemishes will be prevented reducing the signs of aging.

GO ON TO THE NEXT PAGE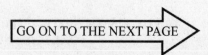

3. Digital music files will soon become the most common form of recorded <u>music, eventually replacing</u> compact discs altogether.

   (A) music, eventually replacing
   (B) music, and eventually replacing
   (C) music that eventually replaces
   (D) music by eventually replacing
   (E) music to eventually replace

4. <u>Appearing to be</u> the only candidate whose views would be acceptable to its membership, the Youth Caucus finally endorsed George Avery for City Council.

   (A) Appearing to be
   (B) Seeming to be
   (C) Because he appeared to be
   (D) Because he seemed
   (E) Being

5. <u>Arturo Toscanini, well-known for his sharp tongue as well as his musical genius, once cowed a famous singer</u> with the remark that there were for him no stars except those in the heavens.

   (A) Arturo Toscanini, well-known for his sharp tongue as well as his musical genius, once cowed a famous singer
   (B) Arturo Toscanini, well-known for his sharp tongue as well than his musical genius, cowed once a famous singer
   (C) Arturo Toscanini's well-known sharp tongue as well as his musical genius once cowed a famous singer
   (D) Arturo Toscanini, who had a well-known sharp tongue as well as musical genius, once cowed a famous singer
   (E) Well-known for his sharp tongue as well as his musical genius, a famous singer was once cowed by Arturo Toscanini

6. Although Beverly Sills never achieved superstar status in Europe or at the Metropolitan Opera, <u>yet she was singing major roles at the City Opera during 20 years</u>.

   (A) yet she was singing major roles at the City Opera during 20 years
   (B) she did sing major roles at the City Opera during 20 years
   (C) she sang major roles at the City Opera for 20 years
   (D) but she sang major roles at the City Opera for 20 years
   (E) yet for 20 years major roles had been sung by her at the City Opera

7. Although Mary Ann is not a great <u>scholar, neither has she published any books, she has and always will be</u> a great teacher and well-loved by her students.

   (A) scholar, neither has she published any books, she has and always will be
   (B) scholar, nor having published any books, she has been and always will be
   (C) scholar and she hasn't published any books, she has been and always will be
   (D) scholar nor published any books, still she had been and always will be
   (E) scholar nor has she published any books, but she has been and always will be

8. Puritan fanatics brought to civil and military affairs a coolness of judgment and mutability of purpose that some writers have thought inconsistent with their religious zeal, <u>but which was in fact a natural outgrowth of it</u>.

   (A) but which was in fact a natural outgrowth of it
   (B) but which were in fact a natural outgrowth of it
   (C) but which were in fact natural outgrowths of it
   (D) but it was in fact a natural outgrowth of them
   (E) which was in fact a natural outgrowth of it

GO ON TO THE NEXT PAGE

9. Unlike the French, the German art songs are dramatic and sometimes almost operatic.

   (A) Unlike the French, the German art songs are dramatic and sometimes almost operatic.
   (B) Unlike the French art songs, the German art songs are dramatic and sometimes almost operatic.
   (C) The German art songs, unlike the French, are dramatic and sometimes almost operatic.
   (D) The German art songs are dramatic and sometimes almost operatic, unlike the French.
   (E) The German art songs, which are dramatic and sometimes almost operatic, are unlike the French.

10. The earliest texts in cuneiform script are about 5,000 years old, having antedated the use of the first alphabets by some 1,500 years.

   (A) old, having antedated the use
   (B) old, having antedated the invention
   (C) old, antedating the use
   (D) old and antedate the use
   (E) old and antedate the invention

11. Henry David Thoreau was a philosopher as well as a naturalist; Gandhi read Civil Disobedience in 1906 and made it a major document in his struggle for Indian independence.

   (A) read Civil Disobedience in 1906 and made it
   (B) read Civil Disobedience in 1906 in order to make it into
   (C) read Civil Disobedience and, in 1906, made it
   (D) would have read Civil Disobedience in 1906 and would have made it
   (E) reading Civil Disobedience in 1906 and making it

12. Some homeowners prefer gas heat to oil because there is no need for deliveries or no large storage tanks, with its being cheaper in most places.

   (A) oil because there is no need for deliveries or no large storage tanks, with its being cheaper in most places
   (B) oil because there is no need for deliveries or large storage tanks, and in most places gas is cheaper
   (C) oil, being that there are no deliveries, no large storage tanks, and it is cheaper in most places
   (D) oil, needing no deliveries or large storage tanks, and anyways gas is cheaper in most places
   (E) oil, since gas is cheaper in most places and has no need of deliveries or large storage tanks

13. Although we now blame most catastrophes on "nature," thinkers in the Middle Ages thought every fire, earthquake, and disease to be the result of divine anger.

   (A) Although we now blame most catastrophes on "nature,"
   (B) Most catastrophes are now blamed on "nature" by us, and
   (C) We now blame "nature" for catastrophes, moreover,
   (D) Although "nature" is now blamed for most catastrophes by us,
   (E) Now blaming most catastrophes on "nature,"

14. A survey of over 1,000 people conducted by a marketing firm determined that people over the age of 40 do not like cherry cola as well as people under the age of 20.

   (A) well as people under the age of 20
   (B) much as people under the age of 20
   (C) many people under the age of 20 do
   (D) well than people under the age of 20 do
   (E) much as people under the age of 20 do

STOP

IF YOU FINISH BEFORE TIME IS CALLED, YOU MAY CHECK YOUR WORK ON THIS SECTION ONLY. DO NOT TURN TO ANY OTHER SECTION IN THE TEST.

Practice Test III

Outline

I. **Section 1:** Writing (p. 545)

II. **Section 2:** Critical Reading (pp. 546–552)

III. **Section 3:** Math (pp. 554–557)

IV. **Section 4:** Writing (pp. 558–563)

V. **Section 5:** Critical Reading (pp. 564–568)

VI. **Section 7:** Math (pp. 570–573)

VII. **Section 8:** Critical Reading (pp. 574–578)

VIII. **Section 9:** Math (pp. 580–582)

IX. **Section 10:** Writing (pp. 584–586)

Practice Test III

SECTION 1—WRITING

Time—25 Minutes

1 Essay

DIRECTIONS: The essay tests your ability to express ideas, develop a point of view, present ideas in a clear and logical fashion, and use language precisely.

Write your essay on the lines provided on your answer sheet—you will receive no other paper on which to write. Do not write your essay in your test book. You will receive credit only for what appears on your answer sheet. Write legibly, and remember that graders must be able to read your handwriting.

You have 25 minutes to plan and write an essay on the topic assigned below. Do not write on any other topic. An essay on another topic is not acceptable. Sample essays and analyses begin on page 699.

Think carefully about the issue presented in the following excerpt and the assignment below.

Some schools and districts have eliminated study hall for their students. The primary drive behind this elimination is to allow students to take additional electives and substantive subjects. Though students might have slightly more work to complete at home, they will leave school much more well-rounded with their added knowledge.

Assignment: Should schools eliminate study hall? Plan and write an essay in which you develop your point of view on this issue. Support your position with reasoning and examples taken from your reading, studies, experience, and observations.

STOP

IF YOU FINISH BEFORE TIME IS CALLED, YOU MAY CHECK YOUR WORK ON THIS SECTION ONLY. DO NOT TURN TO ANY OTHER SECTION IN THE TEST.

Practice Test III

SECTION 2—CRITICAL READING

Time—25 Minutes

24 Items

DIRECTIONS: In this section, solve each item, and choose the correct answer choice. Fill in the corresponding oval on the answer sheet. Answers are on page 702.

Items #1–7: Each item below has one or two blanks, each blank indicating that something has been omitted. Beneath the sentence are five lettered words or sets of words. Choose the word or set of words that best fits the meaning of the sentence as a whole.

Example:

Although its publicity has been -------, the film itself is intelligent, well acted, handsomely produced, and altogether -------.

(A) tasteless . . respectable
(B) extensive . . moderate
(C) sophisticated . . amateur
(D) risqué . . crude
(E) perfect . . spectacular

---

1. The history book, written in 1880, was tremendously -------, unfairly blaming the South for the Civil War.

   (A) biased
   (B) objective
   (C) suppressed
   (D) questionable
   (E) complicated

2. In the Middle Ages, scientists and clergymen thought the universe was well-ordered and -------; today scientists are more likely to see the world as -------.

   (A) baffling . . dogmatic
   (B) harmonious . . chaotic
   (C) transient . . predictable
   (D) emancipated . . intriguing
   (E) divergent . . galling

3. Hot milk has long been a standard cure for insomnia because of its ------- quality.

   (A) malevolent
   (B) amorphous
   (C) soporific
   (D) plaintive
   (E) desultory

4. Since the results of the experiment were ------- the body of research already completed, the committee considered the results to be -------.

   (A) similar to . . speculative
   (B) inconsistent with . . anomalous
   (C) compounded by . . heretical
   (D) dispelled by . . convincing
   (E) contradicted by . . redundant

5. Psychologists believe that modern life ------- neurosis because of the ------- of traditional values that define acceptable behavior.

   (A) copes with . . inundation
   (B) strives for . . condoning
   (C) concentrates on . . plethora
   (D) fosters . . disappearance
   (E) corroborates . . dispelling

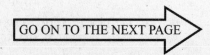
GO ON TO THE NEXT PAGE

6. Peter, ------- by the repeated rejections of his novel, ------- to submit his manuscript to other publishers.

(A) encouraged . . declined
(B) elated . . planned
(C) undaunted . . continued
(D) inspired . . complied
(E) undeterred . . refused

7. All ------- artists must struggle with the conflict between ------- their own talent and knowledge that very few are great enough to succeed.

(A) great . . neglect of
(B) aspiring . . faith in
(C) ambitious . . indifference to
(D) prophetic . . dissolution of
(E) serious . . disregard of

Items #8–24: Each passage below is followed by one or more items based on its content. Answer the items following each passage on the basis of what is stated or implied in the passage.

Item #8 is based on the following passage.

The use of balls probably originated in the Middle East, as an aspect of religious ceremonies. Their use was apparently introduced into Europe by the Moors during the time of their occupation of Spain.
5   The earliest written references to balls of the sort that we associate with games are found in the writings of Christian theologians dating from the period shortly after the Moorish invasion of Europe. These theologians condemned the use of balls as a form of
10 Saturnalia, a pagan festival.

8. The author assumes that the

(A) initial appearance of balls in Europe would have been noted in contemporary writings
(B) use of balls in Europe was originally restricted to religious rites
(C) practices of one religion are often adopted by other religions in the region
(D) games associated with a culture are spread when the influence of that culture grows
(E) writings of a religious movement accurately reflect the practices of its adherents

---

Item #9 is based on the following passage.

Nicholas Nickleby, the second novel of Charles Dickens, has been referred to by some commentators as romantic, but the novel is actually highly realistic. Dickens collected material for his novel on a journey
5   through Yorkshire, during which he investigated for himself the deplorable conditions of the cheap boarding schools that produced broken bones and deformed minds in the name of education.

9. The author's primary purpose is to

(A) expose a pattern of long-standing abuse
(B) prove that novels are either romantic or realistic
(C) revise major commentary of the works of Dickens
(D) propose a new literary theory of the novel
(E) correct a misunderstanding about *Nicholas Nickleby*

GO ON TO THE NEXT PAGE

Item #10 is based on the following passage.

We tend to think of air pollution as a modern problem, but in 1257, when the Queen of England visited Nottingham, she found the smoke so bad that she left for fear of her life. The culprit was soot and
5   smoke that came from the burning of coal. By the nineteenth century, London and other industrialized cities already had serious air pollution problems. By the start of the twentieth century, bronchitis was called the "British disease." England got 30 percent less
10 sunshine than 50 years earlier, and a prominent art critic noted a darkening in the colors used by artists of the time. The Sherlock Holmes stories mention frequently the swirling, yellow-gray fog that enveloped London, and historical records show that buildings
15 were coated with soot almost as soon as they were cleaned and repainted.

10. In developing the passage, the author relies mainly on

(A) statistics to demonstrate that air pollution has serious health consequences
(B) examples to show that air pollution is a long-standing problem
(C) first-hand accounts to refute claims that air pollution is worse now than it was a century ago
(D) inferences from historical records to track the increase in air pollution
(E) opinions from expert authorities to document the significance of air pollution

Item #11 is based on the following passage.

For too many years, communities have been losing public spaces that provide people with an opportunity to meet and exchange ideas. Today, the privately owned shopping mall is often the only
5   remaining gathering space to be found in a community; however, public assembly, speeches, and leafleting can all be legally prohibited by the owners of private property.

11. The author of the passage is primarily concerned with explaining which of the following?

(A) Private places are more convenient than public ones.
(B) Speeches and leafleting are commercial activities.
(C) Freedom of speech is essential to a viable democracy.
(D) Shopping malls are gradually replacing public spaces.
(E) Privately owned shopping malls are not true public spaces.

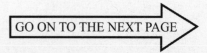 GO ON TO THE NEXT PAGE

Item #12 is based on the following passage.

The cleaning and restoration of Michelangelo's frescoes on the ceiling of the Sistine Chapel were undertaken by some of the world's finest art restorers under the close supervision of an international team of
5 art experts and historians. Nonetheless, the result produced a storm of controversy. Most modern viewers, it seemed, had become accustomed to seeing the frescoes with their colors dulled by layers of yellowing glue and varnish and with the contours of the
10 figures obscured by centuries' accumulation of grime. These viewers thought the restored frescoes no longer looked like "serious art."

12. The author implies that

(A) Michelangelo's frescoes contain subject matter that the public finds objectionable
(B) some people who viewed the restored frescoes thought that they should be restored to their pre-cleaning status
(C) most art works should be cleaned every few years to remove the dirt and grime that accumulates on their surfaces
(D) some viewers expect that high art will be somber to reflect the seriousness of its artistic purpose
(E) the art experts and historians who supervised the cleaning of the frescoes failed to protect the frescoes

Item #13 is based on the following passage.

Protectionists argue that an excess of exports over imports is essential to maintaining a favorable balance of trade. The value of the excess can then be converted to precious metals by demanding gold or silver from
5 the nation or merchants owing the balance. This means, however, that the most favorable of all trade balances would occur when a country exported its entire national output and, in turn, imported only gold and silver. Since one cannot eat gold and silver, the
10 protectionists must surely be incorrect.

13. The author develops the passage primarily by showing that

(A) proponents of protectionism are not completely candid
(B) most economists prefer trade to protectionism
(C) arguments for protectionism lead to an absurd result
(D) economic theories cannot be proved right or wrong
(E) statistics can be manipulated to support any position

GO ON TO THE NEXT PAGE

Item #14 is based on the following passage.

In 1851, the United States established the Puget Sound District of the Bureau of Customs. American settlers, used to the duty-free woolens offered by the British, feared that imposition and enforcement of
5 tariffs would not only increase the cost of woolens imported from the British side of the border but would result in the loss of British markets for American products. Consequently, American and British traders smuggled into the San Juan Islands British wool that
10 was then later sold as domestic wool by American sheepherders. This practice was so widespread and so successful that one naïve textbook writer, dividing the total "domestic" wool production of the islands by the reported number of sheep, credited San Juan's sheep
15 with the world's record for wool production: 150 pounds per sheep per year.

14. It can be inferred that the author refers to the textbook writer as "naïve" (line 12) because the writer

   (A) failed to realize that the total given for domestic wool production included wool that had been smuggled into the islands
   (B) relied on official statistics to determine the number of sheep raised in a particular region of the San Juan islands
   (C) believed that American markets in British territory would not be jeopardized by the imposition of tariffs
   (D) was aware of the possibility of smuggling arrangement but did not investigate further
   (E) refused to believe that San Juan's sheep had actually set a world's record for wool production

Items #15–24 are based on the following passage.

What we expect of translation is a reasonable facsimile of something that might have been said in our language. However, there is debate among critics as to what constitutes a reasonable facsimile. Most of us, at
5 heart, belong to the "soft-line" party: A given translation may not be exactly "living language," but the facsimile is generally reasonable. The "hard-line" party aims only for the best translation. The majority of readers never notice the difference, as they read
10 passively, often missing stylistic integrity as long as the story holds them. Additionally, a literature like Japanese may even be treated to an "exoticism handicap."
   Whether or not one agrees with Roy A. Miller's
15 postulation of an attitude of mysticism by the Japanese toward their own language, it is true that the Japanese have special feelings toward the possibilities of their language and its relation to life and art. These feelings impact what Japanese writers write about and how they
20 write. Many of the special language relationships are not immediately available to the non-Japanese (which is only to say that the Japanese language, like every other, has some unique features). For example, in my own work on Dazai Osamu, I have found that his
25 writing closely mimics the sense of the rhythms of spoken Japanese, and that such a mimicking is difficult to duplicate in English. Juda's cackling hysterically, "Heh, heh, heh" (in *Kakekomi uttae*), or the coy poutings of a schoolgirl (in *Joseito*) have what Masao
30 Miyoshi has called, in *Accomplices of Silence*, an "embarrassing" quality. It is, however, the embarrassment of recognition that the reader of Japanese feels. The moments simply do not work in English.
35   Even the orthography of written Japanese is a resource not open to written English. Tanizaki Jun'ichiro, who elsewhere laments the poverty of "indigenous" Japanese vocabulary, writes in *Bunsho tokuhon* of the contribution to literary effect—to
40 "meaning," if you will—made simply by the way a Japanese author chooses to "spell" a word. In Shiga Naoya's *Kinosaki nite*, for example, the onomatopoeic "bu—n" with which a honeybee takes flight has a different feeling for having been written in *hiragana*
45 instead of *katakana*. I read, and I am convinced. Arishima Takeo uses onomatopoeic words in his children's story *Hitofusa no budo*, and the effect is not one of baby talk, but of gentleness and intimacy that

 GO ON TO THE NEXT PAGE

automatically pulls the reader into the world of
50 childhood fears, tragedies, and consolations, memories
of which lie close under the surface of every adult
psyche.

This, of course, is hard to reproduce in
translation, although translators labor hard to do so.
55 George Steiner speaks of an "intentional strangeness,"
a "creative dislocation," that sometimes is invoked in
the attempt. He cites Chateaubriand's 1836 translation
of Milton's *Paradise Lost*, for which Chateaubriand
"created" a Latinate French to approximate Milton's
60 special English as an example of such a successful act
of creation. He also laments what he calls the "'moon
in pond like blossom weary' school of instant exotica,"
with which we are perhaps all too familiar.

15. The author is primarily concerned with

(A) criticizing translators who do not faithfully
reproduce the style of works written in
another language
(B) suggesting that Japanese literature is more
complex than English literature
(C) arguing that no translation can do justice to a
work written in another language
(D) demonstrating that Japanese literature is
particularly difficult to translate into English
(E) discussing some of the problems of
translating Japanese literature into English

16. In line 30, it can be inferred that *Accomplices of
Silence* is

(A) an English translation of Japanese poetry
(B) a critical commentary on the work of Dazai
Osamu
(C) a prior publication by the author on Japanese
literature
(D) a text on Japanese orthography
(E) a general work on the problem of translation

17. In line 35, the word "orthography" means

(A) poetry
(B) vocabulary
(C) spelling
(D) translation
(E) literature

18. By the phrase "the moments simply do not work
in English" (lines 33–34), the author means that

(A) English speakers are not able to comprehend
the Japanese experience
(B) the Japanese descriptions do not translate
well into English
(C) English is inferior to Japanese for describing
intimate occurrences
(D) stock characters are more familiar to
Japanese readers than to English readers
(E) "hard-line" translators work more diligently
at rendering texts than do "soft-line"
translators

19. In lines 41–45, the author cites Shiga Naoya's
Kinosaki nite in order to

(A) illustrate the effect that Japanese orthography
has on meaning
(B) demonstrate the poverty of indigenous
Japanese vocabulary
(C) prove that it is difficult to translate Japanese
into English
(D) acquaint the reader with an important work
of Japanese literature
(E) impress upon the reader the importance of
faithfully translating a work from one
language into another

20. With which of the following statements would the
author most likely agree?

(A) The Japanese language is the language that is
best suited to poetry.
(B) English is one of the most difficult languages
into which to translate any work written in
Japanese.
(C) It is impossible for a person not fluent in
Japanese to understand the inner meaning of
Japanese literature.
(D) Most Japanese people think that their
language is uniquely suited to conveying
mystical ideas.
(E) Every language has its own peculiar
potentialities that present challenges to a
translator.

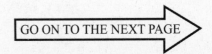

GO ON TO THE NEXT PAGE

21. It can be inferred that the Japanese word "bu—n" (line 43) is most like which of the following English words?

(A) bee
(B) honey
(C) buzz
(D) flower
(E) moon

22. The author uses all of the following EXCEPT

(A) examples to prove a point
(B) citation of authority
(C) analogy
(D) personal knowledge
(E) contrasting two viewpoints

23. It can be inferred that the "exoticism handicap" (lines 12–13) mentioned by the author is

(A) the tendency of some translators of Japanese to render Japanese literature in a needlessly awkward style
(B) the attempt of Japanese writers to create for their readers a world characterized by mysticism
(C) the lack of literal, word-for-word translational equivalents for Japanese and English vocabulary
(D) the expectation of many English readers that Japanese literature can only be understood by someone who speaks Japanese
(E) the difficulty a Japanese reader encounters in trying to penetrate the meaning of difficult Japanese poets

24. The author's attitude toward the "school of instant exotica" (line 62) is one of

(A) endorsement
(B) disapproval
(C) confidence
(D) confusion
(E) courage

STOP

IF YOU FINISH BEFORE TIME IS CALLED, YOU MAY CHECK YOUR WORK ON THIS SECTION ONLY. DO NOT TURN TO ANY OTHER SECTION IN THE TEST.

NO TEST MATERIAL ON THIS PAGE

Practice Test III

SECTION 3—MATH

Time—25 Minutes

18 Items

DIRECTIONS: In this section, solve each item, and choose the correct answer choice. Fill in the corresponding oval on the answer sheet. Use any available space for scratchwork. Answers are on page 702.

Notes:

(1) The use of a calculator is permitted. All numbers used are real numbers.

(2) Figures that accompany problems in this test are intended to provide information useful in solving the problems. They are drawn as accurately as possible EXCEPT when it is stated in a specific problem that the figure is not drawn to scale. All figures lie in a plane unless otherwise indicated.

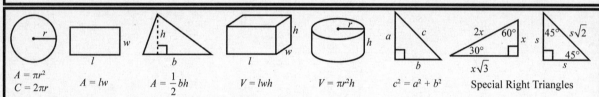

$A = \pi r^2$
$C = 2\pi r$
$A = lw$
$A = \frac{1}{2}bh$
$V = lwh$
$V = \pi r^2 h$
$c^2 = a^2 + b^2$
Special Right Triangles

The number of degrees of arc in a circle is 360.

The sum of the measures in degrees of the angles of a triangle is 180.

---

1. If $5{,}454 = 54(x+1)$, then $x =$

(A)   10
(B)   11
(C)   100
(D)   101
(E)   1001

2. If $k^x \cdot k^9 = k^{21}$ and $\left(m^y\right)^3 = m^{18}$, then $(x - y) =$

(A)   3
(B)   6
(C)   9
(D)   12
(E)   15

3. At the ABC Bulk Mail Center, an old machine stuffs and seals envelopes at a rate of 150 envelopes per minute. A new machine stuffs and seals envelopes at a rate of 350 envelopes per minute. How many minutes will it take both machines working together to seal and stuff a total 750 envelopes?

(A) 0.80
(B) 1.25
(C) 1.50
(D) 1.60
(E) 2.10

GO ON TO THE NEXT PAGE

4. If $x = \dfrac{3y^2}{z}$, what is the result of doubling both y and z?

(A) x is not changed.
(B) x is doubled.
(C) x is tripled.
(D) x is multiplied by 2.
(E) x is multiplied by 6.

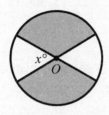

5. The circle with center O has a radius of length 2. If the total area of the shaded regions is 3π, then $x =$

(A) 270
(B) 180
(C) 120
(D) 90
(E) 45

6. If a bar of metal alloy consists of 100 grams of tin and 150 grams of lead, what percent of the entire bar, by weight, is tin?

(A) 10%
(B) 15%
(C) $33\dfrac{1}{3}\%$
(D) 40%
(E) $66\dfrac{2}{3}\%$

7. If $\dfrac{1}{x} + \dfrac{1}{y} = \dfrac{1}{z}$, then $z =$

(A) $\dfrac{1}{xy}$

(B) xy

(C) $\dfrac{x+y}{xy}$

(D) $\dfrac{xy}{x+y}$

(E) $\dfrac{2xy}{x+y}$

8. In a certain clothing store, 60 percent of all the articles are imported and 20 percent of all the articles are priced at \$100 or more. If 40 percent of the total articles priced at \$100 or more are imported, what percent of the articles are priced under \$100 and are not imported?

(A) 28%
(B) 12%
(C) 8%
(D) 4.8%
(E) 2%

GO ON TO THE NEXT PAGE

Each item requires you to solve an item and mark your answer on a special answer grid. For each item, you should write your answer in the boxes at the top of each column and then fill in the ovals beneath each part of the answer you write. Here are some examples:

Answer: 7/2 or 3.5	Answer: 325	Answer: 1/6, .166, or .167
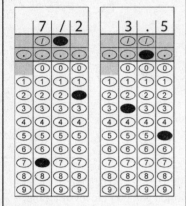	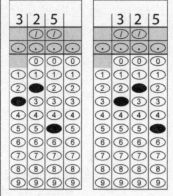	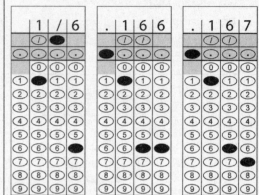

Note: A mixed number such as $3\frac{1}{2}$ must be gridded as 7/2 or as 3.5. If gridded as "31/2," it will be read as "thirty-one halves."

Note: Either position is correct.

Note: A decimal answer with more digits than the grid can accommodate must be truncated. A decimal such as $.16\overline{6}$ must be gridded as .166 or .167. A less accurate value such as .16 or .17 will be scored as incorrect.

---

9. If $3x + 2 = 8$, then $6x =$

10. Members of a civic organization purchase boxes of candy for $1 each and sell them for $2 each. If no other expenses are incurred, how many boxes of candy must they sell to earn a net profit of $500?

11. In a school with a total enrollment of 360 students, 90 students are seniors. What percent of all students enrolled in the school are seniors?

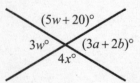

12. If two straight lines intersect as shown, what is the value of x?

GO ON TO THE NEXT PAGE ➡

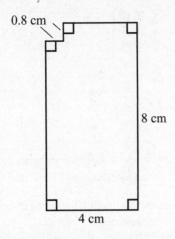

0.8 cm

8 cm

4 cm

13. The figure above is a scale drawing of the floor of a dining hall. If 1 centimeter on the drawing represents 5 meters, what is the area, in square meters, of the floor?

14. A school club spent $\frac{2}{5}$ of its budget for one project and $\frac{1}{3}$ of what remained for another project. If the club's entire budget was equal to $300, how much of the budget, in dollars, was left after the two projects?

15. The average of the following six numbers is 16: 10, 12, 15.1, 15.2, 28, and x. What is the value of x?

16. At the zoo, 25 percent of the animals are birds, 30 percent are reptiles or amphibians, and the rest are mammals. If there are 12 geese, representing 20 percent of the birds, how many mammals are there at the zoo?

17. Jerry grew 5 inches in 1993 and 2 inches more in 1994, before reaching his final height of 5 feet 10 inches. What percentage of his final height did his combined growth for the two year period of 1993 and 1994 represent?

18. A circle with a radius of 2 is superimposed upon a square with sides measuring 5 so that the center of the circle and the center of the square are identical. At how many points will the square and circle intersect?

STOP

IF YOU FINISH BEFORE TIME IS CALLED, YOU MAY CHECK YOUR WORK ON THIS SECTION ONLY. DO NOT TURN TO ANY OTHER SECTION IN THE TEST.

Practice Test III

SECTION 4—WRITING
Time—25 Minutes
35 Items

DIRECTIONS: In this section, solve each item, and choose the correct answer choice. Fill in the corresponding oval on the answer sheet. Answers are on page 702.

Items #1–5: The following sentences test correct, effective expression. Each sentence contains an underlined portion, or the entire sentence may be underlined. Following each sentence are five ways of phrasing the underlined portion. Choice (A) repeats the original; the other four choices are different. If you think the original is better than any of the other choices, choose (A); otherwise, choose one of the other choices.

In choosing answers, follow the conventions of standard written English. Make sure to consider issues of grammar, word choice, sentence construction, and punctuation. Your choice should produce the most effective sentence. It should be clear, precise, and free of ambiguity or awkwardness.

Example:

Allen <u>visiting</u> his cousin in France last summer.

(A) visiting
(B) visited
(C) does visit
(D) a visit
(E) is visiting

---

1. Before the invention of television, <u>radio was the chief form of at-home entertainment</u>.

    (A) radio was the chief form of at-home entertainment
    (B) radio has been the chief form of at-home entertainment
    (C) radio, having been the chief form of at home entertainment
    (D) the chief form of at-home entertainment is the radio
    (E) radio, a form of at-home entertainment, was the chief

2. Once she determined that the muddy conditions <u>will pose</u> a hazard to the players, the athletic director postponed the game.

    (A) will pose
    (B) would pose
    (C) posing
    (D) had posed
    (E) are posing

3. The sustained decline in student enrollment raises doubts about <u>if the highly technical course of instruction is a viable</u> college program.

    (A) if the highly technical course of instruction is a viable
    (B) if there is viability in the highly technical course of instruction as
    (C) whether the highly technical course of instruction is a viable
    (D) the highly technical course of instruction as a viable
    (E) the viability of the highly technical course of instruction as

GO ON TO THE NEXT PAGE

4. <u>In a panicked tone, the duty nurse heard the</u>
<u>mother asking for help for her injured child.</u>

   (A) In a panicked tone, the duty nurse heard the
   mother asking for help for her injured child.
   (B) The duty nurse heard the mother asking for
   help for her injured child, who spoke in a
   panicked tone.
   (C) Her tone being panicked, the mother asked
   the duty nurse for help for her injured child.
   (D) The duty nurse, in a panicked tone, heard the
   mother asking for help for her injured child.
   (E) The duty nurse heard the mother asking in a
   panicked tone for help for her injured child.

5. The CEO of the firm was <u>accused by a group of</u>
<u>opposition shareholders of both diverting</u>
<u>company funds to his private account and sexual</u>
<u>harassment</u> of employees.

   (A) accused by a group of opposition
   shareholders of both diverting company
   funds to his private account and sexual
   harassment
   (B) accused by a group of opposition
   shareholders of diverting company funds to
   his private account and sexual harassment
   (C) being accused by a group of opposition
   shareholders of both diverting company
   funds to his private account and sexual
   harassment
   (D) accused by a group of opposition
   shareholders of diverting both company
   funds to his private account and sexual
   harassment
   (E) diverting company funds to his private
   account and sexual harassment as accused by
   a group of opposition shareholders

Items #6–25: The following sentences test your
knowledge of grammar, usage, diction (choice of
words), and idiom. Each sentence contains either
no error or a single error. If there is an error, it is
underlined and lettered. If the sentence contains
an error, choose the one underlined portion that
must be changed to produce a correct sentence. If
there is no error, choose answer choice (E). In
choosing answers, follow the conventions of
standard written English.

Example:

The principal <u>asked</u> five of <u>we</u> students
       A   B

<u>to enter</u> the <u>public speaking</u> contest.
  C   D

<u>No error</u>
E

6. Khartoum, the <u>capital</u> of Sudan, <u>is</u> situated <u>at</u> the
           A   B   C

   confluence of the Blue Nile and White Nile <u>river</u>.
                                                D

   <u>No error</u>
   E

7. Hieroglyphics and the alphabet <u>are</u> forms of
                                A

   writing <u>that</u> date to the Middle Kingdom of
          B

   Egypt, <u>though</u> the first was fading from use while
           C

   the second was <u>only developing</u>. <u>No error</u>
                   D   E

8. Several of the <u>most influential economists</u> in the
                    A   B

   United States <u>are</u> <u>graduates</u> or teachers at the
               C   D

   University of Chicago. <u>No error</u>
                       E

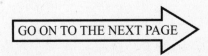
GO ON TO THE NEXT PAGE

9. <u>During</u> his first and <u>only</u> trip to Pennsylvania,
   A   B

   William Penn, Quaker leader and founder of the

   colony, drew up a liberal Frame of Government

   and <u>establishes</u> friendly relations <u>with</u> the
       C   D

   indigenous people. <u>No error</u>
                  E

10. Dynamite, an explosive <u>made from</u> nitroglycerine
                      A

    and various inert fillers, <u>were invented</u> by Alfred
                      B

    Nobel, the Swedish chemist <u>who</u> <u>endowed</u> the
                 C   D

    Nobel prizes. <u>No error</u>
              E

11. <u>When</u> you listen to the music of Khachaturian, a
    A

    Russian composer of Armenian <u>heritage</u>, <u>one</u>
                  B   C

    <u>can hear</u> elements of Armenian and Asian folk
      D

    music. <u>No error</u>
          E

12. A considerable <u>improvement</u> over the Bessemer
              A

    Process, the open-hearth process of <u>producing</u>
                       B

    steel can use up to 100 percent scrap metal, refine

    pig iron with a <u>high</u> phosphorus content, and
           C

    <u>production of</u> less brittle steels. <u>No error</u>
      D   E

13. <u>Usually</u> nocturnal and <u>feeds</u> on small animals
    A   B

    such as insects, the salamander <u>is found</u> in <u>damp</u>
                    C   D

    regions of the northern temperate zone. <u>No error</u>
                       E

14. The first of Kepler's <u>law</u> states <u>that</u> the shape of
                 A   B

    <u>each</u> planet's orbit <u>is</u> an ellipse with the sun at
    C   D

    one focus. <u>No error</u>
           E

15. <u>For</u> someone who enjoys eating in restaurants,
    A

    New York City <u>offers</u> a variety of ethnic cuisines,
            B

    each with <u>their</u> <u>own</u> flavors. <u>No error</u>
          C   D   E

16. <u>While rowing</u>, the direction and speed of the boat
    A

    or shell <u>are</u> controlled by the coxswain, <u>who</u> also
          B   C

    calls the rhythms of the rowers' <u>strokes</u>. <u>No error</u>
                   D   E

17. Rayon, <u>one</u> of the oldest synthetic <u>fibers,</u> is <u>made</u>
         A   B   C

    <u>from</u> cellulose, <u>chiefly</u> derived from wood pulp.
      C   D

    <u>No error</u>
      E

GO ON TO THE NEXT PAGE

18. George Bernard Shaw, the Irish playwright and

critic, was a <u>popular</u> speaker <u>who</u> <u>writes</u> five
            A   B   C

novels before becoming a <u>music</u> critic for London
                          D

newspaper in the late 1890s. <u>No error</u>
                                    E

19. In the 1760s, Adam Smith <u>traveled</u> to France
                                 A

<u>where</u> he met <u>some of</u> the Physiocrats and started
  B   C

<u>to writing</u> his masterpiece, *The Wealth of Nations*.
  D

<u>No error</u>
  E

20. In order <u>to guide</u> a smart bomb, an aircraft pilot
                A

aims a laser beam <u>to</u> the target, <u>which</u> then
                  B   C

reflects the beam back to a computer in the

weapon <u>itself</u>. <u>No error</u>
       D   E

21. Chivalry <u>was</u> the system of ethical ideals that grew
                A

<u>out of</u> feudalism and that reached <u>their</u> high point
  B   C

in the twelfth and thirteenth <u>centuries</u>. <u>No error</u>
                              D   E

22. The area <u>that</u> is now Portugal was added <u>to</u> the
                A   B

Roman Empire <u>around</u> 5 A.D., later overrun
             C

by Germanic tribes in the fifth century, and

finally <u>conquested</u> by the Moors in 711. <u>No error</u>
        D   E

23. Valedictorian of his Rutgers class, an Olympic

gold medalist, and <u>he was</u> an <u>internationally</u>
                   A   B

renowned singer, Paul Robeson <u>was</u> a man of
                                C

<u>many</u> talents. <u>No error</u>
  D   E

24. The cavities of the internal nose, <u>which</u> are lined
                                          A

with a mucous membrane, <u>is covered</u> with fine
                        B

hairs that help <u>to</u> filter dust and impurities <u>from</u>
                C   D

the air. <u>No error</u>
         E

25. It has been noted that <u>when</u> one of the senses
                              A

such as sight, <u>hear,</u> or smell, is <u>seriously</u> degraded
               B   C

the other two become <u>more</u> acute. <u>No error</u>
                      D   E

Items #26–35: The following passages are early drafts of essays. Some portions of the passages need to be revised.

Read each passage and answer the items that follow. Items may be about particular sentences or parts of sentences, asking you to improve the word choice or sentence structure. Other items may refer to parts of the essay or the entire essay, asking you to consider organization or development. In making your decisions, follow the conventions of standard written English.

Items #26–30 refer to the following passage.

(1) My favorite opera is La Bohème by Puccini. **(2)** Why is La Bohème my favorite? **(3)** The action of the opera takes place on the Left Bank of Paris in the 1830s. **(4)** The Left Bank is where the struggling artists

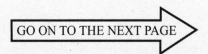
GO ON TO THE NEXT PAGE

and students lived. **(5)** Four of the main characters in the opera are a painter, a philosopher, a musician, and, most important for me, a poet. **(6)** The sets include a sidewalk café and a garret room. **(7)** They even have a passionate romance with a tragic ending.

(8) The opera is based on Scènes de la Vie de Bohème written by Henri Murger. **(9)** When Murger wrote this novel, he himself was a poor writer living in the Latin Quarter in the 1840s. **(10)** The book is a collection of short, funny stories about Henri and his friends.

(11) The individual scenes, on which the novel is based, first appeared as a series of stories in a Parisian newspaper. **(12)** The group of struggling artists that made up Henri's group loved to eat and drink in cafés, but they hardly ever had any money to pay the check. **(13)** They were all very poor, but they will make the most of the present without worrying about the future.

(14) Legend has it that someone once came to visit Murger in his tiny apartment and found Murger in bed. **(15)** When the visitor suggested that Murger get dressed to go to a café, Murger said that he couldn't because he'd lent his only pair of pants to a friend. **(16)** I like to think of this story and imagine myself as Murger, being that he is the struggling writer.

26. The function of sentence 2 is to

 (A) pose a question that the writer will answer
 (B) invite the reader to answer to the question
 (C) signal the writer's confidence about the topic
 (D) imply that "favorite" is a matter of personal choice
 (E) express the writer's doubt about the selection

27. If the writer wanted to add that the Left Bank is also called the Latin Quarter, that purpose could best be accomplished by inserting

 (A) "The Latin Quarter is another name for the Left Bank." after sentence 3
 (B) "The Latin Quarter and the Left Bank are the same thing." after sentence 3
 (C) "(also called the Latin Quarter)" after "Left Bank" in sentence 4
 (D) "The Left Bank is also called the Latin Quarter." after sentence 4
 (E) "The Latin Quarter is another name for the Left Bank." after sentence 4

28. Which of the following is the best revision of the underlined portion of sentence 7 (reproduced below)?

 They even have a passionate romance with a tragic ending.

 (A) Fortunately, they even have
 (B) As a matter of fact, they even have
 (C) It is even that they have
 (D) The opera even has
 (E) It even has

29. In the context of the third paragraph, which revision is most needed in sentence 13?

 (A) Omit "but."
 (B) Change "they" to "struggling artists."
 (C) Change "will make" to "made."
 (D) Start a new sentence with "they."
 (E) Change "but" to "and."

30. In the context of the last paragraph, which revision is most needed in sentence 16?

 (A) Insert "in point of fact" at the beginning
 (B) Omit the word "story."
 (C) Omit the words "being that he is."
 (D) Change the comma to a semicolon
 (E) Change "is" to "was."

Items #31–35 refer to the following passage.

 (1) In 1928, a National Flag Conference adopted the National Flag Code. **(2)** The Code established principles of flag etiquette based upon the practices of the military. **(3)** These principles were eventually enacted into law. **(4)** The Flag Code law does not impose penalties for misuse of the United States Flag, but it is the guide for the proper handling and display of the Stars and Stripes. **(5)** Generally, you should display the flag only from sunrise to sunset on buildings and on stationary flagstaffs in the open. **(6)** You can, however, display the flag twenty-four hours a day if it is properly illuminated during the hours of darkness. **(7)** It is appropriate to display the flag on any day of the year but especially on important holidays such as Memorial Day, Independence Day and Veterans Day. **(8)** The

flag should not be displayed on days when the weather is inclement, unless they're all-weather flags.

(9) When raising the flag, it should be hoisted briskly. **(10)** When you take it down, it should be lowered ceremoniously. **(11)** Take care not to let it touch the ground. **(12)** It should be neatly folded and carefully stored away.

(13) It is all right to clean and mend your flag. **(14)** However, when it becomes so worn that it no longer serves as a proper symbol of the United States, it should be replaced. **(15)** The old flag should be destroyed, preferably by burning.

(16) You may think that displaying the flag just means buying a flag and hanging it on a pole. **(17)** Because the Flag Code covers many other points that you probably don't know about, this will surprise you. **(18)** If you really want to show your patriotism by displaying the flag, then you should be familiar with the rules of flag etiquette.

31. The main idea of the essay is expressed by

(A) sentence 1
(B) sentence 8
(C) sentence 15
(D) sentence 16
(E) sentence 18

32. The overall development of the thesis would be made clearer by beginning a new paragraph with

(A) sentence 2
(B) sentence 3
(C) sentence 5
(D) sentence 6
(E) sentence 8

33. In the context of the first paragraph, which revision is most needed in sentence 8?

(A) Omit the word "unless."
(B) Change "flag" to "flags."
(C) Change "they're" to "it's an" and "flags" to "flag."
(D) Omit the word "when."
(E) Change the comma to a semicolon

34. Which of the following is the best revision of sentence 9 (reproduced below)?

When raising the flag, it should be hoisted briskly.

(A) (As it is now.)
(B) When raising, the flag should be hoisted briskly.
(C) When the flag is rising, it should be done briskly.
(D) When raising the flag, you should hoist it briskly.
(E) When briskly raising the flag, it should be hoisted.

35. Which of the following, in context, is the best way of revising sentence 17 (reproduced below)?

Because the Flag Code covers many other points that you probably don't know about, this will surprise you.

(A) The Flag Code covers many other points that may surprise you.
(B) Because the Flag Code covers many other points that may surprise you.
(C) You may be surprised that the Flag Code covers many other points.
(D) Surprising you, the Flag Code probably covers many other points you don't know about.
(E) Many other points are covered by the Flag Cole that may surprise you.

STOP

IF YOU FINISH BEFORE TIME IS CALLED, YOU MAY CHECK YOUR WORK ON THIS SECTION ONLY. DO NOT TURN TO ANY OTHER SECTION IN THE TEST.

Practice Test III

SECTION 5—CRITICAL READING

Time—25 Minutes

24 Items

DIRECTIONS: In this section, solve each item, and choose the correct answer choice. Fill in the corresponding oval on the answer sheet. Answers are on page 702.

Items #1–8: Each item below has one or two blanks, each blank indicating that something has been omitted. Beneath the sentence are five lettered words or sets of words. Choose the word or set of words that best fits the meaning of the sentence as a whole.

Example:

Although its publicity has been -------, the film itself is intelligent, well acted, handsomely produced, and altogether -------.

(A) tasteless . . respectable
(B) extensive . . moderate
(C) sophisticated . . amateur
(D) risqué . . crude
(E) perfect . . spectacular

1. The millionaire was such a ------- that any appearance he made in public was -------.

   (A) philistine . . negligible
   (B) recluse . . noteworthy
   (C) gourmand . . distorted
   (D) lecher . . unexpected
   (E) traitor . . protracted

2. Because of the ------- of acupuncture therapy in China, Western physicians are starting to learn the procedure.

   (A) veracity
   (B) manipulation
   (C) liquidity
   (D) effectiveness
   (E) inflation

3. Being a celebrity has its -------, one of which is the almost complete lack of -------.

   (A) delusions . . repression
   (B) presumptions . . income
   (C) drawbacks . . privacy
   (D) frustrations . . notoriety
   (E) confrontations . . intimacy

4. The program concluded with a modern symphony that contained chords so ------- that the piece produced sounds similar to the ------- one hears as the individual orchestra members tune their instruments before a concert.

   (A) superfluous . . melody
   (B) pretentious . . roar
   (C) melodious . . applause
   (D) versatile . . harmony
   (E) discordant . . cacophony

5. The king was a haughty aristocrat, but he was not a -------; he ruled his country ------- with genuine affection for his people.

   (A) sycophant . . benevolently
   (B) diplomat . . complacently
   (C) monarch . . stringently
   (D) despot . . magnanimously
   (E) tyrant . . superciliously

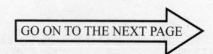

GO ON TO THE NEXT PAGE

6. Although some critics interpret *The Aeneid* as a Christian epic, this interpretation is totally -------, since the epic predates Christianity.

(A) infallible
(B) acceptable
(C) convincing
(D) anachronistic
(E) conventional

7. Black comedy is the combination of that which is humorous with that which would seem ------- to humor: the -------.

(A) apathetic . . ignoble
(B) heretical . . salacious
(C) inferior . . grandiose
(D) extraneous . . innocuous
(E) antithetical . . macabre

8. The original British cast was talented and energetic, while the Broadway cast lacks the ------- of the original players; in fact, the performance is -------.

(A) calmness . . scintillating
(B) splendor . . fallow
(C) verve . . insipid
(D) flexibility . . meticulous
(E) intractability . . quaint

Items #9–24: Each passage below is followed by one or more items based on its content. Answer the items following each passage on the basis of what is stated or implied in the passage.

Item #9 is based on the following passage.

For nearly 250 years, public libraries have afforded patrons, regardless of their economic circumstances, a mind-boggling collection of materials that represents 50 centuries of human thought. Plato
5 and Santayana, Shakespeare and Hemingway, and Bacon and Darwin all stand shoulder to shoulder on their shelves. The library is also a place to learn English, look for a job, read to children, write a term paper, or simply oil a squeaky day. The public library
10 is an American institution older than the American flag; however, this great democratic institution is struggling to survive. This struggle is nothing short of a national calamity.

9. The author of the passage relies extensively on

(A) statistics
(B) authority
(C) examples
(D) deduction
(E) quotations

GO ON TO THE NEXT PAGE

Items #10–24 are based on the following passage.

As long ago as the fifth century B.C., Greek physicians noted that people who had recovered from the "plague" would never get it again—they had acquired immunity. Modern scientists understand that the human immune system is a complex network of specialized cells and organs that protects the body against bacteria, viruses, fungi, and parasites.

Have you ever wondered why you become feverish when you are suffering from the flu? Your body's immune system is simply doing its job. Because the presence of certain organisms in the body is
5 harmful, the immune system will attempt to bar their entry or, failing that, to seek out and destroy them.

At the heart of the immune system is the ability to distinguish between self and non-self. The body's defenses do not normally attack tissues that exhibit a
10 self-marker.* Rather, immune cells and other body cells coexist peaceably. But when immune defenders encounter cells or organisms carrying molecules that say "foreign," the immune troops muster quickly to eliminate the intruders.

15 Any substance that is capable of triggering an immune response is called an antigen. An antigen can be a virus, a bacterium, a fungus, or a parasite; tissues or cells from another individual, except an identical twin, also act as antigens; even otherwise harmless
20 substances such as ragweed pollen or cat hair can set off a misguided response known as an allergy, in which case the substance is called an allergen. An antigen announces its foreignness by means of intricate and characteristic shapes called epitopes, which protrude
25 from its surface.

The immune system controls the production, development, and deployment of white cells called lymphocytes and includes the bone marrow, the thymus (a multi-lobed organ behind the breastbone),
30 and the blood and lymphatic vessels. Like all other blood cells, cells destined to become immune cells are produced in the bone marrow and are called stem cells. Some stem cells develop into lymphocytes while others develop into phagocytes.

35 The two most important classes of lymphocytes are B cells, so called because they mature in the bone marrow, and T cells, which migrate to the thymus. T cells directly attack their targets, which include body cells that have been commandeered by virus or warped
40 by malignancy. (This is called cellular immunity.) B cells, in contrast, work chiefly by secreting

antibodies into the body's fluids. (This is known as humoral immunity.)

The other group of stem cells is the phagocytes;
45 they are large white cannibal cells. A special group of phagocytes, called macrophages (literally, "big eaters"), also have the ability to "display" the antigen after it has been digested.

To fend off the threatening horde, the body has
50 devised astonishingly intricate defenses. Microbes attempting to enter the body must first find a chink in its armor. The skin and the mucous membranes that line the body's portals not only interpose a physical barrier, but they are also rich in scavenger cells and
55 antibodies. Next, invaders must elude a series of non-specific defenses—cells and substances equipped to tackle infectious agents without regard to their antigenic peculiarities. Many potential infections are stopped when microbes are intercepted by patrolling
60 scavenger cells or disabled by enzymes.

Microbes that breach the non-specific barriers are then confronted by weapons that are specifically designed to combat their unique characteristics. This immune system response includes both cellular and
65 humoral components.

The cellular response is initiated by a macrophage. The macrophage digests an antigen and then displays antigen fragments on its own surface. This gives the T cells their marching orders. Some T cells
70 become killer cells and set out to track down body cells that have become infected. Other T cells become communications cells and secrete substances that call other kinds of immune cells, such as fresh macrophages, to the site of the infection. Others coordinate
75 the movements of the various groups of cells once they arrive on the scene. Still others secrete substances that stimulate the production of more T cell troops.

Humoral immunity is primarily the function of B cells, although some help from T cells is almost
80 always needed. B cells, like macrophages, eat antigens. Unlike macrophages, however, a B cell can bind only to an antigen that specifically fits its antibody-like receptor, so the B cell exhibits an antigen fragment that attracts the attention of a T cell. The B cell and T cell interact,
85 and the helper T cell stimulates the B cell to produce clones of itself—each with the highly specific antibody-like receptor. These clones then differentiate into plasma cells and begin producing vast quantities of identical antigen-specific antibodies. Released into the blood-
90 stream, the antibodies lock onto their matching antigens. The antigen-antibody complexes are then cleansed from the circulatory system by the liver and the spleen.

These seemingly chaotic but actually very well-orchestrated maneuvers continue until the attack has

GO ON TO THE NEXT PAGE

95 been repulsed. At that point, specialized T cells, called suppressors, halt the production of antibodies and bring the immune response to a close.

When viewed from a clinical perspective, this process manifests itself in the three classic symptoms
100 of redness, warmth, and swelling. Redness and warmth develop when small blood vessels in the vicinity of the infection become dilated and carry more blood. Swelling results when the vessels, made leaky by yet other immune secretions, allow soluble immune substances
105 to seep into the surrounding tissue. But all of this subsides as the controller T cells begin their mop-up activities. And with that, your illness has run its course.

*Self-markers are distinctive molecules that are carried by virtually all body cells.

10. The passage can best be described as a

(A) refutation of an ancient medical idea
(B) definition of a biological concept
(C) description of a biological process
(D) technical definition of a medical term
(E) treatment for a particular disease

11. According to the third paragraph, an "allergen" differs from "antigens" in that an allergen

(A) does not trigger an immune response
(B) does not exhibit unique epitopes
(C) is not ordinarily harmful
(D) does not announce its foreignness
(E) carries a unique self-marker

12. The passage implies that without the ability to distinguish self from non-self cells, the immune system would

(A) function effectively except against the most powerful threats
(B) still be able to identify various epitopes
(C) no longer require both T cells and B cells
(D) rely exclusively on macrophages for defense against infection
(E) be rendered completely ineffective

13. Which of the following best explains why tissue that is transplanted from an identical twin is not attacked by the immune system?

(A) The transplanted tissue has the same self-identifying molecules as the body.
(B) The transplanted tissue triggers an allergic, not antigenic, reaction.
(C) The transplanted tissue has no unique identifying self or non-self markers.
(D) The body's immune system recognizes the transplanted tissue as foreign but ignores it.
(E) The body's immune system is unable to recognize the self/non-self markers.

14. According to lines 30–43, all of the following statements are true of T cells and B cells EXCEPT

(A) They are two different types of lymphocytes.
(B) B cells mature in the bone marrow, T cells in the thymus.
(C) Both classes of cells are produced by the bone marrow.
(D) Either class can differentiate into a macrophage.
(E) T cells attack other cells; B cells secrete antibodies.

15. As used in this context, "humoral" (line 43) means

(A) comical
(B) latent
(C) fluid
(D) dangerous
(E) infectious

16. The author refers to phagocytes as "cannibal cells" (line 45) because they

(A) are large in size
(B) digest human tissue
(C) display antigen
(D) eat other cells
(E) commandeer viruses

GO ON TO THE NEXT PAGE

17. According to the passage, the body's first line of defense against microbes is

(A) enzymes
(B) scavenger cells
(C) skin and mucous membranes
(D) macrophage cells
(E) T cells

18. The body's "non-specific defenses" (lines 55–56) ignore

(A) antigenic epitopes
(B) foreign substances
(C) physical antibodies
(D) scavenger cells
(E) potential infections

19. According to lines 66–92, cellular and humoral responses are similar in that both

(A) require the presence of a macrophage
(B) commence with one cell's digesting another
(C) are carried out exclusively by one type of cell
(D) necessitate the presence of B cells
(E) result in the production of antibodies

20. The passage mentions all of the following as functions of the T cells EXCEPT

(A) directing cellular activity
(B) communicating with other cells
(C) terminating an immune response
(D) producing other T cells as needed
(E) secreting antibodies into the blood

21. In line 94, "orchestrated" most nearly means

(A) effective
(B) desperate
(C) musical
(D) coordinated
(E) prolonged

22. It can be inferred that without the presence of suppressor T cells

(A) B cells would be unable to clone themselves
(B) non-specific defenses would become ineffective
(C) immune reactions would continue indefinitely
(D) macrophages would not respond to an infection
(E) defenses to infection could not begin

23. Which of the following best describes the function of the final paragraph?

(A) It alerts the reader to the topic that will follow.
(B) It provides further details on functions of immune cells.
(C) It highlights issues that need further research.
(D) It answers the question raised in the first paragraph.
(E) It recapitulates the most important points of the passage.

24. The passage relies upon an extended metaphor of an immune response as a

(A) transaction between business partners
(B) battle between warring camps
(C) struggle against oppressive rule
(D) debate between political candidates
(E) concert by a large group of musicians

STOP

IF YOU FINISH BEFORE TIME IS CALLED, YOU MAY CHECK YOUR WORK ON THIS SECTION ONLY. DO NOT TURN TO ANY OTHER SECTION IN THE TEST.

NO TEST MATERIAL ON THIS PAGE

Practice Test III

SECTION 7—MATH
Time—25 Minutes
20 Items

DIRECTIONS: In this section, solve each item, and choose the correct answer choice. Fill in the corresponding oval on the answer sheet. Use any available space for scratchwork. Answers are on page 702.

Notes:

(1) The use of a calculator is permitted. All numbers used are real numbers.

(2) Figures that accompany problems in this test are intended to provide information useful in solving the problems. They are drawn as accurately as possible EXCEPT when it is stated in a specific problem that the figure is not drawn to scale. All figures lie in a plane unless otherwise indicated.

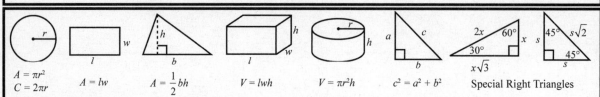

$A = \pi r^2$
$C = 2\pi r$ $A = lw$ $A = \frac{1}{2}bh$ $V = lwh$ $V = \pi r^2 h$ $c^2 = a^2 + b^2$ Special Right Triangles

The number of degrees of arc in a circle is 360.
The sum of the measures in degrees of the angles of a triangle is 180.

---

1. $121,212 + \left(2 \cdot 10^4\right) =$

(A) 321,212
(B) 141,212
(C) 123,212
(D) 121,412
(E) 121,232

2. At a recreation center, it costs \$3 per hour to rent a Ping Pong table and \$12 per hour to rent a lane for bowling. For the cost of renting a bowling lane for two hours, it is possible to rent a Ping Pong table for how many hours?

(A) 4
(B) 6
(C) 8
(D) 18
(E) 36

3. If $6x + 3 = 21$, then $2x + 1 =$

(A) 2
(B) 3
(C) 8
(D) 6
(E) 7

4. Jack, Ken, Larry, and Mike are j, k, l, and m years old, respectively. If $j < k < l < m$, which of the following could be true?

(A) $k = j + l$
(B) $j = k + l$
(C) $j + k = l + m$
(D) $j + k + m = l$
(E) $j + m = k + l$

GO ON TO THE NEXT PAGE

5. The solution set for x in the equation $-|x| = -x$ is

(A) $\{x: x \text{ is a positive integer}\}$
(B) $\{x: x \text{ is either 0 or a positive integer}\}$
(C) $\{x: x > 0\}$
(D) $\{x: x \geq 0\}$
(E) $\{x: x \text{ is a real number}\}$

6. Out of a group of 360 students, exactly 18 are on the track team. What percent of the students are on the track team?

(A) 5%
(B) 10%
(C) 12%
(D) 20%
(E) 25%

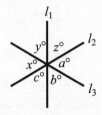

7. In the figure above, three lines intersect as shown. Which of the following must be true?

I. $a = x$
II. $y + z = b + c$
III. $x + a = y + b$

(A) I only
(B) II only
(C) I and II only
(D) I and III only
(E) I, II, and III

8. The sum of the digits of a three-digit number is 11. If the hundreds digit is 3 times the units digit and 2 times the tens digit, what is the number?

(A) 168
(B) 361
(C) 632
(D) 641
(E) 921

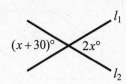

9. In the figure above, $x =$

(A) 15
(B) 30
(C) 45
(D) 60
(E) 90

10. The average (arithmetic mean) height of four buildings is 20 meters. If three of the buildings each has a height of 16 meters, what is the height, in meters, of the fourth building?

(A) 32
(B) 28
(C) 24
(D) 22
(E) 18

11. If x is an odd integer, all of the following expressions are odd EXCEPT

(A) $x + 2$
(B) $3x + 2$
(C) $2x^2 + x$
(D) $2x^3 + x$
(E) $3x^3 + x$

12. What is the sum of the areas of two squares with sides of 2 and 3, respectively?

(A) 1
(B) 5
(C) 13
(D) 25
(E) 36

GO ON TO THE NEXT PAGE

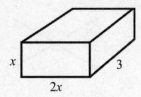

Note: Figure not drawn to scale.

13. In the figure above, the rectangular solid has a volume of 54. What is the value of x?

(A) 2
(B) 3
(C) 6
(D) 9
(E) 12

14. If x is 80 percent of y, then y is what percent of x?

(A) $133\dfrac{1}{3}\%$
(B) 125%
(C) 120%
(D) 90%
(E) 80%

15. From which of the following statements can it be deduced that $m > n$?

(A) $m + 1 = n$
(B) $2m = n$
(C) $m + n > 0$
(D) $m - n > 0$
(E) $mn > 0$

16. If $x \neq 0$, then $\dfrac{8^{2x}}{2^{4x}} =$.

(A) 2^{2x}
(B) 4^{-x}
(C) 4^{2x}
(D) 4^{1-x}
(E) 8^{-x}

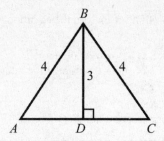

17. If $\sin \angle ABD = \dfrac{\sqrt{7}}{4}$ in the figure above, what is the length of $\overline{AC}$?

(A) 5
(B) 7
(C) $2\sqrt{7}$ (approximately 5.29)
(D) $4\sqrt{3}$ (approximately 6.93)
(E) $3\sqrt{7}$ (approximately 7.94)

18. If functions f, g, and h are defined as $f(x) = \dfrac{x}{2}$, $g(x) = x - 2$, and $h(x) = x^2$, then $f(g(h(4))) =$

(A) 2
(B) 4
(C) 7
(D) 8
(E) 16

19. If $f(3) = 12$ and $f(-2) = 2$, which of the following could represent $f(x)$?

(A) $\dfrac{1}{2}x$
(B) $x + 9$
(C) $2x + 6$
(D) $3x + 8$
(E) $4x + 10$

GO ON TO THE NEXT PAGE

20. Which of the following is true for all x and y such that $x > 0$ and $y < 0$?

(A) $|xy| < x + y$

(B) $|xy| < xy$

(C) $xy < |xy|$

(D) $|x| > |y|$

(E) $|y| > |x|$

STOP

IF YOU FINISH BEFORE TIME IS CALLED, YOU MAY CHECK YOUR WORK ON THIS SECTION ONLY. DO NOT TURN TO ANY OTHER SECTION IN THE TEST.

Practice Test III

SECTION 8—CRITICAL READING
Time—20 Minutes
19 Items

DIRECTIONS: In this section, solve each item, and choose the correct answer choice. Fill in the corresponding oval on the answer sheet. Answers are on page 703.

Items #1–5: Each item below has one or two blanks, each blank indicating that something has been omitted. Beneath the sentence are five lettered words or sets of words. Choose the word or set of words that best fits the meaning of the sentence as a whole.

Example:

Although its publicity has been -------, the film itself is intelligent, well acted, handsomely produced, and altogether -------.

(A) tasteless . . respectable
(B) extensive . . moderate
(C) sophisticated . . amateur
(D) risqué . . crude
(E) perfect . . spectacular

---

1. The judge, after ruling that the article had unjustly ------- the reputation of the architect, ordered the magazine to ------- its libelous statements in print.

   (A) praised . . communicate
   (B) injured . . retract
   (C) sullied . . publicize
   (D) damaged . . disseminate
   (E) extolled . . produce

2. The fact that the office was totally disorganized was one more indication of the ------- of the new manager and of the ------- of the person who had hired him.

   (A) indifference . . conscientiousness
   (B) ignorance . . diligence
   (C) incompetence . . negligence
   (D) tolerance . . viciousness
   (E) propriety . . confidence

3. Since the evidence of the manuscript's ------- is -------, its publication will be postponed until a team of scholars has examined it and declared it to be genuine.

   (A) authenticity . . inconclusive
   (B) truthfulness . . tarnished
   (C) veracity . . indubitable
   (D) legitimacy . . infallible
   (E) profundity . . forthcoming

4. The press conference did not clarify many issues since the President responded with ------- and ------- rather than clarity and precision.

   (A) sincerity . . humor
   (B) incongruity . . candor
   (C) fervor . . lucidity
   (D) animation . . formality
   (E) obfuscation . . vagueness

GO ON TO THE NEXT PAGE

5. Although the novel was not well written, it was such an exciting story that I was completely ------- and could not put it down.

(A) disenchanted
(B) enthralled
(C) indecisive
(D) disgruntled
(E) skeptical

Items #6–7: The passage below is followed by one or more items based on its content. Answer the items following each passage on the basis of what is stated or implied in the passage.

Fifth Avenue and Forty-Fourth Street swarmed with the noon crowd. The wealthy, happy sun glittered in transient gold through the thick windows of the smart shops, lighting upon mesh bags and purses and
5 strings of pearls in gray velvet cases; upon gaudy feather fans of many colors; upon the laces and silks of expensive dresses; upon the bad paintings and the fine period furniture in the elaborate showrooms of interior decorators.
10 Young working women, in pairs and groups and swarms, loitered by these windows, choosing their future boudoirs from some resplendent display that included even a man's silk pajamas laid domestically across the bed. They stood in front of the jewelry
15 stores, picked out their engagement rings and their wedding rings and their platinum wrist watches, and then drifted on to inspect the feather fans and opera cloaks; meanwhile digesting the sandwiches and sundaes they had eaten for lunch.

6. It can be inferred that the women (line 10) are

(A) planning elaborate weddings
(B) window-shopping on their lunch break
(C) eating lunch in the shops in the area
(D) waiting to meet their husbands for lunch
(E) walking briskly as a form of exercise

7. In context, "smart" (line 4) means

(A) intelligent
(B) inexpensive
(C) busy
(D) simple
(E) stylish

Items #8–9: The two passages below are followed by items based on their content and the relationship between the two passages. Answer the items on the basis of what is stated or implied in the passages and in any introductory material that may be provided.

Passage 1

The history of Earth has been punctuated by catastrophic events. Valleys were formed by dramatic plunges of fragments of the Earth's crust; mountains rose in gigantic upheavals of land; rocks formed when
5 one worldwide ocean precipitated out great masses of different materials. The mix of observed animal and plant fossils can be explained only by events such as massive fires or floods that wiped out living forms that were then replaced by other species.

Passage 2

10 Great changes result from gradual processes over long periods of time. Valleys form as constantly flowing water from streams cuts through the sides and bottom of the land. Rocks and mountains are formed, destroyed, and reformed by ongoing volcanic processes
15 and weathering. Different fossil types in successive rock layers represent changes that occur among related organisms due to long-term evolutionary processes.

8. The use of the word "punctuated" in line 1 suggests events that are

(A) observable but gradual
(B) powerful but controlled
(C) known but mysterious
(D) sudden and well-defined
(E) concise and logical

GO ON TO THE NEXT PAGE

9. The two passages develop differing viewpoints about the

(A) observable features of the Earth
(B) time that is spanned by Earth's history
(C) forces that have shaped the Earth
(D) importance of studying geology
(E) nature of scientific inquiry

Items #10–19: The two passages below are followed by items based on their content and the relationship between the two passages. Answer the items on the basis of what is stated or implied in the passages and in any introductory material that may be provided.

Passage 1 is adapted from Henry David Thoreau's Walden *(1854) in which the author discusses his life of solitude in the New England woods. Passage 2 is adapted from* Public Opinion*, published in 1922 by Walter Lippman, a noted journalist and commentator.*

Passage 1

I am sure that I never read any memorable news in a newspaper. If we read of one man robbed or murdered or killed by accident, or one house burned, or one vessel wrecked, or one steamboat blown up, or one
5 cow run over on the railroad, or one mad dog killed, or one lot of grasshoppers in the winter—we never need read of another. One is enough. If you are acquainted with the principle, what do you care for a myriad instances and applications? All news, as it is called, is
10 gossip, even though many people insist on hearing it. If I should pull the bell-rope of the local church to sound a fire alarm, almost everyone in the entire area would stop everything and come running, not mainly to save property from the flames but to see the blaze,
15 especially if it were the parish church itself on fire.

After a night's sleep the news is as indispensable to most people as breakfast: "Pray tell me everything important that has happened anywhere on this globe." They read over coffee and rolls that a man has had his
20 eyes gouged out the previous evening on the Wachito River. There was such a rush the other day at the railway office to learn the foreign news by the last arrival, that several large squares of plate glass were broken—news that I seriously think a ready wit might

25 have written a year or twelve years earlier with surprising accuracy. As for Spain, for instance, if you know how to throw in Don Carlos and the Infanta or Don Pedro and Seville and Granada from time to time in the right proportions—they may have changed the
30 names a little since I last saw the papers—and serve up a bull-fight when other entertainments fail, it will be true to the letter and give as good an idea of the exact state of ruin of things in Spain as the most succinct and lucid reports under this head in the newspapers. And as
35 for England, almost the last significant scrap of news from that quarter was the revolution of 1649; and if you have learned the history of her crops for an average year, you never need attend to that thing again, unless your speculations are of a merely pecuniary
40 character. If one may judge who rarely looks into the newspapers, nothing new does ever happen in foreign parts, a French revolution not excepted.

Passage 2

There is an island in the ocean, where in 1914 a few Englishmen, Frenchmen, and Germans lived. The
45 island was not served by telegraph, and the British mail steamer came once every sixty days. By September, it had not yet come, and the islanders were still talking about the latest newspaper, which told about the approaching trial of Madame Caillaux for the shooting
50 of Gaston Calmette. It was, therefore, with more than usual eagerness that the whole colony assembled at the quay on a day in mid-September to hear from the captain what the verdict had been. Instead, they learned of the start of the war and that for over six weeks those
55 of them who were English and those of them who were French had acted as if they were friends with those of them who were Germans, when in fact they were enemies.

Their plight was not so different from that of
60 most of the population of Europe. They had been mistaken for six weeks; on the continent, the interval may have been only six days or six hours, but there was an interval. There was a moment when the picture of Europe on which business was conducted as usual,
65 and it did not correspond in any way to the Europe that was about to make a jumble of so many lives. There was a time for which each person was still adjusted to an environment that no longer existed. All over the world as late as July 25th people were making goods
70 that they would not be able to ship, and buying goods that they would not be able to import. Careers were planned, enterprises were contemplated, and hopes and

GO ON TO THE NEXT PAGE

expectations were entertained, all in the belief that the world as known was the world as it was. Authors were
75 writing books describing that world. They trusted the picture in their heads. Then, over four years later, on a Thursday morning, came the news of an armistice, and people gave vent to their unutterable relief that the slaughter was over. Yet, in the five days before the real
80 armistice came, though the end of the war had been celebrated, several thousand young men died on the battlefields.

Looking back, we can see how indirectly we know the environment in which we live. We can see
85 that the news of it comes to us sometimes quickly, sometimes slowly, but whatever we believe to be a true picture, we treat as if it were the environment itself. It is harder to remember that about the beliefs upon which we are now acting, but in respect to other
90 peoples and other ages, we flatter ourselves that it is easy to see when they were in deadly earnest about ludicrous pictures of the world. We insist, because of our superior hindsight, that the world as they needed to know it and the world as they did know it were often
95 two quite contradictory things. We can see, too, that while they governed and fought, traded and reformed in the world as they imagined it to be, they produced results, or failed to produce any, in the world as it was. They started for the Indies and found America.

10. The newspaper report that a man has had his eyes gouged out is included by the author of Passage 1 as an example of

   (A) a local event that affects people's lives directly
   (B) an insignificant incident that does not affect the reader
   (C) an unusual occurrence that merits special coverage
   (D) an international incident that warrants detailed description
   (E) a major event that merits national news coverage

11. The author mentions Don Carlos and the Infanta in order to

   (A) demonstrate a thorough familiarity with current events in Spain
   (B) familiarize the reader with recent events that occurred in Spain
   (C) explain how events in Europe affect people all over the world
   (D) illustrate the point that news from Spain repeats itself
   (E) suggest that events in Spain should be reported in greater detail

12. The attitude of the author of Passage 1 towards the news is

   (A) ridicule
   (B) admiration
   (C) indifference
   (D) confidence
   (E) caution

13. As used in this context, "attend to" (line 38) means

   (A) be present at
   (B) be ignorant of
   (C) be concerned with
   (D) grow weary of
   (E) explain about

14. The author adds "especially if it were the parish church" (line 15) in order to

   (A) emphasize that people are fascinated by the bizarre
   (B) prove that citizens do not care about public property
   (C) show that residents take an interest in local events
   (D) stress the importance of the church to community
   (E) refute the notion that more people do not read the news

GO ON TO THE NEXT PAGE

15. According to the author of Passage 2, the people on the island "acted as if they were friends" (line 56) because they

(A) originally came from European countries
(B) were isolated from the rest of the world
(C) disagreed over the outcome of the trial
(D) shared an accurate view of the world
(E) did not realize that war had started

16. The "plight" to which the author refers in line 59 was

(A) incorrect reporting about the progress of the war
(B) lack of accurate information about current conditions
(C) an inability to obtain reports on a regular basis
(D) slanted war news from the European front
(E) need for more details about important events

17. In line 99, the author implies that people of another time

(A) accomplished something significant based upon wrong information
(B) failed to realize that the information available was wrong
(C) could have foreseen that America lay between Europe and India
(D) realized only in hindsight that they had landed in America
(E) appear silly in light of what is now known about the world

18. Which of the following best summarizes the different points of view of the two passages?

(A) The author of Passage 2 believes that news is important while the author of Passage 1 believes it is irrelevant.
(B) The author of Passage 1 believes that news is unreliable while the author of Passage 2 believes that it is accurate.
(C) The author of Passage 1 believes that newspapers provide critical information while the author of Passage 2 believes newspapers are too slow.
(D) The author of Passage 1 believes that news coverage could be improved while the author of Passage 2 believes that it is already adequate.
(E) The author of Passage 2 believes that newspaper should cover important international events while the author of Passage 1 believes local news is more important.

19. If the two authors had been able to write about the internet, they likely would

(A) say that their points apply to the news content on the worldwide web
(B) acknowledge that the new media makes reporting more relevant and more reliable
(C) insist that newspapers remain a better source of information than electronic media
(D) conclude that global news coverage gives readers a more accurate view of the world
(E) argue the quality of news reporting has declined with the development of the web

STOP

IF YOU FINISH BEFORE TIME IS CALLED, YOU MAY CHECK YOUR WORK ON THIS SECTION ONLY. DO NOT TURN TO ANY OTHER SECTION IN THE TEST.

NO TEST MATERIAL ON THIS PAGE

Practice Test III

SECTION 9—MATH
Time—20 Minutes
16 Items

DIRECTIONS: In this section, solve each item, and choose the correct answer choice. Fill in the corresponding oval on the answer sheet. Use any available space for scratchwork. Answers are on page 703.

Notes:

(1) The use of a calculator is permitted. All numbers used are real numbers.

(2) Figures that accompany problems in this test are intended to provide information useful in solving the problems. They are drawn as accurately as possible EXCEPT when it is stated in a specific problem that the figure is not drawn to scale. All figures lie in a plane unless otherwise indicated.

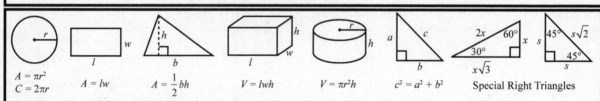

$A = \pi r^2$
$C = 2\pi r$
$A = lw$
$A = \frac{1}{2}bh$
$V = lwh$
$V = \pi r^2 h$
$c^2 = a^2 + b^2$
Special Right Triangles

The number of degrees of arc in a circle is 360.
The sum of the measures in degrees of the angles of a triangle is 180.

---

1. If $p, q, r, s,$ and t are whole numbers and the expression $2[p(q+r)+s]+t$ is even, which of the numbers *must* be even?

   (A) p
   (B) q
   (C) r
   (D) s
   (E) t

2. If the area of a square is $9x^2$, what is the length of its side expressed in terms of x?

   (A) $\frac{x}{3}$
   (B) $3x$
   (C) $9x$
   (D) $\frac{x^2}{3}$
   (E) $3x^2$

GO ON TO THE NEXT PAGE

3. The sum, the product, and the average (arithmetic mean) of three different integers are equal. If two of the integers are x and $-x$, the third integer is

(A) $\dfrac{x}{2}$

(B) $2x$

(C) x

(D) 0

(E) -1

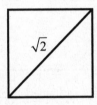

4. The perimeter of the square above is

(A) 1

(B) $\sqrt{2}$

(C) 4

(D) $4\sqrt{2}$

(E) 8

5. A triangle has one side of length 4 and another side of length 11. What are the greatest and least possible integer values for the length of the remaining side?

(A) 7 and 4

(B) 11 and 4

(C) 14 and 8

(D) 15 and 7

(E) 16 and 7

6. If $2x + 3y = 19$, and x and y are positive integers, then x could be equal to which of the following?

(A) 3

(B) 4

(C) 5

(D) 6

(E) 7

7. The scores received by 11 students on a midterm exam are as follows: 45, 57, 75, 80, 80, 81, 83, 88, 91, 93, and 98. What is the median score?

(A) 75

(B) 79

(C) 80

(D) 80.5

(E) 81

8. If $a^2 b^3 c < 0$, then which of the following must be true?

(A) $b^3 < 0$

(B) $b^2 < 0$

(C) $b < 0$

(D) $c < 0$

(E) $bc < 0$

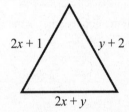

9. In the figure above, what is the perimeter of the equilateral triangle?

(A) 1

(B) 3

(C) 9

(D) 12

(E) 15

GO ON TO THE NEXT PAGE

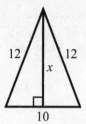

10. In the figure above, what is the value of *x*?

(A) 5
(B) 7.5
(C) $\sqrt{119}$
(D) 13
(E) 17

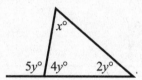

11. In the figure above, what is the value of *x*?

(A) 15
(B) 20
(C) 30
(D) 45
(E) 60

12. In the figure above, what is the length of $\overline{PQ}$?

(A) 0.12
(B) 0.16
(C) 0.13
(D) 0.11
(E) 0.09

2a − 1

3a − 2

13. In the figure above, what is the perimeter of the rectangle?

(A) $10a - 6$
(B) $10a - 3$
(C) $6a - 2$
(D) $5a - 6$
(E) $5a - 3$

14. If the average (arithmetic mean) of *x*, *x*, *x*, 56, and 58 is 51, then *x* =

(A) 43
(B) 47
(C) 49
(D) 51
(E) 53

15. For how many integers *x* is $-2 \le 2x \le 2$?

(A) 1
(B) 2
(C) 3
(D) 4
(E) 5

16. If for any number *n*, [*n*] is defined as the least integer that is greater than or equal to n^2, then [−1.1] =

(A) −2
(B) −1
(C)   0
(D)   1
(E)   2

STOP

IF YOU FINISH BEFORE TIME IS CALLED, YOU MAY CHECK YOUR WORK ON THIS SECTION ONLY. DO NOT TURN TO ANY OTHER SECTION IN THE TEST.

NO TEST MATERIAL ON THIS PAGE

Practice Test III

SECTION 10—WRITING
Time—10 Minutes
14 Items

DIRECTIONS: In this section, solve each item, and choose the correct answer choice. Fill in the corresponding oval on the answer sheet. Answers are on page 703.

Items #1–14: The following sentences test correct, effective expression. Each sentence contains an underlined portion, or the entire sentence may be underlined. Following each sentence are five ways of phrasing the underlined portion. Choice (A) repeats the original; the other four choices are different. If you think the original is better than any of the other choices, choose (A); otherwise, choose one of the other choices.

In choosing answers, follow the conventions of standard written English. Make sure to consider issues of grammar, word choice, sentence construction, and punctuation. Your choice should produce the most effective sentence. It should be clear, precise, and free of ambiguity or awkwardness.

Example:

Allen <u>visiting</u> his cousin in France last summer.

(A) visiting
(B) visited
(C) does visit
(D) a visit
(E) is visiting

1. In no field of history has the search for logical explanation been so diligent <u>so much as</u> the study of the decline and fall of the Roman Empire.

(A) so much as
(B) as in
(C) for
(D) due to
(E) like

2. <u>Letters were received by the editor of the newspaper that complained of its editorial policy.</u>

(A) Letters were received by the editor of the newspaper that complained of its editorial policy.
(B) Letters were received by the editor of the newspaper that complains of its editorial policy.
(C) Letters were received by the editor of the newspaper complaining of their editorial policy.
(D) The editor of the newspaper received letters that were complaining of the paper's editorial policy.
(E) The editor of the newspaper received letters complaining of the paper's editorial policy.

3. Washington Irving's German-influenced stories were profoundly moving to Americans, <u>knowing more than most</u> Britons what it was like to feel the trauma of rapid change, and Americans found in the lazy Rip a model for making a success of failure.

(A) knowing more than most
(B) who knew more then most
(C) knowing more then most
(D) most who knew more about what
(E) who knew more than most

GO ON TO THE NEXT PAGE

4. <u>By law, a qualified physician can only prescribe medicine, protecting the public.</u>

(A) By law, a qualified physician can only prescribe medicine, protecting the public.
(B) By law, only a qualified physician can prescribe medicine, protecting the public.
(C) By law, only a qualified physician can prescribe medicine that protects the public.
(D) In order to protect the public, by law a qualified physician only can prescribe medicine.
(E) In order to protect the public, by law only a qualified physician can prescribe medicine.

5. Improvements in economic theory and data gathering <u>today makes possible more accurate to forecast than was</u> possible even 20 years ago.

(A) today makes possible more accurate to forecast than was
(B) have made possible more accurate forecasts than were
(C) have made possible more accurate forecasts than was
(D) today make possible more accurate forecasts than was
(E) today make possible more accurate forecasting that were

6. It is reported that some tribes in Africa used to eat the livers of their slain <u>enemies which they believed allowed them to ingest their courage.</u>

(A) enemies which they believed allowed them to ingest their courage
(B) enemies which they believed allowed them to ingest their enemies' courage
(C) enemies which would, they believed, allow them to ingest their enemies' courage
(D) enemies, a process they believed allowed them to ingest the courage of their enemies
(E) enemies, a process they believed allowed them to ingest the enemy courage

7. The viola, the alto member of the violin <u>family, having</u> four strings tuned C, G, D, and A, upward from the C below middle C (a fifth lower than the violin's strings).

(A) family, having
(B) family, had
(C) families, having
(D) family, having had
(E) family, has

8. <u>In order to make skiing smoother, safer, and more enjoyable, a number of resorts have hired consultants</u> to design and sculpt the trails.

(A) In order to make skiing smoother, safer, and more enjoyable, a number of resorts have hired consultants
(B) In order to make skiing smoother, safer, and more enjoyable a number of consultants have been hired by resorts
(C) In the interest of making skiing smoother, safer, and able to be enjoyed, a number of resorts have hired consultants
(D) To make skiing smoother, safer, so that you can enjoy it, a number of resorts have hired consultants
(E) To make skiing smoother, also safer and enjoyable, a number of resorts will have hired consultants

9. Horatio Greenough, <u>considering by many to be the first American to become a professional sculptor,</u> executed a bust of then President John Quincy Adams.

(A) considering by many to be the first American to become a professional sculptor
(B) considered by many to be the first American to become a professional sculptor
(C) considering by many to be the first American to have become a professional sculptor
(D) considered by many to be the first professional American sculptor
(E) considered by many to have become the first American professional sculptor

GO ON TO THE NEXT PAGE ⟩

10. Her dissertation was interesting and well-researched, <u>but she lacked the organizational skills to make a convincing argument</u>.

(A) but she lacked the organizational skills to make a convincing argument
(B) lacking the organizational skills making a convincing argument
(C) but she also was lacking in organizational skills which would serve to make her arguments more convincing
(D) but having lacked the organizational skills of a convincing argument
(E) but without a convincing argument as a result of organizational skills

11. Credit card payments are now accepted in exchange for many goods and services around the world and in some countries, <u>like the Americans, is used even more widely than</u> cash.

(A) like the Americans, is used even more widely than
(B) like that of America, is used even more widely than
(C) as in America, are used even more widely than
(D) such as America, are used even more widely than
(E) such as America, are used even more widely as

12. Leprosy is not a highly contagious disease, yet it <u>has always and will continue to be feared until a vaccine will have been developed</u>.

(A) has always and will continue to be feared until a vaccine will have been developed
(B) is and always will continue to be feared until a vaccine is developed
(C) continues being feared and will be feared by people until the development of a vaccine
(D) has always been and will continue to be feared until a vaccine is developed
(E) is always feared and until a vaccine is developed, will continue to be so

13. <u>The delivery in large volume of certain welfare services are costly on account of the large number of public contact employees that are required by this.</u>

(A) The delivery in large volume of certain welfare services are costly on account of the large number of public contact employees that are required by this.
(B) The delivery of a large volume of certain welfare services are costly on account of the large number of public contact employees that this requires.
(C) The delivery in large volume of certain welfare services is costly because of the large number of public contact employees that is required.
(D) The delivery of certain welfare services in large volume is costly on account of the large numbers of public contact employees that is required.
(E) To deliver certain welfare services in large volume is costly on account of that this requires a large number of public service employees.

14. To prove that acridines kill bacteria through asphyxiation rather than starvation (as is the case with sulfa drugs), <u>Dr. Martin nearly spent 10 years building an artificial chemical wall around the bacteria</u> that deprives them of essential food.

(A) Dr. Martin nearly spent 10 years building an artificial chemical wall around the bacteria
(B) building an artificial chemical wall around the bacteria was nearly Dr. Martin's task for 10 years
(C) Dr. Martin spent nearly 10 years building an artificial chemical wall around the bacteria
(D) nearly spending 10 years, Dr. Martin built an artificial chemical wall around the bacteria
(E) 10 years were nearly spent by Dr. Martin building an artificial chemical wall around the bacteria

STOP

IF YOU FINISH BEFORE TIME IS CALLED, YOU MAY CHECK YOUR WORK ON THIS SECTION ONLY. DO NOT TURN TO ANY OTHER SECTION IN THE TEST.

Official Post-Assessment

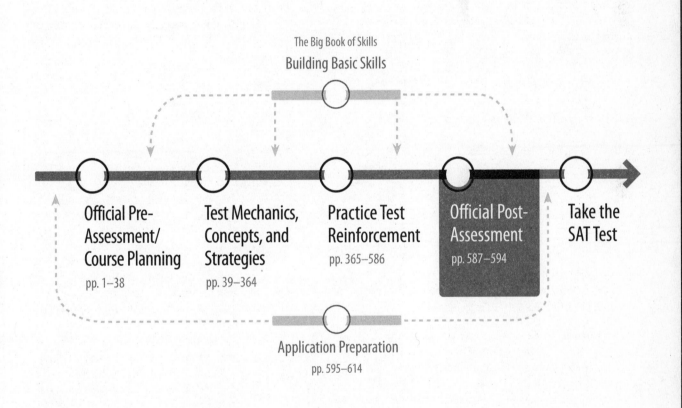

The Big Book of Skills
Building Basic Skills

Official Pre-Assessment/ Course Planning
pp. 1–38

Test Mechanics, Concepts, and Strategies
pp. 39–364

Practice Test Reinforcement
pp. 365–586

Official Post-Assessment
pp. 587–594

Take the SAT Test

Application Preparation
pp. 595–614

CAMBRIDGE
VICTORY FOR THE
SAT TEST

OFFICIAL POST-ASSESSMENT ADMINISTRATION

At the end of the course, you will take a post-assessment. This post-assessment consists of an official, retired SAT test. Perforated test answer sheets for the post-assessment are located in Appendix C of this book for programs not utilizing the Cambridge Platinum Express or Bronze Lite services. When you take the post-assessment, you should bring the following items to the classroom, in addition to anything else your teacher instructs you to bring:

1. Sharpened, soft-lead No. 2 pencils

2. A calculator that is approved for use on the test. This includes any four-function, scientific, or graphing calculator, except for the following:

   - Pocket organizers or PDAs

   - Handheld or laptop computers

   - Electronic writing pad or pen-input devices

   - Calculators built into any electronic communication device, such as a cell phone

   - Models with a QWERTY (typewriter) keypad (Calculators with letters on the keys are permitted as long as the keys are not arranged in a QWERTY keypad.)

   - Models that use paper tape, make noise, or have a power cord

     (For more detailed information on calculator usage, go to *http://www.collegeboard.com/student/testing/sat/testday/bring.html*.)

3. A watch (to pace yourself as you work through each test section)

As you take the test, remember the following points about marking the bubble sheet:

- Completely darken the bubble for each answer choice. If the letter within the bubble can be read through the pencil mark, then it is not dark enough. Mechanical pencils, even with No. 2 pencil lead, often fail to leave a dark mark.

- Stay within the lines.

- When erasing pencil marks, be sure to erase the marks completely. Do not leave any stray marks.

- Circle the answer choices in the test booklet. Towards the end of the section, or after each completed group of items, transfer the selected answers as a group to the answer form. Not only does this minimize erasing on the answer form, but it also saves time and minimizes transcription errors.

- When changing an answer, over-darken the final answer choice after completely erasing the original mark. This extra density tends to offset the residue left over from the original answer choice.

Strategic test-taking:

- Code items in the margin of the test booklet as easy or difficult before beginning to answer them. When pressed for time, you can skip to items that you are more likely to answer correctly.

- Make notes and calculations directly in the test booklet.

- Underline key words in Critical Reading passages.

If your program has ordered post-assessment Student Summary and Item Analysis reports, you will receive one of these reports with your post-assessment results. These reports will help you determine the areas in which you need continued study. You can then utilize your study time to prepare in those areas so that when you take the real test, you are ready to do your best. Refer to the "How to Use the Official Pre-Assessment Reports" (p. 5) to learn more about how to read and use the reports.

HOW TO USE THE OFFICIAL POST-ASSESSMENT REPORTS

You and your teacher will use the results of your post-assessment to recognize your individual strengths and weaknesses. Additionally, be sure at this point in the course that you have not only reviewed the "Setting a Test Score Target," "Overcoming Test Anxiety," and "Overall Test Management" sections in the Official Pre-Assessment/Course Planning part of this book, but that you have also followed through on your schedule for the course.

You will receive the results of your official post-assessment in the form of Student Summary and Student Item Analysis reports approximately 10 days after taking the test. These reports provide details about your performance and will help you to determine where to focus your efforts from now until your official test date by strategically targeting those skills, concepts, and strategies that will help you to improve in your areas of weakness. Just as you did with the pre-assessment, review the details of the sample Student Summary and Student Item Analysis reports on pages 6–7 so that you are familiar with its contents.

Once you have received your post-assessment reports, you can make connections between the reports and the specific skills, concepts, and strategies that you need to study. Review your reports to determine which item-types you need to study. Then, once you have your checklist of items to study, make a "to do" list using the following pages.

TOPIC	START DATE	DATE TO BE COMPLETED	DATE COMPLETED

PLANNING FOR FURTHER STUDY

You have received the results of your post-assessment. You have finished the Cambridge SAT test program. Now what?

In most cases you will have some spare time before the test day, so planning a study schedule between the post-assessment and the real test is critical to reinforce and maintain the skills, concepts, and strategies that you have learned throughout the course. Below are three steps that will help you make the most of your time.

Take the Practice Tests

Most students grasp knowledge of the subjects, but many struggle with time management. If you have not yet done so, take Practice Tests I–III included in the Practice Test Reinforcement part of this book. These practice tests:

1. reinforce skills and strategies,

2. simulate the experience of the real test by using time restrictions to emphasize time management, and

3. are an excellent guide to targeting your study plan.

Create a Written Study Plan

Use the results of your post-assessment and the practice tests to determine a day-by-day schedule that will create a clear and dependable guide for study. Create this plan based on the amount of time you have before the test day.

Several weeks before test day:

- Plan to review all material equally.

- As the test date approaches, devote your time to any particular areas of weakness.

Remember: picking a few subjects to focus on each week will help you manage your time between now and the test.

A few days before test day:

- Focus on core subjects that are giving you difficulty, or areas in which you would like to improve.

- Divide your time proportionally among these subjects based on your assessment of their difficulty.

Determine the topics you will study each day and allot the proper amount of time to study those sections of the book and complete relevant exercises.

Stick to the Plan

Once you have determined your rubric for study, stick to it without fail. Such discipline will surely reward you on the day of the test. Follow these helpful hints:

- Ask your teacher for insight. He or she can help you set goals for each core subject and may be able to suggest further strategies or a re-allotment of your time.

- Do not study too much. An hour or two of studying each day will be more productive than a severe study schedule.

- Practice every day.

Appendix A:
Beyond the SAT Test

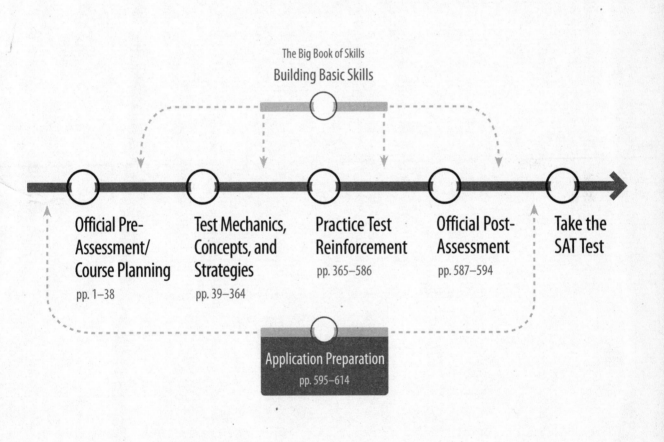

The Big Book of Skills
Building Basic Skills

Official Pre-Assessment/Course Planning
pp. 1–38

Test Mechanics, Concepts, and Strategies
pp. 39–364

Practice Test Reinforcement
pp. 365–586

Official Post-Assessment
pp. 587–594

Take the SAT Test

Application Preparation
pp. 595–614

CAMBRIDGE
VICTORY FOR THE
SAT TEST

APPLICATION PREPARATION

This section echoes our analysis of the admission process in "Setting a Test Score Target" (p. 9). To maximize your chances of success, you must create an admission application that satisfies the needs of the school to which you are applying. This does not mean that you create an application that is fictitious, but it does mean that you organize and present your experiences in a way that depicts you in the most favorable light.

NOTE: As you begin the application process, consider using the *Common Application*[1]. This source allows students to fill out only one application that can be sent to any of the organization's approximately 400 member colleges and universities. If the schools you are interested in attending accept this application, filling it out can save you a lot of time.

Highlight Your Unique Qualities within the Application

You must create an application that satisfies the needs of the school to which you are applying in order to maximize your chances of admissions success. Many times, this means that you should have a certain GPA and SAT test score, while at the same time exhibiting unique characteristics that differentiate you from other students. You should never create a deceptive, fictitious, or over-embellished application, but you should strive to present yourself as well as possible.

Most of the application questions that you will be asked require only short answers. For example:

- Did you work while you were in school?

- What clubs did you join?

- What honors or awards did you receive?

When answering such questions, you do not have much room to maneuver, but you should try to communicate as much information as possible in your short answers. Compare the following pairs of descriptions:

- *Member of Orchestra*
- *Second Violinist of the Orchestra*

- *Played Intra-Mural Volleyball*
- *Co-captain of the Volleyball Team*

- *Member of the AD's CSL*
- *One of three members on the Associate Dean's Committee on Student Life*

- *Worked at Billy's Burger Barn*
- *Weekend Shift Leader at Billy's Burger Barn (12 hours per week)*

In addition to the short-answer questions, some college applications invite or even require you to answer in writing one or more college admissions essay questions. (**NOTE:** The next section, "Six Ways to Jumpstart Your College Admissions Essays," covers in more detail how to write successful admissions essays.) The admissions essay—also called an application essay, personal statement, personal essay, essay question, or admissions

---

[1]The Common Application, https://www.commonapp.org (accessed June 18, 2012).

question—is a written composition from a student, generally submitted to a college at the same time as the application documents. Some college admissions essay questions ask for only a limited degree of additional information. For example:

- In a paragraph, explain to us one reason why you want to attend this college.

Other essay questions are open-ended and require providing more information:

- Tell us additional information about yourself that you think would assist us in the selection process.

Still others are more thought provoking and require a reasoned and clearly articulated answer to the specific question:

- Describe a character in fiction, a historical figure, or a creative work (as in art, music, science, etc.) that has had an influence on you, and explain that influence.

The point of the admissions essay questions is for you to give the admissions decision-makers helpful information that might not be available from your test scores, GPA, and short-answer questions.

You should consider the admissions essay to be a highly significant part of your application for two reasons. First, answers to the essay questions will be your argument to the admissions personnel for your acceptance. The answers will give them additional reasons why they should accept you. Second, the admissions essay is one aspect of the application over which you can exercise real control. Your work experience is established, your GPA is already settled, and your SAT test has been scored. Those aspects of the application cannot easily be manipulated. The writing of the admissions essay, however, is completely under your present control.

What information should be included in an open-ended admissions essay (one that asks generally for more information about yourself)? You should devise arguments that interpret your academic, employment, and personal histories in such a way as to indicate that you have the ability to complete college and that you are committed to studying and later to pursuing a career in a chosen area of study. Clearly, you should stress your strengths. Your essay answer must not be a simple restatement of facts that are already in the application. Imagine, for example, a submitted essay that reads as follows:

I went to high school where I got a 3.5 GPA. I was a member of the Associate Dean's Committee on Student Life, and I worked as the assistant manager on the weekend shift at Billy's Burger Barn. Then, I took the SAT test and got a 1610. I know that I will make a really good B.A. candidate and will enjoy my job.

This essay is not very interesting. Furthermore, all of that information is redundant because it is already included in the answers to the standard questions on the application.

Instead, describe the facts of your life in such a way that they will be interpreted as good reasons for accepting you. The essay below highlights several of the student's strengths:

While many students focused only on their social calendar and extracurricular activities, I learned to manage my academic schedule, work commitments, and social events. As a freshman in high school, I knew my family could not afford the burden of paying for my college education. Unwilling to give up on my dream of going to college, I worked 12 hours each week at Billy's Burger Barn to save money for my education.

At 16, I had to learn how to juggle work, my four honors classes, and my extracurricular activities. My planner became my best friend as it reminded me of where I needed to be and what was due. The organization and time management skills I acquired in high school will greatly benefit my college life, as I plan to be involved in rigorous classes, student organizations, and internships.

Focusing on work experience and the positive lessons you have learned through a job is also a good strategy:

Like many other students, I started working in my junior year to earn money for college tuition. However, my job at Chic Fashion Depot turned out to be more about learning life skills than making money.

I discovered quickly that my work environment was very different from the school environment I was accustomed to. I had to learn how to communicate professionally with customers and my managers. Luckily, I found that helping customers was enjoyable and helped the day pass quickly. My sales skyrocketed as I became more efficient in my duties and more adept at helping customers. I earned "Employee of the Month" four times simply because I took pride in my work and wanted to make customers happy.

Although I enjoyed my job, it was difficult to manage school and work at the same time. However, I knew I had responsibilities at both work and school that needed to be fulfilled. It was all about organizing my time and staying on track. My work experience allowed me to mature and learn important life skills that impacted my social interactions, work ethic and sense of responsibility.

Can you say anything about your test score? Probably not much—the SAT test score is fairly simple and not usually open to interpretation. However, if you feel that your test score does not reflect the level of work of which you are capable, ask a teacher to include a note to this effect in a letter of recommendation that accompanies your application.

Finally, you must also persuade the admissions committee that you are serious about obtaining your college degree. You must be able to give an example of something in your background that explains why you want to go to college. Also, it will help your case if you can suggest what you might do with a college degree. For example:

As a prospective environmental science major, I interned with the Student Environmental Association. Working with private company executives who had themselves satisfied E.P.A. emissions standards, we convinced the University to stop polluting the Ten-Mile Run Creek. From this experience, I learned how business helps to protect our environment. I plan to make environmental resources my area of study, and I hope to work for the government or a private agency to protect the environment.

A word of warning is in order regarding your career objectives: they must be believable. It will not be sufficient to write, "I plan to solve the environmental problems of American industry." Such a statement is much too abstract. College admissions officers are also not interested in a general discourse on the advantages of democracy or the hardship of poverty. If you write, "I want to eliminate damage to the planet and to help private industries help themselves environmentally," then there had better be something in your experience that makes this statement believable.

Thus far, we have discussed the issues of ability and motivation. You may also wish to include information in a general essay answer that demonstrates to the school how you would help create a diverse student body with interesting talents, abilities, and perspectives. This additional information can be something dramatic:

One morning, a patron choked on a burger and lost consciousness. Although my first instinct was to stand paralyzed with fear, I quickly remembered the CPR class I had taken at the local hospital. I used the Heimlich maneuver to dislodge the food and performed CPR until a team of paramedics arrived. Thankfully, the patron recovered fully. This significant event reinforced my interest in the medical profession. The feeling of helping someone in the scariest moment of her life was profound. I want to become an emergency room nurse so that I can help people on a daily basis.

Or, the information may not be so dramatic:

> *My parents are Armenian immigrants, so I am fluent in Armenian as well as English. I would enjoy meeting others who share an interest in the politics, legal developments, and culture of that part of the world.*

Do not underestimate the value of this kind of information. It is, so to speak, the icing on the cake. These details about your life make you a more interesting individual and might tip the scale in your favor when all other things are equal. Keep in mind, though, that it will not get you accepted into a school for which you would not otherwise be competitive in terms of SAT test score and GPA.

Now, we turn our attention to matters of style. Your arguments for acceptance need to be presented in an organized fashion. Use an outline as a tool to help you write consistently and clearly. Once you have organized your thoughts on paper, you should be able to write expressively while staying on topic. Review the following outline and notice the way it guides you while allowing you to write creatively about your experiences.

> I.   *I am committed to extracurricular involvement.*
>   A. *Senior Class Student Council representative*
>   B. *One of two student photographers for the Yearbook*
> II. *I had a high school mentor who encouraged me to pursue my interests.*
>   A. *Mrs. Jensen, my art teacher*
>   B. *Helped develop my passion for photography*
> III. *I want to pursue a teaching career.*
>   A. *Help students pursue their interests*
>   B. *Push students to achieve in academics and extracurricular pursuits*

The prose that you use should display your own natural style of writing. Do not write something that appears contrived or cute. Rather, you should create your outline using as many arguments as possible. Then, you must begin to edit. For most people, the final document should not be more than a page to a page and a half in length—typed, of course! During the editing process, you should strive for an economy of language so that you can convey as much information as possible. Additionally, you will be forced to make considered judgments about the relative importance of various points. You will be forced to delete those ideas that are not really very compelling. In order to compose a really good essay, it may be necessary to reduce five or six pages to a single page, and the process may require more than 20 drafts. Make sure that you have at least one other person look at your essay—a teacher, counselor, or parent would be a good resource.

Because a number of colleges elevate the importance of the college admissions essay, more thorough recommendations are presented in the next section, "Six Ways to Jumpstart Your College Admissions Essays" (p. 603).

Solicit Effective Letters of Recommendation

Perhaps the best advice that we can give you about so-called letters of recommendation is that you should think of them as evaluations rather than recommendations. Indeed, many admissions officers refer to letter-writers as evaluators. These letters can be very important factors in an application, so who should actually write them?

First of all, some schools require a letter from the dean of students (or some similar functionary) at your high school. Essentially, this requirement serves as an inquiry into your behavior. However, colleges do not really expect that this person will have much to say about your application since in many cases students do not become acquainted with their deans. This letter is merely intended to evoke any information about disciplinary problems that might not otherwise surface. So, the best response from a dean, and the one that most people tend to receive, is just a statement to the effect that there is nothing much to say regarding your behavior. In addition to the dean's letter, most schools require, or at least permit, you to submit two or three letters of evaluation from other sources. Who should write these letters? Remember that a letter of evaluation does not necessarily have to come from a well-known person. How effective is the following letter?

> *Francis Scott*
> *Chairperson of the Board*
>
> *To the Admissions Committee:*
>
> *I am recommending Susan Roberts for college. Her mother is a member of our board of directors. Susan's mother earned her doctorate at the University of Chicago and she regularly makes significant contributions to our corporate meetings. Susan, following in her mother's footsteps, will make a fine college candidate.*
>
> *Sincerely,*
> *Francis Scott*

The letterhead holds great promise, but the body of the letter is worthless. It is obvious that Francis Scott does not really have any basis for his conclusion that Susan Roberts "will make a fine college candidate."

Find people who know you very well to write the very best letters of recommendation (e.g., a teacher with whom you took several courses, the sponsor of a club in which you are active, or an employer with whom you have worked closely). A good evaluation will incorporate personal knowledge into the letter and will make references to specific events and activities. For example:

> *White, Weiss, and Blanche*
>
> *To the Admissions Committee:*
>
> *White, Weiss, and Blanche is a consulting firm that advises corporations on environmental concerns. Susan Roberts has worked for us as an intern for the past two summers. Her work is outstanding, and she is an intelligent and genial person.*
>
> *Last summer, as my assistant, Susan edited a five-page report that outlined a way of altering a client's exhaust stack to reduce sulfur emissions. In addition to ensuring that the report was free of spelling and grammar errors, she noticed an important omission in the data table, which we were able to correct before submitting the report. Additionally, Susan assisted with a live presentation during a meeting with the client's board of directors and engineers. She was confident and even answered some questions about the procedures followed in testing the new system.*
>
> *Finally, Susan made an important contribution to our company softball team. The team finished in last place, but Susan played in every game. Her batting average wasn't anything to brag about, but her enthusiasm more than made up for it.*
>
> *Sincerely,*
> *Mary Weiss*

This letter demonstrates that the writer knows the applicant very well. The writer is able to address several aspects of the applicant's character, personality, and work ethic from a position of familiarity. A letter like this one makes for a very meaningful contribution to any college application, so you should strive to receive this type of recommendation as part of your application portfolio.

SIX WAYS TO JUMPSTART YOUR COLLEGE ADMISSIONS ESSAYS

An admissions director sits behind a well-lit desk in a paper-strewn office. Her window overlooks a large, rolling college campus. At mid-morning, students freckle the walkways, ambling to and from the surrounding lecture halls. Of current concern for this college admissions director are not the students already enrolled but the hundreds or even thousands of students who are seeking admission for the fall semester. Near the edge of her desk rises an already teetering stack of college applications, representing the academic hopes and dreams of soon-to-be high school graduates. Students from a wide range of high schools—big, small, public, private, home-based, rural, suburban, urban—have submitted their vital statistics: test score(s); high school transcripts with summaries of classes; GPAs; class rank; extracurricular activities; and references from teachers, coaches, club advisors, and counselors. These application papers assist her in differentiating one level of student from another (e.g., students with "As" and "Bs" versus students with "Bs" and "Cs"). She pulls out two applications with very similar test scores and GPAs and considers which of these two students will receive the coveted stamp of "admitted" on his or her file. Following this task, she will move on to the even more challenging task of mining through applications to find the small percentage of students who are "diamonds in the rough"; these students did not fully flourish in high school for various reasons, but they have the potential to succeed in a college environment.

As a high school student, your goals and aspirations are tightly interwoven with your ability to obtain admission to the college of your choice. Thus, as a student applying to various colleges, it is important for you to understand the selection or admissions process that these institutions of higher education use to narrow the pool of applicants. You should ask a number of probing questions about the process: What criteria do colleges use to admit students? How does the college admissions director decide between the merits of students who hold similar test scores and grades? How does a college discover those rare, under-qualified students who have not fully demonstrated their potential in high school through grades or test scores?

Of course, college admissions directors assess potential students using tools such as GPA, test score(s), teacher references, and extracurricular participation records. But colleges also use an evaluation instrument known as the admissions essay as a significant component in determining which students will or will not receive acceptance letters.

The admissions essay—also referred to as an application essay, a personal statement, or a personal essay—is a written composition from a student, generally submitted to a college at the same time as the application documents. The written essay—typically from 100 to 500 words in length—may answer a directed content question (e.g., an opinion on some current event), or it may respond to a simple "tell us about yourself" question.

The essay prompts listed below reflect actual examples of those delivered alongside recent college admissions applications.

- Write an essay in which you tell us about someone who has made an impact on your life, and explain how and why this person is important to you.

- Choose an issue of importance to you—the issue could be personal, school related, local, political, or international in scope—and write an essay in which you explain the significance of that issue to yourself, your family, your community, or your generation.

- Evaluate a significant experience or achievement, risk you have taken, or ethical dilemma you have faced and its impact on you.

- Discuss some issue of personal, local, national, or international concern and its importance to you.

- Make a rational argument for a position that you do not personally support.

- Share an experience through which you have gained respect for intellectual, social, or cultural differences. Comment on how your personal experiences and achievements would contribute to the diversity of our college.

- As you prepare to pursue a career in music, theatre, or dance, describe your thoughts on the relationship between the arts and today's society. How relevant has your art been to your community and to you?

- What outrages you?

- If you were given a grant to research a scientific or medical issue that you deem important to the world, what would it be, why would you choose it, and what kind of research do you think would have the greatest chance of being productive?

- What have you read recently that you found enlightening?

- Consider the books, essays, poems, or journal articles that you have read over the last year or two, either for school or leisure. Discuss the way in which one of these writings has changed your understanding of the world, of other people, or of yourself.

The admissions essay provides you with an opportunity to "sell" yourself and hopefully elevate your status from a potential student to a future student in the eyes of a college. In submitting this essay, it is important to view the process as a chance to catapult yourself beyond the other candidates. Confidently articulate why a particular college needs you as a student by emphasizing your unique goals, values, aptitudes, and abilities.

What follows are six strategies to help you jumpstart the writing of a college admissions essay. While these strategies can tell you neither exactly what types of questions will be asked (since some colleges ask questions that are quite broad while others ask questions that are very targeted and specific) nor what assessment criteria specific colleges use for evaluating the admissions essay (since each institution tightly guards this type of assessment information), they should provide valuable insights to consider as you begin the essay writing process.

Present Yourself as Unique, Exceptional, or Talented

Because college admissions directors read thousands of essays, you must write in a way that distinguishes you from the crowd of applying students. A large number of college applicants submit adequate to excellent GPAs along with solid test scores. Many have been involved in extracurricular activities, such as athletics, honors clubs, music, or drama. Others have participated in a wide range of leadership or volunteer roles. Given this large pool of truly qualified students, you must leave an impression that makes you positively memorable as a candidate for admission by seizing the opportunity to compose a well-crafted essay that highlights your best characteristics and your achievements.

In preparation for writing the essay, think clearly and creatively about what makes you unique, exceptional, or talented as a potential college student. What unique experiences have you had? Do you have abilities or aptitudes that set you apart from other students? In what special events or activities have you participated? What unique cultural experiences have you encountered? Is there anything special about how or where you grew up? Have you met famous or unique people who have influenced you? Are you exceptionally talented in a particular area, such as music, art, or drama? What motivates you to succeed beyond other students? Do you have atypical work or employment experiences? How have you overcome an individual setback, struggle, or limitation? Have you participated in significant and/or memorable athletic events? Can you identify a unique hobby in which you participate? Have you volunteered or served in your community and made a significant contribution? Do you have a one-of-a-kind talent? Have you received any special awards or commendations? Have you distinguished yourself as a leader in clubs or organizations?

The following are examples of opening essay sentences that include the positive characteristics upon which a student might desire to focus in an essay. Consider how these statements might serve as springboards for powerful admissions essays:

- *Because my grandmother moved into my family's home when I was just ten days old, I have vicariously experienced a distinct and dissimilar culture from my own. I flood my days with friends and activities found in the high-tech, suburban, media-driven, adolescent-controlled culture of Tri-City High School. During the evening hours, however, I wander in a completely different culture immersed in the foods, songs, stories, and language of the "Old World" where my grandmother lived for more than fifty years.*

- *I personally do not know of any other high school student at South High School who has willingly dined on goat intestines, but while traveling over the summer with an international student exchange program, I embraced the opportunity to feast on this unique delicacy.*

- *Senator-elect Jamison shook my hand vigorously and commented to all those within earshot that he was sure my efforts had played a significant role in contributing to his recent election.*

- *Not every seventeen-year-old might jump at the opportunity to witness a three-hour long cardiac surgery from the operating room window of a teaching hospital—but I certainly did. Dr. Rose provided me with just such a privilege in celebration of my fourth year of serving as a volunteer hospital aid at New City Hospital.*

- *Performing with a choir at the governor's mansion may seem like less than a life-changing experience. But after speaking personally with the governor following the performance and asking her one simple question, my perspective regarding the world of women in politics radically changed.*

- *Losing every single game as a senior football player at Old Lake High School may not have taught me much about celebrating victories, but I did learn valuable lessons about perseverance, dedication, and humility.*

- *I never thought I'd write a computer program that other people would regularly use. But after a friend introduced me to the world of open-source coding, I fervently dove into writing new code and improving existing code on a variety of programs that some major companies utilize every day.*

- *Working weekends at Billy B's Barbeque during high school not only allowed me to earn money for college, but it also brought me face-to-face with a host of truly fascinating "regulars" whose life stories I will never forget.*

- *For years, because of my love for reading, each and every librarian at the Key City Public Library knew me by name. But now, because of my love for writing, everyone who reads the Key City Times newspaper also knows me by name.*

- *I was shocked and honored when my name was called as the regional swimmer of the year, especially considering that my pediatrician had warned me that childhood asthma would forever hinder my ability to compete in athletics.*

Remember that the main goal in writing an admissions essay is to distinguish yourself from the other applicants. Note how this next example of a college essay response to the prompt, "What has influenced your desire to study history at New College University?" shines light on a unique relationship that led to exceptional experiences.

At first blush, I look like a typical all-American girl. But I truly live a double identity. From the very day that my grandmother moved into my family's home when I was just ten days old, I have vicariously experienced a distinct and dissimilar culture from my own. I flood my days with friends and activities found in the high-tech, suburban, media-driven, adolescent-controlled culture of Tri-City High School. During the evening hours, however, I wander in a completely different culture immersed in the foods, songs, stories, and language of the "Old World" where my grandmother lived for more than fifty years.

Seeded by the nightly songs and stories of my grandmother, I had for years envisioned scenes of the Italian countryside with narrow streets and quiet villas. In an almost mystical manner, I could smell chickens roasting on open-air fireplaces, feel the breezes off the sea of the Sicilian coast, see the workers harvesting grapes in the hillside vineyards, and hear the after-dinner songs rising from family gatherings. But as a junior at Tri-City High School, those far-away images became reality after I traveled to Italy to spend the summer of my junior year in Sicily as a participant in an International Student Exchange Unlimited program. I was amazed at how my grandmother's stories took tangible shape and substance over twelve memorable and life-transforming weeks.

I knew I would learn valuable lessons traveling the Italian countryside, visiting historical sites, and meeting a rich variety of local characters, but I did not anticipate that this adventure would change my perspective on the world and redirect my future. In my final weeks of the student exchange program, I joined a group digging for archaeological relics just outside the town of Salina. Through listening to the archaeology lectures from local university professors, I discovered that civilizations had for thousands of years settled and resettled the Sicilian shores and hillsides. As I participated in the archaeological dig, I touched shards of pottery left by some of the very earliest inhabitants of the island and helped uncover the burial grounds of ancient people. I read research and became acquainted with civilizations that I never knew had even existed.

This experience, spawned by my grandmother's influence in my life, launched in me a desire to study ancient civilizations and cultures. So, now I'm applying to New College University in order to study history and archaeology. I'm convinced that as a student at New College University I will continue to live a double identity, wonderfully captured between the pull of contemporary and ancient cultures.

Tell an Engaging Story

"The universe is made of stories, not atoms." Muriel Rukeyser

To effectively communicate how you are a unique candidate, tell an engaging story—or stories if word limits permit—of experiences that highlight those personal characteristics that distinguish you from other students.

Think about the last journalistic photograph in a newspaper, magazine, or website that captured your attention. The best photographs tell a story. As you look at a great journalistic picture, you gain an emerging sense of the event, the context, the emotion, the tension, the thrill, or the struggle embedded in the image. In the same manner, the best admissions essays also portray a story that imprints a lasting mark on the reader. When the essay prompts allow, you should consider organizing your essay around meaningful and moving stories that communicate how your hopes and dreams draw you to this particular college and a specific area of study.

Bear in mind this word of warning. As you write your essay, reemphasizing your GPA, SAT test score, or class rank in a bland format does little to draw attention to yourself. Remember that the pages of your college application and high school transcript already list these figures. Yes, these numbers do provide important information to the college. (That, in fact, is why the college requires you to provide them in the first place.) However, these numbers are not central to the purpose of an admissions essay. The core function of this essay is to determine whether you can clearly and concisely articulate, in written fashion, who you are and why you make a great candidate for entrance into a particular college. If your scores are exceptional and you can communicate them in a creative manner, include them in the essay.

Review the following examples of essay paragraphs, and note how telling significant information in a story or narrative form creates a more engaging and readable essay paragraph.

Essay Paragraph 1: Poor Example

As a student at Newbury High School, I was involved in four years of Student Council, Art Club, and the yearbook. My GPA was a 3.9. I graduated in the top 5% of students in my class. I enjoy photography. I want to be an art teacher.

Essay Paragraph 1: Better Example

The janitor laughed loudly as he saw me catapult over the empty wastebaskets strewn in the hall after school. Again, I was literally running (down the school corridor) from my responsibilities as the Student Council representative for the Senior Class to join in assisting the Yearbook production team in hitting another important deadline. As one of two student photographers for Newbury High School, I had worked late into the night selecting the last three pictures to appear on the Yearbook cover. I wanted the three pictures to capture the memories of the school year. Although the pictures were still life, the emotion and movement in each of them was apparent. The crowd cheering at the homecoming football game, the commotion of the hallways during passing period, and the celebration and pride at the senior awards ceremony were the memories forever frozen in time on the yearbook cover.

My passion for photography flourished with the help of Mrs. Jensen, my art teacher and the yearbook advisor. She mentored and encouraged me throughout my four years in high school. She pushed me to achieve to the highest degree not only in academics but also in my extracurricular activities. Because of Mrs. Jensen's example, I too want to be an art teacher who pushes students to take new challenges and to succeed in both academic and extracurricular endeavors.

Essay Paragraph 2: Poor Example

I was selected as the #1 golfer in our state my senior year in high school. In my junior year, I was ranked in the top ten. I think my test scores and my GPA are high enough for you to consider me for a scholarship. I also play in the Jazz Band.

Essay Paragraph 2: Better Example

Innovation. For me, there is a deep sense of satisfaction in finding a unique or creative solution to a problem. In last spring's state high school golf tournament, I was leading the field by a single stroke walking toward the final green. An errant tee shot on my part had landed my ball behind a stand of bushes, and my coaches had groaned when they saw the precarious position of my lie. Thinking quickly— and innovatively—I grabbed my two iron and shot the ball not over the bushes as all would have expected, but under a gap below the bushes, rolling the ball cleanly toward the middle of the green. I sunk a remaining seven-foot putt and won not only the state high school golf tournament but also the #1 ranking that accompanied the win. Throughout my four years of high school varsity golf, I over and over again discovered innovative ways to succeed. It is this deep desire to innovate, to create new avenues to answers, and to find solutions to challenges that drives my love for problem-solving in the areas of mathematics and science. As a member of the Blackstone High School Jazz Band, innovation, too, is what drives my love for creative musical expression. And this love for innovation is what drives me to apply to the honors program at Lake City University, which is known nationally for its unique approach to educating students.

Telling an engaging story about some life experience is a powerful tool in distinguishing yourself from other students. Note that not every essay prompt can be addressed through the use of a story. Some call for a more logical or deductive approach. Nevertheless, when the opportunity to tell a story presents itself within the context of a specific essay prompt, you should seize upon that opportunity to tell why you are a great potential student.

Narrow Your Essay to a Specific Theme

A college admissions essay is typically limited to a certain number of words. As you can imagine, an admissions director does not have the time to read a multiple page treatise covering your entire life story from birth to high school graduation. As you organize your essay, focus your essay on one or two major ideas or themes that express your experiences, abilities, goals, attitudes, ideas, talents, or thoughts. Do not ramble aimlessly or muse recklessly without any focus or overarching structure. Instead, narrow the thrust of your essay to a specific and manageable theme.

Read the following winning essay submitted for a college scholarship contest. Note how the student tells how just one experience in her life—being cast in a play—caused her perspectives on life to mature and grow. Consider how she narrows her theme.

My heart was pounding out of my chest in an unfamiliar rhythm. I longed for water but knew there was not time. In the crowded area, pushed up against others, I could feel their breathing, as rapid and tense as my own. The anticipation was killing me as I swallowed hard and closed my eyes. Overcome with emotion, I cracked my knuckles three times—a habit I perform during extreme nervousness. My mind was flooded with last minute worries, and I tried with difficulty to push them away. I sensed a comforting hand on my shoulder and felt a rush of momentary calmness. "Everything is going to be O.K.," someone said reassuringly.

As the show was about to begin, my anticipation was replaced by excitement. As I looked out tentatively at the audience, I felt strangely secure rather than vulnerable on the stage. Suddenly, as if by magic, my worries were gone. I was no longer Malinda Spry, a seventeen-year-old-girl concerned about monologues, dance routines, and solos; I was someone else. I was Eve, and as the heart-wrenching words to "Children of Eve" escaped my mouth, the scene of expulsion from the beautiful Garden of Eden became my reality.

When I was cast in Children of Eve, *a musical chronicling the events of the Old Testament, I was overwhelmed with giving voice to Eve. I was extremely grateful to be given this unique opportunity to represent such a complex character. As the woman held accountable for the presence of sin in the world, Eve is viewed as the villain in the creation story. However, before long, I saw the other side of Eve, the intelligent, curious, gifted side; the one responsible for humanity's successes in the world rather than its defeat. Although Eve carried the burden of original sin, she was amazingly strong and blessed with an innate desire to learn. I knew that it was my responsibility to portray the story of creation through her eyes. My portrayal of Eve included her passionate response to life in and out of paradise. Inspired, I recognized a parallel between Eve and myself.*

I was exhilarated to bring Eve to life. She was never content with paradise, perfection, or the Garden, as Adam was. Instead, Eve asked the difficult questions and refused to accept life the way it was presented to her. She ardently claimed that it was God's will for humanity to be expelled from Eden in order to discover free will. Although Eve defied God, she found that He never abandoned her, a fact that strengthened my own faith in life.

During the closing moments of the performance, Eve implores God and the rest of creation—her children—for forgiveness. "We were just humans, to error prone," she says, looking around. The song brought tears to my eyes as I realized Eve's influence in all of creation and her profound lesson of forgiveness, not of betrayal, of love, not of hate. As I glanced around the audience, whose faces were filled with sympathy, I knew that they too understood the creation story from Eve's perspective—as it was meant to be told.

Start with an Engaging Hook and End with a Powerful Punch

An effective essay begins with an enticing start. In your essay, write an introduction that hooks the admissions director, compelling him or her to finish reading your composition. Craft your first two or three lines in such a way that they creatively engage the reader. These first sentences are so important that you may need to work and rework them until you find a great combination of words, setting a compelling hook and subsequent direction for your essay.

Here are some tips for creating engaging hooks (not all of them will be used at once, of course):

- Use active verbs (avoid passive verbs).

- Give a sense of feeling or emotion.

- Use a moving literary, historical, or provocative quotation.

- Provide a surprise, logical twist, or emotional shock.

- Use hyperbole.

- Interject a puzzle or riddle.

- Introduce an anecdote.

- Draw an example from a current event.

- Create suspense or drama.

- Convey humor (ONLY if you can do it naturally and tastefully).

- Avoid dull facts and figures.

- Ask a question that cannot be answered.

Remember that your introductory sentences must flow naturally into the entire theme of your essay. The introduction directs the reader toward your remaining thoughts or arguments.

As you develop a powerful hook, do not forget that your essay must answer the question that is asked. Make sure your introductory sentences help you to focus clearly and intentionally on the answer to the essay prompt. No matter how powerful your essay is, if you fail to directly address the prompt that is presented, you fail the essay.

Here are three examples of essay introductions that hook the reader into an engaging story.

Essay Introduction: Example 1

My feet clamped to the floor, immovable, after Mr. Smith called my name as Washington High School's "Student of the Year" at the annual award ceremony. As my shock faded and I coerced my limbs to stand and walk to the stage, I thought of all the people who had helped me achieve this award. There was Mr. Paulsen, my varsity basketball coach, Mrs. Simpson, my orchestra director, and Mr. Smith, the Honor Society advisor who had nominated me for the award.

Essay Introduction: Example 2

"Diplomacy is the art of saying 'Nice doggie' until you can find a rock," quipped Will Rogers, the U.S. humorist and showman. The danger in practicing this particular philosophy of political diplomacy is that

on occasion the dog wakes from its passivity, growls ferociously, and bites aggressively, all before the rock is found and exploited as a defense. Current research in the field of political science provides effective alternatives to this overused passive/aggressive approach to diplomacy that Will Rogers humorously presented.

Essay Introduction: Example 3

Why do I always smell barbequed pork ribs, deep-fried hushpuppies, and large mugs of black coffee in my mind when I think of my love for history? Working weekends at Billy B's Barbeque during high school not only allowed me to save money for college, but it also brought me face to face with a host of truly fascinating "regulars" whose life stories I will never forget. In Mr. Brown's World History class I had studied the causes and results of the Korean War. But it was not until I met Mr. Jacob Abbot—"Jake" to his friends—that I came face-to-face with the real history of that military conflict.

Here is an example of an entire essay that was submitted for a scholarship contest. Observe how this student creatively hooks the reader into the history of her deep desire to become a broadcast journalist.

"Where are my spoons," my mother would ask, commenting on the ever-dwindling supply as she washed dishes. By the time I was seven, my mother discovered that her missing spoons served as microphones, enabling me to host a "live" news show with my younger siblings. With the assistance of my "guests," we performed daily newscasts from our kitchen and living room. As the clock approached our bedtime, I would usher a "breaking news" segment.

Eventually, I learned that the profession of journalism involves more than "breaking news" or playing dress-up for a make-believe camera. As I became a devout viewer of Ted Koppel and 60 Minutes, several things became apparent. Journalism required remaining abreast of both historical and contemporary events, as well as a firm belief that public issues be viewed through the lens of people's everyday experiences.

As a junior in high school, I applied to and was accepted as a student intern at the local television station. This allowed me to move even further from the world of playing broadcast journalism to truly living and breathing it. The weekend news crew took me under their wings and allowed me to try almost every facet of creating the evening news.

While many years have passed since my broadcast days from my living room, I cannot disassociate myself from that little girl and her microphone. Indeed, that girl's dream has not dimmed, nor has the insatiable desire to transform it into reality. As an aspiring broadcast journalist, I hope to ultimately inform and advance larger discourses that affect the social, political, and economic welfare of our society. If admitted to Lincoln University, I want to hone my skills in order to one day tell stories of people at their best and their worst, narratives that speak of our curiosities, our hopes, and our struggles.

You must write your introduction to capture the imagination of the reader. Remember, however, that you must also construct a meaningful ending or conclusion. In the conclusion, attempt to answer the "why," "what next," or "so what" questions of your essay in a meaningful final sentence. Although the conclusion is a summary, do not merely summarize or reword your arguments or thoughts. Give the reader an understanding of the final step or next steps following your essay. Having told a moving story or made a powerful argument, now tell the reader what you want them to remember or do with your essay.

Consider these examples of conclusions:

- *If admitted to Lincoln University, I want to hone my skills in order to one day tell stories of people at their best and their worst, narratives that speak of our curiosities, our hopes, and our struggles.*

- *Now, having held a newborn baby in my hands, I strongly desire to invest my life in preparing to become a caring and skilled pediatrician.*

- *How did meeting Senator Smithson influence my desire to study at Big Valley College? Inspiration, inspiration, inspiration! I, and other women, can indeed succeed in the world of politics.*

- *Yes, my body was still shaking with frustration, anger, and even outrage from the experience. Those memories, to this day, still motivate me to pursue study in the field of clinical psychology.*

Organize the Essay Tightly and Arrange It Meaningfully

Because most essay prompts allow for 500 words or fewer, the organization of your essay answer must be concise and clear. Your introduction should flow smoothly into your first paragraph. Each paragraph must meaningfully follow the previous one. Between the paragraphs there should exist a natural parallelism in the alignment of thoughts, arguments, or ideas.

Prepare for writing your essay by developing a formal outline of your presentation. The elements of the outline must thoughtfully connect. Here are some ways that an essay might be organized.

- Comparison and Contrast

- Point and Counterpoint

- Before and After

- Chronological Sequence

- Cause and Effect

- Logical Progression

- Increasingly Effective Arguments

- Differing Scenes or Locations

- Conflict and Resolution

Read the following example paragraph written in a "before and after" format. Notice how the paragraph is tightly wound around a single theme but moves smoothly from the "before" to the "after."

I failed English class—twice! After the second failure, I sobbed intensely even as my guidance counselor comforted me by explaining this was quite forgivable given that I knew absolutely no English when I had arrived in the United States just two years before. Even in the midst of great compassion, I fretted over my inability to understand a noun from a pronoun, a verb from an adverb, or an infinitive from a gerund. My high school life, so I thought, was doomed to repeating freshman English over and over and over again. But then Mrs. Butler arrived. Like some rare powered superhero, this gifted teacher had the strength to bend my mind to understand not only the basics of the English language but also the complexities of story, poetry, and verse. With her help, I passed not only freshman English, sophomore Composition, and junior Literature with good grades, but I also passed the English Advanced Placement exam with a high score. So now, even as I apply to become an English major at Jefferson State College, I'm determined to return to the high school classroom, and like Mrs. Butler, rescue those who desire not to fail anymore.

Use Proper English

This might sound like overly simplistic advice, but college admissions directors use the essay to determine whether you can write on a college-appropriate level. To impress a college, you must write in a style that follows all the rules of formal English.

As you edit your essay, check for (among other things):

- Proper grammar

- Correct punctuation

- Appropriate word usage

- Normal capitalization

- Proper spelling

- Appropriate abbreviations

- Correct notation of sources (if used)

- Normal pagination and spacing

Find someone to help proofread your essay before you submit it to the college. Consult an English instructor at your high school for direct help in proofreading your essay or for references to someone else who might be available to help.

Bonus Tips

Here are some additional tips to consider as you compose college admissions essays.

- Do not over embellish, lie about, or fabricate your experiences.

- Research and double-check any facts, dates, or numbers that you use.

- Do not overuse words from a thesaurus that you do not normally use.

- Never plagiarize an essay or portions of an essay.

- Do not tell someone else's story or experience as your own.

- Be yourself; find your own voice; be natural.

- Write about something you are passionate about.

- Do not drop names (especially if you do not have a real relationship with the person).

- Avoid clichés and slang.

- Do not try to be overly cute or trite.

- Use specific details, not just generalizations.

- Start the writing process early.

- Write, rewrite, and rewrite again.

- Ask a teacher or advisor to read your essay and provide feedback.

- Do not beg. ("I really, really, really want to attend your college.")

- Avoid odd fonts or unusual paper that might distract from the content of your essay.

- Proofread, proofread, and proofread!

Conclusion

"A finished person is a boring person." Anna Quindlen

For the vast majority of college admissions essays there exist no right or perfect answers. Instead, the college provides you blank space to fill with a well-composed and creative statement reflecting your uniqueness as a person. The questions asked will vary. But always remember that the answers you provide should point to yourself as a future college student who has untapped potential, talent, and ability. Good luck!

Appendix B:
Answers and Explanations

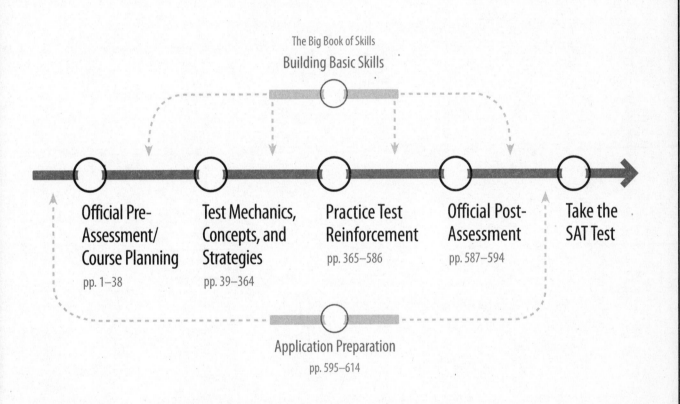

The Big Book of Skills
Building Basic Skills

Official Pre-
Assessment/
Course Planning
pp. 1–38

Test Mechanics,
Concepts, and
Strategies
pp. 39–364

Practice Test
Reinforcement
pp. 365–586

Official Post-
Assessment
pp. 587–594

Take the
SAT Test

Application Preparation
pp. 595–614

CAMBRIDGE
VICTORY FOR THE
SAT TEST

Test Mechanics, Concepts, and Strategies

Outline

I. **Critical Reading: Passages** (pp. 619–620)

    A. Lesson (p. 619)

    B. Quizzes (p. 619)

    C. Review (p. 620)

II. **Critical Reading: Sentence Completions** (pp. 621–622)

    A. Lesson (p. 621)

    B. Quizzes (p. 621)

    C. Review (p. 622)

III. **Math: Multiple Choice** (pp. 623–624)

    A. Calculator Exercise (p. 623)

    B. Lesson (p. 623)

    C. Quizzes (p. 624)

    D. Review (p. 624)

IV. Math: Student-Produced Responses (pp. 625–626)

    A. Calculator Exercise (p. 625)

    B. Lesson (p. 625)

    C. Quizzes (p. 625)

    D. Review (p. 626)

V. Writing (pp. 627–630)

    A. Lesson (p. 627)

    B. Quizzes (p. 628)

    C. Review (p. 629)

CRITICAL READING: PASSAGES

Lesson (p. 53)

1. C	17. C	33. D	49. D	65. B	81. A	97. B
2. A	18. D	34. C	50. B	66. D	82. D	98. D
3. A	19. D	35. B	51. D	67. B	83. A	99. B
4. D	20. E	36. C	52. E	68. A	84. B	100. A
5. B	21. A	37. B	53. C	69. D	85. E	101. B
6. E	22. D	38. B	54. D	70. B	86. B	102. C
7. C	23. E	39. B	55. A	71. A	87. B	103. A
8. C	24. C	40. A	56. B	72. A	88. E	104. A
9. E	25. C	41. C	57. D	73. B	89. E	105. A
10. D	26. A	42. A	58. B	74. A	90. A	106. A
11. A	27. D	43. A	59. A	75. E	91. B	107. D
12. D	28. E	44. C	60. B	76. E	92. B	108. A
13. A	29. C	45. C	61. E	77. D	93. A	109. E
14. C	30. B	46. A	62. C	78. A	94. E	110. C
15. C	31. E	47. A	63. D	79. C	95. D	111. B
16. A	32. A	48. B	64. A	80. C	96. C	112. B

Quizzes (p. 75)

Quiz 1

1. B	10. B
2. A	11. A
3. E	12. C
4. D	13. D
5. B	14. A
6. E	15. B
7. B	16. A
8. A	17. C
9. C	18. D

Quiz II

1. D	10. E
2. A	11. D
3. D	12. B
4. B	13. B
5. A	14. C
6. A	15. A
7. B	16. E
8. E	17. C
9. D	

Quiz III

1. C	10. E
2. B	11. C
3. D	12. B
4. A	13. E
5. A	14. A
6. A	15. B
7. A	16. B
8. B	17. C
9. B	18. A

Quiz IV

1. D	6. B	11. A	16. B	21. A	26. E
2. E	7. D	12. A	17. C	22. C	27. B
3. C	8. C	13. D	18. A	23. B	28. A
4. D	9. A	14. D	19. E	24. B	29. D
5. A	10. C	15. E	20. A	25. A	

Review (p. 103)

1. C	10. D	19. B	28. A	37. E	46. A	55. A
2. A	11. A	20. A	29. C	38. C	47. D	56. B
3. E	12. A	21. C	30. B	39. E	48. D	57. E
4. C	13. C	22. A	31. E	40. A	49. A	58. C
5. A	14. D	23. B	32. A	41. E	50. E	59. E
6. C	15. D	24. B	33. D	42. C	51. C	60. B
7. E	16. B	25. E	34. E	43. E	52. D	
8. B	17. B	26. C	35. C	44. A	53. B	
9. C	18. D	27. C	36. B	45. D	54. B	

CRITICAL READING: SENTENCE COMPLETIONS

Lesson (p. 135)

1. C	18. C	35. E	52. D	69. C	86. A
2. D	19. D	36. E	53. D	70. D	87. C
3. D	20. D	37. C	54. C	71. E	88. D
4. E	21. B	38. B	55. D	72. D	89. E
5. E	22. B	39. E	56. E	73. D	90. E
6. B	23. A	40. A	57. B	74. A	91. B
7. A	24. C	41. E	58. A	75. C	92. B
8. B	25. B	42. B	59. A	76. C	93. E
9. A	26. A	43. B	60. B	77. B	94. E
10. D	27. A	44. A	61. A	78. B	95. B
11. E	28. E	45. A	62. B	79. C	96. C
12. C	29. B	46. E	63. C	80. A	97. B
13. A	30. C	47. E	64. E	81. A	
14. A	31. D	48. D	65. C	82. E	
15. C	32. B	49. C	66. B	83. D	
16. E	33. B	50. D	67. A	84. C	
17. B	34. C	51. D	68. C	85. B	

Quizzes (p. 147)

Quiz I

1. E	9. B
2. B	10. B
3. B	11. E
4. C	12. A
5. A	13. E
6. E	14. D
7. C	15. B
8. C	16. C

Quiz II

1. A	9. C
2. E	10. A
3. D	11. A
4. B	12. E
5. A	13. A
6. C	14. E
7. D	15. B
8. E	16. B

Quiz III

1. C	9. D
2. C	10. E
3. B	11. A
4. C	12. D
5. B	13. E
6. A	14. D
7. D	15. E
8. D	16. E

Quiz IV

1. A		4. B		7. A		10. D		13. D	16. A
2. D		5. C		8. C		11. D		14. B	
3. C		6. B		9. A		12. B		15. B	

Review (p. 157)

1. C	10. E	19. C	28. B	37. D	46. A	55. B
2. A	11. A	20. D	29. D	38. E	47. B	56. B
3. B	12. D	21. B	30. B	39. C	48. D	57. C
4. C	13. A	22. D	31. D	40. C	49. B	
5. A	14. B	23. C	32. A	41. C	50. C	
6. E	15. D	24. D	33. C	42. B	51. E	
7. C	16. B	25. D	34. A	43. A	52. D	
8. A	17. B	26. B	35. C	44. A	53. B	
9. B	18. A	27. B	36. D	45. A	54. A	

MATH: MULTIPLE-CHOICE

Calculator Exercise (p. 180)

1. D; 1   **2.** E; 2   **3.** B; 2   **4.** A; 3   **5.** A; 1

Lesson (p. 183)

1. C	**29.** C	**57.** A	**85.** D	**113.** B	**141.** A
2. C	**30.** A	**58.** E	**86.** D	**114.** D	**142.** C
3. D	**31.** C	**59.** B	**87.** D	**115.** C	**143.** D
4. D	**32.** B	**60.** E	**88.** A	**116.** D	**144.** E
5. C	**33.** C	**61.** C	**89.** D	**117.** D	**145.** D
6. A	**34.** D	**62.** C	**90.** E	**118.** C	**146.** C
7. E	**35.** E	**63.** A	**91.** D	**119.** B	**147.** B
8. B	**36.** A	**64.** A	**92.** D	**120.** C	**148.** A
9. C	**37.** D	**65.** C	**93.** D	**121.** B	**149.** B
10. D	**38.** C	**66.** E	**94.** C	**122.** C	**150.** C
11. D	**39.** D	**67.** B	**95.** B	**123.** A	**151.** C
12. D	**40.** B	**68.** D	**96.** E	**124.** E	**152.** D
13. D	**41.** E	**69.** B	**97.** C	**125.** B	**153.** D
14. E	**42.** E	**70.** B	**98.** D	**126.** A	**154.** B
15. D	**43.** E	**71.** D	**99.** D	**127.** D	**155.** C
16. C	**44.** D	**72.** A	**100.** E	**128.** B	**156.** C
17. E	**45.** C	**73.** C	**101.** C	**129.** C	**157.** E
18. C	**46.** D	**74.** D	**102.** A	**130.** B	**158.** C
19. B	**47.** B	**75.** D	**103.** A	**131.** D	**159.** E
20. D	**48.** E	**76.** D	**104.** E	**132.** C	**160.** E
21. C	**49.** D	**77.** E	**105.** D	**133.** E	**161.** B
22. B	**50.** C	**78.** D	**106.** A	**134.** C	**162.** E
23. C	**51.** C	**79.** C	**107.** C	**135.** E	**163.** A
24. D	**52.** A	**80.** C	**108.** A	**136.** B	**164.** C
25. E	**53.** A	**81.** D	**109.** A	**137.** B	**165.** D
26. E	**54.** D	**82.** E	**110.** E	**138.** B	**166.** C
27. C	**55.** D	**83.** D	**111.** A	**139.** A	**167.** D
28. D	**56.** C	**84.** E	**112.** A	**140.** B	**168.** E

169. C	180. C	191. E	202. C	213. B	224. E
170. D	181. A	192. A	203. D	214. A	225. A
171. D	182. B	193. E	204. B	215. B	226. B
172. B	183. C	194. C	205. B	216. B	227. C
173. A	184. C	195. C	206. C	217. B	228. C
174. A	185. A	196. D	207. C	218. D	229. E
175. E	186. C	197. C	208. D	219. D	230. B
176. E	187. E	198. D	209. C	220. A	231. E
177. C	188. E	199. D	210. D	221. E	
178. C	189. C	200. B	211. D	222. A	
179. C	190. E	201. D	212. B	223. D	

Quizzes (p. 227)

Quiz I

1. A	9. D
2. E	10. B
3. D	11. C
4. C	12. D
5. D	13. D
6. D	14. D
7. D	15. A
8. E	16. A

Quiz II

1. C	11. D
2. A	12. D
3. C	13. D
4. B	14. E
5. C	15. E
6. C	16. C
7. B	17. B
8. D	18. C
9. A	19. E
10. C	20. D

Quiz III

1. C	11. A
2. C	12. A
3. E	13. A
4. B	14. C
5. B	15. B
6. B	16. C
7. A	17. B
8. D	18. E
9. D	19. C
10. D	20. D

Quiz IV

1. C	4. A	7. C	10. D	13. B
2. A	5. D	8. A	11. D	14. A
3. D	6. E	9. E	12. B	15. E

Review (p. 243)

1. B	6. D	11. A	16. E	21. B	26. A
2. C	7. B	12. D	17. B	22. B	27. E
3. C	8. D	13. C	18. B	23. A	28. B
4. E	9. C	14. E	19. C	24. B	29. E
5. D	10. D	15. B	20. C	25. B	

MATH: STUDENT-PRODUCED RESPONSES

Calculator Exercise (p. 265)

1. 3/2 or 1.5; 3 **2.** 24; 3 **3.** 36; 3 **4.** 100; 2 **5.** 3 or 4; 3

Lesson (p. 267)

1. 25
2. 13.6 or 68/5
3. 1/32 or .031
4. 1/24, .041, or .042
5. 650
6. 3/8
7. 50

8. 2
9. 12
10. 8
11. 30
12. 75
13. .25 or 1/4
14. 25

15. 7/12 or .583
16. 16.8 or 84/5
17. 90
18. 7.5 or 15/2
19. 11
20. 6
21. 12

22. 180
23. 2664
24. 4
25. 8/15 or .533
26. 30
27. 50
28. 14

29. 48
30. 3/8 or .375
31. 5/4 or 1.25
32. 60

Quizzes (p. 275)

Quiz I
1. 4 or 5
2. 2
3. 3/2 or 1.5
4. 30
5. 5
6. 3
7. 0
8. 3
9. 8
10. 2

Quiz II
1. 5
2. 10
3. 3/2 or 1.5
4. 0
5. 10
6. 80
7. 1800
8. 15
9. 72
10. 50

Quiz III
1. 9
2. 5/9, .555, or .556
3. 15/2 or 7.5
4. 12/7 or 1.71
5. 45
6. 9
7. 65
8. 20
9. 9/20 or .45
10. 5

Quiz IV
1. 5/3
2. 2
3. 30
4. 8
5. 5

Review (p. 287)

1. 45	**4.** 2	**7.** 72	**10.** 8	**13.** 5
2. 6	**5.** 13	**8.** 7	**11.** 60	
3. 9	**6.** 70	**9.** 8	**12.** 1456	

WRITING

Lesson (p. 315)

1. D	19. B	37. D	55. D	73. D	91. B	109. D
2. D	20. D	38. B	56. B	74. A	92. C	110. A
3. E	21. C	39. B	57. C	75. A	93. E	111. A
4. A	22. C	40. E	58. C	76. A	94. E	112. E
5. B	23. D	41. A	59. D	77. A	95. B	113. B
6. B	24. C	42. C	60. B	78. B	96. C	114. A
7. C	25. A	43. B	61. C	79. B	97. D	115. E
8. D	26. E	44. B	62. C	80. A	98. A	116. B
9. B	27. C	45. D	63. B	81. B	99. A	117. E
10. C	28. E	46. C	64. E	82. E	100. B	118. A
11. C	29. D	47. A	65. E	83. E	101. D	119. A
12. B	30. A	48. C	66. C	84. E	102. B	120. D
13. A	31. A	49. A	67. D	85. A	103. B	
14. A	32. D	50. A	68. B	86. E	104. D	
15. E	33. B	51. D	69. D	87. B	105. B	
16. E	34. D	52. B	70. C	88. C	106. E	
17. A	35. A	53. D	71. C	89. A	107. A	
18. D	36. B	54. D	72. E	90. C	108. –	

Sample Essay Outline

I. Introduction
   A. Thesis statement: Volunteers are a good example of the human capacity for compassion, as demonstrated by their contributions in my school, my community, the country, and the world.
II. In my school, volunteers contribute in many positive ways.
   A. Tutors (Math and English)
   B. Parents (help raise funds and accompany students on field trips)
   C. Students (clean-up days for local waterways)
III. My community would not be the same without the help of volunteers.
   A. Homebound senior citizens need help with transportation, groceries, etc.
   B. Parent volunteers coach sports teams for kids.
IV. The USA and the world have been enriched by compassionate volunteers
   A. March of Dimes
   B. American Cancer Society (my grandmother received support from volunteers)
   C. Mother Teresa

V. Conclusion
    A. Restatement of thesis: Volunteers, citizens who give generously of themselves, help make my community and the world a better and healthier place to live.

Quizzes (p. 333)

Quiz I

1. C	**9.** A
2. D	**10.** D
3. E	**11.** D
4. B	**12.** A
5. D	**13.** C
6. D	**14.** B
7. E	**15.** E
8. E	**16.** C

Quiz II

1. D	**9.** C
2. A	**10.** C
3. E	**11.** B
4. D	**12.** A
5. A	**13.** E
6. B	**14.** B
7. B	**15.** A
8. D	**16.** B

Quiz III

1. B	**9.** E
2. D	**10.** C
3. B	**11.** C
4. B	**12.** B
5. A	**13.** D
6. C	**14.** A
7. D	**15.** C
8. A	**16.** D

Quiz IV

1. A	**4.** C	**7.** D	**10.** B	**13.** B	**16.** D
2. E	**5.** D	**8.** C	**11.** C	**14.** D	
3. D	**6.** D	**9.** C	**12.** B	**15.** A	

Quiz V

Sample Essay—Above Average Response

Professional athletes, media stars, and public leaders choose to put themselves in the public spotlight. They seek the fame and monetary rewards associated with such careers, and they know full well that many supporters, fans, and voters hunger for the most intimate details of their lives. In fact, if public figures were not public, their glamorous careers would not be that much different from other jobs.

Imagine the life of a star baseball player without the attention of the public. To do this, you might think about a situation where the players all wear masks and are known only by numbers, not names. So the star third baseman for the New York Yankees is not Alex Rodriguez but Yankee Number 13. He works at his "office" (Yankee Stadium).

Would as many baseball fans go to the stadium to see Yankee Number 13 as go to see "A Rod?" Probably not. Would a soda company pay top dollar to have faceless #13 endorse its products? Again, the answer is "no." Would fans mob the player on the street seeking autographs? That would be impossible. No one would recognize the anonymous player, and "13" is not an autograph.

Public attention is part of what it means to be a high-profile personality, but that doesn't mean that there are no boundaries between public and private life. Certainly, if it can be said that the public personality accepted the consequences by voluntarily choosing to become a public personality, then it can also be said that this person did not voluntarily relinquish all claims to privacy. In other words, if "A Rod's" decision to play the publicity game was really his decision, then he also decided where the boundary would be drawn. Fans and reporters can discuss and write about what is there for everyone to see, but what Mr. Rodriguez has for breakfast in the privacy of his own home only he can say. If he shares the information, then it's public; if he doesn't, then it's private.

In the final analysis, the fact that someone invites you to his "office" does not mean that you are also entitled to sit in their living room.

Sample Essay—Below Average Response

Regarding public life, I believe that it is important to respect the privacy of others. Privacy is a very important thing because it is necessary to families and individuals alike. Without some privacy, even the most minor details of your life is exposed in the news media.

When privacy is not respected, many things that should not become public are made public. A good example is the President and the First Family. The President has been criticized for at one time maybe having a drinking problem. But now he doesn't. Making this detail of his private life public only muddies the waters and distracts the public's attention from the real issues facing the country. Also, it has been reported that one of the President's daughters has been seen drinking even though she is underaged. But this is a family matter that is between her and her parents, the President and the First Lady. Again, this sort of information just distracts the nation from the really important issues. As a result, some people end up by voting for or against a candidate because that person has or had not used drugs or because a family member is or is not troubled rather than on account of the candidate's position on the issues.

Although some people say that the "public is entitled to know," exposing every little private detail embarrasses the public figure. Additionally, it takes away from the real issues that need to be discussed. So on balance, privacy is a very necessary thing.

Review (p. 351)

1. A	**7.** B	**13.** B	**19.** B	**25.** C	**31.** B	**37.** A
2. E	**8.** D	**14.** A	**20.** E	**26.** A	**32.** D	
3. D	**9.** A	**15.** E	**21.** A	**27.** B	**33.** C	
4. D	**10.** A	**16.** D	**22.** E	**28.** A	**34.** B	
5. A	**11.** C	**17.** B	**23.** E	**29.** D	**35.** E	
6. C	**12.** B	**18.** D	**24.** C	**30.** C	**36.** E	

Sample Essay—Above Average Response

The phrase "the good old days" really begs the question by saying that the time was "good." Whether the "good old days" were really good is the issue, and it can't be decided by simply labeling the time past as good. In fact, the "good old days" were neither "good" nor "old."

In the first place, a closer look will show that the "good old days" really aren't "old." When someone talks about the "good old days," they are usually referring to some period during their lifetime. My grandfather used the phrase to talk about the 1950s and the 1960s. My parents use the phrase to refer to the 1970s and the 1980s. I've even heard people my own age talk about the "good old days" a year or two ago.

Second, the "good old days" weren't particularly good. My grandfather reminisces about the 1950s and the 1960s when there were no interstate traffic jams and no home computers to break down. Of course, what my grandfather fails to mention is that it wasn't until the interstate highway system was built that people could actually drive to many destinations. If everyone still stayed at home, there would be no traffic jams. Plus, even though adding machines and pencils didn't break down very often, the functions done by computers took forever under the old system. Yes, if the bank's computer breaks down, you may have to wait two hours to find out what your balance is, but in the "good old days" you had to wait until the end of the month for your statement.

If the "good old days" were really neither old nor good, why do people think they were so wonderful? Because they are not today. You find that people have the same attitude about the future: tomorrow will be a glorious new day. When people say this, they don't mean literally "tomorrow" but just some time in the future, like the "old" days of the past. Also, they don't necessarily know exactly what the future will bring that is better. Instead, they're hoping that the future will be "glorious," like the "good" times of the past.

Ultimately, the "good old days" are like the "glorious tomorrow." They are another time when, in our imagination, things were much better.

Sample Essay—Below Average Response

The "good old days" were definitely better than they are today. When we compare the "good old days" to these times, we find that many problems that we have did not exist then.

One example of a problem is air pollution. Air pollution is caused by factories and cars. Fifty years ago, there weren't as many factories and cars and so not as much an air pollution problem. Another example is life. It was simpler then. Computers were very limited, and hardly no one had a computer in their home. If you needed to research a topic for school, you had to go to the library where you would find a couple of books. Life is more complicated now because you have the whole worldwide web to choose from.

Some people would say that the good old days were not all that good. There were diseases that didn't have cures. That is true, but there are still diseases with no cures (though who knows what the future may bring). So on balance, the good old days were at least better.

Practice Tests

Outline

I. Practice Test I (pp. 633–664)

    A. Sample Essay Responses and Analyses (p. 633)

    B. Answer Keys (p. 636)

    C. Explanations (p. 638)

II. Practice Test II (pp. 665–697)

    A. Sample Essay Responses and Analyses (p. 665)

    B. Answer Keys (p. 668)

    C. Explanations (p. 670)

III. Practice Test III (pp. 699–731)

    A. Sample Essay Responses and Analyses (p. 699)

    B. Answer Keys (p. 702)

    C. Explanations (p. 704)

PRACTICE TEST I

Sample Essay Responses and Analyses

Section 1—Writing (p. 457)

Above Average Essay Response

The question of what has been the greatest technological advance of the last 125 years can produce a plethora of suggested answers. A 98-year-old farmer could reasonably say "electricity, since it made so many chores easier and faster." He had seen the improvement that electric lighting, electrical pumps and equipment, and modern communications brought to his farm. A 36-year-old executive could similarly vote for the computer, which has brought increased productivity, individual computing capability, and instant communications throughout the business world.

I feel that electricity in all its varied forms is the basis for all technological advances. Electricity has completely transformed life for the individual and family, for our communities, and throughout our world society.

As for individuals, the widespread adoption of electricity has given us light when it is dark. It has enabled us to see and hear news and information instantly from around the world. However, this instant, always-on access can have its downside, keeping us from contact within our community. Some decry the chatter and clutter, and contend we are losing the human contact we need.

In our communities, electrical devices help maintain order in traffic, provide emergency response capability, and provide services such as water and sewage even on hilltops. Worldwide, electricity provides the benefit of global communications and helps make life's tasks less drudgery. Financial markets operate 24 hours a day and reflect news instantly. All investors and governments can have more current information for decisions. The downside can include outsourcing of jobs, which is much discussed lately.

In summary, electricity is the basis of modern technical equipment, research, and advances. Computers are key but useless without electricity through batteries or power lines.

Writing skill and position on issue: This essay displays competent writing skills and a clear sense of organization. Although atypically presented in the first sentence of the second paragraph, the writer's position on the conflicting issues is clearly expressed and well-reasoned.

Development of ideas and organization of essay: Both aspects of the prompt are well presented in the opening paragraph. Some elements of the opposite viewpoint are presented. This contrast adds interest and depth to the essay. The writer also mentions some downsides to electricity, such as the loss of "human contact" and the "outsourcing of jobs." These examples show the writer to be an intelligent thinker who can understand multiple facets of a complex issue. However, ending the second and third paragraphs with these ideas, respectively, detracts from some of the strength of the argument. These ideas should be repositioned so that they do not obscure the writer's argument that electricity is the greatest technological advancement of the last 125 years.

Structure of essay, paragraphs, and transitions: The first paragraph presents the issue to be discussed by reiterating the essay prompt. A short second paragraph effectively introduces the thesis as well as the supporting paragraphs that follow. The supporting paragraphs are appropriate, and each of these paragraphs covers one of the writer's arguments. Transitions between paragraphs are adequate and help give the essay an overall flow and cohesion of thought. Although the conclusion is clear and effective, the transitional phrase "in summary" is low-level usage.

Language usage, sentence structure, and punctuation: There is generally a strong use of language with some minor low-level usage errors, but these errors do not detract from the essay's readability. The sentences are generally strong and effective, but there are too many sentences that contain a three-element series; varying sentence structure adds to the depth and effective presentation of an essay.

Summary and conclusions: Strong written statements of good interest are presented with few distracting errors. The essay would likely receive a reader's score of average to above average (5–6).

Below Average Essay Response

I can see that the students of today would feel that computers are the greatest technical advance of the last 125 years. Home computers are now used for chatting with friends, for research for homework on the Internet, and for entertainment. Computers also hold the data for businesses, government, and airlines. But I feel that electricity is the greatest advance that has occurred.

Computers must have electricity. So must lights and most of the appliances we use every day. My cell phone and Game Boy depend on batteries that provide a basic level of electricity for power. Electricity powers plants, factories, and offices and is even used in planes and cars.

The medical tests and scans I took due to injury all depended on electricity. The advances in medical science are due in part to use of electric driven machines. Much science research involves electricity for equipment to run.

In summary, electricity is obviously the key to modern communications, transportation, and progress. So I feel widespread electrical usage is the greatest advance in technology in 125 years.

Writing skill and position on issue: This essay demonstrates a developing skill in writing. The writer's position is unclear and poorly explained in the first paragraph. In an essay of this length, the thesis must be clearly stated in the opening paragraph; however, the writer does not firmly state his or her position until the last sentence of the first paragraph. By that time, the writer has already written an entire paragraph discussing computers, which he or she considers to be less significant of an advance than electricity. This poor organization of ideas compromises the authority of the writer's position.

Development of ideas and organization of essay: Although the opening paragraph is ambiguous, the main idea is expressed in its last sentence. Good examples, including a personal instance, are presented in the second paragraph. There are two problems in the third paragraph. First, the writer does not explain in detail how electricity was used in medical tests. Second, the last sentence in this paragraph is placed incorrectly within the paragraph. Since this sentence discusses the role of electricity in the general area of science research, it would have better served as the main point and the first sentence of the paragraph. The medical tests and scans could then be presented as examples of the use of electricity in a particular scientific field. Generally, the development of ideas within the essay as a whole and within each paragraph should move from general to specific.

Structure of essay, paragraphs, and transitions: Although poorly developed, the essay does include the basic structural elements: an introduction, a body, and a conclusion. The second and third paragraphs lack introductory material and a clear structure as to how subsequent material will be organized; these paragraphs present a fragmented list of ideas rather than a coherent collection of supporting details that gains strength in developing the thesis. This lack of structure, in turn, detracts from any smooth transitions that should be made between paragraphs. In fact, there is no use of a transitional phrase until the final paragraph, and although effective, "in summary" is low-level usage as a transitional phrase.

Language usage, sentence structure, and punctuation: The essay contains appropriate and understandable language usage. Some errors in noun and adjective forms detract from the essay. "Greatest technological advancement," rather than "greatest technical advance," is the correct expression. "Electricity-driven," rather than "electric driven," is the correct expression. Low-level language and poor sentence structure deter the reader; some of the short sentences tend to express ideas rather abruptly and need improvement.

Summary and conclusions: Overall, there are some good examples listed, but they require more adequate explanation. The essay would likely receive a reader's score of below average (3–4).

Answer Keys

Section 2—Critical Reading (p. 458)

1. B	5. B	9. B	13. D	17. E	21. C
2. C	6. B	10. C	14. A	18. A	22. E
3. B	7. D	11. C	15. A	19. D	23. C
4. C	8. B	12. A	16. C	20. E	24. A

Section 3—Math (p. 466)

1. A	4. E	7. B	10. E	13. C	16. E	19. A
2. B	5. C	8. C	11. C	14. A	17. A	20. B
3. D	6. C	9. D	12. E	15. C	18. D	

Section 5—Critical Reading (p. 470)

1. B	5. C	9. B	13. E	17. E	21. E
2. C	6. A	10. B	14. B	18. C	22. B
3. A	7. A	11. A	15. A	19. B	23. E
4. E	8. E	12. D	16. C	20. A	24. B

Section 6—Math (p. 476)

1. D	5. B	9. 0	11. 8	15. 15.5 or 31/2	18. 2/9
2. A	6. B	10. 12.5, 50/4, or 25/2	12. 8		
3. A	7. A		13. 2	16. 45	
4. C	8. B		14. 72	17. 30	

Section 7—Writing (p. 480)

1. B	6. D	11. B	16. D	21. A	26. B	31. C
2. E	7. E	12. B	17. B	22. B	27. B	32. A
3. C	8. C	13. C	18. E	23. A	28. E	33. C
4. C	9. D	14. A	19. E	24. D	29. D	34. E
5. E	10. C	15. D	20. D	25. B	30. E	35. B

Section 8—Critical Reading (p. 486)

1.	C	4.	A	7.	C	10.	B	13.	D	16.	E	19.	A
2.	A	5.	A	8.	B	11.	B	14.	A	17.	E		
3.	B	6.	E	9.	C	12.	E	15.	E	18.	B		

Section 9—Math (p. 492)

1.	E	4.	D	7.	C	10.	B	13.	E	16.	C
2.	E	5.	E	8.	E	11.	B	14.	E		
3.	E	6.	C	9.	A	12.	D	15.	D		

Section 10—Writing (p. 496)

1.	B	3.	A	5.	B	7.	B	9.	E	11.	D	13.	D
2.	C	4.	E	6.	A	8.	D	10.	E	12.	A	14.	C

Explanations

Section 2—Critical Reading

1. (B) (p. 458) *Critical Reading: Sentence Completions/Thought Extension/Explanatory Phrases*

The only hint in this sentence is the phrase "due to the frigid weather." This phrase indicates that the cabin was probably not warm, or poorly insulated.

2. (C) (p. 458) *Critical Reading: Sentence Completions/Combined Reasoning/Subordinate Conjunctions* and *Coordinate Conjunctions*

In this sentence, a reversal of thought is indicated by the subordinate conjunction "although" and an extension of thought is indicated by the coordinate conjunction "and." What comes after the blank extends the blank, so the blank must somehow parallel the idea of the key word "popular." (A), (B), (D), and (E) all fail on this count. This process of elimination leaves (C) ("personable"), which is compatible with the idea of the candidate's popularity. She may be popular, but she may lose the election, so, you need words that indicate what might cause her to lose the election. The second element of (C) works and confirms the answer choice.

3. (B) (p. 458) *Critical Reading: Sentence Completions/Thought Extension/Explanatory Phrases*

Start with the second half of this sentence. The phrase "without a thorough investigation" implies a sense of reluctance, (B). Further, "elite" is an appropriate word to describe the kind of membership that would have such a reluctance.

4. (C) (p. 458) *Critical Reading: Sentence Completions/Combined Reasoning/Coordinate Conjunctions*

The coordinate conjunction "but" indicates a reversal of thought, and the coordinate conjunction "and" indicates an extension of thought. The blank needs an adjective that is the opposite of "a solid background in theory" or an extension of something that "cannot be taught." This can only be (C), "innate," which means inborn.

5. (B) (p. 459) *Critical Reading: Sentence Completions/Combined Reasoning/Subordinate Conjunctions* and *Key Words*

The sentence begins with the subordinate conjunction "although," which indicates that the first part of the sentence should contrast with the second part of the sentence. The first part of the sentence contains an extension of thought in which the first blank needs a word that parallels the idea of the key words "hostile" or "indifferent." You would not choose (C) or (E); neither "resounding support" nor "bracing support" sounds like "indifference" or "hostility." (D), "adverse support," is a contradiction in terms. (A) and (B) are left, and when you substitute the second element, it is clear that (B) is the correct answer.

6. (B) (p. 459) *Critical Reading: Sentence Completions/Thought Extension/Key Words*

It is best to start this question at the end. Ask yourself what adjective you would need to describe images that are attributed to the key words "illness" or "madness." You might anticipate a word such as "unusual," and (B), "startling," is a good choice.

7. (D) (p. 459) *Critical Reading: Sentence Completions/Combined Reasoning/Explanatory Phrases* and *Subordinate Conjunctions*

As with the previous item, it is best in this case to work backwards, starting at the second blank. Focus on the phrase "never invited back." What would someone have to do to never be invited back? Something negative, obviously. Eliminate (A): if he flattered the hostess, he would surely be invited back. (C) is wrong for a similar reason: it is not negative to enchant someone. (B) and (E) fail to make meaningful statements. That leaves (D), which makes perfect sense: if someone who was typically tactful acted in an insulting way, he would not be invited back. In addition, the first blank must be a word that has an opposite meaning to that of the word in the second blank, as indicated by the subordinate conjunction "although." "Tactful" is sufficiently opposite of "insulted."

8. **(B) (p. 459)** *Critical Reading: Sentence Completions/Thought Extension/Subordinate Conjunctions*

There is not much you can do with this sentence except test the answer choices to fill in the blanks. Eliminate (A) immediately because it does not make any sense to say that a will is sanctimonious by law. Although the other words seem possible on first reading, you can eliminate all but (B). The main clue is the subordinate conjunction "because," which indicates an extension of thought. One blank depends on the other. When you do the substitutions, it becomes apparent that only (B) forms a logical idea.

9. **(B) (p. 459)** *Critical Reading: Passages/Humanities/Application*

The word "likely" signals that this is an Application item. The author states that words function to contribute to the growth of knowledge and art functions to improve human feelings. Words and art operate in different ways, but they share two characteristics: both are cumulative, in that they preserve and transmit the learning of previous generations to the next, and both are progressive, in that they correct "mistakes." (A) is incorrect because art functions not to depict the world but to improve human feelings. (C) is incorrect because the first sentence of the passage states that both art and words are forms of communication. As for (D), while both communication and art may function to improve the human condition, the author does not say that one is more important than the other. Finally, (E) is incorrect because the author neither states nor implies that art depends upon words. Indeed, the passage suggests that art, because it deals with feelings rather than facts, is supreme in its own sphere.

10. **(C) (p. 460)** *Critical Reading: Passages/Social Studies/Main Idea*

The main point is that television cannot adequately depict reality. Television cannot capture the image properly; it cannot reproduce the sound accurately; and it certainly cannot convey taste, smell, or feeling. (A) is incorrect because the author does not offer any suggestions for improving programming. The example of reality TV is designed to show the absurdity of trying to use TV to convey reality. (B) is incorrect because the author does not simply document the differences between reality and TV. The author wants to show that those differences severely mitigate the value of television. (D), on the other hand, overstates the case: the author does not mention any such ill effects of TV on society. Nor does the author suggest any regulation of TV programming, (E).

11. **(C) (p. 460)** *Critical Reading: Passages/Social Studies/Implied Idea*

The last sentence of the passage clearly indicates that the Republicans viewed the 1796 election in terms of "us" versus "them." Since the Republicans were formerly called Anti-Federalists, this suggests they were campaigning against the Federalists. "Monocrat" must have been used by the Republicans to negatively refer to the Federalists. (A) is incorrect because the term was used to describe the 1796 election, not the treaty. (B) is incorrect because the term was created by the Republicans, not the Federalists. (D) is incorrect because the term was used to refer disparagingly to the competing party. Finally, (E) is incorrect because the term was coined by the Republicans.

12. **(A) (p. 461)** *Critical Reading: Passages/Social Studies/Main Idea*

The passage is primarily a discussion of the early days of the Republican Party. Incorrect answers to Main Idea questions are typically either too broad or too narrow. (B) is not broad enough: the passage does mention Jefferson's defeat, but this is a minor point. (C) is too broad: the author does mention the political divisions drawn according to wealth in some cases, but (C) goes beyond that. (D) is incorrect because the author does not criticize anything in the passage. Finally, (E) is incorrect as the passage does not discuss any such misunderstanding.

13. (D) (p. 461) *Critical Reading: Passages/Humanities/Main Idea*

The storyteller interprets the moon landing for the Tanzanian elders using a parable. The United States is like the vain monarch, and the moon is like the lake—uninhabited but worthless. Thus, the storyteller's main point is that the United States' moon landing was a wasted trip to an empty and worthless land, (D). (A) is incorrect because the storyteller is not saying that the moon landing did not occur but rather that it was pointless. (B) is incorrect because there is nothing to suggest that the tribal elders have any influence over the nation's budget or that Tanzania is planning a space program. As for (C), while the statement regarding the parable is true, this is not the storyteller's main point. Since the interpretation is intended to describe the moon landing, the main point will refer to this event and not the parable. Finally, (E) is incorrect because the moon landing, not the U.S. military, is the focus of the story.

14. (A) (p. 461) *Critical Reading: Passages/Social Studies/Implied Idea*

In the second sentence, the author lists "religious organizations, educational institutions, and even businesses" as groups that recruit highly qualified people. The next sentence lists three outstanding examples: the Jesuits, Oxford, and Hudson Bay Company. The parallel structure indicates that the Hudson Bay Company is one such outstanding business. The author goes on to explain the reason for the success of these groups: good management practices. (B) is incorrect because the company is an example of a business that developed a successful management atmosphere. Similarly, (C) is incorrect because the business is a success rather than short-lived. As for (D), while a successful business implies a profitable one, nothing in the passage suggests that the Hudson Bay Company was founded upon religious principles. Finally, (E) is incorrect because the author introduces the company as an "outstanding example" of a business rather than a typical one.

15. (A) (p. 462) *Critical Reading: Passages/Natural Sciences/Implied Idea*

In discussing the sterile insect release strategy in the first paragraph, the author notes that it has had modest success. The next sentence cites two shortcomings: irradiation weakens the insects, making them less likely to breed, and "sterile insects do not search selectively for non-sterile mates." It is this second shortcoming that is the focus of this question. The author explains that those involved in the sterile insect release strategy hope that normal insects will mate with sterile ones. These matings will produce no offspring, resulting in an overall decrease in insect population. However, this strategy depends on the incidence of normal-sterile matings. The sterile insects are as likely to mate with another sterile insect as with a normal insect.

16. (C) (p. 462) *Critical Reading: Passages/Natural Sciences/Vocabulary*

The author explains that the plan for controlling pests by using parasites depends upon releasing the parasites in such a way that they will attack the pest-hosts at the right time, say when they are still in larval form. So, the best choice is "critical." (A) must surely be wrong since the original sentence is clearly not military-related. (B) is surely wrong as well for releasing the parasites at random would not be nearly as effective as applying them at the pre-determined time. The same reasoning applies to (D). As for (D), while you might control pests by "nuking" them with parasites, that is not the procedure described by the author.

17. (E) (p. 463) *Critical Reading: Passages/Natural Sciences/Explicit Detail*

The author specifically says that it is the female of the *B. tryoni* parasite that parasitizes the larvae of the medfly.

18. (A) (p. 463) *Critical Reading: Passages/Natural Sciences/Implied Idea*

The author explains that the parasite release program must cover a 25-square mile area because there is the possibility that medflies will reproduce outside of the one square mile area where they are concentrated. The problem is that this means that a lot of the parasites are being dropped into areas where there are no medflies. But, the author says, not to worry, because they will be attracted by the scent of rotting fruit and migrate to where the infestation is.

19. (D) (p. 463) *Critical Reading: Passages/Natural Sciences/Development*

The word "development" signals that this is a Development item. In the last sentence of the second paragraph, the author states that even though there is usually a balance between parasites and hosts, it is possible to alter that balance by injecting large numbers of parasites into the ecosystem at an opportune moment to reduce the host population. Then, the third paragraph shows how this can be done.

20. (E) (p. 463) *Critical Reading: Passages/Natural Sciences/Implied Idea*

The author states that the medfly population increases tenfold with every generation. So, the 1,000 males and 1,000 females in the population that are first discovered should produce $10 \cdot 2,000 = 20,000$ viable offspring. The passage states that 2,000 medflies will produce 80,000 larvae. So, it can be inferred that the survival rate is 20 out of 80, or 25 percent.

21. (C) (p. 463) *Critical Reading: Passages/Natural Sciences/Implied Idea*

Why would it be necessary to treat the entire 25-square-mile area when, according to the author, most of the medfly reproduction will occur within a one-square-mile area? For the same reason that the parasite release program must cover all 25 square miles: some offspring may reproduce outside of the core region.

22. (E) (p. 463) *Critical Reading: Passages/Natural Sciences/Development*

The purpose of the "even if" is to introduce a worst case scenario: even if the program is as expensive as you can possibly imagine, requiring six batches of parasites. The author goes on to show that the treatment is still cheaper than spraying. (A) is wrong because the assumption made here is the worst case scenario assumption about cost, not an assumption about effectiveness. (B) is simply a misreading of the passage. The reference to damage caused by spraying is found back in the first paragraph. (C) is wrong because the cost point was not previously raised. The author is raising it now: even if it costs as much as it could.... (D) is wrong because by this point the author has finished discussing how the parasite program works.

23. (C) (p. 464) *Critical Reading: Passages/Natural Sciences/Main Idea*

The author begins by mentioning traditional strategies for controlling insect-pests. Then, the author announces that there is a third alternative, and that alternative is the topic of the passage. The second paragraph provides some theoretical background about the relationship between parasites and hosts. Then, the third paragraph gives an example to illustrate the general principles given in the second paragraph and shows how effective this new technique can be. Finally, the last paragraph goes on to say that the new method is not only effective, but it does not harm the environment and it can be cheaper. (C) best describes this development, but you can use the method of elimination to get rid of the other choices. As for (A), the primary purpose is not to criticize anything. As for (B), the author is not defending against an attack, merely explaining. As for (D), while the author says this new method is cost-effective, that is a small point in the last paragraph. Finally, as for (E), though the reproductive habits of the medfly come into play, they are not the focus of the passage.

24. (A) (p. 464) *Critical Reading: Passages/Natural Sciences/Voice*

The author explains how the program works, weighs various pros and cons (such as the number of parasites needed and cost), and concludes that the program is workable and cost-effective. (B) is wrong since the author disposes of the cost objection in the final paragraph. (C) is wrong; it is spraying not parasite release that is harmful to the environment. As for (D), while the program is innovative, it is no longer experimental. Finally, as for (E), while the program is not as simple as swatting the bugs with a flyswatter, it is not all that complicated either—or at least not in the author's opinion.

Section 3—Math

1. **(A) (p. 466)** *Math: Multiple-Choice/Algebra/Solving Algebraic Equations or Inequalities with One Variable/Equations Involving Rational Expressions*

    Solve for N: $\dfrac{1}{2N} + \dfrac{1}{2N} = \dfrac{1}{4} \Rightarrow \dfrac{2}{2N} = \dfrac{1}{4} \Rightarrow \dfrac{1}{N} = \dfrac{1}{4} \Rightarrow N = 4$.

2. **(B) (p. 466)** *Math: Multiple-Choice/Geometry/Lines and Angles*

    $x + 90 + x = 180 \Rightarrow 2x = 90 \Rightarrow x = 45$.

3. **(D) (p. 467)** *Math: Multiple-Choice/Arithmetic/Complicated Arithmetic Application Items*

    Set up an equation: $\dfrac{2J}{3} = 12 \Rightarrow 2J = 36 \Rightarrow J = 18$.

    Alternatively, test the answer choices until you find the one that works. (D): $18 \cdot 2 = 36$, and $36 \div 3 = 12$.

4. **(E) (p. 467)** *Math: Multiple-Choice/Geometry/Spatial Reasoning*

    If the passenger is at station V, he got there either via W or directly from U. If it is the former, he cannot go back to W. If it is the latter, he cannot go to W because that would force him to return to U.

5. **(C) (p. 467)** *Math: Multiple-Choice/Arithmetic/Complicated Arithmetic Application Items*

    $38 \div 4 = 9$ with a remainder of 2. Thus, she will make 9 trips carrying 4 bricks, but she has to make an additional trip with the last 2 bricks.

6. **(C) (p. 467)** *Math: Multiple-Choice/Algebra/Manipulating Algebraic Expressions/Basic Algebraic Manipulations*

    This item can be solved by noting that $b-a$ is the opposite of $a-b$ and $c-b$ is the opposite of $b-c$. Thus, using the rules for signed numbers, $(a-b)(b-c) = (b-a)(c-b)$, and so $(a-b)(b-c) - (b-a)(c-b) = 0$.

    You can also solve this item by evaluating the given expression. Multiply: $(a-b)(b-c) = ab - ac - b^2 + bc$; $(b-a)(c-b) = bc - b^2 - ac + ab$. Subtract the second expression from the first expression: $\left(ab - ac - b^2 + bc\right) - \left(bc - b^2 - ac + ab\right) = 0$.

    Alternatively, substitute numbers: let $a = 5$, $b = 4$, and $c = 3 \Rightarrow 1 \cdot 1 - (-1) \cdot (-1) = 0$.

7. **(B) (p. 467)** *Math: Multiple-Choice/Arithmetic/Common Arithmetic Items/Properties of Numbers*

    List multiples of 9 and test each to see if it is also a multiple of 6: $9(1) = 9$ is not a multiple of 6; $9(2) = 18$ is a multiple of 6: $18 = 6(3)$. Therefore, 18 is the least possible value of n, (B).

    Alternatively, test the choices until you find the smallest value that is divisible by both 6 and 9: 18.

8. **(C) (p. 467)** *Math: Multiple-Choice/Algebra/Expressing and Evaluating Algebraic Functions/Function Notation*

    $f(2) = 2^2 - 2 = 2$. And: $f(f(2)) = f(2) = 2^2 - 2 = 2$.

9. **(D) (p. 467)** *Math: Multiple-Choice/Geometry/Complex Figures*

Since the shaded area, or $2\frac{1}{2}$ squares, is equal to 5 square miles, each full square is equal to 2 square miles.

There are a total of 9 squares, so the area of the entire piece of land is: $9 \text{ squares} \cdot \dfrac{2 \text{ square miles}}{\text{square}} =$

18 square miles.

Alternatively, solve the problem algebraically: if you let $T = \text{total area}$, then $\dfrac{5}{2} \div 9 = \dfrac{5}{T} \Rightarrow \dfrac{5}{18} = \dfrac{5}{T} \Rightarrow T = 18$.

10. **(E) (p. 468)** *Math: Multiple-Choice/Arithmetic/Common Arithmetic Items/Sets: Union, Intersection, and Elements*

Count the pairs that fit the requirement: $(2,1)$, $(3,1)$, $(3,2)$, $(4,1)$, $(4,2)$, and $(4,3)$.

11. **(C) (p. 468)** *Math: Multiple-Choice/Arithmetic/Common Arithmetic Items/Properties of Numbers*

This question becomes easy once you recognize that (C) is the only expression that generates a positive result.

12. **(E) (p. 468)** *Math: Multiple-Choice/Data Analysis/Probability and Statistics/Averages*

Use the technique for finding a missing element in an average. Since the three scores average 75, she earned a total score of $3 \cdot 75 = 225$. Since one score is 75, the remaining scores total $225 - 75 = 150$. The maximum that she could receive on any test is 100, and $150 - 100 = 50$. Thus, the lowest score that she could have received (and still maintain a 75 average) is 50.

13. **(C) (p. 468)** *Math: Multiple-Choice/Geometry/Triangles/Properties of Triangles*

The triangle on the right is an equilateral triangle, so $2x = 8$, which means that $x = 4$. So, the length of side $\overline{AC}$ is $8 + 4 = 12$.

14. **(A) (p. 468)** *Math: Multiple-Choice/Arithmetic/Common Arithmetic Items/Ratios*

Since 6 items out of 30 are inspected, the number of non-inspected items is: $30 - 6 = 24$. Thus, the ratio of inspected items to non-inspected items is: $6:24 = 1:4$.

15. **(C) (p. 469)** *Math: Multiple-Choice/Arithmetic/Common Arithmetic Items/Properties of Numbers*

Test the answer choices. (C): $1 + \dfrac{1}{8} = \dfrac{9}{8}$, and $\dfrac{9}{8} = 9\left(1 \cdot \dfrac{1}{8}\right)$.

16. **(E) (p. 469)** *Math: Multiple-Choice/Arithmetic/Complicated Manipulations*

$\dfrac{1}{2^{-3}} \cdot \dfrac{1}{3^{-2}} = 2^3 \cdot 3^2 = 8 \cdot 9 = 72$.

17. **(A) (p. 469)** *Math: Multiple-Choice/Algebra/Solving Algebraic Equations or Inequalities with One Variable/ Equations Involving Absolute Value*

First, set up the derivative equations: $\dfrac{x-2}{3} = 4$ or $-\left(\dfrac{x-2}{3}\right) = 4$. And solve for x: $x - 2 = 12 \Rightarrow x = 14$ or

$\dfrac{x-2}{3} = -4 \Rightarrow x - 2 = -12 \Rightarrow x = -10$. Then, check $x = 14$ and $x = -10$:

$$\left|\frac{x-2}{3}\right| = 4 \Rightarrow \left|\frac{14-2}{3}\right| = 4 \Rightarrow |4| = 4$$

$$\left|\frac{x-2}{3}\right| = 4 \Rightarrow \left|\frac{-10-2}{3}\right| = 4 \Rightarrow |-4| = 4$$

Alternatively, to save time, this problem is a good opportunity to use the "test-the-test" strategy.

18. (D) (p. 469) *Math: Multiple-Choice/Coordinate Geometry/Slope of a Line*

The given functions $f(-1)=1$ and $f(2)=7$ define two coordinate points included in the graph of $f(x)$: $(-1,1)$ and $(2,7)$. Therefore, the slope of the line is: $m = \frac{7-1}{2-(-1)} = \frac{6}{3} = 2$.

19. (A) (p. 469) *Math: Multiple-Choice/Data Analysis/Data Interpretation/Tables (Matrices)*

The following information is implicit in the table:

STUDENT POPULATION AT SCHOOL X			
	Juniors	Seniors	Total
Women	124	476	600
Men			280
Total			880

So, (A) is already known. But any of the other four numbers will allow you to complete the matrix.

20. (B) (p. 469) *Math: Multiple-Choice/Algebra/Manipulating Algebraic Expressions/Creating Algebraic Expressions*

Since y is the cost of getting in the car plus x miles at $0.4 per mile, $y = 1.5 + 0.4x$.

Section 5—Critical Reading

1. (B) (p. 470) *Critical Reading: Sentence Completions/Thought Extension/Explanatory Phrases*

This sentence is characterized by an extension of thought. First, the second blank must give the reason for what is described by the first blank. Because of this relationship, you can eliminate (A), (D), and (E). However, the second blank also looks forward toward the end of the sentence. It must be something that will become "coherent and concise" when altered. Thus, eliminate (C).

2. (C) (p. 470) *Critical Reading: Sentence Completions/Thought Extension/Key Words*

The only logical feature of the sentence is the extension of thought. The blank must describe changes that are "gradual," a key adjective. Very gradual changes would be almost unnoticeable, or "imperceptible."

3. (A) (p. 470) *Critical Reading: Sentence Completions/Combined Reasoning/Subordinate Conjunctions and Coordinate Conjunctions*

The overall structure of the sentence is a contrast between two ideas, as indicated by the subordinate conjunction "although." However, each of these two ideas is characterized by an extension of thought. Within the first clause, the blank must be consistent with the idea of "adversary," and in the second clause, the coordinate conjunction "or" indicates that the blank must parallel "cruel." Perhaps the easiest way to find the correct choice is to look for an answer having a second element that is parallel to "cruel." Only (A) works. Another key is to focus on the subordinate conjunction "although," which indicates a reversal of thought. The first and second blanks would be contradictory. "Callous" and "sympathetic" fit this requirement.

4. **(E) (p. 470)** *Critical Reading: Sentence Completions/Thought Extension/Key Words*

This sentence contains an extension of thought, as indicated by its logical structure. The second blank must explain or parallel the first blank. Also, the key adjective "incomprehensible" must be a logical result of the two missing words. Only (E) provides the needed continuation: since the translation is idiosyncratic (unusual), it distorts the meaning of the original, making it incomprehensible.

5. **(C) (p. 471)** *Critical Reading: Sentence Completions/Thought Extension/Key Words*

Again, this sentence contains an extension of thought, as indicated by its logical structure. The first blank must explain why the customers were incensed. The second blank must further describe their feelings. The second blank must also describe something that explains why the customers failed to pay the check. On the first score, you can eliminate (A), (B), and (E), for these are not numbered among the characteristics of bad waiters. (D) is close in meaning to a word that might be used to complete that blank. "Lassitude" means "a weary feeling." Logically, it would not be the waiter's feelings but his actions that would offend the customers. (C) is the best choice. Another way to help you tackle this problem is to focus on the key word "incensed" and the second blank. The customers would not be "disconcerted," "condoned," or "thwarted" if they were incensed. This leaves (C) and (E). Again, with (E), a waiter would not be critiqued for his or her "fortitude," a vocabulary word that should be more familiar to you. So, (C) is the logical answer.

6. **(A) (p. 471)** *Critical Reading: Sentence Completions/Combined Reasoning/Coordinate Conjunctions* and *Explanatory Phrases*

To answer this item, you can rely on the coordinate conjunction "and" to find a synonym of "vague" (extension of thought) or use the coordinate conjunction "but" to find an antonym of "clear" and "easily accessible" (reversal of thought). This eliminates every choice but (A).

7. **(A) (p. 471)** *Critical Reading: Sentence Completions/Thought Extension/Coordinate Conjunctions*

There are two logical clues in this item. First, the second blank must extend the idea of the key word "laziness," as indicated by the coordinate conjunction "and." Second, the second clause (everything after the comma) must amplify the idea of not meeting deadlines. (A) does both jobs. Laziness and procrastination are parallel, and the idea of "procrastination" explains why the secretary did not meet her deadlines. Also, "ambition," "zeal," "veracity," and "fortitude," all positive attributes, would not result in a "dismissal."

8. **(E) (p. 471)** *Critical Reading: Sentence Completions/Combined Reasoning/Subordinate Conjunctions* and *Key Words*

The most important logical feature of this sentence is the reversal of thought set up by "although." Additionally, there is the parallel between "depressing" and the second substitution. Thus, a contrast is needed between "seriousness" and something, and a parallel is needed between the key word "depressing" and something. The idea of "morbidity" accomplishes both tasks: the morbid tone contrasts with simple solemnity, and it completes the parallel with "depressing."

9. **(B) (p. 471)** *Critical Reading: Passages/Natural Sciences/Explicit Detail*

The passage specifically states that the shrimp eggs lie inactive in the extreme heat and cold until the rains create the standing pools of water in which the shrimp live out their lives.

10. **(B) (p. 472)** *Critical Reading: Passages/Natural Sciences/Voice*

The author states that there is real danger of a flu epidemic, and to prove this point, he or she cites expert opinion. The author also mentions steps that are being taken to deal with the threat. Therefore, "concerned" is the best description of the author's tone. (A), "alarmed," overstates the case. Although there is inevitable danger, there are also countermeasures that are being taken. (C) is wrong because the author is not "dismissive"; he or she takes the danger seriously. (E), too, overstates the case—but in the opposite direction. The author does mention that steps are being taken, but "optimistic" is too positive a description for this passage. Finally, (D) is wrong because "irreverent" indicates that the author is mocking the problem, but that is not the case. He is seriously discussing the implications of a flu epidemic and the measures currently taken for prevention of such an epidemic.

11. (A) (p. 472) *Critical Reading: Passages/Social Studies/Main Idea*

The passage focuses on Elizabeth and describes her personality in some detail. (B) is incorrect because the passage does not mention any historical events. As for (C), while the passage does speak positively of the policies of Queen Elizabeth, it is only a minor point. (D) is incorrect since the author does not criticize, explicitly or implicitly, government by monarchy. Finally, (E) incorrectly takes the mention of Elizabeth's parents as the focus of the passage.

12. (D) (p. 472) *Critical Reading: Passages/Social Studies/Vocabulary*

The author is describing Elizabeth as frank and confident, so "address" must refer to her manner of speaking, (D). Eliminate (A) because not only does it make no sense in context but the answer to a question of this type is unlikely to be the word's primary meaning. Eliminate the other answer choices, as none make sense in the context of the passage.

13. (E) (p. 473) *Critical Reading: Passages/Natural Sciences/Development*

The author describes the spread of maize and then adds that the same thing happened with wheat and barley thousands of years earlier. The author does this to show that there was nothing surprising in the spread of maize from one region to another, thus making more plausible the theory that maize originated exclusively in the Americas. (A) is incorrect because the author does not compare maize with wheat and barley as a food source. (B) is incorrect because the author believes that the simultaneous origination theory held by some botanists is incorrect. (C) gets the logical connection backwards: the author uses wheat and barley as evidence to support the theory of maize originating solely in the Americas, not the other way around. Finally, (D) is incorrect because wheat and barley moved both from the Middle East westward to Ireland and eastward to Japan.

14. (B) (p. 473) *Critical Reading: Passages/Natural Sciences/Implied Idea*

The author argues that maize spread from Europe through the Middle East to Asia because it followed the links in a chain of favorable climates. The evidence for this is that the regions are all at the same latitudes as the Bahamas, where Columbus presumably acquired maize. This assumes that regions of similar latitudes have similar climates, (B). (A) is incorrect because this is the thesis the author explicitly rejects. (C) is incorrect because the spread of maize depends upon favorable climates, not upon how it compares with other grains. (D) is an interesting choice given that the passage states that the spread began shortly after 1492. However, it does not really matter whether it began in 1493, 1494, or even 1500. Finally, (E) is incorrect since the argument only assumes that Columbus acquired maize in the Bahamas or any other region of similar climate in the Americas.

15. (A) (p. 474) *Critical Reading: Passages/Natural Sciences/Development*

The author begins by theorizing that black holes may represent a possible course in a star's evolution. Then, the author describes the properties of a black hole. Nothing that goes in can get out, so it is impossible to see them. Next, the author asks how one could possibly prove the existence of a black hole (and live to tell about it) and follows this question with a suggestion in the final paragraph: certain natural events might set up a kind of "experiment" that would permit us to determine that black holes do, in fact, exist. (A) correctly describes this development.

16. (C) (p. 474) *Critical Reading: Passages/Natural Sciences/Explicit Detail*

In the first paragraph, the author states that stars the size of our sun or smaller become dwarf stars, and stars with a mass greater than three times that of our sun become black holes. Stars with a mass that is between those two limits become neutron stars.

17. (E) (p. 474) *Critical Reading: Passages/Natural Sciences/Vocabulary*

To be sure, repulsive can mean disgusting and so on, but those meanings are not appropriate here. Rather, in this context, the word has a meaning that is more closely tied to the Latin root "repulses" from "repellere" meaning to drive back. The connotation of disgusting or offensive derives from that more literal meaning.

18. (C) (p. 474) *Critical Reading: Passages/Natural Sciences/Implied Idea*

In describing what a probe might find as it neared a black hole, the author states that it would detect a gravitational field that would be associated with a normal star of the same mass. Thus, you can infer that the black hole keeps the same approximate mass that it had when it was a normal star before it became a black hole.

19. (B) (p. 474) *Critical Reading: Passages/Natural Sciences/Explicit Detail*

In the last sentence of the second paragraph, the author states that the gravitational radius is the "point of no return," or the distance at which objects are irresistibly drawn in by the forces of the black hole. The other choices use language that appears in the selection, but they either represent misreadings of the passage or do not respond to the question asked.

20. (A) (p. 474) *Critical Reading: Passages/Natural Sciences/Vocabulary*

The word "temper" means to add something to a substance to mitigate an excess in that substance, e.g., tempered steel. Here, the word is used figuratively to indicate that skepticism is added to this belief so that it is not so firmly held.

21. (E) (p. 475) *Critical Reading: Passages/Natural Sciences/Explicit Detail*

The author specifically states that nothing (not even light) can escape from a black hole. A probe that is nearing a black hole, he explains, would detect a gravitational field, but it would not see anything.

22. (B) (p. 475) *Critical Reading: Passages/Natural Sciences/Vocabulary*

The word "candidate" can refer to someone who is running for elected office, but that meaning is clearly wrong here. Rather, the author uses the word "candidate" to mean "possibility."

23. (E) (p. 475) *Critical Reading: Passages/Natural Sciences/Explicit Detail*

In the second paragraph, the author describes the "experimental" conditions that might confirm the existence of a black hole, and in the final paragraph, the author describes a star system that seems to fit these conditions. The author mentions that such a system would be a source of X-radiation (A) and that this radiation would exhibit variation (C), as Cygnus X-l does. The author explains that one of the stars is invisible (D)—an important characteristic of a black hole—and that this invisible star has a mass of the requisite weight (B). The author also states that the other star in the system is a blue supergiant, but that is not one of the features of the system that suggests that the system includes a black hole. Thus, (E), while true, does not answer the question.

24. (B) (p. 475) *Critical Reading: Passages/Natural Sciences/Voice*

The author discusses the existence of black holes only in theoretical terms, but gives reason to believe that they might exist and describes the conditions that might prove their existence. (B) best describes this attitude.

Section 6—Math

1. (D) (p. 476) *Math: Multiple-Choice/Data Analysis/Data Interpretation/Pie Charts* and *Arithmetic/Common Arithmetic Items/Proportions and Direct-Inverse Variation*

Begin by writing a simple sentence describing the situation: "150 is equal to 25% of the total." Next, the stem asks for the total number of books sold. Therefore, solve the problem with a simple proportion: 25% over 100% is proportional to the number of Fiction books (150) over the total amount of books (T). First, set up the proportion: $\dfrac{0.25}{1.00} = \dfrac{150}{T}$. Then, cross-multiply and solve for T: $0.25T = 150 \Rightarrow T = 600$.

2. (A) (p. 476) *Math: Multiple-Choice/Coordinate Geometry/The Coordinate System*

A point where two lines on a graph cross is called a point of intersection. This occurs when both equations are equal to each other; the intersection point is the same for both lines. The question asks for the x value, m, of the point of intersection, so, one way to approach this problem is to set the two equations equal to each other and solve for x. Two graphs cross when their y-values, at a single value of x, are equal. To find the points of intersection for two equations, simply set the two equations equal and solve for x. In this instance, $x = m$. So, $x^2 - 4 = -x^2 + 4 \Rightarrow 2x^2 - 8 = 0 \Rightarrow x^2 - 4 = 0 \Rightarrow x^2 = 4 \Rightarrow x = \pm 2$. If $m > 0$, then $m = 2$.

Another way to solve the problem is to set one of the equations equal to zero:
$(m, 0) \Rightarrow 0 = m^2 - 4 \Rightarrow m^2 = 4 \Rightarrow m = \pm 2$. Again, since $m > 0$, $m = 2$. Check that with the other equation: $y = (2)^2 - 4 = 0$.

A third way to solve the problem would be to substitute each of the answer choices for x to find the value for which each equation equals zero. For example: $0 = x^2 - 4 \Rightarrow 0 = (2)^2 - 4 \Rightarrow 0 = 0$ and $0 = -x^2 + 4 \Rightarrow 0 = -(2)^2 + 4 \Rightarrow 0 = 0$.

3. (A) (p. 477) *Math: Multiple-Choice/Data Analysis/Data Interpretation/Tables (Matrices)* and *Probability and Statistics/Averages*

One way to solve this problem is to create an equation using the concept of a weighted average. Here, we divide the total number of dogs by the number of owners. $\text{Average} = 2 = \dfrac{3(1) + 4(2) + x(3) + 1(4)}{3 + 4 + x + 1} \Rightarrow$

$2 = \dfrac{3 + 8 + x(3) + 4}{8 + x} \Rightarrow 2 = \dfrac{15 + x(3)}{8 + x} \Rightarrow 2(8 + x) = 15 + 3x \Rightarrow 16 + 2x = 15 + 3x \Rightarrow x = 1$.

Alternatively, you could test each answer choice, starting with (A). If exactly one owner entered three dogs, that would be a total of 18 dogs and 9 owners—an average of 2 dogs per owner, and the correct answer choice.

4. (C) (p. 477) *Math: Multiple-Choice/Algebra/Manipulating Algebraic Expressions/Evaluating Expressions* and *Arithmetic/Common Arithmetic Items/Ratios*

Using the rule for constructing the sequence, if n is the first term, then, the second term is equal to $\dfrac{1}{2}(n + 4) = \dfrac{n + 4}{2}$. The ratio of the first term, n, to the second term, $\dfrac{n + 4}{2}$, is $\dfrac{n}{\frac{n+4}{2}} = n \cdot \dfrac{2}{n + 4} = \dfrac{2n}{n + 4}$

$\dfrac{n}{\frac{n+4}{2}} = n \cdot \dfrac{2}{n + 4} = \dfrac{2}{n + 4}$.

Alternatively, you can reach the same conclusion by assigning a value to n. To make things easier, use a value that is divisible by 2, such as 4. If the first term of the sequence is 4, then the second term is $\frac{1}{2}(4+4)=4$, and the ratio of the first term to the second term would be $\frac{4}{4}=1$. So, now we substitute 4 for n into the expressions given in each answer choice, and the correct answer will return a value of 1:

(A) $\dfrac{2}{n+4}=\dfrac{2}{4+4}=\dfrac{2}{8}=\dfrac{1}{4}$ ✘

(B) $\dfrac{2}{n+2}=\dfrac{2}{4+2}=\dfrac{2}{6}=\dfrac{1}{3}$ ✘

(C) $\dfrac{2n}{n+4}=\dfrac{2(4)}{4+4}=\dfrac{8}{8}=1$ ✔

(D) $\dfrac{2n}{n+2}=\dfrac{2(4)}{4+2}=\dfrac{8}{6}=\dfrac{4}{3}$ ✘

(E) $\dfrac{2}{4-n}=\dfrac{2}{4-4}=\dfrac{2}{0}$ ✘

5. (B) (p. 477) *Math: Multiple-Choice/Geometry/Circles* and *Arithmetic/Common Arithmetic Items/Percents*

This is not an easy question, so don't be fooled into selecting (D). Let r be the radius of P, the larger circle. It has an area of πr^2. Then, the radius of O, the smaller circle, will be $0.8r$, and it will have an area of $\pi(0.8r)^2=0.64\pi r^2$. So, the area of the smaller circle is only 64 percent of that of the larger circle.

Alternatively, choose some easy numbers to work with. Let the radius of the larger circle equal 10. This means the radius of the smaller circle must be 8. Therefore, $\text{area}_{\text{larger circle}}=\pi(10)^2=100\pi$ and $\text{area}_{\text{smaller circle}}=\pi(8)^2=64\pi$. And 64π is 64% of 100π, (B).

6. (B) (p. 477) *Math: Multiple-Choice/Data Analysis/Probability and Statistics/Averages* and *Algebra/Solving Simultaneous Equations*

Solve using the technique for finding the missing elements of an average. Since the average of the 5 numbers is 26, their sum is $26 \cdot 5=130$. The sum of 20, 23, and 24 is 67, and $130-67=63$. So, $x+y=63$.

Now, you can use the method for solving simultaneous equations. If $x+y=63$ and $x=\frac{3}{4}y$, then $\frac{3}{4}y+y=63$. So, $1.75y=63\Rightarrow y=36$. And $x+36=63\Rightarrow x=27$.

Alternatively, once you know that $x+y=63$, you can eliminate several answers: given that $\frac{x}{y}=\frac{3}{4}$, you know that $y>x$. Thus, x must be less than $63\div 2=31.5$. Therefore, you can eliminate all answer choices that are more than 31.5: (C), (D), and (E). Then, test the remaining answer choices, trying 27 first because it is divisible by 3: $y=\frac{4}{3}\cdot 27=36$, and $27+36=63$. Therefore, the correct answer is (B).

7. (A) (p. 477) *Math: Multiple-Choice/Algebra/Manipulating Algebraic Expressions/Evaluating Expressions*

You can set up the formula in the following way: if the price of 5 boxes of candy is d dollars, then the price of 5 boxes of candy is $100d$ cents. Since each box contains 30 pieces of candy, the price is $100d$ cents per (

$5 \cdot 30 = 150$ pieces), or $\dfrac{100d}{150}$. The cost of 12 pieces of candy is 12 times that, or $\dfrac{100d(12)}{150} = 8d$. You can reach the same result without the algebra by assuming some values and testing the answer choices.

8. **(B) (p. 477) Math: Multiple-Choice/Geometry**

This problem really needs a diagram:

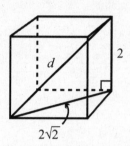

Notice that the diagonal of the face, the edge of the cube, and the diagonal of the cube form a right triangle, the hypotenuse of which is the diagonal of the cube. Since the edge has a length of 2, the diagonal of the face has a length of $2\sqrt{2}$. Now, use the Pythagorean theorem: $d^2 = 2^2 + (2\sqrt{2})^2 = 4 + 8 = 12 \Rightarrow d = \sqrt{12} = 2\sqrt{3}$. This is the length of the diagonal. The distance from any vertex to the center of the cube is one half of that, or $\sqrt{3}$.

9. **(0) (p. 478) Math: Student-Produced Responses/Algebra/Solving Algebraic Equations or Inequalities with One Variable/Simple Equations**

$x + 1 + 2x + 2 + 3x + 3 = 6 \Rightarrow 6x + 6 = 6 \Rightarrow 6x = 0 \Rightarrow x = 0$.

10. **(12.5, $\dfrac{50}{4}$, or $\dfrac{25}{2}$) (p. 478) Math: Student-Produced Responses/Arithmetic/Common Arithmetic Items/Proportions and Direct-Inverse Variation**

Use a direct proportion: $\dfrac{40 \text{ feet}}{500 \text{ feet}} = \dfrac{1 \text{ second}}{x \text{ seconds}} \Rightarrow \dfrac{40}{500} = \dfrac{1}{x} \Rightarrow 40x = 500 \Rightarrow x = \dfrac{500}{40} = \dfrac{50}{4} = \dfrac{25}{2} = 12.5$ seconds. Note that the grid cannot accommodate the fraction 500/40, but that it can accommodate 50/4 or 25/2.

11. **(8) (p. 478) Math: Student-Produced Responses/Arithmetic/Common Arithmetic Items/Properties of Numbers**

We know that $6 < n < 13$ because if $n > 13$, then $13 \div n$ would not have a remainder. Now, plug in numbers.

$13 \div 7 = 1$ with a remainder of 6; $21 \div 7 = 3$ with no remainder ✗
$13 \div 8 = 1$ with a remainder of 5; $21 \div 8 = 2$ with a remainder of 5 ✓

12. **(8) (p. 478) Math: Student-Produced Responses/Algebra/Solving Algebraic Equations or Inequalities with One Variable/Equations Involving Rational Expressions**

Solve for x: $\dfrac{64}{x} - 6 = 2 \Rightarrow \dfrac{64}{x} = 8 \Rightarrow 8x = 64 \Rightarrow x = 8$.

13. **(2) (p. 479)** *Math: Student-Produced Responses/Algebra/Manipulating Algebraic Expressions/Evaluating Expressions*

Since $x, y,$ and z are consecutive integers with $x > y > z$, x is 1 more than y, y is 1 more than z, and x is 2 more than z. Therefore: $y = x - 1$ and $z = x - 2$. Plug these expression for y and z into the given equation and evaluate: $[x - (x-1)][x - (x-2)][(x-1) - (x-2)] = (x - x + 1)(x - x + 2)(x - 1 - x + 2) = 1 + 2 - 1 = 2$.

14. **(72) (p. 479)** *Math: Student-Produced Responses/Arithmetic/Common Arithmetic Items/Properties of Numbers*

Odd numbers less than 10 are 1, 3, 5, 7, and 9. Even numbers less than 10 are 2, 4, 6, and 8. For the greatest value of xy, multiply the greatest numbers in each list: 9 and 8. $9 \cdot 8 = 72$.

15. **(15.5 or $\dfrac{31}{2}$) (p. 479)** *Math: Student-Produced Responses/Arithmetic/Complicated Arithmetic Application Items*

This problem is simplified by writing the information in a table:

Monday	Tuesday	Wednesday	Thursday	Friday
8	$\dfrac{8}{2} = 4$	$\dfrac{4}{2} = 2$	$\dfrac{2}{2} = 1$	$\dfrac{1}{2} = 0.5$

Therefore: $8 + 4 + 2 + 1 + 0.5 = 15.5$. Note that the grid can also accommodate the fraction 31/2.

16. **(45) (p. 479)** *Math: Student-Produced Responses/Geometry/Lines and Angles*

Draw a picture of the triangle described:

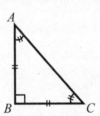

Clearly, the 90° angle must be $\angle ABC$ because the legs of the right triangle must be shorter than the hypotenuse. Thus, the two congruent angles, $\angle BAC$ and $\angle ACB$, must each equal 45°.

17. **(30) (p. 479)** *Math: Student-Produced Responses/Arithmetic/Common Arithmetic Items/Percents*

80 percent of the 150 graduating seniors go to college: $0.8(150) = 120$ seniors go to college. Of those, 75 percent attend school in-state, so 25 percent attend school out-of-state: $0.25(120) = 30$.

18. **($\dfrac{2}{9}$) (p. 479)** *Math: Student-Produced Responses/Arithmetic/Complicated Arithmetic Application Items*

Each big slice equals $\dfrac{1}{6}$ of the whole. Each slice is then cut into thirds: $\dfrac{1}{6} \cdot \dfrac{1}{3} = \dfrac{1}{18}$, so each small slice is $\dfrac{1}{18}$ of the whole. Pete had 4 small slices, or $\dfrac{4}{18} = \dfrac{2}{9}$ of the whole.

Section 7—Writing

1. (B) (p. 480) *Writing/Improving Sentences/Logical Expression/Faulty Comparisons*

The original suffers from a faulty comparison; it attempts to make a comparison between a starting salary and a lawyer. However, the sentence intends to make a comparison between the starting salary of a lawyer in New York and the starting salary of a lawyer in Chicago. (B) makes the needed correction. (C) fails to address the faulty comparison and does not retain the parallel structure of the comparison, introducing a new problem of noun-number agreement. The underlined portion should contain a singular noun ("lawyer"), not a plural noun ("lawyers"). (D) addresses the faulty comparison; however, (D) is wrong because it does not preserve the parallel structure of the comparison: the sentence compares the starting salary of a lawyer to that of lawyers. Finally, (E) is not idiomatic, and it also fails to address the faulty comparison.

2. (E) (p. 480) *Writing/Improving Sentences/Clarity of Expression/Diction and Idioms*

The underlined portion is wrong because the construction "not so much...but instead" is not idiomatic. The correct expression is "not so much...as." (B), (C), and (D) do not provide idiomatic expressions.

3. (C) (p. 480) *Writing/Improving Sentences/Grammar/Pronoun Usage*

The original sentence suffers from a shifting point of view. The first part of the sentence is written from the second person point of view ("you"). However, the underlined portion of the sentence arbitrarily shifts to the third person point of view. Since point of view must always remain consistent, "one meets" should be changed to "you meet." Therefore, (C) is the correct answer choice. (B) fails to address the problem of the original and makes matters worse by introducing a low-level usage expression ("being that") in place of "because." (D) attempts to correct the problem of the original; instead it arbitrarily shifts to the first person point of view. Finally, (E) corrects the problem of the original, but the infinitive verb form "to meet" eliminates the only conjugated verb in the dependent clause.

4. (C) (p. 481) *Writing/Improving Sentences/Grammar/Pronoun Usage*

The original suffers from a lack of pronoun agreement. As written, the singular pronoun "it" incorrectly refers to the plural noun "cameras." (C) solves the problem of the original by simply eliminating the pronoun "it" and using the phrase "in order to" to connect the idea of "recording" to the first part of the sentence in a logical manner. (The purpose of the cameras is to record criminal activities if they should occur.) (B) fails to correct the problem of the original. Finally, (D) and (E) eliminate the problem of the original, but they are unnecessarily awkward and wordy.

5. (E) (p. 481) *Writing/Improving Sentences/Logical Expression/Unintended Meanings*

The original is wrong because it illogically asserts that "Professor Collins" is one of several introductory courses. The sentence intends to say that the introductory biology course taught by Professor Collins is the only one that devotes several class periods to the discussion of Global Warming. (E) makes the needed correction. (B) and (C) fail to address the problem of the original. Finally, (D) not only fails to correct the problem of the original, but it is also unnecessarily awkward and wordy.

6. (D) (p. 481) *Writing/Identifying Sentence Errors/Sentence Structure/Faulty Parallelism*

The error in the original sentence is faulty parallelism. The elements that describe the area should have parallel forms: muck, saw grass, and marshy knolls. All of these are nouns, but in the original sentence, "having marshy knolls" is a verb phrase. As for (A), "southern" is an adjective used correctly to modify the noun "tip." In (B), "tropical" is an adjective used to modify the noun "area." And as for (C), "solidly" is an adverb properly used to modify the verb "packed."

7. **(E) (p. 481)** *Writing/Identifying Sentence Errors/No Error*

The sentence is correct as written. As for (A), "who" is a relative pronoun that refers to Elgar. As for (B), "his" is also a pronoun that correctly refers to Elgar. As for (C), "are" is a plural verb that properly agrees with "marches." And as for (D), "with" is the correct preposition to use in this context.

8. **(C) (p. 481)** *Writing/Identifying Sentence Errors/Clarity of Expression/Diction and Idioms*

"Where" is incorrect: it is a subordinate conjunction that introduces clauses that identify the location of something, but in this sentence, the writer is not trying to identify "where" the water is located. A better construction would be: in which the current is carried. As for (A), "is" is a singular verb that properly agrees with "electrolyte." As for (B), "such as" is an idiomatic expression that has an appropriate meaning in this context. And as for (D), "instead of" is an idiomatic construction that is appropriate in this sentence.

9. **(D) (p. 481)** *Writing/Identifying Sentence Errors/Logical Expression/Illogical Tense Sequence*

"Will rescue" is the future tense, and the choice is inconsistent with the past tense verbs ("were stranded" and "cut off") in the rest of the sentence. The past should be used here as well: rescued. (A) is correct because "during" is a preposition that correctly expresses the idea that the events occurred at some unspecified time throughout the war. "Land retreat," choice (B), has an appropriate meaning here. As for (C), "however" is correctly used to tell the reader that the idea to come (a rescue) contrasts with the idea expressed in the first part of the sentence (the trap).

10. **(C) (p. 482)** *Writing/Identifying Sentence Errors/Grammar/Pronoun Usage*

The problem with the original sentence is that "it" is an extra and unnecessary subject. "Species" is the subject of the sentence, so the "it" has no logical role to play in the structure of the sentence. Therefore, "it" doesn't belong in the sentence at all. (A) is a correct use of the subordinate conjunction "though," which indicates a contrast between two ideas. As for (B), "have" is a plural verb that properly agrees with the subject "dragonflies" and correctly expresses the present tense. And (D) is correct because "more than" is a properly used idiom.

11. **(B) (p. 482)** *Writing/Identifying Sentence Errors/Clarity of Expression/Diction and Idioms*

The problem here is that "solitude" doesn't have an appropriate meaning for the sentence. The correct word would be "solitary." As for (A), "is" is a singular verb that correctly agrees with the singular subject, "eagle." "It" is a singular pronoun that properly agrees with "eagle." And "mates" is a singular verb that correctly agrees with its subject, "it."

12. **(B) (p. 482)** *Writing/Identifying Sentence Errors/Logical Expression/Illogical Tense Sequence*

In the original sentence, "prohibits" indicates an action or condition currently taking place or existing, but the sentence makes it clear that the Act ended in 1809. As a result, "prohibits" should be "prohibited." (A) is correct because "which," a relative pronoun, refers here to "Act" and introduces the clause that tells when the act was in effect. As for (C), "shipping" is a noun that has an appropriate meaning here. And as for (D), the phrase "to and from" has a meaning that is appropriate here.

13. **(C) (p. 482)** *Writing/Identifying Sentence Errors/Grammar/Subject-Verb Agreement*

In the original sentence, the verb "run" is plural, but the subject of the sentence is "Chunnel," a singular noun. "Run" should be "runs." What may make this a little tricky is the proximity of the plural "tubes" to the verb "run." Your ear may think that the word "tubes" is the subject, but it is not. As for (A), "consisting of" is a participle that is used to set up a modifier for "tube," and "central" is an adjective that directly modifies "services," so (B) is not wrong. As for (D), "beneath" is a preposition that creates a phrase modifying "run."

14. (A) (p. 482) *Writing/Identifying Sentence Errors/Sentence Structure/Verb Tense*

"Calling" is the present participle of "to call," but you need the past participle "called" since the sentence is referring to the goddess that the Romans used to refer to as Aurora. As for (B), "by" is idiomatic. As for (C), "was" correctly agrees with its subject, Eos. And in (D), "winds" is a noun and the object of the proposition "of."

15. (D) (p. 482) *Writing/Identifying Sentence Errors/Grammar/Adjectives and Adverbs*

"Imperceptible" is an adjective; what's needed here is the adverb "imperceptibly" to modify the verb "proceed." As for (A), "are" correctly agrees with its subject "enzymes." (B) is acceptable because "that" is a relative pronoun that introduces the clause "that accelerate." And (C) is acceptable since "accelerate" agrees with "enzymes," the antecedent of "that."

16. (D) (p. 482) *Writing/Identifying Sentence Errors/Grammar/Fragments*

The problem with the original sentence is that the main clause lacks a conjugated verb. It should use "is not" rather than "not being." As for (A), "since" is a subordinate conjunction that properly connects the subordinate clause that comes first with the independent clause that follows. As for (B), "arbitrarily," as the "-ly" signals, is an adverb that correctly modifies "have been inserted." And as for (C), "inserted" is the right tense and has an appropriate meaning for this context.

17. (B) (p. 482) *Writing/Identifying Sentence Errors/Grammar/Pronoun Usage*

The original sentence has a second, unnecessary subject: "Hopi, …they resisted…." "They" should be deleted. As for (A), the preposition "of," a word that does a lot of jobs, has an appropriate meaning here. As for (C), "influence" has an appropriate meaning here. And as for (D), the phrasing "than other" is logical since it distinguishes the Hopi from other tribes in the region.

18. (E) (p. 482) *Writing/Identifying Sentence Errors/No Error*

The original sentence is correct. As for (A), "was" agrees with "Hokusai," one painter who lived and worked at the same time in the past. As for (B), "whose" is a relative pronoun that correctly refers to "Hokusai." (C) uses a verb with the correct tense. And (D), "landscapes," is a noun that correctly parallels the other nouns in the series: illustrations, cards, and landscapes.

19. (E) (p. 482) *Writing/Identifying Sentence Errors/No Error*

The original sentence is correct. As for (A), the past tense "developed" correctly describes the process that took place in the past. As for (B), the "in which" introduces the relative clause with "actors" as the subject and "were believed" as the verb. As for (C), as just noted, the verb agrees with the subject. And (D) is acceptable for the same reason that (A) is acceptable.

20. (D) (p. 483) *Writing/Identifying Sentence Errors/Logical Expression/Faulty Comparisons*

The problem with the original sentence is a faulty comparison. The original wording attempts to compare the members of the House with the Senate. What the sentence means to do is compare members of the House with members of the Senate. As for (A), "both" is a plural subject and "are" is the correct verb. As for (B), "members" is plural and refers to the people who are Representatives. And (C) correctly uses the adverb "typically" to modify the verb "are."

21. (A) (p. 483) *Writing/Identifying Sentence Errors/Grammar/Pronoun Usage*

The problem with the original sentence is that "their" is plural and does not agree with its antecedent "university." The phrase ought to read: "its graduates." As for (B), the infinitive "to help" is used here properly. As for (C), "who" refers to students and introduces the clause that has "might be" as the verb. And as for (D), "otherwise" has a meaning appropriate to this context.

22. (B) (p. 483) *Writing/Identifying Sentence Errors/Grammar/Subject-Verb Agreement*

The problem with the original sentence is that the verb "varies" is singular and so does not agree in number with its subject, "flowers." The sentence should read "rayed flowers that vary in color." As for (A), this verb is correct as "which" refers to "aster," a singular noun. You can apply the same reasoning to (C): "grows" correctly agrees with "aster." As for (D), "and" is a coordinate conjunction that is correctly used to join "grows" and "blooms."

23. (A) (p. 483) *Writing/Identifying Sentence Errors/Logical Expression/Unintended Meanings*

The problem with the original sentence is that "calling it" seems to modify the first noun to come after the comma, but the "city" obviously doesn't call itself anything. The problem can be solved by changing (A) to "called." This eliminates the seeming references to someone or something needed to do the calling. As for (B), "was" is appropriately singular and in the past tense. As for (C), "many" has an appropriate meaning in the context. And as for (D), "used" is the correct tense.

24. (D) (p. 483) *Writing/Identifying Sentence Errors/Grammar/Double Negatives*

The "hardly no" is an ungrammatical double negative. The sentence should read either: "is no need for" or "is hardly any need for," depending on the writer's intention. As for (A), "most" has an appropriate meaning here. As for (B), the verb tense is consistent with the overall sentence and "has" correctly agrees with "terrain." Finally, as for (C), "is" is correct since the subject of the clause is "need."

25. (B) (p. 483) *Writing/Identifying Sentence Errors/Grammar/Pronoun Usage*

The problem with the original sentence is that the pronoun "he or she" must refer to a singular person, but "engineers" is plural. The sentence could be corrected by substituting "they" for "he or she." As for (A), "its" is a singular pronoun that correctly agrees with its antecedent, "company." As for (C), "just" is used here idiomatically. And the same reasoning applies to (D); "of solving" is acceptable.

26. (B) (p. 484) *Writing/Improving Paragraphs/Sentence Elements*

The problem with the first paragraph is that the series of short sentences makes it choppy. It's annoying to read because the ideas don't flow. The way to correct this problem is to join some ideas together to create longer sentences, which can be accomplished by connecting sentences 3 and 2: "… a gift from my uncle who taught astronomy at the local college." Connecting the two ideas with "and" won't do the trick, because that will give the reader the impression that the two ideas are of equal importance: it was a gift, and my uncle taught astronomy. What the passage wants to do is make it clear that the phrase "taught astronomy" is a subordinate or secondary idea. So, (D) is wrong. As for (C), relocating the sentence disrupts the logic of the paragraph. (E) is perhaps the second best choice since the paragraph would still make sense and be correct without that sentence, but the paragraph would certainly be weakened. Without a sentence, there is really no reason for mentioning that the telescope was a gift from an uncle.

27. (B) (p. 484) *Writing/Improving Paragraphs/Sentence Elements*

The problem with the referenced part of the paragraph is wrong verb tense. The writer is talking about astronomy as it is, not as it used to be, so the passage should use the present tense. (D) fails to make the needed correction. (C) and (E) eliminate the verb tense problem but introduce a new error: a clause without a main (conjugated) verb.

28. (E) (p. 484) *Writing/Improving Paragraphs/Paragraph Structure*

The difficulty with the original sentence is that the phrase "as such" doesn't have a meaning that is appropriate here, not even if moved to the end of the sentence. And neither "actually" nor "as a matter of fact" is any better. The best choice is (E)—simply delete the phrase. The demonstrative adjective "this," which modifies "system," refers to the "system" that is discussed in the preceding sentence. The two sentences flow well without any additional phrases.

29. (D) (p. 484) *Writing/Improving Paragraphs/Paragraph Structure*

The proposed addition to the passage contains information that would be useful for the reader only if inserted at a logical place. (D) makes a logical insertion. By inserting the new material between sentences 12 and 13, you provide the reader with clarification about the key term "light year."

30. (E) (p. 484) *Writing/Improving Paragraphs/Passage Development*

What should you look for in a good conclusion? You might want a sentence that summarizes the entire passage, but none of the choices offers that option. So, you might look for a sentence that completes the final paragraph, and (E) does that. (E) extends the idea that is developed in sentence 14: we get a good view of a similar galaxy, and this allows us to see ourselves as others might see us. As for (A), the mere fact that this sentence and the first sentence of the passage both mention age and astronomy does not mean that there is a good, logical connection between them. (B) and (C) are weak ideas. Finally, (D) introduces a new topic, which is not a good idea in the last sentence.

31. (C) (p. 485) *Writing/Improving Paragraphs/Passage Development*

The most important organizational feature of the essay is its chronological order marked by the places O'Keeffe lived and worked: from Wisconsin, to various places to study, to New York City and Lake George, to New Mexico. So, any sentence that is inserted in the first paragraph needs to preserve the order, and (C) does. (A) and (B) are way out of sequence. (E) is close, but it puts her moving from the farm before mentioning that her parents were farmers. (D) sounds like it might be appropriate, but in light of the later development, which focuses exclusively on O'Keeffe and not artists generally, it is definitely wrong.

32. (A) (p. 485) *Writing/Improving Paragraphs/Paragraph Structure*

The question asks you to find a word or phrase that will integrate sentence 8 more tightly into the narrative of the second paragraph. According to the passage, Steiglitz exhibited the drawings without permission. O'Keeffe, angry at his having taken this liberty, went to New York with the intention of taking the drawings out of the exhibit, but she spoke with Steiglitz and agreed to let them stay. So, the additional word or phrase should make it clear that one result was expected but another occurred, and "however" nicely signals this reversal. The other choices do not reverse the idea.

33. (C) (p. 485) *Writing/Improving Paragraphs/Sentence Elements*

The word "this" that begins the third paragraph is a demonstrative pronoun, and because it is a pronoun, it needs to have a clear antecedent or referent. If you read carefully, it seems that the author means to say that the dispute and resolution began the relationship, and (C) helps to make this clear. (A) and (E) have to be wrong because neither of these was the direct cause of the relationship. (B) is interesting because the trip did lead to the relationship in the sense that had O'Keeffe not gone, she wouldn't have met Steiglitz, but it wasn't the trip exactly that led to the relationship; it was the dispute over the drawings and its resolution. And (D) is not as good as (C) because "example" is vague.

34. (E) (p. 485) *Writing/Improving Paragraphs/Sentence Elements*

The original sentence needs to be rewritten because it implies that O'Keeffe moved to New Mexico in order to paint specific canvases that would later become famous. What the sentence means to say, however, is that she moved to the area where she would later do this work. (E) makes this clear. (B) is worse than the underlined portion because it still suggests that the move was intended to facilitate the painting of particular canvases, plus the verb tense is inconsistent with the rest of the essay. (C) is wrong because it implies that the two ideas (she moved; she painted) are of equal importance, but the author wants the move to be the important event in the sequence and the paintings to be subordinate, as (E) makes clear. (D) makes the second idea subordinate but creates a contrast that is not appropriate.

35. **(B)** (p. 485) *Writing/Improving Paragraphs/Passage Development*

The author uses the phrase "faraway" twice. One of these is in the last sentence. The other is in sentence 14, where the author explains to the reader the significance of the phrase: O'Keeffe called the landscape in New Mexico "the faraway." The phrase was associated with O'Keeffe's strong feelings about the aura and mystery of New Mexico. So, the author's intention in the final sentence is to tie the ceremony of O'Keeffe's death back to her connection with the landscape, as (B) notes. As for (A), while the author contrasts the cityscapes and the landscapes and the City and New Mexico in general, "the faraway" is not immediately relevant to that distinction. As for (C) and (E), there does not appear to be anything particularly tragic or mysterious about the artist's death at 98. And as for (D), while the author makes this point, it is not connected in the passage to O'Keeffe's death.

Section 8—Critical Reading

1. **(C)** (p. 486) *Critical Reading: Sentence Completions/Combined Reasoning/Explanatory Phrases* and *Key Words*

The key to this sentence is the phrase "for which there is no cure." Whatever can be done to the symptoms is an extension of this thought, which is then contrasted with what cannot be done to the disease itself. You can eliminate (A) on the grounds of usage. Although (B) looks possible at first, the second element does not make sense in the sentence and does not contrast with "disrupt." (D) makes some sense, but again, when you substitute the second element, you get a meaningless sentence. The same is true of (E): "delineate the disease" makes no sense. (C) works perfectly. Since there is no cure, you can only ameliorate the symptoms, "not" eliminate the disease (contrasting idea).

2. **(A)** (p. 486) *Critical Reading: Sentence Completions/Combined Reasoning/Subordinate Conjunctions* and *Explanatory Phrases*

A good approach for this item is to simplify the sentence by eliminating the superfluous details: although he had ____, it was ____ (the reverse) that was important. This sentence begins with the subordinate conjunction "although," which indicates a reversal of thought. All of the first word choices seem plausible with the possible exception of (D), "greed." You can, however, eliminate several choices on the basis of the second element. No one would consider "apathy," "wrongdoing," or "haughtiness" to be a politician's "greatest asset." You are left with (A), which fits the logic of the sentence. It was not credentials (something very tangible) but charisma (something intangible) that was the Senator's greatest asset.

3. **(B)** (p. 486) *Critical Reading: Sentence Completions/Thought Extension/Explanatory Phrases*

This sentence is made difficult by the overall logical structure; "go to pieces," or evaluate the elements separately. Eliminate both (A) and (C) on the basis of their second elements. Cost is not the sort of thing that evolves or relaxes. (D) can be eliminated on the basis of the first element: the phrase "acuity of materials" is meaningless. Now, analyze the overall structure of the sentence. The phrase "due to" signals an extension of thought. What comes before the comma explains the "why" of what comes after the comma. In other words, the "____ of the materials" must explain what happens to the cost. Finally, eliminate (E) because "certainty" does not explain a fluctuation.

4. **(A)** (p. 486) *Critical Reading: Sentence Completions/Combined Reasoning/Subordinate Conjunctions* and *Coordinate Conjunctions*

Again, the sentence begins with the subordinate conjunction "although," which indicates that the first part of the sentence should contrast with the second part of the sentence. The coordinate conjunction "and" indicates that the first blank explains the reasons for what happened in the second blank. Only (A) accomplishes this. Since the remarks were derogatory, they resulted in lawsuits against the comedian. The comedian's remarks would be the opposite of "clever." This eliminates (B). In this context, (C) and (E) do not bring meaning to the sentence. (D) contradicts itself: remarks that were depraved would not assuage lawsuits.

5. **(A) (p. 488)** *Critical Reading: Passages/Social Studies/Vocabulary*

The word "nomological" will not be familiar to most students. The item illustrates, however, that it is possible to use the context in which the word appears to arrive at a good guess as to its meaning. In this case, the Hempel model views history as a science and claims that it can produce conclusions that can be logically deduced from laws. These two elements, logic and laws, are the heart of the theory. Since "deductive-nomological" is intended to describe this view, and since deduction describes the "logical" element, we can infer that "nomological" describes the "law-like" element.

6. **(E) (p. 488)** *Critical Reading: Passages/Social Studies/Vocabulary*

The burden of Passage 1 is that it is not reasonable to expect historical explanations to be as good as scientific explanations because there are so many variables that must be taken into account. However, according to the author of Passage 1, if it were possible to capture and account for all the variables, then a scientifically valid historical conclusion could be drawn—the "if" being an "adequately articulated" set of empirical laws. Thus, in this case, the phrase means "sufficiently detailed," (E). Eliminate (A) as this is the primary and most obvious definition. As for (B) and (C), these choices are not related to the ideas discussed. (D) is a possible distractor because "defined" is related to the idea of "detailed," but it fails since "adequately" is not the same as "precisely."

7. **(C) (p. 488)** *Critical Reading: Passages/Social Studies/Application*

In the second paragraph of Passage 1, the author notes that history may seem to be different from the natural sciences because it does not allow for laboratory experiments. Then, the author mentions a series of revolutions. We can infer that the author thinks that a series of observed historical events can confirm a hypothesis in the same way that a series of laboratory experiments can.

8. **(B) (p. 488)** *Critical Reading: Passages/Social Studies/Explicit Detail*

Toward the end of the third paragraph, the author of Passage 1 specifically states that it is "difficult to find a sufficiently large number of revolutions" to test the validity of a scientific hypothesis, (B). While (A) is true, it does not respond to the question asked. (C) and (D) are both incorrect since they are not mentioned in Passage 1. Finally, (E) confuses Passage 2 with Passage 1. The author of Passage 2 talks about the "inside" of events, meaning the intentions of the actors.

9. **(C) (p. 488)** *Critical Reading: Passages/Social Studies/Voice*

In the second paragraph, the author argues that historical explanations would seem more scientific if data from other disciplines were incorporated into its explanations. To use the example of a revolution, we might expect that a "complete" historical explanation might include information from psychology about something such as a "frustration threshold." For example: the average person is ready to revolt when the standard of living drops by 25 percent. So, the author apparently believes that these disciplines are able to provide reliable data.

10. **(B) (p. 488)** *Critical Reading: Passages/Social Studies/Main Idea*

What is the main theme of the selection? The burden of the author's argument is to demonstrate that history, when properly understood, is as much a science as physics or chemistry.

11. **(B) (p. 489)** *Critical Reading: Passages/Social Studies/Explicit Detail*

Passage 2 mentions *Verstehen* in the third paragraph as the technique that is used by historians to get at the "inside" of an event—the "why," or the motives and intentions, of the actors, (B). (A) and (E) are both incorrect because "understanding" would not apply to the "outside" or physical aspect of an event. As for

(C), while psychology and sociology study intentions and motives they do not employ *Verstehen*. Rather, those disciplines emulate the hard sciences. (D) is incorrect since the whole point of *Verstehen* is that historical laws simply do not exist.

12. **(E) (p. 489)** *Critical Reading: Passages/Social Studies/Explicit Detail*

In the fourth paragraph, the author of Passage 2 explains that the "inside" of an event (thoughts, intentions, motivations) cannot be subsumed under general law of the sort: when the temperature falls below 0°C, water freezes. In principle, this additional "inside" dimension is not something that can be explained by a general law. Thus, the question is whether history is a valid science. The author of Passage 2 says, "Yes, and if you think history is a false science, it is only because you have an unrealistic explanation: why should physics be the model for all science?" (A) and (D) are both incorrect because the author of Passage 2 insists that the deductive-nomological model (like laws of physics) can never be applied fully to historical events. (B) is incorrect because the author of Passage 2 thinks it is possible to make meaningful statements about history—it's simply that the statements will not include ones such as "every time the standard of living drops, a revolution occurs." (C) is incorrect because the author of Passage 2 believes that historical events actually have an additional "inside" dimension.

13. **(D) (p. 489)** *Critical Reading: Passages/Social Studies/Vocabulary*

This item asks about a word with which most students are probably not familiar. A "paradigm" is a model, but even without that knowledge, there is enough information in the context of the passage to reach the right conclusion: it is wrong to liken history to the natural sciences, thus the sciences should not be used as a model, or a paradigm, for human knowledge.

14. **(A) (p. 489)** *Critical Reading: Passages/Social Studies/Application*

The author of Passage 2 is arguing against the position taken by the author of Passage 1, and in the last paragraph, the author of Passage 2 refers to his or her opponent as "the positivist."

15. **(E) (p. 489)** *Critical Reading: Passages/Social Studies/Explicit Detail*

At several points, the author of Passage 2 explicitly points out that historical events involve human thought and action—as opposed to physical events such as falling objects that are literally mindless.

16. **(E) (p. 489)** *Critical Reading: Passages/Social Studies/Vocabulary*

This item tests a particular use of a word that is probably familiar to students. Here, however, it is not the first or most common usage that is intended by the author. Rather, the author uses the word "fable" somewhat derisively to describe the misconceptions of the positivists.

17. **(E) (p. 490)** *Critical Reading: Passages/Social Studies/Application*

The author of Passage 1 argues that both human actions and strictly physical events are governed by scientific laws; the author of Passage 2 argues that human actions are not governed by scientific laws, though purely physical events are. Thus, despite their disagreement, both authors would share the intuition that purely physical events are law-like.

18. **(B) (p. 490)** *Critical Reading: Passages/Social Studies/Application*

The burden of the argument in Passage 2 is that history is not a science (if "science" is used to mean that events occur with law-like regularity). However, Hempel's "deductive-nomological" model of history asserts that its events are law-like and does not distinguish between mental and physical characteristics of a historical event. Therefore, you can infer that the author of Passage 2 would reject Hempel's theory because it fails to make this distinction.

19. (A) (p. 490) *Critical Reading: Passages/Social Studies/Application*

"Inside" is a term used in Passage 2 to refer to intentions or motives of historical actors. The theory advanced in Passage 1 treats these from the standpoint of the social sciences of psychology and sociology. (B) and (C) are incorrect because intentions and motivations are not physical events. (D) is incorrect because this is a technique that might be used by the author of Passage 2. The author of Passage 1 would leave such investigations to the social scientists. Finally, (E) is incorrect; the goal would be to produce an explanation of a historical event, so referring to a previous study would not help.

Section 9—Math

1. (E) (p. 492) *Math: Multiple-Choice/Arithmetic/Common Arithmetic Items/Proportions and Direct-Inverse Variation*

First, find out how many mils there are in 1 cent: $\dfrac{1\ \text{mil}}{0.1\ \text{cents}} = \dfrac{x\ \text{mils}}{1\ \text{cent}} \Rightarrow x = 10$. (There are 10 mils in 1 cent.)

Next, $\$3.13 = 313$ cents, so in $3.13 there are: $313\ \text{cents} \cdot \dfrac{10\ \text{mils}}{1\ \text{cent}} = 3{,}130\ \text{mils}$.

2. (E) (p. 492) *Math: Multiple-Choice/Arithmetic/Common Arithmetic Items/Properties of Numbers*

Simply "test-the-test": $\sqrt{3^2} = 3$, not 9.

3. (E) (p. 493) *Math: Multiple-Choice/Arithmetic/Common Arithmetic Items/Properties of Numbers*

Since $\dfrac{x}{y}$ is an integer, and x and y are different integers so they cannot both be 1, x must be greater than y.

Otherwise, x would not be evenly divisible by y. Thus, (I) is part of the correct answer. As for (II), x and y are positive integers, so $xy > 0$. Finally, $y - x < 0$ is equivalent to $y < x$, which is the same as (I). (E) is the correct answer.

4. (D) (p. 493) *Math: Multiple-Choice/Algebra/Expressing and Evaluating Algebraic Functions/Function Notation*

If n is a prime number greater than 2, then n must be odd and $n-1$ is the next smaller number, which must be an even number. Now, don't be confused by the $n-1$ in the brackets; the defined function tells you to let that quantity be equal to n. Since the quantity is even, n is even, and the function tells you to multiply the quantity by 2: $2(n-1) = 2n - 2$.

5. (E) (p. 493) *Math: Multiple-Choice/Algebra/Expressing and Evaluating Algebraic Functions/Function Notation*

Perform the defined function on the values given: $[3] = 3 \cdot 3 = 9$ and $[4] = 2 \cdot 4 = 8$. $9 \cdot 8 = 72$, so $[3] \cdot [4] = 72$. Now, you can reason that since 72 is an even number, it is the result of performing our defined function on a number equal to one-half of 72, or 36.

Alternatively, test the answer choices until you find one that generates the value 72.

6. **(C) (p. 493)** *Math: Multiple-Choice/Coordinate Geometry/Slope-Intercept Form of a Linear Equation*

Use the slope-intercept method for linear equations ($y = mx + b$), in which m, the slope, is equal to $\dfrac{y_2 - y_1}{x_2 - x_1}$.

Thus, $m = \dfrac{5-1}{7-(-1)} = \dfrac{4}{8} = \dfrac{1}{2}$; the general linear equation is: $y = \dfrac{x}{2} + b$. Inserting one of the given points into

the general linear equation returns a value of $\dfrac{3}{2}$ for b. Therefore, $y = \dfrac{x}{2} + \dfrac{3}{2}$.

Alternatively, it may save time to simply substitute the given points into the equations in the answer choices to find an equation that is true for both points.

7. **(C) (p. 493)** *Math: Multiple-Choice/Geometry/Complex Figures* and *Circles*

Let r be the radius of the smaller circle. Its area is πr^2. Then, the radius of the larger circle is $2r$, and its area is $\pi(2r)^2 = 4\pi r^2$. The shaded part of the diagram is the larger circle minus the smaller one. The area of the shaded part of the diagram is: $4\pi r^2 - \pi r^2 = 3\pi r^2$. The ratio of the shaded area to the unshaded area is:

$\dfrac{3\pi r^2}{\pi r^2} = \dfrac{3}{1}$.

8. **(E) (p. 493)** *Math: Multiple-Choice/Geometry*

A cube has six faces, each with edge-length e, so the surface area of the cube is:

$6(e^2) = 54x^2 \Rightarrow e^2 = 9x^2 \Rightarrow e = \sqrt{9x^2} = 3x$. Thus, the volume of the cube is $(3x)^3 = 27x^3$.

9. **(A) (p. 494)** *Math: Multiple-Choice/Data Analysis/Data Interpretation/Bar, Cumulative, and Line Graphs* and *Arithmetic/Common Arithmetic Items/Percents*

Wages and Salaries + Health Plan + Retirement Benefits + Other = $0.8 + 0.4 + 0.6 + 0.2 = 2$ is the total

compensation. Determine what percent 0.8 is of 2: $\dfrac{x}{100} = \dfrac{0.8}{2} \Rightarrow x = \dfrac{0.8 \cdot 100}{2} = 40\%$.

10. **(B) (p. 494)** *Math: Multiple-Choice/Arithmetic/Complicated Manipulations/Factoring*

Use prime factorization to solve this problem. If x is a multiple of both 5 and 9, then the following are true: $x = 3 \cdot 3 \cdot 5 \cdot a$ (for some other integer, a) and $x \neq 45$ whenever a is any integer other than 1. So (I) is not part of the correct answer. x is even whenever a is even. So (III) is not part of the correct answer. At this point, you can eliminate all answer choices except for (B), but you can prove that (II) is true as well: x is a multiple of 15 because $x = (3 \cdot 5) \cdot 3 \cdot a$.

11. **(B) (p. 494)** *Math: Multiple-Choice/Arithmetic/Complicated Arithmetic Application Items*

Simply work out the calculation. Out of the 24, $\dfrac{1}{3}$, or 8, are rejected without an interview, leaving only 16. If

$\dfrac{1}{4}$ of those are hired, then $\dfrac{1}{4}$ of $16 = 4$ are hired.

12. **(D) (p. 494)** *Math: Multiple-Choice/Geometry/Triangles/Properties of Triangles* and *Rectangles and Squares*

The rectangle has an area of $4 \cdot 9 = 36$. Since the triangle also has that area:

$\dfrac{1}{2} \cdot h \cdot 12 = 36 \Rightarrow 12h = 72 \Rightarrow h = 6$.

13. **(E) (p. 494)** *Math: Multiple-Choice/Geometry/Triangles/Properties of Triangles* and *30°-60°-90° Triangles*

You can solve this problem with or without trigonometry. First, with trigonometry: $\triangle PQR$ is equilateral and therefore equiangular with three 60° angles. And $\angle PQS$ is 30°. Since $\triangle PQS$ is a 30°-60°-90° triangle, you know that it has special properties: $\overline{PQ} = 6$ and $\overline{QS} = 3\sqrt{3}$. Therefore, the altitude $\overline{QS}$ has a length of $3\sqrt{3}$ and the base $\overline{PR}$ has a length of $2 \cdot 3 = 6$, so the area is: $\frac{1}{2}(3\sqrt{3})(6) = 9\sqrt{3}$, which is approximately 15.58.

Note that you can also use the cosine relationship to find the length of $\overline{QS}$: $\cos\angle PQS = \dfrac{\overline{QS}}{\overline{PQ}} \Rightarrow \dfrac{\sqrt{3}}{2} = \dfrac{\overline{QS}}{6} \Rightarrow$

$\overline{QS} = \dfrac{6\sqrt{3}}{2} = 3\sqrt{3}$. And again, the area is: $\frac{1}{2}(3\sqrt{3})(6) = 9\sqrt{3}$.

Alternatively, solve the problem without trigonometry: $\triangle PQS \cong \triangle RQS$, $\overline{PS} = \overline{SR}$, and $\overline{PQ} = \overline{PR} \Rightarrow \overline{PQ} = 2P$. Since $\overline{PS} = 3$, $\overline{PQ} = 6$. $\triangle PQS$ is a right triangle, so by the Pythagorean theorem: $\left(\overline{PQ}\right)^2 = \left(\overline{PS}\right)^2 + \left(\overline{QS}\right)^2 \Rightarrow$

$6^2 = 3^2 + \left(\overline{QS}\right)^2 \Rightarrow \left(\overline{QS}\right)^2 = 36 - 9 = 27 \Rightarrow \overline{QS} = \sqrt{27} = 3\sqrt{3}$. Then, area $= \dfrac{1}{2} \cdot 6 \cdot 3\sqrt{3} = 9\sqrt{3}$.

14. **(E) (p. 495)** *Math: Multiple-Choice/Algebra/Manipulating Algebraic Expressions/Evaluating Expressions*

Set up an equation: Original Price $-\left(\dfrac{1}{3}\right)$Original Price $= B \Rightarrow O - \left(\dfrac{1}{3}\right)O = B \Rightarrow \left(\dfrac{2}{3}\right)O = B \Rightarrow O = \dfrac{3B}{2}$.

Alternatively, you can assume some numbers and "test-the-test."

15. **(D) (p. 495)** *Math: Multiple-Choice/Algebra/Manipulating Algebraic Expressions/Creating Algebraic Expressions*

You can set up the formula by reasoning as follows. Tom's age minus Y years is equal to 3 times Julie's age minus Y years: $T - Y = 3(20 - Y) \Rightarrow T - Y = 60 - 3Y \Rightarrow T = 60 - 2Y$.

Alternatively, you can reach the same conclusion by assuming some values and substituting them into the formulas.

16. **(C) (p. 495)** *Math: Multiple-Choice/Arithmetic/Common Arithmetic Items/Properties of Numbers*

The sum of 4 consecutive integers must always be even. You have two even numbers, and an odd number added to an odd number yields another even number. Therefore, the sum of x consecutive integers must always be even if x is a multiple of 4.

Section 10—Writing

1. **(B) (p. 496)** *Writing/Improving Sentences/Grammar/Adjectives and Adverbs*

The underlined portion contains one error: the adjective "regular" is intended to modify the verb "came," but an adjective cannot modify a verb. The correct word is the adverb "regularly." (B) makes the needed change and introduces no new error. (C), (D), and (E) also make the needed change, but each of them also changes the intended meaning of the original sentence.

2. **(C) (p. 496)** *Writing/Improving Sentences/Sentence Structure/Faulty Parallelism*

The original sentence suffers from a lack of parallelism. The elements that are used to complete the structure, "the one…; the other…," should have parallel parts of speech. Since "proud" and "inflexible" are adjectives, the correct choice of words is "self-abasing" and "penitent." Only (C) and (E) make the needed correction, but (E) eliminates the clear logical connection between the two elements of the sentence.

3. **(A) (p. 496)** *Writing/Improving Sentences/No Error*

The underlined portion is correct. (B) and (C) are incorrect because "beginning" is a participle that is used as an adjective and must modify Marie Curie, but (B) and (C) incorrectly use "beginning" to modify the verb in the main clause, "to study." (D) and (E) both change the meaning of the original sentence.

4. **(E) (p. 497)** *Writing/Improving Sentences/Logical Expression/Unintended Meanings*

The original sentence has an error of logical expression. The sentence means to contrast two ideas. However, by rendering the first idea (priests were forbidden to marry) as a phrase that modifies "priests," the sentence suggests that the two ideas are similar, not dissimilar. (B) is incorrect because it fails to provide the needed contrast between the two ideas. (C), (D), and (E) all provide the needed contrast, but (C) and (D) make other errors. In (C), "they" is intended to refer to "priest," so there is a failure of agreement. And (D) changes the intended meaning of the original sentence by implying that there was a single priest who sired several families.

5. **(B) (p. 497)** *Writing/Improving Sentences/Clarity of Expression/Diction and Idioms*

The underlined portion is not idiomatic. The correct idiom is not "little more but"; it is "little more than." (D) is idiomatic but it changes the intended meaning of the original sentence. The remaining choices are not idiomatic.

6. **(A) (p. 497)** *Writing/Improving Sentences/No Error*

The underlined portion is correct. In (B), the change from the subjunctive "would" to the indicative "will" is incorrect because the original sentence clearly implies that the destruction is contingent, not certain. (C) implies that cutting the trees is a means of exposing the land, a shift from the meaning of the original sentence. (D) is needlessly wordy. (E) changes the intended meaning of the original sentence by implying that the cutting of the trees might or might not expose the land.

7. **(B) (p. 497)** *Writing/Improving Sentences/Logical Expression/Unintended Meanings*

The underlined portion makes an illogical assertion. The placement of the phrase "such as injunctions" suggests that injunctions are a type of court. (B) corrects this false impression by relocating the phrase closer to the noun that it is intended to modify, "equitable remedies." The other three choices correct this problem but introduce new mistakes. (C) changes the intended meaning of the original sentence by implying that the equitable remedies were the only remedies that were available in courts of the Chancery. Additionally, the new placement of "only" isolates the phrase "and not in the courts of law," leaving it disconnected from the rest of the sentence. As for (D), the construction "availability of…" is wordy and awkward. The resulting sentence would read "the availability…was restricted…not to…." This phrasing implies that the availability of equitable remedies was not restricted in courts of law, an extremely awkward sentence that seems to contradict the intended meaning of the original sentence. Finally, (E) makes a similar error. The resulting sentence would read "equitable remedies…were not available…only in courts of Chancery."

8. **(D) (p. 497)** *Writing/Improving Sentences/Logical Expression/Faulty Comparisons*

The original sentence illogically compares the English that is spoken in London and Sydney with two other cities, Boston and Chicago. Additionally, the plural verb "differ" does not agree with its singular subject, "that." (B) corrects the second error but not the first. (C) corrects neither error and creates a non-idiomatic expression. (E) corrects both errors but in doing so makes a new mistake. "Those" incorrectly refers to English.

9. **(E) (p. 497)** *Writing/Improving Sentences/Sentence Structure/Faulty Parallelism*

The original sentence suffers from faulty parallelism. The sequence of ingredients consists of four nouns and a verb, and (E) removes the verb, which makes all elements parallel. Both (D) and (E) solve the problem of parallelism, but the phrase "little amount" is not idiomatic.

10. **(E) (p. 498)** *Writing/Improving Sentences/Logical Expression/Unintended Meanings*

The sentence has an illogical expression—it asserts an equivalence between "literacy" (a thing) and "one" (a person). (B) and (D) fail to correct the problem. (C) creates an illogical expression by asserting an equivalence between literacy and two activities, reading and writing. (E) makes a logical assertion by equating literacy with ability.

11. **(D) (p. 498)** *Writing/Improving Sentences/Grammar/Pronoun Usage*

In the original sentence, "it" lacks a referent. "It" seems to refer to something in the first part of the sentence, but there is no noun there that "it" can replace. (B) has the same problem as the original sentence. As for (C), it is not clear what is reducing. Both (D) and (E) solve the problem of faulty reference, but (E) changes the intended meaning of the original sentence.

12. **(A) (p. 498)** *Writing/Improving Sentences/No Error*

The underlined portion is correct. (B) is ambiguous—it fails to state clearly that overbooking is the means of ensuring a full passenger load. (C) changes the meaning of the original sentence by subordinating the second idea to the first idea. (D) lacks a clear referent. And finally, (E) changes the meaning of the original sentence by implying that an airline overbooks in order to pay compensation to passengers who are bumped.

13. **(D) (p. 498)** *Writing/Improving Sentences/Clarity of Expression/Diction and Idioms*

The original sentence is not idiomatic. "Like" implies a comparison between the high soprano voice and the highest voices in the other ranges, but the sentence means to create a comparison between the typical features of the high soprano voice (lightness and flexibility) and the typical features of the high voices in the other ranges. (D) is the correct idiom for making the comparison.

14. **(C) (p. 498)** *Writing/Improving Sentences/Logical Expression/Unintended Meanings*

The original sentence is ambiguous. It seems to imply that Margaret was the daughter of a childless attorney—a logical contradiction. Only (C) clears up this ambiguity.

PRACTICE TEST II

Sample Essay Responses and Analyses

Section 1—Writing (p. 501)

Above Average Essay Response

Much has been written and debated on the topic of globalization. Trade and improved communications have made the most remote regions and countries a closer part of the world economy and community. However, we cannot ignore the excesses of this trend. Environmental damage, cultural extinction, and even military conflict have occurred along with the globalization benefits.

I feel that globalization cannot be avoided, will continue to expand, and that the positives outweigh the negatives. Globalization has had major effects on individuals, businesses, and governments.

Individuals in both developed and under-developed countries see the effects of globalization each day. As an example, my personal computer software is technically supported by a person I talk with in India. We work together to accomplish a solution. The worker now has a high tech job that previously was done in the USA. In the entertainment field, videos, movies, and music from many cultures is immediately accessible to enrich people in large and small countries.

Businesses in less developed countries have the chance to sell goods and services all over the world. Of course, they now must be "world class" to compete effectively. The positive of this is better products and innovation. A downside is possible failure and loss of even well-known businesses if they cannot meet the higher standards set by globalization.

Governments challenged to provide communications between citizens suddenly have the availability of new technology. Cell phone systems and satellite communications enable rapid installation and connection for even the most remote villages. Of course, government agencies have a major problem in controlling information if that is their past practice. More open information flow to citizens from their own, and other countries should result in a more informed electorate.

Globalization is largely positive bringing more of the world's citizens modern ideas, entertainment, and a wider range of products.

Writing skill and position on issue: This essay reveals clarity of expression and well-developed writing skills. Each side of the issue is presented clearly and succinctly at the beginning of the essay. The writer's position is stated explicitly in the second paragraph with a strong thesis statement. The writer presents both sides of the argument by giving examples of the "pros" and "cons" of globalization. This method of argument is quite effective. However, the writer does not explicitly refute the claims that he or she presents on behalf of the opposing side. This slight oversight undermines the writer's argument, but it is permissible since the writer is only trying to show how the positive effects of globalization outweigh the negative effects. The essay could be improved if the writer concluded by summarizing how the "pros" of globalization outweigh the "cons."

Development of ideas and organization of essay: Ideas introduced in the initial paragraph are clearly presented and supported with arguments. Good examples of personal experience and information gained elsewhere are used to support the writer's position. Although the thesis is atypically introduced in the second paragraph, it is clearly stated and effective. The writer well acknowledges the contrary position, which adds richness of content to his or her argument.

Structure of essay, paragraphs, and transitions: The essay has a clear structure, and good transitions help the reader understand the positions that are argued. The examples provided by the writer are clear and concise. They effectively prove his or her points and are drawn from a wide variety of sources, including personal experience, business, and government. The ideas are adequately explained and consistently follow the logical structure that is laid out by the thesis statement, which is introduced effectively (although atypically) in the second paragraph. The concluding paragraph, however, is too short and therefore less effective.

Language usage, sentence structure, and punctuation: The writer demonstrates a strong control of language usage. Both punctuation and sentence structure are simple and clear, allowing for the writer's strong ideas to shine through. Minor language errors do not detract significantly from the presentation of the ideas and may be the result of the time restrictions that are placed on the writer.

Summary and conclusions: The essay would likely receive a reader's score of average to above average (5–6).

Below Average Essay Response

Some say that there is much benefit in globalization. That the increased trade and better communications everywhere is good. I feel that globalization has been generally bad, especially for smaller and poorer countries. The problems caused by the larger countries include environmental and cultural.

When special resources such as forests or minerals are exploited for world trade, the more backward countries have been hurt. Forests are disappearing to be put into furniture for us to use. Diamonds and gold are mined with little concern for damage or poisoning of the land due to the chemicals used.

The people in less-developed countries are often not ready for modern communications and high tech equipment. Young people who crave modern products run into resistance from elders who value older ways. The less-developed government officials are caught between protecting their country from ruin, and developing it to make needed money. Sometimes corruption results from the new opportunities and hurts the country more.

So globalization may increase the trade and worth of less-developed countries, but at the cost of the environment and the past culture.

Writing skill and position on issue: The essay illustrates some developing skills. The writer's position is stated but not well explained. In the first paragraph, for example, the writer does not offer a reason as to how problems caused by larger countries are detrimental for smaller and poorer countries. There is also no logical connection between problems in larger countries and the topic of globalization in general. In the second paragraph, the writer begins to expand upon his or her thesis but fails to show how "backward countries" are hurt by the mining of special resources. Overall, the essay does not address the problems inherent in globalization with sufficient analysis and clear organization.

Development of ideas and organization of essay: The writer does not provide a well-focused argument. The first paragraph simply equates globalization with the results of actions taken by larger countries. However, these two things are not the same. The examples that are provided have potential, but they require further elaboration. The supporting paragraphs roughly follow the organizational structure offered by the thesis, but many implicit assumptions about the topic (such as that globalization leads to exploitation of natural or special resources, increased communications, and improved equipment) are not discussed in detail and are even confused with the actions of larger countries. This lack of definition blurs the focus of the essay and detracts from the logical consistency of the intended structure. What does globalization have to do with the mining of gold and diamonds? How does globalization increase the worth of less-developed countries while undermining their culture?

Structure of essay, paragraphs, and transitions: The writer includes all of the essential structural elements of an essay: an introduction, a body, and a conclusion. However, the essay is marred by the writer's failure to expand upon good ideas and to clearly define his or her terms. In addition, the writer does a poor job of introducing the topic and stating the thesis. The supporting paragraphs lack adequate explication and transitional material. In fact, the only transitional expression used in the essay ("So") is low-level usage, especially when it is used as a transition into the concluding paragraph. Lastly, the concluding paragraph is too brief.

Language usage, sentence structure, and punctuation: Low-level language usage and some language errors distract from the presentation. The errors include sentence fragments, non-idiomatic language, low-level language, misplaced modifiers, and poor comma usage.

Summary and conclusions: The essay would likely receive a reader's score of below average to average (3–4).

Answer Keys

Section 2—Math (p. 502)

1. C	**4.** E	**7.** D	**10.** E	**13.** E	**16.** A	**19.** C
2. D	**5.** B	**8.** E	**11.** A	**14.** A	**17.** B	**20.** B
3. C	**6.** D	**9.** A	**12.** B	**15.** B	**18.** E	

Section 3—Critical Reading (p. 506)

1. B	**5.** D	**9.** E	**13.** A	**17.** D	**21.** A
2. E	**6.** D	**10.** C	**14.** B	**18.** C	**22.** B
3. B	**7.** E	**11.** C	**15.** A	**19.** C	**23.** C
4. C	**8.** B	**12.** E	**16.** E	**20.** E	**24.** B

Section 4—Math (p. 514)

1. B	**4.** A	**7.** C	**10.** 35	**13.** 30	**16.** 6
2. A	**5.** C	**8.** D	**11.** 10	**14.** 15	**17.** 3
3. D	**6.** D	**9.** 0	**12.** 1	**15.** 9	**18.** 5

Section 6—Writing (p. 518)

1. D	**6.** A	**11.** A	**16.** D	**21.** B	**26.** A	**31.** A
2. C	**7.** D	**12.** D	**17.** C	**22.** D	**27.** A	**32.** B
3. A	**8.** C	**13.** D	**18.** A	**23.** B	**28.** C	**33.** C
4. B	**9.** E	**14.** D	**19.** B	**24.** E	**29.** C	**34.** A
5. A	**10.** E	**15.** D	**20.** D	**25.** D	**30.** C	**35.** A

Section 7—Critical Reading (p. 524)

1. A	**5.** B	**9.** E	**13.** E	**17.** B	**21.** C
2. D	**6.** B	**10.** C	**14.** C	**18.** B	**22.** E
3. A	**7.** B	**11.** C	**15.** C	**19.** D	**23.** A
4. C	**8.** A	**12.** B	**16.** C	**20.** A	**24.** A

Section 8—Math (p. 530)

1. C	4. E	7. C	10. C	13. C	16. E
2. A	5. B	8. D	11. C	14. E	
3. E	6. D	9. D	12. A	15. D	

Section 9—Critical Reading (p. 534)

1. E	4. E	7. B	10. A	13. E	16. C	19. A
2. A	5. E	8. D	11. D	14. B	17. B	
3. B	6. C	9. C	12. D	15. C	18. E	

Section 10—Writing (p. 540)

1. C	3. A	5. A	7. C	9. B	11. A	13. A
2. D	4. C	6. C	8. C	10. E	12. B	14. E

Explanations

Section 2—Math

1. **(C) (p. 502)** *Math: Multiple-Choice/Algebra/Solving Simultaneous Equations*

   Use the technique for solving simultaneous equations: $x + 2 = 7 \Rightarrow x = 5$. Therefore: $5 + y = 11 \Rightarrow y = 6$.

2. **(D) (p. 502)** *Math: Multiple-Choice/Geometry/Lines and Angles*

   The sum of the interior angles of a quadrilateral is 360°, and vertical angles are congruent. Therefore: $x + y + z + 120 = 360 \Rightarrow x + y + z = 240 \Rightarrow x + 150 = 240 \Rightarrow x = 90$.

3. **(C) (p. 503)** *Math: Multiple-Choice/Algebra/Manipulating Algebraic Expressions/Evaluating Expressions*

   The product of x and 5 is $5x$. And the sum of $3x$ and 3 is $3x + 3$. Since the first expression is equal to $\frac{1}{2}$ of the second expression, the entire statement can be written as: $5x = \dfrac{3x + 3}{2}$.

4. **(E) (p. 503)** *Math: Multiple-Choice/Algebra/Expressing and Evaluating Algebraic Functions/Function Notation*

   $-2x^2 + 2 = -2(3)^2 + 2 = -18 + 2 = -16$.

5. **(B) (p. 503)** *Math: Multiple-Choice/Arithmetic/Common Arithmetic Items/Properties and Direct-Inverse Variation*

   Set up a direct proportion: $\dfrac{3}{2} = \dfrac{36}{x} \Rightarrow 3x = 72 \Rightarrow x = 24$.

   Alternatively, assume some values. If the item usually costs $3, two such items cost $6. John can buy three on sale for $6, or $2 each. 36 items at $2 each equals $72. At the regular price, John can buy $72 \div 3 = 24$ items.

6. **(D) (p. 503)** *Math: Multiple-Choice/Geometry/Geometric Notation* and *Triangles*

   Since $\overline{PQ} \cong \overline{QR}$, $\triangle PQR$ is an isosceles triangle and the base angles are congruent, so $\angle PRQ = \angle QPR = 30°$. Therefore: $x + 30 + 30 = 180 \Rightarrow x = 120$.

7. **(D) (p. 503)** *Math: Multiple-Choice/Algebra/Solving Simultaneous Equations*

   To solve a system of simultaneous equations, make a direct substitution of one quantity for another or find a way to compare two quantities directly. In this case, $px = 6$ and $qx = 7$. Thus: $\dfrac{px}{qx} = \dfrac{6}{7} \Rightarrow \dfrac{p}{q} = \dfrac{6}{7}$.

   Alternatively, assume a value for x. If $x = 1$, then $p = 6$ and $q = 7$. Therefore, $\dfrac{p}{q} = \dfrac{6}{7}$.

8. **(E) (p. 503)** *Math: Multiple-Choice/Algebra/Solving Algebraic Equations or Inequalities with One Variable/ Equations Involving Integer and Rational Exponents*

Since $2^x = 16$, $x = 4$. Therefore, $4 = \dfrac{y}{2} \Rightarrow y = 8$.

Alternatively, "test-the-test" with the answer choices. If $y = 8$, then $x = 4$, and since $2^4 = 16$, (E) must be the correct choice.

9. **(A) (p. 504)** *Math: Multiple-Choice/Arithmetic/Common Arithmetic Items/Properties of Numbers*

There is only one digit that, when added to 2, yields 6: 4. Therefore, $\bullet = 4$. Since $4 + 8 = 12$, $\blacklozenge$ must be equal to 2.

10. **(E) (p. 504)** *Math: Multiple-Choice/Algebra/Solving Algebraic Equations or Inequalities with One Variable/ Equations Involving Radical Expressions*

$\sqrt{5x} + 4 = 9 \Rightarrow \sqrt{5x} = 5 \Rightarrow \left(\sqrt{5x}\right)^2 = 5^2 \Rightarrow 5x = 25 \Rightarrow x = 5.$

11. **(A) (p. 504)** *Math: Multiple-Choice/Geometry/Triangles/Properties of Triangles*

The area of the triangle is: $\text{area}_{\text{triangle}} = \dfrac{(\text{base})(\text{height})}{2}$. Therefore: $2 = \dfrac{(\text{base})\left(\dfrac{1}{x}\right)}{2} \Rightarrow \text{base} = 4x.$

12. **(B) (p. 504)** *Math: Multiple-Choice/Data Analysis/Probability and Statistics/Averages*

Use the formula for finding an average: $\text{average} = \dfrac{\text{sum of all numbers}}{\text{total number of numbers}} = \dfrac{4x + 3x}{7} = \dfrac{7x}{7} = x.$

Alternatively, substitute numbers. Assume $x = 10$: the average of 7 numbers would be $\dfrac{4(10) + 3(10)}{7} = \dfrac{70}{7} = 10.$ When you substitute 10 for x into the choices, only (B) returns a value of 10.

13. **(E) (p. 504)** *Math: Multiple-Choice/Geometry/Lines and Angles*

From the three angles in the large triangle, $x + 30 + 90 = 180 \Rightarrow x = 60$. Since $x = y$, $y = 60$, so from the three angles in the smaller triangle, $60 + 30 + z = 180 \Rightarrow z = 90$.

14. **(A) (p. 504)** *Math: Multiple-Choice/Algebra/Manipulating Algebraic Expressions/Evaluating Expressions*

The least possible value for the expression $\dfrac{x + y}{z}$ occurs when x and y are the least and z is the greatest: $\dfrac{6 + 3}{10} = \dfrac{9}{10}.$

15. **(B) (p. 504)** *Math: Multiple-Choice/Algebra/Manipulating Algebraic Expressions/Manipulating Expressions Involving Exponents*

Simply use the laws of exponents: $(-3x)^3 \left(\dfrac{-3x^{-3}}{27}\right) = -27x^3 \left(\dfrac{-3}{27x^3}\right) = 3.$

16. **(A) (p. 505) *Math: Multiple-Choice/Geometry***

After the pieces are cut out, the box will have the following dimensions: length $= 8$, width $= 10$, height $= 1$. $\text{Volume}_{\text{solid}} = \text{length} \cdot \text{width} \cdot \text{height} = 8 \cdot 10 \cdot 1 = 80$.

17. **(B) (p. 505) *Math: Multiple-Choice/Coordinate Geometry/The Coordinate System* and *Geometry/Triangles/ Properties of Triangles***

The base of the triangle is: $3k - k = 2k$. The height of the triangle is: $4k - k = 3k$. Therefore, $\text{area}_{\text{triangle}} = \dfrac{\text{base} \cdot \text{height}}{2} = \dfrac{3k \cdot 2k}{2} = 12 \Rightarrow 3k^2 = 12 \Rightarrow k^2 = 4 \Rightarrow k = 2$.

18. **(E) (p. 505) *Math: Multiple-Choice/Data Analysis/Probability and Statistics/Averages* and *Median***

There is an even number of numbers, so the median is halfway between the two middle numbers: $\text{median} = \dfrac{(b+c)}{2}$. An average is twice the median, so $\dfrac{a+b+c+d}{4} = 2 \cdot \dfrac{b+c}{2} \Rightarrow \dfrac{-2c+0+c+nc}{4} = 0 + c \Rightarrow -c + nc = 4c \Rightarrow nc = 5c \Rightarrow n = 5$.

19. **(C) (p. 505) *Math: Multiple-Choice/Algebra/Solving Simultaneous Equations/Manipulating Algebraic Expressions Involving Exponents***

Use prime factorization to solve: $200 = 2 \cdot 100 = 2 \cdot 2 \cdot 50 = 2 \cdot 2 \cdot 2 \cdot 25 = 2 \cdot 2 \cdot 2 \cdot 5 \cdot 5 = 2^3 \cdot 5^2$. Therefore, $x = 2$ and $y = 5$.

Alternatively, since x and y are positive integers, assume some positive integers for x and y. You will soon discover that the expression, $x^3 y^2 = 200$ is true only when $y = 5$ and $x = 2$. Therefore, the correct answer is $5 \cdot 2 = 10$, (C).

20. **(B) (p. 505) *Math: Multiple-Choice/Arithmetic/Complicated Arithmetic Application Items***

Set up an equation. Let h be the original height of the sapling. From the information given in the item stem, $h = \dfrac{9}{10}(h) + \dfrac{9}{10}$. Now, solve for h: $10h = \dfrac{9}{10}(h)(10) + \dfrac{9}{10}(10) \Rightarrow 10h = 9h + 9 \Rightarrow h = 9$.

Section 3—Critical Reading

1. **(B) (p. 506) *Critical Reading: Sentence Completions/Thought Extension/Subordinate Conjunctions***

This sentence contains an extension of thought, as indicated by the subordinate conjunction "since." You know that because of ____, ____ will be true. The next important clue is the key word "few." Since there are only a few conservatives, their influence must be ____. So, you might anticipate a choice such as "slight" or "insignificant." Eliminate (D) and (E) on the grounds of usage. (A) makes no sense because it is not logical that only a few would have a monumental influence. (C), "discriminatory," doesn't have anything to do with the fact that there are only a few conservatives. You are left with (B). It does make perfect sense to say that the influence of a few would be negligible.

2. **(E) (p. 506) *Critical Reading: Sentence Completions/Thought Extension/Explanatory Phrases***

This sentence contains an extension of thought, as indicated by the phrase clue "not only [this] but [that]." The first blank requires an adjective that extends the idea of a test that maims animals. (D) is not a possible choice because one would not be gratified by the maiming of animals. Although (A) and (B) make some sense, the fact that the key word "maim" is mentioned gives you a clue that the adjective will have a negative connotation. This leaves (C) and (E). Now, look at the second blank that follows the coordinate conjunction "but." This also requires an adjective that summarizes what comes after the blank. Since no two people see the same thing, the test is ____. Only the second element of (E), "unreliable," works.

3. **(B) (p. 506) *Critical Reading: Sentence Completions/Thought Reversal/Subordinate Conjunctions***

This sentence is introduced by the subordinate conjunction "although," which indicates a reversal of thought. Although ____ is horrifying, ____ is worse. The answer choices are easy words. What word is stronger than the key word "horrifying"? (A) and (D) make no sense. (C) and (E) are not adjectives that one would use to describe "torture or dismemberment." (B), "viler," is the only choice.

4. **(C) (p. 506) *Critical Reading: Sentence Completions/Combined Reasoning/Subordinate Conjunctions* and *Punctuation Marks***

This sentence contains both a reversal of thought and an extension of thought as its logical keys. The subordinate conjunction clue "although" tells you that after the comma there will be an idea that is the opposite of "good health." Eliminate (D) and (E) on the grounds of usage. Eliminate (A) because "augment" means to increase, which extends rather than reverses the thought. This leaves (B) and (C). The second part of the sentence is an extension of the first blank, as indicated by the comma (punctuation clue). Eliminate (B), because a body's defenses cannot be indelible. Therefore, (C) must be the correct choice: the body's defenses are impaired if the effectiveness of vitamins is inhibited.

5. **(D) (p. 507) *Critical Reading: Sentence Completions/Thought Extension/Explanatory Phrases***

The first and second blanks must reinforce each other, as indicated by the phrase "to capture." Eliminate (B), (C), and (E), as they create meaningless phrases when they are substituted into the sentence. (A) is not really logical because you cannot capture the significance of something by putting it into a false context. This leaves (D), which clearly works.

6. **(D) (p. 507) *Critical Reading: Sentence Completions/Combined Reasoning/Key Words* and *Subordinate Conjunctions***

This sentence contains both an extension of thought and a reversal of thought as its logical keys. The first blank is an extension of the word "calmly," a key adverb. Eliminate (A), (B), and (C) on the grounds of usage. This leaves (D) and (E). "Scorn" does not extend the idea of calm, but "equanimity" does. Test the second element of (D). The words "without apparent" indicate that the second element should reverse the idea of "equanimity," and it does.

7. **(E) (p. 507) *Critical Reading: Sentence Completions/Combined Reasoning/Punctuation Marks* and *Coordinate Conjunctions***

One way to approach this item is to use the punctuation as a clue: the semicolon indicates a continuation of the first thought. The first blank requires a word that describes someone who is hungry for power. If you know what "cupidity" means, you have the item answered. Otherwise, for the second blank focus on the coordinate conjunction "but," which indicates a reversal of thought. (C) and (D) can be eliminated as they do not reverse "winning." (A) and (B) are also incorrect, as they do not logically complete the sentence. Only (E) effectively completes the sentence.

8. **(B) (p. 507) *Critical Reading: Sentence Completions/Thought Extension/Key Words***

This item is a matter of vocabulary. There are two hints—the adjective "numerous" in conjunction with "evidence." There is only one word (if you know the definitions) that makes any sense in the blank: "You can glean evidence from numerous studies."

9. **(E) (p. 507)** *Critical Reading: Passages/Social Studies/Voice*

After describing several possible uses of technology, the author concludes that the possibilities are "infinite" and limited only by imagination. It is difficult to imagine an attitude that is more optimistic or enthusiastic. The other choices, which range from very negative to neutral, have to be incorrect.

10. **(C) (p. 508)** *Critical Reading: Passages/Social Studies/Development*

Why does the author mention garbage? In essence, the author is reminding the reader that the mayor, and local government in general, is responsible for the routine services that people often take for granted. It is a clever way of emphasizing the importance of the mayor's role as a local official. (A) is incorrect because, while local garbage collection is not a national priority, the purpose is not to show that mayors are insignificant but to show how important they are. As for (B), it is true that government should serve the citizens, but that is not why the writer of this passage mentions garbage. As for (D), the author does not criticize local government. Finally, while the distinction that is noted by (E) is important and assumed for the author's point, proving its existence is not the reason for referring to garbage collection.

11. **(C) (p. 508)** *Critical Reading: Passages/Natural Sciences/Implied Idea*

The author mentions that there are two competing theories—other than the one advanced by the author. The danger might be due to long-term drought, or it might be due to urban sprawl. The author happens to think that the danger comes from buildup of biomass. All three points of view agree that there is a problem and that it is big, so (A), (B), and (D) are incorrect, but they disagree about the cause, which is (C). As for (E), cost is not mentioned.

12. **(E) (p. 509)** *Critical Reading: Passages/Natural Sciences/Explicit Detail*

This item has a thought-reverser (EXCEPT). Four of the five choices are mentioned specifically in the passage; one is not. The one not mentioned is the correct answer. The author mentions in the last sentence that fatal collisions began to occur when ships reached speeds of 13 to 15 knots and that the number of collisions increased as ship speed increased. So, (A) is mentioned and therefore is incorrect. (B), (C), and (D) are mentioned in the fourth sentence—and are also incorrect. (E), however, is not mentioned. The author does not state that the low number of reports was due to poor record keeping.

13. **(A) (p. 509)** *Critical Reading: Passages/Natural Sciences/Main Idea*

(A) is correct because the author is apparently speaking to scientists—to caution them that they must take care to educate the public. (B) is close because the author mentions some health benefits to the public of genetic research. However, the audience to whom the author is speaking is not the public but the doctors. The same analysis applies to (D). As for (C), the author wants to minimize the negative consequences. (E) is incorrect because the audience is not the lay public.

14. **(B) (p. 509)** *Critical Reading: Passages/Natural Sciences/Implied Idea*

In the referenced sentence, the author states that people who are told about the result of the study will be more likely to understand the positive health consequence that could be learned from the study. So, it stands to reason that those who do not have this information will be less likely to get those benefits. As for (A), (C), and (D), the sentence is talking about familiarizing people with results—after the study. Finally, (E) is not supported by the passage.

15. **(A) (p. 510)** *Critical Reading: Passages/Social Studies/Main Idea*

Use the "two-part answers" strategy on this item: first, look at the first word of each answer choice, and second, look at the rest of each choice. The best first word to describe the purpose of the passage is probably "correct" since the author challenges a commonly accepted position. Looking at the rest of (A), it is clear that (A) is the correct answer: the author rejects the common notion that television violence affects the behavior of children.

16. **(E) (p. 511)** *Critical Reading: Passages/Social Studies/Explicit Detail*

In the first paragraph, the author explains that cartoon violence includes three clues that help viewers to know that its violence is not real: animation, humor, and a remote setting. Therefore, using cartoon characters would help children realize that depiction of violence is not real, (I); so too would humor, (III), and a remote setting, (II). Items like this with Roman numerals provide an additional advantage since partial information can be used to eliminate choices. For example, if you are convinced that (III) must be part of the correct choice, then eliminate (A), (B), and (C), making a 50/50 chance of guessing correctly.

17. **(D) (p. 511)** *Critical Reading: Passages/Social Studies/Vocabulary*

This item asks about a common word, so it is likely the author uses it in a nonstandard way. Thus, the correct answer cannot possibly be "chilling," which is the most common meaning of the word. Instead, the author here is saying that fantasy violence inspires exact imitation only in certain exceptional cases.

18. **(C) (p. 511)** *Critical Reading: Passages/Social Studies/Vocabulary*

This item tests a common word, so look for the meaning appropriate to the context. The author means to say that an aggressive action might happen only when it would otherwise be expected or normal.

19. **(C) (p. 511)** *Critical Reading: Passages/Social Studies/Implied Idea*

In the fifth paragraph, the passage states that depiction of violence might have a short-term effect on a child, perhaps for 15 or 20 minutes and then only provided that the situation might call for aggressive behavior anyway. Therefore, you can infer that the child's behavior after a couple of hours is not likely to be affected by the earlier viewing of violence.

20. **(E) (p. 511)** *Critical Reading: Passages/Social Studies/Application*

In the second paragraph, the passage specifically states that young children are able to distinguish the fantasy violence from other types of violence using certain cues. However, they are not able to decide whether the actions are intrinsically right or wrong because they have good or bad effects or because the motives of the actors are good or bad.

21. **(A) (p. 511)** *Critical Reading: Passages/Social Studies/Implied Idea*

The author theorizes that the behavior of children may be changed by watching violence on television, but not for the reason that most people think. According to the author, it is not the violence itself that gets kids worked up but the energy level in the depiction. The author goes on to explain that anything that gets a kid excited may have the same effect, even agitating the kid by turning off the TV set.

22. **(B) (p. 511)** *Critical Reading: Passages/Social Studies/Voice*

In this case, the author is clearly an opponent of the view that fantasy violence on television adversely affects children. (Though the author does say that violence may inspire teenagers or adults to commit violent acts.) In the last paragraph, the author takes on those who hold to the commonly accepted view and accuses them of using television as a scapegoat when the real causes of violence in our society are cultural. The use of the word "scapegoat" is strong and indicates that the author objects to that view.

23. **(C) (p. 512)** *Critical Reading: Passages/Social Studies/Implied Idea*

The author states that of the three types of fantasy violence, the third (realistic violence) has no clues other than the understanding of the viewer that it is intended to be fantasy. Thus, it can be inferred that the failure of children to understand the distinction between real and simulated violence of this sort is primarily due to the lack of clues. (A) is incorrect because the author denies the existence of such a predisposition, and (B) is incorrect because the passage states that children do understand what cartoon figures are supposed to signify. (D) is also incorrect for the same reason. (E) is not mentioned in the passage.

24. (B) (p. 512) *Critical Reading: Passages/Social Studies/Vocabulary*

In the sixth paragraph, the author states that "heavy" viewing of violence on television does not result in "long-term" effects, so "cumulative" must refer to adding up all of the effects over time. For that reason, (A) must be incorrect. The other choices do not explain the use of "cumulative" in this context.

Section 4—Math

1. (B) (p. 514) *Math: Multiple-Choice/Data Analysis/Probability and Statistics/Averages*

Use the concept of an average to create an equation to solve this problem:

$$\text{average} = x = \frac{5+5+10+12+x}{5} \Rightarrow x = \frac{32+x}{5} \Rightarrow 5x = 32+x \Rightarrow 4x = 32 \Rightarrow x = 8.$$

Alternatively, you could test each answer choice, starting with (A). Let $x = 6$. On that assumption, the total of the five elements is 28, and the average is $\frac{28}{5}$, which is not equal to 6, so (A) is wrong. Next, try (B). If $x = 8$, then the total of the five elements is 40, and the average is $\frac{40}{5} = 8$. Since $8 = 8$, (B) is the correct answer choice.

2. (A) (p. 514) *Math: Multiple-Choice/Algebra/Solving Algebraic Equations or Inequalities with One Variable/ Solving Quadratic Equations*

One way of solving this problem is to recognize that one of the two expressions must be equal to 0, or more precisely, since the two expressions are the same, both must equal 0: $3x + 3 = 0 \Rightarrow 3x = -3 \Rightarrow x = -1$.

Alternatively, you could test each answer choice. Starting with (A):
$(3x+3)(3x+3) = 0 \Rightarrow [3(-1)+3][3(-1)+3] = 0 \Rightarrow (-3+3)(-3+3) = 0 \Rightarrow 0 = 0$. This shows that -1 is a possible value of x, and you could then eliminate answer choices (B), (D), and (E). Then, to make the selection between (A) and (C), test 1. Since $x = 1$ doesn't work, the right answer is (A).

3. (D) (p. 514) *Math: Multiple-Choice/Geometry/Triangles/Pythagorean Theorem*

You should first observe that the direct path between Fuller Acres and Farmers' Market is the hypotenuse of a triangle that can be completed as follows:

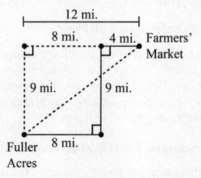

The easiest way to solve the problem is to see that the two known sides of this triangle form a ratio of $\frac{9}{12} = \frac{3}{4}$, suggestive of a $3:4:5$ right triangle. The hypotenuse is determined by the following proportion: if all of the sides are proportional to $3:4:5$, then $\frac{9}{3} = \frac{12}{4} = \frac{x}{5}$, where $x = 15$.

Alternatively, you could find the direct path using the Pythagorean theorem: $a^2 + b^2 = c^2 \Rightarrow 9^2 + 12^2 = x^2 \Rightarrow x = \sqrt{81 + 144} = 15$. Since the indirect path measures $8 + 9 + 4 = 21$ miles and the direct path measure 15 miles, the difference in miles between the two paths is: $21 - 15 = 6$.

4. **(A) (p. 515)** *Math: Multiple-Choice/Algebra/Expressing and Evaluating Algebraic Functions/Function Notation*

According to the item, for all x, $[x] = x^2 + x$. Therefore, $[n] = n^2 + n$ and $[n+2] = (n+2)^2 + (n+2)$. Since $[n] = [n+2]$, $n^2 + n = (n+2)^2 + (n+2)$. Now, solve for n: $\cancel{n^2} + \cancel{n} = \cancel{n^2} + 4n + 4 + \cancel{n} + 2 \Rightarrow 0 = 4n + 6 \Rightarrow -4n = 6 \Rightarrow n = -\dfrac{3}{2}$.

5. **(C) (p. 515)** *Math: Multiple-Choice/Arithmetic/Common Arithmetic Items/Properties of Numbers*

Since 13 is not divisible by 7, t must be divisible by 7 in order for the expression $\dfrac{13x}{7}$ to produce an integer. 3 is the only answer choice that is not divisible by 7.

Alternatively, "test-the-test." Each of the numbers given in the choices will produce an integer except for (C): $\dfrac{13(3)}{7} = \dfrac{39}{7}$, which is not an integer.

6. **(D) (p. 515)** *Math: Multiple-Choice/Algebra/Solving Simultaneous Equations*

Rewrite the equations: $\dfrac{(x+y)}{x} = 4 \Rightarrow x + y = 4x \Rightarrow y = 3x$; $\dfrac{(y+z)}{z} = 5 \Rightarrow y + z = 5z \Rightarrow y = 4z$. Therefore: $3x = 4z \Rightarrow \dfrac{x}{z} = \dfrac{4}{3}$.

7. **(C) (p. 515)** *Math: Multiple-Choice/Arithmetic/Complicated Arithmetic Application Items*

Set up an equation. Let x equal the original amount: $\dfrac{x}{2} - \$60 = \dfrac{x}{5} \Rightarrow \dfrac{x}{2} - \dfrac{x}{5} = \$60 \Rightarrow \dfrac{3x}{10} = 60 \Rightarrow x = 200$.

Alternatively, "test-the-test" with the answer choices.

8. **(D) (p. 515)** *Math: Multiple-Choice/Arithmetic/Complicated Arithmetic Application Items*

Count the different possibilities: RGW, RWG, GRW, GWR, WRG, and WGR.

Alternatively, there are 3 choices for the first house, then 2 choices are left for the second house, and only 1 choice left for the third house: $3 \cdot 2 \cdot 1 = 6$.

9. **(0) (p. 516)** *Math: Student-Produced Responses/Algebra/Manipulating Algebraic Expressions/Evaluating Expressions*

Evaluate the expression for $x = 2$: $x^2 - 2x = (2)^2 - 2(2) = 4 - 4 = 0$.

10. **(35) (p. 516)** *Math: Student-Produced Responses/Arithmetic/Common Arithmetic Items/Proportions and Direct-Inverse Variation*

A 10-pound bag will make five times as much coffee as a 2-pound bag. Thus, $7 \cdot 5 = 35$.

Alternatively, set up a direct proportion and solve for the missing value: $\dfrac{2}{10} = \dfrac{7}{x} \Rightarrow x = \dfrac{7 \cdot 10}{2} = 35$.

11. **(10) (p. 516)** *Math: Student-Produced Responses/Arithmetic/Common Arithmetic Items/Proportions and Direct-Inverse Variation*

$10.00 buys $10.00 ÷ $1.00 = 10 roses or $10.00 ÷ $0.50 = 20 carnations: 20 − 10 = 10.

12. **(1) (p. 516)** *Math: Student-Produced Responses/Algebra/Solving Algebraic Equations with Two Variables*

Perform the indicated operations:

$(x+y)^2 = (x-y)^2 + 4 \Rightarrow x^2 + 2xy + y^2 = x^2 - 2xy + y^2 + 4 \Rightarrow 2xy = -2xy + 4 \Rightarrow xy = 1$.

13. **(30) (p. 517)** *Math: Student-Produced Responses/Geometry/Complex Figures* and *Triangles/Properties of Triangles* and *Rectangles and Squares*

This is a composite figure problem. The shaded area is equal to the sum of the areas of two rectangles and two triangles:

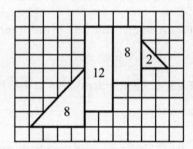

$\text{Area}_{\text{rectangle}} = \text{length} \cdot \text{width}. \quad \text{Area}_{\text{triangle}} = \dfrac{\text{base} \cdot \text{height}}{2}$, or simply analyze the triangles as half-squares:

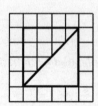

Therefore, $\text{area}_{\text{shaded portion}} = 12 + 8 + 8 + 2 = 30$.

14. **(15) (p. 517)** *Math: Student-Produced Responses/Coordinate Geometry/The Coordinate System* and *Geometry/Triangles/Properties of Triangles*

A sketch will help:

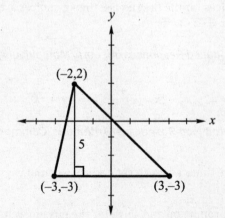

From the diagram, the length of the triangle's base is 6; the height of the triangle is 5. So, the area is $\frac{1}{2}(6)(5)=15$.

15. **(9) (p. 517)** *Math: Student-Produced Responses/Arithmetic/Common Arithmetic Items/Properties of Numbers*

Let n be the smallest integer: $n+(n+1)+(n+2)+(n+3)+(n+4)=55 \Rightarrow 5n+10=55 \Rightarrow 5n=45 \Rightarrow n=9$.

Alternatively, for an odd number of consecutive integers, the middle integer is the sum of the integers divided by the number of integers. So, the middle number is $\frac{55}{5}=11$ and the 5 integers are:

$\{9,10,11,12,13\}$. Therefore, 9 is the smallest integer.

16. **(6) (p. 517)** *Math: Student-Produced Responses/Data Analysis/Data Interpretation/Tables (Matrices)* and *Arithmetic/Simple Manipulations*

Simply do the multiplication and add up the total number of minutes:

ESTIMATED TIME OF CLEANING			
Room	Number	Time per Room	Total Time
Bedroom	4	20 minutes	80 minutes
Bathroom	2	30 minutes	60 minutes
Kitchen	1	45 minutes	45 minutes
Living Area	4	25 minutes	100 minutes
Garage	1	75 minutes	75 minutes
TOTAL			360 minutes

And 360 minutes is 6 hours.

17. **(3) (p. 517)** *Math: Student-Produced Responses/Algebra/Expressing and Evaluating Algebraic Functions/Function Notation*

To find the value of x for which $f(x)=g(x)$: $2x-5=x-2 \Rightarrow x=3$.

18. **(5) (p. 517)** *Math: Student-Produced Responses/Coordinate Geometry/Slope of a Line*

$2=\dfrac{0-(-4)}{x-3} \Rightarrow 2(x-3)=4 \Rightarrow x-3=2 \Rightarrow x=5$.

Section 6—Writing

1. **(D) (p. 518)** *Writing/Improving Sentences/Clarity of Expression/Diction and Idioms* and *Grammar/Pronoun Usage*

The underlined portion of the original sentence contains two errors. First, the construction "not so much this but that" is not idiomatic. The correct idiom is "not so much this *as* that." Second, the underlined part uses the pronoun "one," but "one" is intended to refer to "you." (D) and (E) correct both of these errors. (E), however, changes the intended meaning of the original sentence. It is not the mere fact that someone makes a decision that is important, as (E) implies; rather, the important thing is the outcome of the decision. And the word "choice" refers to the result of the decision, e.g., "her choice was the blue pendant."

2. **(C) (p. 518)** *Writing/Improving Sentences/Logical Expression/Directness*

The original is wrong because it uses the passive voice in a very weak manner. (B), (C), and (D) all use the active voice; however, (B) and (D) are wrong because they also introduce a series of ambiguities. Do members of Kevin's family actually plan on applying to engineering school themselves? Can they not afford to pay for Kevin to go to school or can they not afford to pay for themselves to go to school? The sentence certainly intends to say that Kevin's family cannot afford to pay for him to go to school. Therefore, (C) is the correct answer choice because it restates the underlined portion clearly and concisely in the active voice. (E) is wrong because it is unnecessarily awkward and wordy.

3. **(A) (p. 518)** *Writing/Improving Sentences/No Error*

The original is correct. The singular verb "is" agrees with its singular subject "juxtaposition." (B) is wrong because the plural verb "are" does not agree with the singular subject "juxtaposition." (C) is wrong because "attributable for" is not idiomatic; the correct expression is "attributable to." (D) is wrong because it eliminates the main verb in the sentence, resulting in a sentence fragment. Finally, (E) destroys the logic of the sentence by incorrectly personifying arms and feet; arms and feet cannot "attribute" something.

4. **(B) (p. 519)** *Writing/Improving Sentences/Clarity of Expression/Diction and Idioms*

The original has a problem of word usage. In the underlined portion, "including" is not idiomatic. In this context, "such as" would be the appropriate phrase because the sentence intends to say that both birds ("Northern Bobwhite" and "Red-shouldered Hawk") are examples of rare specimens. So, (D) can be eliminated. Then, the two examples of birds should be joined by the conjunction "or" in order to agree with the singular noun "specimen." So, (C) can be eliminated. (E) is wrong because the plural noun "specimens" would require the use of the conjunction "and" instead of the conjunction "or" to show that both birds (not one or the other bird) are rare specimens. Therefore, (B) is the correct answer choice because it fulfills all of the above conditions.

5. **(A) (p. 519)** *Writing/Improving Sentences/No Error*

The original is correct. In this context, the pronoun "it" serves as part of an accepted idiom (e.g., "It is raining."). (B), (C), and (E) are wrong because the plural pronoun "they" does not serve the same idiomatic function; the pronoun "they" requires a referent, but it does not have a clear referent in this sentence. Finally, (D) is wrong because it creates a fused sentence (two clauses spliced by a comma). In order to properly join the two ideas together, (D) would require either a conjunction to accompany the comma or a semicolon in place of the comma.

6. **(A) (p. 519)** *Writing/Identifying Sentence Errors/Clarity of Expression/Diction and Idioms*

The original sentence contains an instance of non-idiomatic usage. The "being" is not needed and should be eliminated. As for (B), "origins" is correct since etymology is the study of words in general. And (C) and (D) are also written properly since "about" and "ancient" have appropriate meanings in this context.

7. **(D) (p. 519)** *Writing/Identifying Sentence Errors/Grammar/Subject-Verb Agreement*

The original sentence contains an error of subject-verb agreement. The sentence has an inverted structure in which the verb follows the subject. The subject is singular, "new construction," so the verb should be singular, "is." As for (A) and (B), the phrase "most important of all" is idiomatic and acceptable. As for (C), the prepositions "in" has a meaning that is correct in this context.

8. **(C) (p. 519)** *Writing/Identifying Sentence Errors/Grammar/Adjectives and Adverbs*

The problem with (C) is the use of an adjective where an adverb is needed ("easily") to modify the verb "to communicate." As for (A), "development" is a noun that functions as the subject of the first clause. As for (B), "made" is the main verb of that clause, and it correctly describes action that occurred in the past. And (D) is properly written since "everyone" is considered a singular verb.

9. **(E) (p. 519)** *Writing/Identifying Sentence Errors/No Error*

The original sentence is correct as written. As for (A), "threatening" is the present participle form of "to threaten," and it is correctly used as an adjective to modify "problems" (describing what kind of problems are discussed). As for (B), "lists" should be plural since the sentence refers to "various" lists. As for (C), "is" correctly agrees with the singular subject "destruction." And as for (D), since the sentence makes it clear there are more than two threats, "greatest" rather than "greater" is the correct form of the adjective "great."

10. **(E) (p. 519)** *Writing/Identifying Sentence Errors/No Error*

The original sentence is correct as written. As for (A), the introductory phrase "by studying" correctly modifies the first important word that follows the comma: astronomers are the ones who study. (B) is correct: "can determine" shows that the light shift gives astronomers the ability to make this measurement. As for (C), "at which" uses the relative pronoun "which," referring to speed, in order to introduce a relative clause. And as for (D), the singular verb "is" correctly agrees with the singular noun "galaxy."

11. **(A) (p. 520)** *Writing/Identifying Sentence Errors/Grammar/Subject-Verb Agreement*

The original sentence contains an error of subject-verb agreement. The subject of "occur" is "withdrawal," a singular noun, so "occur" should be the plural verb "occurs." As for (B), "when" is a subordinate conjunction that is used here to introduce a clause that explains the conditions under which the events are triggered. As for (C), "are" agrees with its subject "banks." As for (D), "on other investments" is an idiomatic phrase.

12. **(D) (p. 520)** *Writing/Identifying Sentence Errors/Logical Expression/Faulty Comparisons*

The problem with the original sentence is an illogical comparison. It compares the runners from the one club with the other club. (D) should read: "the runners from the Greater City Track Club." As for (A), "who" is the correct relative pronoun, referring to "runners." As for (B), "were" correctly agrees in number with "runners." And as for (C), the "not only...but" is a properly constructed phrase.

13. **(D) (p. 520)** *Writing/Identifying Sentence Errors/Grammar/Pronoun Usage*

The original sentence contains a pronoun, "ones," that does not have a clear and unambiguous referent. "Ones" seems to refer to something like "parties," but that word is not available as a choice. (D) should be "parties" instead of "ones." As for (A), this verb correctly agrees with its subject and has the appropriate tense. As for (B), this is a perfectly good way of joining two clauses together, and the "but" signals that the second and first clauses present conflicting points of view. And as for (C), "have" correctly agrees with the plural "democracies."

14. **(D) (p. 520)** *Writing/Identifying Sentence Errors/Logical Expression/Faulty Comparisons*

The problem with the original sentence is an illogical comparison. The sentence likens the fringe to oriental rugs when the sentence means to say that the fringe is like the fringe on rugs. The correct phrase would be: "resembling that of some oriental rugs." As for (A), "ceremonial" is an adjective that properly modifies the noun "versions." As for (B), this verb agrees with its subject, "versions." And as for (C), "with" is used idiomatically.

15. **(D) (p. 520)** *Writing/Identifying Sentence Errors/Clarity of Expression/Diction and Idioms*

The original sentence contains an error of diction (wrong word). (D) should be "formerly" rather than "formally." As for (A), "that" correctly introduces and functions as the subject of the relative clause, and "becomes" correctly agrees with the singular "subsidiary." As for (B), "less" is the appropriate choice since only two circumstances are compared: before and after. As for (C), "it" clearly refers to "subsidiary."

16. **(D) (p. 520)** *Writing/Identifying Sentence Errors/Grammar/Adjectives and Adverbs*

The original sentence incorrectly uses the adjective "approximate" where the adverb "approximately" is needed. As for (A), the phrase "in order to" is used idiomatically. As for (B), "both" correctly modifies "oxen" and makes sense since the sentence seems to be discussing two animals. As for (C), "must pull" is an acceptable verb, and there is no problem with agreement or tense.

17. **(C) (p. 520)** *Writing/Identifying Sentence Errors/Grammar/Pronoun Usage*

The original sentence shifts from the singular to the plural, which results in a lack of pronoun-antecedent agreement. "They are" is plural, but the first clause uses "apple is." Both phrases must either be singular or plural in order to agree with the subject. As for (A), "not only" is an idiomatic phrase. As for (B), "among" is appropriate here since the sentence is evidently referring to several varieties of apples. And (D) is correct because the "not only" indicates that the sentence is going to make more than one point and "also" effectively connects these two points.

18. **(A) (p. 520)** *Writing/Identifying Sentence Errors/Logical Expression/Unintended Meanings*

The original sentence illogically shifts from the singular to the plural. As written, it seems to say that a single olive grows on more than one tree. The sentence can be corrected by conforming in either direction: "an olive, when picked from the tree...." or "olives, when picked from the trees." In this case, given the rest of the sentence, you'd need to change "trees" to "tree." Then, as for (B), "is" correctly agrees with "olive." As for (C) and (D), these verbs forms are idiomatic.

19. **(B) (p. 520)** *Writing/Identifying Sentence Errors/Grammar/Pronoun Usage*

The original sentence includes an error of pronoun usage: "their" should be "his" in order to correctly refer to "Lincoln." As for (A), "largely" is an adverb and is needed to modify the adjective phrase "on the strength of." As for (C), this verb form correctly expresses the sense of the sentence. And as for (D), "in" is idiomatically used in this context.

20. **(D) (p. 521)** *Writing/Identifying Sentence Errors/Logical Expression/Faulty Comparisons*

The original sentence contains an illogical comparison. The sentence compares the texture and taste of the monkfish to the lobster itself. What the sentence means to say is: the texture and taste of the monkfish resemble those of the more expensive lobster. As for (A), "called" is used idiomatically here to mean "named" or "labeled." And as for (B), "because" correctly introduces the subordinate clause that follows and gives the reason for the first conclusion. And as for (C), "resemble" is plural and correctly agrees with "texture and taste."

21. **(B) (p. 521)** *Writing/Identifying Sentence Errors/Grammar/Pronoun Usage*

The original sentence contains an error of pronoun usage. "I" is intended to be the object of the preposition "except" and should be the objective case "me." As for (A), "everyone" is correctly used here to refer to all contestants with the exception of "Jim and me" stated later. As for (C), "announced" is the past tense of "to announce" and correctly describes the sequence of action. As for (D), the underlined prepositional phrase is correctly used and describes the sequence of events.

22. **(D) (p. 521)** *Writing/Identifying Sentence Errors/Logical Expression/Faulty Comparisons*

The original sentence contains an illogical comparison: he was less successful than his campaigns. What the sentence means to say is: he was less successful than in his earlier campaigns. As for (A), you need an adverb to modify "winning." As for (B), "was appointed" correctly agrees with the singular subject "general." And as for (C), "was" is the correct tense and right number for this context.

23. **(B) (p. 521)** *Writing/Identifying Sentence Errors/Clarity of Expression/Diction and Idioms*

In the original sentence, "required" should be "requiring," an adjective to modify "law." (A) is correctly written using the past tense. (C) correctly conveys the idea that those who were 18 years or older were required to register. And "to register" is used idiomatically.

24. **(E) (p. 521)** *Writing/Identifying Sentence Errors/No Error*

The original sentence is correct as written. As for (A), "during" conveys the sense of an extended period, referred to specifically as the school's "Golden Age." As for (B), the past tense correctly shows that the events belong entirely to the past. (C) is idiomatic. And as for (D), "had been born" effectively conveys that the action comes in the past but before the students "enrolled."

25. **(D) (p. 521)** *Writing/Identifying Sentence Errors/Sentence Structure/Incomplete Split Constructions*

The problem with the original sentence is that "which," a relative pronoun, seems to be introducing a clause by acting as the subject of the clause. But there is another subject, "brother" which agrees with the subject. Instead of "which," (D) should be "for which." As for (A), this past tense verb correctly shows that the action occurred in the past. As for (B), the number of this noun is correct—several films. And as for (C), "including" is used properly in this context.

26. **(A) (p. 522)** *Writing/Improving Paragraphs/Passage Development*

The item asks you to find a sentence that states the main point of the passage, and sentence 1 does a good job: Uranus is strange. Sentence 15 also states the main point by summarizing the development of the selection, but sentence 15 is not a choice. (B) is wrong because sentence 5 talks about only one of the strange features of the planet's atmosphere. The passage also talks about other features of the planet, such as the moons. Sentence 6 is wrong for the same reason: the discussion of the moons is one point among several. And sentence 8 talks about only one of the three moons. And (E) is wrong because sentence 14 is a thought that sets up the conclusion.

27. **(A) (p. 522)** *Writing/Improving Paragraphs/No Error*

The original sentence is correct as written. The other choices rearrange the elements of the sentence but don't improve it. (B) makes it sound as though the most important idea in the sentence is the fact that the poles "point," when the author's main purpose in the sentence is to say that the poles are located on either side of the planet. (C), (D), and (E) are awkward and do not express the thought as clearly and directly as the underlined portion does.

28. **(C) (p. 522)** *Writing/Improving Paragraphs/Sentence Elements*

The phrase "it being" is superfluous and not idiomatic. As for (A), "nevertheless" would create an inappropriate contrast, whereas the passage intends for sentence 10 to continue the idea in sentence 9. (B) changes the intended meaning of the original sentence: it was specifically the impact that caused the indentation. As for (D), a semicolon would inappropriately disrupt the logical flow of the sentence. (E) creates a sentence fragment.

29. **(C) (p. 522)** *Writing/Improving Paragraphs/Paragraph Structure*

Sentences 6 through 10 talk about the moons of Uranus and so, because of structure, these sentences belong in the same paragraph. Sentence 11, however, takes up a new topic: the rings. And the discussion of the rings is continued in paragraph four. All of the sentences about the rings should be in the same paragraph, so sentence 11 should be moved into paragraph three. As for (A) and (B), splitting the second paragraph in either of these ways would fragment the discussion about the moons. As for (D), this would make the original organization worse. And as for (E), as noted, there are two distinct topics here that belong in two different paragraphs.

30. (C) (p. 522) *Writing/Improving Paragraphs/Sentence Elements*

There are two problems with sentence 15. First, the "it" lacks an antecedent. "It" seems to refer to something like "discovery," but there is no noun in the preceding sentence to be the antecedent. (If you're not clear on this, try substituting various words from sentence 14 for "it" in sentence 15 to see whether you get a sentence that makes sense.) Second, the "do" seems to connect with something like "do discover," but again, there is nothing in the preceding sentence to do this job. (C) corrects both of these problems. As for (A), you still have the problem with the vague "it." As for (B), "the discovery" implies that there is a particular event identified, such as "the discovery of radium by the Curies," but there is no such event identified. And (D) and (E) have problems with reference: neither "it" nor "that" refers to anything.

31. (A) (p. 523) *Writing/Improving Paragraphs/Passage Development*

Sentence 1 is a rhetorical question. The author assumes that the reader would answer "Yes," and the point of asking the question is to catch the reader's attention: oh, I like music so I'd better read on. (B) is incorrect since the topics that are listed in sentence 1 are not those discussed in the passage. And (C) is wrong because the author does not take a position in sentence 1. As for (D), while you might ask a question when you need information, the author here is not looking for an answer. As for (E), you might think that the list of topics is included to reassure the reader that he or she will find the passage worth reading. But that is not exactly what (E) says. (A), however, makes this point clearly.

32. (B) (p. 523) *Writing/Improving Paragraphs/Sentence Elements*

Sentence 9 is ambiguous. Although it could probably pass in spoken conversation, writing requires more precision. "That" does not have a clear antecedent. It wants to refer to something like "value," but that word isn't available. So, the ambiguity can be eliminated by substituting "value" for "that." Neither (A) nor (C) makes the change. As for (D) and (E), there is nothing wrong with the "it." "It" is singular and refers in this case to "stamp." Making either of these changes introduces a new error.

33. (C) (p. 523) *Writing/Improving Paragraphs/Passage Development*

There seems to be something missing from the end of the third paragraph. The passage states that the value of a stamp depends on (i) how rare it is and (ii) its condition. Then, the fourth paragraph starts talking about condition. Logically, the passage should discuss rarity first. (C) takes care of this by explaining to the reader how to find out whether a stamp is rare. (A) is irrelevant to the development of the passage. (B) may be true and related generally to stamp collecting, but it doesn't have a place in the logical development of this selection. And (E) is wrong for the same reason that (B) is wrong. (D) is perhaps the second best choice because it mentions the value of stamps. However, (D) is not the most clear and effective way to address the problem—(C) is.

34. (A) (p. 523) *Writing/Improving Paragraphs/No Error*

The original sentence is correct, in part because the author compares three types of stamps in terms of value, so "least" is appropriate. For that reason, (B) is incorrect. (C) is wrong because the pronoun "others" refers to information that has not yet been introduced (mint and unused stamps) and so would be confusing to the reader. (D) is wrong for a similar reason. And (E) is wrong because "least" would be required.

35. (A) (p. 523) *Writing/Improving Paragraphs/Sentence Elements*

The problem with the original sentence is that the pronoun "them" does not agree with its antecedent, "stamp." The pronoun should be singular. (B) is a singular pronoun, but (B) introduces an ambiguity. "It" seems to refer to a particular stamp, but the passage is not about looking for one particular stamp. (C) is wrong because it changes the meaning of the sentence so that it makes no sense. (E) makes the same error as (C) does. And (D) is wrong because in the original sentence, "sure" is an adjective that correctly modifies the subject "you."

Section 7—Critical Reading

1. **(A) (p. 524) Critical Reading: Sentence Completions/Combined Reasoning/Coordinate Conjunctions** and **Key Words**

This sentence contains both an extension of thought and a reversal of thought as its logical keys. The first blank must extend the idea of the key word "casual," as signaled by the coordinate conjunction clue "and." Only (A) can possibly do that. Checking the second element of (A), "belie" means "to disguise," which reverses the "seemingly casual" part of the sentence. He seemed casual but he was not.

2. **(D) (p. 524) Critical Reading: Sentence Completions/Combined Reasoning/Key Words**

This sentence contains both a reversal of thought and an extension of thought as its logical keys. Start with the second blank: you need to describe reviews that border on "cruel" (key word) and only (D) does that. (A) would convey exactly the opposite meaning. (C) has nothing do with cruelty. (B) and (E) do not create meaningful phrases. Based on the second blank alone, the answer is (D). Check the first element of (D): it should reverse the idea of "scathing" reviews, and it does; she has adoring fans, and thus a reputation.

3. **(A) (p. 524) Critical Reading: Sentence Completions/Thought Extension/Subordinate Conjunctions**

This item is largely a test of vocabulary, but there are sufficient clues to point you to the correct answer even if you don't recognize all of the vocabulary. As indicated by the subordinate conjunction "because," the first blank asks for a synonym for the key word "treason." This can only be "perfidy." Even if you do not know the meaning of the correct choice, you can eliminate (B), (D), and (E) because most students would know that neither "grief," "pacifism," nor "patriotism" means "treason." Now, look at the second elements of (A) and (C): both seem to create meaningful phrases. Ultimately, then, the item turns on the meaning of "perfidy." However, even without knowing the meanings of "perfidy" and "veracity," you have a 50/50 chance of answering correctly if you are forced to guess between (A) and (C).

4. **(C) (p. 524) Critical Reading: Sentence Completions/Thought Reversal/Subordinate Conjunctions**

The subordinate conjunction "although" indicates a reversal of thought: the fact that scientists have been able to measure time is subordinate to the main idea, which is that writers and poets have been able to capture time in a more complete way. (A) is incorrect because the sentence does not mean to say that they have neglected time. (D) and (E) fail on the grounds of usage. (C) is the correct answer, since you cannot have a "benign," (B), experience of time.

5. **(B) (p. 524) Critical Reading: Sentence Completions/Combined Reasoning/Subordinate Conjunctions** and **Coordinate Conjunctions**

This sentence contains a reversal of thought, as indicated by the subordinate conjunction "although" and the coordinate conjunction "but." The subordinate conjunction "although" indicates that the conducting was something not expected at a gala or special occasion. Eliminate (C) and (D) since they do not create meaningful phrases. Then, the coordinate conjunction "and" indicates that the first blank is related to the fact that the orchestra was not enthusiastic, so it is not likely that the conducting was "auspicious," (A), or "animated," (E). The coordinate conjunction "but" confirms that with an audience "oblivious" to the "defects" (key word), (B) is the only plausible answer choice.

6. **(B) (p. 525) Critical Reading: Sentence Completions/Combined Reasoning/Key Words** and **Subordinate Conjunctions**

In this sentence, the most obvious logical clue is the parallel between the blank and the key adjective "inferior." You must find something that has similar negative overtones. Of the five choices, only (B) provides the needed parallel. You may also look to the subordinate conjunction "although," which indicates a reversal of thought: that Burns wrote in the Scottish dialect despite negative attitudes toward the practice. Therefore, the blank will be filled with a negative word.

7. **(B) (p. 525)** *Critical Reading: Sentence Completions/Thought Extension/Key Words*

The adjective "given" indicates that the second part of the sentence is an extension of the first part of the sentence. Another key word here is "resign." What is the cause of the Secretary's resignation? It cannot be the fact that the Secretary is in favor of the President's policies, so eliminate (D) and (E). Then, eliminate (A) and (C), because they do not create meaningful statements. (B), however, does provide the reason: "given" the Secretary's disagreement with the President, he will "resign."

8. **(A) (p. 525)** *Critical Reading: Sentence Completions/Thought Extension/Explanatory Phrases*

The phrase "in order to" indicates that the second blank must give the student's reason for doing what is mentioned in the first part of the sentence. Test each choice keeping in mind another key phrase, "additional time." (A) is the only choice that works: the student needs to "extend" the deadline, so he wheedles some extra time. (B) and (C) make the opposite statement. (D) and (E) create phrases that are not idiomatic.

9. **(E) (p. 525)** *Critical Reading: Passages/Social Studies/Vocabulary*

The adverb "however" is an important context clue; it sets up a contrast, indicating that "behind closed doors" and "transparent" have opposite meanings. The opposite of "behind closed doors" is "open to public view."

10. **(C) (p. 525)** *Critical Reading: Passages/Humanities/Application*

This item asks you to consider the meaning of the "old saying" (which captures the message implicit in the passage) and then apply that principle to a new situation. This new situation asks the reader to think critically about the application. "No good deed goes unpunished" is another way of expressing the law of unintended consequences or even the concept of irony. (C) is the correct answer choice because it too expresses irony. Someone who refinishes an antique table is most likely intent on making the table more desirable; depreciation in value would certainly be an unintended consequence. The other answer choices are wrong because they do not express this disjunctive relationship between what is intended and what actually occurs.

11. **(C) (p. 526)** *Critical Reading: Passages/Natural Sciences/Implied Idea*

The author does not specifically state what the most important factor is about the Africanized bee, but you can infer that it is the Africanized bee's aggressiveness. Neither where it originated nor where it is going is the most important factor. As for (D), both Africanized bees and domestic honeybees are able to sting, but the Africanized bee stings "in greater numbers." (E) is not discussed in the passage.

12. **(B) (p. 526)** *Critical Reading: Passages/Social Studies/Development*

The first three sentences include historical background. It is intended to provide the reader with a perspective on the idea of solar access. (A) is incorrect because the mention of various local variations on a theme does not necessarily mean that the author advocates a national program. (C) is incorrect because the author does not mention any limitation. (D) is incorrect because there is no misunderstanding about "distribution" mentioned. (E) is incorrect because the author does not start a debate.

13. **(E) (p. 527)** *Critical Reading: Passages/Natural Sciences/Voice*

The author describes the problem of malformations in amphibians and notes that biologists are concerned. Then, the author goes on to explain that scientists are investigating several possible causes. Finally, the author cautions that the results are not yet final. Therefore, "inconclusive" is a good description of the author's tone. As for (A), (C), and (D), the author does not suggest that the research is incorrect; rather, there is more work to be done before reaching a definitive conclusion. (B) is obviously incorrect.

14. **(C) (p. 527)** *Critical Reading: Passages/Natural Sciences/Vocabulary*

As used in the referenced sentence, "natural" means "normal": this level of malformation is not natural, or not normal. So, (A) must be incorrect because it overstates the severity of the problem: the level of deformities is higher than what is considered to be natural, not higher than what is considered to be elevated. (B) is incorrect since "uncontrived" is an inappropriate meaning of "natural" in this context. Finally, neither (D) nor (E) fits the meaning of the sentence.

15. **(C) (p. 528)** *Critical Reading: Passages/Natural Sciences/Main Idea*

(A) describes a point that the author makes in the selection (in the last sentence in the first paragraph), but that idea is not the main point, or primary concern, of the selection. (B) suggests an idea that is certainly consistent with the overall tone of the passage, but again, the idea is not the main point of the selection. The author is not simply concerned with criticizing those who won't abandon their theories; he is more concerned with demonstrating that those theories are in fact wrong. (C) captures this concern: the main point of the passage is that the popular theories are incorrect. (D) and (E) are like (A): they mention ideas that are covered in the passage, but neither describes the main point.

16. **(C) (p. 528)** *Critical Reading: Passages/Natural Sciences/Vocabulary*

The author distinguishes between behavioral mechanisms for controlling body temperature and other "innate mechanisms." The context suggests that "innate" here means (C) "reflexive."

17. **(B) (p. 528)** *Critical Reading: Passages/Natural Sciences/Explicit Detail*

In the opening sentence, the author establishes that there are two general responses available to warm-blooded animals for regulating body temperature: behavior and innate mechanisms. The author goes on to state that humans rely primarily on the first type of response, but adds that the organism also responds to changes in temperature in the core of the body (the second type of response) and that these changes are triggered by thermoreceptors that are distributed throughout the central nervous system. Thus, statement I must be part of the correct answer choice. In the final sentence of the first paragraph, the author states that the second type of mechanism for regulating temperature is less effective for adjusting to gross changes in temperature than the first type. Thus, II must be part of the correct response. Finally, the author does not state that the internal thermoreceptors are not affected by microwave radiation. The problem that the author cites is not that internal thermoreceptors do not respond to changes in the temperature of the core of the body but that they do not trigger the type of response needed to counteract gross changes in environmental temperatures.

18. **(B) (p. 528)** *Critical Reading: Passages/Natural Sciences/Implied Idea*

In the first sentence of the second paragraph, the author remarks that proponents of the generally accepted theory (which treats microwave radiation like other radiation) simply assumed that one type of radiation would have the same thermal effect as other types of radiation. Then, the author goes on to demonstrate that this assumption is wrong. Thus, (B) is the best description of the error identified by the author. Certainly, there is no suggestion that the proponents of the accepted theory did special laboratory research, control group surveys, or causal investigation. As for (D), while the proponents of the accepted theory may have used deductive reasoning to reach their conclusion, this would not have been the main basis for their conclusions. (Note the wording of the question stem.)

19. **(D) (p. 528)** *Critical Reading: Passages/Natural Sciences/Vocabulary*

The word "appreciate" often means "likes" or "is pleased by," but that meaning is out of place here. Rather, the author uses the word to mean "notice."

20. **(A) (p. 529)** *Critical Reading: Passages/Natural Sciences/Development*

In the lines indicated, the author states that it is possible that an organism could be cooked by microwave radiation (because the radiation penetrates into the core) before it even realizes its temperature is rising. The verb tense here ("could") clearly indicates that the author is introducing a hypothetical possibility. Given the shocking nature of the example, we should conclude that the author has introduced it to dramatize a point.

21. **(C) (p. 529)** *Critical Reading: Passages/Natural Sciences/Vocabulary*

The most common meaning of the word "compromise" (to reach an agreement in which each side gives up something) is not appropriate here. Rather, the author intends a less common meaning: "endanger."

22. **(E) (p. 529)** *Critical Reading: Passages/Natural Sciences/Voice*

The author gives facts and analyzes or discusses a problem, so the tone could be called "scholarly" or "analytical." The author is clearly concerned that other scientists made an error in their assessment of the effects of microwave radiation. (A) is incorrect because the tone is not conversational at all, but expository. (B) is incorrect because although the author seems disturbed by the ignorance of the scientists, he is never disparaging. He is also never facetious or cynical, (C). (D) is close because the tone is scholarly, but (E) is the best choice because the author is more concerned than he is noncommittal.

23. **(A) (p. 529)** *Critical Reading: Passages/Natural Sciences/Development*

The passage explains why microwave radiation is not like other radiation and why microwave radiation is therefore dangerous to warm-blooded species. Since it was until recently assumed that microwave radiation was like other radiation, the author is concerned with pointing out the weaknesses of this theory.

24. **(A) (p. 529)** *Critical Reading: Passages/Natural Sciences/Application*

Since the last paragraph deals with a recent report suggesting that previous assumptions about microwaves were incorrect, the author would probably go on to talk about the need for more research. (B) is incorrect because the author is dealing with microwave radiation and there would be no reason at this point to compare it to other forms of radiation. Besides, the author made the comparison earlier in the passage. (C) is incorrect because it overstates the case. There is no evidence to suggest that microwave radiation is so dangerous that it should be prohibited—just understood and regulated. (D) is incorrect because clearly the author is concerned with new information about microwave radiation. He has already suggested that what we presently know is erroneous. Finally, (E) is incorrect because a discussion of the strategies that are used by various species to control hyperthermia would not follow logically from his remarks that microwave radiation has not been correctly understood. In any event, the discussion of such strategies early in the passage is intended to set the stage for the main point of the selection.

Section 8—Math

1. **(C) (p. 530)** *Math: Multiple-Choice/Geometry*

   You can solve the problem simply by multiplying the dimensions shown to find the volume of each box. Box C, (C), has the largest volume: $3\times4\times5=60$.

   Another strategy is to use a benchmark. Box A, which is $2\times3\times4$, must be larger than Box B, which is $2\times3\times3$, and so on.

2. **(A) (p. 530)** *Math: Multiple-Choice/Arithmetic/Common Arithmetic Items/Properties of Numbers*

   An even number times an odd number yields an even number, and a positive number times a negative number yields a negative number. Thus, the multiplication described in the question stem results in a number that is both negative and even.

3. **(E) (p. 530)** *Math: Multiple-Choice/Algebra/Manipulating Algebraic Expressions/Basic Algebraic Manipulations*

   Apply the distributive property to the given expression: $w(x+y+z)=wx+wy+wz$. (A), (B), (C), and (D) are also equal to $wx+wy+wz$. (E) is incorrect because $w(xy)+w(yz)=wxy+wyz$.

   Alternatively, assume some values. Let $w, x, y,$ and z each be equal to 1. On that assumption: $w(x+y+z)=1(1+1+1)=1(3)=3$. Then, substitute 1 for $w, x, y,$ and z into the answer choices. Every choice yields the value 3 except for (E).

4. **(E) (p. 531)** *Math: Multiple-Choice/Arithmetic/Complicated Arithmetic Application Items*

   If the original prize is x, each student would receive $\frac{x}{11}$. When another student is added, each student would receive $\frac{x}{12}$. Thus, each student would then receive $\frac{x}{12}\div\frac{x}{11}=\frac{11}{12}$ of what he or she would have originally received.

   Alternatively, assume some values. For example, assuming that the prize is worth \$132 (a convenient assumption since $11\cdot12=132$), each student originally receives \$12. After the addition of another student, the prize is worth only \$11. Thus, the second prize must be worth only $\frac{11}{12}$ of the first prize.

5. **(B) (p. 531)** *Math: Multiple-Choice/Geometry/Complex Figures and Circles and Rectangles and Squares and Coordinate Geometry/The Coordinate System*

   This is a shaded area problem: $\text{area}_{\text{shaded portion}} = \text{area}_{\text{square}} - \frac{\text{area}_{\text{circle}}}{4}$. $\text{Area}_{\text{square}} = s^2 = 2^2 = 4$.

   $\text{Area}_{\text{circle}} = \pi r^2 = \pi(2)^2 = 4\pi$. Therefore, $\text{area}_{\text{shaded portion}} = 4 - \frac{4\pi}{4} = 4 - \pi$.

6. **(D) (p. 531)** *Math: Multiple-Choice/Data Analysis/Data Interpretation/Tables (Matrices) and Arithmetic/Common Arithmetic Items/Ratios*

   The number of people having X is: $10+30=40$; the number of people having Y is: $10+40=50$. Thus, the ratio of people having X to people having Y is: $40:50=4:5$.

7. **(C) (p. 531)** *Math: Multiple-Choice/Coordinate Geometry/Slope-Intercept Form of a Linear Equation*

Begin by finding the slope from the two points on the line, $(-1,0)$ and $(2,2)$: $m = \dfrac{y_2 - y_1}{x_2 - x_1} = \dfrac{2-0}{2-(-1)} = \dfrac{2}{3}$. To find b, plug $(-1,0)$ into the general linear equation, $y = mx + b$, where m is the slope. Substitute 0 for y, -1 for x, and $\dfrac{2}{3}$ for m: $0 = \dfrac{2(-1)}{3} + b \Rightarrow b = \dfrac{2}{3}$. Therefore: $y = \dfrac{2x}{3} + \dfrac{2}{3}$.

8. **(D) (p. 532)** *Math: Multiple-Choice/Arithmetic/Common Arithmetic Items/Proportions and Direct-Inverse Variation*

This is a direct variation problem, but you can also use a proportion: $\dfrac{20 \text{ minutes}}{35 \text{ minutes}} = \dfrac{40\%}{x\%} \Rightarrow x = 40\left(\dfrac{35}{20}\right) \Rightarrow x = 70 \Rightarrow x\% = 70\%$.

Alternatively, note that the bushel fills 10 percent every 5 minutes, so it fills another 30 percent in 15 minutes. Therefore, $40\% + 30\% = 70\%$.

9. **(D) (p. 532)** *Math: Multiple-Choice/Arithmetic/Common Arithmetic Items/Percents*

Begin by finding 40 percent of 5: $\dfrac{40}{100} \cdot 5 = \dfrac{200}{100} = 2$. Now, find 50 percent of 2: $\dfrac{50}{100} \cdot 2 = 1$. If 1 person had a score averaging 250 or better, and there are 5 people in all, 4 people had a score averaging below 250.

10. **(C) (p. 532)** *Math: Multiple-Choice/Geometry/Lines and Angles*

A radius drawn from the center O will be perpendicular to $\overline{PQ}$:

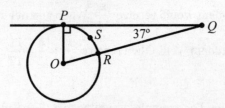

So, $90° + 37° + \angle POR = 180° \Rightarrow \angle POR = 53°$. Since O is the center of the circle and an arc of a circle is equal to its central angle and $\angle POR = 53°$, $\overset{\frown}{PSR} = 53°$.

11. **(C) (p. 532)** *Math: Multiple-Choice/Data Analysis/Data Interpretation/Bar, Cumulative, and Line Graphs* and *Probability and Statistics/Averages* and *Median* and *Mode*

Adding the twelve temperatures and dividing by twelve gives an average slightly greater than 54°F, so (I) is true. Arrange the values in order: 30, 30, 35, 35, 35, 50, 55, 65, 65, 80, 80, and 90. The central values are 50 and 55, so the median (52.5°F) is greater than 50°F, so (II) is true. The mode is 35°F because it is the temperature that appears with the greatest frequency, so (III) is false.

12. **(A) (p. 532)** *Math: Multiple-Choice/Algebra/Solving Algebraic Equations or Inequalities with One Variable/Equations Involving Absolute Value*

Since $\left|\dfrac{1}{3} - \dfrac{1}{2}\right| = \dfrac{1}{6}$, create the derivative equations: $k - \dfrac{1}{8} = \dfrac{1}{6}$ or $-k + \dfrac{1}{8} = \dfrac{1}{6}$. Solve for x: $k = \dfrac{14}{48} = \dfrac{7}{24}$ or $k = -\dfrac{1}{24}$. Remember to check the solutions for all absolute value problems.

Alternatively, use the "test-the-test" strategy.

13. **(C) (p. 533)** *Math: Multiple-Choice/Data Analysis/Data Interpretation/Tables (Matrices)* and *Probability and Statistics/Median*

Determine the "Difference" values:

AGE DIFFERENCE FOR CHILDREN IN FIVE FAMILIES					
Family	Oldest	Age	Youngest	Age	Difference
LaTours	Joan	15	Ed	12	$15-12=3$
Pickett	Harold	17	Claire	8	$17-8=9$
Thibault	Rene	16	Henri	3	$16-3=13$
Barber	Fred	9	Gloria	7	$9-7=2$
Newcomb	Danny	12	Syd	8	$12-8=4$

Arrange the "Difference" values in order: 2, 3, 4, 9, and 13. Therefore, the median age difference is 4.

14. **(E) (p. 533)** *Math: Multiple-Choice/Algebra/Solving Algebraic Equations or Inequalities with One Variable/ Equations Involving Integer and Rational Exponents*

Raise both sides of the equation to the fourth power:

$$\left(x^{\frac{1}{4}}\right)^4 = 20^4 \Rightarrow x = 20^4 = (2\cdot 10)^4 \Rightarrow x = 2^4\cdot 10^4 = 16\cdot 10,000 = 160,000.$$

15. **(D) (p. 533)** *Math: Multiple-Choice/Coordinate Geometry/Graphs of Linear Equations*

This problem can be easily solved if you recall that two lines are perpendicular if the product of their slopes is -1, i.e., if the slopes of the two lines are negative reciprocals of each other, then the two lines are perpendicular. The given line has a slope of $\frac{3}{2}$. The line in (D) has a slope of $-\frac{2}{3}$.

Alternatively, you could sketch the graph of each of the lines.

16. **(E) (p. 533)** *Math: Multiple-Choice/Arithmetic/Common Arithmetic Items/Proportions and Direct-Inverse Variation*

Since $n > m$, the net drain from the tank per minute is: $n - m$. Therefore, the time required to empty the tank is: $\frac{g}{(n-m)}$.

Alternatively, substitute numbers and "test-the-test."

Section 9—Critical Reading

1. **(E) (p. 534)** *Critical Reading: Sentence Completions/Thought Extension/Key Words*

This sentence contains an extension of thought, as indicated by the adverb "thus." So, the missing word must describe the consequences for the poor of high prices in the inner city. Eliminate (A) on the grounds of usage. As for the remaining choices, the strongest connection is between high prices and exploitation.

2. (A) (p. 534) *Critical Reading: Sentence Completions/Thought Reversal/Subordinate Conjunctions*

This sentence contains a reversal of thought, as indicated by the subordinate conjunction "while." Since the legislation is described "as a move to save lives," you should be looking for a word with a positive connotation for the first blank. (B) can be eliminated since no one would want to thwart something that saved lives. (A), (C), (D), and (E) remain possibilities. The second part of the sentence reverses the first part with the word "while." The adjective "alarmist" tells you to look for a word with negative overtones. Thus, eliminate (C), (D), and (E). Therefore, (A) must be the correct choice.

3. (B) (p. 534) *Critical Reading: Sentence Completions/Combined Reasoning/Explanatory Phrases* and *Key Words*

The key to this item is the parallel set up between the key adjective "incomprehensible," which has a negative meaning, and the second blank; the second element of the correct choice must be a word like "incomprehensible." As for the first blank, the missing word must have a positive meaning so that it reverses the idea of something that is "incomprehensible," as indicated by the phrase "including those."(Note that the phrase "including those" functions in the same way as would the phrase "even those.") Only (B) satisfies both of these meanings.

4. (E) (p. 534) *Critical Reading: Sentence Completions/Thought Extension/Explanatory Phrases*

This sentence has several key words and phrase clues to help you find the correct answer. Eliminate (A) because, while a musical style might be famous, unknown, or fading out of memory, you would not likely say that it is foundering. Beyond that, the second substitution must extend the idea of the first: the music is doing ____ thanks to the determined efforts of ____. Given the phrase clue "determined efforts," eliminate (A), (B), and (D) since "foundering," "diminishing," and "waning" are not things that are accomplished by determined efforts. Eliminate (C), since opponents do not create an appreciation for the things that they oppose. Only (E) works: it is due to the efforts of "American" (key adjective) expatriates that jazz is an American art form flourishing in Europe.

5. (E) (p. 536) *Critical Reading: Passages/Social Studies/Development*

The author begins by stating the problem: danger to language and culture. Then, the second paragraph provides some details about the problem. The third paragraph identifies some causes, and the rest of the passage lists some approaches to solve the problem. (B) is incorrect because the author does not pose a dilemma. (A dilemma presents two equally unacceptable alternatives.) (C) is incorrect because the author doesn't sugarcoat the problem in the first place. As for (D), the author never criticizes a plan.

6. (C) (p. 536) *Critical Reading: Passages/Social Studies/Explicit Detail*

In lines 15–16, the author states that rural Tibetans are like foreigners: they lack the language skills that are needed to get jobs. (A) is incorrect because, while the author does draw a distinction between rural workers and city opportunities, the author does not specifically state that unemployment is higher in the city. (B) is incorrect because the author does not say that these workers are entirely lacking in skills, only that they lack linguistic skills. (D) is incorrect and seems to represent a confusion with the information that is given later in that paragraph about monastery schools. As for (E), the fact that employers do not hire the Tibetans who cannot speak a language that is used does not mean that the employers would prefer to hire Chinese workers, as opposed, say, to Tibetan workers who speak Chinese and can communicate.

7. (B) (p. 536) *Critical Reading: Passages/Social Studies/Implied Idea*

The word "inferred" in the stem signals that this is an Implied Idea item. In the second paragraph, the author states that language and culture are important forces for the secularization and modernization of Tibetan society, but many students attend monastery schools because lay schools do not emphasize the study of Tibetan culture. We can infer from this information that modernization and secularization would proceed more rapidly if attendance at lay schools were greater. (A) and (C) are incorrect because the discussion contrasts the two kinds of schools in terms of the emphasis on cultural studies. (D) reaches exactly the incorrect conclusion: monasteries offer cultural studies, and because students are enrolled there, secularization and modernization lag. Finally, (E) has no support in the passage. Of course, the author would like to see lay schools strengthen cultural studies, but the passage does not say that this has already happened.

8. **(D) (p. 537)** *Critical Reading: Passages/Social Studies/Implied Idea*

This item borders on being a Voice item, since it asks about the author's judgment. It doesn't really matter which way you classify it because both types are questions that require you to read "between the lines." At the end of the third paragraph, the author says that the new laws are "encouraging," but adds that the need is urgent. Then, in the next paragraph, the author states that the new law could help promote bilingualism—but only if it is properly implemented. (A) is incorrect because the author thinks that the law has promise. (B), however, overstates the case in the other direction. The author does not think that success is guaranteed. There is nothing in the passage to support (C). Finally, (E) is incorrect both because the author thinks that the new law might work and because the best solution is bilingualism.

9. **(C) (p. 537)** *Critical Reading: Passages/Social Studies/Vocabulary*

The author refers to "standard spoken Tibetan" as being vernacular, so the word must mean "ordinary language." The other answer choices mention ideas that are generally related to the topic of the passage, but none have the correct meaning.

10. **(A) (p. 537)** *Critical Reading: Passages/Social Studies/Explicit Detail*

This item has a thought-reverser, EXCEPT. In the final paragraph, the author suggests literary awards and prizes for Tibetan writers, (B), cultural festivals, (E), competitions of various sorts, (D), and preserving folk culture, (C). Only (A) is not mentioned in the passage: the author does not suggest any way of addressing unemployment.

11. **(D) (p. 537)** *Critical Reading: Passages/Social Studies/Vocabulary*

The author states that there is no standard form of Tibetan but adds that the diasporic community has a proto-version based upon Lhasa. In this context, "emergent" means emerging or developing. As for the other choices, these characteristics might be advantageous for a developing Tibetan, but they do not communicate the idea of "proto" or "emergent."

12. **(D) (p. 537)** *Critical Reading: Passages/Social Studies/Implied Idea*

The author states that classical Tibetan can be read by anyone who is able to read modern Tibetan, yet this is not true of English. This difference exists because English has changed more over the centuries than has Tibetan, effectively making old English a foreign language as far as modern readers are concerned. (A) is incorrect because the author does not comment on the difficulty of learning written English. (B) is incorrect because there is no comparison between the number of different dialects of the two languages. (C) is incorrect because there is no comparison between proto-Tibetan and anything. Finally, (E) has to be incorrect since Passage 2 infers that language, in general, underwrites culture.

13. **(E) (p. 537)** *Critical Reading: Passages/Social Studies/Vocabulary*

The author of Passage 2 states that Tibetan is conservative and then supports the point by noting that a modern speaker of Tibetan can easily read texts that were written 13 centuries ago. In other words, the classical form of the language has not changed much, so one could call it "conservative." (A) is incorrect because classical Tibetan is a literary language. (B) is incorrect because the author talks about the richness of classical Tibetan, so it is not limited. (C) and (D) do not have appropriate definitions.

14. **(B) (p. 537)** *Critical Reading: Passages/Social Studies/Development*

Each of the first three paragraphs of Passage 2 discusses a problem with Tibetan as a language and some developments that may help to correct the problem. The first paragraph states that there is no standard form, but one is developing. The second paragraph states that dialects diverge from classical form—newspapers, etc.—and develop new forms. The third paragraph states that the lack of professional terms promotes the use of Tibetan terms in place of Chinese equivalents. (A), (C), and (D) are incorrect because these discussions are mostly confined to the second paragraph. (E) is incorrect because this notion is developed in the first paragraph.

15. **(C) (p. 538)** *Critical Reading: Passages/Social Studies/Development*

The author spends the first three paragraphs demonstrating that there are serious problems with Tibetan, though there are some encouraging developments. At the beginning of the fourth paragraph, the author asks why people should even bother with Tibetan, given all of the problems associated with it. At this point, the author is addressing another point: why not abandon the language altogether in favor of Chinese? (A) is incorrect because the tone of the question makes things seem worse, not better. As for (B), while both Chinese and Tibetan are intertwined in many ways and are both languages, that is not the reason for the author's question. As for (D), while the author distinguishes language and culture and notes how they are interdependent, this is not why the author asks the question. Finally, (D) also misses the point; if anything, the last paragraph is filled with specific proposals for saving Tibetan.

16. **(C) (p. 538)** *Critical Reading: Passages/Social Studies/Implied Idea*

This item asks for a synthesis of information from the two passages. One of the most important themes in both passages is that language, in this case Tibetan, is essential to the survival of the culture with which it embodies. This shared theme indicates that (B) and (D) are both incorrect. As for (A), no such comparison is suggested in either passage. Finally, (E) is incorrect because both authors seem to believe that Tibetan, which lacks certain modern components, can be supplemented.

17. **(B) (p. 538)** *Critical Reading: Passages/Social Studies/Voice*

The author of Passage 1 says specifically that Tibetan language and culture are threatened with extinction but holds out hope and offers some ideas to promote them in the last paragraph. In the last paragraph of Passage 2, the author mentions the "possible disappearance" of Tibetan but also mentions that this is not inevitable. (B) best summarizes these two attitudes. (A) is overly pessimistic. (C) and (D) are incorrect because the authors have similar opinions. (E) is overly optimistic.

18. **(E) (p. 538)** *Critical Reading: Passages/Social Studies/Explicit Detail*

This item has a thought-reverser, so the correct answer choice is the one exception. (A), (B), (C), and (D) are all discussed by both authors, but only Passage 2 mentions (E).

19. **(A) (p. 539)** *Critical Reading: Passages/Social Studies/Application*

This item asks you to synthesize information from the two passages. Passage 1 talks about Tibetan in terms of the political threat posed by the language of the dominant people, Chinese. For example, the author of Passage 1 says that Tibetans are not allowed to use Tibetan in public meetings but are required to speak Chinese. Passage 2 talks primarily about matters that are internal to the language, e.g., fragmented dialects and problems with spelling. (A) best summarizes this difference. (B) is incorrect because both authors speak favorably about both classical and modern versions of the language. (C) is incorrect for basically the same reason that (B) is incorrect. (D) is incorrect because both authors see language as sustaining culture. (E) misrepresents the first passage.

Section 10—Writing

1. **(C) (p. 540)** *Writing/Improving Sentences/Clarity of Expression/Diction and Idioms*

   The original sentence contains a non-idiomatic expression. "If" does not have the same meaning as "whether." (C) provides the correct expression. The other choices are simply not idiomatic.

2. **(D) (p. 540)** *Writing/Improving Sentences/Logical Expression/Misplaced Modifiers*

   The original sentence contains a misplaced modifier. The proximity of the phrase "when used together" to the phrase "cosmetic company" incorrectly suggests that the introductory phrase is intended to modify "company." An error of this sort can usually be corrected only by restructuring the sentence, as (D) does. As for (B), the modifying phrase is still incorrectly placed. In (B), the phrase seems to modify "appearance." (C) solves the problem of the original sentence, but in doing so (C) changes the intended meaning of the sentence. The original sentence makes it clear that the products are intended to enhance the appearance of the skin by preventing blemishes and reducing the signs of aging, but (C) suggests that these are three separate advantages of the products. (E) makes a similar error.

3. **(A) (p. 541)** *Writing/Improving Sentences/No Error*

   The underlined portion is correct. (B) is incorrect because the two parts of a compound verb must have similar verb forms. (C) and (E) both change the meaning of the original sentence by implying that more than one form of recorded music will replace compact discs. (D), too, changes the meaning of the original sentence because it implies that digital music files will become the most common form of recorded music only by replacing the others. But the original sentence clearly suggests that digital music files will become the most common form of recorded music and then replace compact discs altogether. ("Most common" does not necessarily mean "sole.")

4. **(C) (p. 541)** *Writing/Improving Sentences/Logical Expression/Misplaced Modifiers*

   The original sentence has a dangling modifier and implies that the Youth Caucus was itself a candidate. (B) and (E) fail to correct the error. (C) and (D) both make the needed correction, but "to be" is necessary to complete the predicate that is initiated by "seemed."

5. **(A) (p. 541)** *Writing/Improving Sentences/No Error*

   The underlined portion is correct. (B) introduces two new errors. First, the phrase "as well than" is not idiomatic; and second, the placement of "once" here is not as idiomatic as the placement of "once" in the original sentence. (C) changes the meaning of the original sentence by making "tongue" and "musical genius" the agents who act (instead of the person who acts). (D) is awkward when compared to the underlined portion, and (E) contains a misplaced modifier that changes the meaning of the original sentence by implying that it was the singer who possessed the sharp tongue and musical genius.

6. **(C) (p. 541)** *Writing/Improving Sentences/Logical Expression/Directness* and *Clarity of Expression/Diction and Idioms*

   The original sentence contains two errors. First, a contrast is signaled by "although," so "yet" is superfluous and disrupts the logical flow of the sentence. Second, "during" does not have an appropriate meaning in this sentence. The verb tense of "was singing" could be less ambiguous, as it is in (C). (B) fails to correct the second error. (D) corrects the second error, but substituting "but" for "yet" does not solve the problem of logical structure. Finally, (E) not only fails to solve the problem of logical structure, but it compounds that problem by creating an extremely awkward sentence.

7. **(C) (p. 541)** *Writing/Improving Sentences/Sentence Structure/Problems of Coordination and Subordination and *Incomplete Split Constructions*

The original sentence contains two errors. First, the clause introduced by "neither" has no clear, logical connection to the rest of the sentence. Second, the sentence contains an incomplete construction. It reads "she has…be a great teacher." (C) corrects the incomplete structure and gives the orphaned clause a clear connection to the rest of the sentence. (It is now one of two parallel dependent clauses governed by "although.") (B) and (D) correct the second error but not the first. (E) introduces two new errors: first, the use of "nor" signals a contrast where one is not intended. (The first two ideas about Mary Ann are similar, not different.) Second, "but" is superfluous and disrupts the logical flow of the sentence.

8. **(C) (p. 541)** *Writing/Improving Sentences/Grammar/Subject-Verb Agreement*

The error is one of subject-verb agreement. "Which" refers to "coolness" and to "mutability," and so the sentence requires a plural verb. Additionally, the original sentence sets up an equivalence between those two elements and "a natural outgrowth." Only (B) and (C) correct the first error, and only (C) corrects the second. (D) and (E) are incorrect for the further reason that they distort the intended meaning of the original sentence.

9. **(B) (p. 542)** *Writing/Improving Sentences/Logical Expression/Faulty Comparisons*

The original sentence sets up an illogical comparison between German art songs and the French (people). Only (B) eliminates this problem.

10. **(E) (p. 542)** *Writing/Improving Sentences/Clarity of Expression/Diction and Idioms*

The original sentence contains two problems of diction, or word meaning. First, "antedate" means "to come before"; therefore, "having" is not only superfluous, but the phrase "having antedated" is almost like saying "having had come before," a verb tense that is inconsistent with the rest of the sentence. Additionally, "use" implies an ongoing condition, but the sentence means to say that the cuneiform texts were written before a certain time in history, the date that alphabets were invented or first used.

11. **(A) (p. 542)** *Writing/Improving Sentences/No Error*

The original sentence is correct as written. (B) changes the meaning of the original sentence by implying that Gandhi read *Civil Disobedience* with the objective of making it part of his struggle. (C), too, changes the meaning of the original sentence by implying that it was in 1906 that Gandhi incorporated Thoreau's teachings into his struggle. The original sentence states that it was in 1906 that Gandhi read the work. (D) also changes the meaning of the original sentence. The use of the subjunctive ("would have") implies that Gandhi did not read the work in 1906 because something prevented him from doing so. Finally, (E) eliminates the only conjugated verbs in the sentence. The result is a sentence fragment.

12. **(B) (p. 542)** *Writing/Improving Sentences/Logical Expression/Directness* and *Grammar/Double Negatives*

The original sentence contains two errors. First, there is a lack of logical structure. The "with its being cheaper" is tacked onto the sentence as an afterthought. Second, the original sentence implies that with oil heat there is "no need for…no large storage tanks," a double negative. Only (B) corrects these errors without introducing a new error. (C) is wrong because this use of "being" is not acceptable in standard written English and because the resulting sentence lacks parallelism. As for (D), the placement of the modifier ("needing no deliveries…") implies that it is oil that has these advantages rather than gas. Additionally, "anyways" is colloquial and not acceptable in standard written English. Finally, (E) makes an illogical statement by implying that gas, rather than the homeowner, wishes to avoid the problems associated with oil.

13. **(A) (p. 542)** *Writing/Improving Sentences/No Error*

The original sentence is correct as written. (B) is wrong because it needlessly switches to the passive voice and is awkwardly worded. Additionally, replacing "although" with "and" changes the logical relationship between those two clauses. (C) is incorrect for the reason just mentioned: "moreover" incorrectly expresses the relationship between the clauses. (D) is wrong because it switches needlessly to the passive voice and is awkward. Finally, (E) is incorrect because it changes the meaning of the original sentence and creates an illogical statement.

14. **(E) (p. 542)** *Writing/Improving Sentences/Logical Expression/Faulty Comparisons*

The original sentence is ambiguous. It sets up a comparison between cherry cola and people under the age of 20. (B) fails to eliminate this ambiguity. (C) eliminates the ambiguity but changes the intended meaning of the original sentence. In (D), the phrase "as well than" is not idiomatic. (E) eliminates the ambiguity in the original sentence.

PRACTICE TEST III

Sample Essay Responses and Analyses

Section 1—Writing (p. 545)

Above Average Essay Response

Study hall is beneficial to many students and should therefore not be eliminated from school. It provides the extra time needed to complete homework, review for a test, or even prepare ahead for future assignments. Since students are given the opportunity to take elective classes throughout the school day, study hall should be integrated into their schedule so that they may better manage their studies. Study hall especially helps students in the areas of time management, outside activities, and improved performance in subject areas.

Students under the strains of time management may require study hall to just keep up with their studies. Extracurricular activities, athletics, and after-school jobs can be very time-consuming and tend to distract students from their studies. In order to accommodate these activities, many students deprive themselves of sleep due to late hours of study at home. To a student who works after school to earn some extra spending money, or to help support his or her family, study hall may be the only chance to complete course work.

By allowing for some free time, study hall enables a student to broaden his or her skills and grow as a well-rounded person. Extracurricular activities and after-school jobs provide the necessary outlet for students to relax and socialize with their peers. Many students are even able to apply to their studies new skills learned in other environments.

Study hall is an elective that actually supports the required curriculum. Although many electives may be fun and interesting, students who take study hall can actually devote more time to math, science, and English. Study hall also provides a supportive educational environment that may not be available in every home due to the living arrangements.

In summary, study hall has many more benefits compared to those of having just another subject class. Students under oppressive time pressures can catch up with studies, expand their horizons with reading, and keep up in the face of outside activity demands with the help of study hall.

Writing skill and position on issue: This essay shows good facility with written English and clear organization. The writer offers a great introduction into the subject and presents a strong thesis. His or her position is clearly stated in the opening sentence, and it is supported throughout the essay.

Development of ideas and organization of essay: The overall development of ideas and structure is logical and consistent, going from general to specific; however, some of the generalizations could be improved with more supporting details. The third paragraph, in particular, would benefit from added examples that connect the ideas and make them more effective. The relationship between free time, study hall, and extracurricular activities should be made explicit. Further improvements could be made by presenting an opposing viewpoint and its refutation in order to contrast and in turn reinforce the writer's position.

Structure of essay, paragraphs, and transitions: All of the essential structural elements of an essay are present: an introduction, a body, and a conclusion. The initial paragraph expresses strong ideas and introduces the topic of each of the following paragraphs. The supporting paragraphs are appropriate, each paragraph deals with an argument or position of the writer, and each argument/paragraph is presented in an order that reflects the writer's organizational scheme.

Language usage, sentence structure, and punctuation: Overall, the language usage is appropriate for this type of essay. However, in the second and fifth paragraphs, the word "just" is low-level usage. "In summary" is low-level usage as a transitional phrase for the concluding paragraph.

Summary and conclusions: Overall, the essay is strong in structure and content. The essay would likely receive a reader's score of average to above average (5–6).

Below Average Essay Response

The study hall time I have each day is very important to me. Some schools have cut it out to add another subject to school. We only have so much time in the evening, and without study hall, students might never get their homework done. Study hall really helps students who need to work harder and students with part-time jobs , lots of chores, or athletics.

Students that have to put in a lot of extra work in subjects, really welcome study hall. They may have a poor environment for class work at home. Sometime help is available in study hall for problem subjects. Study hall has reference books not always available in the home. If you have study hall, you at least don't get more homework at that time. Some students just rest in study hall, and don't work on school. That is their choice if they want to waste time.

If you have a part-time job you really need study hall to do at least some homework. This also applies to athletes. They have hours of practice each evening and may be too tired afterwards to study well. Study hall provides a good break in the hard school day, and lets students keep up better in the classroom.

Writing skill and position on issue: This essay demonstrates developing skill. The writer's position is understood, but the essay lacks a clear thesis statement. The essay is simply not sophisticated enough to present the complexity of the issue; it is written with an abrupt and conversational tone that is not appropriate for this type of formal presentation.

Development of ideas and organization of essay: The essay is mostly written from a personal point of view and uses personal experiences to support its position. The ideas presented in the second paragraph are not structured in any particular order and do not follow any organizational scheme; they distract the reader with their choppiness. For example, the second paragraph randomly discusses different points of the argument without giving any consideration to further development or general cohesiveness of thought; the writer discusses both the help that is available during study sessions and the advantage of not being assigned any other homework in study hall. These two ideas do not flow together and should not be included in the same paragraph. The inclusion of the point that some students merely rest during study hall serves no purpose other than to weaken the argument. The essay could be improved by presenting the opposing viewpoint and its refutation in order to contrast and in turn reinforce the writer's position. Also, the last paragraph essentially serves as another body paragraph because it simply discusses several other benefits of study hall.

Structure of essay, paragraphs, and transitions: The structure is too simple. The body of the essay should consist of more than one paragraph. The paragraphs lack good topic sentences and transitions are not used. Since the last paragraph does not adequately provide a conclusion that summarizes the writer's major points, the essay is missing one of its three essential structural elements.

Language usage, sentence structure, and punctuation: The writer shifts between the subjective and objective points of view. This inconsistent voice detracts from the readability of the essay. Low-level language usage and some language errors are present in the essay. For example, "don't work on school" is ambiguous. The writer most likely intends to say that students do not do their schoolwork. "Lots of" is low-level usage.

Summary and conclusions: Major structural and organizational flaws and language usage errors signify a seriously limited essay. The essay would likely receive a reader's score of below average to average (3–4).

Answer Keys

Section 2—Critical Reading (p. 546)

1. A	5. D	9. E	13. C	17. C	21. C
2. B	6. C	10. B	14. A	18. B	22. C
3. C	7. B	11. E	15. E	19. A	23. A
4. B	8. A	12. D	16. B	20. E	24. B

Section 3—Math (p. 554)

1. C	4. B	7. D	10. 500	13. 784	16. 108
2. B	5. E	8. A	11. 25	14. 120	17. 10
3. C	6. D	9. 12	12. 30	15. 15.7	18. 0

Section 4—Writing (p. 558)

1. A	6. D	11. C	16. A	21. C	26. A	31. E
2. B	7. E	12. D	17. E	22. D	27. C	32. C
3. C	8. D	13. B	18. C	23. A	28. D	33. C
4. E	9. C	14. A	19. D	24. B	29. C	34. D
5. A	10. B	15. C	20. B	25. B	30. C	35. A

Section 5—Critical Reading (p. 564)

1. B	5. D	9. C	13. A	17. C	21. D
2. D	6. D	10. C	14. D	18. A	22. C
3. C	7. E	11. C	15. C	19. B	23. D
4. E	8. C	12. E	16. D	20. E	24. B

Section 7—Math (p. 570)

1. B	4. E	7. C	10. A	13. B	16. A	19. C
2. C	5. D	8. C	11. E	14. B	17. C	20. C
3. E	6. A	9. B	12. C	15. D	18. C	

Section 8—Critical Reading (p. 574)

1.	B	4.	E	7.	E	10.	B	13.	C	16.	B
2.	C	5.	B	8.	D	11.	D	14.	A	17.	A
3.	A	6.	B	9.	C	12.	A	15.	E	18.	A

19.	A

Section 9—Math (p. 580)

1.	E	4.	C	7.	E	10.	C	13.	A	16.	E
2.	B	5.	C	8.	E	11.	E	14.	B		
3.	D	6.	C	9.	C	12.	B	15.	C		

Section 10—Writing (p. 584)

1.	B	3.	E	5.	B	7.	E	9.	B	11.	D	13.	C
2.	E	4.	E	6.	D	8.	A	10.	A	12.	D	14.	C

Explanations

Section 2—Critical Reading

1. **(A) (p. 546)** *Critical Reading: Sentence Completions/Thought Extension/Key Words*

   The sentence gives you a very strong adverb clue with the word "unfairly." You can eliminate (B) since something that is unfair could not be objective. You can also eliminate (C) and (D) because they do not create meaningful sentences. (A), "biased," is the best word to convey the idea that the book blamed the South unfairly.

2. **(B) (p. 546)** *Critical Reading: Sentence Completions/Combined Reasoning/Coordinate Conjunctions* and *Explanatory Phrases*

   This sentence contains both an extension of thought and a reversal of thought as its logical keys. The first blank extends the thought that "the universe was well-ordered," as indicated by the coordinate conjunction "and." You can eliminate (A) since it is not logical that something would be well-ordered and baffling. (C), (D), and (E) are not words that you would use to describe the universe. This leaves (B). The contrast between "the Middle Ages" and "today" implies a "but" or "yet" in this sentence, so the second blank will be something opposite to "harmonious." The second element of (B) works because "chaotic" is the opposite of "harmonious."

3. **(C) (p. 546)** *Critical Reading: Sentence Completions/Thought Extension/Subordinate Conjunctions*

   The key logical clue in this sentence is the subordinate conjunction "because," which indicates an extension of thought. The blank extends the first half of the sentence by explaining why hot milk has been a cure for insomnia. If you know that "soporific" means "tending to cause sleep," this is a quick and easy item. If you don't know the word "soporific," but do know the other word choices, each of those can be easily eliminated since none of these extend the intended thought.

4. **(B) (p. 546)** *Critical Reading: Sentence Completions/Thought Extension/Subordinate Conjunctions*

   The subordinate conjunction "since" indicates an extension of thought that links the two blanks, which helps eliminate (A) and (D). Also, given that there is a body of research already existing, the results of the new experiment can only be irrelevant to it, consistent with it, or inconsistent with it. Therefore, eliminate (C). Then, substitute both words of the remaining choices in order to determine the correct answer. (A) cannot be correct since results would not be speculative if they were similar to the research already done. (D) is not possible because the body of research would not be "dispelled by" convincing results. (E) makes no sense because if the results were redundant, then they would not contradict the existing research. This leaves you with (B), which works very well. Results might be considered anomalous if they were inconsistent with the research already done.

5. **(D) (p. 546)** *Critical Reading: Sentence Completions/Thought Extension/Subordinate Conjunctions*

   The logical clue here is the subordinate conjunction "because," which indicates an extension of thought. However, the order in which the ideas are presented in the sentence makes this extension of thought difficult to see. The idea that follows "because" specifies the cause of the first idea: the ____ of traditional values causes modern life to ____ neurosis. Substitute each of the choices into this new sentence. Only (D) produces a sentence that fits the logical structure.

6. **(C) (p. 547)** *Critical Reading: Sentence Completions/Thought Extension/Explanatory Phrases*

   The overall structure of this sentence depends on an extension of thought. The first blank must complete a phrase that is set off by commas that explains why Peter does what he does. Also, the word in the first blank must describe an emotional reaction that is an appropriate response to the phrase clue "repeated rejections." On this ground, eliminate (A), (B), and (D), since it is not logical for anyone to be encouraged, elated, or inspired by rejection. (C) and (E) are both possible reactions to rejection, but (E) does not provide the overall logical continuity that is needed.

7. **(B) (p. 547)** *Critical Reading: Sentence Completions/Thought Reversal/Explanatory Phrases*

This sentence hinges on the second blank. The phrase "conflict between" indicates a contrast between how artists view their own talent and their knowledge that few will succeed. Eliminate (A), (C), and (E) since they fail to provide a contrast. It would not be surprising that an artist who neglected, was indifferent to, or disregarded his talent would not succeed. Eliminate (D), since the phrase "dissolution of their own talent" is not meaningful.

8. **(A) (p. 547)** *Critical Reading: Passages/Social Studies/Development*

Remember that an assumption is most often an unstated premise that underlies the structure of a passage. For example: "Betsy would be the best choice for Student Council President because she is the only candidate with public speaking experience." This line of reasoning assumes, though it does not say so explicitly, that public speaking experience is a good qualification for the office. In this test item, the author assumes, without saying so explicitly, that the first written references to balls would have coincided with the introduction of balls to the region. After all, if writers were likely to mention balls only 500 years after they first appeared, then there would be no reason for the author to date the events in the way they have been dated. The other choices are ideas that are related to the topic of the passage, but they do not function as underlying assumptions in the way that (A) does.

9. **(E) (p. 547)** *Critical Reading: Passages/Humanities/Main Idea*

The author starts by saying that some commentators see the novel as romantic, and then immediately says this is incorrect. The rest of the passage explains why the novel is actually realistic. (E) best describes this development. Now, it is worth looking at the incorrect answers as well. (A) is incorrect because it was Dickens, not the author of this passage, who hoped to expose conditions in the boarding houses. (B) is incorrect because the author does not necessarily believe that this distinction exhausts the possibilities. Rather, the author takes this distinction as a starting point because commentators have tended to regard Nicholas Nickleby as romantic rather than realistic. (C) is similar to (E) but it is too broad and severe in scope: the author wants to correct a misunderstanding, but the author is not trying to revise extensive literary criticism. Finally, while the author is advancing a theory of Nicholas Nickleby, that is not equivalent to proposing a new literary theory of the novel in general.

10. **(B) (p. 548)** *Critical Reading: Passages/Natural Sciences/Development*

The author relies mainly on examples (Nottingham, bronchitis, art, Sherlock Holmes, buildings) to show that air pollution is not a recent phenomenon. As for (A), the author mentions the figure "30 percent," but that does not make the whole passage a discussion of statistics. Similarly, the author mentions the Queen and an art critic, who presumably saw things first hand, but the passage also refers to other evidence as well—so, eliminate (C). (D) is incorrect because there is only one mention of historical records, and (E) is incorrect because the only expert mentioned is the art critic.

11. **(E) (p. 548)** *Critical Reading: Passages/Social Studies/Main Idea*

The author says that public spaces are disappearing and that shopping malls are all that remain. Shopping malls, however, are privately owned properties where freedom of speech is subject to the restrictions of the property owners. So, the shopping mall is not actually a public space. Therefore, (E) is the correct answer choice. (A) is wrong because the author does not mention the idea of convenience. (B) is wrong because the author does not refer to speeches and leafleting as "commercial" activities. (C) is perhaps the second-best answer choice, because this passage might be used in an argument about the importance of public spaces and free speech; however, the passage does not address the issue of democracy or even attempt to characterize freedom of speech as a condition of its viability. Finally, (D) is wrong because it is too narrow:

the author merely mentions how shopping malls are gradually replacing public spaces in order to support the main argument that these malls themselves are not true public spaces.

12. **(D) (p. 549)** *Critical Reading: Passages/Humanities/Implied Idea*

According to the passage, some people who looked at the cleaned frescoes thought that the bright colors were not suitable for serious art. So, we can infer that these people think that high art should be dark and serious to reflect the purpose of art. (That may be a silly expectation, but it is a fair inference about those viewers.) As for (A), it is not the subject matter but appearance of the frescoes that caused controversy. As for (B), though some people apparently objected to the appearance of the cleaned frescoes, nothing in the passage suggests that they thought the dirt should be replaced. As for (C), the author does not discuss when or how often art in general should be cleaned. And as for (E), the author doesn't say that it was a mistake to clean the frescoes nor that the job was done badly—even though some people found the result a little surprising.

13. **(C) (p. 549)** *Critical Reading: Passages/Social Studies/Development*

The writer uses what is called, in technical logical terminology, a *reductio ad absurdum*, or *reductio*. A *reductio* is an argument that shows that the premises or assumptions of a position lead to an absurd result. In this case, the writer shows that protectionism leads to the absurd result of having nothing but gold and silver—no food, no clothes, no heat—only precious metal. (A) describes an attempt to discredit an opponent: we should reject protectionism because the people who support it stand to make a lot of money themselves. In other words, the protectionists have a hidden motive. But that is not what the writer does here. As for (B), the author doesn't say what most economists think. As for (D), while some of us may believe this contention, this particular passage does not address this issue. We may feel the same way about statistics, but this particular author doesn't make that argument.

14. **(A) (p. 550)** *Critical Reading: Passages/Social Studies/Implied Idea*

The textbook writer must have looked at the total wool production reported for the area and the total number of sheep. On dividing "production" by "sheep," the writer determined that production was a record-setting 150 pounds per sheep. The problem with the statistic is that the total wool reported as produced in the islands included a large quantity of smuggled wool that was relabeled "domestic" wool. The textbook writer uncritically accepted the information as reported and announced that these were record-setting sheep. (B) is incorrect because the number of sheep is not the figure that caused the odd result. It was probably accurate. What caused the figure to be so high was the inflated production figure, a figure that included smuggled as well as domestically produced wool. (C) is incorrect because the effect on other markets did not affect the calculation of the bogus number. (D) takes the assumption too far: the implication of the passage is that the writer simply was not aware of the possibility that the production figure included smuggled wool. (E) is incorrect because the writer did accept the figure and was for that very reason considered naïve.

15. **(E) (p. 551)** *Critical Reading: Passages/Social Studies/Main Idea*

(A) is not correct because although the author discusses the difficulty of translation, he does not criticize translators. In fact, he seems sympathetic to their problems since he is a translator himself. (B) is not correct since he mentions the fact that all languages have their particular difficulties and uses the poetry of Milton—an English poet—as an example of a text that is difficult to translate. (C) is wrong because although the author says it is difficult to do justice to a work in another language, he refers to some translations that are successful—those that please the "hard-liners," for instance. He also mentions Chateaubriand's translation of *Paradise Lost* as a successful translation. (D) is incorrect because although the author mentions some of the difficulties of translating Japanese into English, the point of the passage is not that Japanese is particularly difficult, but that it is difficult in some particular ways.

16. (B) (p. 551) *Critical Reading: Passages/Social Studies/Implied Idea*

The author mentions the fact that he has translated some work by Dazai Osamu. He then mentions another book, *Accomplices of Silence*, which discusses certain aspects of Osamu's work. We may infer, then, that the book mentioned is a critical commentary on the work of Osamu. It is certainly not an English translation of Japanese poetry since it is clear that this book talks *about* the literature. It is not a prior publication by the author of the passage because he or she names another author—Masao Miyoshi; thus, (C) is incorrect. (D) is wrong because the author gives examples of the things mentioned in Miyoshi's book, and they have nothing to do with orthography. Finally, (E) is wrong because it is clear that Miyoshi's comments as quoted by the author are about Osamu's effects in Japanese, not in English; therefore, the author is not talking about the problems of translation.

17. (C) (p. 551) *Critical Reading: Passages/Social Studies/Vocabulary*

In the third paragraph, the author discusses the effect of spelling on Japanese literature, and that is what "orthography" means.

18. (B) (p. 551) *Critical Reading: Passages/Social Studies/Implied Idea*

In the second paragraph, the author develops the point that Japanese has some special features that make translation into English difficult. The author offers a couple of examples, concluding that "the moments do not work in English." This means that it is impossible to translate them exactly. (A) is incorrect because it overstates the case. Some aspects of the text cannot be fully rendered, but the author doesn't say that the Japanese experience is completely unavailable to people who do not speak Japanese. As for (C), the author simply says that languages are different, not that one is necessarily superior to the other. As for (D), there is no indication that these are stock characters. And (E) represents a confused reading of the preceding paragraph.

19. (A) (p. 551) *Critical Reading: Passages/Social Studies/Development*

The author uses an example taken from *Kinosaki nite* to illustrate the onomatopoeic effect of writing a word in one system of orthography rather than another. (B) is incorrect because although the author mentions that a Japanese writer laments the poverty of indigenous Japanese vocabulary, this fact is not the point of his example. In fact, the example actually demonstrates a certain richness of the Japanese language. (C) is incorrect because the example has nothing to do with translation. It is an example of an effect that is rendered in Japanese. (D) is not correct since the reader actually learns nothing at all about this work of literature except that this literary device appears in it. Finally, (E) is wrong because, again, the example has nothing to do with translation.

20. (E) (p. 551) *Critical Reading: Passages/Social Studies/Application*

(A) is incorrect because although the author says that the Japanese people have special feelings about the possibilities of their language, he does not say that he shares these feelings. (B) is wrong because although the author discusses the difficulties of translating Japanese, he says that the difficulty stems from the peculiarities of the Japanese language, not from the limitations of the English language. There is no reason to assume that the author thinks it would be easier to translate Japanese into any other language. (C) is wrong because it overstates the case: the author might say that it is difficult, but not necessarily impossible, for someone not fluent in Japanese to understand Japanese literature. (D) is wrong because the author specifically brackets the question of the truth of this hypothesis. (E) is correct because the author states that although Japanese has "special language relationships," he means that like any other language, it has unique features. Thus, the author seems to feel that all languages have special qualities and they all present special challenges to a translator.

21. **(C) (p. 552)** *Critical Reading: Passages/Social Studies/Implied Idea*

Since the author cites this word as an example of onomatopoeia (a poetic device in which the word that is used to describe an action *sounds* like the action itself), the answer can only be (C): buzz. In English, the word "buzz" sounds like the flight of a bee.

22. **(C) (p. 552)** *Critical Reading: Passages/Social Studies/Development*

The author uses many examples to illustrate points: onomatopoeia in *Kinosaki nite*, for instance. The author also cites the particular effects that are difficult to translate in the work of Osamu. The author cites several authorities: Miyoshi on the subject of Osamu, and George Steiner on the subject of translation. As for (D), the author discusses personal experience in translating the work of Osamu. Finally, as for (E), the author also contrasts the entry barriers for business.

23. **(A) (p. 552)** *Critical Reading: Passages/Social Studies/Implied Idea*

(B) cannot be correct since the "handicap" is the result of translating the poetry, not the result of the Japanese writer's intention. (C) is incorrect because although there may be no word-for-word equivalents, that is a general problem of translation, not simply a problem of translating Japanese into English. (D) is incorrect because the handicap is not related to the expectations of the reader. (E) is obviously incorrect since the problem is related to translation and has nothing to do with the problems of a Japanese reader reading in Japanese. The example quoted by the author is obviously a translator's attempt to make the English sound "oriental," or what a Western audience thinks "oriental" sounds like. So, (A) is the correct response.

24. **(B) (p. 552)** *Critical Reading: Passages/Social Studies/Voice*

The author cites Steiner in the final paragraph as "lamenting" or regretting the "instant exotica," and then the author adds: "with which we are perhaps all too familiar." So, the author agrees that the "instant exotica" is a silly way of translating Japanese. Since the author's attitude is negative, (B) is the right response, and the other choices have to be incorrect.

Section 3—Math

1. **(C) (p. 554)** *Math: Multiple-Choice/Algebra/Solving Algebraic Equations or Inequalities with One Variable/Simple Equations*

Solve for x: $5,454 = 54(x+1) \Rightarrow \dfrac{5,454}{54} = x+1 \Rightarrow 101 = x+1 \Rightarrow x = 100$.

2. **(B) (p. 554)** *Math: Multiple-Choice/Algebra/Manipulating Algebraic Expressions/Manipulating Expressions Involving Exponents*

This item tests your understanding of exponents. Use the basic operations of exponents to solve for x and y, and then compute their difference. When multiplying two similar expressions having the same base, k, with differing exponents, the base remains the same and the exponents are added together. So, $x+9 = 21 \Rightarrow x = 12$. Then, raising an exponent to a power is the same as multiplying both exponents. So, $3y = 18 \Rightarrow y = 6$. And $x - y = 12 - 6 = 6$.

3. **(C) (p. 554)** *Math: Multiple-Choice/Arithmetic/Common Arithmetic Items/Proportions and Direct-Inverse Variation*

You can reason verbally to a solution here: the two machines can seal and stuff a total of 500 envelopes per minute: $150 + 350 = 500$. So, it will take a minute and a half to do 750: $500 + 250 = 750$; 250 is half of 500.

Alternatively, you can set up a proportion: $\dfrac{500 \text{ envelopes}}{1 \text{ minute}} = \dfrac{750 \text{ envelopes}}{x \text{ minutes}} \Rightarrow x = \dfrac{750}{500} = 1.5$ minutes.

4. (B) (p. 555) *Math: Multiple-Choice/Algebra/Manipulating Algebraic Expressions/Evaluating Expressions*

You can reason through this problem: because y is squared, doubling y results in a fourfold increase, while doubling z halves the original value. So, the net result is a doubling of x. It is easier, however, to pick a couple of values and see what happens. Let $y = 2$ and $z = 3$. The value of x is originally 4: $x = \dfrac{3(2)^2}{3} = 4$. And

when y is doubled to 4, and z is doubled to 6, x becomes 8: $x = \dfrac{3(4)^2}{6} = 8$. And, 8 is twice as large as 4.

Alternatively, there is another way to approach this problem: $x_0 = \dfrac{3y^2}{z}$ and

$$x_1 = \dfrac{3(2y)^2}{2z} = \dfrac{12y^2}{2z} = \dfrac{6y^2}{z} = 2 \cdot \dfrac{3y^2}{z}.$$

5. (E) (p. 555) *Math: Multiple-Choice/Geometry/Complex Figures* and *Lines and Angles* and *Circles*

First, find the area of the circle: $\pi r^2 = \pi(2)^2 = 4\pi$. Since the shaded area is equal to 3π, it accounts for $\dfrac{3\pi}{4\pi} = \dfrac{3}{4}$ of the circle. Thus, the unshaded area accounts for $\dfrac{1}{4}$ of the circle. This means that angle x plus the angle vertically opposite x are equal to $\dfrac{1}{4}$ of $360° = 90°$. Thus, $2x = 90$, and $x = 45$.

Alternatively, since the figure is drawn to scale, and $x°$ is clearly an acute angle, (E) must be the correct answer since it is the only one that is less than 90°.

6. (D) (p. 555) *Math: Multiple-Choice/Arithmetic/Common Arithmetic Items/Percents*

Use the "is-over-of" strategy: $\dfrac{\text{is}}{\text{of}} = \dfrac{\%}{100} \Rightarrow \dfrac{\text{tin}}{\text{entire bar}} = \dfrac{x}{100} \Rightarrow x = 100 \cdot \dfrac{100}{100 + 150} = 100 \cdot \dfrac{100}{250} = \dfrac{200}{5} = 40\%$.

7. (D) (p. 555) *Math: Multiple-Choice/Arithmetic/Complicated Manipulations/The "Flying-X" Method*

Rewrite the equation: $\dfrac{1}{x} + \dfrac{1}{y} = \dfrac{1}{z}$. Add the fractions using the "flying-x" method: $\dfrac{x+y}{xy} = \dfrac{1}{z}$. Multiply both sides by z: $z \cdot \dfrac{x+y}{xy} = 1$. Multiply both sides by $\dfrac{xy}{x+y}$: $z = \dfrac{xy}{x+y}$.

Alternatively, assume some values. If $x = 1$ and $y = 1$, $z = \dfrac{1}{2}$. Then, substitute 1 for x and 1 for y into the choices. Only (D) generates the value $\dfrac{1}{2}$.

8. **(A) (p. 555)** *Math: Multiple-Choice/Arithmetic/Common Arithmetic Items/Percents*

Set up a table to show the possibilities and fill in the numbers that are given:

	Imported	Not Imported	Total
≥ $100			20%
< $100			
Total	60%		

Since the total must equal 100%:

	Imported	Not Imported	Total
≥ $100			20%
< $100			80%
Total	60%	40%	100%

Next, 40 percent of the articles priced at $100 or more are imported, and 40% of 20% is 8%:

	Imported	Not Imported	Total
≥ $100	8%		20%
< $100			80%
Total	60%	40%	100%

Now, fill in the table:

	Imported	Not Imported	Total
≥ $100	8%	12%	20%
< $100	52%	28%	80%
Total	60%	40%	100%

Alternatively, you can reach the same conclusion by assuming some numbers.

9. **(12) (p. 556)** *Math: Student-Produced Responses/Algebra/Expressing and Evaluating Algebraic Functions/Evaluating Expressions*

Solve for x: $3x + 2 = 8 \Rightarrow 3x = 6 \Rightarrow x = 2$. So, $6(2) = 12$.

10. **(500) (p. 556)** *Math: Student-Produced Responses/Arithmetic/Complicated Arithmetic Application Items*

The profit on each box of candy is $2 - 1 = $1. To earn a total profit of $500, it will be necessary to sell $500 \div $1 = 500$ boxes.

11. (25) (p. 556) *Math: Student-Produced Responses/Arithmetic/Common Arithmetic Items/Percents*

This is a simple percent question. Use the "is-over-of" strategy: $\dfrac{\text{seniors}}{\text{total}} = \dfrac{90}{360} = \dfrac{1}{4} = 25\%$.

12. (30) (p. 556) *Math: Student-Produced Responses/Geometry/Lines and Angles*

The angles labeled $3w°$ and $(5w+20)°$ form a straight line: $3w+(5w+20)=180$. Solve for w: $8w+20=180 \Rightarrow 8w=160 \Rightarrow w=20$. Then, find the measure of the angle that is labeled $(5w+20)°$: $5(20)+20=120$. Since this angle is opposite the angle that is labeled $4x°$, $4x$ must also equal 120. Therefore, $4x=120 \Rightarrow x=30$.

Alternatively, once you have solved for w, solve for x since the angles labeled $3w°$ and $4x°$ also form a straight line: $3w+4x=180 \Rightarrow 3(20)+4x=180$ and $60+4x=180 \Rightarrow 4x=120 \Rightarrow x=30$.

Finally, since the figure is not accompanied by a note stating that it is NOT drawn to scale, you can assume that it is and use "guesstimating" as a strategy of last resort. The angle labeled $4x°$ appears to be 120°, so x must be about 30.

13. (784) (p. 557) *Math: Student-Produced Responses/Geometry/Rectangles and Squares*

If the floor were a perfect rectangle, it would have a width of $4 \cdot 5 = 20$ meters, a length of $8 \cdot 5 = 40$ meters, and a total area of $20 \cdot 40 = 800$ square meters. But the floor is not a perfect rectangle. Its actual area is smaller. Subtract the area of the missing corner. It has dimensions of $0.8 \cdot 5 = 4$. So, its area is 16. The actual area is $800 - 16 = 784$.

14. (120) (p. 557) *Math: Student-Produced Responses/Arithmetic/Complicated Arithmetic Application Items*

If the club spent $\dfrac{2}{5}$ of the budget on the first project, it was left with $\dfrac{3}{5}$ of $\$300 = \$180$. If it spent $\dfrac{1}{3}$ of $\$180$, it was left with $\$180 - \$60 = \$120$.

15. (15.7) (p. 557) *Math: Student-Produced Responses/Data Analysis/Probability and Statistics/Averages*

It is easy enough to figure that for six numbers to average 16, they must add up to $6 \cdot 16 = 96$. The numbers given add up to $10+12+15.1+15.2+28=80.3 \Rightarrow 96-80.3=15.7$, which must be the missing x.

16. (108) (p. 557) *Math: Student-Produced Responses/Arithmetic/Common Arithmetic Items/Percents*

This problem has multiple steps, but the arithmetic is simple. The only amount you have to work with is 12 geese, so start there: $12 \text{ geese} = 20\% \text{ of birds} \Rightarrow 12 = \dfrac{20}{100}x \Rightarrow 12 = \dfrac{1}{5}x \Rightarrow x = 12 \cdot 5 = 60$. Now, you know that there are 60 birds in all. If 25 percent of the animals are birds,

$60 \text{ birds} = 25\% \text{ of the animals} \Rightarrow 60 = \dfrac{25}{100}y \Rightarrow 60 = \dfrac{1}{4}y \Rightarrow y = 60 \cdot 4 = 240$. This is still not the answer—

remember that you want a number representing mammals. You must find what part of this 240-animal total is mammals: % of mammals $= 100\% - (25\% + 30\%) = 45\% \Rightarrow 45\%$ of $240 = 108$ mammals.

17. (10) (p. 557) *Math: Student-Produced Responses/Arithmetic/Common Arithmetic Items/Percents*

First convert Jerry's final height to inches: $5 \cdot 12 = 60 \Rightarrow 60 + 10 = 70$. Jerry's 7-inch growth is 10 percent of 70 inches.

18. **(0) (p. 557)** *Math: Student-Produced Responses/Geometry/Complex Figures* and *Circles* and *Rectangles and Squares*

If you can't picture it in your head, draw it on paper:

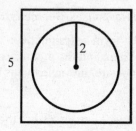

A circle with a radius of 2 has a diameter of 4, so when it is superimposed on a square with sides of 5, it never intersects that square, assuming that the centers are the same.

Section 4—Writing

1. **(A) (p. 558)** *Writing/Improving Sentences/No Error*

The underlined portion is correct. It is best, however, to check the other answer choices to be sure that none of them improve the original sentence. (B) is incorrect because the sentence requires the simple past tense, not the present perfect tense. (C) is incorrect because it results in a sentence fragment without a conjugated verb. (D) is wrong because it is not logical to use the present tense to refer to what is obviously a past event. (E) is not idiomatic English and changes the intended meaning of the original sentence.

2. **(B) (p. 558)** *Writing/Improving Sentences/Logical Expression/Illogical Tense Sequence*

The original suffers from a shifting verb tense. The underlined portion ("will pose") is in the future tense; however, the other verbs in the sentence ("determined" and "postponed") indicate that the events took place in the past. Since muddy conditions existed, and the director postponed the game because of the potential for injury, the subjunctive "would" is required to indicate that these injuries may or may not actually happen. Therefore, (B) is the correct answer choice. (C) is wrong because it eliminates the main verb of the sentence. (D) is wrong because it uses a past participle instead of the subjunctive. Finally, (E) is wrong because it uses a present participle instead of the subjunctive.

3. **(C) (p. 558)** *Writing/Improving Sentences/Clarity of Expression/Diction and Idioms*

The original has a word usage problem. In the underlined portion, "if" is not idiomatic. In this context, "whether" would be the appropriate word choice. Therefore, (C) is the correct answer choice because it simply replaces "if" with "whether." (B) is wrong because it does not address the problem of the original. Also, "instruction as college program" is grammatically incorrect. (D) is wrong because it distorts the intended meaning of the original by implying that there are doubts in terms of the program's merits, rather than doubts in terms of student interest in the program. Finally, (E) is an interesting choice; it simply eliminates "if" altogether, and the resulting sentence makes clear that the doubt is about the viability of the program. However, like (B), (E) is wrong because "instruction as college program" is grammatically incorrect.

4. **(E) (p. 559)** *Writing/Improving Sentences/Logical Expression/Misplaced Modifiers*

The original suffers from the infamous "dangling modifier." As written, the phrase "in a panicked tone" modifies the first important noun that follows it ("the duty nurse"). However, the sentence intends to say that the mother (not the duty nurse) was speaking in a panicked tone. Therefore, "in a panicked tone" should be repositioned so that it is closer to the phrase that it is intended to modify ("the mother"). (E) makes the needed correction. (B) is wrong because it incorrectly implies that the child was speaking in a panicked tone. (C) is wrong because it incorrectly implies that there was some sort of cause and effect relationship between the mother's plea and her tone; however, the mother does not ask for help *because* her tone is panicked. Finally, (D) is wrong for the same reason as the original; the modifying phrase ("in a panicked tone") still seems to apply to "the duty nurse."

5. **(A) (p. 559)** *Writing/Improving Sentences/No Error*

The original is correct. The use of "both" before "diverting" is important because it makes clear that there were two separate and distinct charges against the CEO. (B) is wrong because it eliminates "both," thereby creating an ambiguous sentence; (B) incorrectly implies that the CEO diverted company funds and diverted sexual harassment. (C) is wrong because it unnecessarily changes the main verb to the past progressive tense ("was being accused"). (D) is wrong because it too creates an ambiguous sentence; its placement of "both" incorrectly implies that the CEO diverted both funds and sexual harassment. Finally, (E) is wrong for two reasons. First, it incorrectly implies that the CEO diverted company funds and sexual harassment. Second, it uses the passive voice in a weak manner, making the sentence awkward and confusing.

6. **(D) (p. 559)** *Writing/Identifying Sentence Errors/Grammar*

The problem with the original sentence is that "river" is supposed to refer to both the Blue Nile and the White Nile, so you need the plural: "of the Blue Nile and White Nile rivers." As for (A), "capital" is the correct word (compared with "capitol"). As for (B), "is" correctly agrees with its subject, Khartoum. As for (C), the preposition "at" is the correct one to use here.

7. **(E) (p. 559)** *Writing/Identifying Sentence Errors/No Error*

The original sentence is correct as written. As for (A), the compound subject "hieroglyphics and the alphabet" is plural and needs the plural verb "are." As for (B), "that" correctly connects the first two clauses. As for (C), "though" is correctly used to introduce a subordinate clause. And as for (D), "only developing" completes the second verb of the subordinate clause.

8. **(D) (p. 559)** *Writing/Identifying Sentence Errors/Sentence Structure/Incomplete Split Constructions*

The original sentence includes an incomplete split construction: graduates or teachers at the University of Chicago. The problem is that some words have been omitted: graduates...at the University of Chicago. What the sentence should say is: graduates of or teachers at the University of Chicago. As for (A), "most influential" correctly describes the economists who are very influential. As for (B), "economists" says exactly what the sentence intends. And as for (C), "are" correctly agrees with "economists."

9. **(C) (p. 560)** *Writing/Identifying Sentence Errors/Logical Expression/Illogical Tense Sequence*

The use of the present tense "establishes" is inconsistent with the other verb in the sentence, "drew." Since "drew" is the past tense, (C) should be "established." As for (A), "during" is a preposition that introduces a phrase to modify the verb sequence in the main clause: when did Penn do all of this? As for (B), "only" correctly shows that this was the one trip made. And as for (D), "with" has an appropriate meaning in this context.

10. **(B) (p. 560)** *Writing/Identifying Sentence Errors/Grammar/Subject-Verb Agreement*

The subject of the sentence is the singular "dynamite," so the verb should be the singular "was" rather than the plural "were." As for (A), "made from" is an appropriate idiom, and "made" introduces the phrase that modifies "explosive." As for (C), "who" is the correct choice when referring to people, in this case the chemist named Nobel. And as for (D), "endowed" is correctly in the past tense.

11. (C) (p. 560) *Writing/Identifying Sentence Errors/Grammar/Pronoun Usage*

The problem in the original sentence is its shifting point of view. The sentence switches from the second person to the third person. This could be corrected by changing "one" to "you." As for (A), "when" is a subordinate conjunction that introduces an adverbial clause to tell the reader "when" the reader will be able to hear these elements: when you are listening to Khachaturian. As for (B), "heritage" is used idiomatically. And as for (D), "can hear" is an appropriate verb form.

12. (D) (p. 560) *Writing/Identifying Sentence Errors/Sentence Structure/Faulty Parallelism*

The original sentence exhibits faulty parallelism. The elements in the series should have similar forms: can use, refine, and produce. As for (A), "improvement" functions as an appositive and refers to "open-hearth process." As for (B), "producing" is the right verb form. And as for (C), the adjective "high" correctly modifies "content."

13. (B) (p. 560) *Writing/Identifying Sentence Errors/Sentence Structure/Verb Tense*

The problem in the original sentence is "feeds." "Feeds" is a conjugated verb, that is, it shows person and tense: the salamander feeds every night. But in this sentence, the verb "feed" is not intended to be the main or conjugated verb. Rather, the main verb is "is found." "Usually...insects" is a long adjective that modifies salamander, so "feeds" should be changed to "feeding," a participle. As for (A), "usually" is an adverb that correctly modifies the adjective "nocturnal." As for (C), "is found" is the right number to agree with the singular "salamander." And finally, as for (D), "damp" has a meaning that is appropriate here.

14. (A) (p. 560) *Writing/Identifying Sentence Errors/Clarity of Expression/Diction and Idioms*

The problem with the original sentence is that "law" should be "laws." Your "ear" should tell you that, but you can also reason that "first" implies others to follow, so "law" needs to be plural. As for (B), "that" correctly introduces a dependent clause to act as the object of "states." As for (C), "each" is properly used here to indicate "every one of them." And (D) is correct, since "is" agrees with "orbit."

15. (C) (p. 560) *Writing/Identifying Sentence Errors/Grammar/Pronoun Usage*

The problem with the original sentence is that the plural pronoun "their" does not agree with the singular "each." "Their" should be replaced with "its." As for (A), the preposition "for" introduces an adjective phrase that modifies "New York City." As for (B), "offers" correctly agrees with the singular subject. As for (D), "own" is needed to attribute the flavors to each different cuisine.

16. (A) (p. 560) *Writing/Identifying Sentence Errors/Logical Expression/Misplaced Modifiers*

The original sentence includes a misplaced modifier. "While rowing" seems to modify "direction and speed," but "direction and speed" do not row. The sentence could be completely rewritten to position "rowers" closer to "while rowing," or "while rowing" could be made into a prepositional phrase such as "in rowing." As for (B), "are" correctly agrees with the compound subject "direction and speed." As for (C), "who" correctly refers to the person who is the coxswain. And as for (D), "strokes" correctly refers to the use of the oars by the rowers.

17. (E) (p. 560) *Writing/Identifying Sentence Errors/No Error*

The original sentence is correct as written. "One" is an appositive that modifies "rayon." "Fibers" is correctly plural. "Made from" is idiomatic. And as for (D), "chiefly" is an adverb that properly modifies "derived."

18. (C) (p. 561) *Writing/Identifying Sentence Errors/Logical Expression/Illogical Tense Sequence*

The original sentence contains an incorrect verb tense. The main verb of the sentence ("was") is in the past tense, so everything else has to be built around that time frame. "Writes" should be "wrote." As for (A), "popular" appropriately modifies speaker. As for (B), "who" correctly refers to "speaker," a person. As for (D), "music" can be an adjective as well as a noun, and this usage is appropriate here.

19. **(D) (p. 561)** *Writing/Identifying Sentence Errors/Clarity of Expression/Low-Level Usage*

The original sentence contains an instance of low-level usage. (D) must use either the infinitive (started to write) or the gerund (started writing) but not a combination of the two. As for (A), the past tense "traveled" correctly puts the action in the past and makes it consistent with the other verbs in the sentence. As for (B), "where" introduces a subordinate clause that modifies France. As for (C), "some of" is an idiom that is used correctly here.

20. **(B) (p. 561)** *Writing/Identifying Sentence Errors/Clarity of Expression/Diction and Idioms*

The original sentence contains a non-idiomatic usage of a preposition. The idiomatic phrasing for this context is "aim at" not "aim to." ("Aim to" is sometimes used to mean "intend to.") As for (A), the phrasing is idiomatic. As for (C), "which" is a relative pronoun that introduces and functions as the subject of the relative clause. And as for (D), "itself" correctly refers to "weapon." ("Itself" here is used to stress that it is the weapon that receives the reflected signal.)

21. **(C) (p. 561)** *Writing/Identifying Sentence Errors/Grammar/Pronoun Usage*

The problem with the original sentence is that the pronouns do not agree. The plural pronoun "their" is intended to refer to "system," which is singular; therefore, the singular pronoun "its" is needed. As for (A), "was" is correctly in the past tense and agrees with the singular "chivalry." As for (B), "grew out of" is an idiomatic phrase that has an appropriate meaning in this context. And as for (D), the plural "centuries" is correct since there are two centuries mentioned.

22. **(D) (p. 561)** *Writing/Identifying Sentence Errors/Clarity of Expression/Diction and Idioms*

The problem with the original sentence is one of diction (word choice). The correct word is "conquered." As for (A), "that" is a relative pronoun that refers to "area" and that introduces the clause about Portugal. As for (B), "added to" is the correct idiom. And as for (C), "around," meaning "at approximately" in this case, has the right meaning for this context.

23. **(A) (p. 561)** *Writing/Identifying Sentence Errors/Sentence Structure/Faulty Parallelism*

The three elements in the series should have parallel forms: valedictorian, gold medalist, and internationally renowned singer. The sentence could be corrected by deleting "he was." As for (B), you need the adverb "internationally" to modify the adjective "renowned." As for (C), "was" correctly agrees with "Paul Robeson." And as for (D), "many" is used idiomatically.

24. **(B) (p. 561)** *Writing/Identifying Sentence Errors/Grammar/Subject-Verb Agreement*

The original sentence contains a subject-verb error. The singular "is covered" needs to be plural in order to agree with the plural subject, "cavities." As for (A), "which" is a relative pronoun that refers to "nose." As for (C) and (D), the use of both prepositions is idiomatic.

25. **(B) (p. 561)** *Writing/Identifying Sentence Errors/Sentence Structure/Faulty Parallelism*

The problem with the original sentence is that the three elements in the series should be in similar form: sight, hearing, smell. (A) correctly conveys the notion of time or sequence. As for (C), "seriously" is an adverb that is correctly used to modify "is degraded." Finally, as for (D), "more" is the proper adverb because the two abilities are being compared: normal and more acute.

26. **(A) (p. 562)** *Writing/Improving Paragraphs/Passage Development*

Sentence 2 asks "why?" And the rest of the passage answers that question: the writer likes the idea of struggling artists living in picturesque circumstances. (B) is wrong because the writer intends to answer the question. As for (C), while the writer certainly seems confident, expressing that confidence is not the logical function of sentence 2. (D) is an interesting point, but has no place in this essay. Finally, as for (E), although this is a question, it is not intended to raise doubts. Instead, the author intends to provide an answer.

27. (C) (p. 562) *Writing/Improving Paragraphs/Paragraph Structure*

Inserting the information as a parenthetical expression helps to preserve the flow of the first paragraph. In addition, the information must accurately and effectively refer to "Left Bank." So, (C) is the best choice. The other choices suggest complete sentences, and inserting a whole sentence into the paragraph is likely to be distracting to the reader and give too much importance to a fairly minor detail.

28. (D) (p. 562) *Writing/Improving Paragraphs/Sentence Elements*

The problem with the original sentence is that "they" does not have a referent. Only (D) addresses this issue. But there is another reason to prefer (D). Sentence 6 is not very well integrated into the rest of the paragraph. The reader will likely have trouble understanding the significance of the tragic romance. So, a good revision would make the connection clear, and (D) does.

29. (C) (p. 562) *Writing/Improving Paragraphs/Sentence Elements*

The problem with the original sentence is that the future tense "will make" is inconsistent with the past tense verbs throughout the rest of the paragraph. (C) solves this problem. As for (A), eliminating "but" results in a comma splice—two sentences jammed together, separated by only a comma without a conjunction. As for (B), there is no reason for this change ("they" has a clear antecedent), and the change does not solve the problem just outlined. As for (D), starting a new sentence will not solve the original problem, and creating a new sentence will disrupt the flow of the paragraph. Finally, as for (E), "and" doesn't send the same signal to the reader that "but" does.

30. (C) (p. 562) *Writing/Improving Paragraphs/Sentence Elements*

One problem with the original sentence is that "being that" is low-level usage. Those words should be deleted. Additionally, sentence 16 could be tightened up a bit by making the final phrase an appositive: Murger, the struggling writer. (C) makes both of these revisions. As for (A), "In point of fact" would normally be used to add emphasis to the sentence, but it doesn't appear that any additional emphasis is appropriate here. As for (B), eliminating "story" leaves only "this," a word that is ambiguous in its reference. As for (D), a semicolon signals to the reader that a clause is to follow, but no clause comes. And as for (E), though it is not be wrong to speak of Murger in the past tense, this change does not address the two problems that are mentioned above.

31. (E) (p. 563) *Writing/Improving Paragraphs/Passage Development*

The focus of the essay is on giving the reader some general rules of flag etiquette and then encouraging the reader to look for more information on the topic. Sentence 18 best summarizes this development. Sentence 1, though it is the opening sentence, is not the main point. The reference to the convention is a kind of jumping-off point to get the essay started, but the idea that is stated in sentence 1 is a relatively minor detail. As for (B) and (C), these are relatively minor details. (D) marks the lead-up to the writer's conclusion, but sentence 16 itself does not restate the main point.

32. (C) (p. 563) *Writing/Improving Paragraphs/Paragraph Structure*

The first paragraph actually should be two paragraphs, separated between sentences 4 and 5. The first four sentences provide background for the reader. Starting with sentence 5, the writer gives the reader specific rules for displaying the flag. (A) and (B) are wrong because this would break apart the information about the Flag Code. Finally, (D) and (E) are wrong because this would break apart the information about the general rules for displaying the flag.

33. (C) (p. 563) *Writing/Improving Paragraphs/Sentence Elements*

The difficulty with the original sentence is the inconsistent use of the plural and singular versions of "flag." The rest of the paragraph talks about "the flag," using that term to refer to all U.S. flags in general. So, this sentence needs to be rewritten to conform to the singular. Therefore, (B) is definitely wrong. As for (A), deleting "unless" runs two thoughts together and ignores the fact that the second is subordinate to the first. As for (D), while it would not be incorrect to remove "when" from the sentence, there is no good reason for doing so, and (D) fails to address the real problem with sentence 8. Finally, as for (E), replacing the comma with a semicolon will signal to the reader that another independent clause is coming after the semicolon— but the second idea, as noted, is a subordinate or dependent thought.

34. (D) (p. 563) *Writing/Improving Paragraphs/Sentence Elements*

The original sentence is in need of revision because the "when raising the flag" doesn't have anything to modify. The phrase can't modify "it," because "it" refers to "flag" and causes the sentence to illogically say: when raising the flag, the flag should be hoisted briskly. (D) solves this problem by making it clear that "you" or the "reader" is the one raising the flag. (B), (C), and (E) don't address this problem and actually introduce phrasings that are even more awkward.

35. (A) (p. 563) *Writing/Improving Paragraphs/Sentence Elements*

The original sentence fails to clearly express the relationship between the two ideas that are mentioned. (A) solves the problem by stating directly: the other points may surprise you. (B) is wrong because the result is a dependent clause that is introduced by "because" instead of a complete sentence. (C) is wrong because this version confuses the connection between the ideas that are mentioned in the original passage. It is the various points of etiquette in the Flag Code that may surprise you—not the fact that the Code contains many points. As for (D), this is a weak choice that doesn't clarify matters. Finally, (E) uses the passive voice, making that choice needlessly indirect when compared with (A).

Section 5—Critical Reading

1. (B) (p. 564) *Critical Reading: Sentence Completions/Thought Extension/Explanatory Phrases*

This sentence does not have a logical structure that will help you select the correct answer. The first blank merely asks that you supply an adjective. The first elements of each answer choice are possible descriptions of a millionaire. The second part of the sentence, however, has a key phrase that tells you that something about his "appearance[s] made in public" is an issue. The only word among the first possibilities that has anything to do with going out is "recluse." So, start with that choice and see if it works. If he is a recluse, then his public appearances will indeed be noteworthy. If you check the other possibilities, it is clear that the second word of each choice does not create a meaningful sentence when substituted into the blank.

2. (D) (p. 564) *Critical Reading: Sentence Completions/Thought Extension/Subordinate Conjunctions*

The key clue here is the subordinate conjunction "because," which indicates an extension of thought. This clue tells you that Western physicians are learning a procedure as a result of "the ____ of the acupuncture therapy in China." Logically, they are doing so because the procedure is desirable, so you should look for a noun that has a positive connotation. This eliminates (B) and (E). If you substitute (A) or (C), the sentence is meaningless. So, the answer must be (D).

3. (C) (p. 564) *Critical Reading: Sentence Completions/Thought Extension/Explanatory Phrases*

This sentence really depends on the second blank. Eliminate (A), (B), and (E): "being a celebrity has its presumptions," "being...confrontations," and "being...delusions" are all unlikely. The second part of the sentence tells you to look for a "lack of" something that would create the situation described in the first blank. (D) is wrong because a celebrity does not lack notoriety (fame is part of the definition of celebrity). Thus, the correct choice is (C).

4. (E) (p. 564) *Critical Reading: Sentence Completions/Thought Extension/Explanatory Phrases*

The second blank is an extension of the idea in the first part of the sentence. We know from the key phrase, "sounds similar to the ____ one hears as the individual members tune their instruments before a concert," that this sound will be negative. The only logical answer, even without considering the second blank, is (E). Confirming this, you can eliminate (A) because the idea of hearing a melody does not explain why a chord is superfluous. You can eliminate (B) because the idea of hearing a roar does not explain why a chord might be pretentious. You can eliminate (C) because the idea of hearing applause does not explain why a chord might be melodious. Eliminate (D), because the idea of hearing harmony does not explain why a chord might be versatile. (E) preserves the sense and logic of the sentence. Hearing cacophony explains that the chord is discordant.

5. **(D) (p. 564)** *Critical Reading: Sentence Completions/Combined Reasoning/Coordinate Conjunctions* and *Explanatory Phrases*

The key to the first half of the sentence is the coordinate conjunction "but," which indicates a reversal of thought. The king was not something that is like "a haughty aristocrat." You can eliminate (A) and (C). "Sycophant" does not provide a logical contrast. Since, by definition, a king is a monarch, putting "monarch" into the first blank results in a contradiction. The second blank must be filled by a word that can later be extended by the phrase "genuine affection." Of the remaining choices, only (D) has a second element with the positive overtones needed to complete that extension. Students can also focus on the extending nature of the semicolon, which indicates that the king would rule positively, or "magnanimously."

6. **(D) (p. 565)** *Critical Reading: Sentence Completions/Thought Reversal/Subordinate Conjunctions*

The key to this sentence is the subordinate conjunction "although," which indicates a reversal of thought. The blank would have to be something that connotes falseness or being out of proper order. Only (D), "anachronistic," which means something that is not in chronological order, fits this sentence.

7. **(E) (p. 565)** *Critical Reading: Sentence Completions/Combined Reasoning/Punctuation Marks*

The best way to attack this item is to substitute each pair until you find one that works, keeping in mind that the colon indicates that the second blank extends the first blank. You can immediately eliminate (A) on the grounds of usage as "apathetic to humor" makes no sense. Next, the salacious is not "heretical to humor," so eliminate (B). The grandiose is not "inferior to humor," so eliminate (C). The innocuous is not "extraneous to humor," so eliminate (D). (E) remains, which does make sense. The macabre might be "antithetical to humor."

8. **(C) (p. 565)** *Critical Reading: Sentence Completions/Combined Reasoning/Subordinate Conjunctions* and *Punctuation Marks*

The key word clue in the first part of the sentence is the subordinate conjunction "while." This word tells you that the Broadway cast was the opposite of the British cast. The first blank extends the idea of what the British cast was. Look for a word that goes with "energy" and "talent." (B) and (C) are possibilities; the others do not extend the idea. The word in the second blank must be the opposite of the description of the British cast and extend the faults of the Broadway cast, as the semicolon clue indicates. (D), "meticulous," makes no sense, so the correct answer must be (C).

9. **(C) (p. 565)** *Critical Reading: Passages/Social Studies/Development*

One of the most striking features in this passage is the extensive use of "examples." The author of the passage lists several writers whose books can be found on the shelves of a public library; the author also lists several library activities that might be undertaken by its patrons. (A) and (B) are wrong because the author of the passage neither provides "statistics" nor cites an "authority." As for (D), the author does not engage in any form of logical "deduction." Finally, (E) is wrong because the author does not actually quote from any of the sources that he or she gives as examples; in fact, the author provides no "quotations" at all.

10. **(C) (p. 567)** *Critical Reading: Passages/Natural Sciences/Development*

Use the "two-part answers" strategy, as each choice has two parts: the first word and the rest of the answer. (A) and (E) can be eliminated because "refutation" and "treatment" do not really describe the passage. Then,

(C) must be the right answer since the passage is a description of a biological process. The passage mentions the concept "immune system," but it is primarily concerned with describing how the immune system works and not simply with defining the term.

11. **(C) (p. 567)** *Critical Reading: Passages/Natural Sciences/Explicit Detail*

In the third paragraph, the author states that any substance capable of triggering an immune response is called an antigen, and gives some examples. The author adds that some "otherwise harmless" substances can trigger an immune reaction—things such as pollen or pet hair—and are called allergens.

12. **(E) (p. 567)** *Critical Reading: Passages/Natural Sciences/Implied Idea*

The very basis of the immune system, according to the passage, is the ability to distinguish non-self from self-cells. It is only when the body detects an outsider that the immune system is activated; presumably, without this ability, the system might attack the body itself. In any case, the result would be a real mess. So, the other choices, insofar as they suggest that some part or parts of the system might continue to work, have to be incorrect.

13. **(A) (p. 567)** *Critical Reading: Passages/Natural Sciences/Application*

Since the answer to this item is not specifically stated in the passage, it must be inferred. In the third paragraph, the author states that foreign tissue will trigger an immune reaction unless it comes from an identical twin. Couple this idea with information about self-markers. According to the footnote, the self-marker is a distinctive series of molecules that allow the cells of the immune system to distinguish cells that belong to the body from those that do not. Since an identical twin's tissue is not treated as foreign, you can infer that it must carry the same molecular markers as the body itself.

14. **(D) (p. 567)** *Critical Reading: Passages/Natural Sciences/Explicit Detail*

(D) is the only answer choice that is not a true statement. (A), (B), (C), and (E) are all mentioned in lines 30–43.

(A) Lines 35–37: "The two most important classes of lymphocytes are B cells...and T cells...."
(B) Lines 36–37: "B cells...mature in the bone marrow, and T cells...migrate to the thymus."
(C) Lines 30–37: "...[stem] cells are produced in the bone marrow...Some...develop into lymphocytes...lymphocytes are B cells...and T cells...."
(E) Lines 38–42: "T cells directly attack...body cells....B cells...work chiefly by secreting antibodies...."

15. **(C) (p. 567)** *Critical Reading: Passages/Natural Sciences/Vocabulary*

In the referenced line, the author explains that "humoral" immunity works by way of antibodies in the body's fluids. You know that (A) has to be incorrect since such a connection could not possibly be the key to this kind of item. And the other words have meanings that do not connect to the idea of the fluids and immunity.

16. **(D) (p. 567)** *Critical Reading: Passages/Natural Sciences/Implied Idea*

The obvious meaning of cannibal is "eats its own kind." Therefore, the phagocytes, which are cells, eat other cells. None of the other answer choices capture the meaning of "cannibal."

17. **(C) (p. 568)** *Critical Reading: Passages/Natural Sciences/Explicit Detail*

In the seventh paragraph, the author talks about the body's "astonishingly intricate defenses" and notes that the first line of defense is the body's armor, or skin and mucous membranes. The other mechanisms do not come into play until a microbe has managed to penetrate the first line of defense.

18. (A) *(p. 568) Critical Reading: Passages/Natural Sciences/Explicit Detail*

According to lines 55–57, the nonspecific defenses attack infectious agents without regard to their antigenic peculiarities. That idea is almost enough to get the answer to this item. However, it is necessary to look back earlier in the passage to where the author discusses what gives an antigen its particular characteristics. In the third paragraph, the author explains that an antigen is what it is because of epitopes, intricate and characteristic shapes on the surface of the cell.

19. (B) *(p. 568) Critical Reading: Passages/Natural Sciences/Implied Idea*

The first sentence of the ninth paragraph states that the cellular immune response is started by a macrophage. The first sentence of the tenth paragraph states that a B cell eating some other cell starts not by a macrophage but by the humoral immune response. Therefore, (A) is close but doesn't quite get it right. The correct answer is (B): both processes begin with one cell gobbling up another.

20. (E) *(p. 568) Critical Reading: Passages/Natural Sciences/Explicit Detail*

To answer this item, determine which answer is the exception by verifying which answers are true. Lines 69–75 specifically mention (A), (B,) and (D) as functions of the T cells, and lines 94–96 mention (C). Thus, all of those choices are true. However, secreting antibodies (lines 85–87) is not a function of T cells. Therefore, (E) is not true and is the right answer.

21. (D) *(p. 568) Critical Reading: Passages/Natural Sciences/Vocabulary*

(A), (B), and (E) can be eliminated because they are not synonymous with "orchestrated." Music can certainly be orchestrated; however "orchestrated" does not mean (C),"musical." The author describes the incredibly complex interactions of the various cells of the immune system. Therefore, the best substitute is "coordinated," (D), a synonym for "orchestrated" that suits the content of this passage.

22. (C) *(p. 568) Critical Reading: Passages/Natural Sciences/Implied Idea*

In lines 97–99, the author states that suppressor T cells end the body's immune reaction. Without the T cells, what would happen? Apparently, the immune reaction, with all the various cells doing their jobs, would keep going on.

23. (D) *(p. 568) Critical Reading: Passages/Natural Sciences/Development*

In the first paragraph, the author poses the question: "Have you ever wondered why you become feverish when you are suffering from the flu?" Then, in the last paragraph, the author answers the question: "When viewed from a clinical perspective, this process [the reaction of the immune system] manifests itself in the three classic symptoms [of feverishness]." Now, it may seem as though the last paragraph does something else, such as conclude the essay. However, that is not an answer choice. Even if (D) is not really a good description, it is the best of the available answer choices.

24. (B) *(p. 568) Critical Reading: Passages/Natural Sciences/Implied Idea*

One of the most striking literary features of the passage is the author's extensive reliance on a metaphor of warring camps: the immune cells are the defenders and the infectious agents are the attackers; the body has defenses against the attackers; the immune cells are troops that are assembled to fight the aliens. The author clearly uses images such as troops and battle, etc., so (B) is the best answer choice. None of the other answer choices were metaphors employed by the author.

Section 7—Math

1. (B) (p. 570) *Math: Multiple-Choice/Arithmetic/Simple Manipulations*

Do the indicated operations: $2 \cdot 10^4 = 20{,}000$, and $121{,}212 + 20{,}000 = 141{,}212$.

2. (C) (p. 570) *Math: Multiple-Choice/Arithmetic/Complicated Arithmetic Application Items*

There is no trick to this item. Use "supermarket math." Find out how much the one thing would cost. Then, using that cost, find out how much of the other you can buy. The cost of renting a bowling lane for two hours is $2 \cdot \$12 = \$24$. For $24, you can rent a Ping Pong table for $\$24 \div \$3 = 8$ hours.

3. (E) (p. 570) *Math: Multiple-Choice/Algebra/Manipulating Algebraic Expressions/Evaluating Expressions*

Solve for x: $6x + 3 = 21 \Rightarrow 6x = 18 \Rightarrow x = 3$. Thus: $2x + 1 = 2(3) + 1 = 7$.

Alternatively, recognize that dividing the left side of the first equation by 3 gives you the left side of the second equation: $\dfrac{6x + 3}{3} = 2x + 1$. Therefore, all you have to do to determine the right side of the second equation is divide the right side of the first equation by 3: $\dfrac{21}{3} = 7$.

4. (E) (p. 570) *Math: Multiple-Choice/Algebra/Expressing and Evaluating Algebraic Functions/Functions as Models*

You can reason in general terms to the correct answer. As for (A), since k is less than l and k is less than j, k cannot be equal to l plus j. The same reasoning applies to (B), (C), and (D). (E), however, could be true. For example, if Jack is 5, Ken is 10, Larry is 15, and Mike is 20, then $5 + 20 = 10 + 15$.

5. (D) (p. 571) *Math: Multiple-Choice/Algebra/Solving Algebraic Equations or Inequalities with One Variable/Equations Involving Absolute Value*

For all x, $|x| \geq 0$. Therefore, $-|x| \leq 0$. Since $-x = -|x|$, $-x \leq 0$. So, the solution set is $\{x : x \geq 0\}$.

Alternatively, test each answer choice. (A) is not true, since the equation holds true for not only positive integers but all positive numbers. For example, $-|1| \overset{?}{=} -1 \Rightarrow -1 = -1$ and $-\left|\dfrac{1}{2}\right| \overset{?}{=} -\dfrac{1}{2} \Rightarrow -\dfrac{1}{2} \overset{?}{=} -\dfrac{1}{2}$ are both true. This also eliminates (B). The difference between (C) and (D) is $x = 0$: the equation holds true for 0, so eliminate (C). Finally, the difference between (D) and (E) is negative numbers, so test a negative number: $-|-1| \overset{?}{=} -(-1) \Rightarrow -1 \overset{?}{=} 1$, which isn't true. Therefore, the correct answer is (D), $x \geq 0$.

6. (A) (p. 571) *Math: Multiple-Choice/Arithmetic/Common Arithmetic Items/Percents*

Use the "is-over-of" strategy: $\dfrac{\text{is}}{\text{of}} = \dfrac{\%}{100} \Rightarrow \dfrac{\text{students on track team}}{\text{total students}} = \dfrac{x}{100} \Rightarrow \dfrac{18}{360} = \dfrac{x}{100} \Rightarrow x = 5\%$.

7. (C) (p. 571) *Math: Multiple-Choice/Geometry/Lines and Angles*

(I) must be true because a and x are vertical angles. Similarly, (II) must be true because y and b are equal and z and c are equal. (III), however, is not necessarily true. x and a are equal, y and b are equal, but you do not have information on which to base a conclusion about the relationship between x and y or the relationship between a and b.

8. **(C) (p. 571)** *Math: Multiple-Choice/Arithmetic/Simple Manipulations*

Simply "test-the-test." Only (C) fits the specified conditions: $6+3+2=11$; $6=3\cdot 2$; and $6=2\cdot 3$.

9. **(B) (p. 571)** *Math: Multiple-Choice/Geometry/Lines and Angles*

Set up an equation and solve for x: $x+30=2x \Rightarrow x=30$.

Alternatively, since the figure is not accompanied by a note stating that it is NOT drawn to scale, you can assume that it is and use "guesstimating" as a strategy of last resort. The size of the right-hand angle appears to be about 60°, so half would be about 30°.

10. **(A) (p. 571)** *Math: Multiple-Choice/Data Analysis/Probability and Statistics/Averages*

Use the method for finding the missing element of an average. Since the average height of all four buildings is 20, the sum of the heights of all four is $4\cdot 20=80$. The three known heights total $3\cdot 16=48$, so the missing value is: $80-48=32$.

11. **(E) (p. 571)** *Math: Multiple-Choice/Arithmetic/Common Arithmetic Items/Properties of Numbers*

You can use the properties of odd and even numbers to answer this item. If x is an odd integer, then choices (A) through (D) each represent the addition of an odd number to an even number. (E), however, represents the addition of two odd numbers. Since an odd number plus an odd number equals an even number, (E) is the only expression that does NOT equal an odd number.

Alternatively, substitute a number for x. If $x=1$, an odd number:

(A) $x+2=1+2=3$ (Odd)
(B) $3x+2=3(1)+2=5$ (Odd)
(C) $2x^2+x=2(1)^2+1=2+1=3$ (Odd)
(D) $2x^3+x=2(1)^3+1=2+1=3$ (Odd)
(E) $3x^3+x=3(1)^3+1=3+1=4$ (Even)

12. **(C) (p. 571)** *Math: Multiple-Choice/Geometry/Rectangles and Squares*

One square has an area of $2\cdot 2=4$, and the other has an area of $3\cdot 3=9$. The sum of their areas is: $4+9=13$.

13. **(B) (p. 572)** *Math: Multiple-Choice/Geometry*

Set up an equation and solve for x: $x\cdot 2x\cdot 3=54 \Rightarrow 2x^2=18 \Rightarrow x^2=9 \Rightarrow x=\sqrt{9}=3$.

Alternatively, "test-the-test." Try each answer choice for x until you find one that generates a volume of 54.

14. **(B) (p. 572)** *Math: Multiple-Choice/Arithmetic/Common Arithmetic Items/Percents*

Since x is 80 percent of y, $x=0.8y$, and $y=\dfrac{x}{0.8}=1.25x$. Thus, y is 125 percent of x.

Alternatively, assume some values. If $y=100$, then $x=80\%$ of y, or 80. Finally, find what percent y is of x:
$\dfrac{100}{80}=\dfrac{5}{4}=1.25=125\%$.

15. (D) (p. 572) *Math: Multiple-Choice/Algebra/Manipulating Algebraic Expressions/Basic Algebraic Manipulations*

The given inequality $m > n$ can be deduced only from (D): add n to both sides of $m - n > 0$: $m - n + n > 0 + n \Rightarrow m > n$. As for (A), this proves that $m < n$. As for (B), this proves nothing about m and n, since m and n might be either negative or positive. The same is true of (C), which is equivalent to $m > -n$. Finally, as for (E), you have neither relative values for m and n nor their signs.

16. (A) (p. 572) *Math: Multiple-Choice/Algebra/Manipulating Algebraic Expressions/Manipulating Expressions Involving Exponents*

Remember that the rules of exponents can be applied only to terms of like bases. Here, the numerator has a base of 8 and the denominator has a base of 2. Before we can manipulate the expression, it will be necessary to change one or the other term. There are several different routes that are available. For example: $8^{2x} = (8)^{2x} = (2 \cdot 2 \cdot 2)^{2x} = (2^{2x})(2^{2x})(2^{2x}) = 2^{2x + 2x + 2x} = 2^{6x}$. Finally, complete the division: $2^{6x} \div 2^{4x} = 2^{6x - 4x} = 2^{2x}$. Or, $(8)^{2x} = (2^3)^{2x} = (2)^{(3)(2x)} = 2^{6x}$. And complete the division as shown above. Or, you can choose to work with the denominator.

Alternatively, assume a value for x. Say $x = 1$: $\dfrac{8^{2(1)}}{2^{4(1)}} = \dfrac{8^2}{2^4} = \dfrac{64}{16} = 4$. If 1 is substituted for x into the answer choices, the correct choice will generate the value 4:

(A) $2^{2(1)} = 4$ ✓

(B) $4^{-1} = \dfrac{1}{4}$ ✗

(C) $4^{2(1)} = 16$ ✗

(D) $4^{1-1} = 4^0 = 1$ ✗

(E) $8^{-1} = \dfrac{1}{8}$ ✗

17. (C) (p. 572) *Math: Multiple-Choice/Geometry/Triangles/Pythagorean Theorem*

You can use the Pythagorean theorem to find $\overline{AD}$ and $\overline{DC}$: $(\overline{BD})^2 + (\overline{AD})^2 = (\overline{AB})^2 \Rightarrow 3^2 + (\overline{AD})^2 = 4^2 \Rightarrow (\overline{AD})^2 = 7 \Rightarrow \overline{AD} = \sqrt{7}$. So, the base of the triangle is $2 \cdot \sqrt{7} = 2\sqrt{7}$.

Alternatively, you can also use the trigonometry information that is provided:
$\sin \angle ABD = \dfrac{\overline{AD}}{4} \Rightarrow \dfrac{\sqrt{7}}{4} = \dfrac{\overline{AD}}{4} \Rightarrow \overline{AD} = \sqrt{7}$. And so the base of the triangle is $2 \cdot \sqrt{7} = 2\sqrt{7}$.

18. (C) (p. 572) *Math: Multiple-Choice/Algebra/Expressing and Evaluating Algebraic Functions/Function Notation*

Here we have a group of nested functions. Perform the indicated operations, working from the inside to the outside: $h(4) = (4)^2 = 16 \Rightarrow g(16) = 16 - 2 = 14 \Rightarrow f(14) = \dfrac{14}{2} = 7$.

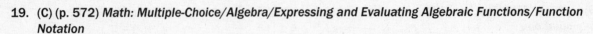

19. **(C) (p. 572)** *Math: Multiple-Choice/Algebra/Expressing and Evaluating Algebraic Functions/Function Notation*

The easiest way to solve this problem is to plug in the given values for x (3 and -2) into the answer choices to find the one that matches the given values for the function (12 and 2):

(A) $x = 3$: $\dfrac{1}{2}x = \dfrac{1}{2}(3) = \dfrac{3}{2} \overset{?}{=} 12$ ✗

(B) $x = 3$: $x + 9 = 3 + 9 = 12 \overset{?}{=} 12$ ✓

   $x = -2$: $x + 9 = -2 + 9 = 7 \overset{?}{=} 2$ ✗

(C) $x = 3$: $2x + 6 = 2(3) + 6 = 12 \overset{?}{=} 12$ ✓

   $x = -2$: $2x + 6 = 2(-2) + 6 = 2 \overset{?}{=} 2$ ✓

Since the expression in (C) holds true for both values of x, we can stop testing the choices: (C) must be correct.

20. **(C) (p. 573)** *Math: Multiple-Choice/Arithmetic/Common Arithmetic Items/Properties of Numbers*

This item tests properties of numbers. Examine each expression. (A) is not necessarily true. $|xy|$ is always a positive number, but $x + y$ could be a negative number—depending on the relative size of x and y. Nor is (B) true. $|xy|$ is always positive, but xy is always negative. For this reason, however, (C) is true. Since $|xy|$ is always positive and xy negative, $|xy|$ is always greater than xy. Finally, (D) and (E) might or might not be true depending on the relative magnitudes of x and y.

Section 8—Critical Reading

1. **(B) (p. 574)** *Critical Reading: Sentence Completions/Thought Extension/Key Words*

First, the overall structure depends on an extension of thought. The second blank must explain the results or consequences of the first blank. Additionally, you can rely on key words such as "unjustly" and "libelous" to help you deduce that the action of the magazine was wrong. On this basis, eliminate (A) and (E); there is nothing wrong with praising or extolling. Eliminate (C) and (D) because they do not explain the natural consequences of the judge's ruling. (C), however, does the job. The judge ruled that the article had wrongly damaged the architect's reputation, so he or she ordered the magazine to make amends by retracting what it had printed.

2. **(C) (p. 574)** *Critical Reading: Sentence Completions/Thought Extension/Coordinate Conjunctions*

This sentence contains a coordinate conjunction "and," which indicates an extension of thought. The blanks must explain why the operation was so "disorganized" (key word). Additionally, the two blanks describe the same kind of behavior and must be parallel. Eliminate (A) and (B), because those word pairs are opposites, not parallels. Eliminate (D) and (E), since they do not supply the needed parallel; they are not related at all. (C) is the choice that supports the overall logical structure of the sentence while providing the parallel between the blanks.

3. **(A) (p. 574)** *Critical Reading: Sentence Completions/Thought Extension/Subordinate Conjunctions*

The subordinate conjunction "since" signals an extension of thought. The blanks must set up the explanation that is given in the part of the sentence following the comma. Why would the publication need to be "postponed" (key word) until further study? Something is missing—the two blanks together must provide it. (A) is the best choice.

4. **(E) (p. 574)** *Critical Reading: Sentence Completions/Combined Reasoning/Coordinate Conjunctions* and *Explanatory Phrases*

This sentence contains both an extension of thought and a reversal of thought as its logical keys. The coordinate conjunction "and" signals that the two missing words are related, and the phrase "rather than" signals that the missing words reverse the idea of "clarity and precision." So, you should look for a pair of similar words that conveys a meaning that is opposite to "clarity and precision." (E) does the job.

5. **(B) (p. 575)** *Critical Reading: Sentence Completions/Combined Reasoning/Subordinate Conjunctions* and *Coordinate Conjunctions*

This sentence contains both a reversal of thought and an extension of thought as its logical keys. First, the subordinate conjunction "although" indicates that the reader's reaction to the novel is opposite to what would be expected if the book were not well-written. Also, the coordinate conjunction "and" indicates that you must extend the thought of the exciting story that the reader "could not put down" (key phrase). Eliminate (A), (D), and (E) because the reader would have put the book down had he or she been any of those things. (C) makes no sense at all, so you are left with (B), which completes the thought perfectly.

6. **(B) (p. 575)** *Critical Reading: Passages/Humanities/Implied Idea*

The passage doesn't specifically say that the young women are window-shopping, but you reach that conclusion by reading carefully. The young women are looking at very expensive merchandise through the shop windows. The passage does not say that the women actually buy anything, so you can infer that they are window-shopping. As for (A), the young women are not really planning anything specific; they are having fun. As for (C) and (D), the passage states that they have already eaten lunch. As for (E), while some people might exercise on their lunch breaks, these young women are digesting their lunches as they window-shop at expensive stores.

7. **(E) (p. 575)** *Critical Reading: Passages/Humanities/Vocabulary*

Since "smart" is a common word, you can pretty much bet that (A) is not the correct answer. Instead, "smart" in this context refers to the fancy stores with their expensive merchandise, so the best choice available is "stylish." As for (B), the stores are expensive, not inexpensive; and as for (D), they are elaborate and not simple. As for (C), the stores are busy, but "smart" in this context refers to the kind of merchandise that the store carries.

8. **(D) (p. 575)** *Critical Reading: Passages/Natural Sciences/Implied Idea*

The author of Passage 1 emphasizes dramatic and sudden forces as the agents of change. "Punctuated" is a word that is related to "punctual" and "point" and so conveys the idea of something that happens suddenly—starts and then stops. This definition is consistent with the author's idea of change as a series of sudden events. (A) is incorrect because the author of Passage 1 emphasizes sudden, not gradual, change. As for (B), while the events are powerful, they are not controllable. As for (C), though the whole story has perhaps not yet been told, there is nothing mysterious about it. As for (E), "concise" and "logical" do not describe physical events.

9. **(C) (p. 576)** *Critical Reading: Passages/Natural Sciences/Explicit Detail*

This item asks you to synthesize information from the two passages. Passage 1 argues that change is dramatic; Passage 2 argues that it is gradual; and (C) summarizes that difference. As for (A), the authors apparently agree on the observable features but disagree on how to explain them. As for (B), the authors may or may not agree entirely on the time that is involved, but they do not disagree about the length of historical time—though they do disagree about the events that fill up that time. As for (D) and (E), both apparently agree that geology and science are important.

10. **(B) (p. 577)** *Critical Reading: Passages/Literary Fiction/Development*

The author is arguing that most of the stories in the newspaper are not really worth reading. He includes this report as an example to show how silly some news coverage is. It is an odd occurrence that does not really affect the person who reads about it—except insofar as it functions as idle gossip. The other choices must be wrong because the event is not significant.

11. **(D) (p. 577)** *Critical Reading: Passages/Literary Fiction/Development*

In the second paragraph, the author of Passage 1 is making the point that the foreign news is not really news and mentions the examples of Spain, England, and France. He writes that it is possible just to toss in some generic information about Spain, and the resulting report will be accurate. (D) best summarizes how the author uses this example. The other choices are wrong because the author is not offering real news, only a parody of the news.

12. **(A) (p. 577)** *Critical Reading: Passages/Literary Fiction/Voice*

The point of Passage 1 is that the reports contained in the newspaper are really worthless, covering all kinds of events that ultimately have no significance. At key points in the passage, the author pokes fun at the news: people would come running in response to a fire alarm in the hope of seeing a good fire, even if it were the church that was burning. Since the author's attitude is negative, you can eliminate (B), (C), and (D). As for (E), while the author might caution readers against the news, his attitude toward the news itself is not mistrust or wariness but ridicule.

13. **(C) (p. 577)** *Critical Reading: Passages/Literary Fiction/Vocabulary*

Because this is a Vocabulary item, you can be pretty sure that the correct answer is not going to be the most common meaning of "attend." As a result, (A) is wrong. In this context, "attend" means to "pay attention to," and (C) is a good match. The other choices do not fit the meaning of the sentence; in fact, (B) and (D) are never synonymous with "attend."

14. **(A) (p. 577)** *Critical Reading: Passages/Literary Fiction/Development*

The author says that people would respond to the fire alarm not because they want to help save property from destruction but because they want to watch a fire. The author adds that this is particularly true if the church itself is on fire. The author is adding emphasis to the point by saying that people would show up to watch their own church burn. As for (B), while it seems that these people might not care enough about property to put out the fire, this is not the point that the author wants to prove. He wants to prove that they would enjoy watching the church burn. (C) is wrong because the point is not that people are legitimately interested in local affairs but that in this case they are fascinated by something unusual. (D) has to be wrong because the point is that people are less interested in the church than in watching a fire. Finally, (E) is far off the mark.

15. **(E) (p. 578)** *Critical Reading: Passages/Literary Fiction/Explicit Detail*

The author states that the people on the island had continued to act as friends even though they were enemies (meaning that the countries from which they originally came were at war). (A) and (B) are ideas mentioned in the selection but do not respond to the question asked. (C) is not discussed in that paragraph, and (D) belongs to another part of the passage altogether.

16. **(B) (p. 578)** *Critical Reading: Passages/Literary Fiction/Explicit Detail*

The "plight" that both the islanders and the residents of Europe shared was the delay in the news reporting. Though the delay may have been longer (in the case of the islander) or shorter (in the case of Europeans nearer to the events), there was still a delay during which people were in the position of acting on outdated and wrong information. As for (A), the reporting was not wrong; it was merely delayed. As for (C), even regular reports can be outdated. As for (D), the problem was not biased news but late news. As for (E), the problem was not partial information but lack of current information.

17. **(A) (p. 578)** *Critical Reading: Passages/Literary Fiction/Implied Idea*

In the final paragraph, the author states that from our perspective we can see that results were achieved even though people were working with outdated or wrong information. The author offers overseas exploration as an example; with the backing of the Spanish government, Columbus set sail for India only to land in what is now the Americas, and to be credited with a significant achievement. As for (B), while the Spanish government and Columbus worked with wrong information, this is not the author's point—the results are what matters. As for (C) and (E), the author talks about hindsight and does not fault those who made errors because their information was limited. (D) represents a misunderstanding of the final paragraph.

18. **(A) (p. 578)** *Critical Reading: Passages/Literary Fiction/Application*

The author of Passage 1 thinks that the news is only gossip. The author of Passage 2 thinks that news is important, even if it arrives a little late. As for (B), the author of Passage 1 does not really care whether news is accurate or not; it's just gossip. As for (C), again, the author of Passage 1 insists that the news has no value at all. As for (D), the author of Passage 2 really does not hold out much hope for the news, though he or she might allow that faster reporting is better than slower reporting. As for (E), while it is true that Passage 1 mentions some local events, the author does not say that one type of event is more suitable for coverage than the other. Similarly, while the second author talks about international events, he does not say that reporting on international events is particularly suited to all newspapers.

19. **(A) (p. 578)** *Critical Reading: Passages/Literary Fiction/Application*

We do not know what the authors would have said about the web because they obviously died before it was invented, but we can make a good guess. The author of Passage 1 would probably say, "See I told you so, more and faster junk." Figuring out author two is a little harder. The point of the second passage is that no matter how fast the news comes, there is always some delay between the event and the report, and during that time, we are operating on wrong information. That point is nicely summarized by the first sentence of the third paragraph: how indirectly we know the environment. Thus, the second author would probably say that while the web closes the gap somewhat, it does not eliminate it. As for (B), there is no way that author one is going to buy into this point. As for (C), surely author two would allow that the web is faster and therefore at least a little better. In any event, author one is going to say that both sources are terrible. The same reasoning applies to (D) and (E).

Section 9—Math

1. **(E) (p. 580)** *Math: Multiple-Choice/Arithmetic/Common Arithmetic Items/Properties of Numbers*

The expression $2[p(q+r)+s]$ will be an even number regardless of the values of $p, q, r,$ or s. But whether the whole expression is even depends on t. If t is even, then the whole expression is even; if t is odd, then the whole expression is odd.

2. **(B) (p. 580)** *Math: Multiple-Choice/Geometry/Rectangles and Squares*

Use the formula for finding the area of a square: area = side • side . $s \cdot s = 9x^2 \Rightarrow s^2 = 9x^2 \Rightarrow s = \sqrt{9x^2} = 3x$.

Alternatively, you can assume some values. If $x = 1$, the area of the square is 9, and its side is 3. Substitute 1 for x in the choices. Both (B) and (E) yield the value 3. So, pick another number, say 3. If $x = 3$, the area of the square is 81, and its side is 9. Substitute 3 for x in both (B) and (E); only (B) yields the correct value 9.

3. **(D) (p. 581)** *Math: Multiple-Choice/Arithmetic/Common Arithmetic Items/Properties of Numbers*

You can arrive at the correct answer in several ways. First, you can reason that if the product of three different integers is 0, one of the integers is 0. Of x and $-x$, one is positive and the other negative, so they cannot be 0. The missing number must be 0. You can also set up equations, but that seems unnecessarily complicated. You would be better off using a third method: substitute some values for x. You'll find that the missing number must be 0.

4. **(C) (p. 581)** *Math: Multiple-Choice/Geometry/Complex Figures* and *Triangles/Properties of Triangles* and *Pythagorean Theorem*

The diagonal of a square creates an isosceles right triangle. Use the Pythagorean theorem, and let the length of each side be s: $s^2 + s^2 = \left(\sqrt{2}\right)^2 \Rightarrow 2s^2 = 2 \Rightarrow s^2 = 1 \Rightarrow s = 1$. Since the side has a length of 1, the perimeter of the square is $4(1) = 4$.

5. **(C) (p. 581)** *Math: Multiple-Choice/Geometry/Triangles/Properties of Triangles*

The sum of the lengths of any two sides of a triangle must be greater than the length of the third side. So, in this case, the third side must be greater than 7 but less than 15. The difference between 11 and 4 is 7, so 7 marks the limit of the shorter side of a triangle with sides of 11 and 4. But the side must be an integer, so the shortest possible side is 8. Conversely, the sum of 4 and 11 is 15. So, 15 marks the limit of the longer side. Since the longer side must have an integral value, its maximum length is 14.

6. **(C) (p. 581)** *Math: Multiple-Choice/Algebra/Solving Algebraic Equations with Two Variables*

You can reason that the only permissible values for x are those which, when multiplied by 2 and subtracted from 19, yield a number that is divisible by 3.

That's a lot of reasoning. Instead, simply "test-the-test." Try (A). If x is 3, then $2x$ is 6, and $3y = 13$. But then y cannot be an integer, so (A) is wrong. The correct answer is (C). If x is 5, then $3y = 9$, and $y = 3$, an integer.

7. **(E) (p. 581)** *Math: Multiple-Choice/Data Analysis/Probability and Statistics/Median*

The median is defined as the value of the center-most number, when arranged numerically. In this case, the numbers are already arranged numerically, and the median is the center number, 81.

8. **(E) (p. 581)** *Math: Multiple-Choice/Algebra/Manipulating Algebraic Expressions/Evaluating Expressions*

The expression is less than zero, so one or three of the factors must be negative. Since $b^3 = b^2 b$, the inequality can be rewritten as $a^2 b^2 bc < 0$. Both a^2 and b^2 are greater than 0. Therefore, $bc < 0$, and (E) must be true.

Alternatively, reason as follows: a^2 cannot be negative, so either b^3 is negative, or c is negative, but not both. This means that either b or c is negative but not both, so, bc must be negative. You can eliminate (A), (B), (C), and (D) since they might be, but are not necessarily, true.

9. **(C) (p. 581)** *Math: Multiple-Choice/Geometry/Triangles/Properties of Triangles*

Since this is an equilateral triangle, the sides are equal. Set up equations: $2x + 1 = 2x + y \Rightarrow y = 1$ and $2x + y = y + 2$. Since one of the sides is $y + 2$, stop after solving the first equation for y. The length of the side is $1 + 2 = 3$. Then, since the three sides are equal in length, the perimeter is $3 \cdot 3 = 9$.

10. **(C) (p. 582)** *Math: Multiple-Choice/Geometry/Triangles/Pythagorean Theorem*

Do not be fooled by the answer "13": this is not a 5-12-13 right triangle. In that case, the side of length 12 would be the second longest leg, not the hypotenuse. You know that in a right triangle, $a^2 + b^2 = c^2$, in which c is the length of the hypotenuse. By plugging in the numbers that you have, you see that $5^2 + b^2 = 12^2$, or $25 + b^2 = 144$. Since $144 - 25 = 119$, b must be the square root of 119.

11. (E) (p. 582) *Math: Multiple-Choice/Geometry/Lines and Angles*

First, find the value of y: $5y + 4y = 180 \Rightarrow 9y = 180 \Rightarrow y = 20$. Next, find the value of x: $4y + 2y + x = 180 \Rightarrow 6y + x = 180$. $6(20) + x = 180 \Rightarrow 120 + x = 180 \Rightarrow x = 60$.

12. (B) (p. 582) *Math: Multiple-Choice/Geometry/Geometric Notation*

The trick here is to recognize that each of the marks between the numbered marks is $\frac{1}{5}$ of the distance between the numbered marks. The distance between each numbered mark is 0.1, so each of the others is worth $0.1 \div 5 = 0.02$. And, given that there are 8 marks between P and Q, $\overline{PQ} = 8(0.02) = 0.16$.

13. (A) (p. 582) *Math: Multiple-Choice/Geometry/Rectangles and Squares*

The perimeter is: $2(3a - 2) + 2(2a - 1) = 6a - 4 + 4a - 2 = 10a - 6$.

Alternatively, assume a value for a. If $a = 2$, then the length of the figure is $3(2) - 2 = 4$, and the width of the figure is $2(2) - 1 = 3$. The perimeter would be: $4 + 4 + 3 + 3 = 14$. Thus, substituting 2 for a into the correct formula will return a value of 14.

14. (B) (p. 582) *Math: Multiple-Choice/Data Analysis/Probability and Statistics/Averages*

Use the technique for finding the missing elements of an average. The average of the 5 numbers is 51, so their sum is $5 \cdot 51 = 255$. The 2 known values total 114, so the remaining 3 numbers total $255 - 114 = 141$. Thus, the missing value is $141 \div 3 = 47$.

Alternatively, set up an algebraic equation for the average and solve for the missing value x:
$$\frac{x + x + x + 56 + 58}{5} = 51 \Rightarrow 3x + 114 = 5(51) \Rightarrow 3x = 255 - 114 = 141 \Rightarrow x = 47.$$

15. (C) (p. 582) *Math: Multiple-Choice/Algebra/Solving Algebraic Equations or Inequalities with One Variable/Simple Equations*

Solve the compound inequality by dividing each part by 2, so −1 is less than or equal to x is less than or equal to 1. Since x is an integer, x could be −1 , 0, or 1.

16. (E) (p. 582) *Math: Multiple-Choice/Algebra/Expressing and Evaluating Algebraic Functions/Function Notation*

Do the indicated operation: $(-1.1)^2 = 1.21$. The smallest integer greater than 1.21 is 2.

Section 10—Writing

1. (B) (p. 584) *Writing/Improving Sentences/Clarity of Expression/Diction and Idioms*

The underlined portion is not idiomatic. The correct expression is "so...as in...." Only (B) conforms to this: "so diligent as in the study...." (A), (C), (D), and (E) all use faulty expressions that do not represent standard English usage.

2. (E) (p. 584) *Writing/Improving Sentences/Logical Expression/Misplaced Modifiers*

The original sentence is incorrect because the modifier "that complained of its editorial policy" is too far removed from the word it modifies, "letters." As written, the sentence seems to imply that the newspaper complained of its editorial policy. (C) fails to eliminate this ambiguity. (B) introduces an error of subject-verb agreement. (D) eliminates the ambiguity but is needlessly wordy. The best choice is (E). (E) corrects the error of the original sentence and has two additional points in its favor. First, the thought is rendered directly with the active voice instead of indirectly with the passive voice. Second, (E) uses the possessive noun "paper's" instead of the possessive pronoun "its," which makes the sentence clearer.

3. **(E) (p. 584)** *Writing/Improving Sentences/Sentence Structure*

(A) is wrong because there is no pronoun to refer to "Americans." (B) corrects that error but introduces the non-idiomatic phrase "more then" instead of "more than." (C) combines the errors of the first two choices. (D) is hopelessly awkward and non-idiomatic. (E) is correct and precise.

4. **(E) (p. 585)** *Writing/Improving Sentences/Logical Expression/Misplaced Modifiers*

The original sentence contains two ambiguities. First, the placement of the modifier "only" implies that the only legal action that a physician can take is prescribing medicine, when the sentence really means to say that it is only physicians who can prescribe medicine. Second, placing the modifier "protecting the public" so close to "medicine" implies that the medicine, not the law, is intended to protect the public. Only (E) corrects both of these errors.

5. **(B) (p. 585)** *Writing/Improving Sentences/Grammar/Subject-Verb Agreement* and *Logical Expression/ Misplaced Modifiers* and *Clarity of Expression/Diction and Idioms*

The underlined portion contains three errors. First, the verb "makes" does not agree with its subject, which is "improvements." Second, "today" introduces a possible ambiguity, because its placement implies that the sentence is talking about data that is gathered on a particular day. In any event, "today" is superfluous. Third, the use of the infinitive "to forecast" is not idiomatic. Only (B) eliminates all three of the errors.

6. **(D) (p. 585)** *Writing/Improving Sentences/Grammar/Pronoun Usage*

The original sentence is incorrect because the relative pronoun "which" lacks a clear referent. "Which" ought to refer to something like "eating," but there is no such noun in the sentence. (B) and (C) fail to correct this error. (D) and (E) both correct the error, but (E), by changing "enemies" to an adjective, creates a non-idiomatic expression. Additionally, (D) is better than the underlined portion because, by using the noun "enemies" instead of the pronoun "their," it avoids a potential ambiguity. (Did the people hope to ingest their own courage or that of the enemy?)

7. **(E) (p. 585)** *Writing/Improving Sentences/Grammar/Fragments*

The original sentence is wrong because it is a sentence fragment—there is no main verb. (B) is incorrect because there is no need to use the past tense. (C) commits the same error as (B) and commits an additional error by making "family" plural. (The resulting phrase is not logical because there is only one violin family.) (D) is wrong because it too is a fragment. (E) is the correct choice because it has a conjugated verb in the correct tense.

8. **(A) (p. 585)** *Writing/Improving Sentences/No Error*

The underlined portion is correct. The sentence maintains parallel structure and the subject agrees with the verb. (B) is incorrect for two reasons. First, (B) switches to the passive voice. As a result, (B) is not as concise as the underlined portion. Second, (B) changes the intended meaning of the original sentence. (C) and (D) are wrong because the resulting sentences would lack parallel structure. (E) also introduces an error of parallelism and compounds the problem by using the future perfect tense.

9. **(B) (p. 585)** *Writing/Improving Sentences/Clarity of Expression/Diction and Idioms*

The use of "considering" in the underlined portion is not idiomatic. (B), (D), and (E) attempt to correct the error, but (D) and (E) make the intended meaning of the original sentence ambiguous. Neither the phrase "first professional American sculptor" nor the phrase "first American professional sculptor" makes clear which of the two elements, American or professional, the speaker considers more important. Only (B) is both consistent with the intended meaning and idiomatically correct.

10. **(A) (p. 586)** *Writing/Improving Sentences/No Error*

The underlined portion is correct. (B) fails to make a logical statement by omitting the conjunction "but," which shows the relationship between the clauses. (C) is wordy; the use of the word "also" is illogical, and (C) changes the intended meaning of the original sentence by introducing the word "more" ("more convincing"). (D) creates an illogical sentence. It is not clear what lacks the organizational skills, and the resulting sentence implies that it is the convincing argument that has organizational skills rather than the person who is making the argument. (E) is also illogical. It implies that it was because of organizational skills that there was no convincing argument. (A) makes it clear that the person doing the writing lacked organizational skills.

11. **(D) (p. 586)** *Writing/Improving Sentences/Logical Expression/Faulty Comparisons* and *Grammar/Subject-Verb Agreement*

The original commits two errors. First, it sets up an illogical comparison between "countries" and "Americans." Second, the verb "is" fails to agree with its subject, "cards." (B) fails to correct the second error. Additionally, (B) is incorrect because "like" is non-idiomatic here and "that" doesn't refer to anything. (C) corrects the problem of agreement, but "as" is not idiomatic. (The "as" implies a similarity between two activities, but the sentence means to create a contrast between America, where credit cards are frequently used, and some other countries.) Finally, (E) implies that credit cards are used as cash more widely in America than in other countries, but the original sentence means to say that in America, credit cards are used more widely than cash.

12. **(D) (p. 586)** *Writing/Improving Sentences/Sentence Structure/Incomplete Split Constructions* and *Logical Expression/Illogical Tense Sequence*

The underlined portion is incorrect because it includes an incomplete construction: "has always…to be feared." Also, the future perfect tense is inappropriate. (B) is incorrect because it has the same incomplete construction as the underlined portion does. (C) is wrong because it is awkward and not idiomatic. (E) changes the meaning of the original sentence: leprosy is not continually being feared. (E) is also awkwardly worded. (D) is the best choice because the construction is complete and the verb tense is appropriate.

13. **(C) (p. 586)** *Writing/Improving Sentences/Clarity of Expression/Diction and Idioms* and *Grammar/Subject-Verb Agreement* and *Pronoun Usage*

The original sentence contains three errors. First, "on account of" is not acceptable in standard written English as a substitute for "because." Second, the verb "are" does not agree with the subject of the sentence, "delivery." Third, "this" does not have a clear referent. Only (C) corrects all three errors.

14. **(C) (p. 586)** *Writing/Improving Sentences/Logical Expression/Misplaced Modifiers*

The underlined portion is incorrect because of a misplaced modifier. The sentence says that Dr. Martin "nearly spent" 10 years doing something. This construction implies that he did not actually embark on the task. (Look closely at the difference between the statements "I nearly spent $10" and "I spent nearly $10.") The sentence means to say that he spent *nearly* 10 years on the task. (B) is wrong because it changes the meaning of the sentence. Here, "nearly" refers to his task and not the length of time he took to accomplish it. (D) is incorrect because it is susceptible to misreading. (D) implies that the process of asphyxiation took almost 10 years. Additionally, the placement of the phrase "nearly spending 10 years" is awkward. Finally, (E) is wrong because it switches to the passive voice, and like the underlined portion, it implies that Dr. Martin did not actually begin the task. (C) is correct because it clearly states that the doctor spent nearly 10 years building the artificial wall.

Appendix C:
Test Answer Sheet

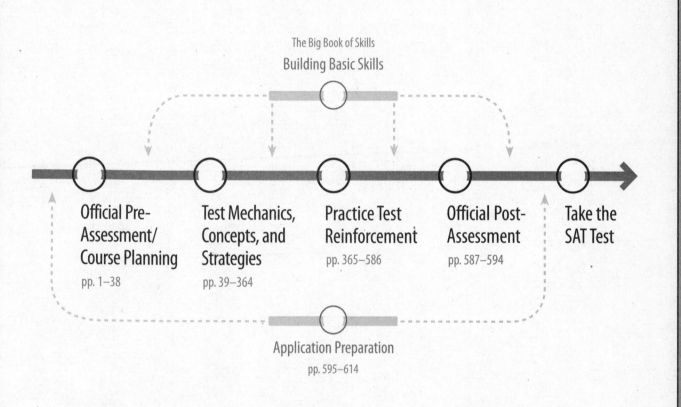

The Big Book of Skills
Building Basic Skills

Official Pre-Assessment/
Course Planning
pp. 1–38

Test Mechanics,
Concepts, and
Strategies
pp. 39–364

Practice Test
Reinforcement
pp. 365–586

Official Post-
Assessment
pp. 587–594

Take the
SAT Test

Application Preparation
pp. 595–614

TEST ANSWER SHEET

Name _____   Student ID Number _____

Date _____   Instructor _____   Course/Session Number _____

Start with number 1 for each new section. If a section has fewer questions than answer spaces, leave the extra answer spaces blank. Be sure to erase any errors or stray marks completely.

Section 2

1 Ⓐ Ⓑ Ⓒ Ⓓ Ⓔ	10 Ⓐ Ⓑ Ⓒ Ⓓ Ⓔ	19 Ⓐ Ⓑ Ⓒ Ⓓ Ⓔ	28 Ⓐ Ⓑ Ⓒ Ⓓ Ⓔ
2 Ⓐ Ⓑ Ⓒ Ⓓ Ⓔ	11 Ⓐ Ⓑ Ⓒ Ⓓ Ⓔ	20 Ⓐ Ⓑ Ⓒ Ⓓ Ⓔ	29 Ⓐ Ⓑ Ⓒ Ⓓ Ⓔ
3 Ⓐ Ⓑ Ⓒ Ⓓ Ⓔ	12 Ⓐ Ⓑ Ⓒ Ⓓ Ⓔ	21 Ⓐ Ⓑ Ⓒ Ⓓ Ⓔ	30 Ⓐ Ⓑ Ⓒ Ⓓ Ⓔ
4 Ⓐ Ⓑ Ⓒ Ⓓ Ⓔ	13 Ⓐ Ⓑ Ⓒ Ⓓ Ⓔ	22 Ⓐ Ⓑ Ⓒ Ⓓ Ⓔ	31 Ⓐ Ⓑ Ⓒ Ⓓ Ⓔ
5 Ⓐ Ⓑ Ⓒ Ⓓ Ⓔ	14 Ⓐ Ⓑ Ⓒ Ⓓ Ⓔ	23 Ⓐ Ⓑ Ⓒ Ⓓ Ⓔ	32 Ⓐ Ⓑ Ⓒ Ⓓ Ⓔ
6 Ⓐ Ⓑ Ⓒ Ⓓ Ⓔ	15 Ⓐ Ⓑ Ⓒ Ⓓ Ⓔ	24 Ⓐ Ⓑ Ⓒ Ⓓ Ⓔ	33 Ⓐ Ⓑ Ⓒ Ⓓ Ⓔ
7 Ⓐ Ⓑ Ⓒ Ⓓ Ⓔ	16 Ⓐ Ⓑ Ⓒ Ⓓ Ⓔ	25 Ⓐ Ⓑ Ⓒ Ⓓ Ⓔ	34 Ⓐ Ⓑ Ⓒ Ⓓ Ⓔ
8 Ⓐ Ⓑ Ⓒ Ⓓ Ⓔ	17 Ⓐ Ⓑ Ⓒ Ⓓ Ⓔ	26 Ⓐ Ⓑ Ⓒ Ⓓ Ⓔ	35 Ⓐ Ⓑ Ⓒ Ⓓ Ⓔ
9 Ⓐ Ⓑ Ⓒ Ⓓ Ⓔ	18 Ⓐ Ⓑ Ⓒ Ⓓ Ⓔ	27 Ⓐ Ⓑ Ⓒ Ⓓ Ⓔ	36 Ⓐ Ⓑ Ⓒ Ⓓ Ⓔ

Section 3

1 Ⓐ Ⓑ Ⓒ Ⓓ Ⓔ	10 Ⓐ Ⓑ Ⓒ Ⓓ Ⓔ	19 Ⓐ Ⓑ Ⓒ Ⓓ Ⓔ	28 Ⓐ Ⓑ Ⓒ Ⓓ Ⓔ
2 Ⓐ Ⓑ Ⓒ Ⓓ Ⓔ	11 Ⓐ Ⓑ Ⓒ Ⓓ Ⓔ	20 Ⓐ Ⓑ Ⓒ Ⓓ Ⓔ	29 Ⓐ Ⓑ Ⓒ Ⓓ Ⓔ
3 Ⓐ Ⓑ Ⓒ Ⓓ Ⓔ	12 Ⓐ Ⓑ Ⓒ Ⓓ Ⓔ	21 Ⓐ Ⓑ Ⓒ Ⓓ Ⓔ	30 Ⓐ Ⓑ Ⓒ Ⓓ Ⓔ
4 Ⓐ Ⓑ Ⓒ Ⓓ Ⓔ	13 Ⓐ Ⓑ Ⓒ Ⓓ Ⓔ	22 Ⓐ Ⓑ Ⓒ Ⓓ Ⓔ	31 Ⓐ Ⓑ Ⓒ Ⓓ Ⓔ
5 Ⓐ Ⓑ Ⓒ Ⓓ Ⓔ	14 Ⓐ Ⓑ Ⓒ Ⓓ Ⓔ	23 Ⓐ Ⓑ Ⓒ Ⓓ Ⓔ	32 Ⓐ Ⓑ Ⓒ Ⓓ Ⓔ
6 Ⓐ Ⓑ Ⓒ Ⓓ Ⓔ	15 Ⓐ Ⓑ Ⓒ Ⓓ Ⓔ	24 Ⓐ Ⓑ Ⓒ Ⓓ Ⓔ	33 Ⓐ Ⓑ Ⓒ Ⓓ Ⓔ
7 Ⓐ Ⓑ Ⓒ Ⓓ Ⓔ	16 Ⓐ Ⓑ Ⓒ Ⓓ Ⓔ	25 Ⓐ Ⓑ Ⓒ Ⓓ Ⓔ	34 Ⓐ Ⓑ Ⓒ Ⓓ Ⓔ
8 Ⓐ Ⓑ Ⓒ Ⓓ Ⓔ	17 Ⓐ Ⓑ Ⓒ Ⓓ Ⓔ	26 Ⓐ Ⓑ Ⓒ Ⓓ Ⓔ	35 Ⓐ Ⓑ Ⓒ Ⓓ Ⓔ
9 Ⓐ Ⓑ Ⓒ Ⓓ Ⓔ	18 Ⓐ Ⓑ Ⓒ Ⓓ Ⓔ	27 Ⓐ Ⓑ Ⓒ Ⓓ Ⓔ	36 Ⓐ Ⓑ Ⓒ Ⓓ Ⓔ

Section 4/5

1 Ⓐ Ⓑ Ⓒ Ⓓ Ⓔ	10 Ⓐ Ⓑ Ⓒ Ⓓ Ⓔ	19 Ⓐ Ⓑ Ⓒ Ⓓ Ⓔ	28 Ⓐ Ⓑ Ⓒ Ⓓ Ⓔ
2 Ⓐ Ⓑ Ⓒ Ⓓ Ⓔ	11 Ⓐ Ⓑ Ⓒ Ⓓ Ⓔ	20 Ⓐ Ⓑ Ⓒ Ⓓ Ⓔ	29 Ⓐ Ⓑ Ⓒ Ⓓ Ⓔ
3 Ⓐ Ⓑ Ⓒ Ⓓ Ⓔ	12 Ⓐ Ⓑ Ⓒ Ⓓ Ⓔ	21 Ⓐ Ⓑ Ⓒ Ⓓ Ⓔ	30 Ⓐ Ⓑ Ⓒ Ⓓ Ⓔ
4 Ⓐ Ⓑ Ⓒ Ⓓ Ⓔ	13 Ⓐ Ⓑ Ⓒ Ⓓ Ⓔ	22 Ⓐ Ⓑ Ⓒ Ⓓ Ⓔ	31 Ⓐ Ⓑ Ⓒ Ⓓ Ⓔ
5 Ⓐ Ⓑ Ⓒ Ⓓ Ⓔ	14 Ⓐ Ⓑ Ⓒ Ⓓ Ⓔ	23 Ⓐ Ⓑ Ⓒ Ⓓ Ⓔ	32 Ⓐ Ⓑ Ⓒ Ⓓ Ⓔ
6 Ⓐ Ⓑ Ⓒ Ⓓ Ⓔ	15 Ⓐ Ⓑ Ⓒ Ⓓ Ⓔ	24 Ⓐ Ⓑ Ⓒ Ⓓ Ⓔ	33 Ⓐ Ⓑ Ⓒ Ⓓ Ⓔ
7 Ⓐ Ⓑ Ⓒ Ⓓ Ⓔ	16 Ⓐ Ⓑ Ⓒ Ⓓ Ⓔ	25 Ⓐ Ⓑ Ⓒ Ⓓ Ⓔ	34 Ⓐ Ⓑ Ⓒ Ⓓ Ⓔ
8 Ⓐ Ⓑ Ⓒ Ⓓ Ⓔ	17 Ⓐ Ⓑ Ⓒ Ⓓ Ⓔ	26 Ⓐ Ⓑ Ⓒ Ⓓ Ⓔ	35 Ⓐ Ⓑ Ⓒ Ⓓ Ⓔ
9 Ⓐ Ⓑ Ⓒ Ⓓ Ⓔ	18 Ⓐ Ⓑ Ⓒ Ⓓ Ⓔ	27 Ⓐ Ⓑ Ⓒ Ⓓ Ⓔ	36 Ⓐ Ⓑ Ⓒ Ⓓ Ⓔ

Section 5/6

1 Ⓐ Ⓑ Ⓒ Ⓓ Ⓔ	10 Ⓐ Ⓑ Ⓒ Ⓓ Ⓔ	19 Ⓐ Ⓑ Ⓒ Ⓓ Ⓔ	28 Ⓐ Ⓑ Ⓒ Ⓓ Ⓔ
2 Ⓐ Ⓑ Ⓒ Ⓓ Ⓔ	11 Ⓐ Ⓑ Ⓒ Ⓓ Ⓔ	20 Ⓐ Ⓑ Ⓒ Ⓓ Ⓔ	29 Ⓐ Ⓑ Ⓒ Ⓓ Ⓔ
3 Ⓐ Ⓑ Ⓒ Ⓓ Ⓔ	12 Ⓐ Ⓑ Ⓒ Ⓓ Ⓔ	21 Ⓐ Ⓑ Ⓒ Ⓓ Ⓔ	30 Ⓐ Ⓑ Ⓒ Ⓓ Ⓔ
4 Ⓐ Ⓑ Ⓒ Ⓓ Ⓔ	13 Ⓐ Ⓑ Ⓒ Ⓓ Ⓔ	22 Ⓐ Ⓑ Ⓒ Ⓓ Ⓔ	31 Ⓐ Ⓑ Ⓒ Ⓓ Ⓔ
5 Ⓐ Ⓑ Ⓒ Ⓓ Ⓔ	14 Ⓐ Ⓑ Ⓒ Ⓓ Ⓔ	23 Ⓐ Ⓑ Ⓒ Ⓓ Ⓔ	32 Ⓐ Ⓑ Ⓒ Ⓓ Ⓔ
6 Ⓐ Ⓑ Ⓒ Ⓓ Ⓔ	15 Ⓐ Ⓑ Ⓒ Ⓓ Ⓔ	24 Ⓐ Ⓑ Ⓒ Ⓓ Ⓔ	33 Ⓐ Ⓑ Ⓒ Ⓓ Ⓔ
7 Ⓐ Ⓑ Ⓒ Ⓓ Ⓔ	16 Ⓐ Ⓑ Ⓒ Ⓓ Ⓔ	25 Ⓐ Ⓑ Ⓒ Ⓓ Ⓔ	34 Ⓐ Ⓑ Ⓒ Ⓓ Ⓔ
8 Ⓐ Ⓑ Ⓒ Ⓓ Ⓔ	17 Ⓐ Ⓑ Ⓒ Ⓓ Ⓔ	26 Ⓐ Ⓑ Ⓒ Ⓓ Ⓔ	35 Ⓐ Ⓑ Ⓒ Ⓓ Ⓔ
9 Ⓐ Ⓑ Ⓒ Ⓓ Ⓔ	18 Ⓐ Ⓑ Ⓒ Ⓓ Ⓔ	27 Ⓐ Ⓑ Ⓒ Ⓓ Ⓔ	36 Ⓐ Ⓑ Ⓒ Ⓓ Ⓔ

Section 6/7

1 Ⓐ Ⓑ Ⓒ Ⓓ Ⓔ	10 Ⓐ Ⓑ Ⓒ Ⓓ Ⓔ	19 Ⓐ Ⓑ Ⓒ Ⓓ Ⓔ	28 Ⓐ Ⓑ Ⓒ Ⓓ Ⓔ
2 Ⓐ Ⓑ Ⓒ Ⓓ Ⓔ	11 Ⓐ Ⓑ Ⓒ Ⓓ Ⓔ	20 Ⓐ Ⓑ Ⓒ Ⓓ Ⓔ	29 Ⓐ Ⓑ Ⓒ Ⓓ Ⓔ
3 Ⓐ Ⓑ Ⓒ Ⓓ Ⓔ	12 Ⓐ Ⓑ Ⓒ Ⓓ Ⓔ	21 Ⓐ Ⓑ Ⓒ Ⓓ Ⓔ	30 Ⓐ Ⓑ Ⓒ Ⓓ Ⓔ
4 Ⓐ Ⓑ Ⓒ Ⓓ Ⓔ	13 Ⓐ Ⓑ Ⓒ Ⓓ Ⓔ	22 Ⓐ Ⓑ Ⓒ Ⓓ Ⓔ	31 Ⓐ Ⓑ Ⓒ Ⓓ Ⓔ
5 Ⓐ Ⓑ Ⓒ Ⓓ Ⓔ	14 Ⓐ Ⓑ Ⓒ Ⓓ Ⓔ	23 Ⓐ Ⓑ Ⓒ Ⓓ Ⓔ	32 Ⓐ Ⓑ Ⓒ Ⓓ Ⓔ
6 Ⓐ Ⓑ Ⓒ Ⓓ Ⓔ	15 Ⓐ Ⓑ Ⓒ Ⓓ Ⓔ	24 Ⓐ Ⓑ Ⓒ Ⓓ Ⓔ	33 Ⓐ Ⓑ Ⓒ Ⓓ Ⓔ
7 Ⓐ Ⓑ Ⓒ Ⓓ Ⓔ	16 Ⓐ Ⓑ Ⓒ Ⓓ Ⓔ	25 Ⓐ Ⓑ Ⓒ Ⓓ Ⓔ	34 Ⓐ Ⓑ Ⓒ Ⓓ Ⓔ
8 Ⓐ Ⓑ Ⓒ Ⓓ Ⓔ	17 Ⓐ Ⓑ Ⓒ Ⓓ Ⓔ	26 Ⓐ Ⓑ Ⓒ Ⓓ Ⓔ	35 Ⓐ Ⓑ Ⓒ Ⓓ Ⓔ
9 Ⓐ Ⓑ Ⓒ Ⓓ Ⓔ	18 Ⓐ Ⓑ Ⓒ Ⓓ Ⓔ	27 Ⓐ Ⓑ Ⓒ Ⓓ Ⓔ	36 Ⓐ Ⓑ Ⓒ Ⓓ Ⓔ

Section 7/8

1 Ⓐ Ⓑ Ⓒ Ⓓ Ⓔ	6 Ⓐ Ⓑ Ⓒ Ⓓ Ⓔ	11 Ⓐ Ⓑ Ⓒ Ⓓ Ⓔ	16 Ⓐ Ⓑ Ⓒ Ⓓ Ⓔ
2 Ⓐ Ⓑ Ⓒ Ⓓ Ⓔ	7 Ⓐ Ⓑ Ⓒ Ⓓ Ⓔ	12 Ⓐ Ⓑ Ⓒ Ⓓ Ⓔ	17 Ⓐ Ⓑ Ⓒ Ⓓ Ⓔ
3 Ⓐ Ⓑ Ⓒ Ⓓ Ⓔ	8 Ⓐ Ⓑ Ⓒ Ⓓ Ⓔ	13 Ⓐ Ⓑ Ⓒ Ⓓ Ⓔ	18 Ⓐ Ⓑ Ⓒ Ⓓ Ⓔ
4 Ⓐ Ⓑ Ⓒ Ⓓ Ⓔ	9 Ⓐ Ⓑ Ⓒ Ⓓ Ⓔ	14 Ⓐ Ⓑ Ⓒ Ⓓ Ⓔ	19 Ⓐ Ⓑ Ⓒ Ⓓ Ⓔ
5 Ⓐ Ⓑ Ⓒ Ⓓ Ⓔ	10 Ⓐ Ⓑ Ⓒ Ⓓ Ⓔ	15 Ⓐ Ⓑ Ⓒ Ⓓ Ⓔ	20 Ⓐ Ⓑ Ⓒ Ⓓ Ⓔ

Section 8/9

1 Ⓐ Ⓑ Ⓒ Ⓓ Ⓔ	6 Ⓐ Ⓑ Ⓒ Ⓓ Ⓔ	11 Ⓐ Ⓑ Ⓒ Ⓓ Ⓔ	16 Ⓐ Ⓑ Ⓒ Ⓓ Ⓔ
2 Ⓐ Ⓑ Ⓒ Ⓓ Ⓔ	7 Ⓐ Ⓑ Ⓒ Ⓓ Ⓔ	12 Ⓐ Ⓑ Ⓒ Ⓓ Ⓔ	17 Ⓐ Ⓑ Ⓒ Ⓓ Ⓔ
3 Ⓐ Ⓑ Ⓒ Ⓓ Ⓔ	8 Ⓐ Ⓑ Ⓒ Ⓓ Ⓔ	13 Ⓐ Ⓑ Ⓒ Ⓓ Ⓔ	18 Ⓐ Ⓑ Ⓒ Ⓓ Ⓔ
4 Ⓐ Ⓑ Ⓒ Ⓓ Ⓔ	9 Ⓐ Ⓑ Ⓒ Ⓓ Ⓔ	14 Ⓐ Ⓑ Ⓒ Ⓓ Ⓔ	19 Ⓐ Ⓑ Ⓒ Ⓓ Ⓔ
5 Ⓐ Ⓑ Ⓒ Ⓓ Ⓔ	10 Ⓐ Ⓑ Ⓒ Ⓓ Ⓔ	15 Ⓐ Ⓑ Ⓒ Ⓓ Ⓔ	20 Ⓐ Ⓑ Ⓒ Ⓓ Ⓔ

Section 10

1 Ⓐ Ⓑ Ⓒ Ⓓ Ⓔ	6 Ⓐ Ⓑ Ⓒ Ⓓ Ⓔ	11 Ⓐ Ⓑ Ⓒ Ⓓ Ⓔ	16 Ⓐ Ⓑ Ⓒ Ⓓ Ⓔ
2 Ⓐ Ⓑ Ⓒ Ⓓ Ⓔ	7 Ⓐ Ⓑ Ⓒ Ⓓ Ⓔ	12 Ⓐ Ⓑ Ⓒ Ⓓ Ⓔ	17 Ⓐ Ⓑ Ⓒ Ⓓ Ⓔ
3 Ⓐ Ⓑ Ⓒ Ⓓ Ⓔ	8 Ⓐ Ⓑ Ⓒ Ⓓ Ⓔ	13 Ⓐ Ⓑ Ⓒ Ⓓ Ⓔ	18 Ⓐ Ⓑ Ⓒ Ⓓ Ⓔ
4 Ⓐ Ⓑ Ⓒ Ⓓ Ⓔ	9 Ⓐ Ⓑ Ⓒ Ⓓ Ⓔ	14 Ⓐ Ⓑ Ⓒ Ⓓ Ⓔ	19 Ⓐ Ⓑ Ⓒ Ⓓ Ⓔ
5 Ⓐ Ⓑ Ⓒ Ⓓ Ⓔ	10 Ⓐ Ⓑ Ⓒ Ⓓ Ⓔ	15 Ⓐ Ⓑ Ⓒ Ⓓ Ⓔ	20 Ⓐ Ⓑ Ⓒ Ⓓ Ⓔ

Student-Produced Responses

Only answers entered in the circles in each grid will be scored. You will not receive credit for anything written in the boxes above the circles.

Appendix D:
Progress Reports

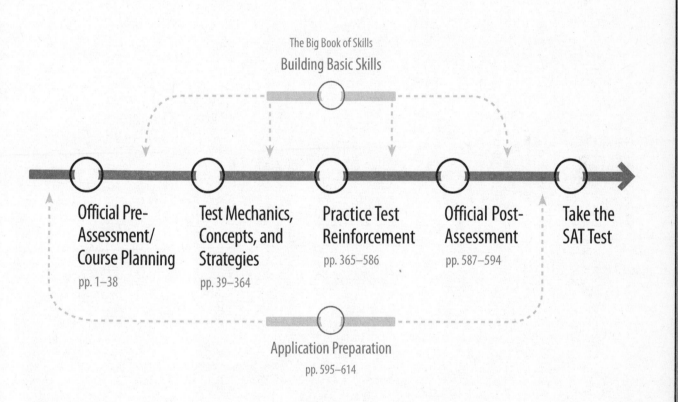

The Big Book of Skills
Building Basic Skills

Official Pre-Assessment/ Course Planning
pp. 1–38

Test Mechanics, Concepts, and Strategies
pp. 39–364

Practice Test Reinforcement
pp. 365–586

Official Post-Assessment
pp. 587–594

Take the SAT Test

Application Preparation
pp. 595–614

TEST MECHANICS, CONCEPTS, AND STRATEGIES

The progress reports on the following pages are designed to help you monitor your progress on the "Lesson," "Review," and "Quizzes" sections in each lesson of the "Test Mechanics, Concepts, and Strategies" part of this book. Complete the assigned items by the due date given by your instructor. Check your answers using the answer keys in Appendix B of this book*, and record both the number and percentage of items answered correctly on the *student copies* of the progress reports. Identify the date on which you completed each section. List the numbers of any items that you would like your instructor to review in class. Then, transfer this information to the corresponding *instructor copies* of the reports and give them to your instructor. Be sure to leave the last three columns of the *instructor copies* blank; these are for your instructor's use in evaluating your progress.

*Consult with your instructor to determine whether you will use Appendix B to complete the Test Mechanics, Concepts, and Strategies Progress Reports.

Test Mechanics, Concepts, and Strategies
(Student Copy)

Exercise	Total # of Items			% of Items Correct	Date Completed	Item #s to Review
	Possible	Assigned	Correct			
CRITICAL READING: PASSAGES						
Lesson (p. 53)	112					
Quiz I (p. 75)	18					
Quiz II (p. 82)	17					
Quiz III (p. 88)	18					
Quiz IV (p. 94)	29					
Review (p. 103)	60					
CRITICAL READING: SENTENCE COMPLETIONS						
Lesson (p. 135)	97					
Quiz I (p. 147)	16					
Quiz II (p. 149)	16					
Quiz III (p. 151)	16					
Quiz IV (p. 153)	16					
Review (p. 157)	57					
MATH: MULTIPLE-CHOICE						
Lesson (p. 183)	231					
Quiz I (p. 227)	16					
Quiz II (p. 231)	20					
Quiz III (p. 235)	20					
Quiz IV (p. 240)	15					
Review (p. 243)	29					

Exercise	Total # of Items			% of Items Correct	Date Completed	Item #s to Review
	Possible	Assigned	Correct			
MATH: STUDENT-PRODUCED RESPONSES						
Lesson (p. 267)	32					
Quiz I (p. 275)	10					
Quiz II (p. 278)	10					
Quiz III (p. 282)	10					
Quiz IV (p. 285)	5					
Review (p. 287)	13					
WRITING						
Lesson (Multiple-Choice) (p. 315)	120					
Lesson (Essay) (p. 332)	1		N/A	N/A		
Quiz I (Multiple-Choice) (p. 333)	16					
Quiz II (Multiple-Choice) (p. 337)	16					
Quiz III (Multiple-Choice) (p. 341)	16					
Quiz IV (Multiple-Choice) (p. 344)	16		N/A	N/A		
Quiz V (Essay) (p. 348)	1					
Review (Multiple-Choice) (p. 351)	37					
Review (Essay) (p. 358)	1		N/A	N/A		

Test Mechanics, Concepts, and Strategies
(Instructor Copy)

Name _____

Student ID Number _____

Date _____

Instructor _____

Course/Session Number _____

Exercise	Total # of Items			% of Items Correct	Date Completed	Item #s to Review	Instructor Skill Evaluation (Check One Per Section)		
	Possible	Assigned	Correct				Mastered	Partially Mastered	Not Mastered
CRITICAL READING: PASSAGES									
Lesson (p. 53)	112								
Quiz I (p. 75)	18								
Quiz II (p. 82)	17								
Quiz III (p. 88)	18								
Quiz IV (p. 94)	29								
Review (p. 103)	60								
CRITICAL READING: SENTENCE COMPLETIONS									
Lesson (p. 135)	97								
Quiz I (p. 147)	16								
Quiz II (p. 149)	16								
Quiz III (p. 151)	16								
Quiz IV (p. 153)	16								
Review (p. 157)	57								
MATH: MULTIPLE-CHOICE									
Lesson (p. 183)	231								
Quiz I (p. 227)	16								
Quiz II (p. 231)	20								
Quiz III (p. 235)	20								
Quiz IV (p. 240)	15								
Review (p. 243)	29								

Exercise	Total # of Items			% of Items Correct	Date Completed	Item #s to Review	Instructor Skill Evaluation (Check One Per Section)		
	Possible	Assigned	Correct				Mastered	Partially Mastered	Not Mastered
MATH: STUDENT-PRODUCED RESPONSES									
Lesson (p. 267)	32								
Quiz I (p. 275)	10								
Quiz II (p. 278)	10								
Quiz III (p. 282)	10								
Quiz IV (p. 285)	5								
Review (p. 287)	13								
WRITING									
Lesson (Multiple-Choice) (p. 315)	120								
Lesson (Essay) (p. 332)	1		N/A	N/A		N/A			
Quiz I (Multiple-Choice) (p. 333)	16								
Quiz II (Multiple-Choice) (p. 337)	16								
Quiz III (Multiple-Choice) (p. 341)	16								
Quiz IV (Multiple-Choice) (p. 344)	16								
Quiz V (Essay) (p. 348)	1								
Review (Multiple-Choice) (p. 351)	37								
Review (Essay) (p. 358)	1		N/A	N/A		N/A			

PRACTICE TEST REINFORCEMENT

The progress reports on the following pages are designed to help you monitor your progress on the multiple-choice portions of the practice tests in the "Practice Test Reinforcement" part of this book. Complete the assigned items by the due date given by your instructor. The Self-Guided Practice Test should be done *without* time restrictions; the explanations are included in the presentation of the exam. Timed Practice Tests I–III should be done *with* time restrictions. Correct your answers using the answers and explanations in Appendix B of this book*, and record both the number and percentage of items answered correctly on the *student copies* of the progress reports. Identify the date on which you completed each test. List the numbers of any items that you would like your instructor to review in class. Then, transfer this information to the corresponding *instructor copies* of the reports and give them to your instructor. Be sure to leave the last three columns of the *instructor copies* blank; these are for your instructor's use in evaluating your progress. (**NOTE:** In the first column of each report, the numbering refers to the test sections and the page numbers refer to the locations of those sections in the "Practice Test Reinforcement" part of this book.)

*Consult with your instructor to determine whether you will use Appendix B to complete the Practice Test Reinforcement Progress Reports.

Practice Test Reinforcement

(Student Copy)

Exercise	Total # of Items			% of Items Correct	Date Completed	Item #s to Review
	Possible	Assigned	Correct			
PRACTICE TEST I						
1. Writing—Essay (p. 457)	1		N/A	N/A		
2. Critical Reading (p. 458)	24					
3. Math (p. 466)	20					
5. Critical Reading (p. 470)	24					
6. Math (p. 476)	18					
7. Writing (p. 480)	35					
8. Critical Reading (p. 486)	19					
9. Math (p. 492)	16					
10. Writing (p. 496)	14					
PRACTICE TEST II						
1. Writing—Essay (p. 501)	1		N/A	N/A		
2. Math (p. 502)	20					
3. Critical Reading (p. 506)	24					
4. Math (p. 514)	18					
6. Writing (p. 518)	35					
7. Critical Reading (p. 524)	24					
8. Math (p. 530)	16					
9. Critical Reading (p. 534)	19					
10. Writing (p. 540)	14					

Exercise	Total # of Items			% of Items Correct	Date Completed	Item #s to Review
	Possible	Assigned	Correct			
PRACTICE TEST III						
1. Writing—Essay (p. 545)	1		N/A	N/A		
2. Critical Reading (p. 546)	24					
3. Math (p. 554)	18					
4. Writing (p. 558)	35					
5. Critical Reading (p. 564)	24					
7. Math (p. 570)	20					
8. Critical Reading (p. 574)	19					
9. Math (p. 580)	16					
10. Writing (p. 584)	14					

Practice Test Reinforcement
(Instructor Copy)

Name _____   Student ID Number _____

Date _____   Instructor _____   Course/Session Number _____

Exercise	Total # of Items			% of Items Correct	Date Completed	Item #s to Review	Instructor Skill Evaluation (Check One Per Section)		
	Possible	Assigned	Correct				Mastered	Partially Mastered	Not Mastered
PRACTICE TEST I									
1. Writing—Essay (p. 457)	1		N/A	N/A		N/A			
2. Critical Reading (p. 458)	24								
3. Math (p. 466)	20								
5. Critical Reading (p. 470)	24								
6. Math (p. 476)	18								
7. Writing (p. 480)	35								
8. Critical Reading (p. 486)	19								
9. Math (p. 492)	16								
10. Writing (p. 496)	14								
PRACTICE TEST II									
1. Writing—Essay (p. 501)	1		N/A	N/A		N/A			
2. Math (p. 502)	20								
3. Critical Reading (p. 506)	24								
4. Math (p. 514)	18								
6. Writing (p. 518)	35								
7. Critical Reading (p. 524)	24								
8. Math (p. 530)	16								
9. Critical Reading (p. 534)	19								
10. Writing (p. 540)	14								

Exercise	Total # of Items			% of Items Correct	Date Completed	Item #s to Review	Instructor Skill Evaluation (Check One Per Section)		
	Possible	Assigned	Correct				Mastered	Partially Mastered	Not Mastered
PRACTICE TEST III									
1. Writing—Essay (p. 545)	1		N/A	N/A		N/A			
2. Critical Reading (p. 546)	24								
3. Math (p. 554)	18								
4. Writing (p. 558)	35								
5. Critical Reading (p. 564)	24								
7. Math (p. 570)	20								
8. Critical Reading (p. 574)	19								
9. Math (p. 580)	16								
10. Writing (p. 584)	14								

ITEM INDEX

In the following index, all of the numeric references are designed as follows: **Page #**/Item #. The parenthetical information beside each item category refers to the subject–area in which that item category appears.

30°-60°-90° Triangles (Math: Multiple-Choice and Student-Produced Responses)

Lesson (MC): **214**/183–184; **215**/189; **216**/196; **219**/207; **220**/210
Quiz I (MC): **229**/12
Quiz IV (MC): **241**/8
Practice Test 1, Section 9 (MC): **494**/13

45°-45°-90° Triangles (Math: Multiple-Choice and Student-Produced Responses)

Lesson (MC): **214**/181–182, 185; **216**/196; **219**/206, 208–209

Absolute Value (Math: Multiple-Choice and Student-Produced Responses)

Lesson (MC): **192**/55–57

Adjectives and Adverbs (Writing)

Lesson: **318**/25–30
Quiz IV: **345**/7
Review: **352**/8
Directed–Study Practice Test, Section 3: **386**/12
Practice Test 1, Section 7: **482**/15
Practice Test I, Section 10: **496**/1
Practice Test II, Section 6: **519**/8; **520**/16

Algebra (Math: Multiple-Choice and Student-Produced Responses)

Lesson (MC): **183–184**/2–6; **190**/41; **195–205**/82–150; **217**/200
Lesson (SPR): **268**/1; **269**/9; **270**/10; **271**/17–20
Quiz I (MC): **228**/4; **229**/10; **230**/13, 15–16
Quiz I (SPR): **276**/3; **277**/10
Quiz II (MC): **231**/3; **232**/6, 8, 10; **233**/15–16
Quiz II (SPR): **279**/2
Quiz III (MC): **236**/8, 11; **237**/13
Quiz III (SPR): **283**/1; **283**/3–4, 6
Quiz IV (MC): 240/1; **241**/3–4; **241**/6; **242**/11, 14
Quiz IV (SPR): **286**/1, 4–5
Review (MC): **246**/14; **246**/17; **247**/23; **248**/26
Review (SPR): **288**/4; **290–291**/12–13

Directed–Study Practice Test, Section 2 (MC): **372**/1–3; **375**/8
Directed–Study Practice Test, Section 2 (SPR): **377**/12
Directed–Study Practice Test, Section 5 (MC): **408**/2–3; **410**/8; **411**/10; **412**/12; **414**/17; **415**/20
Directed–Study Practice Test, Section 8 (MC): **430**/3–4; **431**/6; **432**/8–9; **434**/14–16
Practice Test 1, Section 3 (MC): **466**/1; **467**/6, 8; **469**/17, 20
Practice Test I, Section 6 (MC): **477**/4; **477**/6–7
Practice Test 1, Section 6 (SPR): **478**/9; **478–479**/12–13
Practice Test I, Section 9 (MC): **493**/4–5; **495**/14–15
Practice Test II, Section 2 (MC): **502**/1; **503**/3–4; **503**/7–8; **504**/10, 14–15; **505**/19
Practice Test II, Section 4 (MC): **514**/2; **515**/4; **515**/6
Practice Test II, Section 4 (SPR): **516**/9; **516**/12; **517**/17
Practice Test II, Section 8 (MC): **530**/3; **532**/12; **533**/14
Practice Test III, Section 3 (MC): **554**/1–2; **555**/4
Practice Test III, Section 3 (SPR): **556**/9
Practice Test III, Section 7 (MC): **570–571**/3–5; **572**/15–16; **572**/18–19
Practice Test III, Section 9 (MC): **581**/6, 8; **582**/15–16

Ambiguity in Scope (Writing)

Lesson: **324**/79
Quiz IV: **346**/8

Application (Critical Reading: Passages)

Lesson: **56**/12–13; **57**/21; **58**/28; **59**/34; **60**/40; **63**/54; **64**/59; **67**/75; **70**/90; **71**/95; **72**/100
Quiz I: **78**/8; **80**/16; **81**/18
Quiz II: **85**/10; **87**/16–17
Quiz III: **92**/12;
Quiz IV: **98**/17; **102**/29
Review: **104**/5; **106**/13; **108**/20; **111**/32; **112**/37; **114**/42; **116**/52; **118**/58
Directed–Study Practice Test, Section 4: **404**/17; **406**/20
Directed–Study Practice Test, Section 6: **422**/13; **426**/21
Directed–Study Practice Test, Section 9: **446**/19
Practice Test 1, Section 2: **459**/9
Practice Test I, Section 8: **488**/7; **489**/14; **490**/17–19
Practice Test II, Section 3: **511**/20
Practice Test II, Section 7: **525**/10; **529**/24

Practice Test II, Section 9: **539**/19
Practice Test III, Section 2: **551**/20
Practice Test III, Section 5: **567**/13
Practice Test III, Section 8: **578**/18–19

Approximation (Math: Multiple-Choice and Student-Produced Responses)

Lesson (MC): **189**/35–36

Arithmetic (Math: Multiple-Choice and Student-Produced Responses)

Lesson (MC): **183**/1; **186–187**/16–25; **188–195**/30–81; **205**/149–150; **217**/201
Lesson (SPR): **268–269**/3–7; **270**/14; **271**/15; **273**/25, 28; **274**/29–30
Quiz I (MC): **227**/2; **228**/5; **229**/7–8; **230**/14
Quiz I (SPR): **276**/1–2; **277**/6, 8
Quiz II (MC): **231**/4; **232**/11; **233**/14
Quiz II (SPR): **279–280**/3–5; **280**/7; **281**/9
Quiz III (MC): **235**/2; **235**/4; **236**/5, 10; **237**/15; **238**/16
Quiz III (SPR): **284**/9–10
Quiz IV (MC): **240**/1–2; **241**/5; **242**/10, 12
Quiz IV (SPR): **285**/2
Review (MC): **244**/3, 5; **245**/9–10, 12–13; **247**/20–22, 24–25; **248**/27–28
Review (SPR): **288**/1–2; **290**/9
Directed–Study Practice Test, Section 2 (MC): **373**/4; **374**/5, 7
Directed–Study Practice Test, Section 2 (SPR): **376**/9–10; **380–381**/16–18
Directed–Study Practice Test, Section 5 (MC): **408**/1; **409**/5; **410**/6; **411**/10; **412**/11, 13; **413**/15; **414**/16
Directed–Study Practice Test, Section 8 (MC): **429**/1; **430**/2; **433**/11; **434**/13
Practice Test 1, Section 3 (MC): **467**/3, 5, 7; **468**/10–11, 14; **469**/15–16
Practice Test I, Section 6 (MC): **476**/1; **477**/4–5
Practice Test 1, Section 6 (SPR): **478**/10–11; **479**/14–15, 17–18
Practice Test I, Section 9 (MC): **492**/1–3; **494**/9–11; **495**/16
Practice Test II, Section 2 (MC): **503**/5; **504**/9; **505**/20
Practice Test II, Section 4 (MC): **515**/5, 7–8
Practice Test II, Section 4 (SPR): **516**/10–11; **517**/15–16
Practice Test II, Section 8 (MC): **530**/2; **531**/4, 6; **532**/8–9; **533**/16
Practice Test III, Section 3 (MC): **554**/3; **555**/6–8
Practice Test III, Section 3 (SPR): **556**/10–11; **557**/14, 16–17
Practice Test III, Section 7 (MC): **570**/1–2; **571**/6, 8, 11; **572**/14; **573**/20
Practice Test III, Section 9 (MC): **580**/1; **581**/3

Arithmetic Probability (Math: Multiple-Choice and Student-Produced Responses)

Lesson (MC): **224–225**/227–229
Quiz III (MC): **238**/18
Quiz III (SPR): **283**/2

Averages (Math: Multiple-Choice and Student-Produced Responses)

Lesson (MC): **185**/11; **223–224**/220–224
Lesson (SPR): **269**/8; **273**/27
Quiz I (MC): **229**/9
Quiz I (SPR): **277**/7
Quiz II (MC): **232**/9
Quiz III (MC): **235**/1; **236**/6
Quiz IV (MC): **242**/11
Review (MC): **244**/7
Directed–Study Practice Test, Section 2 (SPR): **379**/14
Directed–Study Practice Test, Section 8 (MC): **433**/10
Practice Test 1, Section 3 (MC): **468**/12
Practice Test I, Section 6 (MC): **477**/3, 6
Practice Test II, Section 2 (MC): **504**/12; **505**/18
Practice Test II, Section 4 (MC): **514**/1
Practice Test II, Section 8 (MC): **532**/11
Practice Test III, Section 3 (SPR): **557**/15
Practice Test III, Section 7 (MC): **571**/10
Practice Test III, Section 9 (MC): **582**/14

Bar, Cumulative, and Line Graphs (Math: Multiple-Choice and Student-Produced Responses)

Lesson (MC): **220–222**/211–215
Quiz II (MC): **234**/20
Practice Test 1, Section 9 (MC): **494**/9
Practice Test II, Section 8 (MC): **532**/11

Basic Algebraic Manipulations (Math: Multiple-Choice and Student-Produced Responses)

Lesson (MC): **195**/82–83
Lesson (SPR): **268**/1
Directed–Study Practice Test, Section 5 (MC): **410**/8
Directed–Study Practice Test, Section 8 (MC): **431**/4, 6; **432**/9
Practice Test 1, Section 3 (MC): **467**/6
Practice Test II, Section 8 (MC): **530**/3
Practice Test III, Section 7 (MC): **572**/15

Circles (Math: Multiple-Choice and Student-Produced Responses)

Lesson (MC): **184**/8; **185**/9; **188**/26; **215**/188; **216**/191–194; **217**/197
Quiz II (MC): **233**/12
Quiz III (MC): **236**/9; **237**/14; **239**/20
Quiz IV (MC): **242**/9, 13
Review (MC): **244**/8
Review (SPR): **288**/3; **289**/5, 7; **290**/10
Directed–Study Practice Test, Section 5 (MC): **413**/14
Practice Test 1, Section 6 (MC): **477**/5
Practice Test 1, Section 9 (MC): **493**/7
Practice Test II, Section 8 (MC): **531**/5
Practice Test III, Section 3 (MC): **555**/5
Practice Test III, Section 3 (SPR): **557**/18

Clarity of Expression (Writing)

Lesson: **323**/73–80
Quiz I: **333**/6–8
Quiz II: **337**/1; 337/4
Quiz III: **341**/3; **341**/7; **342**/9
Quiz IV: **345**/4; **346**/8–10; **347**/16
Review: 352/6; **353**/17–19; **354**/22; **355**/31; **356**/33
Directed–Study Practice Test, Section 3: **386**/11; **388**/17; **389**/20; **390**/22
Directed–Study Practice Test, Section 10: **448**/3; **449**/5
Practice Test I, Section 7: **480**/2; **481**/8; **482**/11
Practice Test I, Section 10: **497**/5; **498**/13
Practice Test II, Section 6: **518**/1; **519**/4; **519**/6; **520**/15; **521**/23
Practice Test II, Section 10: **540**/1; **541**/6; 542/10
Practice Test III, Section 4: **558**/3; **560**/14; **561**/19–20; **561**/22
Practice Test III, Section 10: **584**/1; **585**/5; **585**/9; **586**/13

Colons (Writing)

Lesson: **327**/102–103

Combined Reasoning (Critical Reading: Sentence Completions)

Lesson: **135**/3; **143**/83–92; **145**/95, 97
Quiz I: **147**/2, 4; **148**/8, 14
Quiz II: **149**/2; **150**/13–14
Quiz III: **151**/7; **152**/16
Quiz IV: **153**/1; **154**/7
Review: 158/7–9; **160**/33; **161**/44; **162**/46–48, 50–53; **163**/55–57
Directed–Study Practice Test, Section 4: **398–399**/3–6
Directed–Study Practice Test, Section 6: **416**/1; **417**/2, 4; **418**/5, 7; **419**/8
Directed–Study Practice Test, Section 9: **436**/1; **437**/5

Practice Test 1, Section 2: **458**/2, 4; **459**/5, 7
Practice Test I, Section 5: **470**/3; **471**/6, 8
Practice Test I, Section 8: **486**/1–2, 4
Practice Test II, Section 3: **506**/4; **507**/6–7
Practice Test II, Section 7: **524**/1–2, 5; **525**/6
Practice Test II, Section 9: **534**/3
Practice Test III, Section 2: **546**/2
Practice Test III, Section 5: **564**/5; **565**/7–8
Practice Test III, Section 8: **574**/4; **575**/5

Commas (Writing)

Lesson: **324–326**/81–97

Common Arithmetic Items (Math: Multiple-Choice and Student-Produced Responses)

Lesson (MC): **186**/16–18; **187**/19, 22, 24; **188**/27–28; **190–194**/42–73; **195**/81; **205**/149; **217**/201
Lesson (SPR): **269**/6–7; **270**/14; **271**/15; **273**/28; **274**/29
Quiz I (MC): **228**/5; **229**/7; **230**/14
Quiz I (SPR): **276**/1–2; **277**/8
Quiz II (MC): **233**/14
Quiz II (SPR): **279–280**/3–5; **281**/9
Quiz III (MC): **235**/2, 4; **236**/10; **237**/15; **238**/16
Quiz III (SPR): **284**/10
Quiz IV (MC): **240**/2; **242**/10, 12
Quiz IV (SPR): **285**/2
Review (MC): 244/3, 5; **245**/9–10, 12–13; **247**/20, 24–25; **248**/27–28
Review (SPR): **290**/9
Directed-Study Practice Test, Section 2 (MC): **373**/4; **374**/5, 7
Directed-Study Practice Test, Section 2 (SPR): **376**/10; **380**/17; **381**/18
Directed-Study Practice Test, Section 5 (MC): **409**/5; **410**/6; **411**/10; **412**/13
Directed-Study Practice Test, Section 8 (MC): **429**/1; **433**/11; **434**/13
Practice Test 1, Section 3 (MC): **467**/7; **468**/10–11, 14; **469**/15
Practice Test I, Section 6 (MC): **476**/1; **477**/4–5
Practice Test 1, Section 6 (SPR): **478**/10–11; **479**/14, 17
Practice Test I, Section 9 (MC): **492–493**/1–3; **494**/9; **495**/16
Practice Test II, Section 2 (MC): **503**/5; **504**/9
Practice Test II, Section 4 (MC): **515**/5
Practice Test II, Section 4 (SPR): **516**/10–11; **517**/15
Practice Test II, Section 8 (MC): **530**/2; **531**/6; **532**/8–9; **533**/16
Practice Test III, Section 3 (MC): **554**/3; **555**/6, 8
Practice Test III, Section 3 (SPR): **556**/11; **557**/16–17
Practice Test III, Section 7 (MC): **571**/6, 11; **572**/14; **573**/20
Practice Test III, Section 9 (MC): **580**/1; **581**/3

Complex Figures (Math: Multiple-Choice and Student-Produced Responses)

Lesson (MC): **185**/9; **216–217**/193–198; **218**/205; **219**/206, 209; **220**/210
Lesson (SPR): **268**/2; **270**/13; **272**/23–24; **273**/26
Quiz I (MC): **229**/11
Quiz II (MC): **233**/12
Quiz III (MC): **237**/14; **238**/17; **239**/20
Quiz IV (MC): **241**/8
Review (MC): **245**/11; **246**/15, 18
Review (SPR): **288**/3; **289**/7; **290**/10
Directed-Study Practice Test, Section 2 (MC): **374**/6
Directed-Study Practice Test, Section 5 (MC): **413**/14
Practice Test 1, Section 3 (MC): **467**/9
Practice Test I, Section 9 (MC): **493**/7
Practice Test II, Section 4 (SPR*):* **517**/13
Practice Test II, Section 8 (MC): **531**/5
Practice Test III, Section 3 (MC): **555**/5
Practice Test III, Section 3 (SPR): **557**/18
Practice Test III, Section 9 (MC): **581**/4

Complicated Arithmetic Application Items (Math: Multiple-Choice and Student-Produced Responses)

Lesson (MC): **183**/1; **187**/20, 23, 25; **188**/29; **190**/39–41; **195**/80; **205**/150
Lesson (SPR): **268**/3; **273**/25; **274**/30
Quiz I (MC): **227**/2; **229**/8
Quiz II (MC): **231**/4
Quiz II (SPR): **280**/7
Quiz III (MC): **236**/5
Quiz IV (MC): **240**/1*Review (MC):* **247**/21–22
Review (SPR): **288**/1–2
Directed-Study Practice Test, Section 2 (SPR): **380**/16
Directed-Study Practice Test, Section 5 (MC): **413**/15
Practice Test 1, Section 3 (MC): **467**/3, 5
Practice Test 1, Section 6 (SPR): **479**/15, 18
Practice Test I, Section 9 (MC): **494**/11
Practice Test II, Section 2 (MC): **505**/20
Practice Test II, Section 4 (MC): **515**/7–8
Practice Test II, Section 8 (MC): **531**/4
Practice Test III, Section 3 (SPR): **556**/10; **557**/14
Practice Test III, Section 7 (MC): **570**/2

Complicated Manipulations (Math: Multiple-Choice and Student-Produced Responses)

Lesson (MC): **189**/32–38
Lesson (SPR): **269**/4–5
Quiz II (MC): **232**/11
Directed Study Practice Test, Section 5 (MC): **412**/11
Directed Study Practice Test, Section 8 (MC): **430**/2
Practice Test 1, Section 3 (MC): **469**/16

Practice Test I, Section 9 (MC): **494**/10
Practice Test III, Section 3 (MC): **555**/7

Concepts of Domain and Range (Math: Multiple-Choice and Student-Produced Responses)

Lesson (MC): **201–202**/126–129
Directed Study Practice Test, Section 5 (MC): **415**/20

Coordinate Conjunctions (Combined Reasoning)

Lesson: **135**/3; **144**/85; **145**/89–90, 92; **146**/97
Quiz IV: **153**/1; **154**/7
Review: **158**/7–9; **162**/47–48, 50, 53; **163**/55–57
Directed Study Practice Test, Section 4: **398**/3; **399**/5–6; **400**/9
Directed Study Practice Test, Section 6: **417**/2; **418**/4
Directed Study Practice Test, Section 9: **437**/5
Practice Test 1, Section 2: **458**/2, 4
Practice Test I, Section 5: **470**/3; **471**/6
Practice Test I, Section 8: **486**/4
Practice Test II, Section 3: **507**/7
Practice Test II, Section 7: **524**/1, 5
Practice Test III, Section 2: **546**/2
Practice Test III, Section 5: **564**/5
Practice Test III, Section 8: **574**/4–5

Coordinate Conjunctions (Thought Extension)

Lesson: **137**/18, 20–21; **138**/22, 28
Quiz I: **148**/12, 16
Quiz III: **152**/13
Review: **157**/1; **160**/35; **162**/49
Directed Study Practice Test, Section 4: **400**/9
Practice Test 1, Section 5: **471**/7
Practice Test III, Section 8: **574**/2

Coordinate Conjunctions (Thought Reversal)

Lesson: **135**/4; **136**/10; **137**/19; **138**/23–27
Quiz II: **149**/3–4
Quiz III: **151**/3
Quiz IV: **154**/13–14; **155**/16

Coordinate Geometry (Math: Multiple-Choice and Student-Produced Responses)

Lesson (MC): **184**/7; **205–212**/151–174
Lesson (SPR): **274**/31
Quiz I (SPR): **277**/5
Quiz II (MC): **232**/7; **233**/13; **234**/19
Quiz II (SPR): **281**/10
Quiz III (MC): **237**/12; **238**/19
Quiz IV (MC): **242**/13; **242**/15

Review (MC): **244**/6
Review (SPR): **289**/8
Directed-Study Practice Test, Section 2 (MC): **375**/8
Directed-Study Practice Test, Section 5 (MC): **414**/18; **415**/19
Directed-Study Practice Test, Section 8 (MC): **432**/7
Practice Test 1, Section 3 (MC): **469**/18
Practice Test I, Section 6 (MC): **476**/2
Practice Test I, Section 9 (MC): **493**/6
Practice Test II, Section 2 (MC): **505**/17
Practice Test II, Section 4 (SPR): **517**/14, 18
Practice Test II, Section 8 (MC): **531**/5, 7; **533**/15

The Coordinate System (Math: Multiple-Choice and Student-Produced Responses)

Lesson (MC): **205–206**/151–154
Quiz IV (MC): **242**/13
Review (MC): **244**/6
Directed-Study Practice Test, Section 2 (MC): **375**/8
Directed-Study Practice Test, Section 8 (MC): **432**/7
Practice Test 1, Section 6 (MC): **476**/2
Practice Test II, Section 2 (MC): **505**/17
Practice Test II, Section 4 (SPR): **517**/14
Practice Test II, Section 8 (MC): **531**/5

Creating Algebraic Expressions (Math: Multiple-Choice and Student-Produced Responses)

Lesson (MC): **184**/4; **197**/93–94; **203–205**/141–150
Quiz III (MC): **237**/13
Quiz IV (MC): **241**/3–4; **242**/11
Review (MC): **246**/14
Directed-Study Practice Test, Section 2 (MC): **375**/8
Directed-Study Practice Test, Section 8 (MC): **435**/16
Practice Test 1, Section 3 (MC): **469**/20
Practice Test I, Section 9 (MC): **495**/15
Practice Test II, Section 2 (MC): **505**/17

Dashes (Writing)

Lesson: **327**/105

Data Analysis (Math: Multiple-Choice and Student-Produced Responses)

Lesson (MC): **185**/11; **220–226**/211–231
Lesson (SPR): **269**/8; **273**/27; **274**/32
Quiz I (MC): **228**/6; **229**/9
Quiz I (SPR): **277**/7
Quiz II (MC): **232**/9; **234**/18, 20
Quiz III (MC): **235**/1; **236**/6; **238**/16, 18
Quiz III (SPR): **283**/2
Quiz IV (MC): **240**/2; **242**/11
Review (MC): **244**/7; **248**/27–29

Directed-Study Practice Test, Section 2 (SPR): **379**/14–15
Directed-Study Practice Test, Section 8 (MC): **429**/1; **433**/10
Practice Test 1, Section 3 (MC): **468**/12; **469**/19
Practice Test I, Section 6 (MC): **476**/1; **477**/3, 6
Practice Test I, Section 9 (MC): **494**/9
Practice Test II, Section 2 (MC): **504**/12; **505**/18
Practice Test II, Section 4 (MC): **514**/1
Practice Test II, Section 4 (SPR): **517**/16
Practice Test II, Section 8 (MC): **531**/6; **532**/11; **533**/13
Practice Test III, Section 3 (SPR): **557**/15
Practice Test III, Section 7 (MC): **571**/10
Practice Test III, Section 9 (MC): **581**/7; **582**/14

Data Interpretation (Math: Multiple-Choice and Student-Produced Responses)

Lesson (MC): **220–223**/211–219
Lesson (SPR): **274**/32
Quiz I (MC): **228**/6; **229**/9
Quiz II (MC): **232**/9; **234**/20
Quiz III (MC): **236**/6; **238**/16
Quiz IV (MC): **240**/2
Review (MC): **248**/27–29
Directed-Study Practice Test, Section 8 (MC): **429**/1
Practice Test 1, Section 3 (MC): **469**/19
Practice Test I, Section 6 (MC): **476**/1; **477**/3
Practice Test I, Section 9 (MC): **494**/9
Practice Test II, Section 4 (SPR): **679**/16
Practice Test II, Section 8 (MC): **531**/6; **532**/11; **533**/13

Decimal–Fraction Equivalents (Math: Multiple-Choice and Student-Produced Responses)

Lesson (MC): **189**/38;
Quiz II (MC): **232**/11

Development (Critical Reading: Passages)

Lesson: **55**/7–8; **57**/19; **58**/26; 59/32; **60**/38; **62**/50–51; **64**/62; **66**/67; **66**/71; **67**/73; **68**/78; **69**/82; **70**/89; **71**/93; **71**/96; **72**/101
Quiz II: **82**/1; **82**/3; **87**/15
Quiz III: **89**/3; **90**/5; **91**/9; **92**/15; **93**/17
Quiz IV: **97**/12; **102**/28
Review: **103**/1–2; **106**/11; **114**/44; **115**/47; **119**/60
Directed Study Practice Test, Section 4: **407**/24
Directed Study Practice Test, Section 6: **420**/10; **423**/14; **425**/16; **427**/22
Directed Study Practice Test, Section 9: **444**/14–15
Practice Test 1, Section 2: **463**/19; **463**/22
Practice Test I, Section 5: **473**/13; **474**/15
Practice Test II, Section 3: **508**/10
Practice Test II, Section 7: **526**/12; **529**/20; **529**/23
Practice Test II, Section 9: **536**/5; **537**/14–15

Practice Test III, Section 2: **547**/8; **548**/10; **549**/13; **551**/19; **552**/22
Practice Test III, Section 5: **565**/9–10; **568**/23
Practice Test III, Section 8: **577**/10–11, 14

Diction and Idioms (Writing)

Lesson: **323**/73–78
Quiz I: **333**/6–8
Quiz II: **337**/1
Quiz III: **341**/7; **342**/9
Quiz IV: **345**/4; **346**/9–10; **347**/16
Review: **352**/6; **353**/17–19; **355**/31; **356**/33
Directed Study Practice Test, Section 3: **390**/22
Directed Study Practice Test, Section 10: **448**/3; **449**/5
Practice Test 1, Section 7: **480**/2; **481**/8; **482**/11
Practice Test I, Section 10: **497**/5; **498**/13
Practice Test II, Section 6: **518**/1; **519**/4; **519**/6; **520**/15; **521**/23
Practice Test II, Section 10: **540**/1; **541**/6; **542**/10
Practice Test III, Section 4: **558**/3; **560**/14; **561**/20; **561**/22
Practice Test III, Section 10: **584**/1; **585**/5; **585**/9; **586**/13

Directness (Writing)

Lesson: **322**/62–69
Quiz I: **334**/10
Review: **354**/20; **354**/23
Practice Test II, Section 6: **518**/2
Practice Test II, Section 10: **541**/6; **542**/12

Distance Formula (Math: Multiple-Choice and Student-Produced Responses)

Lesson (MC): **207**/160–162; **212**/173
Quiz I (SPR): **277**/5
Quiz II (SPR): **281**/10
Quiz IV (MC): **242**/15
Review (SPR): **289**/8

Double Negatives (Writing)

Lesson: **318**/31–32
Practice Test 1, Section 7: **483**/24
Practice Test II, Section 10: **542**/12

End–Stop Punctuation (Writing)

Lesson: **327**/104

Equations Involving Absolute Value (Math: Multiple-Choice and Student-Produced Responses)

Lesson (MC): **184**/6; **200**/113–114
Quiz I (MC): **230**/15
Directed-Study Practice Test, Section 2 (MC): **373**/3
Practice Test 1, Section 3 (MC): **469**/17
Practice Test II, Section 8 (MC): **532**/12
Practice Test III, Section 7 (MC): **571**/5

Equations Involving Integer and Rational Exponents (Math: Multiple-Choice and Student-Produced Responses)

Lesson (MC): **199–200**/109–112
Quiz II (MC): **231**/3
Practice Test II, Section 2 (MC): **503**/8
Practice Test II, Section 8 (MC): **533**/14

Equations Involving Radical Expressions (Math: Multiple-Choice and Student-Produced Responses)

Lesson (MC): **199**/105–108
Quiz II (MC): **233**/16
Practice Test II, Section 2 (MC): **504**/10

Equations Involving Rational Expressions (Math: Multiple-Choice and Student-Produced Responses)

Lesson (MC): **184**/3; **198**/101–103
Quiz II (MC): **233**/15
Quiz III (SPR): **283**/4
Practice Test 1, Section 3 (MC): **466**/1
Practice Test 1, Section 6 (SPR): **478**/12

Evaluating Expressions (Math: Multiple-Choice and Student-Produced Responses)

Lesson (MC): **196**/84–87
Lesson (SPR): **269**/9; **271**/17
Quiz I (SPR): **276**/3
Quiz II (MC): **232**/8
Quiz III (MC): **236**/8
Quiz III (SPR): **283**/1
Review (MC): **248**/26
Review (SPR): **288**/4
Directed-Study Practice Test, Section 5 (MC): **408**/2; **411**/10; **414**/17
Practice Test 1, Section 6 (MC): **477**/4, 7
Practice Test 1, Section 6 (SPR): **479**/13
Practice Test I, Section 9 (MC): **495**/14
Practice Test II, Section 2 (MC): **503**/3; **504**/14
Practice Test II, Section 4 (MC): **516**/9

Practice Test III, Section 3 (MC): **555**/4
Practice Test III, Section 3 (SPR): **556**/9
Practice Test III, Section 7 (MC): **570**/3
Practice Test III, Section 9 (MC): **581**/8

Evaluating Sequences Involving Exponential Growth (Math: Multiple-Choice and Student-Produced Responses)

Lesson (MC): **183**/2; **198**/95–98
Quiz I (MC): **230**/13

Explanatory Phrases (Combined Reasoning)

Lesson: **144**/83–84
Quiz I: **147**/2, 4
Quiz II: **149**/2; **150**/13–14
Review: **158**/7; **160**/33; **162**/46, 50–53
Directed Study Practice Test, Section 6: **416**/1; **417**/2; **418**/5; **419**/8
Directed Study Practice Test, Section 9: **436**/1
Practice Test 1, Section 2: **459**/7
Practice Test I, Section 5: **471**/6
Practice Test I, Section 8: **486**/1–2
Practice Test II, Section 9: **534**/3
Practice Test III, Section 2: **546**/2
Practice Test III, Section 5: **564**/5
Practice Test III, Section 8: **574**/4

Explanatory Phrases (Thought Extension)

Lesson: **135**/1, 5; **136**/12–13; **143–144**xxx/72–82
Quiz I: **147**/1, 6; **148**/7, 13
Quiz II: **149**/1; **150**/8, 15
Quiz III: **152**/9, 15
Quiz IV: **153**/5–6; **154**/8, 11–12
Review: **157**/2–4, 6, 13, 15; **159**/16–17, 20, 22, 24; **160**/30, 32, 34; **161**/38–43, 45
Directed Study Practice Test, Section 6: **417**/3; **418**/6
Directed Study Practice Test, Section 9: **437**/2
Practice Test 1, Section 2: **458**/1, 3
Practice Test I, Section 5: **470**/1
Practice Test I, Section 8: **486**/3
Practice Test II, Section 3: **506**/2; **507**/5
Practice Test II, Section 7: **525**/8
Practice Test II, Section 9: **534**/4
Practice Test III, Section 2: **547**/6
Practice Test III, Section 5: **564**/1, 3–4

Explanatory Phrases (Thought Reversal)

Lesson: **137**/16
Quiz II: **149**/7; **150**/11–12
Quiz III: **151**/1, 8; **152**/11
Quiz IV: **154**/10

Practice Test III, Section 2: **547**/7

Explicit Detail (Critical Reading: Passages)

Lesson: **54**/3–5; **56**/17; **57**/24; **59**/33; **60**/36; **62**/44; **64**/60; **65**/66; **66**/68; **66**/70; **69**/80; **69**/85; **71**/92; **72**/103; **74**/108–110
Quiz I: **75**/2; **78**/7; **80**/15
Quiz II: **84**/7
Quiz III: **92**/13
Quiz IV: **95**/2–4; **96**/8; **97**/11; **98**/16; **100**/20–21; **102**/25–27
Review: **107**/15; **108**/18–19; **109**/21–22; **109**/24; **111**/29; **112**/34; **113**/39; **114**/41; **114**/43; **116**/50–51; **117**/54
Directed Study Practice Test, Section 4: **402**/11; **403**/14; **407**/23
Directed Study Practice Test, Section 6: **421**/12; **425**/17
Directed Study Practice Test, Section 9: **439**/7–8; **442**/10; **445**/18
Practice Test 1, Section 2: **463**/17
Practice Test I, Section 5: **471**/9; **474**/16; **474**/19; **475**/21; **475**/23
Practice Test I, Section 8: **488**/8; **489**/11–12; **489**/15
Practice Test II, Section 3: **509**/12; **511**/16
Practice Test II, Section 7: **528**/17
Practice Test II, Section 9: **536**/6; **537**/10; **538**/18
Practice Test III, Section 5: **567**/11; **567**/14; **568**/17–18; **568**/20
Practice Test III, Section 8: **576**/9; **578**/15–16

Expressing and Evaluating Algebraic Functions (Math: Multiple-Choice and Student-Produced Responses)

Lesson (MC): **184**/5; **200–202**/118–130
Lesson (SPR): **271**/18
Quiz I (MC): **230**/16
Quiz I (SPR): **277**/10
Quiz II (MC): **232**/6
Quiz III (MC): **236**/11
Quiz III (SPR): **283**/3
Quiz IV (SPR): **285**/1; **285**/4
Directed-Study Practice Test, Section 5 (MC): **415**/20
Directed-Study Practice Test, Section 8 (MC): **432**/8; **434**/14
Practice Test 1, Section 3 (MC): **467**/8
Practice Test 1, Section 9 (MC): **493**/4–5
Practice Test II, Section 2 (MC): **503**/4
Practice Test II, Section 4 (MC): **515**/4
Practice Test II, Section 4 (SPR): **517**/17
Practice Test III, Section 3 (SPR): **556**/9
Practice Test III, Section 7 (MC): **570**/4; **572**/18–19
Practice Test III, Section 9 (MC): **582**/16

Factoring (Math: Multiple-Choice and Student-Produced Responses)

Lesson (MC): **189**/33–34
Lesson (SPR): **269**/5
Directed-Study Practice Test, Section 8 (MC): **430**/2
Practice Test I, Section 9 (MC): **494**/10

Factoring Expressions (Math: Multiple-Choice and Student-Produced Responses)

Lesson (MC): **196**/90–92
Quiz IV (MC): **241**/6
Quiz IV (SPR): **286**/5
Review (MC): **247**/23
Directed-Study Practice Test, Section 5 (MC): **412**/12
Directed-Study Practice Test, Section 8 (MC): **434**/15

Faulty Comparisons (Writing)

Lesson: **321**/51–56
Quiz I: **333**/2
Quiz III: **342**/9
Quiz IV: **344**/2; 347/13
Review: **353**/16
Directed Study Practice Test, Section 3: **384**/5
Practice Test 1, Section 7: **480**/1; 483/20
Practice Test I, Section 10: **497**/8
Practice Test II, Section 6: **520**/12; **520**/14; **521**/20; **521**/22
Practice Test II, Section 10: **542**/9; **542**/14
Practice Test III, Section 10: **586**/11

Faulty Parallelism (Writing)

Lesson: **320**/43–45
Quiz I: **333**/5
Quiz III: **341**/6
Quiz IV: **345**/5; 346/11
Review: **351**/4
Directed Study Practice Test, Section 10: **447**/1–2; **452**/11; **453**/14
Practice Test 1, Section 7: **481**/6
Practice Test I, Section 10: **496**/2; **497**/9
Practice Test III, Section 4: **560**/12; **561**/23; **561**/25

The "Flying–X" Method (Math: Multiple-Choice and Student-Produced Responses)

Lesson (MC): **189**/37
Practice Test III, Section 3 (MC): **555**/7

Fragments (Writing)

Lesson: **315**/1–3
Review: **352**/12

Directed Study Practice Test, Section 3: **383**/3
Practice Test 1, Section 7: **482**/16
Practice Test III, Section 10: **585**/7

Function Notation (Math: Multiple-Choice and Student-Produced Responses)

Lesson (MC): **184**/5; **200–201**/118–125
Lesson (SPR): **271**/18
Quiz I (MC): **230**/16
Quiz II (MC): **232**/6
Quiz III (MC): **236**/11
Quiz IV (SPR): **285**/1
Directed-Study Practice Test, Section 8 (MC): **432**/8; **434**/14
Practice Test 1, Section 3 (MC): **467**/8
Practice Test I, Section 9 (MC): **493**/4–5
Practice Test II, Section 2 (MC): **503**/4
Practice Test II, Section 4 (MC): **515**/4
Practice Test II, Section 4 (SPR): **517**/17
Practice Test III, Section 7 (MC): **572**/18–19
Practice Test III, Section 9 (MC): **582**/16

Functions as Models (Math: Multiple-Choice and Student-Produced Responses)

Lesson (MC): **202**/130
Practice Test III, Section 7 (MC): **570**/4

Geometric Notation (Math: Multiple-Choice and Student-Produced Responses)

Practice Test II, Section 2 (MC): **503**/6
Practice Test III, Section 9 (MC): **582**/12

Geometric Probability (Math: Multiple-Choice and Student-Produced Responses)

Lesson (MC): **225**/230–231
Quiz II (MC): **234**/18

Geometry (Math: Multiple-Choice and Student-Produced Responses)

Lesson (MC): **184**/8; **185**/9–10, 12–15; **187**/26; **212–219**/175–210
Lesson (SPR): **268**/2; **270**/11–13; **271**/16; **272**/21–24; **273**/26
Quiz I (MC): **227**/1; **228**/3; **229**/11–12
Quiz I (SPR): **276**/4; **277**/9
Quiz II (MC): **231**/1–2; **232**/5; **233**/12, 17
Quiz II (SPR): **279**/1; **280**/6, 8
Quiz III (MC): **235**/3; **236**/7, 9; **237**/14; **238**/17; **239**/20
Quiz III (SPR): **283**/5; **284**/7–8
Quiz IV (MC): **241**/7–8; **242**/9, 13

Quiz IV (SPR): **285**/3
Review (MC): **243**/1–2; **244**/4–5, 8; **245**/10–11; **246**/15–16, 18–19; **247**/24–25
Review (SPR): **288**/3; **289**/5–7; **290**/10–11
Directed-Study Practice Test, Section 2 (MC): **374**/6
Directed-Study Practice Test, Section 2 (SPR): **377**/11; **378**/13
Directed-Study Practice Test, Section 5 (MC): **409**/4; **410**/7; **411**/9; **413**/14
Directed-Study Practice Test, Section 8 (MC): **431**/5; **433**/12
Practice Test 1, Section 3 (MC): **466**/2; **467**/4, 9; **468**/13
Practice Test I, Section 6 (MC): **477**/5, 8
Practice Test 1, Section 6 (SPR): **479**/16
Practice Test I, Section 9 (MC): **493**/7–8; **494**/12–13
Practice Test II, Section 2 (MC): **502**/2; **503**/6; **504**/11, 13; **505**/16–17
Practice Test II, Section 4 (MC): **514**/3
Practice Test II, Section 4 (SPR): **517**/13–14
Practice Test II, Section 8 (MC): **530**/1; **531**/5; **532**/10
Practice Test III, Section 3 (MC): **555**/5
Practice Test III, Section 3 (SPR): **556**/12–13; **557**/18
Practice Test III, Section 7 (MC): **571**/7, 9, 15; **572**/13, 17
Practice Test III, Section 9 (MC): **580**/2; **581**/4–5, 9; **582**/10–13

Grammar (Writing)

Lesson: **315–319**/1–37
Quiz I: **333**/1; **334**/7–8
Quiz II: **337**/2; **337**/5–8
Quiz III: **341**/1–2; **341**/4; **341**/7
Quiz IV: **344**/2; **345**/6; **346**/10
Review: **351**/3; **351**/5; **352**/7–8; **352**/10–13; **354**/20; **354**/24; **356**/33
Directed Study Practice Test, Section 3: **383**/3; **384**/5–6; **386**/10; **386**/12–13; **387**/15–16; **388**/18–19; **390**/23; **391**/25
Directed Study Practice Test, Section 10: **449**/5; **451**/9; **453**/13
Practice Test 1, Section 7: **480**/3–4; **482**/10; **482**/13; **482**/15–17; **483**/21–22; **483**/24–25
Practice Test I, Section 10: **496**/1; **498**/11
Practice Test II, Section 6: **518**/1; **519**/7–8; **520**/11; **520**/13; **520**/16–17; **520**/19; **521**/21
Practice Test II, Section 10: **541**/8; **542**/12
Practice Test III, Section 4: **559**/6; **560**/10–11; **560**/15; **561**/21; **561**/24
Practice Test III, Section 10: **585**/5–7; **586**/11; **586**/13

Graphs of First–Degree Inequalities
(Math: Multiple-Choice and Student-Produced Responses)

Lesson (MC): **209**/164

Graphs of Linear Equations (Math: Multiple-Choice and Student-Produced Responses)

Lesson (MC): **208**/163; **212**/174
Directed-Study Practice Test, Section 5 (MC): **415**/19
Practice Test II, Section 8 (MC): **533**/15

Graphs of Quadratic Equations and Relations (Math: Multiple-Choice and Student-Produced Responses)

Lesson (MC): **209**/165–166
Quiz IV (MC): **242**/15
Directed-Study Practice Test, Section 5 (MC): **414**/18

Humanities (Critical Reading: Passages)

Lesson: **56**/16–22; **63–67**/56–75
Quiz I: **78**/8
Quiz II: **85**/8
Quiz III: **88**/1–2
Quiz IV: **99**/18–23
Review: **107**/15
Directed Study Practice Test, Section 6: **421**/12; **423**/14
Directed Study Practice Test, Section 9: **438**/6–7
Practice Test 1, Section 2: **459**/9; **461**/13
Practice Test II, Section 7: **525**/10
Practice Test III, Section 2: **547**/9; **549**/12
Practice Test III, Section 8: **575**/6–7

Hyphens (Writing)

Lesson: **327**/106

Identifying Sentence Errors (Writing)

Lesson: **315**/4–8; **316**/11–15; **317**/17–24; **318**/29–33; **319**/35–37; **320**/43–51; **321**/53–55; **321**/57–59; **322**/67–69; **323**/73–78; **324**/80; **324**/82–84; **325**/86–88; **326**/91; **326**/93–97; **327**/101–103; **327**/106
Quiz I: **333**/1–6
Quiz II: **337**/1–6
Quiz III: **341**/1–6
Quiz IV: **344**/1–16
Review: **351–353**/1–19
Directed Study Practice Test, Section 3: **384**/6–25
Practice Test 1, Section 7: **481**/6–25
Practice Test II, Section 6: **519**/6–25
Practice Test III, Section 4: **559**/6–25

Illogical Tense Sequence (Writing)

Lesson: **321**/57–60
Quiz I: **333**/4
Quiz III: **341**/5
Directed Study Practice Test, Section 3: **385**/8

Directed Study Practice Test, Section 10: **451**/10; **452**/12
Practice Test 1, Section 7: **481**/9; **482**/12
Practice Test III, Section 4: **558**/2; **560**/9; **561**/18
Practice Test III, Section 10: **586**/12

Implied Idea (Critical Reading: Passages)

Lesson: **55**/9–11; **57**/20; **58**/27; **59**/31; **60**/39; **63**/52–53; **64**/58; **65**/64; **67**/72; **69**/81; **69**/84; **70**/87; **71**/94; **73**/104; **73**/106–107
Quiz I: **76**/4–5; **79**/10; **80**/14
Quiz II: **82**/2; **85**/8; **86**/12–13
Quiz III: **88**/2; **91**/10; **92**/14; **92**/16
Quiz IV: **95**/5–7; **97**/13; **98**/15; **99**/19; **100**/23
Review: **106**/9–10; **106**/12; **107**/16; **109**/25; **110**/27; **111**/30–31; **112**/36; **113**/40; **117**/55
Directed Study Practice Test, Section 4: **405**/19
Directed Study Practice Test, Section 6: **421**/11; **427**/23
Directed Study Practice Test, Section 9: **443**/11
Practice Test 1, Section 2: **460**/11; **461**/14–15; **463**/18; **463**/20–21
Practice Test I, Section 5: **473**/14; **474**/18
Practice Test II, Section 3: **508**/11; **509**/14; **511**/19; **511**/21; **512**/23
Practice Test II, Section 7: **526**/11; **528**/18
Practice Test II, Section 9: **536**/7–8; **537**/12; **538**/16
Practice Test III, Section 2: **549**/12; **550**/14; **551**/16; **551**/18; **552**/21; **552**/23
Practice Test III, Section 5: **567**/12; **567**/16; **568**/19; **568**/22; **568**/24
Practice Test III, Section 8: **575**/6; **575**/8; **578**/17

Improving Paragraphs (Writing)

Lesson: **329–331**/109–120
Quiz I: **335**/11–16
Quiz II: **339**/11–16
Quiz III: **342**/11–16
Review: **356**/34–37
Directed Study Practice Test, Section 3: **393**/26–35
Practice Test 1, Section 7: **484**/26–35
Practice Test II, Section 6: **522**/26–35
Practice Test III, Section 4: **562**/26–35

Improving Sentences (Writing)

Lesson: **315**/1–3; **316**/9–10; **317**/16; **318**/25–28; **319**/34; **319**/38–42; **321**/52; **321**/56; **321**/60–66; **323**/70–72; **324**/79; **324**/81; **325**/85; **325**/89–90; **326**/92; **326**/98–100; **327**/104–105; **328**/107
Quiz I: **334**/7–10; **334**/9–10
Quiz II: **338**/7–10
Quiz III: **341**/7–10
Review: **354**/20–33
Directed Study Practice Test, Section 3: **382**/1–5

Directed Study Practice Test, Section 10: **447**/1–14
Practice Test 1, Section 7: **480**/1–5
Practice Test I, Section 10: **496**/1–14
Practice Test II, Section 6: **518**/1–5
Practice Test II, Section 10: **540**/1–14
Practice Test III, Section 4: **558**/1–5
Practice Test III, Section 10: **584**/1–14

Incomplete Split Constructions (Writing)

Lesson: **320**/46–47
Review: **356**/32
Practice Test II, Section 6: **521**/25
Practice Test II, Section 10: **541**/7
Practice Test III, Section 4: **559**/8
Practice Test III, Section 10: **586**/12

Inequalities Involving Absolute Value
(Math: Multiple-Choice and Student-Produced Responses)

Lesson (MC): **200**/115–117

Inequalities Involving Rational Expressions
(Math: Multiple-Choice and Student-Produced Responses)

Lesson (MC): **199**/104

Key Words (Combined Reasoning)

Lesson: **135**/3; **144**/83, 85–87; **145**/88–89, 91; **146**/97
Quiz I: **148**/8, 14
Quiz II: **150**/14
Quiz III: **151**/7
Review: **162**/47–48, 51
Directed Study Practice Test, Section 4: **399**/4; **400**/8
Directed Study Practice Test, Section 6: **417**/4; **418**/7
Directed Study Practice Test, Section 9: **436**/1
Practice Test 1, Section 2: **459**/5
Practice Test I, Section 5: **471**/8
Practice Test I, Section 8: **486**/1
Practice Test II, Section 3: **507**/6
Practice Test II, Section 7: **524**/1–2; **525**/6
Practice Test II, Section 9: **534**/3

Key Words (Thought Extension)

Lesson: **136**/6, 11; **139**/40; **140**/41–43, 46–47; **141**/51–60; **142**/61–65; **145**/94
Quiz I: **148**/9–10, 16
Quiz III: **151**/4
Quiz IV: **153**/2
Review: **158**/12; **159**/19, 25; **160**/27–28; **161**/36
Directed Study Practice Test, Section 9: **437**/3

Practice Test 1, Section 2: **459**/6
Practice Test I, Section 5: **470**/2, 4; **471**/5
Practice Test II, Section 3: **507**/8
Practice Test II, Section 7: **525**/7
Practice Test II, Section 9: **534**/1
Practice Test III, Section 2: **546**/1
Practice Test III, Section 8: **574**/1

Key Words (Thought Reversal)

Lesson: **136**/9; **140**/44–45, 48–50; **146**/96
Quiz II: **149**/6; **150**/9
Quiz III: **151**/6
Review: **157**/5; **158**/14; **159**/18; **161**/37

Lines and Angles (Math: Multiple-Choice and Student-Produced Responses)

Lesson (MC): **185–186**/12–15; **212**/175–179;
218/202, 204
Lesson (SPR): **272**/22
Quiz I (MC): **227**/1; **228**/3
Quiz I (SPR): **276**/4
Quiz II (MC): **231**/2
Quiz II (SPR): **279**/1; **280**/6
Quiz III (MC): **236**/7; **238**/17; **239**/20
Quiz III (SPR): **284**/7
Quiz IV (SPR): **285**/3
Review (MC): **246**/18–19; **247**/25
Review (SPR): **289**/6; **290**/11
Directed-Study Practice Test, Section 2 (SPR): **377**/11
Directed-Study Practice Test, Section 5 (MC): **409**/4
Practice Test 1, Section 2 (MC): **466**/2
Practice Test 1, Section 6 (SPR): **479**/16
Practice Test II, Section 2 (MC): **502**/2; **504**/13
Practice Test II, Section 8 (MC): **532**/10
Practice Test III, Section 3 (MC): **555**/5
Practice Test III, Section 3 (SPR): **556**/12
Practice Test III, Section 7 (MC): **571**/7, 9
Practice Test III, Section 9 (MC): **582**/11

Literary Fiction (Critical Reading: Passages)

Lesson: **68**/76–90
Practice Test III, Section 8: **577**/10–19

Logical Expression (Writing)

Lesson: **321–323**/51–72
Quiz I: **333**/2; **333**/4; **334**/8; **334**/10
Quiz II: **338**/8–10
Quiz III: **341**/5; **342**/9; **342**/10
Quiz IV: **344**/2–3; **345**/7; **347**/13
Review: **353**/16; **354**/20; **354**/23; **355**/25; **355**/27;
355/29–30

Directed Study Practice Test, Section 3: **382**/1; **384**/5;
385/8
Directed Study Practice Test, Section 10: **449**/4; **450**/6;
451/10; **452**/12
Practice Test 1, Section 7: **480**/1; **481**/5; **481**/9; **482**/12;
483/20; **483**/23
Practice Test I, Section 10: **497**/4; **497**/7–8; **498**/10;
498/14
Practice Test II, Section 6: **518**/2; **520**/12; **520**/14;
520/18; **521**/20; **521**/22
Practice Test II, Section 10: **540**/2; **541**/4; **541**/6; **542**/9;
542/12; **542**/14
Practice Test III, Section 4: **558**/2; **559**/4; **560**/9;
560/16; **561**/18
Practice Test III, Section 10: **584**/2; **585**/4–5; **586**/11–12;
586/14

Low–Level Usage (Writing)

Lesson: **324**/80
Quiz II: **337**/4
Quiz III: **341**/3
Review: **354**/22
Directed Study Practice Test, Section 3: **386**/11; **388**/17;
389/20
Practice Test III, Section 4: **561**/19

Main Idea (Critical Reading: Passages)

Lesson: **54**/1–2; **56**/16; **57**/23; **59**/30; **60**/35; **61**/42–43;
64/61; **65**/65; **71**/97–98; **74**/111
Quiz I: **77**/6; **80**/12–13
Quiz II: **83**/4; **86**/11
Quiz III: **88**/1; **89**/4; **93**/18
Quiz IV: **94**/1; **97**/10; **100**/22; **101**/24
Review: **104**/4; **104**/6; **106**/8; **109**/23; **111**/33;
114/45–46; **116**/49; **118**/57
Directed Study Practice Test, Section 4: **402**/10; **405**/18
Directed Study Practice Test, Section 6: **425**/15; **428**/24
Practice Test 1, Section 2: **460**/10; **461**/12–13; **464**/23
Practice Test I, Section 5: **472**/11
Practice Test I, Section 8: **488**/10
Practice Test II, Section 3: **509**/13; **510**/15
Practice Test II, Section 7: **528**/15
Practice Test III, Section 2: **547**/9; **548**/11; **551**/15

Manipulating Algebraic Expressions (Math: Multiple-Choice and Student-Produced Responses)

Lesson (MC): **184**/4; **195–197**/82–94;
203–204/141–150
Lesson (SPR): **268**/1; **269**/9; **271**/17
Quiz I (SPR): **276**/3
Quiz II (MC): **232**/8

Quiz III (MC): **236**/8
Quiz III (SPR): **283**/1
Quiz IV (MC): **241**/3–4, 6; **242**/11
Quiz IV (SPR): **286**/5
Review (MC): **247**/23; **248**/26
Review (SPR): **288**/4
Directed-Study Practice Test, Section 2 (MC): **375**/8
Directed-Study Practice Test, Section 5 (MC): **408**/2; **410**/8; **411**/10; **412**/12; **414**/17
Directed-Study Practice Test, Section 8 (MC): **431**/4, 6; **432**/9; **434**/15; **435**/16
Practice Test 1, Section 2 (MC): **467**/6; **469**/20
Practice Test I, Section 6 (MC): **477**/4, 7
Practice Test 1, Section 6 (SPR): **479**/13
Practice Test I, Section 9 (MC): **495**/14–15
Practice Test II, Section 2 (MC): **503**/3; **504**/14–15
Practice Test II, Section 4 (MC): **516**/9
Practice Test II, Section 8 (MC): **530**/3
Practice Test III, Section 3 (MC): **554**/2; **555**/4
Practice Test III, Section 7 (MC): **570**/3; **572**/15–16
Practice Test III, Section 9 (MC): **581**/8

Manipulating Expressions Involving Exponents (Math: Multiple-Choice and Student-Produced Responses)

Lesson (MC): **196**/88–89
Directed-Study Practice Test, Section 2 (MC): **372**/1
Practice Test II, Section 2 (MC): **504**/15
Practice Test III, Section 3 (MC): **554**/2
Practice Test III, Section 7 (MC): **572**/16

Median (Math: Multiple-Choice and Student-Produced Responses)

Lesson (MC): **224**/225
Practice Test II, Section 2 (MC): **505**/18
Practice Test II, Section 8 (MC): **532**/11; **533**/13
Practice Test III, Section 9 (MC): **581**/7

Misplaced Modifiers (Writing)

Lesson: **323**/70–72
Quiz I: **334**/10
Quiz II: **338**/10
Quiz IV: **344**/3
Review: **354**/23; 355/25
Directed Study Practice Test, Section 3: **382**/1
Directed Study Practice Test, Section 10: **449**/4
Practice Test II, Section 10: **540**/2; **541**/4
Practice Test III, Section 4: **559**/4; **560**/16
Practice Test III, Section 10: **584**/2; **585**/4–5; **586**/14

Mode (Math: Multiple-Choice and Student-Produced Responses)

Lesson (MC): **224**/226
Practice Test II, Section 8 (MC): **532**/11

Natural Sciences (Critical Reading: Passages)

Lesson: **59**/35–41; **72**/98–112
Quiz I: **77**/5–7
Quiz II: **82**/3–4; **85**/9–17
Quiz III: **89**/3–4; **90**/7–8
Quiz IV: **97**/10–17; **101**/24–29
Review: **104**/4–5; **105**/7–14; **108**/17–25; **112**/37; **117**/56–60
Directed Study Practice Test, Section 4: **405**/18–24
Directed Study Practice Test, Section 6: **420**/9–11
Practice Test 1, Section 2: **462**/15–24
Practice Test I, Section 5: **471**/9–10; **473**/13–24
Practice Test II, Section 3: **508**/11–14
Practice Test II, Section 7: **526**/11; **527**/13–24
Practice Test III, Section 2: **548**/10
Practice Test III, Section 5: **567**/10–24
Practice Test III, Section 8: **575**/8–9

Nouns and Noun Clauses (Writing)

Lesson: **319**/33–37
Review: **354**/24

Paragraph Structure (Writing)

Quiz III: **343**/13
Review: 356/34
Directed Study Practice Test, Section 3: **394**/29; **396**/34
Practice Test 1, Section 7: **484**/28–29; **485**/32
Practice Test II, Section 6: **522**/29
Practice Test III, Section 4: **562**/27; **563**/32

Passage Development (Writing)

Lesson: **329**/111; **330**/114; **331**/120
Quiz I: **336**/15–16
Quiz II: **339**/13; **340**/16
Quiz III: **343**/13; **343**/16
Review: 357/37
Directed Study Practice Test, Section 3: **394**/31–33; **396**/35
Practice Test 1, Section 7: **484**/30–31; **485**/35
Practice Test II, Section 6: **522**/26; **523**/31; **523**/33
Practice Test III, Section 4: **562**/26; **563**/31

Percents (Math: Multiple-Choice and Student-Produced Responses)

Lesson (MC): **187**/24; **188**/27; **192**/58–64; **204**/149; **217**/201
Lesson (SPR): **269**/7; **270**/14; **274**/29
Quiz IV (MC): **240**/2
Review (MC): **244**/3, 5; **245**/13; **247**/24; **248**/27–28
Directed-Study Practice Test, Section 2 (SPR): **380**/17
Directed-Study Practice Test, Section 8 (MC): **433**/11
Practice Test 1, Section 6 (MC): **477**/5
Practice Test 1, Section 6 (SPR): **479**/17
Practice Test I, Section 9 (MC): **494**/9
Practice Test II, Section 8 (MC): **532**/9
Practice Test III, Section 3 (MC): **555**/6, 8
Practice Test III, Section 3 (SPR): **556**/11; **557**/16–17
Practice Test III, Section 7 (MC): **571**/6; **572**/14

Pie Charts (Math: Multiple-Choice and Student-Produced Responses)

Lesson (MC): **222**/216–217
Lesson (SPR): **274**/32
Quiz I (MC): **228**/6
Practice Test 1, Section 6 (MC): **476**/1

Probability and Statistics (Math: Multiple-Choice and Student-Produced Responses)

Lesson (MC): **185**/11; **223–235**/220–231
Lesson (SPR): **269**/8; **273**/27
Quiz I (SPR): **277**/7
Quiz II (MC): **234**/18
Quiz III (MC): **235**/1; **238**/18
Quiz III (SPR): **283**/2
Quiz IV (MC): **242**/11
Review (MC): **244**/7
Directed-Study Practice Test, Section 2 (SPR): **379**/14–15
Directed-Study Practice Test, Section 8 (MC): **433**/10
Practice Test 1, Section 3 (MC): **468**/12
Practice Test I, Section 6 (MC): **477**/3, 6
Practice Test II, Section 2 (MC): **504**/12; **505**/18
Practice Test II, Section 4 (MC): **514**/1
Practice Test II, Section 8 (MC): **532**/11; **533**/13
Practice Test III, Section 3 (SPR): **557**/15
Practice Test III, Section 7 (MC): **571**/10
Practice Test III, Section 9 (MC): **581**/7; **582**/14

Problems of Coordination and Subordination (Writing)

Lesson: **319**/39–42
Quiz IV: **347**/12; **347**/14
Practice Test II, Section 10: **541**/7

Pronoun Usage (Writing)

Lesson: **317–318**/16–24
Quiz I: **334**/8
Quiz II: **337**/5; **338**/8
Quiz III: **341**/1–2; **341**/4; **341**/7
Quiz IV: **344**/2
Review: **351**/5; **352**/7; **352**/10; **354**/20; **354**/24; **356**/33
Directed Study Practice Test, Section 3: **384**/5–6; **386**/10; **387**/15; **388**/18–19; **390**/23
Directed Study Practice Test, Section 10: **449**/5; **451**/9; **453**/13
Practice Test 1, Section 7: **480**/3–4; **482**/10; **482**/17; **483**/21; **483**/25
Practice Test I, Section 10: **498**/11
Practice Test II, Section 6: **518**/1; **520**/13; **520**/17; **520**/19; **521**/21
Practice Test III, Section 4: **560**/11; **560**/15; **561**/21
Practice Test III, Section 10: **585**/6; **586**/13

Properties of Numbers (Math: Multiple-Choice and Student-Produced Responses)

Lesson (MC): **186**/18; **188**/28; **190**/42–49; **194**/74–79; **195**/81
Lesson (SPR): **273**/28
Quiz I (SPR): **276**/1–2
Quiz II (MC): **233**/14
Quiz II (SPR): **279**/3
Quiz III (MC): **235**/2; **236**/10; **237**/15
Quiz IV (MC): **242**/10, 12
Quiz IV (SPR): **285**/2
Review (MC): **245**/12
Directed-Study Practice Test, Section 2 (MC): **373**/4 ; **374**/5, 7
Directed-Study Practice Test, Section 5 (MC): **409**/5; **410**/6; **411**/10; **412**/13
Practice Test 1, Section 3 (MC): **467**/7; **468**/11; **469**/15
Practice Test 1, Section 6 (SPR): **478**/11; **479**/14
Practice Test I, Section 9 (MC): **492**/2; **493**/3; **495**/16
Practice Test II, Section 2 (MC): **504**/9
Practice Test II, Section 4 (MC): **515**/5
Practice Test II, Section 4 (SPR): **517**/15
Practice Test II, Section 8 (MC): **530**/2
Practice Test III, Section 7 (MC): **571**/11; **573**/20
Practice Test III, Section 9 (MC): **580**/1; **581**/3

Properties of Tangent Lines (Math: Multiple-Choice and Student-Produced Responses)

Lesson (MC): **185**/10; **215**/189–192

Properties of Triangles (Math: Multiple-Choice and Student-Produced Responses)

Lesson (MC): **214**/184–185; **215**/187, 189; **216**/194–195; **217**/198; **218**/203

Proportions and Direct–Inverse Variation (Math: Multiple-Choice and Student-Produced Responses)

Lesson (MC): **187**/19; **193**/67–73
Quiz I (MC): **228**/5
Quiz I (SPR): **277**/8
Quiz II (SPR): **279**/4; **281**/9
Quiz III (MC): **235**/4; **238**/16
Review (MC): **245**/9–10; **247**/20
Review (SPR): **290**/9
Directed-Study Practice Test, Section 2 (SPR): **376**/10; **381**/18
Directed-Study Practice Test, Section 8 (MC): **429**/1; **434**/13
Practice Test 1, Section 6 (MC): **476**/1
Practice Test 1, Section 6 (SPR): **478**/10
Practice Test I, Section 9 (MC): **492**/1
Practice Test II, Section 2 (MC): **503**/5
Practice Test II, Section 4 (SPR): **516**/10–11
Practice Test II, Section 8 (MC): **532**/8; **533**/16
Practice Test III, Section 3 (MC): **554**/3

Punctuation (Writing)

Lesson: **324**/81–107

Punctuation Marks (Combined Reasoning)

Lesson: **144**/84, 86
Quiz I: **148**/8
Quiz II: **149**/2; **150**/13
Quiz IV: **154**/7
Review: **161**/44
Directed Study Practice Test, Section 6: **418**/7
Practice Test II, Section 3: **506**/4; **507**/7
Practice Test III, Section 5: **565**/7–8

Punctuation Marks (Thought Extension)

Lesson: **142–143**/66–76
Quiz I: **147**/3, 5; **148**/15
Quiz II: **150**/16
Quiz IV: **153**/6; **154**/11
Review: **159**/21, 23; **163**/54
Directed Study Practice Test, Section 9: **437**/4

Pythagorean Theorem (Math: Multiple-Choice and Student-Produced Responses)

Lesson (MC): **185**/9; **213**/180; **215**/187; **218**/205; **219**/209; **220**/210
Lesson (SPR): **270**/11
Quiz II (MC): **233**/17
Quiz IV (MC): **241**/7
Practice Test II, Section 4 (MC): **514**/3
Practice Test III, Section 7 (MC): **572**/17
Practice Test III, Section 9 (MC): **581**/4; **582**/10

Qualitative Behavior of Graphs of Functions (Math: Multiple-Choice and Student-Produced Responses)

Lesson (MC): **210**/167–168
Quiz III (MC): **238**/19

Quotation Marks (Writing)

Lesson: **328**/107

Ratios (Math: Multiple-Choice and Student-Produced Responses)

Lesson (MC): **186**/16–17; **187**/22; **193**/65–66
Lesson (SPR): **269**/6; **271**/15
Quiz I (MC): **229**/7
Quiz II (SPR): **280**/5
Quiz III (SPR): **284**/10
Review (MC): **247**/25
Directed-Study Practice Test, Section 5 (MC): **410**/6
Practice Test 1, Section 3 (MC): **468**/14
Practice Test I, Section 6 (MC): **477**/4
Practice Test II, Section 8 (MC): **531**/6

Rectangles and Squares (Math: Multiple-Choice and Student-Produced Responses)

Lesson (MC): **215**/186–187, 192; **216**/193, 195–197; **217**/200–201; **219**/206, 209
Lesson (SPR): **270**/12; **271**/16
Quiz III (MC): **235**/3; **237**/14
Quiz III (SPR): **283**/5
Review (MC): **243**/1–2; **246**/15, 18
Review (SPR): **289**/7; **290**/10
Directed-Study Practice Test, Section 5 (MC): **410**/7; **413**/14
Directed-Study Practice Test, Section 8 (MC): **431**/5
Practice Test 1, Section 9 (MC): **494**/12
Practice Test II, Section 4 (SPR): **517**/13
Practice Test II, Section 8 (MC): **531**/5
Practice Test III, Section 3 (SPR): **557**/13, 18
Practice Test III, Section 7 (MC): **571**/12
Practice Test III, Section 9 (MC): **580**/2; **582**/13

Run–on Sentences (Writing)

Lesson: **319**/38

Scatterplots (Math: Multiple-Choice and Student-Produced Responses)

Lesson (MC): **223**/219

Semicolons (Writing)

Lesson: **326**/98–101

Sentence Elements (Writing)

Lesson: **329**/109–110; **329**/112–113; **330**/115–119
Quiz I: **335**/11–14
Quiz II: **339**/11–12; **340**/14–15
Quiz III: **342**/11–12; **343**/14–15
Review: **357**/35–36
Directed Study Practice Test, Section 3: **393**/26–28;
394/30
Practice Test 1, Section 7: **484**/26–27; **485**/33–34
Practice Test II, Section 6: **522**/28; **522**/30; **523**/32;
523/35
Practice Test III, Section 4: **562**/28–30; **563**/33–35

Sentence Structure (Writing)

Lesson: **319–320**/38–50
Quiz I: **333**/5
Quiz III: **341**/6
Quiz IV: **345**/5–6; **346**/11–12; **347**/14
Review: **351**/1; **351**/4; **352**/9; **353**/14; **356**/32
Directed Study Practice Test, Section 3: **385**/9
Directed Study Practice Test, Section 10: **447**/1–2;
452/11; **453**/14
Practice Test 1, Section 7: **481**/6; **482**/14
Practice Test I, Section 10: **496**/2; **497**/9
Practice Test II, Section 6: **521**/25
Practice Test II, Section 10: **541**/7
Practice Test III, Section 4: **559**/8; **560**/12–13; **561**/23;
561/25
Practice Test III, Section 10: **584**/3; **586**/12

Sets: Union, Intersection, and Elements
(Math: Multiple-Choice and Student-Produced
Responses)

Lesson (MC): **191**/50–54
Quiz I (MC): **230**/14
Quiz IV (SPR): **285**/2
Practice Test 1, Section 3 (MC): **468**/10

Simple Equations (Math: Multiple-Choice and Student-Produced Responses)

Lesson (MC): **198**/99
Quiz I (MC): **228**/4; **229**/10
Quiz IV (MC): **240**/1
Practice Test III, Section 3 (MC): **554**/1
Practice Test III, Section 9 (MC): **582**/15
Practice Test 1, Section 6 (SPR): **478**/9

Simple Inequalities (Math: Multiple-Choice and Student-Produced Responses)

Lesson (MC): **198**/100
Quiz IV (MC): **241**/3

Simple Manipulations (Math: Multiple-Choice and Student-Produced Responses)

Lesson (MC): **187**/21; **188**/30–31; **194**/74–79
Quiz I (SPR): **277**/6
Quiz III (SPR): **284**/9
Quiz IV (MC): **241**/5
Directed-Study Practice Test, Section 2 (SPR): **376**/9
Directed-Study Practice Test, Section 5 (MC): **408**/1;
414/16
Practice Test II, Section 4 (SPR): **517**/16
Practice Test III, Section 7 (MC): **570**/1; **571**/8

Simplifying (Math: Multiple-Choice and Student-Produced Responses)

Lesson (MC): **189**/32
Lesson (SPR): **269**/4
Directed-Study Practice Test, Section 5 (MC): **412**/11

Slope of a Line (Math: Multiple-Choice and Student-Produced Responses)

Lesson (MC): **206**/155–157
Lesson (SPR): **274**/31
Quiz II (MC): **232**/7; **233**/13
Quiz III (MC): **237**/12
Practice Test 1, Section 3 (MC): **469**/18
Practice Test II, Section 4 (SPR): **517**/18

Slope–Intercept Form of a Linear Equation
(Math: Multiple-Choice and Student-Produced
Responses)

Lesson (MC): **184**/7; **207**/158–159; **212**/171–172
Quiz II (MC): **234**/19
Practice Test 1, Section 9 (MC): **493**/6
Practice Test II, Section 8 (MC): **531**/7

Social Studies (Critical Reading: Passages)

Lesson: **54**/1–15; **57**/23–34; **61**/42–55; **70**/91–97
Quiz I: **75**/1–4; **79**/9–18
Quiz II: **82**/1–2; **83**/5–7
Quiz III: **90**/5–6; **91**/9–18
Quiz IV: **94**/1–9
Review: **103**/1–3; **104**/6; **107**/16; **110**/26–36;
113/38–55
Directed Study Practice Test, Section 4: **402**/10–17
Directed Study Practice Test, Section 6: **422**/13;
425/15–24
Directed Study Practice Test, Section 9: **439**/8–19
Practice Test 1, Section 2: **460**/10–12; **461**/14
Practice Test I, Section 5: **472**/11–12
Practice Test I, Section 8: **488**/5–19
Practice Test II, Section 3: **507**/9–10; **510**/15–24
Practice Test II, Section 7: **525**/9; **526**/12
Practice Test II, Section 9: **536**/5–19
Practice Test III, Section 2: **547**/8; **548**/11; **549**/13–24
Practice Test III, Section 5: **565**/9

Solving Algebraic Equations or Inequalities with One Variable (Math: Multiple-Choice and Student-Produced Responses)

Lesson (MC): **184**/3, 6; **190**/41; **198–200**/99–117;
203/141, 143; **217**/200
Quiz I (MC): **228**/4; **229**/10; **230**/15
Quiz II (MC): **231**/3; **233**/15–16
Quiz III (SPR): **283**/4
Quiz IV (MC): **240**/1; **241**/3
Review (MC): **246**/17
Directed-Study Practice Test, Section 2 (MC): **372**/1;
373/3
Directed-Study Practice Test, Section 5 (MC): **409**/3
Practice Test 1, Section 3 (MC): **466**/1; **469**/17
Practice Test 1, Section 6 (SPR): **478**/9, 12
Practice Test II, Section 2 (MC): **503**/8; **504**/10
Practice Test II, Section 4 (MC): **514**/2
Practice Test II, Section 8 (MC): **532**/12; **533**/14
Practice Test III, Section 3 (MC): **554**/1
Practice Test III, Section 7 (MC): **571**/5
Practice Test III, Section 9 (MC): **582**/15

Solving Algebraic Equations with Two Variables (Math: Multiple-Choice and Student-Produced Responses)

Lesson (MC): **201**/131
Directed-Study Practice Test, Section 2 (SPR): **377**/12
Practice Test II, Section 4 (SPR): **516**/12
Practice Test III, Section 9 (MC): **581**/6

Solving Quadratic Equations and Relations (Math: Multiple-Choice and Student-Produced Responses)

Lesson (MC): **203**/136–140
Quiz IV (MC): **242**/14
Practice Test II, Section 4 (MC): **514**/2

Solving Simultaneous Equations (Math: Multiple-Choice and Student-Produced Responses)

Lesson (MC): **202**/132–135; **203**/142
Lesson (SPR): **270**/10; **271**/19–20
Quiz II (MC): **232**/10
Quiz II (SPR): **279**/2
Quiz III (SPR): **283**/6
Quiz IV (MC): **241**/4
Review (SPR): **245**/12–13
Directed-Study Practice Test, Section 2 (MC): **373**/2
Directed-Study Practice Test, Section 8 (MC): **430**/3
Practice Test 1, Section 6 (MC): **477**/6
Practice Test II, Section 2 (MC): **502**/1; **503**/7; **505**/19
Practice Test II, Section 4 (MC): **515**/6

Spatial Reasoning (Math: Multiple-Choice and Student-Produced Responses)

Lesson (MC): **217**/199
Quiz II (MC): **231**/1
Quiz II (SPR): **280**/8
Directed-Study Practice Test, Section 5 (MC): **411**/9
Practice Test 1, Section 3 (MC): **467**/4

Subject–Verb Agreement (Writing)

Lesson: **315–317**/4–15
Quiz I: **333**/1; **334**/7
Quiz II: **337**/2; **337**/6–7
Quiz III: **341**/7
Quiz IV: **345**/6; **346**/10
Review: **351**/3; **352**/11; **352**/13; **354**/24
Directed Study Practice Test, Section 3: **387**/13; **388**/16
Practice Test 1, Section 7: **482**/13; **483**/22
Practice Test II, Section 6: **519**/7; **520**/11
Practice Test II, Section 10: **541**/8
Practice Test III, Section 4: **560**/10; **561**/24
Practice Test III, Section 10: **585**/5; **586**/11; **586**/13

Subordinate Conjunctions (Combined Reasoning)

Lesson: **145**/90–92, 95
Quiz I: **147**/2
Quiz III: **151**/7

Review: **158**/8–9; **160**/33; **161**/44; **162**/46, 52; **163**/55, 57
Directed Study Practice Test, Section 4: **398**/3; **399**/5–6
Directed Study Practice Test, Section 6: **416**/1; **419**/8
Directed Study Practice Test, Section 9: **437**/5
Practice Test 1, Section 2: **458**/2; **459**/5, 7
Practice Test I, Section 5: **470**/3; **471**8
Practice Test I, Section 8: **486**/2; **486**/4
Practice Test II, Section 3: **506**/4; **507**/6
Practice Test II, Section 7: **524**/5; **525**/6
Practice Test III, Section 5: **565**/8
Practice Test III, Section 8: **575**/5

Subordinate Conjunctions (Thought Extension)

Lesson: **136**/8; **137**/14; **139**/36–37, 39
Quiz I: **148**/11
Quiz II: **149**/5; **150**/10
Quiz III: **151**/2, 5; **152**/10
Quiz IV: **154**/9
Review: **158**/11
Directed Study Practice Test, Section 4: **398**/2; **400**/7
Practice Test 1, Section 2: **459**/8
Practice Test II, Section 3: **506**/1
Practice Test II, Section 7: **524**/3
Practice Test III, Section 2: **546**/3–5
Practice Test III, Section 5: **564**/2
Practice Test III, Section 8: **574**/3

Subordinate Conjunctions (Thought Reversal)

Lesson: **135**/2; **137**/15, 17; **138**/29–30; **139**/31–35, 38
Quiz III: **152**/12, 14
Quiz IV: **153**/3–4; **155**/15
Review: **160**/26, 31
Directed Study Practice Test, Section 4: **397**/1
Practice Test II, Section 3: **506**/3
Practice Test II, Section 7: **524**/4
Practice Test II, Section 9: **534**/2
Practice Test III, Section 5: **565**/6

Tables (Matrices) (Math: Multiple-Choice and Student-Produced Responses)

Lesson (MC): **223**/218
Quiz III (MC): **238**/16
Quiz IV (MC): **240**/2
Review (MC): **248**/27–29
Directed-Study Practice Test, Section 8 (MC): **429**/1
Practice Test 1, Section 3 (MC): **469**/19
Practice Test I, Section 6 (MC): **477**/3
Practice Test II, Section 4 (SPR): **517**/16
Practice Test II, Section 8 (MC): **531**/6; **533**/13

Thought Extension (Critical Reading: Sentence Completions)

Lesson: **135**/1, 5; **136**/6, 8, 11–13; **137**/18, 20–21; **138**/22, 28; **139**/36–37, 39–40; **140**/41–43, 46–47; **141-144**/51–82; **145**/93–94
Quiz I: **147**/1, 3, ; **147-148**/5–7; **148**/9–13; **148**/15–16
Quiz II: **149**/1; **149**/5; **150**/8; **150**/10; **150**/15–16
Quiz III: **151**/2; **151**/4–5; **152**/9–10; **152**/13; **152**/15
Quiz IV: **153**/2; **153**/5–6; **154**/8–9; **154**/11–12
Review: **157**/1–4; **157**/6; **258**/10–13; **158-159**/15–17; **159**/19–25; **160**/27–30; **160**/32; **160-161**/34–36; **161**/38–43; **161**/45; **162**/49; **163**/54
Directed-Study Practice Test, Section 4: **398**/2; **400**/7; **400**/9
Directed-Study Practice Test, Section 6: **417**/3; **418**/6
Directed-Study Practice Test, Section 9: **437**/2–4
Practice Test 1, Section 2: **458**/1; **458**/3; **459**/6; **459**/8
Practice Test I, Section 5: **470**/1–2; **470-471**/4–5; **471**/7
Practice Test I, Section 8: **486**/3
Practice Test II, Section 3: **506**/1–2; **507**/5; **507**/8
Practice Test II, Section 7: **524**/3; **525**/7–8
Practice Test II, Section 9: **534**/1; **534**/4
Practice Test III, Section 2: **546**/1; **546-547**/3–6
Practice Test III, Section 5: **564**/1–4
Practice Test III, Section 8: **574**/1–3

Thought Reversal (Critical Reading: Sentence Completions)

Lesson: **135**/2, 4; **136**/7, 9–10; **137**/15–17, 19; **138**/23–27, 29–30; **139**/31–35, 38; **140**/44–45, 48–50; **146**/96
Quiz II: **149**/3–4; **149**/6–7; **150**/9; **150**/11–12
Quiz III: **151**/1; **151**/3; 151/6; **151**/8; **152**/11–12; **152**/14
Quiz IV: **153**/3–4; **154**/10; **154-155**/13–16
Review: **157**/5; **158**/14; **159**/18; **160**/26; **160**/31; **161**/37
Directed-Study Practice Test, Section 4: **397**/1; **400**/8
Practice Test II, Section 3: **506**/3
Practice Test II, Section 7: **524**/4
Practice Test II, Section 9: **534**/2
Practice Test III, Section 2: **547**/7
Practice Test III, Section 5: **565**/6

Transformations and Their Effects on Graphs of Functions (Math: Multiple-Choice and Student-Produced Responses)

Lesson (MC): **211**/169–170

Triangles (Math: Multiple-Choice and Student-Produced Responses)

Lesson (MC): **184**/9; **213-214**/180–185; **215**/187, 189; **216**/194–196, 198; **218**/203; **218-219**/205–210

Lesson (SPR): **270**/11; **272**/21
Quiz I (MC): **229**/11–12
Quiz I (SPR): **277**/9
Quiz II (MC): **232**/5; **233**/12, 17
Quiz II (SPR): **280**/6
Quiz III (SPR): **284**/8
Quiz IV (MC): **241**/7–8
Review (MC): **244**/4; **245**/10–11; **246**/15, 18; **247**/24
Review (SPR): **290**/11
Directed-Study Practice Test, Section 2 (SPR): **378**/13
Directed-Study Practice Test, Section 8 (MC): **433**/12
Practice Test 1, Section 3 (MC): **468**/13
Practice Test I, Section 9 (MC): **494**/12–13
Practice Test II, Section 2 (MC): **503**/6; **504**/11; **505**/17
Practice Test II, Section 4 (MC): **514**/3
Practice Test II, Section 4 (SPR): **517**/13–14
Practice Test III, Section 7 (MC): **572**/17
Practice Test III, Section 9 (MC): **581**/4–5, 9; **582**/10

Unintended Meanings (Writing)

Lesson: **322**/61
Quiz I: **334**/8; **334**/10
Quiz II: **338**/8–9
Quiz III: **342**/9
Quiz IV: **345**/7
Review: **355**/27; **355**/30
Directed Study Practice Test, Section 10: **450**/6
Practice Test I, Section 7: **481**/5; **483**/23
Practice Test I, Section 10: **497**/4; **497**/7; **498**/10; **498**/14
Practice Test II, Section 6: **520**/18

Verb Tense (Writing)

Lesson: **320**/48–50
Quiz IV: **345**/6
Review: **351**/1; **352**/9; **353**/14
Directed Study Practice Test, Section 3: **385**/9
Practice Test 1, Section 7: **482**/14
Practice Test III, Section 4: **560**/13

Vocabulary (Critical Reading: Passages)

Lesson: **54**/6; **57**/18; **58**/25; **60**/37; **62**/45–49; **64**/57; **65**/63; **67**/74; **68**/76–77; **69**/79; **69**/83; **70**/88; **71**/91; **72**/99; **73**/105
Quiz I: **75**/1; **79**/9; **80**/11
Quiz II: **83**/5; **85**/9; **87**/14
Quiz III: **90**/6; **90**/8; **92**/11
Review: **105**/7; **108**/17; **111**/28; **113**/38; **116**/48; **118**/59
Directed Study Practice Test, Section 4: **402**/13; **403**/15–16; **406**/21
Directed Study Practice Test, Section 6: **426**/20

Directed Study Practice Test, Section 9: **438**/6; **440**/9; **443**/13; **445**/17
Practice Test 1, Section 2: **462**/16
Practice Test I, Section 5: **472**/12; **474**/17; **474**/20; **475**/22
Practice Test I, Section 8: **488**/5–6; **489**/13; **489**/16
Practice Test II, Section 3: **511**/17–18; **512**/24
Practice Test II, Section 7: **525**/9; **527**/14; **528**/16; **528**/19; **529**/21
Practice Test II, Section 9: **537**/9; **537**/11; **537**/13
Practice Test III, Section 2: **551**/17
Practice Test III, Section 5: **567**/15; **568**/21
Practice Test III, Section 8: **575**/7; **577**/13

Voice (Critical Reading: Passages)

Lesson: **56**/14–15; **57**/22; **58**/29; **60**/41; **63**/55–56; **66**/69; **69**/86; **72**/102; **74**/112
Quiz I: **76**/3; **80**/17
Quiz II: **84**/6
Quiz III: **90**/7
Quiz IV: **96**/9; **97**/14; **99**/18
Review: **103**/3; **106**/14; **110**/26; **112**/35; **116**/53; **117**/56
Directed Study Practice Test, Section 4: **402**/12; **406**/22
Directed Study Practice Test, Section 6: **420**/9; **425**/18–19
Directed Study Practice Test, Section 9: **443**/12; **445**/16
Practice Test 1, Section 2: **464**/24
Practice Test I, Section 5: **472**/10; **475**/24
Practice Test I, Section 8: **488**/9
Practice Test II, Section 3: **507**/9; **511**/22
Practice Test II, Section 7: **527**/13; **529**/22
Practice Test II, Section 9: **538**/17
Practice Test III, Section 2: **552**/24
Practice Test III, Section 8: **577**/12

Working with Triangles (Math: Multiple-Choice and Student-Produced Responses)

Lesson (SPR): **272**/21
Quiz I (MC): **229**/11
Quiz II (MC): **232**/5; **233**/12
Quiz II (SPR): **280**/6
Quiz III (SPR): **284**/8
Review (MC): **244**/4; **245**/10–11; **246**/15, 18; **247**/24
Review (SPR): **290**/11
Directed-Study Practice Test, Section 2 (SPR): **378**/13
Directed-Study Practice Test, Section 8 (MC): **433**/12
Practice Test 1, Section 3 (MC): **468**/13
Practice Test I, Section 9 (MC): **494**/12–13
Practice Test II, Section 2 (MC): **504**/11; **505**/17
Practice Test II, Section 4 (SPR): **517**/13–14
Practice Test III, Section 9 (MC): **581**/4–5, 9